Advanced Spanish

Edited by
Enrique Montes

LIVING LANGUAGE®

Content in this program has been modified and enhanced from *Starting Out in Spanish* and *Complete Course Spanish: The Basics*, both published in 2008.

Published in the United States by Living Language, an imprint of Random House, Inc.

www.livinglanguage.com

Editor: Suzanne McQuade
Production Editor: Carolyn Roth
Production Manager: Tom Marshall
Interior Design: Sophie Chin
Illustrations: Sophie Chin

First Edition

Library of Congress Cataloging-in-Publication Data

Advanced Spanish / edited by Enrique Montes. -- 1st ed.
p. cm.
ISBN 978-0-307-97164-7
1. Spanish language--Textbooks for foreign speakers--English. 2. Spanish language--Grammar. 3. Spanish language--Spoken Spanish. I. Montes, Enrique.
PC4129.E5A38 2011
468.2'421--dc23
2011021882

PRINTED IN THE UNITED STATES OF AMERICA

10 9 8 7 6

Acknowledgments

Thanks to the Living Language team: Amanda D'Acierno, Christopher Warnasch, Suzanne McQuade, Laura Riggio, Erin Quirk, Amanda Munoz, Fabrizio LaRocca, Siobhan O'Hare, Sophie Chin, Sue Daulton, Alison Skrabek, Carolyn Roth, Ciara Robinson, and Tom Marshall.

COURSE

OUTLINE

COURSE

OUTLINE

How to Use This Course

¡Bienvenidos! Welcome to *Living Language Advanced Spanish*!

Before we begin, let's take a quick look at what you'll see in this course.

CONTENT

Advanced Spanish is a continuation of *Intermediate Spanish*. Now that you've mastered the basics with *Essential* and *Intermediate Spanish*, you'll take your Spanish even further with a comprehensive look at irregular verbs, advanced verb tenses, and complex sentences.

UNITS

There are four units in this course. Each unit has four lessons arranged in a "building block" structure: the first lesson will present essential *words*, the second will introduce longer *phrases*, the third will teach *sentences*, and the fourth will show how everything works together in everyday *conversations*.

At the beginning of each unit is an introduction highlighting what you'll learn in that unit. At the end of each unit you'll find the Unit Essentials, which reviews the key information from that unit, and a self-graded Unit Quiz, which tests what you've learned.

LESSONS

There are four lessons per unit for a total of 16 lessons in the course. Each lesson has the following components:

- **Introduction** outlining what you will cover in the lesson.
- **Word Builder 1** (first lesson of the unit) presenting key words and phrases.
- **Phrase Builder 1** (second lesson of the unit) introducing longer phrases and expressions.
- **Sentence Builder 1** (third lesson of the unit) teaching sentences.
- **Conversation 1** (fourth lesson of the unit) for a natural dialogue that brings together important vocabulary and grammar from the unit.
- **Take It Further** providing extra information about the new vocabulary you just saw, expanding on certain grammar points, or introducing additional words and phrases.
- **Word/Phrase/Sentence/Conversation Practice 1** practicing what you learned in Word Builder 1, Phrase Builder 1, Sentence Builder 1, or Conversation 1.
- **Grammar Builder 1** guiding you through important Spanish grammar that you need to know.
- **Work Out 1** for a comprehensive practice of what you saw in Grammar Builder 1.
- **Word Builder 2/Phrase Builder 2/Sentence Builder 2/Conversation 2** for more key words, phrases, or sentences, or a second dialogue.
- **Take It Further** for expansion on what you've seen so far and additional vocabulary.
- **Word/Phrase/Sentence/Conversation Practice 2** practicing what you learned in Word Builder 2, Phrase Builder 2, Sentence Builder 2, or Conversation 2.
- **Grammar Builder 2** for more information on Spanish grammar.
- **Work Out 2** for a comprehensive practice of what you saw in Grammar Builder 2.
- **Tip** or **Culture Note** for a helpful language tip or useful cultural information related to the lesson or unit.

- **Drive It Home** reviewing important grammar and vocabulary from the lesson.
- **How Did You Do?** outlining what you learned in the lesson.

UNIT ESSENTIALS

You will see the **Unit Essentials** at the end of every unit. This section summarizes and reviews the key information from the unit, but with missing vocabulary information for you to fill in. In other words, each Unit Essentials works as both a study guide and a blank "cheat sheet." Once you complete it, you'll have your very own reference for the most essential vocabulary and grammar from the unit.

UNIT QUIZ

After each Unit Essentials, you'll see a **Unit Quiz**. The quizzes are self-graded so it's easy for you to test your progress and see if you should go back and review.

PROGRESS BAR

You will see a **Progress Bar** on each page that has course material. It indicates your current position within the unit and lets you know how much progress you're making. Each line in the bar represents a Grammar Builder section.

AUDIO

Look for the symbol ▶ to help guide you through the audio as you're reading the book. It will tell you which track to listen to for each section that has audio. When you see the symbol, select the indicated track and start listening! If you don't see the symbol, then there isn't any audio for that section. You'll also see ⏸, which will tell you where that track ends.

The audio can be used on its own—in other words, without the book—when you're on the go. Whether in your car or at the gym, you can listen to the audio on its own to brush up on your pronunciation or review what you've learned in the book.

PRONUNCIATION GUIDE, GRAMMAR SUMMARY, GLOSSARY

At the back of this book you will find a **Pronunciation Guide**, **Grammar Summary**, and **Glossary**. The Pronunciation Guide provides information on Spanish pronunciation and the phonetics system used in this course. The Grammar Summary contains a helpful, brief overview of key points in the Spanish grammar system. The Glossary (Spanish–English and English–Spanish) includes all of the essential words from the four units of *Advanced Spanish*, as well as some additional vocabulary.

FREE ONLINE TOOLS

Go to **www.livinglanguage.com/languagelab** to access your free online tools. The tools are organized around the units in this course, with audiovisual flashcards, as well as interactive games and quizzes for each unit. These tools will help you to review and practice the vocabulary and grammar that you've seen in the units, as well as provide some bonus words and phrases related to the unit's topic.

Unit 1: Shopping

In this unit, you'll learn vocabulary related to clothing and colors, as well as some useful shopping expressions. You'll also learn how to make comparisons and how to talk about future plans. By the end of this unit, you should be able to:

- ☐ Name articles of clothing and talk about shopping
- ☐ Conjugate common stem-changing verbs
- ☐ Compare things using adjectives and adverbs
- ☐ Describe how clothing fits and looks
- ☐ Use direct object pronouns
- ☐ Talk about the near future
- ☐ Conjugate reflexive verbs
- ☐ Use reflexive pronouns

Lesson 1: Words

By the end of this lesson, you will be able to:

- □ Understand how to conjugate common stem-changing verbs
- □ Name articles of clothing

Word Builder 1

1A Word Builder 1 (CD 7, Track 1)

el cinturón	*belt*
los pantalones	*pants*
el traje	*suit*
la camisa	*shirt*
la corbata	*tie*
los calcetines	*socks*
los vaqueros	*jeans*
la camiseta	*T-shirt*
la gabardina	*raincoat*
el saco/la chaqueta	*jacket*
el jersey/el suéter	*sweater*
los zapatos	*shoes*
la falda	*skirt*

Word Practice 1

1. ______________________
2. ______________________
3. ______________________
4. ______________________

Identify the correct items on the clothesline.

ANSWER KEY

1. **la camisa**/**la camiseta**; 2. **los calcetines**; 3. **la falda**; 4. **los zapatos**

Grammar Builder 1

STEM-CHANGING VERBS

1B Grammar Builder 1 (CD 7, Track 2)

In previous units in both *Essential Spanish* and *Intermediate Spanish*, you learned the conjugations of a few irregular verbs. Remember stem-changing verbs from Lesson 10 of *Essential Spanish*? Let's take another look at these verbs. The first group includes verbs in which the **o** of the infinitive changes to **ue**, as in

almorzar (*to have lunch*). Notice that this change happens in all the forms except **nosotros** and **vosotros**.

ALMORZAR (*TO HAVE LUNCH*)	
yo almuerzo	**nosotros/as almorzamos**
tú almuerzas	**vosotros/as almorzáis**
él/ella/usted almuerza	**ellos/ellas/ustedes almuerzan**

Here are a few more common **o** to **ue** verbs.

costar	*to cost*
dormir	*to sleep*
encontrar	*to find, to meet*
morir	*to die*
mostrar	*to show*
volver	*to return*
volar	*to fly*
oler	*to smell*
recordar	*to remember*
soñar	*to dream*
mover	*to move*
poder	*can, to be able*

Notice that **h-** is added to **oler** (*to smell*) in the forms where the vowel changes.

OLER (*TO SMELL*)	
yo huelo	**nosotros/as olemos**
tú hueles	**vosotros/as oléis**
él/ella/usted huele	**ellos/ellas/ustedes huelen**

A second common stem change is -**e** to -**ie**, as in **pensar** (*to think*). Again, the **nosotros** and **vosotros** forms are not affected.

PENSAR ***(TO THINK)***	
yo pienso	**nosotros/as pensamos**
tú piensas	**vosotros/as pensáis**
él/ella/usted piensa	**ellos/ellas/ustedes piensan**

Here are some other **e** to **ie** verbs.

mentir	*to lie, to tell lies*
entender	*to understand*
sentir	*to feel*
cerrar	*to close*
comenzar	*to begin*
despertarse	*to wake up*
sentarse	*to sit down*

¿Cuánto cuesta esa camisa?
How much does that shirt cost?

Ellos sueñan con tener mucho dinero.
They dream of having a lot of money.

La clase comienza en veinte minutos.
The class begins in twenty minutes.

No entiendo lo que estás dicendo.
I don't understand what you are saying.

Work Out 1

Complete the following sentences with one of the following verbs: **pensar**, **dormir**, **sentir**, **costar**, **comenzar**, **cerrar**, **encontrar**, **entender**, **mostrar**, **volar**.

1. **Yo** ________________ **dolor en la espalda.**
2. **Yo no** ________________**. ¿Puede hablar más despacio por favor?**
3. **Las tiendas abren a las nueve y media de la mañana y** ________________ **a las ocho de la noche.**
4. **Ella** ________________ **las camisetas de algodón al cliente.**
5. **¿Cuánto** ________________ **esa blusa roja?**
6. **Tú no** ________________ **una corbata que combine con la camisa.**
7. **Mi bebita** ________________ **once horas todas las noches.**
8. **Nosotros siempre** ________________ **con la misma aerolínea.**
9. **La película** ________________ **a las cinco.**
10. **Tú** ________________ **demasiado en tus problemas.**

ANSWER KEY

1. **siento**; 2. **entiendo**; 3. **cierran**; 4. **muestra**; 5. **cuesta**; 6. **encuentras**; 7. **duerme**; 8. **volamos**; 9. **comienza**; 10. **piensas**

Word Builder 2

1C Word Builder 2 (CD 7, Track 3)

el vestido	*dress*
el abrigo	*overcoat*
la blusa	*blouse*
el bolso	*handbag*

el traje de baño/el bañador	*bathing suit*
la bata	*robe*
las sandalias	*sandals*
la bufanda	*scarf*
los guantes	*gloves*
las medias	*stockings*

Word Practice 2

Match the Spanish word with its appropriate English translation.

1. las medias	a. *gloves*
2. el bolso	b. *dress*
3. el vestido	c. *blouse*
4. los guantes	d. *stockings*
5. el abrigo	e. *handbag*
6. la blusa	f. *overcoat*

ANSWER KEY

1. d; 2. e; 3. b; 4. a; 5. f; 6. c

Grammar Builder 2

MORE STEM-CHANGING VERBS

1D Grammar Builder 2 (CD 7, Track 4)

There is another group of verbs with stems that change from **-e** to **-i**. **Pedir** (*to ask for*) is one example.

PEDIR *(TO ASK FOR)*	
yo pido	nosotros/as pedimos

PEDIR ***(TO ASK FOR)***	
tú pides	**vosotros/as pedís**
él/ella/usted pide	**ellos/ellas/ustedes piden**

Here are some other common **-e** to-**i** verbs.

conseguir	*to find, to obtain, to get*
medir	*to measure*
reír	*to laugh*
repetir	*to repeat*
servir	*to serve*
impedir	*to prevent*
sonreír	*to smile*

Take a look at **sonreír** (*to smile*), which is just like **reír** (*to laugh*). Notice where the accent goes.

SONREÍR ***(TO SMILE)***	
yo sonrío	**nosotros/as sonreímos**
tú sonríes	**vosotros/as sonreís**
él/ella/usted sonríe	**ellos/ellas/ustedes sonríen**

Finally, some verbs ending in **-cer** or **-cir** have the irregularity of adding a **-z** before the ending in the first person singular. Take **agradecer** (*to be thankful, to thank*) as an example.

AGRADECER ***(TO BE THANKFUL, TO THANK)***	
yo agradezco	**nosotros/as agradecemos**
tú agradeces	**vosotros/as agradecéis**
él/ella/usted agradece	**ellos/ellas/ustedes agradecen**

Other common examples include the following.

ofrecer	*to offer*
producir	*to produce*
conducir	*to drive*
traducir	*to translate*

Verbs ending in **-ger** and **-gir** change the **-g** to **-j** in the first person singular. One example is **escoger** (*to choose*).

ESCOGER *(TO CHOOSE)*	
yo escojo	**nosotros/as escogemos**
tú escoges	**vosotros/as escogéis**
él/ella/usted escoge	**ellos/ellas/ustedes escogen**

Here are some other examples.

elegir	*to choose*
exigir	*to demand*
proteger	*to protect*
dirigir	*to direct*

Él no consigue trabajo.
He doesn't find work.

Tú sonríes poco.
You don't smile a lot.

Yo conduzco un auto verde.
I drive a green car.

Yo exijo una explicación.
I demand an explanation.

Work Out 2

Conjugate the verb in parentheses.

1. **La maestra** ______________ **las oraciones varias veces. (repetir)**
2. **Yo** ______________ **un auto viejo. (conducir)**
3. **El presidente** ______________ **la reunión. (dirigir)**
4. **Ella siempre** ______________ **películas extranjeras. (escoger)**
5. **Tú** ______________ **demasiado de tus empleados. (exigir)**
6. **Ellos** ______________ **la mesa. (medir)**
7. **La estación de televisión** ______________ **siete series cada año. (producir)**
8. **Ellos** ______________ **una película de cine. (escoger)**

ANSWER KEY

1. **repite**; 2. **conduzco**; 3. **dirige**; 4. **escoge**; 5. **exiges**; 6. **miden**; 7. **produce**; 8. **escogen**

Take It Further

There will be times when you're speaking to a native Spanish speaker when you will simply not understand what he or she has just said. The best thing you can do in such circumstances is to let the person know that you are having a bit of trouble. Here are a few phrases—some you already know, and some are new—that can help you.

Disculpe, ¿puede repetir lo que acaba de decir, por favor?
Sorry, could you please repeat what you just said?

No entiendo.
I don't understand.

¿Qué significa . . . ?
What does . . . mean?

Disculpe, ¿cómo dijo?

Sorry, what did you say?

Drive It Home

Write the correct form of the verb in parentheses.

1. **Tú** ______________________ **la lección. (entender)**
2. **Ella** ______________________ **la lección. (entender)**
3. **Nosotros** ______________________ **la lección. (entender)**
4. **Ellos** ______________________ **la lección. (entender)**
5. **Yo** ______________________ **en mi familia. (pensar)**
6. **Ustedes** ______________________ **en su familia. (pensar)**
7. **Usted** ______________________ **en su familia. (pensar)**
8. **Vosotros** ______________________ **en vuestra familia. (pensar)**

ANSWER KEY

1. **entiendes**; 2. **entiende**; 3. **entendemos**; 4. **entienden**; 5. **pienso**; 6. **piensan**; 7. **piensa**; 8. **pensáis**

How Did You Do?

By now, you should be able to:

- ☐ Understand how to conjugate common stem-changing verbs (Still unsure? Jump back to pages 14 and 18.)
- ☐ Name articles of clothing (Still unsure? Jump back to pages 13 and 17.)

Lesson 2: Phrases

By the end of this lesson, you should be able to:

- ☐ Talk about shopping
- ☐ Compare things using *more/-er* or *less than*
- ☐ Compare two people or things that are equal
- ☐ Use superlatives like *the best*, and *the worst*

Phrase Builder 1

2A Phrase Builder 1 (CD 7, Track 5)

ir de compras	*to go shopping*
llevar una prenda puesta	*to wear something*
ir de escaparates	*to go window-shopping*
buscar gangas	*to look for bargains*
comprar en rebaja	*to buy on sale*
comprar en el mercadillo	*to buy at the flea market*
probarse algo	*to try something on*
hacer a la medida	*to custom sew*
lavar en seco	*to dry-clean*
lavar a mano	*to hand wash*

Phrase Practice 1

Match the Spanish with its appropriate English translation.

1. **lavar en seco**
2. **lavar a mano**
3. **ir de escaparates**
4. **ir de compras**
5. **buscar gangas**
6. **comprar en rebaja**

a. *to buy on sale*
b. *to dry-clean*
c. *to look for bargains*
d. *to hand wash*
e. *to go shopping*
f. *to go window-shopping*

ANSWER KEY
1. b; 2. d; 3. f; 4. e; 5. c; 6. a

Grammar Builder 1

COMPARATIVES

2B Grammar Builder 1 (CD 7, Track 6)

In English, you can compare things with the formula *more/-er* or *less* + adjective/adverb/noun + *than*. In Spanish, the *more* comparative formula is:

más + adjective/adverb/noun + **que**

Mi hermana es más alta que mi madre.
My sister is taller than my mother.

Juan tiene más camisas que su hermano.
Juan has more shirts than his brother.

But just like in English, there are a few exceptions. The following adjectives have a different form for the comparative.

ADJECTIVE		COMPARATIVE	
bueno/a	*good*	**mejor**	*better*
malo/a	*bad*	**peor**	*worse*
grande	*big*	**mayor**	*bigger/older*
pequeño/a	*small*	**menor**	*smaller/younger*

Esta camisa me queda mejor que la azul.
This shirt fits me better than the blue one.

Esta corbata se ve peor que la otra.
This tie looks worse than the other.

Ella es mayor que nuestra hija.
She is older than our daughter.

Mi hermana es dos años menor que yo.
My sister is two years younger than I (am).

When you want to show inferiority, you will use the following formula:

menos + adjective/adverb/noun + **que**

Yo soy menos tímida que mi amiga Rocío.
I am less shy than my friend Rocío.

Nosotros vamos al cine menos frecuentemente que vosotros.
We go to the movies less often than you (do).

Pedro tiene menos dinero que su esposa.

Pedro has less money than his wife.

Work Out 1

Fill in the blank with the appropriate Spanish translation of the words in parentheses.

1. **Yo trabajo** ______________________ **tú.** *(fewer hours than)*
2. **Vosotros viajáis** ______________________ **nosotros.** *(more frequently than)*
3. **Esa película es** ______________________ **la de las once y media.** *(longer than)*
4. **Este bolso es** ______________________ **el negro.** *(more expensive than)*
5. **Tú lees** ______________________ **yo.** *(fewer books than)*
6. **Ellos tienen** ______________________ **sus padres.** *(more problems than)*
7. **Esta chaqueta es** ______________________ **la otra.** *(more elegant than)*
8. **Carlos es** ______________________ **su esposa.** *(ten years older than)*

ANSWER KEY

1. **menos horas que**; 2. **más frecuentemente que**; 3. **más larga que**; 4. **más costoso que**; 5. **menos libros que**; 6. **más problemas que**; 7. **más elegante que**; 8. **diez años mayor que**

Phrase Builder 2

2C Phrase Builder 2 (CD 7, Track 7)

¿Qué desea?	*What would you like?*
¿De qué color?	*What color?*
¿Cuánto vale?	*How much is it?*
¿Algo más?	*Anything else?*
No, gracias, eso es todo.	*No, thanks; that's all.*
Me queda mal.	*It doesn't fit me.*
Te quedan bien.	*They fit you well.*
¡Qué elegante!	*How elegant!*
Me lo llevo.	*I'll take it.*
Es muy costoso.	*It's very expensive.*

Phrase Practice 2

Match the Spanish with its appropriate English translation.

1. **Me lo llevo.**
2. **Me queda mal.**
3. **¿De qué color?**
4. **¿Cuánto vale?**
5. **¿Qué desea?**
6. **¿Algo más?**

a. *What color?*
b. *How much is it?*
c. *I'll take it.*
d. *What would you like?*
e. *Anything else?*
f. *It doesn't fit me.*

ANSWER KEY

1. c; 2. f; 3. a; 4. b; 5. d; 6. e

Grammar Builder 2

EQUAL COMPARISONS AND SUPERLATIVES

2D Grammar Builder 2 (CD 7, Track 8)

There will be times when you want to compare two people or things that are equal. In this case, you will use the following formula:

tan + adjective/adverb + **como**

Madrid es tan interesante como Nueva York.
Madrid is as interesting as New York.

La vida en Madrid es tan rápida como en Nueva York.
Life in Madrid is as fast as in New York.

To compare two phrases, you need to use **tanto**, which will agree in gender and number with the noun it precedes.

Carmen tiene tanta paciencia como tú.
Carmen has as much patience as you (do).

Ella tiene tanto dinero como su padre.
She has as much money as her father (does).

Ella tiene tantos gastos como ustedes.
She has as many expenses as you (do).

Ella tiene tantas sandalias como yo.
She has as many sandals as I (do).

When you use expressions like *the biggest*, *the worst*, *the most exciting*, and *the least difficult*, you are using superlatives. Forming superlatives in Spanish is very easy: simply add the corresponding definite article (**el**, **la**, **los**, **las**) to the patterns you've already learned, and use the preposition **de** when you want to express *in/of*.

Este vestido es el más costoso (de todo).
This dress is the most expensive (of all).

La falda roja es la más fea.
The red skirt is the ugliest.

Marta es la menos extrovertida de la familia.
Marta is the least extroverted in the family.

Ellos son los menos puntuales de todos mis amigos.
They are the least punctual of all my friends.

Mis hermanas son las más altas de la clase.
My sisters are the tallest in the class.

Ese edificio es el más alto.
That building is the highest.

Work Out 2

Fill in the blanks with the Spanish equivalents of the words in parentheses.

1. **Mi oficina es** ____________________ **la tuya.** *(as big as)*
2. **Estos tiquetes son** ____________________. *(the least expensive)*

3. **Nuestra habitación es** ______________________ **las tres.** *(the smallest of)*

4. **Es** ______________________ **película del año.** *(the worst)*

5. **Ella lleva el vestido** ______________________ **.** *(the prettiest)*

6. **Los zapatos de color café son** ______________________ **.** *(the most comfortable)*

7. **Me gusta el chocolate** ______________________ **a ti.** *(as much as)*

8. **Él tiene** ______________________ **trabajo del mundo.** *(the best)*

ANSWER KEY

1. **tan grande como**; 2. **los menos costosos**; 3. **la más pequeña de**; 4. **la peor**; 5. **más bonito**; 6. **los más cómodos**; 7. **tanto como**; 8. **el mejor**

Tip!

A good way to improve your Spanish vocabulary is to read short passages from newspapers or magazines, many of which you can, of course, find online. Before you begin to read an article, it is important that you focus on the title of the article and look at any pictures that are attached to it. Skim quickly over the entire text, looking for information that will help you get the gist of the content. In this way, you can familiarize yourself with the topic and begin to anticipate the information that you'll read. Read the text only a couple of times, and don't focus on each individual word. It's more important that you get the overall picture. Trying to understand and learn each little word will only cause you to give up and feel frustrated. For now, focus on the big picture, and then move on to something else. Soon enough, you'll be able to worry about all the little details! To find some practice material, go to your favorite search engine and type in **revistas en español** (*magazines in Spanish*) or **periódicos en español** (*newspapers in Spanish*).

Drive It Home

Make comparative sentences using the adjective in parentheses. Follow the model by saying that the first person is more of the quality mentioned than the second one.

example: **María (inteligente) Jorge**
María es más inteligente que Jorge.

1. **Mi hermana (tímida) mi prima.** ______________________
2. **Mi hermana (alta) mi prima.** ______________________
3. **Mi hermana (morena) mi prima.** ______________________
4. **Mi hermana (elegante) mi prima.** ______________________
5. **La comedia (buena) el drama.** ______________________
6. **La comedia (malo) el drama.** ______________________

ANSWER KEY

1. **Mi hermana es más tímida que mi prima.** 2. **Mi hermana es más alta que mi prima.** 3. **Mi hermana es más morena que mi prima.** 4. **Mi hermana es más elegante que mi prima.** 5. **La comedia es mejor que el drama.** 6. **La comedia es peor que el drama.**

How Did You Do?

By now, you should be able to:

- ☐ Talk about shopping (Still unsure? Jump back to page 23.)
- ☐ Compare things using *more/-er* or *less than* (Still unsure? Jump back to page 24.)
- ☐ Compare two people or things that are equal (Still unsure? Jump back to page 28.)
- ☐ Use superlatives like *the best*, and *the worst* (Still unsure? Jump back to page 29.)

Lesson 3: Sentences

By the end of this lesson, you should be able to:

- ☐ Talk about what size you wear
- ☐ Describe how clothing fits and looks
- ☐ Use direct object pronouns
- ☐ Talk about things you are planning to do in the near future

Sentence Builder 1

3A Sentence Builder 1 (CD 7, Track 9)

¿Qué número calza?	*What shoe size do you wear?*
Calzo el número treinta y siete.	*I wear shoe size 37.*
¿Qué talla lleva usted?	*What size do you wear?*
No estoy seguro/a.	*I'm not sure.*
Mi talla es cuarenta.	*I wear size 40.*

¿Le gustaría probarse este suéter?	*Would you like to try this sweater on?*
¿Ya lo atendieron?	*Has someone helped you? (lit., Have you been helped?)*
Gracias, sólo estoy mirando.	*Thanks, I'm just looking.*
¿Dónde está el probador?	*Where is the dressing room?*
Estoy buscando un vestido de noche informal.	*I'm looking for a casual evening dress.*

Sentence Practice 1

Fill in the blanks in each sentence based on the English translation.

1. **¿Qué talla** ______________ **usted?** *What size do you wear?*
2. **No estoy** ______________ **.** *I'm not sure.*
3. ______________ **es cuarenta.** *I wear size 40.*
4. **Gracias,** ______________ **.** *Thanks, I'm just looking.*
5. **Estoy buscando** ______________ **.** *I'm looking for a casual evening dress.*
6. **¿Dónde está** ______________ **?** *Where is the dressing room?*

ANSWER KEY

1. **lleva**; 2. **seguro/a**; 3. **Mi talla**; 4. **sólo estoy mirando**; 5. **un vestido de noche informal**; 6. **el probador**

Grammar Builder 1

DIRECT OBJECT PRONOUNS

3B Grammar Builder 1 (CD 7, Track 10)

A direct object is a noun (or pronoun) that shows you what the verb is acting on. For example, in the sentence *Manuel is buying a sweater*, the direct object is the noun *sweater*—it's the answer to the question *what is Manuel buying?* A direct object can also be a person, as in *Manuel sees the salesperson*, in answer to the question *who does Manuel see?*

Direct object pronouns are the pronouns used to replace direct object nouns, such as *sweater* or *salesperson* in our examples above. In English, there are some different pronouns used as direct objects: *me* instead of *I*, *her* instead of *she*, *him* instead of *he*, etc. Spanish is no different. Let's look at the direct object pronouns in Spanish.

DIRECT OBJECT PRONOUNS			
me	*me*	**nos**	*us*
te	*you (infml.)*	**os**	*all of you (infml.)*
lo	*him, it, you (fml.)*	**los**	*them, you*
la	*her, it, you (fml.)*	**las**	*them, you*

Don't forget that nouns in Spanish can be feminine or masculine, even if they're inanimate. So, lo can mean *he* or *it* for a masculine noun, and la can mean *she* or *it* for a feminine noun. The same is true of los and las, in the plural. The direct object pronouns that correspond to **usted** are lo and la, and the ones that correspond to **ustedes** are los and las. The difference depends on whether you are talking to a man or a woman.

Yo amo a María.
I love María.

Yo la amo.
I love her.

Manuela llama a Pedro.
Manuela calls Pedro.

Manuela lo llama.
Manuela calls him.

Ellos visitan a María y Clara.
They visit María and Clara.

Ellos las visitan.
They visit them.

Now let's look at how direct object pronouns are used. In Spanish, as you saw in the examples above, they come right before the verb.

Carlos no te conoce.
Carlos doesn't know you.

Los oigo pero no los veo.
I hear them, but I don't see them.

Nosotros no la olvidamos.
We don't forget her.

However, if the main verb appears in the infinitive form (ending in **-ar**, **-er**, or **-ir**), the direct object pronoun can come either before the verbal phrase or after the infinitive, in which case the pronoun is attached to it.

Carlos te quiere conocer.
Carlos wants to meet you.

Carlos quiere conocerte.
Carlos wants to meet you.

Los puedo oír, pero no los puedo ver.

I can hear them, but I can't see them.

Puedo oírlos, pero no puedo verlos.

I can hear them, but I can't see them.

Nosotros no queremos olvidarla.

We don't want to forget her.

Nosotros no la queremos olvidar.

We don't want to forget her.

A similar thing happens with the present participle (**-ando**, **-iendo**) form. Notice the use of the accent mark, which ensures that the stress remains on the same syllable as it would if there were no participial ending.

Te estoy ayudando.

I am helping you.

Estoy ayudándote.

I am helping you.

Work Out 1

Replace the direct object noun with a pronoun.

1. **La señorita atiende al cliente.** ______________________

____

2. Ella está comprando unos zapatos. ______________________________

____

3. Mis hijas van a dar una fiesta el viernes. ______________________________

____

4. Yo voy a traer unas flores. ______________________________

____

5. Vais a escribir una carta. ______________________________

____

6. Estoy enviando un mensaje a Roberto. ______________________________

____

7. Manuel conoce a tu familia. ______________________________

____

8. Mis amigos llaman a María todos los días. ______________________________

____

ANSWER KEY

1. La señorita lo atiende. 2. Ella los está comprando./Ella está comprándolos. 3. Mis hijas la van a dar el viernes. 4. Yo las voy a traer./Yo voy a traerlas. 5. Vais a escribirla./La vais a escribir. 6. Estoy enviándolo a Roberto./Lo estoy enviando a Roberto. 7. Manuel la conoce. 8. Mis amigos la llaman todos los días.

Sentence Builder 2

3C Sentence Builder 2 (CD 7, Track 11)

¿Puedo probarme esta falda?	*Can I try this skirt on?*
¿Me puede hacer un descuento?	*Can you give me a discount?*
¿Está rebajado?	*Is it reduced/on sale?*

¿Cómo le quedan?	*How do they fit?*
Me quedan un poco cortos.	*They are a bit short.*
Ese color es el último grito de la moda.	*That color is very trendy right now.*
¿Cuánto cuesta la cartera negra de cuero?	*How much is the black leather handbag?*
¿Dónde se encuentran chaquetas para caballero?	*Where can I find men's jackets?*
La chaqueta no combina bien con los pantalones.	*The jacket doesn't go well with the pants.*

Sentence Practice 2

Fill in the blanks in each sentence based on the English translation.

1. **¿Puedo** ________________ **esta falda?** *Can I try this skirt on?*
2. **¿Me puede** ________________**?** *Can you give me a discount?*
3. **¿Está** ________________**?** *Is it reduced/on sale?*
4. **Me quedan** ________________ **.** *They are a bit short.*
5. **¿Cuánto cuesta** ________________ **?**

   How much is the black leather handbag?
6. **La chaqueta** ________________ **los pantalones.**

   The jacket doesn't go well with the pants.

ANSWER KEY

1. **probarme**; 2. **hacer un descuento**; 3. **rebajado**; 4. **un poco cortos**; 5. **la cartera negra de cuero**; 6. **no combina bien con**

Grammar Builder 2

THE FUTURE WITH IR A (*GOING TO*)

3D Grammar Builder 2 (CD 7, Track 12)

Now let's take a look at how we can talk about things we are planning on doing tomorrow or in the near future. In Spanish, there is a very simple formula:

ir (*to go*) + **a** (*to*) + verb in the infinitive

This is the equivalent of *going to* in English.

Yo voy a comprar un traje.
I am going to buy a suit.

Tú vas a ir de compras por la tarde.
You are going to go shopping in the afternoon.

Ella va a estrenar su chaqueta el martes.
She is going to wear her jacket for the first time on Tuesday.

Usted va a viajar a España.
You are going to travel to Spain.

Nosotros vamos a mirar escaparates.
We are going to go window-shopping.

Vosotros vais a buscar zapatos.
You are going to look for shoes.

Ustedes van a descansar.
You are going to rest.

Here are some useful time expressions that you can use to show a time in the future.

hoy	*today*
hoy por la tarde	*today in the afternoon*
hoy por la noche	*today in the evening*
mañana	*tomorrow*
mañana por la mañana	*tomorrow morning*
mañana por la tarde	*tomorrow afternoon*
mañana por la noche	*tomorrow evening*
más tarde	*later*
esta tarde	*this afternoon*
esta noche	*this evening*
la semana que viene	*next week*
el mes que viene	*next month*
el año que viene	*next year*

Work Out 2

Answer the following questions using the information in parentheses.

1. **¿Cuándo van a ir a Los Ángeles? (ellos, en diciembre)** ________________
____
2. **¿Qué vas a comprar? (yo, unos pantalones y unos zapatos)** ________________
____
3. **¿Adónde vais de vacaciones? (nosotros, Costa Rica)** ________________
____

4. ¿Cuántas personas va a invitar a la fiesta? (ella, 45 personas) ____________

____

5. ¿Qué película van a ver? (nosotros, una película de Almodóvar) ____________

____

6. ¿A qué hora vas a salir de la oficina? (yo, a las 3:30 de la tarde) ____________

____

7. ¿Cuántas camisas tengo que comprar? (tú, tres) ____________

____

8. ¿Cuándo van a hacer la presentación? (ellas , el martes por la tarde) ____________

____

ANSWER KEY

1. Ellos van a ir en diciembre. 2. Voy a comprar unos pantalones y unos zapatos. 3. Vamos a ir a Costa Rica. 4. Ella va a invitar a cuarenta y cinco personas. 5. Vamos a ver una película de Almodóvar. 6. Voy a salir a las tres y media de la tarde. 7. Tienes que comprar tres camisas. 8. Ellas van a hacer la presentación el martes por la tarde.

Take It Further

You're probably going to need a few more adjectives to describe the way clothes and shoes fit. Here is a very useful list.

ajustado/a	*tight*
suelto/a	*loose, flowing*
escotado/a	*low-cut*
ancho/a	*baggy, wide*
enterizo/a	*one-piece*
de dos piezas	*two-piece*
cómodo/a	*comfortable*
incómodo/a	*uncomfortable*

suave	*soft*
duro/a	*hard*

Los vestidos sueltos y escotados son perfectos para noches de verano.
Loose and low-cut dresses are perfect for summer nights.

Estos zapatos no son tan suaves como los negros.
These shoes are not as soft as the black ones.

Los trajes de baño enterizos son más cómodos que los de dos piezas.
One-piece bathing suits are more comfortable than two-piece ones.

Estos pantalones están muy ajustados.
These pants are very tight.

Drive It Home

A. Change each sentence by replacing **el helado** with the object pronoun **lo**.

1. **Yo pruebo el helado.** ______
2. **Ella prueba el helado.** ______
3. **Tú pruebas el helado.** ______
4. **Nosotros probamos el helado.** ______

B. Now rewrite the sentences that you created above using the future with **ir a**.

1. ______
2. ______

3. ______________________________

4. ______________________________

ANSWER KEY

A. 1. **Yo lo pruebo.** 2. **Ella lo prueba.** 3. **Tú lo pruebas.** 4. **Nosotros lo probamos.**

B. 1. **Yo lo voy a probar./Yo voy a probarlo.** 2. **Ella lo va a probar./Ella va a probarlo.** 3. **Tú lo vas a probar./Tú vas a probarlo.** 4. **Nosotros lo vamos a probar./Nosotros vamos a probarlo.**

How Did You Do?

By now, you should be able to:

- ☐ Talk about what size you wear (Still unsure? Jump back to page 32.)
- ☐ Describe how clothing fits and looks (Still unsure? Jump back to page 41.)
- ☐ Use direct object pronouns (Still unsure? Jump back to page 33.)
- ☐ Talk about things you are planning to do in the near future (Still unsure? Jump back to page 39.)

Lesson 4: Conversations

By the end of this lesson, you should be able to:

- ☐ Conjugate reflexive verbs
- ☐ Use reflexive pronouns
- ☐ Talk about colors, patterns, and fabrics

Conversation 1

4A Conversation 1 (CD 7, Track 13 - Spanish Only; Track 14 - Spanish and English)

Juan is at a men's shop trying on some clothes, because he is going on vacation with his girlfriend next week and he needs a few things.

Vendedora:	**¿Qué tal le quedan los pantalones, señor?**
Juan:	**Estos vaqueros azul claro son muy anchos y estos negros son demasiado ajustados. ¿Tiene una talla intermedia?**
Vendedora:	**Espere un momento. Voy a buscar a ver qué encuentro. Y las camisetas, ¿qué tal?**
Juan:	**La anaranjada parece ser de un material más ligero que la verde, ¿no es verdad?**
Vendedora:	**Sí, la anaranjada es cien por ciento de algodón. El color es el último grito de la moda y le queda mejor que la verde. Claro, es también más costosa.**
Juan:	**¿Tiene más en mi talla?**
Vendedora:	**Sí, creo que sí. ¿Tiene algún color en mente?**
Juan:	**Me gustaría llevar dos blancas, una azul oscura y otra en amarillo o rojo.**
Vendedora:	**Si gusta esperar un momento, voy a buscar los vaqueros y otras camisetas. Ya regreso.**
Juan:	**Mientras espero, voy a mirar por ahí a ver qué más encuentro.**
Vendedora:	**Muy bien. Hay pantalones cortos y bañadores en descuento allá enfrente.**

Saleswoman:	*Do the pants fit, sir?*
Juan:	*These light blue jeans are too loose, and these black ones are too tight. Do you have something in between?*
Saleswoman:	*Wait a moment. I'll take a look and see what I can find. What about the T-shirts?*
Juan:	*The orange one seems to be made of a lighter material than the green one, right?*
Saleswoman:	*Yes, the orange one is one hundred percent cotton. The color is very trendy nowadays, and it suits you better than the green one. Of course, it's more expensive.*
Juan:	*Do you have more in my size?*
Saleswoman:	*Yes, I think so. Do you have a color in mind?*

Juan:	*I'd like to take two white ones, a dark blue one, and another one in yellow or red.*
Saleswoman:	*If you'd like to wait a moment, I'll go get the jeans and the T-shirts. I'll be back soon.*
Juan:	*While I wait, I'll take a look over there to see what else I find.*
Saleswoman:	*Very well. There are shorts and bathing suits on sale over there in the front.*

Take It Further

When it comes to clothes, you'll find that in the Spanish-speaking world, there are different words for the same thing. In Latin America, for example, blue jeans are **los jeans**, sweater is **un suéter**, and jacket is **una chaqueta**, **un saco**, or **una americana**. But in Spain, a pair of blue jeans is **unos vaqueros**, a sweater is **un suéter** or **un jersey**, and a jacket may be referred to as **una chaqueta**. And when it comes to talking about underwear, no one seems to agree: women's underwear can be **bragas**, **bombachas**, **calzoncitos**, or **pantis**, and men's undergarments are **calzones** or **calzoncillos**. Stockings are **medias** or **pantymedias**, and socks are **calcetines** or **medias**. Slippers are known as **zapatillas**, **pantuflas**, or **chinelas**, and a robe as **bata**, **albornoz**, or **deshabillé**. So, what to do? When in Rome, do as the Romans, and simply use the words people use where you are!

Conversation Practice 1

Fill in the blank with the correct word from the conversation.

1. **Estos vaqueros** ______________ **son muy anchos y estos negros son demasiado** ______________. *These light blue jeans are too loose, and these black ones are too tight.*

2. __________ **buscar a ver qué encuentro.** *I'll take a look and see what I can find.*

3. **Sí, la anaranjada es cien por ciento de** ________________ **.** *Yes, the orange one is one hundred percent cotton.*

4. **Claro, también es más** _______________ **.** *Of course, it's more expensive.*

5. ______________________ **llevar dos blancas, una azul oscura y otra en amarillo o rojo.** *I'd like to take two white ones, a dark blue one, and another one in yellow or red.*

6. **Si gusta esperar un momento, voy a buscar los** ______________________ **y otras** __________________ **.** *If you'd like to wait a moment, I'll go get the jeans and the T-shirts. I'll be back soon.*

ANSWER KEY

1. **azul claro**/**ajustados**; 2. **Voy a**; 3. **algodón**; 4. **costosa**; 5. **Me gustaría** 6. **vaqueros**/**camisetas**

Grammar Builder 1

REFLEXIVE VERBS

4B Grammar Builder 1 (CD 7, Track 15)

Reflexive verbs are verbs in which the subject performs the action on him- or herself. Spanish reflexive verbs often correspond to English verbs that use reflexive pronouns, like *to wash oneself*, *to dress oneself*, and so on. But there are also many verbs that are reflexive in Spanish but are not reflexive in English. Spanish reflexive verbs are conjugated following the same rules as **-ar**, **-er**, **-ir**, or irregular verbs, but their infinitives always end in **-se**. When reflexive verbs are conjugated, they always take the following reflexive pronouns.

REFLEXIVE PRONOUNS	
me (*myself*)	**nos** (*ourselves*)

REFLEXIVE PRONOUNS	
te *(yourself)*	**os** *(yourselves)*
se *(himself, herself, itself, yourself)*	**se** *(themselves, yourselves)*

These pronouns come before the conjugated verb. Let's take a look at **levantarse**, which means *to get up*.

LEVANTARSE *(TO GET UP)*			
(yo) me levanto	*I get up*	**(nosotros/as) nos levantamos**	*we get up*
(tú) te levantas	*you get up*	**(vosotros/as) os levantáis**	*you get up*
(él/ella/usted) se levanta	*he/she/it gets up*	**(ellos/ellas/ ustedes) se levantan**	*they/you get up*

When a reflexive verb is used with other verbs, like in the present continuous with **estar** or the immediate future with **ir**, the reflexive pronoun can be placed either before the verb phrase or after it. If it comes after, it's attached to the end of the main verb.

(Yo) me levanto a las seis todos los días.
I get up at six every day.

En este momento me estoy levantando.
Right now, I am getting up.

En este momento estoy levantándome.
Right now, I am getting up.

Mañana me voy a levantar tarde.
Tomorrow I'm going to get up late.

Mañana voy a levantarme tarde.
Tomorrow I'm going to get up late.

Here are some more common reflexive verbs in Spanish. Again, notice that some of them can be translated reflexively in English, but not all of them.

REFLEXIVE VERBS	
acostarse	*to go to bed*
llamarse	*to be called*
vestirse	*to get dressed*
ponerse	*to put (something) on*
divertirse	*to have fun*
ducharse	*to shower*
bañarse	*to bathe*
sentarse	*to sit down*
sentirse	*to feel*
despedirse	*to say good-bye*

You've probably noticed that if you take off the **-se** ending of the reflexive infinitive, you're left with another, non-reflexive verb. Our first example, **levantarse**, is like this. **Levantarse** means *to get up, to rise*, or *to lift oneself from a seated or reclining position*, but **levantar** simply means *to lift* or *to raise (something else)*. Similar pairs are **llamar** (*to call*) and **llamarse** (*to call oneself, to be called*), **vestir** (*to dress [someone else]*) and **vestirse** (*to get dressed, to dress oneself*), and so on. Here are some more examples of reflexive verbs.

Me siento muy feliz.
I feel very happy.

Ella se va a despedir de su familia esta tarde.
She's going to say good-bye to her family this afternoon.

Ellos se están vistiendo para la fiesta.
They are getting dressed for the party.

Also note that reflexives can have a reciprocal sense. In the plural form, the reflexive pronoun can sometimes mean *each other* or *one another*, as in these sentences.

Nos miramos.
We look at each other.

Ellos se están besando.
They are kissing each other.

Los perros se huelen.
The dogs smell one another.

Work Out 1

Combine the following words to form sentences, conjugating the verbs as necessary.

1. **Yo/llamarse/Pedro Campos.** ______________________________

2. **Ellos/ir a divertirse/en la fiesta de esta noche.** ______________________________

3. **Él/ir a sentarse/a leer el periódico.** ______________________________

4. **En este momento yo/estar probándose/el vestido.** ______________________

5. **¿A qué hora/levantarse/usted todos los días?** ______________________

6. **Ellos/acostarse/muy tarde los fines de semana.** ______________________

7. **¿Vosotros/estar mirando/en el espejo ahora?** ______________________

8. **Después de/trotar/ella/ir a bañarse.** ______________________

ANSWER KEY

1. **Yo me llamo Pedro Campos.** 2. **Ellos van a divertirse/se van a divertir en la fiesta de esta noche.** 3. **Él se va a sentar/va a sentarse a leer el periódico.** 4. **En este momento me estoy probando/estoy probándome el vestido.** 5. **¿A qué hora se levanta usted todos los días?** 6. **Ellos se acuestan muy tarde los fines de semana.** 7. **¿Os estáis mirando en el espejo ahora?** 8. **Después de trotar, ella se va a bañar/va a bañarse.**

Conversation 2

4C Conversation 2 (CD 7, Track 16 - Spanish Only; Track 17 - Spanish and English)

Now listen in as Sara, Juan's girlfriend, does some shopping of her own.

Vendedora: **¿Ya la atendieron?**

Sara: **Gracias. ¿Cuánto cuesta la cartera negra de cuero? No tiene una etiqueta con el precio.**

Vendedora: **Vamos a ver … Tiene razón. Estos bolsos están rebajados y tienen un treinta por ciento de descuento.**

Sara: **¡Es una ganga! Me lo llevo. También me gustaría probarme unos zapatos.**

Vendedora:	**¿Qué número calza?**
Sara:	**Treinta y siete.**
Vendedora:	**La talla treinta y siete está en esta sección. ¿Busca algún color en particular?**
Sara:	**Sí, quiero unos zapatos que vayan con el bolso negro.**
Vendedora:	**Aquí hay unos muy bonitos y con un tacón no muy alto. Son muy cómodos. ¿Le gustan?**
Sara:	**A ver ... me los voy a probar. ¡Me quedan como anillo al dedo! ¡Me los llevo! ¿Están también rebajados?**
Vendedora:	**Soñar no cuesta nada, ¿verdad? Desafortunadamente, no.**
Sara:	**Bueno, no importa. Son bonitos y me quedan bien.**

Saleswoman:	*Is someone helping you?*
Sara:	*Thank you. How much is the black leather bag? It doesn't have a price tag.*
Saleswoman:	*Let's see ... You're right. These handbags are on sale, and they are thirty percent off.*
Sara:	*That's a bargain! I'll take it. I'd also like to try on some shoes.*
Saleswoman:	*What size do you wear?*
Sara:	*Thirty-seven.*
Saleswoman:	*Size thirty-seven is in this section. Are you looking for any particular color?*
Sara:	*Yes, I'd like a pair of shoes that go with the black bag.*
Saleswoman:	*Here are some very pretty ones with a not-so-high heel. They are very comfortable. Do you like them?*
Sara:	*Let's see ... I'm going to try them on. They fit me like a glove! I'll take them! Are they also on sale?*
Saleswoman:	*It doesn't hurt to ask! (lit., "To dream doesn't cost anything, right?") Unfortunately, no ...*
Sara:	*Well, it doesn't matter. They're pretty and they fit me well.*

Take It Further

As you learn Spanish, you'll see that there's a saying for just about anything and everything. There are two sayings in the above dialogue. The first one, **Me queda como anillo al dedo**, is equivalent of the English saying *It fits me like a glove*. The second one, **Soñar no cuesta nada**, literally means *To dream doesn't cost anything*, but in this context, you can translate it as *It doesn't hurt to ask.*

Conversation Practice 2

Unscramble the Spanish sentences below from the dialogue above. The English sentence is unscrambled.

1. **¿la/atendieron/ya?** *Is someone helping you?* ____________________

2. **¿cuero/cuesta/la/cuánto/negra/cartera/de?** *How much is the black leather bag?* ____________________

3. **¿calza/número/qué?** *What size do you wear?* ____________________

4. **probarme/gustaría/zapatos/unos/me/también.** *I'd also like to try on some shoes.* ____________________

5. **no/nada/¿verdad?/soñar/cuesta** *It doesn't hurt to ask! (lit., "To dream doesn't cost anything, right?")* ____________________

6. **bonitos/son/me/y/bien/quedan.** *They're pretty and they fit me well.* ____________________

ANSWER KEY

1. **¿Ya la atendieron?** 2. **¿Cuánto cuesta la cartera negra de cuero?** 3. **¿Qué número calza?** 4. **También me gustaría probarme unos zapatos.** 5. **Soñar no cuesta nada, ¿verdad?** 6. **Son bonitos y me quedan bien.**

Grammar Builder 2

COLORS, PATTERNS, AND FABRICS

4D Grammar Builder 2 (CD 7, Track 18)

Here are the colors in Spanish.

amarillo	*yellow*
azul	*blue*
celeste	*sky blue*
azul marino	*navy blue*
rojo	*red*
verde	*green*
marrón/café	*brown*
negro	*black*
blanco	*white*
gris	*gray*
naranja/anaranjado	*orange*
morado	*purple*
rosa/rosado	*pink*
dorado	*gold*
plateado	*silver*

Remember that most colors have to agree in gender and number with the noun they modify. Exceptions are those ending in **-e** or in a consonant like, **verde**, **azul**, **marrón**, **café**, and **celeste**, which only have to agree in number.

Este vestido plateado no combina con esos zapatos rojos.
This silver dress doesn't match those red shoes.

Las camisas amarillas son más costosas que las azules.
The yellow shirts are more expensive than the blue ones.

Los zapatos café no me gustan.
I don't like the brown shoes.

Here are a few more adjectives you can use with colors to describe clothes.

a rayas	*striped*
a cuadros	*plaid*
estampado	*with a pattern, patterned*
de lunares	*polka-dotted*
oscuro	*dark*
claro	*light*

And here are some types of fabric.

algodón	*cotton*
lana	*wool*
lino	*linen*
seda	*silk*
cuero	*leather*
plástico	*plastic*
gamuza	*suede*
poliéster	*polyester*

Me gusta la camisa de algodón de rayas azules y grises.
I like the blue and gray striped cotton shirt.

Quiero una chaqueta de gamuza café.

I want a brown suede jacket.

La falda roja a cuadros de lana es muy costosa.

The red plaid wool skirt is very expensive.

Work Out 2

Answer using complete sentences. **¿De qué color son estas cosas?**

1. **las naranjas** ______
2. **el océano** ______
3. **la luna** ______
4. **los limones** ______
5. **el sol** ______
6. **la sangre** ______
7. **el césped** ______
8. **el carbón** ______

ANSWER KEY

1. **Las naranjas son anaranjadas.** 2. **El océano es azul.** 3. **La luna es blanca.** 4. **Los limones son amarillos.** 5. **El sol es amarillo.** 6. **La sangre es roja.** 7. **El césped es verde.** 8. **El carbón es negro.**

Take It Further

Just like in English, there are many idiomatic expressions in Spanish using colors. Here are a few.

ponerse rojo como un tomate	*to be embarrassed (lit., to turn red like a tomato)*
ponerse colorado	*to be embarrassed (lit., to turn red)*
estar rojo de la ira	*to be very angry (lit., to be red with fury)*
contar un chiste verde	*to tell an obscene joke (lit., to tell a green joke)*
ver todo negro	*to be a pessimist (lit., to see everything as black)*
ver todo color de rosa	*to be an optimist, to wear rose-colored glasses (lit., to see everything pink)*
ir de punta en blanco	*to be dressed to the nines (lit., to go from the tip in white)*
ser de sangre azul	*to have blue blood (lit., to be of blue blood)*
estar negro de la risa	*to laugh very hard (lit., to turn black with laughter)*

Drive It Home

Give the complete conjugation of the following reflexive verbs:

DUCHARSE ***(TO SHOWER)***	
yo ______________	**nosotros/as** ______________
tú ______________	**vosotros** ______________
él/ella/Ud. ______________	**ellos/ellas/Uds.** ______________

PONERSE ***(TO PUT ON)***	
yo ______	**nosotros/as** ______
tú ______	**vosotros** ______
él/ella/Ud. ______	**ellos/ellas/Uds.** ______

ANSWER KEY

ducharse: me ducho, te duchas, se ducha, nos duchamos, os ducháis, se duchan

ponerse: me pongo, te pones, se pone, nos ponemos, os ponéis, se ponen

How Did You Do?

By now, you should be able to:

- ☐ Conjugate reflexive verbs (Still unsure? Jump back to page 46.)
- ☐ Use reflexive pronouns (Still unsure? Jump back to page 46.)
- ☐ Talk about colors, patterns, and fabrics (Still unsure? Jump back to page 53.)

Don't forget to practice and reinforce what you've learned by visiting **www.livinglanguage.com/languagelab** for flashcards, games, and quizzes for Unit 1!

Unit 1 Essentials

Vocabulary Essentials

ITEMS OF CLOTHING

	belt
	jacket
	pants
	suit
	shirt
	tie
	socks
	jeans
	T-shirt
	raincoat
	jacket
	sweater
	shoes
	skirt
	dress
	overcoat
	blouse
	handbag
	bathing suit
	robe

	sandals
	scarf
	gloves
	stockings

[Pgs. 13 and 17]

CLOTHING VERBS

	to go shopping
	to wear something
	to go window-shopping
	to look for bargains
	to buy on sale
	to buy at the flea market
	to try something on
	to custom sew
	to dry-clean
	to hand wash

[Pg. 23]

SHOPPING EXPRESSIONS

	What would you like?
	What color?
	How much is it?
	Anything else?
	No, thanks; that's all.
	It doesn't fit me.

	They fit you well.
	How elegant!
	I'll take it.
	It's very expensive.
	What shoe size do you wear?
	I wear shoe size 37.
	What size do you wear?
	I'm not sure.
	I wear size 40.
	Would you like to try this sweater on?
	Is someone helping you?
	Thanks, I'm just looking.
	Where is the dressing room?
	I'm looking for a casual evening dress.
	Can I try this skirt on?
	Can you give me a discount?
	Is it reduced/on sale?
	How do they fit?
	They are a bit short.
	That color is very trendy right now.
	How much is the black leather handbag?
	Where can I find men's jackets?
	The jacket doesn't go well with the pants.

[Pgs. 27, 32, and 37]

FUTURE TIME EXPRESSIONS

	today
	today in the afternoon
	today in the evening
	tomorrow
	tomorrow morning
	tomorrow afternoon
	tomorrow evening
	later
	this afternoon
	this evening
	next week
	next month
	next year

[Pg. 40]

CLOTHING ADJECTIVES

	tight
	loose/flowing
	low-cut
	baggy/wide
	one-piece
	two-piece
	comfortable
	uncomfortable
	soft

	hard

[Pg. 41]

COLORS

	yellow
	blue
	sky blue
	navy blue
	red
	green
	brown
	black
	white
	gray
	orange
	purple
	pink
	gold
	silver

[Pg. 53]

PATTERNS

	striped
	plaid
	with a pattern, patterned
	polka-dotted

	dark
	light

[Pg. 54]

FABRICS

	cotton
	wool
	linen
	silk
	leather
	plastic
	suede
	polyester

[Pg. 54]

IDIOMATIC EXPRESSIONS USING COLORS

	to be embarrassed (lit., to turn red like a tomato)
	to be embarrassed (lit., to turn red)
	to be very angry (lit., to be red with fury)
	to tell an obscene joke (lit., to tell a green joke)
	to be a pessimist (lit., to see everything as black)
	to be an optimist, to wear rose-colored glasses (lit., to see everything pink)

	to be dressed to the nines (lit., to go from the tip in white)
	to have blue blood (lit., to be of blue blood)
	to laugh very hard (lit., to turn black with laughter)

[Pg. 56]

Grammar Essentials

O TO UE STEM-CHANGING VERBS

ALMORZAR *(TO HAVE LUNCH)*	
yo almuerzo	nosotros/as almorzamos
tú almuerzas	vosotros/as almorzáis
él/ella/usted almuerza	ellos/ellas/ustedes almuerzan
Similar verbs: costar *(to cost)*, dormir *(to sleep)*, encontrar *(to find, to meet)*, morir *(to die)*, mostrar *(to show)*, volver *(to return)*, volar *(to fly)*, oler *(to smell)*, recordar *(to remember)*, soñar *(to dream)*, mover *(to move)*, poder *(can, to be able)*	

E TO IE STEM-CHANGING VERBS

PENSAR *(TO THINK)*	
yo pienso	nosotros/as pensamos
tú piensas	vosotros/as pensáis
él/ella/usted piensa	ellos/ellas/ustedes piensan
Similar verbs: mentir *(to lie, to tell lies)*, entender *(to understand)*, sentir *(to feel)*, cerrar *(to close)*, comenzar *(to begin)*, despertarse *(to wake up)*, sentarse *(to sit down)*	

E TO I STEM-CHANGING VERBS

PEDIR *(TO ASK FOR)*	
yo pido	nosotros/as pedimos
tú pides	vosotros/as pedís
él/ella/usted pide	ellos/ellas/ustedes piden
Similar verbs: conseguir (*to find*), medir (*to measure*), reír (*to laugh*), repetir (*to repeat*), servir (*to serve*), impedir (*to prevent*), sonreír (*to smile*)	

CER VERBS ADDING Z IN FIRST PERSON SINGULAR

AGRADECER *(TO BE THANKFUL)*	
yo agradezco	nosotros/as agradecemos
tú agradeces	vosotros/as agradecéis
él/ella/usted agradece	ellos/ellas/ustedes agradecen
Similar verbs: ofrecer (*to offer*), producir (*to produce*), conducir (*to drive*), traducir (*to translate*), conocer (*to know*)	

GER AND GIR VERBS ADDING J IN FIRST PERSON SINGULAR

ESCOGER *(TO CHOOSE)*	
yo escojo	nosotros/as escogemos
tú escoges	vosotros/as escogéis
él/ella/usted escoge	ellos/ellas/ustedes escogen
Similar verbs: elegir (*to choose*), exigir (*to demand*), proteger (*to protect*), dirigir (*to direct*)	

COMPARATIVES AND SUPERLATIVES

To form a comparative:

más + adjective/adverb/noun + que

Some adjectives have irregular comparatives.

ADJECTIVE		COMPARATIVE	
bueno/a	*good*	mejor	*better*
malo/a	*bad*	peor	*worse*
grande	*big*	mayor*	*bigger/older*
pequeño/a	*small*	menor	*smaller/younger*
* Note that mayor can also mean *older*, and menor can also mean *younger*.			

To make equal comparisons:

tan + adjective/adverb + como

To form the superlative:

el/la/los/las + comparative adjective/adverb

DIRECT OBJECT PRONOUNS

DIRECT OBJECT PRONOUNS			
me	*me*	nos	*us*
te	*you (infml.)*	os	*all of you (infml.)*
lo	*him, it, you (fml.)*	los	*them, you*
la	*her, it, you (fml.)*	las	*them, you*

Remember that direct pronouns come right before the verb, unless the verb appears in the infinitive, in which case the direct object pronoun can come before the verbal phrase, or after the infinitive, in which case the pronoun is attached to the infinitive.

FUTURE WITH IR A (*TO GO TO*)

ir (*to go*) + a (*to*) + verb in the infinitive

REFLEXIVE PRONOUNS

REFLEXIVE PRONOUNS	
me (*myself*)	nos (*ourselves*)
te (*yourself*)	os (*yourselves*)
se (*himself, herself, itself, yourself*)	se (*themselves, yourselves*)

REFLEXIVE VERBS

LEVANTARSE ***(TO GET UP)***	
(yo) me levanto	(nosotros/as) nos levantamos
(tú) te levantas	(vosotros/as) os levantáis
(él/ella/usted) se levanta	(ellos/ellas/ustedes) se levantan
Similar verbs: acostarse (*to go to bed*), llamarse (*to be called*), vestirse (*to get dressed*), ponerse (*to put something on*), divertirse (*to have fun*), ducharse (*to shower*), bañarse (*to bathe*), sentarse (*to sit down*), sentirse (*to feel*), despedirse (*to say good-bye*)	

VERBS

AGRADECER ***(TO BE THANKFUL)***	
yo agradezco	nosotros/as agradecemos
tú agradeces	vosotros/as agradecéis
él/ella/usted agradece	ellos/ellas/ustedes agradecen

ALMORZAR ***(TO HAVE LUNCH)***	
yo almuerzo	nosotros/as almorzamos
tú almuerzas	vosotros/as almorzáis
él/ella/usted almuerza	ellos/ellas/ustedes almuerzan

ESCOGER ***(TO CHOOSE)***	
yo escojo	nosotros/as escogemos
tú escoges	vosotros/as escogéis
él/ella/usted escoge	ellos/ellas/ustedes escogen

LEVANTARSE ***(TO GET UP)***	
(yo) me levanto	(nosotros/as) nos levantamos
(tú) te levantas	(vosotros/as) os levantáis
(él/ella/usted) se levanta	(ellos/ellas/ustedes) se levantan

OLER ***(TO SMELL)***	
yo huelo	nosotros/as olemos
tú hueles	vosotros/as oléis
él/ella/usted huele	ellos/ellas/ustedes huelen

PEDIR ***(TO ASK FOR)***	
yo pido	nosotros/as pedimos
tú pides	vosotros/as pedís
él/ella/usted pide	ellos/ellas/ustedes piden

PENSAR ***(TO THINK)***	
yo pienso	nosotros/as pensamos
tú piensas	vosotros/as pensáis
él/ella/usted piensa	ellos/ellas/ustedes piensan

SONREÍR ***(TO SMILE)***	
yo sonrío	nosotros/as sonreímos
tú sonríes	vosotros/as sonreís
él/ella/usted sonríe	ellos/ellas/ustedes sonríen

Unit 1 Quiz

A. Fill in the blanks by conjugating the verb in parentheses.

1. Ella ______________________________ hablar varios idiomas. (poder)
2. El estudiante le ______________________________ a la profesora. (mentir)
3. Yo ______________________________ un dolor de cabeza muy fuerte. (tener)
4. Los niños ______________________________ cuando están contentos. (sonreír)
5. Nosotros ______________________________ mucho los fines de semana. (dormir)
6. Los camareros ______________________________ la comida. (servir)
7. Ustedes ______________________________ un carro muy rápido. (conducir)
8. Usted ______________________________ al trabajo en una semana. (volver)

B. Match the column on the left with the English word on the right.

1. la corbata	a. *worse*
2. la falda	b. *to try on*
3. probar	c. *wide*
4. la bufanda	d. *tie*
5. ajustado	e. *tight*
6. ancho	f. *shoe*
7. peor	g. *skirt*
8. el zapato	h. *scarf*

C. Fill in the blanks with the Spanish equivalents of the words in parentheses.

1. **Tu casa es** ________________ **la mía.** *(bigger than)*

2. **Esta ciudad es** ________________. *(the most expensive)*

3. **Esta película es** ________________ **del año.** *(the best)*

4. **Mi trabajo es** ________________ **el tuyo.** *(as good as)*

5. **Estos pantalones son** ________________ **los otros pantalones.** *(uglier)*

6. **Este restaurante es** ________________ **el otro.** *(better than)*

7. **Mi padre es** ________________ **yo.** *(taller)*

8. **Esta blusa es** ________________. *(the least expensive)*

D. Choose the vocabulary word that fits the sentence.

1. **Ella se (ducha/pone) ropa muy elegante.**

2. **El (algodón/marrón) es un color muy bonito.**

3. **Nosotros llamamos a Clarisa y Mirna pero no (la/las) visitamos.**

4. **Tú te (acuestas/llamas) en una cama muy cómoda.**

5. **La comedia es mejor (como/que) el drama.**

6. **La comedia es tan buena (como/que) el drama.**

7. **¿Cuánto (comienza/cuesta) esta camiseta?**

8. **Yo me (acuesto/levanto) temprano por la mañana.**

ANSWER KEY

A. 1. **puede**; 2. **miente**; 3. **tengo**; 4. **sonríen**; 5. **dormimos**; 6. **sirven**; 7. **conducen**; 8. **vuelve**

B. 1. d; 2. g; 3. b; 4. h; 5. e; 6. c. 7. a; 8. f

C. 1. **más grande que**; 2. **la más cara**; 3. **la mejor**; 4. **tan bueno como**; 5. **más feos que**; 6. **mejor que**; 7. **más alto que**; 8. **la menos cara**

D. 1. **pone**; 2. **marrón**; 3. **las**; 4. **acuestas**; 5. **que**; 6. **como**; 7. **cuesta**; 8. **levanto**

How Did You Do?

Give yourself a point for every correct answer, then use the following key to determine whether or not you're ready to move on:

0–7 points: It's probably best to go back and study the lessons again to make sure you understood everything completely. Take your time; it's not a race! Make sure you spend time reviewing vocabulary with the flashcards and reading through each grammar note carefully.

8–16 points: If the questions you missed were in sections A or B, you may want to review the vocabulary again; if you missed answers mostly in sections C or D, check the unit essentials to make sure you have your conjugations and other grammar basics down.

17–20 points: Feel free to move on to the next unit! You're doing a great job.

points

Unit 2:
Let's Eat!

In this unit, you'll learn how to order food at a restaurant and how to do some grocery shopping in Spanish. You will also learn how to talk about things that happened in the past. By the end of this unit, you should be able to:

- ☐ Name and describe types of food
- ☐ Use indirect object pronouns
- ☐ Form adverbs by adding **-mente**
- ☐ Order food in a restaurant
- ☐ Use expressions of quantity
- ☐ Talk about things that happened in the past
- ☐ Shop for food in a grocery store
- ☐ Conjugate the past tense of irregular verbs

Lesson 5: Words

By the end of this lesson, you should be able to:

- ☐ Name and describe types of food
- ☐ Use indirect object pronouns
- ☐ Form adverbs

Word Builder 1

5A Word Builder 1 (CD 7, Track 19)

el desayuno	*breakfast*
el almuerzo	*lunch*
la merienda	*snack time*
la cena	*dinner*
la comida	*food, dinner*
la cuchara	*spoon*
el tenedor	*fork*
el cuchillo	*knife*
el vaso	*glass*
la copa	*wineglass*
la taza	*cup*
el plato	*plate, dish*
la servilleta	*napkin*
la carta/el menu	*menu*
la cuenta	*bill, check*
la propina	*tip*

Word Practice 1

Match each Spanish word below to its appropriate English translation.

1. **el desayuno** — a. *lunch*
2. **la cuenta** — b. *dinner*
3. **la copa** — c. *menu*
4. **la carta** — d. *bill, check*

5. **la cena** e. *breakfast*

6. **el almuerzo** f. *wineglass*

ANSWER KEY

1. e; 2. d; 3. f; 4. c; 5. b; 6. a

Grammar Builder 1

INDIRECT OBJECT PRONOUNS

5B Grammar Builder 1 (CD 7, Track 20)

Take a look at this sentence: *I gave him the book.* You already know that *the book* is the thing given; it's the direct object. But there's a second type of object in that sentence, too. *Him* is an indirect object pronoun. It could also be expressed as *to him*, as in *I gave the book to him*. Indirect object pronouns tell us to whom or for whom an action is done. Let's take a look at them in Spanish.

INDIRECT OBJECT PRONOUNS			
me	*(to/for) me*	**nos**	*(to/for) us*
te	*(to/for) you (infml. sg.)*	**os**	*(to/for) you (infml. pl.)*
le	*(to/for) him, her, it, you (fml. sg.)*	**les**	*(to/for) them, you (fml. pl.)*

Indirect object pronouns can be used to replace indirect object nouns.

¿Qué les vas a ofrecer a tus invitados?
What are you going to offer your guests?

Les voy a ofrecer champaña.
I'm going to offer them champagne.

¿Qué le vas a regalar a Pablo?
What are you going to give Pablo?

Le voy a regalar una guitarra.
I'm going to give him a guitar.

Notice that since **le** and **les** can refer to several things, you can also use them along with a phrase like **a él**, **a ella**, **a usted**, **a ellos**, **a ellas**, or **a ustedes** to avoid misunderstanding.

No les voy a comprar nada a ellos.
I'm not going to buy anything for them.

Le dijimos la verdad a él.
We told him the truth.

In addition, you'll see that Spanish speakers often like to emphasize the indirect object pronoun by using **a mí**, **a ti**, **a nosotros/as**, **a vosotros/as**, and so on, even when these expressions are not necessary for clarification.

Ellas nos dan la receta a nosotros.
They give us the recipe.

Tú me escribes una carta a mí.
You write a letter to me.

¿Qué nos vas a comprar a nosotros?
What are you going to buy for us?

Les voy a enviar unas tarjetas a mis primos.
I'm going to send some cards to my cousins.

Just like direct object pronouns, indirect object pronouns are placed before a single conjugated verb or verb phrase; or attached to the end of a verbal phrase.

Margarita le da el plato a Laura.
Margarita gives Laura the dish.

Margarita le está dando el plato a Laura.
Margarita is giving Laura the dish.

Margarita está dándole el plato a Laura.
Margarita is giving Laura the dish.

Margarita le va a dar el plato a Laura.
Margarita is going to give Laura the dish.

Margarita va a darle el plato a Laura.
Margarita is going to give Laura the dish.

With commands, the indirect object pronoun is attached to affirmative commands, but placed before negative ones.

Por favor, póngame tres kilos de limones.
Please give me three kilos of lemons.

No nos dé leche en polvo.
Do not give us powdered milk.

Tráigame una servilleta.
Bring me a napkin.

No me sirva el almuerzo frío.
Don't serve me a cold lunch.

Work Out 1

Fill in the blank with the appropriate indirect object pronoun.

1. **Ella ______ sirve la comida a él.**
2. **Él ______ regala unas flores a ella.**
3. **Voy a escribir ______ una carta a ellas.**
4. **El mesero ______ trae la carta a nosotras.**
5. **Ella ______ trae un regalo a ustedes.**
6. **Tú ______ das los dos litros de leche a mí.**
7. ______ **vamos a enviar una invitación muy especial a vosotros.**
8. **Por favor, traiga ______ un cuchillo a nosotros.**

ANSWER KEY

1. **le**; 2. **le**; 3. **(escribir)les**; 4. **nos**; 5. **les**; 6. **me**; 7. **Os**; 8. **(tráiga)nos**

Word Builder 2

5C Word Builder 1 (CD 7, Track 21)

Here is some more useful vocabulary you can use to talk about food.

la comida	*food*
el pan	*bread*
la carne	*meat*
el pollo	*chicken*
el cerdo	*pork*
el vegetal	*vegetable*
el tomate	*tomato*
el fríjol	*bean*

la mantequilla	*butter*
el jugo	*juice*
el arroz	*rice*
duro/a	*hard*
sobrecocido/a	*overcooked*
quemado/a	*burnt*
picante	*spicy*
podrido/a	*bad, rotten*
pasado/a	*spoiled*
agrio/a	*sour*
dulce	*sweet*
salado/a	*salty*
amargo/a	*bitter*
a la parrilla	*grilled*
frito/a	*fried*
ahumado/a	*smoked*

Word Practice 2

Match the Spanish adjective on the left with its appropriate English translation on the right.

1. **amargo/a** — a. *sour*
2. **agrio/a** — b. *bitter*
3. **ahumado/a** — c. *spoiled*
4. **duro/a** — d. *smoked*
5. **podrido/a** — e. *hard*
6. **pasado/a** — f. *bad, rotten*

ANSWER KEY
1. b; 2. a; 3. d; 4. e; 5. f; 6. c

Grammar Builder 2

ADVERBS

5D Grammar Builder 2 (CD 7, Track 22)

Adverbs are words that are used to describe a verb, an adjective, or another adverb, like the word *happily*. In English, a lot of adverbs are formed by adding *-ly* to the end of an adjective, as in *happy–happily*. Similarly, in Spanish, adverbs are formed by adding **-mente** to the feminine form of adjectives ending in **-o** and to the final **-e** or consonant of any other adjective. Here are a few adjective-adverb pairs.

feliz	*happy*	**felizmente**	*happily*
triste	*sad*	**tristemente**	*sadly*
lento	*slow*	**lentamente**	*slowly*
rápido	*quick*	**rápidamente/ rápido**	*quickly*
nuevo	*new*	**nuevamente**	*once again, anew*
frecuente	*frequent*	**frecuentemente**	*frequently*
normal	*normal*	**normalmente**	*normally*

When an adverb is describing a verb, telling you how something is done, it's placed after the verb, regardless of whether it is a single verb or a verb phrase.

Ella come lentamente.
She eats slowly.

Ellos trabajan rápidamente.
They work quickly.

Nosotros vamos a comer rápidamente.
We're going to eat quickly.

But an adverb can also come at the beginning of a sentence if it describes a characteristic of, or expresses an attitude toward, the whole sentence.

Normalmente trabajo ocho horas diarias.
I normally work eight hours a day.

Tristemente no podemos viajar el mes entrante.
Sadly, we won't be able to travel next month.

When an adverb describes an adjective or another adverb, it's placed in front of the word it is modifying.

Sus respuestas son completamente absurdas.
Your answers are completely absurd.

Yo duermo muy bien.
I sleep very well.

Tienes que trabajar más rápidamente.
You need to work more quickly.

When using two or more adverbs in a series, the suffix **-mente** is dropped from all except the very last one.

Ella trabaja rápida, diligente y eficientemente.
She works quickly, diligently, and efficiently.

La serpiente se mueve lenta y silenciosamente.
The snake moves slowly and quietly.

Work Out 2

Fill in the blank with the appropriate adverb.

1. Necesito el informe (inmediato). ____________
2. Marcos hace su trabajo (rápido y eficiente). ____________

   ____
3. (Frecuente) corremos por las mañanas en el parque. ____________
4. Marta habla (lento y claro). ____________
5. Ella no contesta el teléfono (rápido). ____________
6. (Nuevo) tenemos un problema con la computadora. ____________
7. El problema se va a resolver (fácil). ____________
8. Vosotros (normal) vais al cine los sábados por la tarde. ____________

ANSWER KEY

1. inmediatamente; 2. rápida y eficientemente; 3. Frecuentemente; 4. lenta y claramente; 5. rápidamente; 6. Nuevamente; 7. fácilmente; 8. normalmente

Take It Further

Watch out for those false cognates! False cognates are words that look the same or similar in English and in Spanish but actually have very different meanings. Here are three examples of adverbs that look the same but mean different things (immediately after each is the English equivalent of the Spanish word).

actualmente	*at the present time*
efectivamente/realmente	*actually*
en absoluto	*absolutely not*

totalmente	*absolutely*
sensiblemente	*perceptibly*
sensatamente	*sensibly*

Here are a few other words that are false cognates.

embarazada	*pregnant*
el delito	*crime*
contestar	*to answer*
atender	*to take care of*
asistir	*to be present; to attend*
éxito	*success*
suceso	*an event or happening*

Drive It Home

Replace the indirect object pronoun **me** with the indirect object pronoun indicated on each line.

A. **Carlita me da la servilleta.**

1. *to you (infml.)* ____________________

2. *to him/to her/to you (fml.)* ____________________

3. *to us* ____________________

4. *to them* ______________________________

____

B. **Juan me ofrece una copa de vino.**

1. *to you (infml.)* ______________________________

____

2. *to him/to her/to you (fml.)* ______________________________

____

3. *to us* ______________________________

____

4. *to them* ______________________________

____

ANSWER KEY

A. 1. **Carlita te da la servilleta.** 2. **Carlita le da la servilleta.** 3. **Carlita nos da la servilleta.** 4. **Carlita les da la servilleta.**

B. 1. **Juan te ofrece una copa de vino.** 2. **Juan le ofrece una copa de vino.** 3. **Juan nos ofrece una copa de vino.** 4. **Juan les ofrece una copa de vino.**

How Did You Do?

By now, you should be able to:

□ Name and describe types of food (Still unsure? Jump back to page 77.)

□ Use indirect object pronouns (Still unsure? Jump back to page 74.)

□ Form adverbs (Still unsure? Jump back to page 79.)

Lesson 6: Phrases

By the end of this lesson, you should be able to:

- ☐ Describe how food tastes
- ☐ Use expressions of quantity
- ☐ Form adverbs that don't end in **-mente**
- ☐ Talk about things that happened in the past

Phrase Builder 1

6A Phrase Builder 1 (CD 8, Track 1)

Me gustaría …	*I would like …*
Me puede traer …	*Could you bring me …*
Tengo ganas de …	*I feel like …*
No huele bien.	*It doesn't smell good.*
Huele mal.	*It smells bad.*
Sabe a vinagre.	*It tastes like vinegar.*
La leche está cortada.	*The milk is sour.*
¿Algo más?	*Anything else?*
No, nada más, gracias.	*No, nothing else, thanks.*
Las papayas tienen buena pinta.	*The papayas look good.*
¿Cuánto es?	*How much is it?*

Phrase Practice 1

Match the Spanish phrase on the left with its appropriate English translation on the right.

1. **¿Algo más?**	a. *How much is it?*
2. **¿Cuánto es?**	b. *Could you bring me …*
3. **Tengo ganas de …**	c. *It smells bad.*
4. **Me gustaría …**	d. *I feel like …*
5. **Me puede traer …**	e. *Anything else?*
6. **Huele mal.**	f. *I would like …*

ANSWER KEY

1. e; 2. a; 3. d; 4. f; 5. b; 6. c

Grammar Builder 1

MORE ON ADVERBS

6B Grammar Builder 1 (CD 8, Track 2)

There are, of course, a few adverbs that do not follow the pattern described in the previous lesson. Let's break them down into groups, starting with adverbs of quantity or degree.

bastante	*quite, enough*
poco	*a few, a little*
mucho	*a lot*
demasiado	*too much*
muy	*very*
tanto	*as much, as many*
más	*more*
menos	*less*
nada	*nothing*

algo	*somewhat*

And here are adverbs of time that don't end in **-mente**.

ahora	*now*
ya	*already, now*
tarde	*late*
temprano	*early*
pronto	*soon*
por fin	*finally*

And finally, here are adverbs of manner that don't end in **-mente**.

bien	*well*
mal	*badly, poorly*
mejor	*better*
peor	*worse*

Ella siempre se sirve demasiada comida.
She always serves herself too much food.

La comida está muy condimentada.
The food is very spicy.

Tengo poco tiempo para almorzar.
I have little time for lunch.

Yo desayuno temprano.
I have an early breakfast.

Work Out 1

Give the adverb that means the opposite of each of the adverbs below.

1. **mal** ______________________
2. **felizmente** ______________________
3. **poco** ______________________
4. **lentamente** ______________________
5. **temprano** ______________________
6. **algo** ______________________
7. **más** ______________________
8. **mejor** ______________________

ANSWER KEY

1. **bien**; 2. **tristemente**; 3. **mucho**; 4. **rápidamente**; 5. **tarde**; 6. **nada;** 7. **menos**; 8. **peor**

Phrase Builder 2

6C Phrase Builder 2 (CD 8, Track 3)

la lata de atún	*can of tuna*
la tajada de jamón	*slice of ham*
la pieza de pollo	*piece of chicken*
la bolsa de papas	*sack of potatoes*
la botella de agua mineral	*bottle of mineral water*
el cartón de jugo	*carton of juice*
el racimo de uvas	*bunch of grapes*
el frasco de mermelada	*jar of jam*
el manojo de zanahorias	*handful of carrots*

el paquete de galletas	*package of cookies*
la rebanada de pan	*slice of bread*
un litro de leche	*a liter of milk*
dos kilos de naranjas	*two kilos of oranges*

Phrase Practice 2

Fill in the blanks in each phrase based on the English translation.

1. **la** ______________________ **de atún** *can of tuna*
2. **la** ______________________ **de jamón** *slice of ham*
3. **la** ______________________ **de pollo** *piece of chicken*
4. **la** ______________________ **de papas** *sack of potatoes*
5. **la** ______________________ **de agua mineral** *bottle of mineral water*
6. **el** ______________________ **de uvas** *bunch of grapes*
7. **el** ______________________ **de mermelada** *jar of jam*
8. **el** ______________________ **de zanahorias** *handful of carrots*
9. **el** ______________________ **de galletas** *package of cookies*
10. **la** ______________________ **de pan** *slice of bread*

ANSWER KEY

1. **lata**; 2. **tajada**; 3. **pieza**; 4. **bolsa**; 5. **botella**; 6. **racimo**; 7. **frasco**; 8. **manojo**; 9. **paquete**; 10. **rebanada**

Grammar Builder 2

THE PRETERITE OF -AR VERBS AND ESTAR

6D Grammar Builder 2 (CD 8, Track 4)

Now that you're able to talk about things that are happening in the present and discuss plans for the future, it's time to learn how to talk about things that happened in the past. To do this, you will be using what's called the preterite tense. As with the present tense, in the preterite, Spanish verbs follow a pattern according to whether they end in **-ar**, **-er**, or **-ir**. Let's first take a look at regular verbs ending in **-ar**, like **estudiar**. To form the preterite, take the root of the verb and add the following endings.

PRETERITE ENDINGS OF REGULAR -AR VERBS	
yo -é	**nosotros/as -amos**
tú -aste	**vosotros/as -asteis**
él/ella/usted -ó	**ellos/ellas/ustedes -aron**

ESTUDIAR *(TO STUDY)* - PRETERITE	
yo estudié	**nosotros/as estudiamos**
tú estudiaste	**vosotros/as estudiasteis**
él/ella/usted estudió	**ellos/ellas/ustedes estudiaron**

You might have noticed that the conjugation of **-ar** verbs in the first person plural (**nosotros/as**) is the same in the present and in the preterite. Thus, **estudiamos** can mean *we speak* or *we spoke*; the context should always make it clear whether it is present or past.

Ayer hablé con mis padres por teléfono.
Yesterday, I spoke to my parents over the phone.

La semana pasada viajamos a París.
Last week we traveled to Paris.

Viajamos a las Bahamas para nuestras vacaciones.
We're traveling to the Bahamas on our vacation.

Ella terminó el informe anoche.
She finished the report last night.

Here are some useful time expressions you can use with the preterite.

ayer	*yesterday*
anoche	*last night*
la semana pasada	*last week*
el mes pasado	*last month*
el año pasado	*last year*
luego	*then*
entonces	*then*
después	*afterwards*
más tarde	*later*
una vez	*once*

Hablamos por teléfono y después tomamos un café.
We talked on the phone and then had a cup of coffee.

Caminamos por el parque y luego desayunamos en el hotel.
We walked through the park and then had breakfast at the hotel.

Even though the verb estar is an -ar verb, it follows an irregular pattern.

ESTAR *(TO BE)* - PRETERITE			
yo estuve	*I was*	nosotros/as estuvimos	*we were*
tú estuviste	*you were*	vosotros/as estuvisteis	*you were*
él/ella/usted estuvo	*he/she was, you were*	ellos/ellas/ustedes estuvieron	*they/you were*

Work Out 2

Change the following sentences to the preterite.

1. Tú caminas mucho. ______________________________

____

2. Ella saborea el vino tinto. ______________________________

____

3. Ella toca el piano. ______________________________

____

4. Ustedes hablan por teléfono con su jefe. ______________________________

____

5. Vosotros escucháis música clásica. ______________________________

____

6. **Él está en Nueva York.** ______________________________

____

7. **Hoy estamos en un restaurante italiano.** ______________________________

____

8. **Esta semana contestamos sus preguntas.** ______________________________

____

ANSWER KEY

1. **Tú caminaste mucho.** 2. **Ella saboreó el vino tinto.** 3. **Ella tocó el piano.** 4. **Ustedes hablaron por teléfono con su jefe.** 5. **Vosotros escuchasteis música clásica.** 6. **Él estuvo en Nueva York.** 7. **Ayer estuvimos en un restaurante italiano.** 8. **La semana pasada contestamos sus preguntas.**

Take It Further

Shopping for food can sometimes be an adventure, for not in every country will you find **supermercados** (*supermarkets*) like in the United States. Many times you will find that there are **plazas de mercado** (*outdoor markets*) where you can find just about anything from fruits and vegetables to cleaning products and even clothes. Going to the market is not only about buying; it's about socializing and interacting with other people. Of course, there are also food stores, and many of them tend to be smaller stores that specialize in a particular category of food.

la panadería	*bread bakery*
la pastelería	*bakery (for pastries, etc.)*
la lechería	*dairy store*
la carnicería	*butcher shop*
la pescadería	*fish shop, fish market*
la tienda	*convenience store*
la charcutería	*delicatessen (for cold cuts, etc.)*

Drive It Home

Let's practice the preterite of **-ar** verbs. Change the sentences below according to the subject indicated on each line.

A. **Yo viajé el mes pasado.**

1. **Tú** ______________________________
2. **Usted** ______________________________
3. **Él** ______________________________
4. **Nosotros** ______________________________

B. **Yo hablé por teléfono anoche.**

1. **Tú** ______________________________
2. **Usted** ______________________________
3. **Ella** ______________________________
4. **Ellos** ______________________________

ANSWER KEY

A. 1. **Tú viajaste el mes pasado.** 2. **Usted viajó el mes pasado.** 3. **Él viajó el mes pasado.** 4. **Nosotros viajamos el mes pasado.**

B. 1. **Tú hablaste por teléfono anoche.** 2. **Usted habló por teléfono anoche.** 3. **Ella habló por teléfono anoche.** 4. **Ellos hablaron por teléfono anoche.**

How Did You Do?

By now, you should be able to:

- ☐ Describe how food tastes (Still unsure? Jump back to page 84.)
- ☐ Use expressions of quantity (Still unsure? Jump back to page 87.)

- ☐ Form adverbs that don't end in **-mente** (Still unsure? Jump back to page 85.)
- ☐ Talk about things that happened in the past (Still unsure? Jump back to page 89.)

Lesson 7: Sentences

By the end of this lesson, you should be able to:

- ☐ Order food in a restaurant
- ☐ Shop for food in a grocery store
- ☐ Talk about things that happened in the past, using **-er** and **-ir** verbs
- ☐ Conjugate the past tense of irregular verbs

Sentence Builder 1

7A Sentence Builder 1 (CD 8, Track 5)

¿Cuál es el plato del día?	*What is the special of the day?*
¿Qué desea (usted) pedir?	*What would you like to order?*
¿Qué me recomienda?	*What do you recommend?*
¿Me podría traer la cuenta, por favor?	*Could you please bring me the check?*
¿Está incluida la propina en la cuenta?	*Is the tip included in the bill?*
¿Qué ingredientes tiene este plato?	*What ingredients are in this dish?*
¿Cómo quiere la carne?	*How would you like the meat?*
La quiero término medio, por favor.	*I want it medium-rare, please.*
La quiero término tres cuartos, por favor.	*I want it medium, please.*
La quiero bien asada, por favor.	*I want it well-done, please.*

Sentence Practice 1

Fill in the blanks in each sentence based on the English translation.

1. **¿Cuál es** ________________ **?** *What is the special of the day?*
2. **¿** ________________ **(usted) pedir?** *What would you like to order?*
3. **¿Qué me** ________________ **?** *What do you recommend?*
4. **La quiero** ________________ **, por favor.** *I want it medium-rare, please.*
5. **La quiero** ________________ **, por favor.** *I want it medium, please.*
6. **La quiero** ________________ **, por favor.** *I want it well-done, please.*

ANSWER KEY

1. el plato del día; 2. Qué desea; 3. recomienda; 4. término medio; 5. término tres cuartos; 6. bien asada

Grammar Builder 1

THE PRETERITE OF -ER AND -IR VERBS

7B Grammar Builder 1 (CD 8, Track 6)

Now let's look at the preterite of **-er** and **-ir** verbs, which follow the same pattern.

PRETERITE ENDINGS OF REGULAR -ER/-IR VERBS	
yo -í	nosotros/as -imos
tú -iste	vosotros/as -isteis
él/ella/usted -ió	ellos/ellas/ustedes -ieron

COMER *(TO EAT)* - PRETERITE	
yo comí	nosotros/as comimos
tú comiste	vosotros/as comisteis
él/ella/usted comió	ellos/ellas/ustedes comieron

ESCRIBIR *(TO WRITE)* - PRETERITE	
yo escribí	nosotros/as escribimos
tú escribiste	vosotros/as escribisteis
él/ella/usted escribió	ellos/ellas/ustedes escribieron

Take a look at how the verb oír (*to hear*) is conjugated in the preterite.

OÍR *(TO HEAR)* - PRETERITE	
yo oí	nosotros/as oímos
tú oíste	vosotros/as oísteis
él/ella/usted oyó	ellos/ellas/ustedes oyeron

You already know that there are several verbs that are irregular in the present tense, and, in fact, you've already learned the conjugation of estar in the preterite, which is also irregular. We'll take a look at a few irregular verbs in the preterite over the next couple of lessons. Just keep in mind that a verb's being irregular in the present does not necessarily mean that it will be irregular in the preterite. The verbs despertar(se), volver, almorzar, and salir are examples of this. They have some irregularity in the present, but they're perfectly regular in the preterite.

Yo me despierto a las ocho todos los días.
I get up at eight every day.

Yo me desperté a las nueve ayer.
Yesterday, I got up at nine.

Ellos vuelven esta tarde.
They come back this afternoon.

Ellos volvieron ayer por la noche.
They came back yesterday evening.

Tú almuerzas a la misma hora siempre.
You always have lunch at the same time.

Tú almorzaste más temprano ayer.
You had lunch earlier yesterday.

Yo salgo de la oficina a las tres.
I leave the office at three.

Ayer salí a las cinco.
Yesterday, I left at five.

Work Out 1

Rewrite the following sentences in the preterite. Use the clues given in parentheses when necessary.

1. **Yo bebo café y jugo de naranja con el desayuno.** ______________________

____

2. **Ella te escribe una carta todos los días. (ayer)** ______________________

____

3. **Vosotros coméis tostadas con mermelada.** ______________________

____

4. **Mañana vamos a salir tarde de la oficina. (ayer)** ______________________

____

5. **Ella come chocolate todo el día.** ______________________________

____

6. **Yo no oigo nada.** ______________________________

____

7. **Ellas parten para México.** ______________________________

____

ANSWER KEY

1. **Yo bebí café y jugo de naranja con el desayuno.** 2. **Ella te escribió una carta ayer.** 3. **Vosotros comisteis tostadas con mermelada.** 4. **Ayer salimos tarde de la oficina.** 5. **Ella comió chocolate todo el día.** 6. **Yo no oí nada.** 7. **Ellas partieron para México.**

Sentence Builder 2

7C Sentence Builder 2 (CD 8, Track 7)

¿En qué puedo servirle?	*How may I help you?*
Necesito un litro de leche.	*I need a liter of milk.*
¿Me puede dar un kilo de patatas?	*Could you give me a kilo of potatoes?*
¿Cuántas naranjas quiere?	*How many oranges do you want?*
Póngame dos chuletas de cordero, por favor.	*Give me two lamb chops, please.*
¿Quiere usted algo más?	*Would you like anything else?*
Eso es todo.	*That's all.*
¿Cuánto pesan las chuletas?	*How much do the chops weigh?*
¿Cómo están las papayas?	*How are the papayas?*
Deme tres botellas de vino tinto.	*Give me three bottles of red wine.*
¿Cuánto le debo?	*How much do I owe you?*

Sentence Practice 2

Fill in the blanks in each sentence based on the English translation.

1. Necesito ______________________. *I need a liter of milk.*
2. ______________________. *That's all.*
3. ¿______________ las chuletas? *How much do the chops weigh?*
4. ______________________ de vino tinto.

   Give me three bottles of red wine.
5. ______________________, por favor.

   Give me two lamb chops, please.
6. ¿______________________? *How much do I owe you?*

ANSWER KEY

1. un litro de leche; 2. Eso es todo; 3. Cuánto pesan; 4. Deme tres botellas; 5. Póngame dos chuletas de cordero; 6. Cuánto le debo

Grammar Builder 2

THE PRETERITE OF SER, IR, TENER, AND HACER

7D Grammar Builder 2 (CD 8, Track 8)

As we mentioned before, there are a few verbs that are irregular in the preterite. The verbs ser (*to be*) and ir (*to go*) take identical forms in the preterite.

SER *(TO BE)*/IR *(TO GO)* - PRETERITE	
yo fui	nosotros/as fuimos
tú fuiste	vosotros/as fuisteis
él/ella/usted fue	ellos/ellas/ustedes fueron

It is easy to distinguish ser from ir by context.

Ella fue profesora de inglés. (ser)

She was an English teacher.

Ella fue a Chile de vacaciones. (ir)

She went to Chile on vacation.

The verbs **tener** and **hacer** are also irregular in the preterite.

TENER *(TO HAVE)* - PRETERITE	
yo tuve	**nosotros/as tuvimos**
tú tuviste	**vosotros/as tuvisteis**
él/ella/usted tuvo	**ellos/ellas/ustedes tuvieron**

HACER *(TO DO, TO MAKE)* - PRETERITE	
yo hice	**nosotros/as hicimos**
tú hiciste	**vosotros/as hicisteis**
él/ella/usted hizo	**ellos/ellas/ustedes hicieron**

Tuvimos que esperar cuatro horas en el aeropuerto.

We had to wait four hours at the airport.

Yo hice un viaje muy largo.

I took (lit., made) a very long trip.

Work Out 2

Fill in the blanks with the correct form of the preterite of **ser**, **hacer**, **ir**, or **tener**.

1. **Yo** ____________________ **al supermercado esta mañana.**

2. **Tú** ______________________ **una familia pequeña.**

3. **Ellos** ______________________ **una presentación muy buena.**

4. **Ella** ______________________ **una cantante famosa.**

5. **Él** ______________________ **una llamada por teléfono al exterior.**

6. **Ellos** ______________________ **felices.**

7. **Ustedes** ______________________ **un apartamento en Nueva York.**

8. **Vosotros** ______________________ **a Costa Rica de vacaciones.**

ANSWER KEY

1. fui; 2. tuviste; 3. hicieron; 4. fue; 5. hizo; 6. fueron; 7. tuvieron; 8. fuisteis

Culture Note

In the Spanish-speaking world, eating habits are a bit different from those in the United States. In most countries, people follow the European way of eating; that is, they don't switch the fork from the left to the right hand when eating; the right hand is not kept on the lap, but rather on the table; and people usually wish each other **¡Buen provecho!** (*Enjoy your meal!*) before beginning to eat. Another custom is known as **la sobremesa**, or *after-dinner conversation*. Usually people stay seated around the table after lunch or dinner to chat while having a drink or a cup of coffee.

Let's practice the preterite of **-er** and **-ir** verbs. Change the sentence below according to the subject indicated on each line.

A. **Yo bebí una limonada ayer.**

1. **Tú** ______________________

2. **Usted** ______________________

3. **Él** ______________________

4. **Nosotros** ____________________

B. **Yo viví en España el año pasado.**

1. **Tú** ____________________

2. **Usted** ____________________

3. **Ella** ____________________

4. **Ellos** ____________________

ANSWER KEY

A. 1. **Tú bebiste una limonada ayer.** 2. **Usted bebió una limonada ayer.** 3. **Él bebió una limonada ayer.** 4. **Nosotros bebimos una limonada ayer.**

B. 1. **Tú viviste en España el año pasado.** 2. **Usted vivió en España el año pasado.** 3. **Ella vivió en España el año pasado.** 4. **Ellos vivieron en España el año pasado.**

How Did You Do?

By now, you should be able to:

- ☐ Order food in a restaurant (Still unsure? Jump back to page 94.)
- ☐ Shop for food in a grocery store (Still unsure? Jump back to page 98.)
- ☐ Talk about things that happened in the past using **-er** and **-ir** verbs (Still unsure? Jump back to page 95.)
- ☐ Conjugate the past tense of irregular verbs (Still unsure? Jump back to page 99.)

Lesson 8: Conversations

By the end of this lesson, you should be able to:

- ☐ Confidently make spelling changes in the preterite
- ☐ Conjugate irregular verbs in the preterite

Conversation 1

8A Conversation 1 (CD 8, Track 9 - Spanish Only; Track 10 - Spanish and English)

Roberto is travelling through Colombia. He is now in Villa de Leyva, at a local restaurant, ordering something for lunch.

Mesero:	**Buenas tardes, ¿qúe desea pedir?**
Roberto:	**¿Cuál es el plato del día?**
Mesero:	**Como entrada tenemos un ceviche de pescado; el plato principal es ajiaco con pollo, y de postre le podemos ofrecer arroz con leche, natilla o cuajada con melado.**
Roberto:	**¿Qué ingredientes tiene el ajiaco?**
Mesero:	**El ajiaco es una sopa espesa a base de pollo, diferentes tipos de papa y guascas, una hierba típica de la región. Se sirve con mazorca y aguacate.**
Roberto:	**Bueno, suena muy bien. Tráigame el ajiaco solamente.**
Mesero:	**¿Y de postre?**
Roberto:	**¿Cuál me recomienda?**
Mesero:	**La cuajada con melado está muy buena.**
Roberto:	**Muy bien.**
Mesero:	**¿Algo más?**
Roberto:	**Una cerveza, por favor.**

Waiter:	*Good afternoon, what would you like to order?*
Roberto:	*What's the special of the day?*
Waiter:	*As an appetizer we have ceviche de pescado; the main dish is ajiaco con pollo, and as a dessert we can offer you arroz con leche, natilla, or cuajada con melado.*
Roberto:	*What are the ingredients in ajiaco?*
Waiter:	*Ajiaco is a type of thick soup with chicken, different kinds of potatoes, and guascas, a typical herb of the region. It's served with corn and avocado.*
Roberto:	*Well, it sounds good. Bring me the ajiaco by itself.*
Waiter:	*And for dessert?*
Roberto:	*Which one do you recommend?*
Waiter:	*The cuajada con melado is very good.*
Roberto:	*Very good.*
Waiter:	*Anything else?*
Roberto:	*A beer, please.*

Culture Note

Villa de Leyva is probably one of the finest colonial towns in Colombia. It is located in Boyacá, a department in the center of the country. Founded in 1572, Villa de Leyva has a very small population—not more than 4,500 inhabitants—and is considered a national monument to colonial architecture. It is a popular recreational destination for people living in Bogotá because it is only a couple of hours away by car.

Conversation Practice 1

Fill in the blanks below with the appropriate word based on the English translations and the dialogue above.

1. **De postre** ________________ **arroz con leche, natilla o cuajada con melado.**

   As a dessert we can offer you arroz con leche, natilla, or cuajada con melado.

2. **¿Qué** ________________ **tiene el ajiaco?** *What are the ingredients in ajiaco?*

3. ________________ **con mazorca y aguacate.** *It's served with corn and avocado.*

4. **Bueno,** ________________ **muy bien.** *Well, it sounds good.*

5. **¿Cuál** ________________**?** *Which one do you recommend?*

ANSWER KEY

1. **le podemos ofrecer**; 2. **ingredientes**; 3. **Se sirve**; 4. **suena**; 5. **me recomienda**

Grammar Builder 1

SPELLING CHANGES IN THE PRETERITE

8B Grammar Builder 1 (CD 8, Track 11)

Most of the time, irregularities in the preterite have to do with spelling changes. For example, verbs ending in **-car** change the **c** to **qu** before **e**; verbs ending in **-gar** change the **g** to **gu** before **e**; and verbs ending in **-zar** change the **z** to **c** before **e**.

SACAR *(TO TAKE OUT)* - PRETERITE	
yo saqué	**nosotros/as sacamos**
tú sacaste	**vosotros/as sacasteis**
él/ella/usted sacó	**ellos/ellas/ustedes sacaron**

LLEGAR *(TO ARRIVE)* - PRETERITE	
yo llegué	**nosotros/as llegamos**
tú llegaste	**vosotros/as llegasteis**
él/ella/usted llegó	**ellos/ellas/ustedes llegaron**

EMPEZAR ***(TO BEGIN)*** **- PRETERITE**	
yo empecé	**nosotros/as empezamos**
tú empezaste	**vosotros/as empezasteis**
él/ella/usted empezó	**ellos/ellas/ustedes empezaron**

Often, **i** is changed to **y**.

LEER ***(TO READ)*** **- PRETERITE**	
yo leí	**nosotros/as leímos**
tú leíste	**vosotros/as leísteis**
él/ella/usted leyó	**ellos/ellas/ustedes leyeron**

CREER ***(TO BELIEVE)*** **- PRETERITE**	
yo creí	**nosotros/as creímos**
tú creíste	**vosotros/as creísteis**
él/ella/usted creyó	**ellos/ellas/ustedes creyeron**

The verbs **decir** (*to say*) and **traer** (*to bring*) take a **j** between the vowels.

DECIR ***(TO SAY)*** **- PRETERITE**	
yo dije	**nosotros/as dijimos**
tú dijiste	**vosotros/as dijisteis**
él/ella/usted dijo	**ellos/ellas/ustedes dijeron**

TRAER ***(TO BRING)*** **- PRETERITE**	
yo traje	**nosotros/as trajimos**
tú trajiste	**vosotros/as trajisteis**
él/ella/usted trajo	**ellos/ellas/ustedes trajeron**

¿Llegaste a tiempo a tu cita?
Did you get to your appointment on time?

Leyó el periódico y se marchó al trabajo.
She/He read the newspaper and left for work.

Le dije la verdad a él.
I told him the truth.

Nos trajeron un vino excelente.
They brought us an excellent wine.

Work Out 1

Change the sentence using the pronoun given in parentheses.

1. **Marqué las cajas con nuestros nombres y dirección. (usted)** ______________
2. **No creí lo que dijo. (vosotros)** ______________
3. **Ellas dijeron la verdad. (nosotras)** ______________
4. **Pagamos la cuenta. (yo)** ______________
5. **¿Trajeron lápiz y papel para tomar nota? (usted)** ______________

6. Él apagó la luz muy tarde. (ellas) ______

______

7. Ustedes comenzaron a estudiar italiano. (él) ______

______

8. No leísteis el periódico esta mañana. (tú) ______

______

ANSWER KEY

1. Usted marcó las cajas con nuestros nombres y dirección. 2. No creísteis lo que dijo. 3. Nosotras dijimos la verdad. 4. Pagué la cuenta. 5. ¿Trajo lápiz y papel para tomar nota? 6. Ellas apagaron la luz muy tarde. 7. Él comenzó a estudiar italiano. 8. No leíste el periódico esta mañana.

Conversation 2

8C Conversation 2 (CD 8, Track 12 - Spanish Only; Track 13 - Spanish and English)

Roberto has decided to help his friend Marisa, who is busy working, with grocery shopping. He's at a local grocery store, getting a few things.

Tendero:	¿En qué puedo servirle?
Roberto:	Necesito dos litros de leche.
Tendero:	¿Entera o descremada?
Roberto:	Entera. También quiero un kilo de naranjas, una lata de atún, una bolsa de papas y un manojo de zanahorias.
Tendero:	¿Algo más?
Roberto:	Las papayas tienen buena pinta.
Tendero:	Sí, están muy dulces. ¿Quiere llevar una?
Roberto:	Sí, pero no muy grande.
Tendero:	¿Qué le parece ésta?
Roberto:	Sí, se ve bien. ¿Cuánto le debo?
Tendero:	Son diez mil trescientos pesos.
Roberto:	Aquí tiene. Muchas gracias. Hasta luego.

Shopkeeper:	*How may I help you?*
Roberto:	*I need two liters of milk.*
Shopkeeper:	*Whole or skim milk?*
Roberto:	*Whole. I also want a kilo of oranges, a can of tuna, a bag of potatoes, and a handful of carrots.*
Shopkeeper:	*Anything else?*
Roberto:	*The papayas look good.*
Shopkeeper:	*Yes, they're very sweet. Would you like to take one?*
Roberto:	*Yes, but not a very big one.*
Shopkeeper:	*How about this one?*
Roberto:	*Yes, it looks good. How much do I owe you?*
Shopkeeper:	*That's ten thousand, three hundred pesos.*
Roberto:	*Here you are. Thanks. Good-bye.*

Take It Further

The metric system is almost always used in the Spanish-speaking world. So you will hear people buying things like:

cuatro onzas de queso	*four ounces of cheese*
media libra de naranjas	*a half pound of oranges*
dos litros de leche	*two liters of milk*
cien gramos de crema	*a hundred grams of cream*
una libra de arroz	*a pound of rice*
un kilo de patatas	*a kilo of potatoes*

Conversation Practice 2

Fill in the blanks below with the appropriate word based on the English translations and the dialogue above.

1. **¿En qué** ________________? *How may I help you?*
2. **También quiero** ________________**, una lata de atún,** ________________ **y un manojo de zanahorias.** *I also want a kilo of oranges, a can of tuna, a bag of potatoes, and a handful of carrots.*
3. **Las papayas tienen** ________________. *The papayas look good.*
4. **¿Qué** ________________ **ésta?** *How about this one?*
5. **Sí,** ________ **bien.** *Yes, it looks good.*

ANSWER KEY

1. **puedo servirle**; 2. **un kilo de naranjas**/**una bolsa de papas**; 3. **buena pinta**; 4. **le parece**; 5. **se ve**

Grammar Builder 2

IRREGULAR VERBS IN THE PRETERITE

8D Grammar Builder 2 (CD 8, Track 14)

The following verbs follow a slightly different pattern of conjugation in the preterite.

PODER *(TO BE ABLE)* - PRETERITE	
yo pude	nosotros/as pudimos
tú pudiste	vosotros/as pudisteis
él/ella/usted pudo	ellos/ellas/ustedes pudieron

PONER ***(TO PUT)*** **- PRETERITE**	
yo puse	**nosotros/as pusimos**
tú pusiste	**vosotros/as pusisteis**
él/ella/usted puso	**ellos/ellas/ustedes pusieron**

SABER ***(TO KNOW)*** **- PRETERITE**	
yo supe	**nosotros/as supimos**
tú supiste	**vosotros/as supisteis**
él/ella/usted supo	**ellos/ellas/ustedes supieron**

QUERER ***(TO WANT)*** **- PRETERITE**	
yo quise	**nosotros/as quisimos**
tú quisiste	**vosotros/as quisisteis**
él/ella/usted quiso	**ellos/ellas/ustedes quisieron**

ANDAR ***(TO WALK)*** **- PRETERITE**	
yo anduve	**nosotros/as anduvimos**
tú anduviste	**vosotros/as anduvisteis**
él/ella/usted anduvo	**ellos/ellas/ustedes anduvieron**

VENIR ***(TO COME)*** **- PRETERITE**	
yo vine	**nosotros/as vinimos**
tú viniste	**vosotros/as vinisteis**
él/ella/usted vino	**ellos/ellas/ustedes vinieron**

Él no pudo comer.

He couldn't eat.

Ella puso el pollo en agua caliente.

She put the chicken in hot water.

Ayer supimos la noticia.

Yesterday we learned the news.

Note that **saber** used in the preterite changes its meaning: *to learn, to find out.*

Nosotros no quisimos pagar la cuenta.

We didn't want to pay the bill.

Anduviste por todo el museo.

You walked through the entire museum.

Mi esposo vino a casa tarde.

My husband came home late.

Work Out 2

Fill in the blanks with the correct Spanish preterite form of the English verb in parentheses.

1. **¿Dónde** ________________ **él mi suéter?** *(to put)*
2. **Ella no** ________________ **llamar a sus padres.** *(to want)*
3. **Usted no** ________________ **completar el cuestionario.** *(to be able)*
4. **Él** ________________ **de Argentina.** *(to come)*
5. **Yo no** ________________ **comer en ese restaurante.** *(to be able)*

6. **Ayer nosotros** ______________ **dos horas por el parque.** *(to walk)*

7. **¿Vosotros** ______________ **cómo llegar a la casa de Juan?** *(to find out)*

8. **Ellos** ______________ **ayer por la noche.** *(to come)*

ANSWER KEY

1. **puso**; 2. **quiso**; 3. **pudo**; 4. **vino**; 5. **pude**; 6. **anduvimos**; 7. **supisteis**; 8. **vinieron**

Culture Note

Many people think that food in all of the Spanish-speaking world is hot and spicy. Well, that is perhaps the case in Mexico and a few other countries in Central America. But the truth is, the cuisines of Spanish-speaking countries are as varied as the people who enjoy them. In Spain, you will find **paella** (a saffron-spiced rice with different kinds of meat and seafood) and the traditional **tortilla de patatas** (potato omelet). Argentina is known for the excellent quality of its beef; steaks are usually served with **chimichurri**, a green sauce of herbs and chilies, and **empanadas** (meat and cheese pastries) are very popular for lunch. In Venezuela and Colombia, **arepas** (baked cornmeal cakes) are traditionally served with breakfast, and, on the Caribbean coast, **arroz con coco** (coconut rice) is a typical side dish. Popular desserts in Colombia are **arroz con leche** (rice pudding), **cuajada con melado** (soft cheese with melted sugar), and **natilla** (soft custard). And in Peru, **ceviche** (raw fish marinated in lime juice) is one of the country's staple dishes.

Drive It Home

Give the preterite **yo** form of the following irregular verbs:

1. **poder** ______________

2. **poner** ______________

3. **saber** ______________

4. **querer** ______________

5. **andar** ______________________

6. **venir** ______________________

ANSWER KEY

1. **Yo pude.** 2. **Yo puse.** 3. **Yo supe.** 4. **Yo quise.** 5. **Yo anduve.** 6. **Yo vine.**

How Did You Do?

By now, you should be able to:

- ☐ Confidently make spelling changes in the preterite
  (Still unsure? Jump back to page 105.)
- ☐ Conjugate irregular verbs in the preterite
  (Still unsure? Jump back to page 110.)

Don't forget to practice and reinforce what you've learned by visiting **www.livinglanguage.com/languagelab** for flashcards, games, and quizzes for Unit 2!

Unit 2 Essentials

Vocabulary Essentials

MEALS AND UTENSILS

	breakfast
	lunch
	snack time
	dinner
	food, dinner
	spoon
	fork
	knife
	glass
	wineglass
	cup
	plate, dish
	napkin
	menu
	bill, check
	tip

[Pg. 73]

FOOD VOCABULARY

	food
	bread
	meat
	chicken
	pork
	vegetable
	tomato
	bean
	butter
	juice
	rice
	hard
	overcooked
	burnt
	spicy
	bad, rotten
	spoiled
	sour
	sweet
	salty
	bitter
	grilled
	fried
	smoked

[Pg. 77]

FOOD EXPRESSIONS

	I would like . . .
	Could you bring me . . .
	I feel like . . .
	It doesn't smell good.
	It smells bad.
	It tastes like vinegar.
	The milk is sour.
	Anything else?
	No, nothing else, thanks.
	The papayas look good.
	How much is it?

[Pg. 84]

FOOD QUANTITY EXPRESSIONS

	can of tuna
	slice of ham
	piece of chicken
	sack of potatoes
	bottle of mineral water
	carton of juice
	bunch of grapes
	jar of jam
	handful of carrots
	package of cookies
	slice of bread

	a liter of milk
	two kilos of oranges
	four ounces of cheese
	a half pound of oranges
	two liters of milk
	a hundred grams of cream
	a pound of rice
	a kilo of potatoes

[Pgs. 87 and 109]

FOOD VENDORS

	bread bakery
	bakery (for pastries, etc.)
	dairy store
	butcher shop
	fish shop, fish market
	convenience store
	delicatessen

[Pg. 92]

RESTAURANT EXPRESSIONS

	What is the special of the day?
	What would you like to order?
	What do you recommend?
	Could you please bring me the check?
	Is the tip included in the bill?

	What ingredients are in this dish?
	How would you like the meat?
	I want it medium-rare, please.
	I want it medium, please.
	I want it well-done, please.

[Pg. 94]

FOOD SHOPPING EXPRESSIONS

	How may I help you?
	I need a liter of milk.
	Could you give me a kilo of potatoes?
	How many oranges do you want?
	Give me two lamb chops, please.
	Would you like anything else?
	That's all.
	How much do the chops weigh?
	How are the papayas?
	Give me three bottles of red wine.
	How much do I owe you?

[Pg. 98]

ADVERBS ENDING IN –MENTE

	happily
	sadly
	slowly
	quickly

	anew, once again
	frequently
	normally
	at the present time
	actually
	absolutely
	perceptibly
	sensibly

[Pgs. 79 and 81]

ADVERBS NOT ENDING IN –MENTE

	quite, enough
	a few, a little
	a lot
	too much
	very
	as much/as many
	more
	less
	very
	nothing
	somewhat
	now
	already, now
	late
	early

	soon
	finally
	well
	badly, poorly
	better
	worse

[Pg. 85]

TIME EXPRESSIONS USED TO TALK ABOUT THE PAST

	yesterday
	last night
	last week
	last month
	last year
	then
	then
	afterwards
	later
	once

[Pg. 90]

Grammar Essentials

INDIRECT OBJECT PRONOUNS			
me	*(to/for) me*	**nos**	*(to/for) us*
te	*(to/for) you (infml. sg.)*	**os**	*(to/for) you (infml. pl.)*
le	*(to/for) him, her, it, you (fml. sg.)*	**les**	*(to/for) them, you (fml. pl.)*

Indirect object pronouns are placed before a single conjugated verb or verb phrase, or attached to the end of a verbal phrase.
Indirect object pronouns are attached to affirmative commands, but placed before negative ones.

ADVERBS

Adverbs are formed by adding -mente to the feminine form of adjectives ending in -o and to the final -e or consonant of any other adjective.
When used to describe a verb, adverbs come after the verb they modify.
When used to describe an adjective or another adverb, adverbs come in front of the word they modify.
An adverb can come at the beginning of a sentence if it describes a characteristic of, or expresses an attitude toward, the whole sentence.
When using two or more adverbs in a series, the suffix -mente is dropped from all except the very last one.

THE PRETERITE

The preterite is used to describe actions in the past. To form the preterite, take the root of the verb and add the following endings.

PRETERITE ENDINGS OF REGULAR -AR VERBS	
yo -é	nosotros/as -amos
tú -aste	vosotros/as -asteis
él/ella/usted -ó	ellos/ellas/ustedes -aron

PRETERITE ENDINGS OF REGULAR -ER/-IR VERBS	
yo -í	nosotros/as -imos
tú -iste	vosotros/as -isteis
él/ella/usted -ió	ellos/ellas/ustedes -ieron

VERBS

ANDAR *(TO WALK)* - PRETERITE	
yo anduve	nosotros/as anduvimos
tú anduviste	vosotros/as anduvisteis
él/ella/usted anduvo	ellos/ellas/ustedes anduvieron

COMER *(TO EAT)* - PRETERITE	
yo comí	nosotros/as comimos
tú comiste	vosotros/as comisteis
él/ella/usted comió	ellos/ellas/ustedes comieron

CREER *(TO BELIEVE)* - PRETERITE	
yo creí	nosotros/as creímos
tú creíste	vosotros/as creísteis
él/ella/usted creyó	ellos/ellas/ustedes creyeron

DECIR *(TO SAY)* - PRETERITE	
yo dije	nosotros/as dijimos
tú dijiste	vosotros/as dijisteis
él/ella/usted dijo	ellos/ellas/ustedes dijeron

EMPEZAR *(TO BEGIN)* - PRETERITE	
yo empecé	nosotros/as empezamos
tú empezaste	vosotros/as empezasteis
él/ella/usted empezó	ellos/ellas/ustedes empezaron

ESCRIBIR *(TO WRITE)* - PRETERITE	
yo escribí	nosotros/as escribimos
tú escribiste	vosotros/as escribisteis
él/ella/usted escribió	ellos/ellas/ustedes escribieron

ESTAR *(TO BE)* - PRETERITE	
yo estuve	nosotros/as estuvimos
tú estuviste	vosotros/as estuvisteis
él/ella/usted estuvo	ellos/ellas/ustedes estuvieron

ESTUDIAR *(TO STUDY)* - PRETERITE	
yo estudié	nosotros/as estudiamos
tú estudiaste	vosotros/as estudiasteis
él/ella/usted estudió	ellos/ellas/ustedes estudiaron

HACER *(TO DO, TO MAKE)* - PRETERITE	
yo hice	nosotros/as hicimos
tú hiciste	vosotros/as hicisteis
él/ella/usted hizo	ellos/ellas/ustedes hicieron

IR *(TO GO)* - PRETERITE	
yo fui	nosotros/as fuimos
tú fuiste	vosotros/as fuisteis
él/ella/usted fue	ellos/ellas/ustedes fueron

LEER *(TO READ)* - PRETERITE	
yo leí	nosotros/as leímos
tú leíste	vosotros/as leísteis
él/ella/usted leyó	ellos/ellas/ustedes leyeron

LLEGAR *(TO ARRIVE)* - PRETERITE	
yo llegué	nosotros/as llegamos
tú llegaste	vosotros/as llegasteis
él/ella/usted llegó	ellos/ellas/ustedes llegaron

OÍR *(TO HEAR)* - PRETERITE	
yo oí	nosotros/as oímos
tú oíste	vosotros/as oísteis
él/ella/usted oyó	ellos/ellas/ustedes oyeron

PODER *(TO BE ABLE)* - PRETERITE	
yo pude	nosotros/as pudimos
tú pudiste	vosotros/as pudisteis
él/ella/usted pudo	ellos/ellas/ustedes pudieron

PONER *(TO PUT)* - PRETERITE	
yo puse	nosotros/as pusimos
tú pusiste	vosotros/as pusisteis
él/ella/usted puso	ellos/ellas/ustedes pusieron

QUERER *(TO WANT)* - PRETERITE	
yo quise	nosotros/as quisimos
tú quisiste	vosotros/as quisisteis
él/ella/usted quiso	ellos/ellas/ustedes quisieron

SABER *(TO KNOW)* - PRETERITE	
yo supe	nosotros/as supimos
tú supiste	vosotros/as supisteis
él/ella/usted supo	ellos/ellas/ustedes supieron

SACAR *(TO TAKE OUT)* - PRETERITE	
yo saqué	nosotros/as sacamos
tú sacaste	vosotros/as sacasteis
él/ella/usted sacó	ellos/ellas/ustedes sacaron

SER *(TO BE)* - PRETERITE	
yo fui	nosotros/as fuimos
tú fuiste	vosotros/as fuisteis
él/ella/usted fue	ellos/ellas/ustedes fueron

TENER *(TO HAVE)* - PRETERITE	
yo tuve	nosotros/as tuvimos
tú tuviste	vosotros/as tuvisteis
él/ella/usted tuvo	ellos/ellas/ustedes tuvieron

TRAER *(TO BRING)* - PRETERITE	
yo traje	nosotros/as trajimos
tú trajiste	vosotros/as trajisteis
él/ella/usted trajo	ellos/ellas/ustedes trajeron

VENIR *(TO COME)* - PRETERITE	
yo vine	nosotros/as vinimos
tú viniste	vosotros/as vinisteis
él/ella/usted vino	ellos/ellas/ustedes vinieron

Unit 2 Quiz

A. Rewrite the sentence with the subject in parentheses.

1. Yo traje un racimo de uvas. (Ella) ____________________

2. Patricia viajó a las Bahamas el año pasado. (Patricia y Pablo) ____________________

3. Ella fue al parque por la noche. (Ustedes) ____________________

4. Tú hiciste un viaje muy largo. (Yo) ____________________

5. Mateo sacó un libro de la biblioteca. (Tú) ____________________

6. Ellos volvieron ayer por la noche. (Usted) ____________________

7. Ayer salí a las seis de la tarde. (Nosotros) ____________________

8. Hablamos por teléfono y después tomamos un café. (Él) ____________________

B. Replace the underlined indirect object pronoun with the clue in parentheses.

1. **Ella te da el desayuno.** *(to me)* ____________________

____

2. **Él me ofrece un regalo.** *(to you, infml. sg.)* ____________________

____

3. **El doctor me da la receta.** *(to you, fml. sg.)* ____________________

____

4. **Ella le escribe una carta.** *(to me)* ____________________

____

5. **Mi amiga me compró un regalo.** *(to us)* ____________________

____

6. **Él nos da una copa de vino.** *(to her)* ____________________

____

7. **Nosotros te damos las gracias.** *(to them)* ____________________

____

8. **Yo te digo la verdad.** *(to you, infml. pl.)* ____________________

____

C. Choose the appropriate vocabulary word.

1. **Por la mañana como el desayuno y al mediodía tomo** ____________________ **.** **(el almuerzo/la cena)**

2. **Yo le doy al camarero** ____________________ **. (el cuchillo/la propina)**

3. **Yo compré dos** ____________________ **de vino tinto. (botellas/piezas)**

4. Nosotros bebimos café y ______________ con el desayuno. (jugo/vino)

5. Él ______________ un libro interesante. (creyó/leyó)

6. Es bueno ______________ la verdad. (decir/traer)

7. La comida de la noche es ______________. (la cena/el desayuno)

8. Yo ______________ a Chile el año pasado. (fui/oí)

D. Fill in the blanks by conjugating the verb in parentheses in the *preterite*.

1. Ella ______________ por la ciudad. (andar)

2. El estudiante ______________ completar su tarea a tiempo. (poder)

3. Usted ______________ el periódico sobre la mesa. (poner)

4. Yo ______________ a tiempo al restaurante. (llegar)

5. Nosotros ______________ ir al parque de diversiones. (querer)

6. Los camareros ______________ con la comida (venir)

7. Ustedes ______________ regalos para las fiesta. (traer)

8. Usted ______________ siempre cosas interesantes. (decir)

ANSWER KEY

A. 1. Ella trajo un racimo de uvas. 2. Patricia y Pablo viajaron a las Bahamas el año pasado. 3. Ustedes fueron al parque por la noche. 4. Yo hice un viaje muy largo. 5. Tú sacaste un libro de la biblioteca. 6. Usted volvió ayer por la noche. 7. Ayer salimos a las seis de la tarde. 8. Habló por teléfono y después tomó un café.

B. 1. Ella me da el desayuno. 2. Él te ofrece un regalo. 3. El doctor le da la receta. 4. Ella me escribe una carta. 5. Mi amiga nos compró un regalo. 6. Él le da una copa de vino. 7. Nosotros les damos las gracias. 8. Yo os digo la verdad.

C. 1. el almuerzo; 2. la propina; 3. botellas; 4. jugo; 5. leyó; 6. decir; 7. la cena; 8. fui

D. 1. anduvo; 2. pudo; 3. puso; 4. llegué; 5. quisimos; 6. vinieron; 7. trajeron; 8. dijo

How Did You Do?

Give yourself a point for every correct answer, then use the following key to determine whether or not you're ready to move on:

0–7 points: It's probably best to go back and study the lessons again to make sure you understood everything completely. Take your time; it's not a race! Make sure you spend time reviewing vocabulary with the flashcards and reading through each grammar note carefully.

8–16 points: If the questions you missed were in sections A or B, you may want to review the vocabulary again; if you missed answers mostly in sections C or D, check the unit essentials to make sure you have your conjugations and other grammar basics down.

17–20 points: Feel free to move on to the next unit! You're doing a great job.

points

Unit 3: School and Work

In this unit, you'll learn more about expressing the past. You will also learn lots of useful vocabulary related to school and work. By the end of this unit, you should be able to:

- □ Talk confidently about school and work
- □ Know how to use direct and indirect objects in a sentence
- □ Talk about the recent past
- □ Express obligation and necessity
- □ Identify when to use the imperfect or the preterite
- □ Conjugate regular and irregular verbs in the imperfect

Lesson 9: Words

By the end of this lesson, you should be able to:

- □ Talk generally about school and work
- □ Use more irregular verbs in the preterite
- □ Use both indirect and direct object pronouns in one sentence

Word Builder 1

9A Word Builder 1 (CD 8, Track 15)

la materia	*school subject*
la(s) matemática(s)	*mathematics*
la historia	*history*
la literatura	*literature*
la ciencia	*science*
la biología	*biology*
la química	*chemistry*
la geografía	*geography*
la filosofía	*philosophy*
la asignatura	*course*
los estudios	*studies*
la beca	*scholarship*
matricularse	*to register*
la biblioteca	*library*
la sala de conferencias	*lecture hall, conference room*
graduarse	*to graduate*
los derechos de matrícula	*tuition*
la tesis	*dissertation*
la licenciatura	*master's degree (a degree between a bachelor's degree and a master's degree)*
el título académico	*academic degree*

Word Practice 1

Match the Spanish word on the left with its appropriate English translation on the right.

1. **la materia** a. *studies*
2. **los estudios** b. *course*
3. **la asignatura** c. *library*
4. **la tesis** d. *school subject*
5. **la biblioteca** e. *scholarship*
6. **la beca** f. *dissertation*

ANSWER KEY

1. d; 2. a; 3. b; 4. f; 5. c; 6. e

Grammar Builder 1

MORE IRREGULAR VERBS IN THE PRETERITE

9B Grammar Builder 1 (CD 8, Track 16)

Here are the irregular preterite forms of **dar** (*to give*), **pedir** (*to ask for*), and **ver** (*to see*).

DAR *(TO GIVE)* - PRETERITE	
yo di	**nosotros/as dimos**
tú diste	**vosotros/as disteis**
él/ella/usted dio	**ellos/ellas/ustedes dieron**

PEDIR *(TO ASK FOR)* - PRETERITE	
yo pedí	**nosotros/as pedimos**
tú pediste	**vosotros/as pedisteis**
él/ella/usted pidió	**ellos/ellas/ustedes pidieron**

VER *(TO SEE)* - PRETERITE	
yo vi	nosotros/as vimos
tú viste	vosotros/as visteis
él/ella/usted vio	ellos/ellas/ustedes vieron

Ella nos dio una noticia muy buena.
She gave us very good news.

Él me pidió mi número de teléfono.
He asked me for my phone number.

Vimos una película romántica.
We saw a romantic movie.

In Spanish, we use the verb **haber** to say *there is/there are*. In the present tense, the form is **hay**, and in the preterite, it is **hubo**.

Hubo mucha gente en la fiesta de anoche.
There were a lot of people at last night's party.

Hubo solamente una película extranjera en el festival de cine.
There was only one foreign movie in the film festival.

Work Out 1

Fill in the blank with the correct preterite form of **dar**, **pedir**, **ver**, or **haber**.

1. **Ella nos** ______________________ **disculpas.**

2. **Tú me ________________ un libro muy interesante para leer.**

3. **________________ una reunión extraordinaria ayer.**

4. **Ustedes ________________ el accidente.**

5. **________________ cinco personas para la entrevista.**

6. **Ella le ________________ una carta de referencia.**

7. **Yo no ________________ al ladrón.**

8. **Nosotros te ________________ la carta la semana pasada.**

ANSWER KEY

1. **pidió**; 2. **diste**; 3. **Hubo**; 4. **vieron**; 5. **Hubo**; 6. **pidió**; 7. **vi**; 8. **dimos**

Word Builder 2

9C Word Builder 2 (CD 8, Track 17)

la cita	*appointment*
la reunión	*meeting*
la sala de conferencias	*conference room, lecture hall*
el contrato	*contract*
el/la empleado/a	*employee*
el sindicato	*union*
el seguro	*insurance*
la entrevista	*interview*
la cualificación	*qualification*
la hoja de vida/la historia de trabajo	*résumé*
las referencias	*references*
el/la jubilado/a	*retired person*

Word Practice 2

Match the Spanish word on the left with its appropriate English translation on the right.

1. **el seguro** a. *employee*
2. **el sindicato** b. *insurance*
3. **la reunión** c. *union*
4. **el/la empleado/a** d. *meeting*
5. **la entrevista** e. *appointment*
6. **la cita** f. *interview*

ANSWER KEY

1. b; 2. c; 3.d ; 4. a; 5. f; 6. e

Grammar Builder 2

DOUBLE OBJECT PRONOUNS

9D Grammar Builder 2 (CD 8, Track 18)

In Units 1 and 2, you learned about direct and indirect object pronouns. They are basically not much different from one another, except for the third person singular and plural.

INDIRECT OBJECT PRONOUNS	DIRECT OBJECT PRONOUNS
me (a mí)	**me**
te (a ti)	**te**
le (a él/ella/usted)	**lo/la**
nos (a nosotros/as)	**nos**
os (a vosotros/as)	**os**
les (a ellos/ellas/ustedes)	**los/las**

Just as in English, it's possible to have both a direct object pronoun and an indirect object pronoun in the same sentence in Spanish. In that case, the indirect object pronoun comes first. To avoid the awkward repetition of the same sounds, use **se** instead of **le** or **les** preceding **lo(s)/la(s)**. In order to clarify the meaning of **se**, use **a él/a ella/a usted/a ellos/a ellas/a ustedes**.

Ellos me dan un libro (a mí).
They give me a book.

Ellos me lo dan (a mí).
They give it to me.

Nosotros le entregamos el informe a ella.
We gave the report to her.

Nosotros se lo entregamos a ella.
We gave it to her.

When the pronouns appear in sentences with more than one verb, they can be placed either before the verbs or attached to the end of the main verb.

Él está entregando su examen al profesor.
He is giving his test to the teacher.

Él se lo está entregando.
He is giving it to him.

Él está entregándoselo.
He is giving it to him.

Vosotros vais a dar una sorpresa a Juan.
You are going to give Juan a surprise.

Vosotros se la vais a dar.

You are going to give it to him.

Vosotros vais a dársela.

You are going to give it to him.

Work Out 2

Replace the direct object in these sentences with the corresponding direct object pronoun.

1. **Ella nos está vendiendo una radio.** ______________________

____

2. **El estudiante hace el trabajo.** ______________________

____

3. **Yo me compré unos pantalones negros.** ______________________

____

4. **Vosotros os tomáis una medicina.** ______________________

____

5. **Él le va a decir la verdad a Sofía.** ______________________

____

6. **Ellas le trajeron un regalo.** ______________________

____

7. Él no puede comer carne. ______________________________

____

8. Ellos le están enviando un correo a su jefe. ______________________________

____

ANSWER KEY

1. Ella nos la está vendiendo. 2. El estudiante lo hace. 3. Yo me los compré. 4. Vosotros os la tomáis. 5. Él se la va a decir. 6. Ellas se lo trajeron. 7. Él no la puede comer. 8. Ellos se lo están enviando.

Take It Further

Here are a few more false cognates that you should be aware of.

la conferencia	*lecture*
la lectura	*a reading*
la librería	*bookstore*
el colegio	*elementary or secondary school*
la facultad	*department*
el profesorado	*faculty*

Drive It Home

Write the correct *preterite* form of the verb indicated in parentheses.

1. Yo ______________________________ la cuenta. (pedir)
2. Ella ______________________________ la cuenta. (pedir)
3. Nosotros ______________________________ la cuenta. (pedir)
4. Ustedes ______________________________ la cuenta. (pedir)
5. Rogelio ______________________________ una película fantástica. (ver)

6. **Rogelio y Carmen** ______________________ **una película fantástica. (ver)**

7. **Tú** ______________________ **una película fantástica. (ver)**

8. **Tú y yo** ______________________ **una película fantástica. (ver)**

ANSWER KEY

1. **pedí**; 2. **pidió**; 3. **pedimos**; 4. **pidieron**; 5. **vio**; 6. **vieron**; 7. **viste**; 8. **vimos**

How Did You Do?

By now, you should be able to:

- ☐ Talk generally about school and work
  (Still unsure? Jump back to pages 132 and 135.)
- ☐ Use more irregular verbs in the preterite
  (Still unsure? Jump back to page 133.)
- ☐ Use both indirect and direct object pronouns in one sentence
  (Still unsure? Jump back to page 136.)

Lesson 10: Phrases

By the end of this lesson, you should be able to:

- ☐ Talk more specifically about being a student
- ☐ Talk about the recent past using **hace** and **acabar de**
- ☐ Converse about applying for a job
- ☐ Express a strong necessity (*to have to, must, should*)

Phrase Builder 1

10A Phrase Builder 1 (CD 8, Track 19)

aprobar un curso	*to pass a course*
tomar un examen	*to take a test*
aprobar/suspender un examen	*to pass/fail a test*
escribir un trabajo de investigación	*to write a research paper*
estudiante a tiempo completo	*full-time student*
estudiante a tiempo parcial	*part-time student*
especializarse en ...	*to major in ...*
sacar buenas/malas notas	*to get good/bad grades*
el horario de clases	*class schedule*
me interesa(n) ...	*I'm interested in ...*
No estoy seguro/a todavía.	*I'm not sure yet.*
¿Qué te parece ... ?	*What do you think of ... ?*
Y tú, ¿qué piensas?	*And how about you? What do you think?*

Phrase Practice 1

Match the Spanish phrase on the left with its appropriate English translation on the right.

1. **aprobar un curso**	a. *to write a research paper*
2. **hacer un examen**	b. *to pass a course*
3. **escribir un trabajo de investigación**	c. *to pass a test*
4. **suspender un examen**	d. *to major in*
5. **especializarse en**	e. *to fail a test*
6. **aprobar un examen**	f. *to take a test*

ANSWER KEY

1. b; 2. f; 3. a; 4. e; 5. d; 6. c

Grammar Builder 1

EXPRESSING PAST ACTIONS WITH HACE AND ACABAR DE

10B Grammar Builder 1 (CD 8, Track 20)

The verb **acabar** means *to finish* something. But you will hear it often in the expression **acabar de** + infinitive, which is equivalent to saying *to have just* in English. It refers to something that happened recently. Here are a few examples of how it is used.

Acabo de terminar el informe.

I have just finished the report.

Ella acaba de hacer una llamada a Ecuador.

She has just made a phone call to Ecuador.

Nosotros acabamos de terminar la entrevista.

We've just finished (concluded) the interview.

To express an action that began in the past and continues into the present, use **hace** + time + **que** + present tense. Note that the verb in Spanish is in the present tense, but in English, it's translated as the present perfect progressive (*have/has been doing*).

Hace un año que estudio español.
I've been studying Spanish for a year.

Hace cinco años que ella trabaja aquí.
She's been working here for five years.

¿Cuánto hace que estudia arquitectura?
How long have you been studying architecture?

To express *ago,* use **hace** + time + **que** + preterite. In this case, the verb tense in both languages is the simple past.

Hace un año que estudié español.
I studied Spanish a year ago.

Hace cinco años que ella trabajó aquí.
She worked here five years ago.

¿Cuánto hace que estudió arquitectura?
How long ago did you study architecture?

Work Out 1

Use the English translations to help fill in the blanks.

1. **Hace tres semanas que** ______________________ **en el informe.**
   (She's been working on the report for three weeks.)
2. ______________ **mi matrícula hace un mes.** *(I paid my tuition a month ago.)*
3. **Ella** ______________ **aquí hace dos años.** *(She worked here two years ago.)*
4. **María acaba de** ______________ **un libro.** *(María has just read a book.)*
5. **Ellos acaban de** ______________________ **una nueva computadora.**
   (They've just bought a new computer.)
6. **Nosotros** ______________ **hace una hora.** *(We ate an hour ago.)*
7. **Hace tres meses que** ______________________ **español.**
   (I've been studying Spanish for three months.)
8. **Acaban de** ______________ **de vacaciones.** *(They've just left on vacation.)*

ANSWER KEY

1. **trabaja**; 2. **Pagué**; 3. **trabajó**; 4. **leer**; 5. **comprar**; 6. **comimos**; 7. **estudio**; 8. **partir**

Phrase Builder 2

10C Phrase Builder 2 (CD 8, Track 21)

la solicitud de empleo	*job application*
La jornada es de treinta y siete horas.	*It is a thirty-seven-hour workweek.*
¿Cuándo comienzo?	*When do I start?*
Hay un período de prueba de seis meses.	*There's a probationary period of six months.*
un mes de vacaciones	*a month's vacation*

¿Hay incentivos?	*Are there any incentives?*
No tengo referencias.	*I don't have references.*
contribuciones a la pensión y el seguro	*pension and insurance contributions*
Domino el francés.	*I speak French fluently.*
¿Cuántos años de experiencia tiene?	*How many years of experience do you have?*

Phrase Practice 2

Fill in the blanks in each sentence based on the English translation.

1. ________________ **es de treinta y siete horas.** *It is a thirty-seven-hour workweek.*

2. **¿**____**?** *When do I start?*

3. **¿Hay** ________________________________**?** *Are there any incentives?*

4. **Hay** ______________ **de seis meses.** *There's a probationary period of six months.*

5. ____**.** *I don't have references.*

6. **¿Cuántos** ________________ **tiene?** *How many years of experience do you have?*

ANSWER KEY

1. **La jornada**; 2. **Cuándo comienzo**; 3. **incentivos**; 4. **un período de prueba**; 5. **No tengo referencias**; 6. **años de experiencia**

Grammar Builder 2

EXPRESSING OBLIGATION OR NECESSITY

10D Grammar Builder 2 (CD 8, Track 22)

In English, when you want to express obligation or strong necessity, you use *to have to*, *must*, or *should*. In Spanish, use **tener que** + infinitive or **deber** + infinitive, as you learned in Lesson 17 of Intermediate Spanish. You can also use the construction **hay que** + infinitive, which is a bit more impersonal.

Ella tiene que estudiar para el examen.
She has to study for the test.

Debemos hacer una lista de invitados.
We must make a guest list.

Hay que hablar claramente.
It is necessary to speak clearly.

Work Out 2

Fill in the blanks with the appropriate form of the verb in parentheses.

1. **Ellos** ______ **tener en cuenta la situación. (deber)**
2. **Yo** ______ **que vender mi apartamento. (tener)**
3. **Ella no** ______ **venir a la oficina hoy. (deber)**
4. ______ **que consultar a un abogado. (haber)**
5. **Él** ______ **que llamar al hospital. (tener)**

6. ________________ que llamar a Juan inmediatamente. (haber)

7. Nosotros ________________ hacer una excepción en este caso. (deber)

8. Ellos ________________ que enviar el informe lo antes posible. (tener)

ANSWER KEY

1. deben; 2. tengo; 3. debe; 4. Hay; 5. tiene; 6. Hay; 7. debemos; 8. tienen

Take It Further

Take a look at the following words. They are all related to an amount of money, but they are not necessarily synonyms.

el sueldo	*pay*
el salario	*salary*
el jornal/la paga	*wage*
el pago	*payment*
la retribución	*repayment*
los honorarios	*fees*
los ingresos	*earnings*

Drive It Home

Change the sentences below by replacing the subject with the one indicated in each line.

A. Yo acabo de terminar el examen.

1. (Tú) ________________

2. (Nosotros) ________________

3. (Usted) ________________

4. **(Ellas)** ____________________

B. **Hace un año que tú vives en España.**

1. **(yo)** ____________________
2. **(vosotros)** ____________________

____

3. **(Marta)** ____________________

____

4. **(Marta y Eloy)** ____________________

____

ANSWER KEY

A. 1. **Tú acabas de terminar el examen.** 2. **Nosotros acabamos de terminar el examen.** 3. **Usted acaba de terminar el examen.** 4. **Ellas acaban de terminar el examen.**

B. 1. **Hace un año que yo vivo en España.** 2. **Hace un año que vosotros vivís en España.** 3. **Hace un año que Marta vive en España.** 4. **Hace un año que Marta y Eloy viven en España.**

How Did You Do?

By now, you should be able to:

- ☐ Talk more specifically about being a student
  (Still unsure? Jump back to page 141.)
- ☐ Talk about the recent past using **hace** and **acabar de**
  (Still unsure? Jump back to page 142.)
- ☐ Converse about applying for a job
  (Still unsure? Jump back to page 144.)
- ☐ Express a strong necessity (*to have to, must, should*)
  (Still unsure? Jump back to page 146.)

Lesson 11: Sentences

By the end of this lesson, you should be able to:

- ☐ Talk about being a student
- ☐ Use the imperfect when describing actions of the past
- ☐ Confidently express your job qualifications

Sentence Builder 1

11A Sentence Builder 1 (CD 8, Track 23)

¿Cuál es tu carrera?	*What is your major?*
¿Cuál es tu especialidad?	*What is your major?*
¿En qué año estás?	*What year are you in?*
Se gradúa el año que viene.	*He/She graduates next year.*
¿Qué clases tomas este semestre?	*What classes are you taking this semester?*
¿Qué notas sacaste?	*What grades did you get?*
¿Qué planes tienes para el futuro?	*What are your plans for the future?*
Pienso ser periodista.	*I'm thinking about being a journalist.*
Acaba de graduarse en medicina.	*He/She just graduated in medicine.*
Tenemos que escribir un trabajo de investigación.	*We have to write a research paper.*

Sentence Practice 1

Fill in the blanks in each sentence based on the English translation.

1. **¿Cuál es** __________________________**?** *What is your major?*
2. **¿**______________________________**?** *What year are you in?*
3. **¿**_______________________ **este semestre?** *What classes are you taking this semester?*
4. **¿Qué notas** ______________________**?** *What grades did you get?*
5. **¿**_________________________________ **para el futuro?** *What are your plans for the future?*

ANSWER KEY

1. **tu carrera/ tu especialidad**; 2. **En qué año estás**; 3. **Qué clases tomas**; 4. **sacaste**; 5. **Qué planes tienes**

Grammar Builder 1

THE IMPERFECT OF -AR VERBS

11B Grammar Builder 1 (CD 8, Track 24)

So far, you've learned how to express actions that happened in the past with the preterite tense. There is, however, another past tense, called the imperfect, which is used to describe actions in the past that do not have a clear beginning or end, or are part of a routine or habit. The imperfect often corresponds to the English habitual past, with *used to* + verb, or to the past progressive *was/were* + *-ing*.

Durante el verano, me levantaba a las nueve.
During the summer, I used to get up at nine.

Después del desayuno, caminaba por la playa.
After breakfast, I would walk along the beach.

To form the imperfect of **-ar** verbs, simply take the root of the verb and add the following endings.

REGULAR IMPERFECT ENDINGS FOR -AR VERBS	
yo -aba	**nosotros/as -ábamos**
tú -abas	**vosotros/as -abais**
él/ella/usted -aba	**ellos/ellas/ustedes -aban**

Let's look at how this works with the verb **pagar** (*to pay*).

PAGAR (*TO PAY*) - IMPERFECT	
yo pagaba	**nosotros/as pagábamos**
tú pagabas	**vosotros/as pagabais**
él/ella/usted pagaba	**ellos/ellas/ustedes pagaban**

Work Out 1

Complete the following paragraph with the verbs in the imperfect tense.

Cuando tenía nueve años me 1 ________________ **(yo/gustar) jugar con mis amigos en el parque. A veces** 2 ________________ **(nosotros/montar) en bicicleta, otras veces** 3 ________________ **(nosotros/jugar) al fútbol. El tiempo** 4 ____________ **(pasar) muy rápido porque nos divertíamos mucho. Cuando** 5 ________________ **(llegar) la noche,** 6 ________________ **(nosotros/jugar) a las escondidas. En el verano,** 7 ________________________ **(nosotros/acostarse) muy tarde y** 8 ________________________ **(nosotros/levantarse) muy tarde también.**

ANSWER KEY

1. **gustaba**; 2. **montábamos**; 3. **jugábamos**; 4. **pasaba**; 5. **llegaba**; 6. **jugábamos**; 7. **nos acostábamos**; 8. **nos levantábamos**

Sentence Builder 2

11C Sentence Builder 2 (CD 8, Track 25)

¿En qué trabaja?	*What do you do for a living?*
Le ofrecemos un contrato por un año.	*We're offering you a one-year contract.*
Hay que trabajar horas extras.	*You have to work overtime.*
Tengo una especialización en farmacia clínica.	*I have a master's degree in clinical pharmacy.*
¿Cuál es su objetivo en solicitar este puesto?	*What is your aim in applying for this job?*
Su oferta es muy interesante.	*Your offer is very interesting.*
¿Cuándo comienzo?	*When do I start?*
¿Qué otras cualificaciones posee?	*What other qualifications do you have?*
Soy bueno/a trabajando en equipo.	*I'm good at working on a team.*
Sé trabajar bajo presión.	*I know how to work under pressure.*

Sentence Practice 2

Fill in the blanks in each sentence based on the English translation.

1. **¿** ____________________ **?** *What do you do for a living?*
2. **¿** ____________________ **en solicitar este puesto?**
   What is your aim in applying for this job?
3. ____________________ **es muy interesante.** *Your offer is very interesting.*
4. **¿** ____________________ **posee?**
   What other qualifications do you have?

5. ______________________ **en equipo.** *I'm good at working on a team.*

6. **Sé trabajar** ______________________. *I know how to work under pressure.*

ANSWER KEY

1. **En qué trabaja**; 2. **Cuál es su objetivo**; 3. **Su oferta**; 4. **Qué otras cualificaciones**; 5. **Soy bueno/a trabajando**; 6. **bajo presión**

Grammar Builder 2

THE IMPERFECT OF -ER AND -IR VERBS

11D Grammar Builder 2 (CD 8, Track 26)

The same set of endings is used in the imperfect of **-er** and **-ir** verbs.

REGULAR IMPERFECT ENDINGS FOR -ER/-IR VERBS	
yo -ía	**nosotros/as -íamos**
tú -ías	**vosotros/as -íais**
él/ella/usted -ía	**ellos/ellas/ustedes -ían**

VENDER *(TO SELL)* - IMPERFECT	
yo vendía	**nosotros/as vendíamos**
tú vendías	**vosotros/as vendíais**
él/ella/usted vendía	**ellos/ellas/ustedes vendían**

ESCRIBIR *(TO WRITE)* - IMPERFECT	
yo escribía	**nosotros/as escribíamos**
tú escribías	**vosotros/as escribíais**
él/ella/usted escribía	**ellos/ellas/ustedes escribían**

The imperfect doesn't always correspond to habitual or progressive past actions. Sometimes it's translated as the simple past when it describes a number of conditions and qualities, such as physical appearance, age, occupation, traits or characteristics, mental and emotional states, location, beliefs, opinions, and wishes. Notice that all of these conditions and qualities are things that you can think of as "background" information—not some action that happened at a specific point in time in the past, but rather, characteristics that have lasted over a period.

Ella tenía el pelo rojo y largo.
She had long red hair.

Mi abuelo tenía setenta años, estaba triste, y no quería hablar.
My grandfather was seventy years old, he was sad, and he didn't want to talk.

Su casa estaba lejos de las montañas y estaba en mal estado.
His house was far away from the mountains and in bad shape.

Work Out 2

Fill in the blanks with the imperfect form of the verb(s) given.

1. **Ella siempre ________________ tarde del trabajo. (salir)**
2. **Mi tío Alfonso ________________ una casa cerca al mar. (tener)**
3. **Ella ________________ en Brasil. (vivir)**
4. **Ella ________________ cincuenta años pero ________________ más vieja. (tener/parecer)**
5. **Ellos ________________ novelas rosa. (escribir)**
6. **Vosotros ________________ hasta tarde los fines de semana. (dormir)**

7. **Nosotros ______ que ella no ______ dinero. (saber/tener)**

8. **Yo no ______ lo que ______. (creer/oír)**

ANSWER KEY

1. salía; 2. tenía; 3. vivía; 4. tenía/parecía; 5. escribían; 6. dormíais; 7. sabíamos/tenía; 8. creía/oía

Culture Note

Some universities in Latin America and Spain are quite different from those in the United States. There may be no on-campus housing, because students generally live at home with their parents or rent and share apartments or houses with other students. Even though students do play a number of different sports, there are often no teams associated with any one university, nor are there scholarships offered to these athletes. Furthermore, there are no fraternities or sororities; students meet more informally at cafés or at home.

Drive It Home

Replace the underlined part of the sentence with the words in parentheses.

1. **Durante el verano yo caminaba en la playa con mis amigos. (en el parque)**

______

2. **Durante el verano yo caminaba en la playa con mis amigos. (mi familia)**

______

3. **Durante el verano yo caminaba en la playa con mis amigos. (la primavera)**

______

4. **Durante el verano yo caminaba en la playa con mis amigos. (jugar)**

______

5. **Durante el verano <u>yo caminaba</u> en la playa con mis amigos. (ella + caminar)**

____

6. **Durante el verano <u>yo caminaba</u> en la playa con mis amigos. (tú + caminar)**

____

7. **Durante el verano <u>yo caminaba</u> en la playa con mis amigos. (ustedes + caminar)**

____

8. **Durante el verano <u>yo caminaba</u> en la playa con mis amigos. (nosotros + caminar)**

____

ANSWER KEY

1. **Durante el verano yo caminaba en el parque con mis amigos.** 2. **Durante el verano yo caminaba en la playa con mi familia.** 3. **Durante la primavera yo caminaba en la playa con mis amigos.** 4. **Durante el verano yo jugaba en la playa con mis amigos.** 5. **Durante el verano ella caminaba en la playa con mis amigos.** 6. **Durante el verano tú caminabas en la playa con mis amigos.** 7. **Durante el verano ustedes caminaban en la playa con mis amigos.** 8. **Durante el verano nosotros caminábamos en la playa con mis amigos.**

How Did You Do?

By now, you should be able to:

- ☐ Talk about being a student
  (Still unsure? Jump back to page 149.)
- ☐ Use the imperfect when describing actions of the past
  (Still unsure? Jump back to pages 150 and 153.)
- ☐ Confidently express your job qualifications
  (Still unsure? Jump back to page 152.)

Lesson 12: Conversations

By the end of this lesson, you should be able to:

- ☐ Use **ir**, **ser**, and **ver** in the imperfect
- ☐ Use the imperfect to express two simultaneous actions in the past
- ☐ Use the imperfect and the preterite in one sentence

Conversation 1

12A Conversation 1 (CD 8, Track 27 - Spanish Only; Track 28 - Spanish and English)

Isabel and Olga have been friends since high school, but they haven't seen each other in months. They've just bumped into each other at the university bookstore.

Isabel:	**¡Hola, Olga! ¡Qué sorpresa! ¿Cómo estás?**
Olga:	**¡Lo mismo digo! ¿Cómo te ha ido? ¡No sabía que estudiabas en esta universidad también!**
Isabel:	**Sí, decidí especializarme en ingeniería mecánica y me gané una beca para estudiar aquí. Y tú, ¿cuál es tu carrera?**
Olga:	**¡Felicitaciones! Estoy estudiando pediatría.**
Isabel:	**¿En qué año estás?**
Olga:	**Me gradúo en dos años. Pero no estoy segura si voy a continuar.**
Isabel:	**¿Por qué no? Siempre te gustó trabajar con niños.**
Olga:	**Ya lo sé. Pero estoy pensando especializarme en sicología infantil. Y a ti, ¿cuánto te falta?**
Isabel:	**Tres semestres más. Ya estoy lista para empezar a trabajar.**
Olga:	**Sí, te entiendo. Bueno, y ¿qué te parece está universidad?**
Isabel:	**Me gusta mucho. Estoy muy contenta aquí.**

Isabel:	*Hi, Olga! What a surprise! How are you?*

Olga: *Same here! How have you been? I didn't know that you studied here as well!*

Isabel: *Yes, I decided to major in mechanical engineering and I was awarded a scholarship to study here. And you, what's your major?*

Olga: *Congratulations! I'm studying to be a pediatrician.*

Isabel: *What year are you in?*

Olga: *I'll graduate in two years. But I'm not sure whether I am going to continue.*

Isabel: *Why not? You always liked working with kids.*

Olga: *I know. But I am thinking about majoring in child psychology. And you, how much more do you have to go?*

Isabel: *Three more semesters. I'm ready to start working.*

Olga: *Yes, I understand. Well, so, what do you think of the university?*

Isabel: *I like it a lot. I'm very happy here.*

Culture Note

More and more women in Latin America and Spain are studying to go into fields that were once associated with men only, such as engineering or physics. Despite this, employment opportunities are not the same, varying from country to country and across social backgrounds.

Conversation Practice 1

Fill in the blanks below with the appropriate word based on the English translations and the dialogue above.

1. **¡No ______________ que ______________ en esta universidad también!** *I didn't know that you studied here as well!*

2. **Sí, ____________ especializarme en ingeniería mecánica y ____________ una beca para estudiar aquí.** *Yes, I decided to major in mechanical engineering and I was awarded a scholarship to study here.*

3. **Y tú, ¿cuál es tu ____________?** *And you, what's your major?*

4. **Siempre ____________ trabajar con niños.** *You always liked working with kids.*

5. **Pero estoy pensando especializarme en ____________.** *But I am thinking about majoring in child psychology.*

ANSWER KEY

1. **sabía/estudiabas**; 2. **decidí, me/gané**; 3. **carrera**; 4. **te gustó**; 5. **sicología infantil**

Grammar Builder 1

IR, SER, AND VER IN THE IMPERFECT

12B Grammar Builder 1 (CD 9, Track 1)

The good news about the imperfect tense is that there are only three irregular verbs.

IR *(TO GO)* - IMPERFECT	
yo iba	**nosotros/as íbamos**
tú ibas	**vosotros/as ibais**
él/ella/usted iba	**ellos/ellas/ustedes iban**

SER *(TO BE)* - IMPERFECT	
yo era	**nosotros/as éramos**
tú eras	**vosotros/as erais**
él/ella/usted era	**ellos/ellas/ustedes eran**

VER *(TO SEE)* - IMPERFECT	
yo veía	**nosotros/as veíamos**
tú veías	**vosotros/as veíais**
él/ella/usted veía	**ellos/ellas/ustedes veían**

Here are some examples of these three irregular verbs in sentences. Note that the imperfect in each of the examples below describes a background setting against which the main events of a story take place.

Eran las once de la noche y nevaba.

It was eleven at night and it was snowing.

Era un día de invierno y no se veía a nadie en la calle.

It was a winter day and there was no one to be seen on the street.

Estaba nublado e iba a llover.

It was cloudy and it was going to rain.

Work Out 1

Change the underlined phrases using the pronoun given in parentheses.

1. **Era viernes por la noche y Miguel estaba en una fiesta. (nosotros)** ____________

____

2. **Eran las once de la mañana y yo tenía mucho frío. (tú)** ____________

____

3. **Una vez cuando nadábamos en la piscina . . . (ellos)** ________________

____

4. **Era un día muy bonito y ellos querían ir al campo. (nosotros)** ________________

____

5. **Una noche, cuando caminaba a casa . . . (vosotros)** ________________

____

6. **Era tarde y ella caminaba sola. (ellos)** ________________

____

ANSWER KEY

1. **Era viernes por la noche y nosotros estábamos en una fiesta.** 2. **Eran las once de la mañana y tú tenías mucho frío.** 3. **Una vez cuando nadaban en la piscina . . .** 4. **Era un día muy bonito y decidimos ir al campo.** 5. **Una noche, cuando caminabais a casa . . .** 6. **Era tarde y ellos caminaban solos.**

Conversation 2

12C Conversation 2 (CD 9, Track 2 - Spanish Only; Track 3 - Spanish and English)

Hernando is applying for a job as a pharmacist and is being interviewed for the position by the head of pharmacology of a well-known hospital in Buenos Aires.

Doctor:	**Su hoja de vida es impresionante. Está muy cualificado. ¿Cuál es su objetivo en solicitar este puesto?**
Hernando:	**Quiero vincularme con un hospital prestigioso para desarrollarme profesionalmente.**
Doctor:	**Y, ¿qué es lo que nos ofrece usted a nosotros?**
Hernando:	**Gran capacidad para el trabajo. Sé manejar situaciones estresantes, y soy bueno trabajando en equipo.**
Doctor:	**¿Domina el inglés?**
Hernando:	**Claro que sí. Tengo una especialización en farmacia clínica de la universidad de Brighton en Inglaterra. Además hablo francés e italiano.**

Doctor:	**Bueno, le podemos ofrecer un contrato por un año con jornada de treinta y siete horas y un mes de vacaciones.**
Hernando:	**Su oferta es muy interesante. ¿Cuándo comienzo?**
Doctor:	**Nos gustaría que empezara tan pronto como sea posible.**
Hernando:	**Estoy disponible a partir del quince de este mes, ¿le parece bien?**
Doctor:	**Perfecto. ¡Bienvenido a bordo!**

Doctor:	*Your résumé is impressive. You're very well qualified. What's your aim in applying for this job?*
Hernando:	*I want to join a prestigious hospital in order to advance professionally.*
Doctor:	*And, what do you offer us?*
Hernando:	*Great work capacity. I know how to handle stressful situations, and I'm a good team worker.*
Doctor:	*Do you speak English?*
Hernando:	*Yes, of course. I have a specialized degree in clinical pharmacy from Brighton University in England. Plus, I speak French and Italian.*
Doctor:	*Well, we can offer you a one-year contract with a thirty-seven-hour workweek and a month of vacation.*
Hernando:	*Your offer is very interesting. When do I start?*
Doctor:	*We would like you to start as soon as possible.*
Hernando:	*I'm available as of the fifteenth of this month. How does that sound?*
Doctor:	*Perfect! Welcome!*

Take It Further

There are a number of English words that the Royal Academy of Spanish Language has accepted into the Spanish language. Today these words are so common that Spanish speakers might not even realize that they're borrowed from English. This misimpression is made easier by the spelling of the words, which has often been adapted for the Spanish language.

estresante	*stressing*
fútbol	*soccer*
parqueadero	*parking lot*
computadora	*computer*

Conversation Practice 2

Fill in the blanks below with the appropriate word based on the English translations and the dialogue above.

1. **Está muy** ________________. *You're very well qualified.*
2. **¿Cuál es su objetivo en** ________________**?** *What's your aim in applying for this job?*
3. **Y, ¿qué es lo que nos ofrece usted** ________________**?** *And, what do you offer us?*
4. **Sé manejar situaciones** ________________**, y soy bueno trabajando en equipo.** *I know how to handle stressful situations, and I'm a good team worker.*
5. **Bueno, le podemos ofrecer un** ________________ **por un año con** ________________ **de treinta y siete horas y un mes de vacaciones.** *Well, we can offer you a one-year contract with a thirty-seven-hour workweek and a month of vacation.*
6. **Estoy** ________________ **a partir del quince de este mes, ¿le parece bien?** *I'm available as of the fifteenth of this month. How does that sound?*

ANSWER KEY

1. **cualificado**; 2. **solicitar este puesto**; 3. **a nosotros**; 4. **estresantes**; 5. **contrato/jornada**; 6. **disponible**

Grammar Builder 2

USING THE PRETERITE AND THE IMPERFECT

12D Grammar Builder 2 (CD 9, Track 4)

You can use the imperfect to express two or more actions that were going on at the same time. Simultaneous actions are often linked with words like **mientras** (*while*) or **mientras tanto** (*meanwhile*).

Ella leía el periódico mientras yo cocinaba.
She read the newspaper while I cooked.

Mientras nosotros mirábamos televisión, ellos se vestían.
While we watched television, they got dressed.

To indicate that two or more actions happened sequentially, use the preterite.

Ella desayunó y luego fue a trabajar.
She had breakfast and then went to work.

Yo leí el periódico, tomé mi café y miré la tele.
I read the newspaper, drank my coffee, and watched TV.

In cases where you have an ongoing action that is interrupted by another action, use the imperfect to describe the action that was in progress and the preterite to describe the action that interrupted it.

Yo dormía cuando sonó el teléfono.
I was sleeping when the phone rang.

Empezó a llover cuando jugábamos en el parque.
It began to rain while we were playing in the park.

Work Out 2

Form sentences using the preterite and/or the imperfect, following the clues given:

1. **Ella/leer/una novela/mientras/yo/jugar/a las cartas.** *(simultaneous actions)*

   ____

2. **Ellos/trabajar/en el jardín/después/ir/de compras.** *(one action happens after the other)* ______________________________

   ____

3. **Nosotros/cocinar/cuando/ella/llamar/por teléfono.** *(one action interrupts the other)* ______________________________

   ____

4. **Mientras/yo/dormir/vosotros/mirar/la tele**. *(simultaneous actions)* __________

   ____

5. **Vosotros/almorzar/luego/ir de compras**. *(one action happens after the other)*

   ____

6. **Ella/llorar/él/gritar**. *(simultaneous actions)* ______________________________

   ____

7. **Yo/cantar/cuando/ellos/llamar a la puerta.** *(one action interrupts the other)*

   ____

ANSWER KEY

1. **Ella leía una novela mientras yo jugaba a las cartas.** 2. **Ellos trabajaron en el jardín y después fueron de compras.** 3. **Nosotros cocinábamos cuando ella llamó por teléfono.** 4. **Mientras yo dormía, vosotros mirabais la tele.** 5. **Vosotros almorzasteis y luego fuisteis de compras.** 6. **Ella lloraba y él gritaba.** 7. **Yo cantaba cuando ellos llamaron a la puerta.**

Take It Further

Back in Lesson 4 of *Intermediate Spanish*, we touched on accent marks and how they're used in Spanish. Now that you have some more experience under your belt, let's take a closer look. If a word ends in a vowel (**a**, **e**, **i**, **o**, **u**) or the letters **n** or **s**, and the stress falls on the last syllable, an accent mark is required.

caminó	*(he/she) walked*
dormí	*I slept*
canción	*song*
verás	*you will see*

If the word ends in a consonant other than **n** or **s** and the stress falls on the next-to-last syllable, an accent mark is also required.

lápiz	*pencil*
difícil	*difficult*
cárcel	*prison*
mártir	*martyr*

Sometimes, accent marks are used only to differentiate between words that would otherwise look identical.

él	*he*	**el**	*the*
qué	*what*	**que**	*that*
más	*more*	**mas**	*but*
tú	*you*	**tu**	*your*
sé	*I know*	**se**	*himself/herself, etc.*
sí	*yes*	**si**	*if*

Remember that question words have an accent when used in a question but the corresponding relative pronouns or connecting words do not.

¿cómo?	*how?*	**como**	*as, like*

¿cuál?	*which?*	**cual**	*which, as*
¿cuándo?	*when?*	**cuando**	*when*
¿dónde?	*where?*	**donde**	*where*
¿qué?	*what?*	**que**	*which, that*
¿quién?	*who? whom?*	**quien**	*who, whom*
¿cuánto?	*how much?*	**cuanto**	*as much, as many*

For example, in the first sentence below, **¿cómo?** is a question word, and in the second, **como** is a relative pronoun, introducing another sentence within the main one.

¿Cómo funciona?
How does it work?

No funciona como yo me imaginaba.
It doesn't work like (lit., how) I thought.

Demonstrative pronouns (**éste**, **ése**, **aquél**) have an accent, while demonstrative adjectives (**este**, **ese**, **aquel**) don't. Of course, if all of this is a bit overwhelming, don't worry. As with everything else, the more you read and write in Spanish, the easier this will become, and you'll get used to seeing certain words with an accent mark.

Drive It Home

In the following sentences an ongoing action is interrupted by another action. Replace the action in progress with the imperfect form of the verb indicated on each line.

A. **Yo dormía cuando sonó el teléfono.**

1. **cocinar** ______________________________

2. **hablar** ______________________________

3. **leer** ______________________________

4. **trabajar** ______________________________

B. **Ella trabajaba cuando llegó su amigo.**

1. **escribir** ______________________________

2. **bailar** ______________________________

3. **comer** ______________________________

4. **bañarse** ______________________________

ANSWER KEY

A. 1. **Yo cocinaba cuando sonó el teléfono.** 2. **Yo hablaba cuando sonó el teléfono.** 3. **Yo leía cuando sonó el teléfono.** 4. **Yo trabajaba cuando sonó el teléfono.**

B. 1. **Ella escribía cuando llegó su amigo.** 2. **Ella bailaba cuando llegó su amigo.** 3. **Ella comía cuando llegó su amigo.** 4. **Ella se bañaba cuando llegó su amigo.**

How Did You Do?

By now, you should be able to:

- ☐ Use **ir**, **ser**, and **ver** in the imperfect (Still unsure? Jump back to page 159.)
- ☐ Use the imperfect to express two simultaneous actions in the past (Still unsure? Jump back to page 164.)
- ☐ Use the imperfect and the preterite in one sentence (Still unsure? Jump back to page 164.)

Don't forget to practice and reinforce what you've learned by visiting **www.livinglanguage.com/languagelab** for flashcards, games, and quizzes for Unit 3!

Unit 3 Essentials

Vocabulary Essentials

SCHOOL SUBJECTS

	school subject
	mathematics
	history
	literature
	science
	biology
	chemistry
	geography
	philosophy

[Pg. 132]

SCHOOL VERBS AND PHRASES

	to pass a course
	to take a test
	to pass/fail a test
	to write a research paper
	full-time student
	part-time student
	to major in …
	to get good/bad grades

	class schedule
	I'm interested in ...
	I'm not sure yet.
	What do you think of ... ?
	And how about you? What do you think?
	What is your major?
	What is your major?
	What year are you in?
	He/She graduates next year.
	What classes are you taking this semester?
	What grades did you get?
	What are your plans for the future?
	I'm thinking about being a journalist.
	He/She just graduated in medicine.
	We have to write a research paper.

[Pgs. 141 and 149]

WORKPLACE VOCABULARY

	appointment
	meeting
	conference room
	contract
	employee
	union
	insurance
	interview

	qualification
	résumé
	references
	retired person

[Pg. 135]

WORKPLACE PHRASES

	job application
	It is a thirty-seven-hour workweek.
	When do I start?
	There's a probationary period of six months.
	a month's vacation
	Are there any incentives?
	I don't have references.
	pension and insurance contributions
	I speak French fluently.
	How many years of experience do you have?
	What do you do for a living?
	We're offering you a one-year contract.
	You have to work overtime.
	I have a master's degree in clinical pharmacy.
	What is your aim in applying for this job?
	Your offer is very interesting.
	When do I start?
	What other qualifications do you have?
	I'm good at working on a team.

	I know how to work under pressure.

[Pgs. 144 and 152]

Grammar Essentials

DOUBLE OBJECT PRONOUNS

When two object pronouns appear in a sentence, the indirect object pronoun comes first. Use **se** instead of **le** or **les** preceding **lo(s)/la(s)**.

In order to clarify the meaning of **se**, use **a él/a ella/a usted/a ellos/a ellas/a ustedes.**

When the pronouns appear with more than one verb, they can be placed either before the verbs or attached to the end of the main verb.

EXPRESSING PAST ACTIONS WITH HACE AND ACABAR DE

To express *to have just*, use:

acabar de + infinitive

To express an action that began in the past and continues into the present, use:

hace + time + **que** + present tense

To express *ago*, use:

hace + time + **que** + preterite

EXPRESSING OBLIGATION OR NECESSITY

tener que + infinitive

deber + infinitive

hay que + infinitive

THE IMPERFECT

Use the imperfect tense to describe actions in the past that do not have a clear beginning or end, or are part of a routine or habit. To form the imperfect of -ar verbs, simply take the root of the verb and add the following endings.

REGULAR IMPERFECT ENDINGS FOR -AR VERBS	
yo -aba	**nosotros/as -ábamos**
tú -abas	**vosotros/as -abais**
él/ella/usted -aba	**ellos/ellas/ustedes -aban**

REGULAR IMPERFECT ENDINGS FOR -ER/-IR VERBS	
yo -ía	**nosotros/as -íamos**
tú -ías	**vosotros/as -íais**
él/ella/usted -ía	**ellos/ellas/ustedes -ían**

VERBS

DAR *(TO GIVE)* - PRETERITE	
yo di	**nosotros/as dimos**
tú diste	**vosotros/as disteis**
él/ella/usted dio	**ellos/ellas/ustedes dieron**

ESCRIBIR *(TO WRITE)* - IMPERFECT	
yo escribía	**nosotros/as escribíamos**
tú escribías	**vosotros/as escribíais**
él/ella/usted escribía	**ellos/ellas/ustedes escribían**

IR *(TO GO)* - IMPERFECT	
yo iba	**nosotros/as íbamos**
tú ibas	**vosotros/as ibais**
él/ella/usted iba	**ellos/ellas/nosotros/as iban**

PAGAR *(TO PAY)* - IMPERFECT	
yo pagaba	nosotros/as pagábamos
tú pagabas	vosotros/as pagabais
él/ella/usted pagaba	ellos/ellas/ustedes pagaban

PEDIR *(TO ASK FOR)* - PRETERITE	
yo pedí	nosotros/as pedimos
tú pediste	vosotros/as pedisteis
él/ella/usted pidió	ellos/ellas/ustedes pidieron

SER *(TO BE)* - IMPERFECT	
yo era	nosotros/as éramos
tú eras	vosotros/as erais
él/ella/usted era	ellos/ellas/ustedes eran

VENDER *(TO SELL)* - IMPERFECT	
yo vendía	nosotros/as vendíamos
tú vendías	vosotros/as vendíais
él/ella/usted vendía	ellos/ellas/ustedes vendían

VER *(TO SEE)* - PRETERITE	
yo vi	nosotros/as vimos
tú viste	vosotros/as visteis
él/ella/usted vio	ellos/ellas/ustedes vieron

VER *(TO SEE)* - IMPERFECT	
yo veía	nosotros/as veíamos
tú veías	vosotros/as veíais
él/ella/usted veía	ellos/ellas/ustedes veían

Unit 3 Quiz

A. Fill in the blank with the correct form of the verb in the imperfect tense.

1. **Yo me ________________________ mucho en la playa. (divertir)**
2. **Mi amigo siempre __________________ a todas las reuniones. (asistir)**
3. **Ellos ______________ un informe al profesor todas las semanas. (entregar)**
4. **Usted _____________ un trabajo de investigación cuando lo visité. (escribir)**
5. **Cuando éramos niños nosotros _______________ a Disneylandia con toda la familia. (viajar)**
6. **Ustedes siempre ____________ las vacaciones de verano en la playa. (pasar)**
7. **Ellas ______________________ en esa universidad también. (estudiar)**
8. **¿Tú no ____________________ seguros de autos en la agencia ? (vender)**

B. Decide whether to use the preterite or the imperfect and write the appropriate form in the blank.

1. **Yo bailaba mientras ella ____________________________ . (cantar)**
2. **Ella escuchaba la música cuando José ________________ a la casa. (llegar)**
3. **Nosotros ______________________ cuando el profesor entró en el aula de clases. (estudiar)**
4. **Juanita escribía mientras Josefa ____________________ la novela. (leer)**
5. **Ustedes asistían a la universidad mientras yo _____________alumno. (ser)**

6. Primero yo visité la tienda y después yo ______________ al supermercado. (ir)

7. Ustedes entraban al cine cuando yo los ______________________ . (encontrar)

8. Mis padres cocinaban cuando ellos ________________ con la comida. (llegar)

C. Select the correct term from the word list below:

la biblioteca, salarios, suspendo, la librería, la ciencia, el título académico, apruebo, la entrevista

1. La biología y la química son materias en el mundo de ____________________ .

2. En __________________________________ es posible estudiar y sacar libros.

3. Después de graduarse, el estudiante recibe ____________________________ .

4. Durante _____________________ los candidatos discuten sus cualificaciones.

5. En ____ puedo comprar los libros.

6. Yo _______________________________ el examen porque tengo malas notas.

7. La compañía ofrece beneficios buenos y __________________________ altos.

8. Yo _____________________________________ el curso con notas muy buenas.

D. Unscramble the following sentence fragments. Then give the English translation.

1. dos años/hace/yo/aquí/que/trabajé ____________________________________

____

____

2. ellas/de/escribir/acaban/un trabajo de investigación ______________________

____

____

3. **dos meses/soy/estudiante/que/hace/a tiempo completo** ____________________

____

____

4. **acabamos/aprobar/el examen/nosotros/de** ____________________

____

____

5. **que/ella/física/estudia/hace/tres meses** ____________________

____

____

6. **un correo electrónico/acabo/enviar/yo/de** ____________________

____

____

7. **acaba/de/una entrevista/ella/tener** ____________________

____

____

8. **viven/en los Estados Unidos/diez años/hace/que/mis primos** ____________________

____

____

ANSWER KEY

A. 1. **divertía**; 2. **asistía**; 3. **entregaban**; 4. **escribía**; 5. **viajábamos**; 6. **pasaban**; 7. **estudiaban**; 8. **vendías**
B. 1. **cantaba**; 2. **llegó**; 3. **estudiábamos**; 4. **leía**; 5. **era**; 6. **fui**; 7. **encontré**; 8. **llegaron**
C. 1. **la ciencia**; 2. **la biblioteca**; 3. **el título académico**; 4. **la entrevista**; 5. **la librería**; 6. **suspendo**; 7. **salarios**; 8. **apruebo**
D. 1. **Hace dos años que yo trabajé aquí.** *I worked here two years ago.* 2. **Ellas acaban de escribir un trabajo de investigación.** *They have just written a research paper.* 3. **Hace dos meses que soy estudiante a tiempo completo.** *I've been a full-time student for two months.* 4. **Nosotros acabamos de aprobar el examen.** *We have just passed the exam.* 5. **Hace tres meses que ella estudia física.** *She's been studying physics for three months.* 6. **Yo acabo de enviar un correo electrónico.** *I've just sent an e-mail.* 7. **Ella acaba de tener una entrevista.** *She's just had an interview.* 8. **Hace diez años que mis primos viven en los Estados Unidos.** *My cousins have been living in the United States for ten years.*

How Did You Do?

Give yourself a point for every correct answer, then use the following key to determine whether or not you're ready to move on:

0–7 points: It's probably best to go back and study the lessons again to make sure you understood everything completely. Take your time; it's not a race! Make sure you spend time reviewing vocabulary with the flashcards and reading through each grammar note carefully.

8–16 points: If the questions you missed were in sections A or B, you may want to review the vocabulary again; if you missed answers mostly in sections C or D, check the unit essentials to make sure you have your conjugations and other grammar basics down.

17–20 points: Feel free to move on to the next unit! You're doing a great job.

points

Unit 4:
Sports and Hobbies

In this unit, you'll learn how to express doubt, denial, and emotions in Spanish. You'll also learn how to talk about the hobbies you have and the sports you enjoy. By the end of this unit, you should be able to:

- ☐ Name and talk about different hobbies and sports
- ☐ Express the probability or possibility that something would happen
- ☐ Describe what you enjoy doing in your free time
- ☐ Identify verbs and expressions that require the use of the subjunctive
- ☐ Form the subjunctive of regular and irregular verbs
- ☐ Identify the difference in using the subjunctive and the indicative
- ☐ Use relative pronouns to create clauses

Lesson 13: Words

By the end of this lesson, you should be able to:

- ☐ Name different types of hobbies and sports
- ☐ Express the probability or possibility that something would happen
- ☐ Use **se** to make general statements

Word Builder 1

13A Word Builder 1 (CD 9, Track 5)

la afición	*hobby*
el/la aficionado/a	*fan*
el pasatiempo	*hobby*
el tiempo libre	*free time*
coleccionar	*to collect*
la artesanía	*craft*
la fotografía	*photography*
la música	*music*
la pintura	*painting*
el baile	*dancing*
la filatelia	*stamp collecting*
las antigüedades	*antiques*
la cocina	*cooking*
la costura	*sewing*
la lectura	*reading*

Word Practice 1

Match the Spanish word on the left with its appropriate English translation on the right.

1. **la lectura**	a. *painting*
2. **la pintura**	b. *craft*
3. **la afición**	c. *hobby*
4. **la artesanía**	d. *sewing*

5. **la cocina** e. *reading*

6. **la costura** f. *cooking*

ANSWER KEY

1. e; 2. a; 3. c; 4. b; 5. f; 6. d

Grammar Builder 1

THE CONDITIONAL

13B Grammar Builder 1 (CD 9, Track 6)

The present conditional is used to express the probability or possibility that something would happen, depending on specific circumstances. In most cases where *would* is used in English, the conditional is used in Spanish. To form the conditional, simply add the following endings to the infinitive form of any verb.

CONDITIONAL ENDINGS	
yo -ía	**nosotros/as -íamos**
tú -ías	**vosotros/as -íais**
él/ella/usted -ía	**ellos/ellas/ustedes -ían**

Notice that these are the same as the endings that were used for **-er/-ir** verbs in the imperfect, but these are added to the entire infinitive, not the verb root, and are also used for conditional **-ar** verbs. Let's see how this works with the following example verbs: **hablar** (*to talk*), **ser** (*to be*), and **abrir** (*to open*).

HABLAR *(TO TALK)* - CONDITIONAL	
yo hablaría	**nosotros/as hablaríamos**
tú hablarías	**vosotros/as hablaríais**
él/ella/usted hablaría	**ellos/ellas/ustedes hablarían**

SER *(TO BE)* - CONDITIONAL	
yo sería	**nosotros/as seríamos**
tú serías	**vosotros/as seríais**
él/ella/usted sería	**ellos/ellas/ustedes serían**

ABRIR *(TO OPEN)* - CONDITIONAL	
yo abriría	**nosotros/as abriríamos**
tú abrirías	**vosotros/as abriríais**
él/ella/usted abriría	**ellos/ellas/ustedes abrirían**

The following verbs have irregular stems.

saber	**sabr-ía**	*to know*
tener	**tendr-ía**	*to have*
salir	**saldr-ía**	*to go out*
poder	**podr-ía**	*to be able to*
hacer	**har-ía**	*to make*
decir	**dir-ía**	*to say*
haber	**habr-ía**	*there is/there are*
querer	**querr-ía**	*to want*
venir	**vendr-ía**	*to come*

Let's look at some examples of the conditional.

Yo estudiaría ruso, pero no tengo tiempo.
I would study Russian, but I don't have time.

En tu caso, yo no diría nada.
In your case, I wouldn't say anything.

Con más dinero, ella haría maravillas.

With more money, she would perform miracles.

Work Out 1

Form sentences with the verbs in parentheses, using the conditional.

1. **Nosotros** ______________ **algo pero no hay nada en la nevera. (comer)**
2. **Yo** ______________ **medicina pero no me gusta ver sangre. (estudiar)**
3. **Nadie** ______________ **en esa casa tan vieja. (vivir)**
4. **Ella** ______________ **la verdad, pero no puede. (decir)**
5. **Ellos** ______________ **temprano, pero tienen que terminar el informe. (salir)**
6. **Los chicos** ______________ **su tarea, pero olvidaron sus libros. (hacer)**
7. **Vosotros** ______________ **al cine, pero ya es muy tarde. (ir)**
8. **Tú** ______________ **una computadora, pero no tienes el dinero. (comprar)**

ANSWER KEY

1. **comeríamos**; 2. **estudiaría**; 3. **viviría**; 4. **diría**; 5. **saldrían**; 6. **harían**; 7. **iríais**; 8. **comprarías**

Word Builder 2

13C Word Builder 2 (CD 9, Track 7)

el deporte	*sport*
el atleta	*athlete*
el deportista	*person who plays sports*
el jugador	*player*
el ciclismo	*biking, cycling*

el fútbol	*soccer*
el béisbol	*baseball*
la natación	*swimming*
el buceo	*diving*
la equitación	*horseback riding*
la caza	*hunting*
el baloncesto	*basketball*
el ajedrez	*chess*

Word Practice 2

Match the Spanish word on the left with its appropriate English translation on the right.

1. **la caza** — a. *swimming*
2. **el jugador** — b. *sport*
3. **la natación** — c. *diving*
4. **el buceo** — d. *basketball*
5. **el baloncesto** — e. *hunting*
6. **el deporte** — f. *player*

ANSWER KEY

1. e; 2. f; 3. a; 4. c; 5. d; 6. b

Grammar Builder 2

IMPERSONAL SE

13D Grammar Builder 2 (CD 9, Track 8)

In English, we can make general statements with words like *you*, *people*, or *one*: *You shouldn't drink in public. In Spain, people eat supper very late. One shouldn't swim right after eating.* In all of these sentences, words like *you*, *people*, and *one* are used to mean *people in general*, rather than any particular person. These sentences are impersonal because we don't have anyone specific in mind. In Spanish, the impersonal **se** is used in front of verbs to make general statements like these. Generally, you use **se** with either the third person singular or the third person plural of the verb.

Se dice que va a llover.
They say it's going to rain.

En España, se cena muy tarde.
In Spain, people eat supper very late.

Las oficinas se cierran a las tres.
The offices close at three.

¿Cómo se dice "helado" en francés?
How do you say "ice cream" in French?

No se debe comer a prisa.
One shouldn't eat quickly.

Work Out 2

Form sentences using the impersonal **se**. Conjugate the verb in the present tense.

1. **En ese lugar no (poder) pagar con tarjetas de crédito.** ______________________

____

2. **En la universidad no (deber) llegar tarde a una clase.** ______________________

____

3. **En Cuba (conseguir) buenos cigarros.** ______________________

____

4. **Para sacar buenas notas (tener) que estudiar mucho.** ______________________

____

5. **(Pensar) que aprender otro idioma es importante.** ______________________

____

6. **(Decir) que es mala suerte viajar en martes trece.** ______________________

____

7. **¿Cómo (decir) "buenos días" en ruso?** ______________________

____

8. **¿Cómo (escribir) esa palabra?** ______________________

____

ANSWER KEY

1. **En ese lugar no se puede pagar con tarjetas de crédito.** 2. **En la universidad no se debe llegar tarde a una clase.** 3. **En Cuba se consiguen buenos cigarros.** 4. **Para sacar buenas notas se tiene que estudiar mucho.** 5. **Se piensa que aprender otro idioma es importante.** 6. **Se dice que es mala suerte viajar en martes trece.** 7. **¿Cómo se dice "buenos días" en ruso?** 8. **¿Cómo se escribe esa palabra?**

Tip!

Reading newspaper and magazine articles in Spanish might turn out to be a frustrating experience at first because of the number of new words and expressions. Some of the tips described in this course will help you decipher the meanings of many words without having to look them up in the dictionary. However, there will be times, especially when a word or expression keeps coming up in the text, that you'll need to look it up. When looking up words in a dictionary, it's important to remember that verbs are listed in the infinitive form, not the conjugated form. Don't always take the first definition you find listed; many words have multiple meanings and functions. You need to decide which one is the best for the context of the sentence. And a very important rule when dealing with two languages is to be extremely suspicious of word-for-word translations. Idiomatic expressions are often completely different across languages (and sound funny when translated literally!), but even "regular" expressions can be constructed in very different ways with very different words. So, don't abuse your dictionary; it is a tool that can provide you with a wealth of information, but it can lead you astray if you use it in the wrong way.

Drive It Home

Silvina always plays the lottery. What would she do if she won the top prize? Make conditional sentences with the clues in parentheses.

1. **Silvina (ser más generosa)** ____________________

2. **Silvina (viajar mucho)** ____________________

3. **Silvina (tener tiempo libre)** ____________________

4. **Silvina (comprar un apartamento en la playa)** ____________________

5. **Silvina (dar mucho dinero a su familia)** ____________________

6. **Silvina (comer en muchos restaurantes)** ____________________

7. **Silvina (estudiar otros idiomas)** ______________________________

____

8. **Silvina (coleccionar antigüedades)** ______________________________

____

ANSWER KEY

1. **Silvina sería más generosa.** 2. **Silvina viajaría mucho.** 3. **Silvina tendría tiempo libre.** 4. **Silvina compraría un apartamento en la playa.** 5. **Silvina daría mucho dinero a su familia.** 6. **Silvina comería en muchos restaurantes.** 7. **Silvina estudiaría otros idiomas.** 8. **Silvina coleccionaría antigüedades.**

How Did You Do?

By now, you should be able to:

- ☐ Name different types of hobbies and sports
(Still unsure? Jump back to pages 180 and 183.)
- ☐ Express the probability or possibility that something would happen
(Still unsure? Jump back to page 181.)
- ☐ Use **se** to make general statements
(Still unsure? Jump back to page 184.)

Lesson 14: Phrases

By the end of this lesson, you should be able to:

- ☐ Describe what you enjoy doing in your free time
- ☐ Identify the subjunctive and when to use it
- ☐ Talk about a game like soccer
- ☐ Use the subjunctive to express things or events

Phrase Builder 1

14A Phrase Builder 1 (CD 9, Track 9)

The following phrases will help you describe what you enjoy doing in your free time.

coleccionar objetos de arte	*to collect pieces of art*
visitar tiendas de antigüedades	*to visit antique shops*
asistir a una subasta	*to attend an auction*
descansar	*to rest*
tener un pasatiempo costoso	*to have an expensive hobby*
pasar el día en la piscina	*to spend the day at the swimming pool*
ser perezoso	*to be lazy*
escuchar música	*to listen to music*
practicar un deporte	*to play sports*
hacer ejercicio	*to exercise*
llevar un diario	*to keep a diary*

Phrase Practice 1

Match the Spanish phrase on the left with its appropriate English translation on the right.

1. **practicar un deporte**
2. **hacer ejercicio**
3. **llevar un diario**
4. **descansar**
5. **ser perezoso**
6. **escuchar música**

a. *to be lazy*
b. *to listen to music*
c. *to rest*
d. *to keep a diary*
e. *to exercise*
f. *to play sports*

ANSWER KEY

1. f; 2. e; 3. d; 4. c; 5. a; 6. b

Grammar Builder 1

THE SUBJUNCTIVE

14B Grammar Builder 1 (CD 9, Track 10)

Up to this point, you've been studying ways to express facts related to time (present, past, and future) in what is known as the *indicative mood*. All this means is that you have been learning how to present information in a factual and objective way; you're *indicating* how things are (or how you think they are). However, there are ways of expressing things that aren't necessarily part of the world as it is. These may include things like emotions, persuasion, doubt, denial, and uncertainty. In the next few lessons, we'll be looking at the *subjunctive mood*, a way to express things or events that are not factual or concrete, but rather, hypothetical or subjective. In Spanish, the subjunctive is usually introduced by **que**. Take a look at these examples.

Espero que mi equipo gane el partido.
I hope my team wins the match.

Ojalá que no llueva hoy.
I hope it doesn't rain today.

Both examples express a hope for something that may or may not turn out to be true or to happen, so the subjunctive is used instead of the indicative. To form the present subjunctive of regular verbs, take the conjugation of the verb in the first person singular (**yo**) of the present tense, drop the final **-o**, and add the following endings. Note the use of opposite vowels: **-ar** verbs use **-e** endings, and **-er** and **-ir** verbs use **-a** endings.

SUBJUNCTIVE ENDINGS OF REGULAR -AR VERBS	
yo -e	**nosotros/as -emos**
tú -es	**vosotros/as -éis**
él/ella/usted -e	**ellos/ellas/ustedes -en**

SUBJUNCTIVE ENDINGS OF REGULAR -ER/-IR VERBS	
yo -a	**nosotros/as -amos**
tú -as	**vosotros/as -áis**
él/ella/usted -a	**ellos/ellas/ustedes -an**

Let's see how that looks with some example verbs: **comprar** (*to buy*), **comer** (*to eat*), and **escribir** (*to write*).

COMPRAR *(TO BUY)* - SUBJUNCTIVE	
yo compre	**nosotros/as compremos**
tú compres	**vosotros/as compréis**
él/ella/usted compre	**ellos/ellas/ustedes compren**

COMER *(TO EAT)* - SUBJUNCTIVE	
yo coma	**nosotros/as comamos**
tú comas	**vosotros/as comáis**
él/ella/usted coma	**ellos/ellas/ustedes coman**

ESCRIBIR *(TO WRITE)* - SUBJUNCTIVE	
yo escriba	**nosotros/as escribamos**
tú escribas	**vosotros/as escribáis**
él/ella/usted escriba	**ellos/ellas/ustedes escriban**

Verbs with an irregular stem in the **yo** form keep that stem in all forms of the present subjunctive, such as the following verbs.

tener (yo tengo)	**teng-a**	*to have*
hacer (yo hago)	**hag-a**	*to make*
venir (yo vengo)	**veng-a**	*to come*

salir (yo salgo)	**salg-a**	*to go out*
poner (yo pongo)	**pong-a**	*to put*
decir (yo digo)	**dig-a**	*to say*
traer (yo traigo)	**traig-a**	*to bring*
conocer (yo conozco)	**conozc-a**	*to know*

Verbs with a stem change in the present indicative have the same kind of stem change in the present subjunctive. In **-ar** and **-er** verbs, the stem change occurs in all persons except **nosotros(as)** and **vosotros(as)**. On the other hand, **-ir** verbs undergo the stem change in all persons. Here are three examples.

PENSAR ***(TO THINK)*** **- SUBJUNCTIVE**	
yo piense	**nosotros/as pensemos**
tú pienses	**vosotros/as penséis**
él/ella/usted piense	**ellos/ellas/ustedes piensen**

PODER ***(TO BE ABLE TO)*** **- SUBJUNCTIVE**	
yo pueda	**nosotros/as podamos**
tú puedas	**vosotros/as podáis**
él/ella/usted pueda	**ellos/ellas/ustedes puedan**

SERVIR ***(TO SERVE)*** **- SUBJUNCTIVE**	
yo sirva	**nosotros/as sirvamos**
tú sirvas	**vosotros/as sirváis**
él/ella/usted sirva	**ellos/ellas/ustedes sirvan**

Work Out 1

Give the corresponding subjunctive form of the following verbs.

1. que tú (querer) ______
2. que él (oír) ______
3. que yo (venir) ______
4. que nosotros (salir) ______
5. que ellas (traer) ______
6. que vosotras (comer) ______
7. que ustedes (pedir) ______
8. que él (hablar) ______
9. que usted (partir) ______
10. que ella (sentir) ______

ANSWER KEY

1. que tú quieras; 2. que él oiga; 3. que yo venga; 4. que nosotros salgamos; 5. que ellas traigan; 6. que vosotras comáis; 7. que ustedes pidan; 8. que él hable; 9. que usted parta; 10. que ella sienta

Phrase Builder 2

14C Phrase Builder 2 (CD 9, Track 11)

The following phrases will help you when talking about a game such as soccer.

ganar un partido	*to win a game*
perder un partido	*to lose a game*
llenar un estadio	*to fill up a stadium*
el número de espectadores	*the number of spectators*
marcar/hacer/anotar un gol	*to score a goal*

intercambiar camisetas	*to exchange T-shirts*
comprar boletos en la taquilla	*to buy tickets at the gate*
quedar empatados	*to be tied*
hacer una cola/fila	*to stand in line*
el medio tiempo	*halftime*
vitorear a un equipo	*to cheer for a team*
el campeonato mundial de fútbol	*the world soccer championship*

Phrase Practice 2

Fill in the blanks in each phrase based on the English translation.

1. ______________ **un partido** *to win a game*
2. ______________ **un partido** *to lose a game*
3. ______________ **un estadio** *to fill up a stadium*
4. ______________ **camisetas** *to exchange T-shirts*
5. ______________ **una cola/fila** *to stand in line*
6. ______________ **a un equipo** *to cheer for a team*

ANSWER KEY

1.**ganar** ; 2.**perder** ; 3.**llenar** ; 4.**intercambiar** ; 5.**hacer** ; 6.**vitorear**

Grammar Builder 2

USING THE SUBJUNCTIVE

14D Grammar Builder 2 (CD 9, Track 12)

So, how do you use the subjunctive? Whenever you want to express a request, a desire, or a demand, or give advice, you will be using the subjunctive mood. Usually, when the verb in the main clause of the sentence expresses any of these, the verb that comes after (in the dependent **que** clause) must be in the subjunctive. The following verbs and phrases are usually followed by another verb in the subjunctive.

aconsejar que ...	*to advise that/to ...*
querer que ...	*to want that/to ...*
desear que ...	*to wish that ...*
pedir que ...	*to request that ...*
insistir que ...	*to insist that ...*
recomendar que ...	*to recommend that ...*
sugerir que ...	*to suggest that ...*
preferir que ...	*to prefer that ...*
prohibir que ...	*to forbid that/to ...*
Es preferible que ...	*It's preferable that ...*
Es mejor que ...	*It's better that ...*
Es necesario que ...	*It's necessary that ...*

Here are a few examples to illustrate how the subjunctive is used.

Quiero que se vaya inmediatamente.
I want him to leave right now.

Te prohíbo que hables con ellos.
I forbid you to talk to them.

Es preferible que nos llame mañana.
It is preferable that you call us tomorrow.

Ella desea que tú vuelvas pronto.
She wishes that you come back soon.

Ustedes sugieren que se cambie la fecha.
You suggest that the date be changed.

Notice that where Spanish uses the subjunctive, English often uses infinitives, such as *I want him to leave now* or *I want you to talk to them*. But English also has a subjunctive, as shown in the last three examples: *that you call us*, *that you come back*, and *that the date be changed* are all examples of the English subjunctive. It may sound stuffy and formal in English, because the subjunctive is dying out in English. But in Spanish, it's alive and well, and it doesn't sound overly formal.

Work Out 2

Fill in the blanks with the correct form of the verb in the subjunctive mood.

1. **Es mejor que tú ________________ (venir) más temprano.**
2. **Le recomiendo a usted que ________________ (traer) los documentos necesarios.**
3. **Yo insisto en que los niños ________________ (comer) todas sus verduras.**
4. **Nosotros preferimos que ellos ________________ (salir) de viaje el lunes.**
5. **Te aconsejo que no ________________ (mirar) tanta televisión.**
6. **Les sugerimos que ________________ (llamar) antes de venir.**
7. **Te prohíbo que ________________ (fumar).**

8. **Les pedimos que** ________________ **(escribir) una carta.**

ANSWER KEY

1. **Es mejor que tú vengas más temprano.** 2. **Le recomiendo a usted que traiga los documentos necesarios.** 3. **Yo insisto en que los niños coman todas sus verduras.** 4. **Nosotros preferimos que ellos salgan de viaje el lunes.** 5. **Te aconsejo que no mires tanta televisión.** 6. **Les sugerimos que llamen antes de venir.** 7. **Te prohíbo que fumes.** 8. **Les pedimos que escriban una carta.**

Tip!

A good way of learning the subjunctive is to remember that it is always introduced by the word **que**. When you ask a Spanish speaker how to conjugate a verb in this mood, they will always respond by using **que** plus the verb. It simply sounds correct and it is an easier way to remember how to conjugate the verbs.

Drive It Home

Use the subjunctive form to tell a friend that you're hoping that these actions happen. Use **Espero que ...** (*I hope that ...*) to introduce the phrase followed by the **tú** form of the subjunctive.

1. **ganar el partido de fútbol** ________________

2. **comprar un coche nuevo** ________________

3. **cocinar una cena fantástica** ________________

4. **hablar español bien** ________________

5. **vivir en una casa más grande** ____

____

6. **salir a tiempo** ____

____

7. **tener vacaciones pronto** ____

____

8. **venir a mi casa** ____

____

ANSWER KEY

1. **Espero que ganes el partido de fútbol.** 2. **Espero que compres un coche nuevo.** 3. **Espero que cocines una cena fantástica.** 4. **Espero que hables español bien.** 5. **Espero que vivas en una casa más grande.** 6. **Espero que salgas a tiempo.** 7. **Espero que tengas vacaciones pronto.** 8. **Espero que vengas a mi casa.**

How Did You Do?

By now, you should be able to:

- ☐ Describe what you enjoy doing in your free time
  (Still unsure? Jump back to page 189.)
- ☐ Identify the subjunctive and when to use it
  (Still unsure? Jump back to page 190.)
- ☐ Talk about a game like soccer
  (Still unsure? Jump back to page 193.)
- ☐ Use the subjunctive to express things or events
  (Still unsure? Jump back to page 195.)

Lesson 15: Sentences

By the end of this lesson, you should be able to:

- ☐ Confidently converse about hobbies and sports
- ☐ Form the subjunctive of some irregular verbs
- ☐ Identify verbs and expressions that require the use of the subjunctive.

Sentence Builder 1

15A Sentence Builder 1 (CD 9, Track 13)

Los discos de vinilo tienen su encanto.	*LPs have a certain charm.*
¿Eres un aficionado al fútbol?	*Are you a soccer fan?*
Me gusta el sonido que hace la aguja.	*I like the sound the needle makes.*
Tengo una colección enorme.	*I have a huge collection.*
Lo cual quiere decir que no te gusta mi música.	*Which means you don't like my music.*
Prefiero la música clásica.	*I prefer classical music.*
Tenemos gustos muy diferentes.	*We have very different tastes.*
Es el deporte que menos me gusta.	*It's the sport that I like the least.*
La tecnología nos permite escuchar la música de forma tan clara.	*Technology allows us to listen to music in such a clear way.*

Sentence Practice 1

Fill in the blanks in each sentence based on the English translation.

1. **¿Eres** ______________________ **al fútbol?** *Are you a soccer fan?*
2. ______________________ **que hace la aguja.** *I like the sound the needle makes.*
3. **Lo cual quiere decir que** ______________________**.**

   Which means you don't like my music.
4. ______________________ **la música clásica.** *I prefer classical music.*
5. ______________________ **muy diferentes.** *We have very different tastes.*
6. **Es el deporte** ______________________. *It's the sport I like the least.*

ANSWER KEY

1. **un aficionado**; 2. **Me gusta el sonido**; 3. **no te gusta mi música**; 4. **Prefiero**; 5. **Tenemos gustos**; 6. **que menos me gusta**

Grammar Builder 1

IRREGULAR VERBS IN THE SUBJUNCTIVE

15B Grammar Builder 1 (CD 9, Track 14)

A few verbs have an irregular present subjunctive form.

ESTAR *(TO BE)* - SUBJUNCTIVE	
yo esté	**nosotros/as estemos**
tú estés	**vosotros/as estéis**
él/ella/usted esté	**ellos/ellas/ustedes estén**

SER *(TO BE)* - SUBJUNCTIVE	
yo sea	nosotros/as seamos
tú seas	vosotros/as seáis
él/ella/usted sea	ellos/ellas/ustedes sean

SABER *(TO KNOW)* - SUBJUNCTIVE	
yo sepa	nosotros/as sepamos
tú sepas	vosotros/as sepáis
él/ella/usted sepa	ellos/ellas/ustedes sepan

DAR *(TO GIVE)* - SUBJUNCTIVE	
yo dé	nosotros/as demos
tú des	vosotros/as deis
él/ella/usted dé	ellos/ellas/ustedes den

IR *(TO GO)* - SUBJUNCTIVE	
yo vaya	nosotros/as vayamos
tú vayas	vosotros/as vayáis
él/ella/usted vaya	ellos/ellas/ustedes vayan

Es mejor que todos sepan los resultados del examen.
It is better that everyone know the results of the test.

Ella prefiere que estemos en su casa a las ocho.
She prefers us to be at her house at eight. (She wants us to be at her house at eight.)

Te sugiero que seas más puntual.
I suggest you be more punctual.

The present subjunctive of the verb **haber** (*there is/there are*) is **haya**.

Es mejor que haya suficiente comida.
It is better that there be enough food.

Sugiero que haya más invitados.
I suggest there be more guests.

Verbs ending in **-car**, **-gar**, and **-zar** undergo small spelling changes in all persons of the present subjunctive.

BUSCAR *(TO LOOK FOR)* - SUBJUNCTIVE	
yo busque	nosotros/as busquemos
tú busques	vosotros/as busquéis
él/ella/usted busque	ellos/ellas/ustedes busquen

PAGAR *(TO PAY)* - SUBJUNCTIVE	
yo pague	nosotros/as paguemos
tú pagues	vosotros/as paguéis
él/ella/usted pague	ellos/ellas/ustedes paguen

COMENZAR *(TO BEGIN)* - SUBJUNCTIVE	
yo comience	nosotros/as comencemos
tú comiences	vosotros/as comencéis
él/ella/usted comience	ellos/ellas/ustedes comiencen

Te recomiendo que busques tu pasaporte.
I recommend that you look for your passport.

Es mejor que pagues esa cajetilla de cigarrillos.
It is better that you pay for that pack of cigarettes.

Nos sugieren que comencemos de inmediato.
They suggest that we begin immediately.

Work Out 1

Fill in the blanks with the correct form of the present subjunctive of the verbs in parentheses.

A mí me gusta coleccionar violines, pero mi esposa me prohíbe que los 1 ________________ **(poner) en la sala de nuestra casa. Ella prefiere que** 2 ________________ **(ellos/estar) en el sótano. Ella me prohíbe que** 3 ________________ **(yo/comprar) más violines. Insiste en que** 4 ________________ **(yo/buscar) otra afición. Ella me sugiere que** 5 ________________ **(yo/coleccionar) algo más pequeño y fácil de guardar. Deseo que nosotros** 6 ________________ **(ganar) la lotería para comprar una casa muy grande donde pueda poner mis violines. Pero es mejor que yo** 7 ________________ **(ser) más realista y** 8 ________________ **(comenzar) a buscar otra afición. Voy a sugerirle que** 9 ________________ **(nosotros/ir) al Museo de Historia Natural. Tal vez ella prefiera que** 10 ________________ **(yo/saber) más de fósiles y los empiece a coleccionar.**

ANSWER KEY

1. **ponga**; 2. **estén**; 3. **compre**; 4. **busque**; 5. **coleccione**; 6. **ganemos**; 7. **sea**; 8. **comience**; 9. **vayamos**; 10. **yo sepa**

Sentence Builder 2

15C Sentence Builder 2 (CD 9, Track 15)

¡Ni lo sueñes!	*Don't even dream about it!*
No nos lo podemos perder.	*We can't miss it.*
¿Quieres ir al partido el sábado?	*Would you like to go to Saturday's game?*
Es mejor que pase por tu apartamento más tarde.	*It is better that I drop by your apartment later on.*
Te apuesto a que el Boca gana.	*I bet you Boca will win.*
El marcador va a ser dos a cero.	*The score will be two to zero.*
¿Quieres que te recoja en tu casa?	*Would you like me to pick you up at your place?*
Tengo unos boletos para el partido.	*I have a few tickets for the game.*
Soy un hincha de ese equipo.	*I'm a fan of that team.*

Sentence Practice 2

Fill in the blanks in each sentence based on the English translation.

1. **¡** ______________________ **!** *Don't even dream about it!*
2. ______________________ **perder.** *We can't miss it.*
3. ______________________ **el Boca gana.** *I bet you Boca will win.*
4. ______________________ **va a ser dos a cero.** *The score will be two to zero.*
5. **Tengo** ______________ **para el partido.** *I have a few tickets for the game.*
6. ______________________ **de ese equipo.** *I'm a fan of that team.*

ANSWER KEY

1. **Ni lo sueñes**; 2. **No nos lo podemos**; 3. **Te apuesto a que**; 4. **El marcador**; 5. **unos boletos**; 6. **Soy un hincha**

Grammar Builder 2

VERBS FOLLOWED BY THE SUBJUNCTIVE

15D Grammar Builder 2 (CD 9, Track 16)

The subjunctive mood is also used to express feelings, emotions, and personal perceptions. Here are a few verbs and expressions that require the use of the subjunctive. They're all followed by the word **que** + the verb in the subjunctive mood (notice that some verbs are reflexive).

sentir que ...	*to regret that ...*
esperar que ...	*to hope that ...*
tener miedo de que ...	*to be afraid that ...*
gustar que ...	*to like (it) that ...*
enfadarse que ...	*to be angry that ...*
alegrarse de que ...	*to be glad that ...*
preocuparse de que ...	*to worry that ...*
sorprenderse que ...	*to be surprised that ...*
molestarse que ...	*to be bothered that ...*
Es una lástima que ...	*It's a pity that ...*
Es triste que ...	*It's sad that ...*
Es bueno que ...	*It's good that ...*

Let's take a look at some examples, and again, notice the different ways that the subjunctive can be translated into English.

Nos enfada que (ellas) lleguen tarde.
We're angry that they arrive late.

Me preocupa que (él) viaje de noche.
It worries me that he travels at night.

Le gusta que lo despierten temprano.
He likes to be woken up early.

Tengo miedo de que (ella) sepa la verdad.
I'm afraid of her learning the truth.

Es una lástima que (ustedes) no estén aquí.
It's a pity that you aren't here.

Notice in the above examples, that subject pronouns (for both the indicative and the subjunctive verbs) are usually omitted. Because most sentences occur in a context, it's easy to know who the subject of each verb is. The subject pronoun is specified only when it's necessary to make the meaning clear.

Work Out 2

Answer the following questions using the words provided.

1. **¿De qué te alegras? Yo/alegrarse/tú/estar aquí.** ______________________

   ____

2. **¿Qué le preocupa a Martín? Él/preocuparse/no haber/boletos para el cine.**

   ____

3. **¿Qué espera usted que ella haga? Yo/esperar/ella/llegar temprano.** __________

   ____

4. **¿Qué le sorprende a ella de él? Ella/sorprenderse/él/coleccionar rocas.**

   ____

5. **¿Qué temen ellos? Ellos/temer/su equipo/perder/el partido.** ____________

____

6. **¿Qué alegra a tus padres? Ellos/alegrarse/yo/llamarlos por teléfono.**

____

7. **¿Qué os molesta de Enrique? Nosotros/molestarse/él/fumar.** ____________

____

8. **¿Qué te enfada? Yo/enfadarse/la gente/decir/mentiras.** ____________

____

ANSWER KEY

1. **Me alegro de que estés aquí.** 2. **Le preocupa que no haya boletos para el cine.** 3. **Espero que ella llegue temprano.** 4. **A ella le sorprende que él coleccione rocas.** 5. **Ellos temen que su equipo pierda el partido.** 6. **Les alegra que yo los llame por teléfono.** 7. **Nos molesta que él fume.** 8. **Me enfada que la gente diga mentiras.**

Tip!

Explore the internet to find more examples of the subjunctive at work. In a search engine, type the phrases **que él sea** or **que ella vaya** or any other examples of the subjunctive. Collect three or four sentences and see if you can figure out why the subjunctive is used. What is the speaker conveying? Is it emotion, doubt, uncertainty, desire, etc.? The more examples of the subjunctive you see, the easier it will be for you to master it.

Drive It Home

You have a lot of suggestions for your friend. Use the subjunctive form of the verb to give your recommendation. Start each sentence with **Te sugiero que …** (*I suggest that you …*) followed by the **tú** form in the subjunctive.

1. **ser honesto** ____________________

____

2. **estar a tiempo** ____________________

____

3. **saber otro idioma** ____________________

____

4. **dar tu abrigo** ____________________

____

5. **ir al cine** ____________________

____

6. **pagar con tarjeta de crédito** ____________________

____

7. **comenzar inmediatamente** ____________________

____

8. **buscar los resultados** ____________________

____

ANSWER KEY

1. **Te sugiero que seas honesto.** 2. **Te sugiero que estés a tiempo.** 3. **Te sugiero que sepas otro idioma.** 4. **Te sugiero que des tu abrigo.** 5. **Te sugiero que vayas al cine.** 6. **Te sugiero que pagues con tarjeta de crédito.** 7. **Te sugiero que comiences inmediatamente.** 8. **Te sugiero que busques los resultados.**

How Did You Do?

By now, you should be able to:

- ☐ Confidently converse about hobbies and sports
  (Still unsure? Jump back to pages 199 and 204.)
- ☐ Form the subjunctive of some irregular verbs
  (Still unsure? Jump back to page 200.)
- ☐ Identify verbs and expressions that require the use of the subjunctive.
  (Still unsure? Jump back to page 205.)

Lesson 16: Conversations

By the end of this lesson, you should be able to:

- ☐ Identify the difference in using the subjunctive and the indicative
- ☐ Use relative pronouns to create clauses

Conversation 1

16A Conversation 1 (CD 9, Track 17 - Spanish Only; Track 18 - Spanish and English)

Clarisa is on a date with Manuel. They are getting to know each other and are talking about each other's interests.

Clarisa: **Tengo una colección enorme de discos de vinilo.**
Manuel: **Es un poco extraño hoy en día en que la tecnología nos permite escuchar la música de una forma más clara con los discos compactos.**

Clarisa: **Para mí, los discos de vinilo tienen su encanto. Me encanta escuchar el sonido que hace la aguja cuando se termina el disco. No sé ... me parece que hoy todo tiene que ser tan perfecto, que las cosas pierden su gracia.**

Manuel: **¿Y coleccionas toda clase de música?**

Clarisa: **No, no toda. Me gusta mucho la música clásica y me encanta el jazz. También tengo discos de los años cicuenta y sesenta.**

Manuel: **Lo cual quiere decir que no te gusta la música más moderna.**

Clarisa: **No, no mucho ... Y a ti, ¿qué música te gusta?**

Manuel: **Bueno, pues yo tengo una colección de guitarras eléctricas.**

Clarisa: **Así que te gusta el "heavy metal".**

Manuel: **Sí, así es. Tenemos gustos muy diferentes en cuanto a música.**

Clarisa: **No me dirás que también eres un aficionado al fútbol, porque es el deporte que menos me gusta.**

Manuel: **Mmm ... ¿Te gustaría otro martini?**

Clarisa: *I have an enormous collection of LPs.*

Manuel: *That's a bit strange nowadays when technology allows us to listen to music in such a clear way with CDs.*

Clarisa: *LPs have a certain charm for me. I love to hear the sound the needle makes once the record is over. I don't know ... I think that today, everything has to be so perfect that things lose their appeal.*

Manuel: *Do you collect all kinds of music?*

Clarisa: *No, not all. I like classical music very much and I love jazz. I also have records from the fifties and sixties.*

Manuel: *So, that means you don't like more modern music.*

Clarisa: *No, not really ... And you, what kind of music do you like?*

Manuel: *I have a collection of electric guitars.*

Clarisa: *So you like heavy metal.*

Manuel: *Yes, that's right. We have very different tastes regarding music.*

Clarisa: *Don't tell me that you're a soccer fan, because it's the sport I like the least.*

Manuel: *Mmm ... Would you like another martini?*

Culture Note

Soccer, or **fútbol** in Spanish, is a multibillion-dollar business in Latin America, Spain and throughout the world, and it moves millions of fans to follow their teams wherever they go. Brazil, Argentina, and Uruguay are the Latin American countries with the longest soccer traditions. Regardless of the political instability of some countries and the deep economic and social differences that exist, soccer has the power to bring people closer together like no other sport or event.

When you talk about **fútbol**, you are talking about some of the greatest athletes in the world. Players such as Pelé (Edson Arantes do Nascimento), also known as the King of Soccer in Brazil, the country's top goal scorer; Diego Armando Maradona, Argentina's greatest soccer player and perhaps one of the most controversial; Brazilians Ronaldo, Ronaldinho, and Kaká; young Spanish stars from the 2010 World Cup winning squad such as David Villa, Xabi Alonso, and Cesc Fàbregas; and others such as the Colombian goalkeeper Huiguita and el Pibe Valderrama are every kid's role model and every adult's hero. Soccer is played on neighborhood streets, parks, and beaches all over Latin America. It's a sport that knows no social class, race, or age. It can bring people together in a way that no other sport can, filling stadiums the size of the Estadio Maracana in Rio de Janeiro, which, in the 1950 World Championship, held 199,548 fans to see the final between Uruguay and Brazil. To learn more about **fútbol**, and to practice your Spanish, check out ***es.fifa.com***.

Conversation Practice 1

Fill in the blanks below with the appropriate word based on the English translations and the dialogue above.

1. **Para mí, los discos de vinilo ____________________ .**

   LPs have a certain charm for me.

2. **No sé … me parece que hoy todo ________________ tan perfecto, que las cosas pierden su gracia.** *I don't know … I think that today, everything has to be so perfect that things lose their appeal.*

3. **Lo cual ________________ que no te gusta la música más moderna.**

   So, that means you don't like more modern music.

4. **Tenemos ________________ muy diferentes en cuanto a música.**

   We have very different tastes regarding music.

5. **No me dirás que también eres ________________ al fútbol, porque es el deporte que menos me gusta.** *Don't tell me that you're a soccer fan, because it's the sport I like the least.*

ANSWER KEY

1. **tienen su encanto**; 2. **tiene que ser**; 3. **quiere decir**; 4. **gustos**; 5. **un aficionado**

Grammar Builder 1

THE SUBJUNCTIVE VS. THE INDICATIVE

16B Grammar Builder 1 (CD 9, Track 19)

The subjunctive is also used to express disbelief, doubt, denial, and uncertainty.

Dudo que nuestro equipo gane.
I doubt our team will win.

Es posible que me trasladen a Nueva York.
It's possible that I'll be transferred to New York.

However, if the verb in the main clause expresses certainty, belief, or affirmation, the indicative is used.

Creo que nuestro equipo va a ganar.
I believe our team will win.

Es verdad que me han trasladado a Nueva York.
It's true that I've been transferred to New York.

The following verbs and phrases are commonly used to express disbelief, doubt, denial, and uncertainty.

no creer que …	*not to believe that …*
no pensar que …	*not to think that …*
Es posible que …	*It is possible that …*
dudar que …	*to doubt that …*
No es verdad que …	*It is not true that …*
No es cierto que …	*It is not true that …*
Es imposible que …	*It is impossible that …*
No hay nada que …	*There's nothing that …*
No hay nadie que …	*There's no one who…*
No hay ningún/ninguna … que …	*There's no (thing) that…/There's no (person) who…*
negar que …	*to deny that …*

Work Out 1

Change the following sentences using the clues given.

Example: Creo que van a comprar un apartamento en Lima. (yo no creer que)
No creo que vayan a comprar un apartamento en Lima.

1. Es cierto que Ana está embarazada. (No es cierto que) ______________________

____

2. Vamos a sacar una buena nota en el examen. (Es posible que) ______________________

____

3. Es seguro que el equipo está retrasado. (Es posible que) ______________________

____

4. Es verdad que en esa compañía pagan un sueldo muy alto. (No es verdad que)

____

5. Ellos están buscando trabajo. (yo dudar) ______________________

____

6. Estoy seguro de que va a llover. (yo no creer) ______________________

____

7. Hay otro deporte más exigente que el fútbol. (nosotros dudar) ______________________

____

8. Todo en esta vida es difícil. (yo negar) ______________________

____

ANSWER KEY

1. No es cierto que Ana esté embarazada. 2. Es posible que saquemos una buena nota en el examen. 3. Es posible que el equipo esté retrasado. 4. No es verdad que en esa compañía paguen un sueldo muy

alto. 5. **Dudo que ellos estén buscando trabajo.** 6. **No creo que vaya a llover.** 7. **Nosotros dudamos que haya otro deporte más exigente que el fútbol.** 8. **Niego que todo en esta vida sea difícil.**

Conversation 2

16C Conversation 2 (CD 9, Track 20 - Spanish Only; Track 21 - Spanish and English)

Carlos and Manuel are making plans for the weekend and are talking about their favorite sport.

Carlos: **Oye, Manuel, ¿quieres ir al partido del sábado?**
Manuel: **¡Me encantaría! ¿Tienes boletos?**
Carlos: **Sí, precisamente tengo dos boletos para el partido entre Boca Juniors y el Atlético River Plate.**
Manuel: **Bueno, pues es un partido que no nos lo podemos perder. Tú sabes que yo soy un hincha del Boca. ¿A qué hora juegan?**
Carlos: **El partido empieza a las siete de la noche. ¿Quieres que te recoja en tu casa a eso de las cinco y media?**
Manuel: **No, creo que estaré en la oficina trabajando. Es mejor que me pase por tu apartamento cuando termine.**
Carlos: **Está bien. Y . . . ¿cómo van a ser nuestras apuestas esta vez?**
Manuel: **Te apuesto a que el Boca gana uno a cero en los primeros treinta minutos de juego.**
Carlos: **¡Ni lo sueñes! El River Plate está jugando muy bien y creo que va a ganar. Te apuesto a que el marcador va a ser dos a cero. Además, tu equipo tiene un portero pésimo.**
Manuel: **Bueno, ya veremos. Nosotros vamos a llegar a la Copa Libertadores. Hasta el sábado.**

Carlos: *Hey, Manuel, would you like to go to the soccer game on Saturday?*
Manuel: *I'd love to! Do you have tickets?*
Carlos: *Yes, I have two tickets for the game between Boca Juniors and Atlético River Plate.*

Manuel:	*Well, it's a game we can't miss. You know I'm a big fan of Boca. What time do they play?*
Carlos:	*The game starts at seven in the evening. Do you want me to pick you up at your place at around five thirty?*
Manuel:	*No, I think I'll be at work. I'll drop by your apartment when I'm done.*
Carlos:	*Okay. So what are our bets going to be this time?*
Manuel:	*I bet you Boca will win one to nothing in the first thirty minutes of the game.*
Carlos:	*In your dreams! River Plate is playing very well and I think they'll win. I bet you the score will be two to zero. Plus, your team has a terrible goalkeeper.*
Manuel:	*We'll see. We'll make it to the Copa Libertadores. See you Saturday.*

Culture Note

The soccer club **Atlético Boca Juniors** is one of the most popular and successful in Argentina. It's located in **La Boca**, a neighborhood in Buenos Aires. This club, along with its rival, **Atlético River Plate**, can fill up entire stadiums in Argentina. The **Boca Juniors** have won several soccer cups, including the Intercontinental Cup in 1978, 2000, and 2003; and the **Copa Libertadores** in 1977, 1978, 2000, 2001, 2003, and 2007. To read more about both clubs, check out ***www.bocajuniors.com.ar*** and ***www.cariverplate.com.ar***.

Conversation Practice 2

Fill in the blanks below with the appropriate word based on the English translations and the dialogue above.

1. **Bueno, pues es un partido que no ________________ perder.**

   Well, it's a game we can't miss.

2. **El partido** ______________________ **a las siete de la noche.**

The game starts at seven in the evening.

3. **¿Quieres que te** ______________ **en tu casa a eso de las cinco y media?**

Do you want me to pick you up at your place at around five thirty?

4. **Te apuesto a que el Boca** ____________________ **en los primeros treinta minutos de juego.** *I bet you Boca will win one to nothing in the first thirty minutes of the game.*

5. **Además, tu equipo tiene** ________________________ **pésimo.**

Plus, your team has a terrible goalkeeper.

ANSWER KEY

1. **nos lo podemos**; 2. **empieza**; 3. **recoja**; 4. **gana uno a cero**; 5. **un portero**

Grammar Builder 2

RELATIVE PRONOUNS AND CLAUSES

16D Grammar Builder 2 (CD 9, Track 22)

Relative pronouns, such as *that*, *which*, and *who(m)*, are used to refer back to a previous noun in a sentence. They introduce relative clauses, which are mini-sentences that give more information about that previous noun: *The book that I read is very interesting. The team that I like the most just won.* In many cases in English, we can even omit relative pronouns like *who* and *that*. In Spanish, however, relative pronouns cannot be left out, and there is a wider variety to choose from.

The two most common relative pronouns are **que** and **quien**. **Que** is used to refer to both people and things. **Quien** (plural form **quienes**) is used only to refer to people, and it's preceded by the prepositions **a**, **con**, **para**, or **de**.

El equipo que acaba de ganar es mi favorito.
The team that has just won is my favorite.

El jugador con quien hablaste es muy famoso.
The player you talked to is very famous.

El hombre que está afuera es su esposo.
The man who's outside is her husband.

Las mujeres a quienes entrevistaste son atletas profesionales.
The women you interviewed are professional athletes.

When the relative pronoun must specify one among several previously mentioned nouns, a compound form using the definite article (**el**, **la**, **los**, **las**) + **que** or **cual(es)** is used. They are generally used after prepositions, such as **en**, **sin**, **por**, and **para**. Notice that the definite article agrees in number and gender with the noun it refers to.

No es el auto en el que viajé la semana pasada.
It's not the car that I traveled in last week. (... in which I traveled last week.)

Es la calle por la que caminamos ayer.
It's the street we walked along yesterday. (... along which we walked yesterday.)

Son los sueños en los cuales siempre piensas.
They are the dreams that you always think of. (... in which you always think.)

Es la mujer de la cual está enamorado.
She's the woman he's in love with. (... with whom he's in love.)

Cuyo (cuya, cuyos, cuyas) is also a relative pronoun but looks more like an adjective, because it agrees in gender and number with the person or thing possessed, not with the person or thing it refers to.

El autor, cuyo nombre no recuerdo, vivió en esta ciudad.
The author, whose name I don't remember, lived in this city.

Los niños, cuyas manos están sucias, no quieren lavarse.
The children, whose hands are dirty, don't want to wash up.

Work Out 2

Choose the relative pronoun that best completes the sentence.

1. **Los pasajes __________ compré son solamente de ida. (los cuales, que, los que)**
2. **La cantante, ______________ fama es mundial, viene a finales de septiembre. (que, quien, cuya)**
3. **El apartamento en ______________ quiero vivir está en el último piso de ese edificio. (la cual, el cual, los cuales)**
4. **Las mujeres ______________ nos visitaron eran espías. (quienes, que, cuyas)**
5. **Los chicos, __________ nombres desconozco, son los hijos de nuestra vecina. (cuyos, que, quienes)**
6. **Esos son los documentos con ____________________ te debes presentar ante el juez. (quienes, los cuales, cuyos)**
7. **El hombre con _________________ nos encontramos era el esposo de Maura. (los cuales, quienes, quien)**
8. **Las estampillas ________ compré son para mi colección. (la cual, quien, que)**

ANSWER KEY

1. **que**; 2. **cuya**; 3. **el cual**; 4. **que**; 5. **cuyos**; 6. **los cuales**; 7. **quien**; 8. **que**

Culture Note

One of the most prestigious soccer trophies is without doubt **La Copa Libertadores de América**. It's an international cup organized by **CONMEBOL** (**Confederación Sudaméricana de Fútbol**) and is played for by the leading clubs in South America. Teams from Argentina have been the most successful in the competition, earning a total of twenty-two trophies over the course of the **Copa**'s history. A Brazilian team has won the trophy fourteen times. For more information, visit www.conmebol.com.

The **Copa América** is another important national competition in South America. It's played every two years. Twelve countries participate: Argentina, Brazil, Bolivia, Chile, Colombia, Ecuador, Paraguay, Peru, Uruguay, and Venezuela, along with two additional guests from other soccer confederations.

Drive It Home

Change each sentence from the indicative to the subjunctive. Start each sentence by saying **Yo no creo que él …** (*I don't think that he …*)

1. **Creo que él compra un apartamento nuevo.** ______________________

____

2. **Creo que él vive en Miami.** ______________________

____

3. **Creo que él habla inglés.** ______________________

____

4. **Creo que él estudia otros idiomas.** ______________________

____

5. Creo que él va a Nueva York. ______________________________

____

6. Creo que él dice la verdad. ______________________________

____

7. Creo que él saca buenas notas en los exámenes. ______________________________

____

8. Creo que él viene a visitarnos. ______________________________

____

ANSWER KEY

1. Yo no creo que él compre un apartamento nuevo. 2. Yo no creo que él viva en Miami. 3. Yo no creo que él hable inglés. 4. Yo no creo que él estudie otros idiomas. 5. Yo no creo que él vaya a Nueva York. 6. Yo no creo que él diga la verdad. 7. Yo no creo que él saque buenas notas en los exámenes. 8. Yo no creo que él venga a visitarnos.

How Did You Do?

By now, you should be able to:

- □ Identify the difference in using the subjunctive and the indicative. (Still unsure? Jump back to page 212.)
- □ Use relative pronouns to create clauses (Still unsure? Jump back to page 217.)

Don't forget to practice and reinforce what you've learned by visiting **www.livinglanguage.com/languagelab** for flashcards, games, and quizzes for Unit 4!

Unit 4 Essentials

Vocabulary Essentials

LEISURE VOCABULARY

	hobby
	fan
	hobby
	free time
	to collect
	craft
	photography
	music
	painting
	dancing
	stamp collecting
	antiques
	cooking
	sewing
	reading

[Pg. 180]

LEISURE VERBS

	to collect pieces of art
	to visit antique shops

	to attend an auction
	to rest
	to have an expensive hobby
	to spend the day at the swimming pool
	to be lazy
	to listen to music
	to play sports
	to do exercise
	to keep a diary

[Pg. 189]

LEISURE EXPRESSIONS

	LPs have a certain charm.
	Are you a soccer fan?
	I like the sound the needle makes.
	I have a huge collection.
	Which means you don't like my music.
	I prefer classical music.
	We have very different tastes.
	It's the sport I like the least.
	Technology allows us to listen to music in such a clear way.

[Pg. 199]

SPORTS VOCABULARY

	sport
	athlete
	person who plays sports
	player
	biking, cycling
	soccer
	baseball
	swimming
	diving
	horseback riding
	hunting
	basketball
	chess

[Pg. 183]

SPORTS VERBS

	to win a game
	to lose a game
	to fill up a stadium
	to score a goal
	to exchange T-shirts
	to buy tickets at the gate
	to be tied
	to stand in line
	to cheer for a team

[Pg. 193]

SPORTS EXPRESSIONS

	Don't even dream about it!
	We can't miss it.
	Would you like to go to Saturday's game?
	It is better that I drop by your apartment later on.
	I bet you Boca will win.
	The score will be two to zero.
	Would you like me to pick you up at your place?
	I have a few tickets for the game.
	I'm a fan of that team.

[Pg. 204]

Grammar Essentials

IMPERSONAL SE

The impersonal **se** is used in front of verbs to make general statements referring to *people in general* or *one*.

Use **se** with either the third person singular or the third person plural of the verb.

RELATIVE PRONOUNS

Relative pronouns are used to refer back to a previous noun in a sentence. They introduce relative clauses, which are mini-sentences that give more information about that previous noun. In Spanish, relative pronouns cannot be omitted.

que *(that, which, who, whom)*	*Refers to people and things*
quien/quienes *(that, which, who, whom)*	*Refers to people, usually preceded by the prepositions* **a**, **con**, **para**, *or* **de**

cuyo/cuya/cuyos/cuyas (*whose*)	*agrees in gender and number with the person or thing possessed, not with the person or thing it refers to*

When the relative pronoun must specify one among several previously mentioned nouns, a compound form using the definite article (**el**, **la**, **los**, **las**) + **que** or **cual(es)** is used, generally after prepositions, such as **en**, **sin**, **por**, and **para**.

THE CONDITIONAL

The present conditional is used to express the probability or possibility that something would happen, depending on specific circumstances. To form the conditional, simply add the following endings to the infinitive form of any verb.

CONDITIONAL ENDINGS	
yo -ía	**nosotros/as -íamos**
tú -ías	**vosotros/as -íais**
él/ella/usted -ía	**ellos/ellas/ustedes -ían**

IRREGULAR CONDITIONAL VERB STEMS

saber	**sabr-ía**	*to know*
tener	**tendr-ía**	*to have*
salir	**saldr-ía**	*to go out*
poder	**podr-ía**	*to be able to*
hacer	**har-ía**	*to make*
decir	**dir-ía**	*to say*
haber	**habr-ía**	*there is/there are*
querer	**querr-ía**	*to want*
venir	**vendr-ía**	*to come*

THE SUBJUNCTIVE

The subjunctive mood expresses things or events that are not factual or concrete, but rather, hypothetical or subjective.

The subjunctive is usually introduced by **que**.

To form the present subjunctive of regular verbs, take the conjugation of the verb in the first person singular (**yo**) of the present tense, drop the final **-o**, and add the following endings.

SUBJUNCTIVE ENDINGS OF REGULAR -AR VERBS	
yo -e	**nosotros/as -emos**
tú -es	**vosotros/as -éis**
él/ella/usted -e	**ellos/ellas/ustedes -en**

SUBJUNCTIVE ENDINGS OF REGULAR -ER/-IR VERBS	
yo -a	**nosotros/as -amos**
tú -as	**vosotros/as -áis**
él/ella/usted -a	**ellos/ellas/ustedes -an**

EXPRESSIONS THAT REQUIRE THE SUBJUNCTIVE

Es preferible que ...	*It's preferable that ...*
Es mejor que ...	*It's better that ...*
Es necesario que ...	*It's necessary that ...*
Es posible que ...	*It is possible that ...*
No es verdad que ...	*It is not true that ...*
No es cierto que ...	*It is not true that ...*
Es imposible que ...	*It is impossible that ...*
No hay nada que ...	*There's nothing that ...*
No hay nadie que ...	*There's no one who that ...*
No hay ningún/ninguna ... que ...	*There's no ... that/who ...*

Es una lástima que ...	*It's a pity that ...*
Es triste que ...	*It's sad that ...*
Es bueno que ...	*It's good that ...*

VERBS THAT REQUIRE THE SUBJUNCTIVE

aconsejar que ...	*to advise that/to ...*
alegrarse de que ...	*to be glad that ...*
desear que ...	*to wish that ...*
dudar que ...	*to doubt that ...*
enfadarse que ...	*to be angry that ...*
esperar que ...	*to hope that ...*
gustar que ...	*to like (it) that ...*
insistir en que ...	*to insist that ...*
molestarse que ...	*to be bothered that ...*
negar que ...	*to deny that ...*
no creer que ...	*not to believe that ...*
no pensar que ...	*not to think that ...*
pedir que ...	*to request that ...*
preferir que ...	*to prefer that ...*
preocuparse de que ...	*to worry that ...*
prohibir que ...	*to forbid that/to ...*
querer que ...	*to want that/to ...*
recomendar que ...	*to recommend that ...*
sentir que ...	*to regret that ...*
sorprenderse de que ...	*to be surprised that ...*
sugerir que ...	*to suggest that ...*
tener miedo de que ...	*to be afraid that ...*

VERBS

ABRIR *(TO OPEN)* - CONDITIONAL	
yo abriría	nosotros/as abriríamos
tú abrirías	vosotros/as abriríais
él/ella/usted abriría	ellos/ellas/ustedes abrirían

BUSCAR *(TO LOOK FOR)* - SUBJUNCTIVE	
yo busque	nosotros/as busquemos
tú busques	vosotros/as busquéis
él/ella/usted busque	ellos/ellas/ustedes busquen

COMENZAR *(TO BEGIN)* - SUBJUNCTIVE	
yo comience	nosotros/as comencemos
tú comiences	vosotros/as comencéis
él/ella/usted comience	ellos/ellas/ustedes comiencen

COMER *(TO EAT)* - SUBJUNCTIVE	
yo coma	nosotros/as comamos
tú comas	vosotros/as comáis
él/ella/usted coma	ellos/ellas/ustedes coman

COMPRAR *(TO BUY)* - SUBJUNCTIVE	
yo compre	nosotros/as compremos
tú compres	vosotros/as compréis
él/ella/usted compre	ellos/ellas/ustedes compren

DAR *(TO GIVE)* - SUBJUNCTIVE	
yo dé	nosotros/as demos
tú des	vosotros/as deis
él/ella/usted dé	ellos/ellas/ustedes den

ESTAR *(TO BE)* - SUBJUNCTIVE	
yo esté	nosotros/as estemos
tú estés	vosotros/as estéis
él/ella/usted esté	ellos/ellas/ustedes estén

HABLAR *(TO TALK)* - CONDITIONAL	
yo hablaría	nosotros/as hablaríamos
tú hablarías	vosotros/as hablaríais
él/ella/usted hablaría	ellos/ellas/ustedes hablarían

IR *(TO GO)* - SUBJUNCTIVE	
yo vaya	nosotros/as vayamos
tú vayas	vosotros/as vayáis
él/ella/usted vaya	ellos/ellas/ustedes vayan

PAGAR *(TO PAY)* - SUBJUNCTIVE	
yo pague	nosotros/as paguemos
tú pagues	vosotros/as paguéis
él/ella/usted pague	ellos/ellas/ustedes paguen

PENSAR *(TO THINK)* - SUBJUNCTIVE	
yo piense	nosotros/as pensemos
tú pienses	vosotros/as penséis
él/ella/usted piense	ellos/ellas/ustedes piensen

PODER *(TO BE ABLE TO)* - SUBJUNCTIVE	
yo pueda	nosotros/as podamos
tú puedas	vosotros/as podáis
él/ella/usted pueda	ellos/ellas/ustedes puedan

SABER *(TO KNOW)* - SUBJUNCTIVE	
yo sepa	nosotros/as sepamos
tú sepas	vosotros/as sepáis
él/ella/usted sepa	ellos/ellas/ustedes sepan

SER *(TO BE)* - CONDITIONAL	
yo sería	nosotros/as seríamos
tú serías	vosotros/as seríais
él/ella/usted sería	ellos/ellas/ustedes serían

SER *(TO BE)* - SUBJUNCTIVE	
yo sea	nosotros/as seamos
tú seas	vosotros/as seáis
él/ella/usted sea	ellos/ellas/ustedes sean

SERVIR *(TO SERVE)* - SUBJUNCTIVE	
yo sirva	nosotros/as sirvamos
tú sirvas	vosotros/as sirváis
él/ella/usted sirva	ellos/ellas/ustedes sirvan

Unit 4 Quiz

A. Give the corresponding subjunctive form of the verb in parentheses.

1. **Te recomiendo que (tú buscar) tu pasaporte pronto.** ______________________

____

2. **Es posible que (ellos pasar) mucho tiempo buscándolo.** ______________________

____

3. **Me sorprende que (ella no encontrar) las llaves.** ______________________

____

4. **Te aconsejo que (tú hacer) fila.** ______________________

____

5. **Me molesta que (ellos fumar).** ______________________

____

6. **Espero que (ustedes ir) al aeropuerto.** ______________________

____

7. **Es mejor que (ellos tener) más cuidado con sus bicicletas.** ______________________

____

8. **Es preferible que (nosotros visitar) a la familia mañana.** ______________________

____

B. Match the column on the left with the English word on the right.

1. **perder un partido**
2. **quedar empatados**
3. **descansar**
4. **la natación**
5. **la caza**
6. **el ajedrez**
7. **el pasatiempo**
8. **la lectura**

a. *swimming*
b. *to be tied*
c. *chess*
d. *to rest*
e. *hobby*
f. *to lose a game*
g. *reading*
h. *hunting*

C. Determine whether each verb should be in the indicative or subjunctive form. Then conjugate each verb in the blanks below.

1. **Yo no __________ (creer) que tú ________________ (llegar) a tiempo.**
2. **Es posible que él te __________ su plato favorito. (servir)**
3. **Nosotros ______________________ (esperar) que ella ________________ (asistir) a la subasta.**
4. **Ojalá que ellos _________________ a tiempo. (llegar)**
5. **Él me __________________ (aconsejar) que yo __________________ (ir) al estadio temprano.**
6. **Ella ____________ (desear) que usted ____________ (comer) toda la comida.**
7. **Ellos __________________ (sugerir) que nosotros ____________________ (pagar) con tarjeta de crédito.**
8. **Es posible que ellos _________________ el campeonato mundial. (perder)**

D. Select the correct term from each pair:

1. Paquito es ______________________________ a los deportes. (afición/aficionado)

2. La música, la pintura y ____________________ son mis formas de arte favoritas. (el baile/la cocina)

3. Cuando tengo ________________________________ voy a comprar antigüedades. (la costura/tiempo libre)

4. Yo __________________________ una computadora nueva pero no tengo dinero. (compraría/compro)

5. Me gusta mucho el agua, por eso prefiero ____________________ y la natación. (el buceo/la equitación)

6. Mi ______________________________ favorito es el fútbol. (deporte/deportista)

7. El equipo ganó el partido porque ______________________________ un gol más. (intercambió/marcó)

8. Voy ahora a comprar los boletos en ____. (la camiseta/la taquilla)

ANSWER KEY

A. 1. Te recomiendo que tú busques tu pasaporte pronto. 2. Es posible que ellos pasen mucho tiempo buscándolo. 3. Me sorprende que ella no encuentre las llaves. 4. Te aconsejo que tú hagas fila. 5. Me molesta que ellos fumen. 6. Espero que ustedes vayan al aeropuerto. 7. Es mejor que ellos tengan más cuidado con sus bicicletas. 8. Es preferible que nosotros visitemos a la familia mañana.

B. 1. f; 2. b; 3. d; 4. a; 5. h; 6. c; 7. e; 8. g

C. 1. creo/llegues; 2. sirva; 3. esperamos/asista; 4. lleguen; 5. aconseja/vaya; 6. desea/coma; 7. sugieren/paguemos; 8. pierdan

D. 1. aficionado; 2. el baile; 3. tiempo libre; 4. compraría; 5. el buceo; 6. deporte; 7. marcó; 8. la taquilla

How Did You Do?

Give yourself a point for every correct answer, then use the following key to determine whether or not you're ready to move on:

0–7 points: It's probably best to go back and study the lessons again to make sure you understood everything completely. Take your time; it's not a race! Make sure you spend time reviewing vocabulary with the flashcards and reading through each grammar note carefully.

8–16 points: If the questions you missed were in sections A or B, you may want to review the vocabulary again; if you missed answers mostly in sections C or D, check the unit essentials to make sure you have your conjugations and other grammar basics down.

17–20 points: Great! Your Spanish has come a long way! Even though you've reached the end of this course, there's no reason to stop learning.

points

Consider some of these activities to keep your Spanish fresh, and to continue learning.

- ☐ Watch Spanish language movies.
- ☐ Download (legally!) a few Spanish songs and pay attention to the lyrics or look up the lyrics online to read along.
- ☐ Bookmark an online Spanish language newspaper or magazine. Read a little bit every day.
- ☐ Buy a book in Spanish and try to read it every day.
- ☐ Check out chatrooms or other online communities in Spanish.
- ☐ Remember to visit **www.livinglanguage.com/languagelab** for further practice, and return to this book to review any time you want.
- ☐ Use your imagination! You can tailor your Spanish exposure to your interests—food, music, theater, music, sports: the path is up to you. Enjoy, and **buena suerte**!

Pronunciation Guide

If you've ever had trouble with English spelling, or if you've ever come across an unfamiliar word and had no idea how to pronounce it, you'll be happy to know that neither of these things is likely to be an issue in Spanish. Spanish spelling is phonetic, meaning that things are pronounced the way they're written. The rules for stress—which SYL-la-ble gets the EM-pha-sis—are very regular in Spanish, and any irregularities are marked in spelling with an accent mark. We'll cover all of that little by little, but let's get started with an overview of Spanish pronunciation.

1. VOWELS

Each vowel in Spanish is pronounced clearly and distinctly, and each vowel has one and only one pronunciation. A vowel may be written with an accent, as in **sí** or **América**, but this never changes the pronunciation of that vowel. It may mark stress, as in **América**, or it may only serve to distinguish between two words, as in **sí** (*yes*) and **si** (*if*). Let's look at each vowel, starting with simple vowels.

a	like *a* in *father*	**a, amigo, la, las, pan, habla, Santiago**
e	like *ay* in *day*, but cut off before the *ee*	**él, de, en, padre, tren, este, Mercedes**
i	like *i* in *police*	**mí, amiga, hiciste, cinco, Chile, Sevilla**
o	like *o* in *no*, but cut off before the *oo*	**no, dos, hombre, costar, ocho, teléfono, Colombia**
u	like *u* in *rule*	**uno, tú, mucho, azúcar, Honduras, puro**

Vowels can also appear in pairs, which are called diphthongs. A diphthong is usually a combination of a weaker vowel (**i** or **u**) and a more prominent one.

ai, ay	like *i* in *bide*	**aire, hay, traigo, ¡ay!**

au	like *ou* in *house*	**restaurante, autobús, automóvil, Mauricio**
ei, ey	like *ay* in *day*	**seis, ley, treinta, rey**
ia, ya	like *ya* in *yard*	**gracias, comercial, estudiar, ya**
ie, ye	like *ye* in *yet*	**pie, quiero, tiene, yerba, abyecto**
io, yo	like *yo* in *yoga*	**yo, acción, despacio, estudio**
iu, yu	like *u* in *united*	**ciudad, yuca, yugo, yunta**
oi, oy	like *oy* in *toy*	**estoy, hoy, oiga, voy**
ua	like *wa* in *want*	**cuatro, Juan, ¿cuál?, ¿cuánto?**
ue	like *we* in *west*	**nueve, fuego, puerta, cuesta, bueno**
uo	like *wo* in *woe*	**continuo, antiguo, mutuo, superfluo**
ui, uy	like *we* in *week*	**muy, ruido, cuidado, huir**

2. CONSONANTS

b	like *b* in *boy* at the beginning of a word	**bueno, brazo, bajo, barca, bocadillo**
b	between vowels for some speakers, as above, but the lips don't touch	**Cuba, haber, beber, cobayo, deber, ubicar**
c	like *k* in *kite* before consonants, **a**, **o**, and **u**	**Cristóbal, cosa, casa, cuánto, cuál, truco**

c	like *s* in *sea* before **e** and **i**	**cerca, servicio, cierto, fácil, posición**
ch	like *ch* in *choose*	**charlar, chico, muchacho, ocho, mucho**
d	at the beginning of a word or after **n**, like *d* in *day*, but with the tongue touching the back of the upper teeth	**día, despegar, durante, cuándo, donde, mando**
d	between vowels, like *th* in *thin*	**media, nada, todo, poder, freiduría, prometido**
f	like *f* in *father*	**familia, Francisco, Federico, formulario**
g	like *g* in *go* before consonants, **a**, **o**, and **u**	**grande, Gloria, gustar, gusano, goloso, ganar, vengo**
g	like the strong *h* in *hope* before **e** or **i**	**general, Gibraltar, girar, rígido, urgente**
gü	like *gw* in *Gwen*	**vergüenza, lengüeta, cigüeña**
h	silent	**hablo, hay, hubo, ahora, hombre, deshonroso**
j	like the strong *h* in *hope*	**julio, jabón, mejor, José, tarjeta, jefe, trujar**
ll	like *y* in *yes*	**llamo, pollo, llama, llover, allí, llaves, trulla**
m	like *m* in *met*	**mismo, Marco, mano, Manuel, pluma, mandar**

n	like *n* in *not*	**nunca, no, Nicaragua, Argentina, nombre**
ñ	like *ni* in *onion*	**español, mañana, muñeca, ñame, gañir**
p	like *p* in *pear*	**para, pueblo, postre, Panamá, Perú**
qu	like *k* in *kite*	**que, querer, paquete, saquen, quemar, quizás**
r	at the beginning of a word, a trilled sound made with the tongue against the ridge behind the upper teeth	**rico, rubio, Ramón, Rosa, rincón, red, risa**
r	otherwise like the tapped *d* in *ladder*	**América, pero, quisiera, aire, libre, brazo, caro**
rr	like word-initial **r**, a trilled sound made with the tongue against the ridge behind the upper teeth	**perro, carro, tierra, horror, irritar, terrible**
s	like *s* in *see* (never like *z* in *zone*)	**casa, sucio, San Salvador, soltero, vasto, rosa**
t	like *t* in *take*, but with the tongue touching the back of the upper teeth	**tocar, fruta, tú, teclado, traje, tener**
v	like *b* in *boy* at the beginning of a word	**vaso, veinte, vivir, vivo, veramente**
y	like *y* in *yes*; on its own, like *ee* in *teen*	**ayer, ayudo, Bayamo, poyo**

z	like *s* in *see*	**zona, diez, luz, marzo, azul, azúcar**

3. STRESS

There are three simple rules to keep in mind when it comes to stress. First, if a word ends in any consonant other than **-n** or **-s**, the last syllable receives the stress.

cuidad, capaz, notabilidad, navegar, familiar, refrigerador

Second, if a word ends in a vowel or in **-n** or **-s**, the penultimate (second-to-last) syllable receives the stress.

amigo, hablan, derechos, cubierto, portorriqueño, examen, libros

Note that diphthongs with the weak vowels **i** or **u** count as one syllable, so the stress will regularly fall before them.

academia, continuo, manubrio, sanitario, justicia

Combinations with two strong vowels count as two syllables.

tarea, menudeo, banqueteo, barbacoa

Any time stress doesn't follow these rules, an accent is used.

inglés, teléfono, tomó, práctico, drogaría, todavía, título, farmacéutico, petróleo, revés, apagón

4. REGIONAL SPANISH PRONUNCIATION

The Spanish pronunciation that you'll learn in this course is standard Latin American Spanish. There are certainly some local differences in pronunciation that you will probably come across, the most commonly known being the difference between Latin American and European Spanish. The major difference in pronunciation is that the sound *th,* as in *thin,* is much more common in Spain. In Latin America, this sound is typically only found in *d* when it comes between vowels.

media, nada, todo, poder, puedo

These words are pronounced with a *th* in Spain, too. But in Spain, **c** before **i** or **e** and **z** is also pronounced like *th* in *thin.*

cerca, servicio, cierto, fácil, docena, diez, voz, luz, marzo, azul, razón

There are some noticeable differences in local varieties of Spanish found in Latin America and Spain, as well. You don't need to worry about imitating these differences; the standard pronunciation you'll learn in this course will serve you perfectly well. But you may notice, for example, that in some countries or regions the combination **ll** is pronounced like the *lli* in *million,* the *j* in *juice,* the *sh* in *show,* or the *s* in *pleasure.* The semivowel **y** may have a similar range of pronunciation. In some countries, particularly in the Caribbean, final **s** may be dropped altogether, if not the entire last syllable! You may even hear **r** pronounced as something similar to **l**. There's certainly nothing wrong with any of these variations, although as a student, you'll probably find it useful to concentrate on the standard pronunciation offered in this course first.

Grammar Summary

Keep in mind that there are always at least some exceptions to every grammar rule.

1. ARTICLES

	DEFINITE		INDEFINITE	
	Singular	Plural	Singular	Plural
Masculine	**el**	**los**	**un**	**unos**
Feminine	**la**	**las**	**una**	**unas**

Note: **El** is used before a feminine noun beginning with stressed **a** (or **ha**). The article **lo** is used before parts of speech other than nouns when they are used as nouns. **Unos** (**unas**) is often used to mean *some* or *a few*.

2. CONTRACTIONS

de + **el** = **del** (*from/of the*)

a + **el** = **al** (*to the*)

3. PLURALS

a. Nouns ending in an unstressed vowel or diphthong add **-s**.

b. Nouns ending in a stressed vowel or diphthong add **-es**.

c. Nouns ending in a consonant add **-es**.

d. Nouns ending in **-z** change the **z** to **c** and then add **-es**.

4. POSSESSION

Possession is shown by the preposition **de**: **el libro de Juan** (*Juan's book*).

5. ADJECTIVES

Adjectives agree with the nouns they modify in both gender and number.

a. If the masculine singular ending is **-o**, the feminine singular is **-a**, the masculine plural is **-os**, and the feminine plural is **-as**.
b. If the masculine singular ending is not **-o**, there is no change in the feminine singular, and both genders are **-es** in the plural.

6. COMPARISON

The regular comparative is formed with **más** (*more*) or **menos** (*less*), and the regular superlative is formed with the definite article + **más** (*the most*) or **menos** (*the least*).

7. PRONOUNS

	SUBJECT	DIRECT OBJECT	INDIRECT OBJECT	PREPOSITIONAL	REFLEXIVE
1st sg.	**yo**	**me**	**me**	**mí**	**me**
2nd sg.	**tú**	**te**	**te**	**ti**	**te**
3rd m. sg.	**él**	**lo**	**le**	**él**	**se**
3rd f. sg.	**ella**	**la**	**le**	**ella**	**se**
2nd sg., fml.	**usted**	**lo/la**	**le**	**usted**	**se**
1st pl.	**nosotros/ nosotras**	**nos**	**nos**	**nosotros**	**nos**
2nd pl.	**vosotros/ vosotras**	**os**	**os**	**vosotros**	**os**
3rd m. pl.	**ellos**	**los**	**les**	**ellos**	**se**

	SUBJECT	DIRECT OBJECT	INDIRECT OBJECT	PREPOSITIONAL	REFLEXIVE
3rd f. pl.	**ellas**	**las**	**les**	**ellas**	**se**
2nd pl., fml.	**ustedes**	**los/las**	**les**	**ustedes**	**se**

8. QUESTION WORDS

¿Qué?	*What?*	**¿Cuál?** **¿Cuáles?**	*What?/ Which one?*
¿Por qué?	*Why?*	**¿Quién?** **¿Quiénes?**	*Who?*
¿Cómo?	*How?*	**¿Dónde?**	*Where?*
¿Cuánto? **¿Cuánta?** **¿Cuántos?** **¿Cuántas?**	*How much?/How many?*	**¿Cuándo?**	*When?*

9. ADVERBS

Spanish **-mente** corresponds to *-ly* in English. It is added to the feminine form of the adjective.

10. DEMONSTRATIVES

ADJECTIVES		PRONOUNS			
Masculine	Feminine	Masculine	Feminine	Neuter	
este	**esta**	**éste**	**ésta**	**esto**	*this*
ese	**esa**	**ése**	**ésa**	**eso**	*that*
aquel	**aquella**	**aquél**	**aquélla**	**aquello**	*that (farther removed)*
estos	**estas**	**éstos**	**éstas**	**estos**	*these*
esos	**esas**	**ésos**	**ésas**	**esos**	*those*
aquellos	**aquellas**	**aquéllos**	**aquéllas**	**aquellos**	*those (farther removed)*

11. *IF* SENTENCES

IF THE MAIN CLAUSE HAS A VERB IN THE:	THE **SI** *(IF)* CLAUSE HAS A VERB IN THE:
Present	*Present/Future*
Future	*Present*
Imperfect	*Imperfect*
Preterite	*Preterite*
Conditional	*Imperfect Subjunctive (**-ra** or **-se**)*
Past Conditional	*Past Perfect Subjunctive (**hubiera** or **hubiese**)*

If the subject of the main clause and the subject of the *if* clause are the same, it's possible to replace a verb in the subjunctive with an infinitive. In this case **si** is replaced by **de**.

12. SUBJUNCTIVE

The subjunctive is used:

a. with verbs of desire, request, suggestion, permission, approval and disapproval, judgment, opinion, uncertainty, emotion, surprise, fear, denial, and so on. It is often used in a dependent clause introduced by **que** (*that*).
b. in affirmative or negative commands in the polite form, in negative commands in the familiar form, in *let's* suggestions, and in indirect or third person commands with *let* (*him/her/them*).
c. in **si** (*if*) conditional clauses that are unreal or contrary to fact.
d. after impersonal verbs that do not express certainty.
e. after certain conjunctions that never introduce statements of accomplished fact (**antes de que**, **aunque**, **como si**, etc.). Other conjunctions may or may not introduce a statement of accomplished fact. When they do, they take the indicative; otherwise they take the subjunctive (**a menos que**, **a pesar de que**, etc.).
f. to refer to indefinites like **ningún** (*no*) or **alguien** (*someone*) when there's a doubt about that person's existence.
g. after compounds with **-quiera** (*-ever*): **quienquiera** (*whoever*), **dondequiera** (*wherever*), **cualquier** (*whatever, whichever*).

comer

to eat

yo	nosotros/as
tú	vosotros/as
él/ella/usted	ellos/ellas/ustedes

Present		Present Progressive	
como	comemos	estoy comiendo	estamos comiendo
comes	coméis	estás comiendo	estáis comiendo
come	comen	está comiendo	están comiendo

Preterite		Imperfect	
comí	comimos	comía	comíamos
comiste	comisteis	comías	comíais
comió	comieron	comía	comían

Future		Conditional	
comeré	comeremos	comería	comeríamos
comerás	comeréis	comerías	comeríais
comerá	comerán	comería	comerían

Imperative		Subjunctive	
		coma	comamos
come	comed	comas	comáis
coma		coma	coman

conducir

to drive

yo	nosotros/as
tú	vosotros/as
él/ella/usted	ellos/ellas/ustedes

Present		Present Progressive	
conduzco	conducimos	estoy conduciendo	estamos conduciendo
conduces	conducís	estás conduciendo	estáis conduciendo
conduce	conducen	está conduciendo	están conduciendo

Preterite		Imperfect	
conduje	condujimos	conducía	conducíamos
condujiste	condujisteis	conducías	conducíais
condujo	condujeron	conducía	conducían

Future		Conditional	
conduciré	conduciremos	conduciría	conduciríamos
conducirás	conduciréis	conducirías	conduciríais
conducirá	conducirán	conduciría	conducirían

Imperative		Subjunctive	
		conduzca	conduzcamos
conduce	conducid	conduzcas	conduzcáis
conduzca		conduzca	conduzcan

conocer
to know

yo	nosotros/as
tú	vosotros/as
él/ella/usted	ellos/ellas/ustedes

Present	
conozco	conocemos
conoces	conocéis
conoce	conocen

Present Progressive	
estoy conociendo	estamos conociendo
estás conociendo	estáis conociendo
está conociendo	están conociendo

Preterite	
conocí	conocimos
conociste	conocisteis
conoció	conocieron

Imperfect	
conocía	conocíamos
conocías	conocíais
conocía	conocían

Future	
conoceré	conoceremos
conocerás	conoceréis
conocerá	conocerán

Conditional	
conocería	conoceríamos
conocerías	conoceríais
conocería	conocerían

Imperative	
conoce	conoced
conozca	

Subjunctive	
conozca	conozcamos
conozcas	conozcáis
conozca	conozcan

dar
to give

yo	nosotros/as
tú	vosotros/as
él/ella/usted	ellos/ellas/ustedes

Present		Present Progressive	
doy	damos	estoy dando	estamos dando
das	dais	estás dando	estáis dando
da	dan	está dando	están dando

Preterite		Imperfect	
di	dimos	daba	dábamos
diste	disteis	dabas	dabais
dio	dieron	daba	daban

Future		Conditional	
daré	daremos	daría	daríamos
darás	daréis	darías	daríais
dará	darán	daría	darían

Imperative		Subjunctive	
		dé	demos
da	dad	des	deis
dé		dé	den

deber

to have to, must

yo	nosotros/as
tú	vosotros/as
él/ella/usted	ellos/ellas/ustedes

Present		Present Progressive	
debo	debemos	estoy debiendo	estamos debiendo
debes	debéis	estás debiendo	estáis debiendo
debe	deben	está debiendo	están debiendo

Preterite		Imperfect	
debí	debimos	debía	debíamos
debiste	debisteis	debías	debíais
debió	debieron	debía	debían

Future		Conditional	
deberé	deberemos	debería	deberíamos
deberás	deberéis	deberías	deberíais
deberá	deberán	debería	deberían

Imperative		Subjunctive	
		deba	debamos
debe	debed	debas	debáis
deba		deba	deban

escoger
to choose

yo	nosotros/as
tú	vosotros/as
él/ella/usted	ellos/ellas/ustedes

Present		Present Progressive	
escojo	escogemos	estoy escogiendo	estamos escogiendo
escoges	escogéis	estás escogiendo	estáis escogiendo
escoge	escogen	está escogiendo	están escogiendo

Preterite		Imperfect	
escogí	escogimos	escogía	escogíamos
escogiste	escogisteis	escogías	escogíais
escogió	escogieron	escogía	escogían

Future		Conditional	
escogeré	escogeremos	escogería	escogeríamos
escogerás	escogeréis	escogerías	escogeríais
escogerá	escogerán	escogería	escogerían

Imperative		Subjunctive	
		escoja	escojamos
escoge	escoged	escojas	escojáis
escoja		escoja	escojan

estar
to be

yo	nosotros/as
tú	vosotros/as
él/ella/usted	ellos/ellas/ustedes

Present		Present Progressive	
estoy	estamos	estoy estando	estamos estando
estás	estáis	estás estando	estáis estando
está	están	está estando	están estando

Preterite		Imperfect	
estuve	estuvimos	estaba	estábamos
estuviste	estuvisteis	estabas	estábais
estuvo	estuvieron	estaba	estaban

Future		Conditional	
estaré	estaremos	estaría	estaríamos
estarás	estaréis	estarías	estaríais
estará	estarán	estaría	estarían

Imperative		Subjunctive	
		esté	estemos
está	estad	estés	estéis
esté		esté	estén

hablar

to speak, to talk

yo	nosotros/as
tú	vosotros/as
él/ella/usted	ellos/ellas/ustedes

Present		Present Progressive	
hablo	hablamos	estoy hablando	estamos hablando
hablas	habláis	estás hablando	estáis hablando
habla	hablan	está hablando	están hablando

Preterite		Imperfect	
hablé	hablamos	hablaba	hablábamos
hablaste	hablasteis	hablabas	hablabais
habló	hablaron	hablaba	hablaban

Future		Conditional	
hablaré	hablaremos	hablaría	hablaríamos
hablarás	hablaréis	hablarías	hablaríais
hablará	hablarán	hablaría	hablarían

Imperative		Subjunctive	
		hable	hablemos
habla	hablad	hables	habléis
hable		hable	hablen

hacer
to do, to make

yo	nosotros/as
tú	vosotros/as
él/ella/usted	ellos/ellas/ustedes

Present		Present Progressive	
hago	hacemos	estoy haciendo	estamos haciendo
haces	hacéis	estás haciendo	estáis haciendo
hace	hacen	está haciendo	están haciendo

Preterite		Imperfect	
hice	hicimos	hacía	hacíamos
hiciste	hicisteis	hacías	hacíais
hizo	hicieron	hacía	hacían

Future		Conditional	
haré	haremos	haría	haríamos
harás	haréis	harías	haríais
hará	harán	haría	harían

Imperative		Subjunctive	
		haga	hagamos
haz	haced	hagas	hagáis
haga		haga	hagan

ir
to go

yo	nosotros/as
tú	vosotros/as
él/ella/usted	ellos/ellas/ustedes

Present		Present Progressive	
voy	vamos	estoy yendo	estamos yendo
vas	vais	estás yendo	estáis yendo
va	van	está yendo	están yendo

Preterite		Imperfect	
fui	fuimos	iba	íbamos
fuiste	fuisteis	ibas	ibais
fue	fueron	iba	iban

Future		Conditional	
iré	iremos	iría	iríamos
irás	iréis	irías	iríais
irá	irán	iría	irían

Imperative		Subjunctive	
		vaya	vayamos
ve	id	vayas	vayáis
vaya		vaya	vayan

pedir
to ask for

yo	nosotros/as
tú	vosotros/as
él/ella/usted	ellos/ellas/ustedes

Present		Present Progressive	
pido	pedimos	estoy pidiendo	estamos pidiendo
pides	pedís	estás pidiendo	estáis pidiendo
pide	piden	está pidiendo	están pidiendo

Preterite		Imperfect	
pedí	pedimos	pedía	pedíamos
pediste	pedisteis	pedías	pedíais
pidió	pidieron	pedía	pedían

Future		Conditional	
pediré	pediremos	pediría	pediríamos
pedirás	pediréis	pedirías	pediríais
pedirá	pedirán	pediría	pedirían

Imperative		Subjunctive	
		pida	pidamos
pide	pedid	pidas	pidáis
pida		pida	pidan

pensar
to think

yo	nosotros/as
tú	vosotros/as
él/ella/usted	ellos/ellas/ustedes

Present		Present Progressive	
pienso	pensamos	estoy pensando	estamos pensando
piensas	pensáis	estás pensando	estáis pensando
piensa	piensan	está pensando	están pensando

Preterite		Imperfect	
pensé	pensamos	pensaba	pensábamos
pensaste	pensasteis	pensabas	pensabais
pensó	pensaron	pensaba	pensaban

Future		Conditional	
pensaré	pensaremos	pensaría	pensaríamos
pensarás	pensaréis	pensarías	pensaríais
pensará	pensarán	pensaría	pensarían

Imperative		Subjunctive	
		piense	pensemos
piensa	pensad	pienses	penséis
piense		piense	piensen

poder
to be able to, can

yo	nosotros/as
tú	vosotros/as
él/ella/usted	ellos/ellas/ustedes

Present

puedo	podemos
puedes	podéis
puede	pueden

Present Progressive

estoy pudiendo	estamos pudiendo
estás pudiendo	estáis pudiendo
está pudiendo	están pudiendo

Preterite

pude	pudimos
pudiste	pudisteis
pudo	pudieron

Imperfect

podía	podíamos
podías	podíais
podía	podían

Future

podré	podremos
podrás	podréis
podrá	podrán

Conditional

podría	podríamos
podrías	podríais
podría	podrían

Imperative

puede	poded
pueda	

Subjunctive

pueda	podamos
puedas	podáis
pueda	puedan

poner
to put

yo	nosotros/as
tú	vosotros/as
él/ella/usted	ellos/ellas/ustedes

Present		Present Progressive	
pongo	ponemos	estoy poniendo	estamos poniendo
pones	ponéis	estás poniendo	estáis poniendo
pone	ponen	está poniendo	están poniendo

Preterite		Imperfect	
puse	pusimos	ponía	poníamos
pusiste	pusisteis	ponías	poníais
puso	pusieron	ponía	ponían

Future		Conditional	
pondré	pondremos	pondría	pondríamos
pondrás	pondréis	pondrías	pondríais
pondrá	pondrían	pondría	pondrían

Imperative		Subjunctive	
		ponga	pongamos
pon	poned	pongas	pongáis
ponga		ponga	pongan

querer

to want

yo	nosotros/as
tú	vosotros/as
él/ella/usted	ellos/ellas/ustedes

Present		Present Progressive	
quiero	queremos	estoy queriendo	estamos queriendo
quieres	queréis	estás queriendo	estáis queriendo
quiere	quieren	está queriendo	están queriendo

Preterite		Imperfect	
quise	quisimos	quería	queríamos
quisiste	quisisteis	querías	queríais
quiso	quisieron	quería	querían

Future		Conditional	
querré	querremos	querría	querríamos
querrás	querréis	querrías	querríais
querrá	querrán	querría	querrían

Imperative		Subjunctive	
		quiera	queramos
quiere	quered	quieras	queráis
quiera		quiera	quieran

saber
to know

yo	nosotros/as
tú	vosotros/as
él/ella/usted	ellos/ellas/ustedes

Present		Present Progressive	
sé	sabemos	estoy sabiendo	estamos sabiendo
sabes	sabéis	estás sabiendo	estáis sabiendo
sabe	saben	está sabiendo	están sabiendo

Preterite		Imperfect	
supe	supimos	sabía	sabíamos
supiste	supisteis	sabías	sabíais
supo	supieron	sabía	sabían

Future		Conditional	
sabré	sabremos	sabría	sabríamos
sabrás	sabréis	sabrías	sabríais
sabrá	sabrán	sabría	sabrían

Imperative		Subjunctive	
		sepa	sepamos
sabe	sabed	sepas	sepáis
sepa		sepa	sepan

salir
to go out

yo	nosotros/as
tú	vosotros/as
él/ella/usted	ellos/ellas/ustedes

Present		Present Progressive	
salgo	salimos	estoy saliendo	estamos saliendo
sales	salís	estás saliendo	estáis saliendo
sale	salen	está saliendo	están saliendo

Preterite		Imperfect	
salí	salimos	salía	salíamos
saliste	salisteis	salías	salíais
salió	salieron	salía	salían

Future		Conditional	
saldré	saldremos	saldría	saldríamos
saldrás	saldréis	saldrías	saldríais
saldrá	saldrán	saldría	saldrían

Imperative		Subjunctive	
		salga	salgamos
sal	salid	salgas	salgáis
salga		salga	salgan

ser
to be

yo	nosotros/as
tú	vosotros/as
él/ella/usted	ellos/ellas/ustedes

Present		Present Progressive	
soy	somos	estoy siendo	estamos siendo
eres	sois	estás siendo	estáis siendo
es	son	está siendo	están siendo

Preterite		Imperfect	
fui	fuimos	era	éramos
fuiste	fuisteis	eras	erais
fue	fueron	era	eran

Future		Conditional	
seré	seremos	sería	seríamos
serás	seréis	serías	seríais
será	serán	sería	serían

Imperative		Subjunctive	
		sea	seamos
sé	sed	seas	seáis
sea		sea	sean

tener
to have

yo	nosotros/as
tú	vosotros/as
él/ella/usted	ellos/ellas/ustedes

Present		Present Progressive	
tengo	tenemos	estoy teniendo	estamos teniendo
tienes	tenéis	estás teniendo	estáis teniendo
tiene	tienen	está teniendo	están teniendo

Preterite		Imperfect	
tuve	tuvimos	tenía	teníamos
tuviste	tuvisteis	tenías	teníais
tuvo	tuvieron	tenía	tenían

Future		Conditional	
tendré	tendremos	tendría	tendríamos
tendrás	tendréis	tendrías	tendríais
tendrá	tendrán	tendría	tendrían

Imperative		Subjunctive	
		tenga	tengamos
ten	tened	tengas	tengáis
tenga		tenga	tengan

traer
to bring

yo	nosotros/as
tú	vosotros/as
él/ella/usted	ellos/ellas/ustedes

Present		Present Progressive	
traigo	traemos	estoy trayendo	estamos trayendo
traes	traéis	estás trayendo	estáis trayendo
trae	traen	está trayendo	están trayendo

Preterite		Imperfect	
traje	trajimos	traía	traíamos
trajiste	trajisteis	traías	traíais
trajo	trajeron	traía	traían

Future		Conditional	
traeré	traeremos	traería	traeríamos
traerás	traeréis	traerías	traeríais
traerá	traerán	traería	traerían

Imperative		Subjunctive	
		traiga	traigamos
trae	traed	traigas	traigáis
traiga		traiga	traigan

venir
to come

yo	nosotros/as
tú	vosotros/as
él/ella/usted	ellos/ellas/ustedes

Present		Present Progressive	
vengo	venimos	estoy viniendo	estamos viniendo
vienes	venís	estás viniendo	estáis viniendo
viene	vienen	está viniendo	están viniendo

Preterite		Imperfect	
vine	vinimos	venía	veníamos
viniste	vinisteis	venías	veníais
vino	vinieron	venía	venían

Future		Conditional	
vendré	vendremos	vendría	vendríamos
vendrás	vendréis	vendrías	vendríais
vendrá	vendrán	vendría	vendrían

Imperative		Subjunctive	
		venga	vengamos
ven	venid	vengas	vengáis
venga		venga	vengan

ver
to see

yo	nosotros/as
tú	vosotros/as
él/ella/usted	ellos/ellas/ustedes

Present		Present Progressive	
veo	vemos	estoy viendo	estamos viendo
ves	veis	estás viendo	estáis viendo
ve	ven	está viendo	están viendo

Preterite		Imperfect	
vi	vimos	veía	veíamos
viste	visteis	veías	veíais
vio	vieron	veía	veían

Future		Conditional	
veré	veremos	vería	veríamos
verás	veréis	verías	veríais
verá	verán	vería	verían

Imperative		Subjunctive	
		vea	veamos
ve	ved	veas	veáis
vea		vea	vean

vivir
to live

yo	nosotros/as
tú	vosotros/as
él/ella/usted	ellos/ellas/ustedes

Present		Present Progressive	
vivo	vivimos	estoy viviendo	estamos viviendo
vives	vivís	estás viviendo	estáis viviendo
vive	viven	está viviendo	están viviendo

Preterite		Imperfect	
viví	vivimos	vivía	vivíamos
viviste	vivisteis	vivías	vivíais
vivió	vivieron	vivía	vivían

Future		Conditional	
viviré	viviremos	viviría	viviríamos
vivirás	viviréis	vivirías	viviríais
vivirá	vivirán	viviría	vivirían

Imperative		Subjunctive	
		viva	vivamos
vive	vivid	vivas	viváis
viva		viva	vivan

Glossary

Note that the following abbreviations will be used in this glossary: (m.) = masculine, (f.) = feminine, (sg.) = singular, (pl.) = plural, (fml.) = formal/polite, (infml.) = informal/familiar. If a word has two grammatical genders, (m./f.) or (f./m.) is used.

Spanish-English

A

a *to, at*
a las cinco *at five (o'clock)*
¿A qué hora es? *At what time is it?*
A ver ... *Let's see ...*
de ... a ... *from ... through ...*
abdomen (m.) *abdomen*
abogado/abogada (m./f.) *lawyer*
abonado/abonada (m./f.) *subscriber*
línea (f.) **de abonado digital (DSL)** *DSL*
abrigo (m.) *overcoat*
abril (m.) *April*
abrir *to open*
abrir la puerta *to open the door*
abrochar *to fasten*
abrocharse el cinturón de seguridad *to buckle up*
absolutamente *absolutely*
absoluto/absoluta (m./f.) *absolute*
en absoluto *absolutely not*
absurdo/absurda (m./f.) *absurd*
abuela (f.) *grandmother*
abuelo (m.) *grandfather*
abuelos (pl.) *grandfathers, grandparents*
aburrido/aburrida (m./f.) *bored, boring*
aburrir *to bore*
aburrirse *to be bored, to get bored*
Me aburre/aburren ... (sg./pl.) *I'm bored by ...*
acabar *to finish*
acabar de ... *to have just ... (done something)*
academia (f.) *school, academy*
académico/académica (m./f.) *academic*
accidente (m.) *accident*
aceite (m.) *oil*
aceptar *to accept*
acera (f.) *sidewalk*
aconsejar *to advise*
aconsejar que ... *to advise that/to ...*
acostarse *to go to bed*
actor (m.) *actor*
actriz (f.) *actress*
actualmente *at the present time*
acuerdo (m.) *agreement*
De acuerdo. *All right.*
acupuntura (f.) *acupuncture*
además *moreover*
Adiós. *Good-bye.*
adjuntar *to attach*
adjuntar un documento *to attach a file*
adjunto/adjunta (m./f.) *enclosed*
documento (m.) **adjunto** *attachment*
adolescente (m.) *adolescent, teenager*
adulto/adulta (m./f.) *adult*
aerolínea (f.) *airline*
aeropuerto (m.) *airport*
afeitar *to shave*
navaja (f.) **de afeitar** *razor*
afeitarse *to shave (oneself)*
afición (f.) *hobby*
aficionado/aficionada (m./f.) *fan*
afuera *outside*
afueras (f. pl.) *outskirts*
agencia (f.) *agency*
agente (m./f.) *agent*
agitado/agitada (m./f.) *agitated, rough*
agosto (m.) *August*
agradable (m./f.) *pleasant*
agradecer *to be thankful*
Le agradezco su ayuda. *Thank you for your help.*
agrio/agria (m./f.) *sour*
agua (f.) *water*

agua mineral *mineral water*
el agua *the water*
las aguas *the waters*
aguacate (m.) *avocado*
aguja (f.) *needle*
ahí *there*
ahora *now*
ahora mismo *right now*
ahorrar *to save*
ahumado/ahumada (m./f.) *smoked*
ajedrez (m.) *chess*
ajustado/ajustada (m./f.) *tight*
al (a + el) *to the* (m.)*/at the* (m.)
albornoz (m.) *robe*
alcalde (m.) *mayor*
alcaldía (f.) *municipal building*
alcoba (f.) *bedroom, room*
aldea (f.) *village*
alegrarse *to be glad*
alegrarse de que ... *to be glad that ...*
alegre (m./f.) *happy*
alemán (m.) *German (language)*
alemán/alemana (m./f.) *German*
alergia (f.) *allergy*
alérgico/alérgica (m./f.) *allergic*
alfombra (f.) *carpet*
álgebra (f.) *algebra*
algo *something, somewhat*
¿Algo más? *Anything else?*
algodón (m.) *cotton*
alguien *somebody, someone*
alguien más *somebody else*
algún/alguno/alguna (before m. sg. nouns/m. sg./f. sg.) *some, something*
algunos/algunas (m. pl./f. pl.) *some, something*
allí *there*
almorzar *to have lunch*
almuerzo (m.) *lunch*
¿Aló? *Hello? (on the phone)*
alquilar *to rent*
alto (m.) *stop, height*
¡Alto! *Stop!*
alto/alta (m./f.) *tall, high*
tener la tensión alta *to have high blood pressure*
alumno/alumna (m./f.) *student*
amanecer (m.) *dawn*
al amanecer *at dawn*
amar *to love*
amargo/amarga (m./f.) *bitter, sour*
amarillo/amarilla (m./f.) *yellow*
páginas (f. pl.) **amarillas** *yellow pages*
americana (f.) *jacket*
americano/americana (m./f.) *American*
amigo/amiga (m./f.) *friend*
amueblado/amueblada (m./f.) *furnished*
anaranjado/anaranjada (m./f.) *orange (color)*
ancho/ancha (m./f.) *wide, baggy*
andar *to walk*
andén (m.) *sidewalk, platform*
por el andén *on the sidewalk*
anexo (m.) *attachment*
anexo al correo electrónico *e-mail attachment*
angosto/angosta (m./f.) *narrow*
anillo (m.) *ring*
año (m.) *year*
año pasado *last year*
año que viene *next year*
año entrante *next year*
¿Cuántos años tiene? *How old are you (sg. fml.)/is he/is she?*
este año *this year*
los años cincuenta *the fifties*
segundo año *second year*
tercer año *third year*
tener ... años *to be ... years old*
anoche *last night*
anotar *to record, to write down*
anotar un gol *to score a goal*
antes *before*
antes de ... *before ...*
lo antes posible *as soon as possible*
antigüedad (f.) *antique*
tienda (f.) **de antigüedades** *antique store*
antigüedades (f. pl.) *antiques*
antiguo/antigua (m./f.) *old*
antipático/antipática (m./f.) *unfriendly*
apagar *to turn off*
apagar las luces *to turn off the lights*
aparador (m.) *cupboard*
apartamento (m.) *apartment*
apetito (m.) *appetite*
apostar *to bet*
apuesto a que ... *to bet that ...*
aprender *to learn*

aprender a ... *to learn how to ...*
Estoy aprendiendo español. *I'm learning Spanish.*
aprobar *to pass*
aprobar un curso *to pass a course*
aprobar un examen *to pass a test*
apuesta (f.) *bet*
apuro (m.) *difficult situation*
aquel/aquella (m. sg./f. sg.) *that (far from the speaker and the listener)*
aquél/aquélla (m. sg./f. sg.) *that (one) over there (far from the speaker and the listener)*
aquello (neuter) *that (one, thing) over there (far from the speaker and the listener)*
aquellos/aquellas (m. pl./f. pl.) *those (far from the speaker and the listener)*
aquéllos/aquéllas (m. pl./f. pl.) *those (ones) over there (far from the speaker and the listener)*
aquí *here*
Aquí está ... *Here is ...*
Aquí tiene. *Here you are.*
árbol (m.) *tree*
archivo (m.) *file*
área (m.) *area*
arena (f.) *sand*
Argentina (f.) *Argentina*
argentino/argentina (m./f.) *Argentinian*
armario (m.) *closet, filing cabinet*
arquitecto/arquitecta (m./f.) *architect*
arquitectura (f.) *architecture*
arroz (m.) *rice*
arte (m.) *art*
artesanía (f.) *craft*
artista (m./f.) *artist*
asar *to grill*
bien asada *well-done*
así *so*
Así es. *That's right.*
Así que ... *So ...*
por así decir *so to speak*
asignatura (f.) *subject, course*
asistente (m./f.) *assistant*
asistir *to attend, to be present*
astronauta (m./f.) *astronaut*
atardecer (m.) *dusk*
al atardecer *at dusk*
atención (f.) *attention*
atender *to attend to, to serve, to take care of*
atentamente *carefully*
atleta (m./f.) *athlete*
atlético/atlética (m./f.) *athletic*
atracción (f.) *attraction*
atractivo/atractiva (m./f.) *attractive*
atrás *behind, back*
atún (m.) *tuna*
audífonos (m. pl.) *headphones*
aula (m.) *classroom*
auto (m.) *car*
autobús (m.) *bus*
recorrido (m.) **por autobús** *tour bus*
automático/automática (m./f.) *automatic*
contestador (m.) **automático** *answering machine*
automóvil (m.) *car*
autopista (f.) *highway, freeway*
autor/autora (m./f. less common) *author*
autovía (f.) *highway, freeway*
avenida (f.) *avenue*
aventura (f.) *adventure*
películas (pl.) **de aventuras** *adventure films*
avión (m.) *airplane*
ayer *yesterday*
ayuda (f.) *help*
Le agradezco su ayuda. *Thank you for your help.*
ayudar *to help*
¿Puede ayudarme? *Can you help me?*
ayuntamiento (m.) *city hall*
azúcar (m.) *sugar*
azul (m.) **claro** *the color light blue*
azul (m./f.) *blue*
azul claro *light blue*
azul marino *navy blue*
azul oscuro *dark blue*
ser de sangre azul *to have blue blood (lit., to be of blue blood)*

B

bailar *to dance*
baile (m.) *dancing*
bajar *to lower, to download*
bajo *under, below*
bajo/baja (m./f.) *short*
tener la tensión baja *to have low blood pressure*
balcón (m.) *balcony*

balón (m.) *ball*
baloncesto (m.) *basketball*
bañador (m.) *bathing trunks*
banana (f.) *banana*
bañarse *to take a bath, to bathe*
banco (m.) *bank*
banda (f.) *band*
bañera (f.) *bathtub*
baño (m.) *bathroom*
  traje (m.) **de baño** *bathing suit*
banquero/banquera (m./f.) *banker*
bar (m.) *bar*
barato/barata (m./f.) *cheap*
barbería (f.) *barbershop*
barbilla (f.) *chin*
barrio (m.) *neighborhood*
base (f.) *base*
bastante *quite, enough, quite a lot*
bata (f.) *robe*
batidora (f.) *blender*
bebé (m./f.) *baby*
beber *to drink*
bebida (f.) *drink*
bebito/bebita (m./f.) *little baby*
beca (f.) *scholarship*
béisbol (m.) *baseball*
  partido (m.) **de béisbol** *baseball game*
beneficio (m.) *benefit*
besar *to kiss*
biblioteca (f.) *library*
bicicleta (f.) *bicycle*
bien *well*
  Estoy bien. *I'm fine.*
  Que esté bien. *May you be well.*
  Que estés bien. *Take care.*
  ¡Qué bien! *How nice!*
Bienvenido./Bienvenida. (m./f.) *Welcome.* (to a man/to a woman)
billar (m.) *pool, billiards*
billete (m.) *ticket*
biología (f.) *biology*
blanco/blanca (m./f.) *white*
  ir de punta en blanco *to be dressed to the nines (lit., to go from the tip in white)*
  vino (m.) **blanco** *white wine*
bloquear *to block*
blusa (f.) *blouse*
bobo/boba (m./f.) *fool, idiot*
boca (f.) *mouth*
boleto (m.) *ticket*
bolígrafo (m.) *pen*
Bolivia (f.) *Bolivia*
boliviano/boliviana (m./f.) *Bolivian*
bolsa (f.) *bag, sack*
bolso (m.) *handbag*
bombachas (f. pl.) *women's underwear*
bonito/bonita (m./f.) *nice, pretty*
bordo (m.) *board*
  a bordo *on board*
  Bienvenidos a bordo. *Welcome aboard.*
borracho/borracha (m./f.) *drunk*
borrar *to erase*
bosque (m.) *forest*
bote (m.) *carton*
botella (f.) *bottle*
botiquín (m.) *medicine cabinet*
bragas (f. pl.) *women's underwear*
Brasil (m.) *Brazil*
brasileño/brasileña (m./f.) *Brazilian* (noun)
brasilero/brasilera (m./f.) *Brazilian* (adjective)
brazo (m.) *arm*
brote (m.) *rash*
buceo (m.) *diving*
buen/bueno/buena (before m. sg. nouns/ m./f.) *good*
  Buenas noches. *Good evening./Good night.*
  Buenas tardes. *Good afternoon.*
  Buenos días. *Good morning.*
  ¡Buen provecho! *Enjoy the meal!*
  ¡Buen trabajo! *Good job!*
  El tiempo es bueno. *The weather is good.*
  Es bueno que ... *It's good that ...*
  Hace muy buen tiempo. *It's beautiful.*
  Nochebuena (f.) *Christmas Eve*
bufanda (f.) *scarf*
buscar *to look for, to pick up*
buzón (m.) *mailbox*
  buzón de voz *voice mail*

C

caballero (m.) *gentleman*
caballo (m.) *horse*
cabecera (f.) *head*
  pediatra (m./f.) **de cabecera** *regular pediatrician*
cabeza (f.) *head*

pararse de cabeza *to go crazy, to go out of one's mind*
perder la cabeza *to lose one's head*
tener dolor de cabeza *to have a headache*
tener la cabeza fría *to keep a cool head*
cabina (f.) *booth, cabin*
cabina telefónica *telephone booth*
cable (m.) *cable*
cada (m./f.) *each, every*
cadera (f.) *hip*
caer *to fall*
café (m.) *coffee*
café (m./f.) *coffee-colored*
cafetera (f.) *coffeemaker*
cafetería (f.) *café, coffee shop, cafeteria, diner*
caja (f.) *cash register, box*
cajetilla (f.) *packet*
cajetilla de cigarrillos *pack of cigarettes*
cajón (m.) *drawer*
calcetines (m. pl.) *socks*
caliente (m./f.) *hot*
calificaciones (f. pl.) *grades*
calle (f.) *street*
luz (f.) **de la calle** *streetlight*
callejón (m.) *alley*
calor (m.) *heat*
Hace calor. *It's hot.*
tener calor *to be hot, to be warm*
calvo/calva (m./f.) *bald*
calzar *to wear (shoes)*
¿Qué número calza? *What shoe size do you wear?*
calzoncillos (m. pl.) *men's underpants*
calzoncitos (m. pl.) *women's underwear*
calzones (m. pl.) *men's undergarments*
cama (f.) *bed*
cámara (f.) *camera*
camarera (f.) *waitress*
camarero (m.) *waiter*
camarón (m.) *shrimp*
cambiar *to change, to exchange*
cambio (m.) *change*
caminar *to walk*
camino (m.) *way, path*
camisa (f.) *shirt*
camiseta (f.) *T-shirt, undershirt*
camisilla (f.) *undershirt*
campeón/campeona (m./f.) *champion*
campeonato (m.) *championship*
camping (m.) *camping*
ir de camping *to go camping*
campo (m.) *field, camp*
Canadá (m.) *Canada*
canadiense (m./f.) *Canadian*
canal (m.) *channel*
cancelar *to cancel*
canción (f.) *song*
candidato/candidata (m./f.) *candidate*
cansado/cansada (m./f.) *tired*
cansancio (m.) *fatigue*
tener cansancio *to be tired*
cantante (m./f.) *singer*
cantar *to sing*
capacidad (f.) *capacity*
cara (f.) *face*
dar la cara *to face the circumstances*
ser caradura *to be shameless*
carbón (m.) *coal*
cárcel (f.) *prison*
carnaval (m.) *carnival*
carne (f.) *meat, beef*
carne de cerdo (f.) *pork*
carnicería (f.) *butcher shop*
caro/cara (m./f.) *expensive*
carpeta (f.) *file*
carpintero/carpintera (m./f.) *carpenter*
carpio (m.) *carpus*
síndrome (m.) **del túnel del carpio** *carpal tunnel syndrome*
carrera (f.) *major, university course*
carretera (f.) *highway, freeway*
carril (m.) *lane*
Siga por el carril de la derecha. *Stay in the right lane.*
carro (m.) *car*
carta (f.) *menu, letter*
cartas (f. pl.) *playing cards*
cartelera (f.) *billboard, list of plays*
cartelera de cine *movie listing*
cartera (f.) *wallet, handbag*
cartón (m.) *carton, cardboard*
casa (f.) *house*
casado/casada (m./f.) *married*
casarse *to get married*
casarse con *to marry (someone)*
casi *almost*

casi nunca *seldom, almost never*
caso (m.) *case*
casualidad (f.) *chance, coincidence*
por casualidad *by chance*
catedral (f.) *cathedral*
catorce *fourteen*
caza (f.) *hunting*
CD (m.) *CD*
CD rom (m.) *CD-ROM*
lector (m.) **de CD** *CD player*
lector (m.) **de CD rom** *CD-ROM drive*
cebolla (f.) *onion*
ceja (f.) *eyebrow*
celeste (m./f.) *sky blue*
celoso/celosa (m./f.) *jealous*
celular (m.) *cell phone*
cena (f.) *dinner*
cenar *to eat dinner*
centralita (f.) *switchboard*
centro (m.) *center*
centro comercial *shopping mall*
centro de información *information center*
cerca *close, near*
cerca de ... *close to/near ...*
cerdo (m.) *pork*
carne (f.) **de cerdo** *pork*
cerdo/cerda (m./f.) *pig*
carne (f.) **de cerdo** *pork*
cerebro (m.) *brain*
cero *zero*
cerrar *to close*
cerro (m.) *hill*
cerveza (f.) *beer*
cesar *to stop*
cesar de ... *to stop ... (doing something)*
césped (m.) *lawn, grass*
champaña (m.) *champagne*
champú (m.) *shampoo*
chanchito/chanchita (m./f.) *piglet*
Chao. *Bye.*
chaqueta (f.) *jacket*
charcutería (f.) *delicatessen*
charla (f.) *chat*
espacio (m.) **para charla** *chat room*
chat (m.) *chat room*
che *hey (filler word, Argentina)*
cheque (m.) *check*
chica (f.) *girl*
chico (m.) *boy*
Chile (m.) *Chile*
chileno/chilena (m./f.) *Chilean*
chinelas (f. pl.) *slippers*
chino (m.) *Chinese (language)*
chiste (m.) *joke*
contar un chiste verde *to tell an obscene joke (lit., to tell a green joke)*
chocolate (m.) *chocolate*
chuleta (f.) *chop*
chuleta de cordero *lamb chop*
ciclismo (m.) *biking, cycling*
cielo (m.) *sky*
cien/ciento (before a noun/before a number except mil) *one hundred*
cien personas *one hundred people*
cien por ciento *one hundred percent*
ciento tres dólares *one hundred and three dollars*
por ciento *percent*
ciencia (f.) *science*
cierto/cierta (m./f.) *true*
No es cierto que ... *It is not true that ...*
cigarrillo (m.) *cigarette*
cajetilla (f.) **de cigarrillos** *pack of cigarettes*
cinco *five*
a las cinco *at five (o'clock)*
cuarenta y cinco *forty-five*
cincuenta *fifty*
cine (m.) *movie*
cinturón (m.) *belt*
abrocharse el cinturón de seguridad *to buckle up*
circo (m.) *circus*
cita (f.) *appointment*
ciudad (f.) *city, town*
claramente *clearly*
claro *clearly*
¡Claro que sí! *Of course!*
Sí, claro. *Yes, of course.*
claro/clara (m./f.) *light*
azul (m./f.) **claro** *light blue*
clase (f.) *class, kind*
toda clase *all kinds*
clásico/clásica (m./f.) *classic*
música (f.) **clásica** *classical music*
cliente (m./f.) *customer*
clínica (f.) *clinic*

farmacia (f.) **clínica** *clinical pharmacy*
club (m.) *club*
coca (f.) *coca*
coche (m.) *car*
cocina (f.) *kitchen, stove, cooking*
cocinar *to cook*
código (m.) *code*
codo (m.) *elbow*
coger *to catch, to pick up, to take*
coger fuerzas (f. pl.) *to regain strength*
coger un examen *to take a test*
coincidencia (f.) *coincidence*
¡Qué coincidencia! *What a coincidence!*
cola (f.) *tail, line*
hacer una cola *to stand in line*
colección (f.) *collection*
coleccionar *to collect*
colega/colega (m./f.) *colleague*
colegio (m.) *elementary/secondary school*
colgar *to hang*
colgar el teléfono *to hang up the phone*
colina (f.) *hill*
collar (m.) *necklace*
Colombia (f.) *Colombia*
colombiano/colombiana (m./f.) *Colombian*
colonia (f.) *cologne*
color (m.) *color*
¿De qué color es ... ? *What color is ... ?*
ver todo color de rosa *to be an optimist, to wear rose colored glasses*
colorado/colorada (m./f.) *red*
ponerse colorado *to be embarrassed (lit., to turn red)*
columna (f.) *column*
columna vertebral *backbone, spinal column*
coma (f.) *comma*
combinar *to combine, to match*
combinar con ... *to go with ...*
comedia (f.) *comedy*
comedor (m.) *dining room*
comenzar *to start, to begin*
comenzar a ... *to start ... (doing something)*
comer *to eat*
comercial (m./f.) *commercial*
centro (m.) **comercial** *shopping mall*
comida (f.) *food, dinner*
como *as, like*
como ya sabes *as you already know*
cómo *how* (question)
¿Cómo? *What?/Pardon me?*
¿Cómo estás (tú)? *How are you?* (infml.)
¿Cómo estás de tiempo? *Do you have time?/ How are you doing for time?*
¿Cómo está usted? *How are you?* (fml.)
¿Cómo se llama usted? *What's your name?* (fml.)
¿Cómo te llamas? *What's your name?* (infml.)
¿Cómo te trata la vida? *How's life treating you?*
¿Cómo va todo? *How is everything going?*
¿Sabe cómo ... ? *Do you know how to ... ?*
cómodo/cómoda (m./f.) *comfortable*
compañía (f.) *company*
completamente *completely*
completar *to complete*
completo/completa (m./f.) *full*
a tiempo completo *full-time*
compra (f.) *purchase*
ir de compras *to go shopping*
comprar *to buy, to shop*
comprar en rebaja *to buy on sale*
comprender *to understand*
computadora (f.) *computer*
comunicar *to communicate*
Está comunicando. *The line is busy.*
con *with, to*
concierto (m.) *concert*
condimentado/condimentada (m./f.) *spicy*
conducir *to drive*
conectar *to connect*
conexión (f.) *connection*
conferencia (f.) *conference, meeting, lecture*
sala (f.) **de conferencias** *meeting room*
conjunto (m.) *band (music)*
conocer *to know (people, places), to meet*
conocer de vista *to know by sight*
conocer palmo a palmo *to know like the back of one's hand*
dar a conocer *to make known*
Gusto en conocerlo/la. *Pleased to meet you.* (to a man/to a woman)
consultar *to look up, to consult*
consultorio (m.) *office*
consultorio del médico *doctor's office*
contable (m./f.) *accountant*
contar *to count, to tell*

contar un chiste verde *to tell an obscene joke (lit., to tell a green joke)*
contento/contenta (m./f.) *happy*
contestador (m.) **(automático)** *answering machine*
contestar *to reply to, to answer*
contestar el teléfono *to answer the phone*
contigo *with you*
continuar *to continue*
Continúa recto. *Continue straight.*
contra *against*
contrato (m.) *contract*
contribución (f.) *contribution*
copa (f.) *wineglass*
copa de vino *glass of wine*
copia (f.) *copy*
copiar *to copy*
corazón (m.) *heart*
corbata (f.) *tie*
cordero/cordera (m./f.) *lamb*
chuleta (f.) **de cordero** *lamb chop*
coro (m.) *choir*
correo (m.) *post office*
correo electrónico (correo-e) *e-mail*
dirección (f.) **de correo electrónico** *e-mail address*
correr *to run*
cortado/cortada (m./f.) *sour*
cortina (f.) *curtain*
corto/corta (m./f.) *short*
cosa (f.) *thing*
¿Cómo van las cosas? *How are things?*
cosquilleo (m.) *tingling feeling*
costar *to cost*
¿Cuánto cuesta? *How much does it cost?*
costoso/costosa (m./f.) *expensive*
costura (f.) *sewing*
crédito (m.) *loan, credit*
tarjeta (f.) **de crédito** *credit card*
creer *to believe, to think*
Creo que sí. *I think so.*
no creer que ... *not to believe that ...*
¿No crees? *Don't you think?*
crema (f.) *creme*
crema de afeitar *shaving cream*
crío/cría (m./f.) *kid*
cruce (m.) *intersection*
cruzar *to cross*
cuaderno (m.) *notebook*
cuadra (f.) *block*
Está a dos cuadras de aquí. *It's two blocks from here.*
cuadro (m.) *painting, picture, square*
a cuadros *plaid*
cual/cuales (sg./pl.) *which* (relative pronoun), *as*
cuál/cuáles (sg./pl.) *which, what* (question)
cualificación (f.) *qualification, skill*
cualificado/cualificada (m./f.) *qualified*
cualquier *any*
cuando *when* (relative adverb)
cuándo *when* (question)
cuanto/cuanta/cuantos/cuantas (m. sg./f. sg./m. pl./f. pl.) *as much, as many*
en cuanto a ... *regarding ...*
cuánto/cuánta/cuántos/cuántas (m. sg./f. sg./m. pl./f. pl.) *how much, how many*
¿Cuántos años tiene? *How old are you* (sg. fml.)*/is he/is she?*
¿Cuánto cuesta? *How much does it cost?*
¿Cuánto es? *How much is it?*
cuarenta *forty*
cuarenta y cinco *forty-five*
cuarto (m.) *quarter, room, bedroom*
a las seis menos cuarto *at a quarter to six*
a las seis y cuarto *at a quarter past six*
término (m.) **tres cuartos** *medium (cooked meat)*
cuatro *four*
cuatrocientos/cuatrocientas (m./f.) *four hundred*
cuchara (f.) *spoon*
cuchillo (m.) *knife*
cuello (m.) *neck*
cuenco (m.) *bowl*
cuenta (f.) *bill, check, account*
tener en cuenta *to take into account*
pagar la cuenta *to check out*
cuero (m.) *leather*
cuerpo (m.) *body*
cuerpo humano *human body*
cuestionario (m.) *questionnaire*
cuñada (f.) *sister-in-law*
cuñado (m.) *brother-in-law*
currículum (m.) *curriculum*
currículum vítae *résumé, CV*
curso (m.) *course*

cuyo/cuya/cuyos/cuyas (m. sg./f. sg./m. pl./f. pl.) *whose, of which* (relative pronoun)

D

dar *to give, to show*
dar a conocer *to make known*
dar a luz *to give birth*
dar con *to find (something)*
dar de narices *to fall flat on one's face*
dar la cara *to face the circumstances*
dar la hora *to tell time*
dar la mano *to shake hands*
dar la vuelta *to turn around*
dar (las) gracias *to give thanks*
de *of, from, about*
de . . . a . . . *from . . . through . . .*
¿De dónde eres? *Where are you from?*
de la madrugada *in the early morning (before daybreak)*
de la mañana *in the morning*
de la noche *in the evening, at night*
de la tarde *in the afternoon*
De nada. *You're welcome.*
¿De qué color es . . . ? *What color is . . . ?*
debajo *underneath*
debajo de . . . *underneath . . .*
deber *must, to owe*
débil (m./f.) *weak*
década (f.) *decade*
decidir *to decide*
decir *to tell, to say*
¿Cómo se dice " . . . " en . . . ? *How do you say " . . . " in . . . ?*
¿Díga(me)? *Hello? (on the phone)*
No me digas. *Really?*
por así decir *so to speak*
¿Qué quiere decir eso? *What does that mean?*
decisión (f.) *decision*
dedicar *to dedicate*
dedo (m.) *finger*
dedo del pie *toe*
dejar *to leave*
dejar un mensaje después de oír la señal *to leave a message after the tone*
del (de + el) *of the* (m.)*, from the* (m.)*, about the* (m.)
delante *in front*
delante de . . . *in front of . . .*
delgado/delgada (m./f.) *thin*
delicioso/deliciosa (m./f.) *delicious*
delito (m.) *crime*
demasiado/demasiada (m./f.) *too much, too many*
dentista (m./f.) *dentist*
dentro *inside*
dentro de . . . *inside of . . .*
departamento (m.) *department*
tienda (f.) **por departamentos** *department store*
depender *to depend*
depender de . . . *to depend on . . .*
dependiente/dependienta (m./f.) *store clerk*
deporte (m.) *sport*
deportista (m./f.) *person who plays sports*
deportivo/deportiva (m./f.) *athletic*
zapatillas (f. pl.) **deportivas** *sneakers, tennis shoes*
derecha (f.) *right side*
a la derecha *on the right*
Gira a la derecha. *Turn right.*
derecho *straight*
Siga derecho. *Go straight.*
derecho (m.) *law, right, duty*
derechos (pl.) **de matrícula** *tuition*
derecho/derecha (m./f.) *right-side*
a mano derecha *on the right-hand side*
desafortunadamente *unfortunately*
desagradable (m./f.) *unpleasant*
desarrollar *to develop*
desastre (m.) *disaster*
desayuno (m.) *breakfast*
descansar *to rest*
desconocer *not to know*
descremado/descremada (m./f.) *skimmed*
leche (f.) **descremada** *skim milk*
describir *to describe*
descripción (f.) *description*
descuento (m.) *discount*
hacer un descuento *to give a discount*
treinta por ciento de descuento *thirty percent off*
desde *since, from*
desear *to want, to wish*
desear que . . . *to wish that . . .*
¿Qué desea? *What would you like?*
desgracia (f.) *misfortune*
por desgracia *unfortunately*

deshabillé (m.) *robe*
desierto (m.) *desert*
desodorante (m.) *deodorant*
despacho (m.) *office*
despacio *slowly*
  Hable más despacio, por favor. *Speak more slowly, please.*
despedirse *to say good-bye*
despertarse *to wake up, to get up*
después *afterwards*
  después de ... *after ...*
detalle (m.) *detail*
detergente (m.) *detergent*
  detergente de ropa *laundry detergent*
  detergente de vajilla *dishwashing detergent*
detestar *to detest*
detrás *behind*
  detrás de ... *behind ...*
día (m.) *day*
  Buenos días. *Good morning.*
  día festivo *holiday*
  dos días a la semana *twice a week*
  este día *this day*
  hoy en día *nowadays*
  Que tenga un buen día. *Have a nice day.*
  todo el día *all day*
  todos los días *every day*
diario (m.) *diary*
  llevar un diario *to keep a diary*
diario/diaria (m./f.) *daily*
diarrea (f.) *diarrhea*
diciembre (m.) *December*
diecinueve *nineteen*
dieciocho *eighteen*
dieciséis *sixteen*
diecisiete *seventeen*
diente (m.) *tooth*
diez *ten*
  a las ocho y diez *at eight ten (8:10)*
  diez mil *ten thousand*
  diez y seis *sixteen*
  diez y siete *seventeen*
  diez y ocho *eighteen*
  diez y nueve *nineteen*
diferencia (f.) *difference*
diferente (m./f.) *different*
difícil (m./f.) *difficult*
digital (m./f.) *digital*
  línea (f.) **de suscriptor/abonado digital (DSL)** *DSL*
diligentemente *diligently*
dinero (m.) *money*
Dios (m.) *God*
  ¡Por Dios! *For God's sake!*
diploma (m.) *diploma*
dirección (f.) *address, direction*
  dirección de correo electrónico *e-mail address*
dirigir *to direct*
disco (m.) *disk, record*
  disco de vinilo *vinyl record, LP*
disculpa (f.) *excuse, apology*
disculpar *to excuse*
  Disculpa./Disculpe. *Excuse me.* (infml./fml.)
discutir *to discuss*
diseño (m.) *design*
Disneylandia *Disneyland*
disponible (m./f.) *available*
diversión (f.) *amusement*
  parque (m.) **de diversiones** *amusement park*
divertido/divertida (m./f.) *fun*
divertirse *to have fun*
divorciado/divorciada (m./f.) *divorced*
divorciarse *to get a divorce*
  divorciarse de ... *to divorce (someone)*
doblar *to turn*
doce *twelve*
doctor/doctora (m./f.) *doctor*
documental (m.) *documentary*
documento (m.) *document, file*
  documento adjunto *attachment*
dólar (m.) *dollar*
dolor (m.) *pain*
  tener dolor de cabeza *to have a headache*
  tener dolor de garganta *to have a sore throat*
dominar *to dominate, to master*
  Domino el francés. *I speak French fluently.*
domingo (m.) *Sunday*
don (m.) *Mr.*
doña (f.) *Mrs.*
donde *where* (relative adverb)
dónde *where* (question)
  ¿De dónde eres? *Where are you from?*
dorado/dorada (m./f.) *gold (color)*
dormir *to sleep*
dormitorio (m.) *bedroom*

dos *two*
dos días a la semana *twice a week*
doscientos/doscientas (m./f.) *two hundred*
dotado/dotada (m./f.) *talented*
drama (m.) *drama*
dramático/dramática (m./f.) *dramatic*
obra (f.) **dramática** *drama*
ducha (f.) *shower*
ducharse *to take a shower/bath*
dudar *to doubt*
dudar que ... *to doubt that ...*
dulce (m.) *sweet, pastry*
dulce (m./f.) *sweet*
durante *during*
duro/dura (m./f.) *hard*
ser caradura *to be shameless*
DVD (m.) *DVD*
lector (m.) **de DVD** *DVD player*

E

economía (f.) *economics*
económico/económica (m./f.) *economical, low-cost*
precio (m.) **económico** *reasonable price*
Ecuador (m.) *Ecuador*
ecuatoriano/ecuatoriana (m./f.) *Ecuadorian*
edad (f.) *age*
edificio (m.) *building*
efectivamente *actually*
efectivo (m.) *cash*
pagar en efectivo *to pay cash*
eficientemente *efficiently*
ejercicio (m.) *exercise*
el *the* (m. sg.)
el de ella *hers*
el de ellas *theirs* (f. pl.)
el de ellos *theirs* (m. pl./mixed group)
el de él *his*
el de usted *yours* (sg. fml.)
el de ustedes *yours* (pl.)
él *he*
el de él (m. sg.) *his*
la de él (f. sg.) *his*
eléctrico/eléctrica (m./f.) *electric, electrical*
electricista/electricista (m./f.) *electrician*
electrodoméstico (m.) *electrical appliance*
tienda (f.) **de electrodomésticos** *electronics store*
electrónico/electrónica (m./f.) *electronic*
correo (m.) **electrónico** *e-mail*
dirección (f.) **de correo electrónico** *e-mail address*
elefante (m.) *elephant*
elegante (m./f.) *elegant*
elegir *to choose*
eliminar *to delete, to eliminate*
ella *she*
el de ella (m. sg.) *hers*
la de ella (f. sg.) *hers*
ellas *they* (f. pl.)
el de ellas (m. sg.) *theirs* (f. pl.)
la de ellas (f. sg.) *theirs* (f. pl.)
ellos *they* (m. pl./mixed group)
el de ellos (m. sg.) *theirs* (m. pl./mixed group)
la de ellos (m. sg.) *theirs* (m. pl./mixed group)
embarazada (f.) *pregnant*
embotellamiento (m.) *traffic jam*
emocionante (m./f.) *exciting*
empatado/empatada (m./f.) *tied*
quedar empatados *to be tied*
empatar *to draw, to tie*
empezar *to begin*
empleado/empleada (m./f.) *employee*
empleo (m.) *job, employment*
en *in, at, by (means), on*
enamorado/enamorada (m./f.) *in love*
encantar *to enchant*
Encantado./Encantada. *Pleased to meet you.* (said by a man/said by a woman)
Me encanta/encantan ... (sg./pl.) *I really like ...*
¡Me encantaría! *I'd love to!*
encanto (m.) *charm*
encima *above*
encima de ... *above ...*
y encima ... *and on top of that ...*
encontrar *to meet up with, to find*
encontrarse con ... *to meet ... (somebody)*
enero (m.) *January*
enfadarse *to get angry*
enfadarse de que ... *to be angry that ...*
enfermedad (f.) *illness, disease*
enfermo/enferma (m./f.) *sick*
enfrente *opposite*
enfrente de ... *across from ... , in front of ...*
enhorabuena (f.) *congratulations*

enorme (m./f.) *huge*
ensalada (f.) *salad*
entender *to understand*
enterizo/enteriza (m./f.) *one-piece*
entero/entera (m./f.) *whole*
  leche (f.) **entera** *whole milk*
entonces *then*
  Hasta entonces. *Until then.*
entrada (f.) *entrance, ticket, appetizer*
entrante (m./f.) *coming*
  mes (m.) **entrante** *next month*
entrar *to enter*
entre *between*
  entre ... y ... *between ... and ...*
entregar *to submit*
entrenador/entrenadora (m./f.) *coach*
entretenimiento (m.) *entertainment*
entrevista (f.) *interview*
  programa (m.) **de entrevistas** *talk show*
entrevistar *to interview*
enviar *to send*
equipo (m.) *team*
equitación (f.) *horseback riding*
equivocado/equivocada (m./f.) *wrong*
  número (m.) **equivocado** *wrong number*
escaleras (f. pl.) *stairs*
escaparate (m.) *display window*
  ir de escaparates *to go window-shopping*
escoba (f.) *broom*
escoger *to choose*
escondidas (f. pl.) *hide-and-seek*
escotado/escotada (m./f.) *low-cut*
escribir *to write*
escritor/escritora (m./f.) *writer*
escritorio (m.) *desk, study*
escuchar *to listen to*
escuela (f.) *school*
escultura (f.) *sculpture*
ese/esa (m. sg./f. sg.) *that (near the listener)*
ése/ésa (m. sg./f. sg.) *that (one) (near the listener)*
eso (neuter) *that (one, thing) (near the listener)*
  a eso de *about, around*
  a eso de las nueve *at about nine o'clock*
  por eso *for this reason*
esos/esas (m. pl./f. pl.) *those (near the listener)*
ésos/ésas (m. pl./f. pl.) *those (ones) (near the listener)*
espacio (m.) *space*
  espacio para charla *chat room*
espalda (f.) *back*
España (f.) *Spain*
español (m.) *Spanish (language)*
  Estoy aprendiendo español. *I'm learning Spanish.*
  Hablo un poco de español. *I speak a little Spanish.*
español/española (m./f.) *Spanish*
espantoso/espantosa (m./f.) *scary*
especialidad (f.) *specialty, major*
especialización (f.) *specialization, master's degree*
especializarse *to specialize*
  especializarse en ... *to major in ...*
espectador/espectadora (m./f.) *spectator*
espejo (m.) *mirror*
espera (f.) *wait*
  poner en espera *to put on hold*
esperar *to hope, to wait*
  esperar que ... *to hope that ...*
  Espere, por favor. *Hold on, please.*
  ¡Yo espero que sí! *I hope so!*
espeso/espesa (m./f.) *thick*
espía (m./f.) *spy*
esposa (f.) *wife*
esposo (m.) *husband*
esquiar *to ski*
esquina (f.) *corner*
  a la vuelta de la esquina *around the corner*
estación (f.) *station*
  estación de ferrocarril *train station*
  estación de tren *train station*
estación (f.) *season*
estadio (m.) *stadium*
estado (m.) *state*
  los Estados Unidos *the United States*
estadounidense (m./f.) *American*
estampado/estampada (m./f.) *with a pattern, patterned*
estampilla (f.) *postage stamp*
estanque (m.) *pond*
estante (m.) *shelf, bookshelf*
estar *to be*
  Aquí está ... *Here is ...*
  ¿Cómo estás (tú)? *How are you?* (infml.)
  ¿Cómo estás de tiempo? *Do you have time?/ How are you doing for time?*

¿Cómo está usted? *How are you?* (fml.)
Está granizando. *It's hailing.*
Está lloviendo. *It's raining.*
Está nevando. *It's snowing.*
Está nublado. *It's cloudy.*
estar en buenas manos *to be in good hands*
estar mal *to be not doing well*
Estoy aprendiendo español. *I'm learning Spanish.*
Estoy bien. *I'm fine.*
No está mal. *It's not bad.*
Que esté bien. *May you be well.*
Que estés bien. *Take care.*
este (m.) *east*
este/esta (m. sg./f. sg.) *this (near the speaker)*
esta noche (f.) *this evening, tonight*
éste/ésta (m. sg./f. sg.) *this (one) (near the speaker)*
estilo (m.) *style*
esto (neuter) *this (one, thing) (near the speaker)*
estómago (m.) *stomach*
tener mal de estómago *to have an upset stomach*
estos/estas (m. pl./f. pl.) *these (near the speaker)*
éstos/éstas (m. pl./f. pl.) *these (ones) (near the speaker)*
estrecho/estrecha (m./f.) *narrow*
estrella (f.) *star*
estrenar *to use for the first time*
estresante (m./f.) *stressing, stressful*
estudiante/estudiante (m./f.) *student*
estudiar *to study*
estudio (m.) *study, office*
estudios (pl.) *studies*
estupendo/estupenda (m./f.) *fine, wonderful, marvelous*
¡Estupendo! *Great!*
etiqueta (f.) *tag, label*
etiqueta con el precio *price tag*
ex *ex-*
exacto/exacta (m./f.) *exact*
Exacto. *Exactly.*
examen (m.) *test*
aprobar un examen *to pass a test*
hacer un examen, presentarse a un examen *to take a test*
hacerse un examen de sangre *to take a blood test*
suspender un examen *to fail a test*
exceder *to exceed*
excelente (m./f.) *excellent*
excepción (f.) *exception*
excursionismo (m.) *hiking*
hacer excursionismo *to go hiking*
exigente (m./f.) *demanding*
exigir *to demand*
éxito (m.) *success*
experiencia (f.) *experience*
explicación (f.) *explanation*
exterior (m.) *outside*
extra (m./f.) *extra*
horas (f. pl.) extras *extra hours, overtime*
extranjero/extranjera (m./f.) *foreign, foreigner*
extraño/extraña (m./f.) *strange*
persona (f.) extraña *strange person*
extraordinario/extraordinaria (m./f.) *extraordinary*
extrovertido/extrovertida (m./f.) *extroverted*

F

fábrica (f.) *factory*
fácil (m./f.) *easy*
fácilmente *easily*
facultad (f.) *department (at college/university)*
falda (f.) *skirt*
faltar *to miss, to be lacking, to be necessary*
fama (f.) *fame*
familia (f.) *family*
familiar (m./f.) *(of) family, familiar*
famoso/famosa (m./f.) *famous*
fantástico/fantástica (m./f.) *fantastic*
farmacéutico/farmacéutico (m./f.) *pharmacist*
farmacia (f.) *drugstore, pharmacy*
farmacia clínica *clinical pharmacy*
farola (f.) *lamppost*
favor (m.) *favor*
Hágame el favor de ... *Do me the favor of ...*
Por favor. *Please.*
favorito/favorita (m./f.) *favorite*
fax (m.) *fax machine*
febrero (m.) *February*
fecha (f.) *date*
felicitar *to congratulate*
¡Felicitaciones! *Congratulations!*
feliz (m./f.) *happy*
felizmente *happily*

feo/fea (m./f.) *ugly*
ferrocarril (m.) *railroad, train*
  estación (f.) **de ferrocarril** *train station*
festivo/festiva (m./f.) *festive*
  día (m.) **festivo** *holiday*
fiebre (f.) *fever*
  tener fiebre *to have a fever*
fiesta (f.) *party, holiday*
fijo/fija (m./f.) *fixed, permanent*
  trabajo (m.) **fijo** *steady job*
fila (f.) *line*
  hacer una fila *to stand in line*
filatelia (f.) *stamp collecting*
filosofía (f.) *philosophy*
fin (m.) *end*
  fin de semana *weekend*
  por fin *finally, at last*
final (m.) *end*
finanzas (f. pl.) *finance*
firma (f.) *signature*
física (f.) *physics*
flor (f.) *flower*
folleto (m.) *brochure*
fontanero/fontanera (m./f.) *plumber*
forma (f.) *way, manner*
fósil (m.) *fossil*
foto (f.) *picture, photograph*
  hacer una foto *to take a picture*
fotografía (f.) *photography*
francés (m.) *French (language)*
francés/francesa (m./f.) *French*
frasco (m.) *jar, bottle*
frase (f.) *phrase*
frecuencia (f.) *frequency*
  con frecuencia *frequently, often*
frecuente (m./f.) *frequent*
frecuentemente *frequently*
fregadero (m.) *(kitchen) sink*
freno (m.) *brake (automobile)*
  poner el pie en el freno *to hit the brakes*
frente (f.) *forehead*
fríjol (m.) *bean*
frío (m.) *cold temperature/sensation*
  Hace frío. *It's cold.*
  tener frío *to be cold*
frío/fría (m./f.) *cold*
  tener la cabeza fría *to keep a cool head*
frito/frita (m./f.) *fried*
fruta (f.) *fruit*
fuera *outside*
  fuera de . . . *outside of . . .*
fuerte (m./f.) *strong*
fuerza (f.) *strength*
  coger fuerzas (f. pl.) *to regain strength*
fumar *to smoke*
funcionar *to work, to function*
fútbol (m.) *soccer*
  fútbol americano *football*
futuro (m.) *future*

G

gabardina (f.) *raincoat*
gafas (f. pl.) *eyeglasses*
  gafas de sol *sunglasses*
galería (f.) *gallery*
galleta (f.) *cookie*
gamba (f.) *shrimp*
gamuza (f.) *suede*
gana (f.) *wish, desire*
  tener ganas de . . . *to feel like . . .*
ganar *to earn, to win*
  ¡Ojalá que ganen! *I hope they win!*
ganga (f.) *bargain*
garaje (m.) *garage*
garganta (f.) *throat*
  tener dolor de garganta *to have a sore throat*
gasolinera (f.) *gas station*
gasto (m.) *expense*
gato (m.) *cat*
gel (m.) *gel*
generalmente *generally*
generoso/generosa (m./f.) *generous*
gente (f.) *people*
geografía (f.) *geography*
gerente (m.) *manager*
gimnasia (f.) *gymnastics*
gimnasio (m.) *gymnasium*
girar *to turn*
  Gira a la derecha. *Turn right.*
  Gira a la izquierda. *Turn left.*
gol (m.) *goal*
  anotar/hacer/marcar un gol *to score a goal*
gordo/gorda (m./f.) *fat, big*
gracia (f.) *grace, appeal*
  dar (las) gracias *to give thanks*
  gracias (pl.) *thanks*

Gracias. *Thank you.*
Muchas gracias. *Thanks a lot.*
gracioso/graciosa (m./f.) *funny*
grado (m.) *degree*
graduarse *to graduate*
gráfico/gráfica (m./f.) *graphic*
gramo (m.) *gram*
gran/grande (before sg. nouns/all other cases) *big, large, great*
granizar *to hail*
Está granizando. *It's hailing.*
granjero/granjera (m./f.) *farmer*
gratis *free*
grave (m./f.) *serious*
gris (m.) *the color gray*
gris (m./f.) *gray*
gritar *to shout, to scream*
grito (m.) *cry, scream*
último grito *the very latest*
guantes (m. pl.) *gloves*
guardar *to save, to keep*
guayaba (f.) *guava*
guía (f.) *(guide) book*
guía telefónica *phone book*
guitarra (f.) *guitar*
tocar la guitarra *to play the guitar*
gustar *to please*
gustar que ... *to like (it) that ...*
Me gusta/gustan ... (sg./pl.) *I like ...*
Me gustaría ... *I'd like ...*
gusto (m.) *pleasure, taste*
Gusto en conocerlo/la. *Pleased to meet you.* (to a man/to a woman)
Mucho gusto. *It's a pleasure.*

H

haber *to have*
¿Cómo te ha ido? *How have you been?*
Hay ... *There is .../There are ...*
Hay que ... *It is necessary to ...*
No hay nada que ... *There's nothing that ...*
No hay nadie que ... *There's no one who/that ...*
No hay ningún ... que ... *There's no ... that/who ...*
¿Qué hay? *What's up?/What's going on?*
habitación (f.) *room, bedroom*
hablar *to speak, to talk*
hablar con .... *to speak to ...*
¿Hablas inglés? *Do you speak English?* (infml.)
¿Habla usted inglés? *Do you speak English?* (fml.)
Hable más despacio, por favor. *Speak more slowly, please.*
Hablo un poco de español. *I speak a little Spanish.*
hacer *to do, to make*
Hace calor. *It's hot.*
Hace frío. *It's cold.*
Hace muy buen tiempo. *It's beautiful.*
hacer a la medida *to custom sew*
hacer deporte *to play sports*
hacer una cola/fila *to stand in line*
hacer un descuento *to give a discount*
hacer excursionismo *to go hiking*
hacer senderismo *to go hiking*
hacer una foto *to take a picture*
hacer una llamada internacional/local/nacional *to make an international/local/national call*
hacerse un examen de sangre *to take a blood test*
Hace sol. *It's sunny.*
Hace viento. *It's windy.*
Hágame el favor de ... *Do me the favor of ...*
Se me hace tarde. *I'm late.*
hacha (f.) *axe*
hacia *toward*
hambre (f.) *hunger*
tener hambre *to be hungry*
hasta *until, even*
Hasta entonces. *Till then.*
Hasta luego. *I'll see you later.*
Hasta mañana. *Until tomorrow./See you tomorrow.*
Hasta más tarde. *Until later.*
Hasta pronto. *See you soon.*
hecho/hecha (m./f.) *made, done*
heladería (f.) *ice cream parlor*
helado (m.) *ice cream*
heredar *to inherit*
hermana (f.) *sister*
hermano (m.) *brother*
hermanos (pl.) *brothers, brothers and sisters, siblings*
hielo (m.) *ice*

hierba (f.) *herb*
higiénico/higiénica (m./f.) *hygienic*
  papel (m.) **higiénico** *toilet paper*
hija (f.) *daughter*
hijastra (f.) *stepdaughter*
hijastro (m.) *stepson*
hijo (m.) *son*
  hijos (pl.) *sons, children (sons and daughters)*
hincha (m./f.) *fan, supporter*
hincharse *to swell*
historia (f.) *history*
historial (m.) *background, record*
  historial de trabajo *résumé*
hockey (m.) *hockey*
hoja (f.) *sheet (of paper)*
  hoja de vida *résumé*
Hola. *Hello.*
hombre (m.) *man*
  hombre de negocios *businessman*
hombro (m.) *shoulder*
homeopatía (f.) *homeopathy*
honesto/honesta (m./f.) *honest*
honorarios (m. pl.) *fees*
hora (f.) *time, hour*
  ¿A qué hora es? *At what time is it?*
  dar la hora *to tell time*
  horas (f. pl.) **extras** *extra hours, overtime*
  ¿Qué hora es? *What time is it?*
  ¿Qué horas son? *What time is it?*
  ¿Qué hora tiene? *What time do you have?*
horario (m.) *schedule*
horno (m.) *oven*
horror (m.) *horror*
hospital (m.) *hospital*
hostal (m.) *youth hostel*
hotel (m.) *hotel*
hoy *today*
  hoy en día *nowadays*
hueso (m.) *bone*
huevo (m.) *egg*
humano/humana (m./f.) *human*
  cuerpo (m.) **humano** *human body*
huracán (m.) *hurricane*

I

ida (f.) *outbound journey*
idea (f.) *idea*
ideal (m./f.) *ideal*
idioma (m.) *language*
iglesia (f.) *church*
igual (m./f.) *equal*
  ... es igual a ... *... equals (=) ...*
igualmente *also, likewise*
  Igualmente. *The same to you.*
imaginar *to imagine*
impedir *to prevent*
importante (m./f.) *important*
importar *to matter*
  No importa. *It doesn't matter.*
imposible (m./f.) *impossible*
  Es imposible que ... *It is impossible that ...*
impresionante (m./f.) *impressive*
impresora (f.) *printer*
impuesto (m.) *tax*
  planilla (f.) **de impuestos** *tax return*
incentivo (m.) *incentive*
incluir *to include*
  ¿Está incluido el servicio? *Is service included?*
incómodo/incómoda (m./f.) *uncomfortable*
infantil (m./f.) *children's*
  sicología (f.) **infantil** *child psychology*
información (f.) *information*
  centro (m.) **de información** *information center*
informal (m./f.) *casual*
informe (m.) *report*
ingeniería (f.) *engineering*
  ingeniería mecánica *mechanical engineering*
ingeniero/ingeniera (m./f.) *engineer*
Inglaterra (f.) *England*
inglés (m.) *English (language)*
  ¿Hablas inglés? *Do you speak English?* (infml.)
  ¿Habla usted inglés? *Do you speak English?* (fml.)
inglés/inglesa (m./f.) *English*
ingrediente (m.) *ingredient*
ingreso (m.) *earnings*
inmediatamente *immediately*
inmediato/inmediata (m./f.) *immediate*
  de inmediato *immediately*
inodoro (m.) *toilet*
insistir *to insist*
  insistir en que ... *to insist that ...*
instantáneo/instantánea (m./f.) *instantaneous*
  mensaje (m.) **instantáneo** *instant message*

inteligente (m./f.) *intelligent, smart*
intercambiar *to exchange*
interés (m.) *interest*
  tener interés en ... *to be interested in ...*
  visitar los lugares de interés *to go sightseeing*
interesante (m./f.) *interesting*
interesar *to interest*
  Me interesa/interesan ... (sg./pl.) *I'm interested in ...*
intermedio/intermedia (m./f.) *intermediate*
internacional (m./f.) *international*
  llamada (f.) **internacional** *international call*
Internet *internet*
  por Internet *online*
intersección (f.) *intersection*
investigación (f.) *research, investigation*
  trabajo (m.) **de investigación** *research paper*
invierno (m.) *winter*
invitación (f.) *invitation*
invitado/invitada (m./f.) *guest*
invitar *to invite*
ir *to go*
  ¿Cómo te ha ido? *How have you been?*
  ¿Cómo van las cosas? *How are things?*
  ir a ... *to go to (a place), to be going to (do)*
  ir a pie/caminar *to walk*
  ir de camping *to go camping*
  ir de compras *to go shopping*
  ir de escaparates *to go window-shopping*
  ir de punta en blanco *to be dressed to the nines (lit., to go from the tip in white)*
ira (f.) *anger*
  estar rojo de la ira *to be very angry (lit., to be red with fury)*
italiano (m.) *Italian (language)*
italiano/italiana (m./f.) *Italian*
izquierda (f.) *left side*
  a la izquierda *on the left*
  Gira a la izquierda. *Turn left.*
izquierdo/izquierda (m./f.) *left*
  a mano izquierda *on the left-hand side*

J

jabón (m.) *soap*
jamón (m.) *ham*
jardín (m.) *garden*
jazz (m.) *jazz*
jeans (m. pl.) *jeans*
jefe/jefa (m./f.) *boss*
jersey (m.) *sweater*
jornada (f.) *working day*
jornal (m.) *wage*
jota (f.) *the letter j*
  no saber ni jota de ... *to not have a clue about ...*
joven (m./f.) *young*
jubilado/jubilada (m./f.) *retired, retired person*
juego (m.) *game*
jueves (m.) *Thursday*
juez (m.) *judge*
jugador/jugadora (m./f.) *player*
jugar *to play*
jugo (m.) *juice*
julio (m.) *July*
junio (m.) *June*
junto/junta (m./f.) *together*
juzgado (m.) *court*

K

kilo (m.) *kilo, kilogram*
kilómetro (m.) *kilometer*

L

la *the* (f. sg.)*; it* (f.)*, her, you (f. sg. fml.)* (direct object pronoun)
  la de ella *hers*
  la de ellas *theirs* (f. pl.)
  la de ellos *theirs* (m. pl./mixed group)
  la de él *his*
  la de usted *yours* (sg. fml.)
  la de ustedes *yours* (pl.)
labio (m.) *lip*
lado (m.) *side*
  al lado de ... *next to ...*
ladrón (m./f.) *thief*
lago (m.) *lake*
lámpara (f.) *lamp*
lana (f.) *wool*
langosta (f.) *lobster*
lápiz (m.) *pencil*
largo/larga (m./f.) *long*
las *the* (f. pl.)*; them* (f.)*, you* (f. pl.) (direct object pronoun)
lástima (f.) *pity*
  Es una lástima que ... *It's a pity that ...*
lata (f.) *can*

lavabo (m.) *sink, wash basin*
lavadora (f.) *washing machine*
lavaplatos (m.) *dishwasher*
lavar *to wash*
lavar a mano *to hand wash*
lavar en seco *to dry-clean*
lavar la ropa *to do the laundry*
lavar los platos *to do the dishes*
lavarse *to wash oneself*
le *(to/for) him, her, it, you* (fml. sg.) (indirect object pronoun)
lección (f.) *lesson*
leche (f.) *milk*
leche en polvo *powdered milk*
lechería (f.) *dairy store*
lechuga (f.) *lettuce*
lector (m.) *reader*
lector de CD *CD player*
lector de CD rom *CD-ROM drive*
lector de DVD *DVD player*
lectura (f.) *reading*
leer *to read*
lejía (f.) *bleach*
lejos *far*
lejos de ... *far from ...*
lengua (f.) *tongue, language*
lentamente *slowly*
lento/lenta (m./f.) *slow*
les *(to/for) them, you* (fml. pl.) (indirect object pronoun)
lesión (f.) *injury*
levantar *to raise, to lift*
levantarse *to get up, to rise*
Me levanto. *I get up.*
libra (f.) *pound*
media libra *half pound*
libre (m./f.) *free*
librería (f.) *bookstore*
libro (m.) *book*
libro de texto *textbook*
licenciatura (f.) *bachelor's degree*
ligero/ligera (m./f.) *light, thin*
límite (m.) *limit*
limón (m.) *lemon*
limonada (f.) *lemonade*
limpio/limpia (m./f.) *clean*
línea (f.) *line*
línea de suscriptor/abonado digital (DSL) *DSL*
lino (m.) *linen*
lista (f.) *list*
listo/lista (m./f.) *ready*
¿Listos? *Ready?*
literatura (f.) *literature*
litro (m.) *liter*
llamada (f.) *phone call*
hacer una llamada internacional/local/nacional *to make an international/local/national call*
llamar *to call*
llamar por teléfono *to make a phone call*
llamar por teléfono a ... *to call ... on the phone*
¿Quién lo llama? *Who's calling?*
llamarse *to be called*
¿Cómo se llama usted? *What's your name?* (fml.)
¿Cómo te llamas? *What's your name?* (infml.)
Me llamo ... *My name is ...*
llave (f.) *key*
llegar *to arrive*
llegar a ... *to get to ..., to arrive at ...*
llenar *to fill*
llevar *to wear, to carry, to take, to keep*
llevar un diario *to keep a diary*
llorar *to cry*
llover *to rain*
Está lloviendo. *It's raining.*
lluvia (f.) *rain*
lo *it* (m.), *him, you (m. sg. fml.)* (direct object pronoun)
Lo siento. *I'm sorry.*
local (m./f.) *local*
llamada (f.) **local** *local call*
Londres *London*
los *the* (m. pl.); *them* (m.), *you* (m. pl.) (direct object pronoun)
Los Ángeles *Los Angeles*
lotería (f.) *lottery*
luego *later, then*
Hasta luego. *I'll see you later.*
lugar (m.) *place*
visitar los lugares de interés *to go sightseeing*
luna (f.) *moon*
lunar (m.) *mole, beauty mark*
de lunares *polka-dotted*

lunes (m.) *Monday*
luz (f.) *light*
  apagar las luces *to turn off the lights*
  dar a luz *to give birth*
  luz de la calle *streetlight*

M

madera (f.) *wood*
  de madera *wooden*
madrastra (f.) *stepmother*
madre (f.) *mother*
madrugada (f.) *late night, early morning (from midnight till daybreak)*
  de la madrugada *in the early morning*
  Es la una y diez de la madrugada. *It's ten after one in the morning.*
maestro/maestra (m./f.) *teacher*
mágico/mágica (m./f.) *magical*
magnífico/magnífica (m./f.) *magnificent, great*
mal *bad(ly), poorly*
  estar mal *to be not doing well*
  No está mal. *It's not bad.*
mal (m.) *illness*
  estar mal del estómago *to have an upset stomach*
maleta (f.) *suitcase*
malo/mala (m./f.) *bad*
mamá (f.) *mom*
mami (f.) *mom*
mañana (f.) *morning, tomorrow*
  a las nueve de la mañana *at nine a.m.*
  de la mañana *in the morning*
  esta mañana *this morning*
  Hasta mañana. *Until tomorrow./See you tomorrow.*
manejar *handle*
mano (f.) *hand*
  a la mano *at hand*
  a mano derecha *on the right-hand side*
  a mano izquierda *on the left-hand side*
  dar la mano *to shake hands*
  estar en buenas manos *to be in good hands*
  lavar a mano *to hand wash*
manojo (m.) *handful, bunch*
mantequilla (f.) *butter*
manzana (f.) *apple, block*
mapa (m.) *map*
mar (m.) *sea, ocean*
maravilla (f.) *wonder, miracle*
marcador (m.) *scoreboard*
marcar *to mark, to dial*
  marcar un gol *to make a goal*
  marcar un número de teléfono *to dial a phone number*
marchar *to go, to leave*
mareado/mareada (m./f.) *dizzy*
mareo (m.) *sickness*
  tener mareo *to be dizzy*
marido (m.) *husband*
marino/marina (m./f.) *marine*
  azul (m./f.) **marino** *navy blue*
marrón (m./f.) *brown*
martes (m.) *Tuesday*
martini (m.) *martini*
mártir (m./f.) *martyr*
marzo (m.) *March*
mas *but*
más *more, plus (+)*
  alguien más *somebody else*
  el/la/los/las (m. sg./f. sg./m. pl./f. pl.) **más … de …** *the most … in/of …*
  Hasta más tarde. *Until later.*
  más o menos *more or less, so-so, just okay*
  más … que … *more …/-er than …*
  más tarde *later*
matemáticas (f. pl.) *mathematics*
materia (f.) *school subject*
material (m.) *material*
matrícula (f.) *registration*
  derechos (m. pl.) **de matrícula** *tuition*
matricularse *to register*
matrimonio (m.) *marriage*
mayo (m.) *May*
mayor (m./f.) *older, bigger*
  el/la/los/las (m. sg./f. sg./m. pl./f. pl.) **mayor** *the oldest, the biggest*
mazorca (f.) *corncob*
me *me* (direct object pronoun)*; (to/for) me* (indirect object pronoun)*; myself*
  Me aburre/aburren … (sg./pl.) *I'm bored by …*
  Me encanta/encantan … (sg./pl.) *I really like …*
  Me gusta/gustan … (sg./pl.) *I like …*
  Me gustaría … *I'd like …*
  Me interesa/interesan … (sg./pl.) *I'm interested in …*
  Me levanto. *I get up.*

Me llamo ... *My name is ...*
¿Me permite ... ? *May I please ... ?* (fml.)
¿Me permites ... ? *May I please ... ?* (infml.)
mecánico/mecánica (m./f.) *mechanical*
ingeniería (f.) **mecánica** *mechanical engineering*
mediano/mediana (m./f.) *medium*
medianoche (f.) *midnight*
a medianoche *at midnight*
medias (f. pl.) *stockings, socks*
medicamento (m.) *medication*
tomar un medicamento *to take medication*
medicina (f.) *medicine*
médico/médica (m./f.) *doctor*
consultorio (m.) **del médico** *doctor's office*
medida (f.) *measurement*
hacer a la medida *to custom sew*
medio/media (m./f.) *half, midway*
a las cinco y media *at five thirty*
medianoche (f.) *midnight*
medio tiempo (m.) *halftime*
término (m.) **medio** *medium-rare*
mediodía (m.) *noon*
a mediodía *at noon*
Son las doce del mediodía. *It's twelve noon.*
medir *to measure*
mejilla (f.) *cheek*
mejor (m./f.) *better*
el/la/los/las (m. sg./f. sg./m. pl./f. pl.) **mejor** *the best*
Es mejor que ... *It's better that ...*
memoria (f.) *memory*
menor (m./f.) *younger, smaller*
el/la/los/las (m. sg./f. sg./m. pl./f. pl.) **menor** *the youngest, the smallest*
menos *less, minus (-)*
a las seis menos cuarto *at a quarter to six*
el/la/los/las (m. sg./f. sg./m. pl./f. pl.) **menos ... de ...** *the least ... in/of ...*
Es la una menos cinco. *It's five to one. (12:55)*
más o menos *more or less, so-so, just okay*
menos ... que ... *less ... than ...*
mensaje (m.) *message*
dejar un mensaje después de oír la señal *to leave a message after the tone*
mensaje instantáneo *instant message*
mente (f.) *mind*
mentir *to lie*
mercadillo (m.) *flea market*
mercado (m.) *market*
merienda (f.) *snack time*
mermelada (f.) *jam*
mes (m.) *month*
este mes *this month*
mes entrante *next month*
mes pasado *last month*
mes que viene *next month*
mesa (f.) *table*
mesera (f.) *waitress*
mesero (m.) *waiter*
metro (m.) *metro, subway*
mexicano/mexicana (m./f.) *Mexican*
México (m.) *Mexico*
mezquita (f.) *mosque*
mí *me* (after a preposition)
mi/mis (sg./pl.) *my*
microondas (m.) *microwave*
miedo (m.) *fear*
tener miedo *to be scared/afraid*
tener miedo de que ... *to be scared/afraid that ...*
miel (f.) *honey*
mientras *while*
mientras tanto *meanwhile*
miércoles (m.) *Wednesday*
mil *one thousand*
cien mil *hundred thousand*
diez mil *ten thousand*
veinte mil *twenty thousand*
millón *one million*
un millón de casas *one million houses*
minuto (m.) *minute*
mío/mía/míos/mías (m. sg./f. sg./m. pl./f. pl.) *mine*
mirar *to watch, to look at*
mirar la televisón *to watch television*
Mire ... *Hmm .../Look ...*
mismo/misma (m./f.) *same*
ahora mismo *right now*
mixto/mixta (m./f.) *mixed*
moda (f.) *fashion*
de moda *in fashion, in style*
módem (m.) *modem*
moderno/moderna (m./f.) *modern*
molestarse *to be bothered*
molestarse de que ... *to be bothered that ...*

momento (m.) *moment*
en este momento *at this moment, right now*
Un momento. *Hold on./One moment.*
monitor (m.) *monitor*
montaña (f.) *mountain*
montar *to ride*
monumento (m.) *monument*
morado/morada (m./f.) *purple*
moreno/morena (m./f.) *dark-haired, dark-skinned*
morir *to die*
Moscú *Moscow*
mostrador (m.) *counter*
mostrar *to show*
mover *to move*
móvil (m.) *mobile phone*
muchacha (f.) *girl*
muchacho (m.) *boy*
mucho *a lot, much, very*
mucho/mucha (m./f.) *a lot of*
Mucho gusto. *It's a pleasure.*
muchos/muchas (m. pl./f. pl.) *many, a lot of*
Muchas gracias. *Thanks a lot.*
muebles (m. pl.) *furniture*
muela (f.) *molar*
muerto/muerta (m./f.) *dead person, dead*
mujer (f.) *woman, wife*
mujer de negocios *businesswoman*
mujer policía *policewoman*
muletilla (f.) *filler word/phrase*
multa (f.) *fine*
mundial (m./f.) *worldwide, worldly*
campeonato (m.) **mundial** *world championship*
mundo (m.) *world*
muñeca (f.) *wrist*
músculo (m.) *muscle*
museo (m.) *museum*
música (f.) *music*
música clásica *classical music*
musical (m.) *musical*
músico (m./f.) *musician*
muy *very*

N

nacional (m./f.) *national*
llamada (f.) **nacional** *national call*
nacionalidad (f.) *nationality*
nada *nothing*
De nada. *You're welcome.*
nada más *nothing else*
No hay nada que ... *There's nothing that ...*
No, para nada. *No, not at all.*
nadar *to swim*
nadie *nobody, no one*
No hay nadie que ... *There's no one who/that ...*
naipes (m. pl.) *(playing) cards*
naranja (f.) *orange (fruit)*
nariz (f.) *nose*
dar de narices *to fall flat on one's face*
natación (f.) *swimming*
natural (m./f.) *natural*
naturaleza (f.) *nature*
náusea (f.) *nausea, sickness*
tener náusea(s) *to be nauseated, to have nausea*
navaja (f.) *pocket-knife*
navaja de afeitar *razor*
necesario/necesaria (m./f.) *necessary*
Es necesario que ... *It's necessary that ...*
necesitar *to need*
negar *to deny*
negar que ... *to deny that ...*
negocio (m.) *business*
hombre (m.) **de negocios** *businessman*
mujer (f.) **de negocios** *businesswoman*
negro/negra (m./f.) *black*
estar negro de la risa *to laugh very hard (lit., to turn black with laughter)*
ver todo negro *to be a pessimist (lit., to see everything as black)*
nervio (m.) *nerve*
nevar *to snow*
Está nevando. *It's snowing.*
nevera (f.) *refrigerator*
ni *nor*
ni ... ni *neither ... nor*
niebla (f.) *fog*
niebla tóxica/con humo *smog*
nieta (f.) *granddaughter*
nieto (m.) *grandson*
nietos (pl.) *grandsons, grandchildren*
nieve (f.) *snow*
niña (f.) *young girl, female child*
ningún/ninguno/ninguna (before m. sg.

nouns/m. sg./f. sg.) *no, none*
No hay ningún ... que ... *There's no ... that/ who ...*
niño (m.) *young boy, male child*
no *not, no*
No, para nada. *No, not at all.*
noche (f.) *evening, night*
a las siete de la noche *at seven p.m.*
Buenas noches. *Good evening./Good night.*
de la noche *at night, in the evening*
esta noche *tonight*
medianoche *midnight*
Nochebuena *Christmas Eve*
por la noche *at night*
nombre (m.) *name*
normal (m./f.) *normal*
normalmente *normally*
norte (m.) *north*
nos *us* (direct object pronoun)*; (to/for) us* (indirect object pronoun)*; ourselves*
nosotras *we* (f. pl.)
nosotros *we* (m. pl./mixed group)
nota (f.) *note, grade*
sacar buenas/malas notas *to get good/bad grades*
tomar nota *to take note*
noticia (f.) *a piece of news*
noticias (pl.) *news*
novecientos/novecientas (m./f.) *nine hundred*
novela (f.) *novel*
novela rosa *romance novel*
noventa *ninety*
novia (f.) *girlfriend, fiancée*
noviembre (m.) *November*
novio (m.) *boyfriend, fiancé*
nube (f.) *cloud*
nublado/nublada (m./f.) *cloudy*
Está nublado. *It's cloudy.*
nuera (f.) *daughter-in-law*
nuestro/nuestra/nuestros/nuestras (m. sg./f. sg./m. pl./f. pl.) *our*
nuestro/nuestra/nuestros/nuestras (m. sg./f. sg./m. pl./f. pl.) *ours*
Nueva York *New York*
nuevamente *once again*
nueve *nine*
nuevo/nueva (m./f.) *new*
número (m.) *number*
número de teléfono *telephone number*
nunca *never*
casi nunca *seldom, almost never*

O

o *or*
más o menos *more or less, so-so, just okay*
o ... o *either ... or*
objetivo (m.) *objective, aim*
objeto (m.) *object*
obra (f.) *play (theater)*
obra dramática *drama*
obrero/obrera (m./f.) *construction worker*
occidente (m.) *west*
océano (m.) *ocean*
ochenta *eighty*
ocho *eight*
a las ocho y diez *at eight ten (8:10)*
ochocientos/ochocientas (m./f.) *eight hundred*
octubre (m.) *October*
ocupado/ocupada (m./f.) *busy*
oeste (m.) *west*
oferta (f.) *offer*
oficina (f.) *office*
oficinista (m./f.) *office worker*
ofrecer *to offer*
oír *to hear*
Ojalá que ... *I hope/wish ...*
ojo (m.) *eye*
ojo por ojo *an eye for an eye*
oler *to smell*
olvidar *to forget*
once *eleven*
onza (f.) *ounce*
ópera (f.) *opera*
operadora (f.) *operator*
operarse *to have an operation*
opuesto/opuesta (m./f.) *opposite*
oración (f.) *prayer*
ordenador (m.) *computer*
oreja (f.) *ear*
oriente (m.) *east*
os *all of you* (infml.) (direct object pronoun)*; (to/for) you* (infml. pl.)*(indirect object pronoun); yourselves* (infml.)
oscuro/oscura (m./f.) *dark*
azul (m./f.) **oscuro** *dark blue*
verde (m./f.) **oscuro** *dark green*

otoño (m.) *fall*
otro/otra (m./f.) *another*

P

paciencia (f.) *patience*
tener paciencia *to be patient*
padrastro (m.) *stepfather*
padre (m.) *father*
padres (pl.) *fathers, parents*
paga (f.) *wage*
pagar *to pay*
pagar en efectivo *to pay cash*
pagar la cuenta *to check out, to pay the bill/check*
página (f.) *page*
páginas (pl.) **amarillas** *yellow pages*
página web *webpage*
pago (m.) *payment*
país (m.) *country*
palabra (f.) *word*
palacio (m.) *palace*
palmo (m.) *palm*
conocer palmo a palmo *to know like the back of one's hand*
palo (m.) *stick*
pan (m.) *bread*
panadería (f.) *bakery*
panameño/panameña (m./f.) *Panamanian*
pantalla (f.) *screen*
pantalones (m. pl.) *pants*
pantis (m. pl.) *women's underwear*
pantuflas (f. pl.) *slippers*
pantymedias (f. pl.) *stockings*
papa (f.) *potato*
papá (m.) *dad*
papi (m.) *dad*
papaya (f.) *papaya*
papel (m.) *paper*
papel higiénico *toilet paper*
paquete (m.) *package*
para *for, towards, in order to, intended for, by/until a certain time*
espacio (m.) **para charla** *chat room*
No, para nada. *No, not at all.*
parada (f.) *stop, bus stop*
parado/parada (m./f.) *unemployed*
paraguas (m.) *umbrella*
Paraguay (m.) *Paraguay*
parar *to stop, to leave*
pararse de cabeza *to go crazy, to go out of one's mind*
parcial (m./f.) *partial*
a tiempo parcial *part-time*
pardo/parda (m./f.) *grayish brown*
parecer *to look like, to seem*
¿Qué te parece . . . ? *What do you think of . . . ?*
¿Qué te parece si . . . ? *How about if . . . ?*
pared (f.) *wall*
pariente (m./f.) *relative*
París *Paris*
parque (m.) *park*
parqueadero (m.) *parking lot*
parrilla (f.) *grill*
a la parrilla *grilled*
parte (f.) *part, side*
¿De parte de quién? *Who's calling?*
por otra parte *on the other hand*
por una parte *on the one hand*
particular (m./f.) *particular*
partido (m.) *(sport) game*
partido de béisbol *baseball game*
partir *to leave, to set off*
partir de . . . *to start from . . .*
párvulo/párvula (m./f.) *young child*
pasado/pasada (m./f.) *spoiled*
pasado/pasada (m./f.) *past*
año (m.) **pasado** *last year*
mes (m.) **pasado** *last month*
semana (f.) **pasada** *last week*
pasaje (m.) *ticket*
pasaporte (m.) *passport*
pasar *to pass, to forward, to go by, to happen, to spend*
Le paso. *I'm putting you through. (on the phone)*
pasar el día *to spend the day*
¿Qué pasa? *How's it going?*
pasatiempos (m.) *hobby*
Pascua (f.) *Easter*
pastelería (f.) *bakery (for pastries, etc.)*
pastilla (f.) *pill*
patata (f.) *potato*
patio (m.) *backyard*
peaje (m.) *toll*
peatón (m.) *pedestrian*
pecho (m.) *breast, chest*

pediatra (m./f.) *pediatrician*
pediatría (f.) *pediatrics*
pedir *to order, to ask for*
  pedir que . . . *to request that . . .*
película (f.) *movie, film*
  películas (pl.) **de aventuras** *adventure films*
  películas de horror *horror films*
  películas de suspenso *suspense films*
  películas románticas *romantic films*
pelo (m.) *hair*
pelota (f.) *ball*
peluquería (f.) *hair salon*
pena (f.) *pain, pity*
  ¡Qué pena! *That's too bad!*
pendientes (m. pl.) *earrings*
penicilina (f.) *penicillin*
pensar *to think*
  no pensar que . . . *not to think that . . .*
pensión (f.) *pension*
peor (m./f.) *worse*
  el/la/los/las (m. sg./f. sg./m. pl./f. pl.) **peor** *the worst*
pepino (m.) *cucumber*
pequeño/pequeña (m./f.) *small*
pera (f.) *pear*
percibir *to perceive*
perder *to lose, to miss*
  perder la cabeza *to lose one's head*
Perdón. *Excuse me.*
perezoso/perezosa (m./f.) *lazy*
  ser perezoso *to be lazy*
perfecto/perfecta (m./f.) *perfect*
perfume (m.) *perfume*
periódico (m.) *newspaper*
periodista (m./f.) *journalist*
período (m.) *period*
  período de prueba *probationary period*
permitir *to allow*
  ¿Me permite . . . ? *May I please . . . ?* (fml.)
  ¿Me permites . . . ? *May I please . . . ?* (infml.)
pero *but*
perro (m.) *dog*
persona (f.) *person*
  persona extranjero *stranger*
personal (m.) *staff*
Perú (m.) *Peru*
peruano/peruana (m./f.) *Peruvian*
pesar *to weigh*
pescadería (f.) *fish shop, fish market*
pescado (m.) *fish*
pésimo/pésima (m./f.) *terrible*
peso (m.) *peso*
pestañas (f. pl.) *eyelashes*
piano (m.) *piano*
picante (m./f.) *spicy*
pie (m.) *foot*
  dedo (m.) **del pie** *toe*
  ir a pie *to walk*
  poner el pie en el freno *to hit the brakes*
  tener los pies en la tierra *to have both feet on the ground*
piel (f.) *skin*
pierna (f.) *leg*
pieza (f.) *piece*
  de dos piezas *two-piece*
pijama (m.) *pajamas*
pimienta (f.) *pepper (spice)*
pimiento (m.) *pepper (vegetable)*
pinta (f.) *spot, appearance*
pintor/pintora (m./f.) *painter*
pintura (f.) *painting*
piscina (f.) *swimming pool*
piso (m.) *floor, apartment*
placer (m.) *pleasure*
plan (m.) *plan*
plancha (f.) *iron*
planchar *to iron*
  tabla (f.) **de planchar** *ironing board*
planilla (f.) *form*
  planilla de impuestos *tax return*
plano (m.) *map*
plano/plana (m./f.) *flat*
planta (f.) *plant*
plantilla (f.) *staff*
plástico (m.) *plastic*
plátano (m.) *banana*
plateado/plateada (m./f.) *silver (color)*
plato (m.) *plate, dish*
  lavar los platos *to do the dishes*
  plato del día *special of the day*
  plato principal *main dish*
playa (f.) *beach*
plaza (f.) *plaza, square*
  plaza de mercado *outdoor market*
pluma (f.) *pen*
pobre (m./f.) *poor, poor person*

los pobres *the poor*
poco *little*
Hablo un poco de español. *I speak a little Spanish.*
un poco *a little*
pocos/pocas (m. pl./f. pl.) *few*
poder *can, to be able to, to have permission to*
¿Podría . . . ? *Could you . . . ?*
podrido/podrida (m./f.) *bad, rotten*
policía (m./f.) *police officer*
mujer (f.) **policía** *policewoman*
poliéster (m.) *polyester*
pollo (m.) *chicken*
polvo (m.) *dust, powder*
leche (f.) **en polvo** *powdered milk*
poner *to put, to place*
poner el pie en el freno *to hit the brakes*
poner en espera *to put on hold*
ponerse *to become, to turn, to put something on*
ponerse colorado *to be embarrassed (lit., to turn red)*
por *for, by, around, at, because of, due to, in place of, in exchange for, through*
por casualidad *by chance*
por desgracia *unfortunately*
¡Por Dios! *For God's sake!*
por eso *for this reason*
Por favor. *Please.*
por fin *finally, at last*
por la noche *at night*
por la radio *on the radio*
por lo tanto *therefore*
por lo visto *apparently*
por otra parte *on the other hand*
por qué *why*
por supuesto *of course*
por teléfono *on the phone*
por una parte *on the one hand*
porque *because*
portero (m.) *goalkeeper*
portugués/portuguesa (m./f.) *Portuguese*
poseer *to own, to hold*
posible (m./f.) *possible*
Es posible que . . . *It is possible that . . .*
lo antes posible *as soon as possible*
postre (m.) *dessert*
practicar *to practice, to play (sports)*
precio (m.) *price*
etiqueta (f.) **con el precio** *price tag*
precio económico *reasonable price*
precisamente *precisely*
preferible (m./f.) *preferable*
Es preferible que . . . *It's preferable that . . .*
preferir *to prefer*
preferir que . . . *to prefer that . . .*
pregunta (f.) *question*
preguntar *to ask*
premio (m.) *prize*
prenda (f.) *garment*
preocuparse *to worry*
No se preocupe. *Don't worry.*
preocuparse de que . . . *to worry that . . .*
preparado/preparada (m./f.) *ready, prepared*
¿Preparados? *Ready?*
presentación (f.) *presentation*
presentar *to introduce*
Te presento a . . . *Let me introduce you to . . .*
presidente/presidenta (m./f.) *president*
presión (f.) *pressure*
prestigioso/prestigiosa (m./f.) *prestigious*
primavera (f.) *spring*
primer/primero/primera (before m. sg. nouns/m./f.) *first*
primo/prima (m./f.) *cousin*
primos (pl.) *cousins*
principal (m./f.) *main*
plato (m.) **principal** *main dish*
prisa (f.) *hurry*
aprisa *quickly*
tener prisa *to be in a hurry*
probador (m.) *dressing room*
probar *to try, to taste*
probarse *to try on (clothes)*
problema (m.) *problem*
producir *to produce*
producto (m.) *product*
profesión (f.) *profession*
profesional (m./f.) *professional*
profesionalmente *professionally*
profesor/profesora (m./f.) *professor*
profesorado (m.) *faculty*
programa (m.) *program*
programa de entrevistas *talk show*
programa de televisión *television program*
prohibir *to forbid, to prohibit*
prohibir que . . . *to forbid that/to . . .*

prometer *to promise*
prometido/prometida (m./f.) *fiancé(e)*
pronto *soon*
propina (f.) *tip*
proteger *to protect*
provecho (m.) *benefit*
  ¡Buen provecho! *Enjoy the meal!*
próximo/próxima (m./f.) *near, next*
  próxima semana (f.) *next week*
proyecto (m.) *project*
prueba (f.) *proof, test, probation*
  período (m.) **de prueba** *probationary period*
pueblo (m.) *town*
puente (m.) *bridge, long weekend*
puerta (f.) *door*
  abrir la puerta *to open the door*
pues *so, since, therefore, well, then*
  Pues, aquí estamos. *Here we are.*
  Pues bien. *Fine.*
  Pues, nada. *Not much.*
puesto (m.) *(job) position, post*
pulmones (m. pl.) *lungs*
pulsera (f.) *bracelet*
punta (f.) *tip, end*
  ir de punta en blanco *to be dressed to the nines (lit., to go from the tip in white)*
punto (m.) *point*
  en punto *exactly*
  Son las tres en punto. *It's three o'clock sharp.*
puntual (m./f.) *punctual*
púrpura (m./f.) *purple*

Q

que *which, that* (relative pronoun, conjunction)
qué *what* (question)
  ¿A qué hora es? *At what time is it?*
  ¿De qué color es . . . ? *What color is . . . ?*
  por qué *why*
  ¡Qué . . . ! *How . . . !*
  ¡Qué bien! *How nice!*
  ¿Qué hay? *What's up?/What's going on?*
  ¿Qué hora es? *What time is it?*
  ¿Qué horas son? *What time is it?*
  ¿Qué pasa? *How's it going?*
  ¡Qué pena! *That's too bad!*
  ¿Qué quiere decir eso? *What does that mean?*
  ¿Qué tal? *What's happening?*
  ¿Qué tal si . . . ? *How about if . . . ?*
  ¿Qué te parece si . . . ? *How about if . . . ?*
  ¡Yo qué sé! *How do I know!?/How should I know!?*
quedar *to remain, to retain, to fit*
  quedar empatados *to be tied*
quemado/quemada (m./f.) *burnt*
querer *to want, to love*
  querer que . . . *to want that/to . . .*
  ¿Qué quiere decir eso? *What does that mean?*
  Quisiera . . . *I'd like . . .*
  Te quiero. *I love you.*
queso (m.) *cheese*
quien/quienes (sg./pl.) *who, whom* (relative pronoun)
quién/quiénes (sg./pl.) *who, whom* (question)
  ¿De parte de quién? *Who's calling?*
  ¿De quién . . . ? *Whose . . . ?*
  ¿Quién lo llama? *Who's calling?*
química (f.) *chemistry*
quince *fifteen*
quinientos/quinientas (m./f.) *five hundred*

R

racimo (m.) *bunch (of grapes)*
  racimo de uvas *bunch of grapes*
radio (f.) *radio*
  por la radio *on the radio*
rampa (f.) *ramp*
rápidamente *fast, quickly*
rápido *fast, quickly*
rápido/rápida (m./f.) *fast, quick*
ratón (m.) *mouse*
raya (f.) *stripe*
  a rayas *striped*
razón (f.) *reason*
  tener razón *to be right*
realismo (m.) *realism*
realista (m./f.) *realistic*
realmente *actually*
rebaja (f.) *discount*
  comprar en rebaja *to buy on sale*
rebajado/rebajada (m./f.) *reduced*
rebanada (f.) *slice*
recepción (f.) *reception desk*
recepcionista (m./f.) *receptionist*
receso (m.) *recess*
receta (f.) *recipe*
recibir *to receive*

recoger *to pick up*
recomendar *to recommend*
  recomendar que . . . *to recommend that . . .*
reconocer *to recognize*
recordar *to remember*
recorrido (m.) *route*
  recorrido por autobús *tour bus trip*
recreo (m.) *recreation*
recto *straight*
  Continúa recto. *Continue straight.*
redondo/redonda (m./f.) *round*
reducir *to reduce*
referencia (f.) *reference*
refresco (m.) *soft drink, soda*
regalar *to give (a gift)*
regalo (m.) *gift*
región (f.) *region*
regional (m./f.) *regional*
registrarse *to check in*
regresar *to return*
reír *to laugh*
relación (f.) *relationship*
relámpago (m.) *lightening*
relleno (m.) *stuffing, filling*
  frase (f.) **de relleno** *filler phrase*
reloj (m.) *watch, clock*
repetir *to repeat*
  Repita, por favor *Repeat, please.*
representante (m.) *representative*
reserva (f.) *reservation*
reservación (f.) *reservation*
resolver *to resolve*
responder *to answer*
responsable (m./f.) *responsible*
respuesta (f.) *answer*
restaurante (m.) *restaurant*
resto (m.) *rest*
resultado (m.) *result*
retransmitir *to forward*
retrasado/retrasada (m./f.) *slow, behind*
retrasar *to delay, to postpone*
retribución (f.) *repayment*
reunión (f.) *meeting*
reunir *to gather, to meet*
revista (f.) *magazine*
rico/rica (m./f.) *rich*
río (m.) *river*
risa (f.) *laughter*
  estar negro de la risa *to laugh very hard (lit., to turn black with laughter)*
roca (f.) *rock*
rodilla (f.) *knee*
rojo/roja (m./f.) *red*
  estar rojo de la ira *to be very angry (lit., to be red with fury)*
romántico/romántica (m./f.) *romantic*
ropa (f.) *clothing*
  detergente (m.) **de ropa** *laundry detergent*
  lavar la ropa *to do the laundry*
  tienda (f.) **de ropa** *clothing store*
rosa (f.) *rose*
  novela (f.) **rosa** *romance novel*
  ver todo color de rosa *to be an optimist, to wear rose colored glasses (lit., to see everything pink)*
rosado/rosada (m./f.) *pink*
rubio/rubia (m./f.) *blonde*
rural (m./f.) *rural*
ruso (m.) *Russian (language)*

S

sábado (m.) *Saturday*
saber (intransitive verb) *to taste*
saber (transitive verb) *to know (facts, information), to learn*
  no saber ni jota de . . . *to not have a clue about . . .*
  ¿Quién sabe? *Who knows?*
  ¿Sabe cómo . . . ? *Do you know how to . . . ?*
  ¡Yo qué sé! *How do I know!?/How should I know!?*
saborear *to taste*
sacar *to take out, to get*
  sacar buenas notas *to get good grades*
  sacar malas notas *to get bad grades*
saco (m.) *jacket*
sal (f.) *salt*
sala (f.) *living room*
  sala de conferencias *meeting room, conference room, lecture hall*
salado/salada (m./f.) *salty*
salario (m.) *salary*
salida (f.) *exit*
salir *to leave, to go out*
  salir de viaje *to go on a trip*
salsa (f.) *sauce, salsa*

saltar *to skip*
saltarse el semáforo *to go through a light*
saludable (m./f.) *healthy*
saludo (m.) *greeting*
¡Saludos! *Hello!*
sandalias (f. pl.) *sandals*
sangre (f.) *blood*
hacerse un examen de sangre *to take a blood test*
ser de sangre azul *to have blue blood (lit., to be of blue blood)*
se *himself, herself, itself, yourself* (fml.), *themselves, yourselves* (fml.); *(to/for) him, her, it, you* (fml. sg./pl.), *them* (indirect object pronoun, used in place of le/les when preceding lo/la/los/las); *you, people, one* (impersonal pronoun)
secadora (f.) *dryer*
sección (f.) *section*
seco/seca (m./f.) *dry*
lavar en seco *to dry-clean*
secretaria (m./f.) *secretary*
secreto (m.) *secret*
sed (f.) *thirst*
tener sed *to be thirsty*
seda (f.) *silk*
seguir *to follow*
Siga derecho. *Go straight.*
Siga por el carril de la derecha. *Stay in the right lane.*
segundo/segunda (m./f.) *second*
segundo año *second year*
seguridad (f.) *safety, security*
abrocharse el cinturón de seguridad *to buckle up*
seguro (m.) *insurance*
seguro/segura (m./f.) *sure, safe*
Seguro/Segura que sí. *I'm sure.*
seis *six*
seiscientos/seiscientas (m./f.) *six hundred*
semáforo (m.) *traffic light*
saltarse el semáforo *to go through a light*
semana (f.) *week*
dos días a la semana *twice a week*
esta semana *this week*
fin (m.) **de semana** *weekend*
próxima semana *next week*
semana pasada *last week*
semana que viene *next week*
todas las semanas *every week*
semanal (m./f.) *weekly*
semestre (m.) *semester*
señal (f.) *signal*
dejar un mensaje después de oír la señal *to leave a message after the tone*
senderismo (m.) *hiking*
hacer senderismo *to go hiking*
seno (m.) *breast*
señor (m.) *Mr.*
señora (f.) *Mrs.*
sensatamente *sensibly*
sensiblemente *perceptibly*
sentar *to seat*
estar sentado *to be seated*
sentarse *to sit down*
sentido (m.) *sense, direction*
de sentido único *one-way*
sentir *to feel*
Lo siento. *I'm sorry.*
sentir que ... *to regret that ...*
sentirse *to feel*
septiembre (m.) *September*
ser *to be*
Es la una. *It's one o'clock.*
Son las tres. *It's three o'clock.*
Son las tres en punto. *It's three o'clock sharp.*
ser caradura *to be shameless*
serie (f.) *series*
serio/seria (m./f.) *serious*
serpiente (f.) *snake*
servicio (m.) *service*
¿Está incluido el servicio? *Is service included?*
servilleta (f.) *napkin*
servir *to serve*
¿En qué puedo servirle? *How may I help you?*
sesenta *sixty*
sesión (f.) *session*
setecientos/setecientas (m./f.) *seven hundred*
setenta *seventy*
si *if*
¿Qué tal si ...? *How about if ...?*
¿Qué te parece si ...? *How about if ...?*
sí *yes*
¡Claro que sí! *Of course!*
Creo que sí. *I think so.*
Seguro/segura que sí. *I'm sure.*

¡Yo espero que sí! *I hope so!*
sicología (f.) *psychology*
siempre *always*
siesta (f.) *nap*
siete *seven*
siglo (m.) *century*
este siglo *this century*
significar *to mean*
silenciosamente *quietly*
silla (f.) *chair, seat*
simpático/simpática (m./f.) *friendly*
simplemente *simply, only*
sin *without*
sindicato (m.) *union*
síndrome (m.) *syndrome*
síndrome del túnel del carpio *carpal tunnel syndrome*
síntoma (m.) *symptom*
sistema (m.) *system*
sistema de sonido *sound system*
sitio (m.) *place*
sitio web *website*
situación (f.) *situation*
sobre *on top of, over, above, about*
sobre todo *especially*
sobrecocido/sobrecocida (m./f.) *overcooked*
sobremesa (f.) *after-dinner conversation*
sobrina (f.) *niece*
sobrino (m.) *nephew*
sofá (m.) *sofa, couch*
sol (m.) *sun*
gafas (f. pl.) **de sol** *sunglasses*
Hace sol. *It's sunny.*
solamente *only*
soledad (f.) *solitude*
solicitar *to apply for, to request*
solicitud (f.) *application*
sólo *merely, solely, only*
solo/sola (m./f.) *sole, only, alone*
soltero/soltera (m./f.) *single*
solución (f.) *solution*
sombrero (m.) *hat*
sonar *to sound, to ring*
soñar *to dream*
¡Ni lo sueñes! *Don't even dream about it!*
soñar con … *to dream about …*
sonido (m.) *sound*
sistema (m.) **de sonido** *sound system*
sonido (m.) *sound*
sonreír *to smile*
sopa (f.) *soup*
sorprenderse *to be surprised*
sorprenderse de que … *to be surprised that …*
sorpresa (f.) *surprise*
sótano (m.) *basement*
su/sus (sg./pl.) *his, her, its, their, your* (pl./sg. fml.)
suave (m./f.) *soft*
subasta (f.) *auction*
subterráneo (m.) *subway*
suburbano/suburbana (m./f.) *suburban*
suceso (m.) *event, happening*
sucio/sucia (m./f.) *dirty*
Sudamérica *South America*
suegra (f.) *mother-in-law*
suegro (m.) *father-in-law*
sueldo (m.) *pay*
suelo (m.) *floor*
suelto/suelta (m./f.) *loose, flowing*
sueño (m.) *sleepiness, sleep*
tener sueño *to be sleepy*
suerte (f.) *luck*
suéter (m.) *sweater*
suficiente (m./f.) *enough*
sufrir *to suffer*
sugerir *to suggest*
sugerir que … *to suggest that …*
supermercado (m.) *supermarket*
supuesto (m.) *supposition*
por supuesto *of course*
sur (m.) *south*
suscriptor/suscriptora (m./f.) *subscriber*
línea (f.) **de suscriptor digital (DSL)** *DSL*
suspender *to fail, to suspend*
suspender un examen *to fail a test*
suspenso (m.) *suspense*
películas (f. pl.) **de suspenso** *suspense films*
suyo/suya/suyos/suyas (m. sg./f. sg./m. pl./f. pl.) *his, hers, theirs, yours*

T

tabla (f.) *table, board*
tabla de planchar *ironing board*
tacón (m.) *heel*
tajada (f.) *slice*
tal *such*

¿Qué tal? *How's it going?*
¿Qué tal si . . . ? *How about if . . . ?*
tal vez *perhaps*
talla (f.) *size*
tamaño (m.) *size*
también *also, too*
tampoco *neither, not either*
tan *so (very)*
tan . . . como *as . . . as* (comparison)
tanto *in such a manner*
mientras tanto *meanwhile*
por lo tanto *therefore*
tanto/tanta (m./f.) *as much, as many*
tanto/tanta/tantos/tantas (m. sg./f. sg./m. pl./f. pl.) **. . . como** *as . . . as* (comparison)
taquilla (f.) *box office*
tarde *late*
Hasta más tarde. *Until later.*
más tarde *later*
Se me hace tarde. *I'm late.*
tarde (f.) *afternoon*
a las cuatro de la tarde *at four p.m.*
Buenas tardes. *Good afternoon.*
de la tarde *in the afternoon*
esta tarde *this afternoon*
tarea (f.) *homework*
tarjeta (f.) *card*
tarjeta de crédito *credit card*
taxi (m.) *taxi*
taxista (m./f.) *taxi driver*
taza (f.) *cup*
tazón (m.) *bowl*
te *you* (infml. sg.) (direct object pronoun); *(to/for) you* (infml. sg.) (indirect object pronoun); *yourself* (infml.)
Te presento a . . . *Let me introduce you to . . .*
té (m.) *tea*
teatro (m.) *theater*
techo (m.) *ceiling*
teclado (m.) *keyboard*
tecnología (f.) *technology*
tejanos (m. pl.) *jeans*
telefónico/telefónica (m./f.) *(of) telephone, telephonic*
cabina (f.) **telefónica** *telephone booth*
guía (f.) **telefónica** *phone book*
teléfono (m.) *telephone*
colgar el teléfono *to hang up the phone*
contestar el teléfono *to answer the phone*
llamar por teléfono *to make a phone call*
llamar por teléfono a . . . *to call . . . on the phone*
marcar un número de teléfono *to dial a phone number*
número (m.) **de teléfono** *telephone number*
televisión (f.) *television*
mirar la televisón *to watch television*
programa (m.) **de televisión** *television program*
televisor (m.) *television (set)*
temer *to fear, to be afraid of*
temperatura (f.) *temperature*
templo (m.) *temple*
temprano *early* (adverb)
temprano/temprana (m./f.) *early*
tendón (m.) *tendon*
tenedor (m.) *fork*
tener *to have*
Aquí tiene. *Here you are.*
¿Cuántos años tiene? *How old are you* (sg. fml.)*/is he/is she?*
Que tenga un buen día. *Have a nice day.*
tener . . . años *to be . . . years old*
tener calor *to be hot, to be warm*
tener cansancio *to be tired*
tener dolor de cabeza *to have a headache*
tener dolor de garganta *to have a sore throat*
tener fiebre *to have a fever*
tener frío *to be cold*
tener ganas de . . . *to feel like . . .*
tener hambre *to be hungry*
tener interés en . . . *to be interested in . . .*
tener la cabeza fría *to keep a cool head*
tener la tensión alta/baja *to have high/low blood pressure*
tener los pies en la tierra *to have both feet on the ground*
tener mareo *to be dizzy*
tener miedo *to be scared*
tener náusea(s) *to be nauseated, to have nausea*
tener paciencia *to be patient*
tener prisa *to be in a hurry*
tener que . . . *to have to . . .*
tener razón *to be right*
tener sed *to be thirsty*

tener sueño *to be sleepy*
tener tos *to have a cough*
tenis (m.) *tennis*
tensión (f.) *tension*
tener la tensión alta/baja *to have high/low blood pressure*
tomar la tensión *to take the blood pressure*
tercero/tercer/tercera (m. sg./m. sg. before a m. noun/f.) *third*
tercer año *third year*
terminar *to finish*
término (m.) *term, period, point*
término medio *medium-rare*
término tres cuartos *medium*
tesis (f.) *dissertation*
tetera (f.) *teakettle*
texto (m.) *text*
libro (m.) **de texto** *textbook*
ti *you* (infml. sg.) (after a preposition)
tía (f.) *aunt, woman*
tiempo (m.) *time, weather*
a tiempo *on time, in time*
a tiempo completo *full-time*
a tiempo parcial *part-time*
El tiempo es bueno. *The weather is good.*
¿Cómo estás de tiempo? *Do you have time?/ How are you doing for time?*
Hace muy buen tiempo. *It's beautiful.*
medio tiempo *halftime*
tienda (f.) *store, convenience store*
tienda de antigüedades *antique store*
tienda de electrodomésticos *appliances store*
tienda de ropa *clothing store*
tienda por departamentos *department store*
Tienes que ... *You have to ...*
tierra (f.) *land*
tener los pies en la tierra *to have both feet on the ground*
tímido/tímida (m./f.) *shy*
tinto/tinta (m./f.) *dark red*
vino (m.) **tinto** *red wine*
tío (m.) *uncle, man*
típico/típica (m./f.) *typical*
tipo (m.) *type*
tiquete (m.) *ticket*
título (m.) *degree, diploma*
toalla (f.) *towel*
tobillo (m.) *ankle*
tocar *to touch, to play an instrument*
tocar el piano *to play the piano*
tocar la guitarra *to play the guitar*
todavía *still, yet*
todo (m.) *everything*
sobre todo *especially*
todo/toda (m./f.) *all, every*
todas las semanas *every week*
todo el día *all day*
todos los días *every day*
tomar *to take, to have (food and drink)*
tomar la tensión *to take the blood pressure*
tomar un medicamento *to take medication*
tomate (m.) *tomato*
tono (m.) *tone, dial tone*
tormenta (f.) *storm*
torta (f.) *cake*
tos (f.) *cough*
tener tos *to have a cough*
tostada (f.) *toast*
totalmente *absolutely*
tóxico/tóxica (m./f.) *toxic*
niebla (f.) **tóxica** *smog*
trabajador/trabajadora (m./f.) *hardworking*
trabajar *to work*
¿En qué trabaja? *What do you do for a living?*
trabajo (m.) *job, work*
¡Buen trabajo! *Good job!*
historial (m.) **de trabajo** *résumé*
trabajo de investigación *research paper*
trabajo de verano *summer job*
trabajo fijo *steady job*
traducir *to translate*
traer *to bring, to get, to take*
tráfico (m.) *traffic*
traje (m.) *suit*
traje de baño *bathing suit*
tranquilo/tranquila (m./f.) *quiet, calm*
trasladar *to transfer*
tratamiento (m.) *treatment*
tratar *to treat*
¿Cómo te trata la vida? *How's life treating you?*
tratar *to try*
tratar de ... *to try ... (to do something)*
trece *thirteen*
treinta *thirty*
tren (m.) *train*

estación (f.) **de tren** *train station*
tres *three*
trescientos/trescientas (m./f.) *three hundred*
triste (m./f.) *sad*
Es triste que ... *It's sad that ...*
tristemente *sadly*
trotar *to jog*
trueno (m.) *thunder*
tú *you* (sg. infml.) (subject pronoun)
tu/tus (sg./pl.) *your* (sg. infml.)
túnel (m.) *tunnel*
síndrome (m.) **del túnel del carpio** *carpal tunnel syndrome*
turismo (m.) *tourism*
turista (m./f.) *tourist*
tuyo/tuya/tuyos/tuyas (m. sg./f. sg./m. pl./f. pl.) *yours* (infml.)

U

último/última (m./f.) *last*
último grito (m.) *the very latest*
un *a* (m.)
una *a* (f.), *one (o'clock)*
Es la una. *It's one o'clock.*
It's one o'clock.
uña (f.) *nail, claw*
unas *some* (f. pl.)
único/única (m./f.) *only, unique, single*
de sentido (m.) **único** *one-way*
unido/unida (m./f.) *united*
los Estados Unidos *the United States*
universidad (f.) *university*
uno *one*
unos *some* (m. pl.)
urbano/urbana (m./f.) *urban*
urgentemente *urgently*
Uruguay (m.) *Uruguay*
uruguayo/uruguaya (m./f.) *Uruguayan*
usar *to use, to take*
usted *you* (sg. fml.) (subject pronoun)
el de usted (m. sg.) *yours* (sg. fml.)
la de usted (f. sg.) *yours* (sg. fml.)
ustedes *you* (pl.) (subject pronoun)
el de ustedes (m. sg.) *yours* (pl.) (referring to a masculine singular object)
la de ustedes (f. sg.) *yours* (pl.) (referring to a feminine singular object)
uvas (f. pl.) *grapes*
racimo (m.) **de uvas** *bunch of grapes*

V

vacaciones (f. pl.) *vacation*
de vacaciones *on vacation*
vajilla (f.) *tableware*
detergente (m.) **de vajilla** *dishwashing detergent*
vale (m.) *coupon, voucher*
¿Cuánto vale? *How much is it?*
Vamos ... *Let's go ...*
vaqueros (m. pl.) *jeans*
variedad (f.) *variety*
varios/varias (m./f.) *several*
vaso (m.) *glass*
vecino/vecina (m./f.) *neighbor*
vegetal (m.) *vegetable*
veinte *twenty*
veinticinco *twenty-five*
veinticuatro *twenty-four*
veintidós *twenty-two*
veintinueve *twenty-nine*
veintiocho *twenty-eight*
veintiséis *twenty-six*
veintisiete *twenty-seven*
veintitrés *twenty-three*
veintiuno *twenty-one*
velocidad (f.) *speed*
vendaje (m.) *bandage*
vendedor/vendedora (m./f.) *salesman/saleswoman*
vender *to sell*
venezolano/venezolana (m./f.) *Venezuelan*
Venezuela (f.) *Venezuela*
venir *to come, to fit (somebody)*
año (m.) **que viene** *next year*
mes (m.) **que viene** *next month*
Me viene bien. *It suits me fine.*
semana (f.) **que viene** *next week*
venta (f.) *sale*
ventana (f.) *window*
ver *to see*
A ver ... *Let's see ...*
Nos vemos. *See you. (lit., We see each other.)*
por lo visto *apparently*
ver todo negro *to be a pessimist (lit., to see everything as black)*
verano (m.) *summer*

trabajo (m.) **de verano** *summer job*
verdad (f.) *truth*
Es verdad. *That's right.*
No es verdad que … *It is not true that …*
¿verdad? *right?*
verde (m./f.) *green*
contar un chiste verde *to tell a dirty joke (lit., to tell a green joke)*
verde oscuro *dark green*
verdura (f.) *vegetable*
vertebral (m./f.) *vertebral*
columna (f.) **vertebral** *backbone, spinal column*
vestíbulo (m.) *hall*
vestido (m.) *dress*
vestido de noche *evening dress*
vestir *to dress (someone)*
vestirse *to get dressed*
veterinario/veterinaria (m./f.) *veterinarian*
vez (f.) *time*
a veces *sometimes*
dos veces por semana *twice a week*
una vez *once*
tal vez *perhaps*
vía (f.) *lane*
viajar *to travel*
viaje (m.) *travel, trip*
Buen viaje. *Have a good trip.*
salir de viaje *to go on a trip*
vida (f.) *life*
¿Cómo te trata la vida? *How's life treating you?*
hoja (f.) **de vida** *résumé*
viejo/vieja (m./f.) *old*
viento (m.) *wind*
Hace viento. *It's windy.*
viento (m.) *wind*
viernes (m.) *Friday*
vincularse *to form links*
vincularse con … *to form links with …*
vinilo (m.) *vinyl*
disco (m.) **de vinilo** *vinyl record*
vino (m.) *wine*
vino blanco *white wine*
vino tinto *red wine*
violeta (m./f.) *violet (color)*
violín (m.) *violin*
visita guiada (f.) *guided tour*
visitante (m./f.) *visitor*
visitar *to visit*
visitar los lugares de interés *to go sightseeing*
vista (f.) *view*
conocer de vista *to know by sight*
vitorear *to cheer*
vivir *to live*
volar *to fly*
volver *to turn, to return*
vosotras *you* (f. pl. infml.) (subject pronoun) *(used in Spain)*
vosotros *you* (m. pl. infml./mixed group infml.) (subject pronoun) (used in Spain)
voz (f.) *voice*
buzón (m.) **de voz** *voice mail*
vuelo (m.) *flight*
vuelta (f.) *turn*
a la vuelta de la esquina *around the corner*
vuestro/vuestra/vuestros/vuestras (m. sg./f. sg./m. pl./f. pl.) *your/yours* (pl. infml.) (used in Spain)

W

web (f.) *web (internet)*
página (f.) **web** *webpage*
sitio (m.) **web** *website*

Y

y *and*
a las ocho y diez *at eight ten (8:10)*
a las cinco y media *at a half past five*
treinta y uno *thirty-one*
ya *already, now, right*
Ya está. *That's it.*
yerno (m.) *son-in-law*
yo *I*

Z

zanahoria (f.) *carrot*
zapatería (f.) *shoe store*
zapatillas (f. pl.) *slippers*
zapatillas deportivas *sneakers, tennis shoes*
zapatos (m. pl.) *shoes*
zumo (m.) *juice*

English-Spanish

A

a *un/una* (m./f.)
  a lot *mucho*
  a lot of *mucho/mucha* (m./f.), *muchos/muchas* (m. pl./f. pl.)
abdomen *abdomen* (m.)
about *de, sobre, a eso de*
  about the (m.) *del (de + el)*
  at about nine o'clock *a eso de las nueve*
  dream about . . . *soñar con . . .*
  How about if . . . ? *¿Qué tal si . . . ?/¿Qué te parece si . . . ?*
  not have a clue about . . . (to) *no saber ni jota de . . .*
above *encima, sobre*
  above . . . *encima de . . .*
absolute *absoluto/absoluta* (m./f.)
absolutely *absolutamente, totalmente*
  absolutely not *en absoluto*
absurd *absurdo/absurda* (m./f.)
academic *académico/académica* (m./f.)
academy *academia* (f.)
accept (to) *aceptar*
accident *accidente* (m.)
account *cuenta* (f.)
accountant *contable* (m./f.)
across from . . . *enfrente de . . .*
actor *actor* (m.)
actress *actriz* (f.)
actually *efectivamente, realmente*
acupuncture *acupuntura* (f.)
address *dirección* (f.)
adult *adulto/adulta* (m./f.)
adventure *aventura* (f.)
  adventure films *películas* (pl.) *de aventuras*
advise (to) *aconsejar*
  advise that/to . . . (to) *aconsejar que . . .*
after . . . *después de . . .*
  after-dinner conversation *sobremesa* (f.)
  It's ten after one in the morning. *Es la una y diez de la madrugada.*
afternoon *tarde* (f.)
  Good afternoon. *Buenas tardes.*
  in the afternoon *de la tarde*
  this afternoon *esta tarde*
afterwards *después*
against *contra*
age *edad* (f.)
agency *agencia* (f.)
agent *agente* (m./f.)
agitated *agitado/agitada* (m./f.)
agreement *acuerdo* (m.)
aim *objetivo* (m.)
airline *aerolínea* (f.)
airplane *avión* (m.)
airport *aeropuerto* (m.)
algebra *álgebra* (f.)
all *todo/toda* (m./f.)
  all day *todo el día*
  All right. *De acuerdo.*
  No, not at all. *No, para nada.*
allergic *alérgico/alérgica* (m./f.)
allergy *alergia* (f.)
alley *callejón* (m.)
allow (to) *permitir*
almost *casi*
  almost never *casi nunca*
alone *solo/sola* (m./f.)
already *ya*
  as you already know *como ya sabes*
also *igualmente, también*
always *siempre*
a.m. *de la mañana, de la madrugada*
  at nine a.m. *a las nueve de la mañana*
American *americano/americana* (m./f.), *estadounidense* (m./f.)
amusement *diversión* (f.)
  amusement park *parque* (m.) *de diversiones*
and *y*
  and on top of that . . . *y encima . . .*
anger *ira* (f.)
ankle *tobillo* (m.)
another *otro/otra* (m./f.)
answer *respuesta* (f.)
answer (to) *responder, contestar*
  answer the phone (to) *contestar el teléfono*
answering machine *contestador* (m.) *(automático)*
antique *antigüedad* (f.)
antiques *antigüedades* (f. pl.)
  antique store *tienda* (f.) *de antigüedades*
any *cualquier*
Anything else? *¿Algo más?*

apartment *apartamento* (m.), *piso* (m.)
apology *disculpa* (f.)
apparently *por lo visto*
appeal *gracia* (f.)
appearance *pinta* (f.)
appetite *apetito* (m.)
appetizer *entrada* (f.)
apple *manzana* (f.)
application *solicitud* (f.)
apply for (to) *solicitar*
appointment *cita* (f.)
April *abril* (m.)
architect *arquitecto/arquitecta* (m./f.)
architecture *arquitectura* (f.)
area *área* (m.)
Argentina *Argentina* (f.)
Argentinian *argentino/argentina* (m./f.)
arm *brazo* (m.)
around *por, a eso de*
  around the corner *a la vuelta de la esquina*
  around town *por la ciudad*
arrive (to) *llegar*
  arrive at ... (to) *llegar a ...*
art *arte* (m.)
artist *artista* (m./f.)
as *como, cual/cuales* (sg./pl.)
  as ... as *tan ... como (comparisons), tanto/tanta/tantos/tantas* (m. sg./f. sg./m. pl./f. pl.) *... como (comparisons)*
  as many/much *cuanto/cuanta/cuantos/cuantas* (m. sg./f. sg./m. pl./f. pl.), *tanto/tanta* (m./f.)
  as soon as possible *lo antes posible*
  as you already know *como ya sabes*
ask (to) *preguntar*
ask for (to) *pedir*
assistant *asistente* (m./f.)
astronaut *astronauta* (m./f.)
at *a, en, por*
  arrive at ... (to) *llegar a ...*
  at a quarter to six *a las seis menos cuarto*
  at about nine o'clock *a eso de las nueve*
  at dawn *al amanecer*
  at dusk *al atardecer*
  at five (o'clock) *a las cinco*
  at hand *a la mano*
  at last *por fin*
  at midnight *a medianoche*
  at night *por la noche*
  at noon *a mediodía*
  at the (m.) *al (a + el)*
  at the present time *actualmente*
  at this moment *en este momento*
  At what time is it? *¿A qué hora es?*
  look at (to) *mirar*
  No, not at all. *No, para nada.*
athlete *atleta* (m./f.)
athletic *atlético/atlética* (m./f.), *deportivo/deportiva* (m./f.)
attach (to) *adjuntar*
  attach a file (to) *adjuntar un documento/archivo*
attachment *anexo* (m.), *archivo* (m.), *documento* (m.) *adjunto*
attend (to) *asistir*
  attend to (to) *atender*
attention *atención* (f.)
attraction *atracción* (f.)
attractive *atractivo/atractiva* (m./f.)
auction *subasta* (f.)
August *agosto* (m.)
aunt *tía* (f.)
author *autor* (m.)
automatic *automático/automático* (m./f.)
available *disponible* (m./f.)
avenue *avenida* (f.)
avocado *aguacate* (m.)
axe *hacha* (f.)

B

baby *bebé* (m./f.)
  little baby *bebito/bebita* (m./f.)
bachelor's degree *licenciatura* (f.)
back *espalda* (f.), *atrás*
  know like the back of one's hand (to) *conocer palmo a palmo*
backbone *columna* (f.) *vertebral*
background *historial* (m.)
backyard *patio* (m.)
bad *malo/mala* (m./f.), *podrido/podrida* (m./f.)
  It's not bad. *No está mal.*
bad(ly) *mal*
bag *bolsa* (f.)
baggy *ancho/ancha* (m./f.)
bakery *panadería* (f.), *pastelería* (f.) *(for pastries, etc.)*

balcony *balcón* (m.)
bald *calvo/calva* (m./f.)
ball *balón* (m.), *pelota* (f.)
banana *plátano* (m.), *banana* (f.)
band *banda* (f.), *conjunto* (m.) *(music)*
bandage *vendaje* (m.)
bank *banco* (m.)
banker *banquero/banquera* (m./f.)
bar *bar* (m.)
barbershop *barbería* (f.)
bargain *ganga* (f.)
base *base* (f.)
baseball *béisbol* (m.)
  baseball game *partido* (m.) *de béisbol*
basement *sótano* (m.)
basketball *baloncesto* (m.)
bathe (to) *bañarse*
bathing suit *traje* (m.) *de baño*
bathing trunks *bañador* (m.)
bathroom *baño* (m.)
bathtub *bañera* (f.)
be (to) *estar, ser*
  be ... years old (to) *tener ... años*
  be a pessimist (to) *ver todo negro (lit., to see everything as black)*
  be able to (to) *poder*
  be afraid (to) *tener miedo*
  be afraid of (to) *temer*
  be afraid that ... (to) *tener miedo de que ...*
  be an optimist (to) *ver todo color de rosa (lit., to see everything pink)*
  be angry that ... (to) *enfadarse de que ...*
  be bored (to) *aburrirse*
  be bothered (to) *molestarse*
  be bothered that ... (to) *molestarse de que ...*
  be called (to) *llamarse*
  be cold (to) *tener frío*
  be dizzy (to) *tener mareo*
  be dressed to the nines (to) *ir de punta en blanco (lit., to go from the tip in white)*
  be embarrassed (to) *ponerse colorado (lit., to turn red)*
  be glad (to) *alegrarse*
  be glad that ... (to) *alegrarse de que ...*
  be going to (do) (to) *ir a ...*
  be hot (to) *tener calor*
  be hungry (to) *tener hambre*
  be in a hurry (to) *tener prisa, tener cansancio*
  be in good hands (to) *estar en buenas manos*
  be interested in ... (to) *tener interés en ...*
  be lacking (to) *faltar*
  be lazy (to) *ser perezoso*
  be nauseated (to) *tener náusea(s)*
  be necessary (to) *faltar*
  be not doing well (to) *estar mal*
  be patient (to) *tener paciencia*
  be present (to) *asistir*
  be right (to) *tener razón*
  be scared (to) *tener miedo*
  be scared that ... (to) *tener miedo de que ...*
  be seated (to) *estar sentado*
  be shameless (to) *ser caradura*
  be sleepy (to) *tener sueño*
  be surprised (to) *sorprenderse*
  be surprised that ... (to) *sorprenderse de que ...*
  be thankful (to) *agradecer*
  be thirsty (to) *tener sed*
  be tied (to) *quedar empatados*
  be tired (to) *tener consancio*
  be very angry (to) *estar rojo de la ira (lit., to be red with fury)*
  be warm (to) *tener calor*
  May you be well. *Que esté bien.*
beach *playa* (f.)
bean *fríjol* (m.)
beauty mark *lunar* (m.)
because *porque*
  because of *por*
become (to) *ponerse*
bed *cama* (f.)
bedroom *dormitorio* (m.), *alcoba* (f.), *cuarto* (m.)
beef *carne* (f.)
beer *cerveza* (f.)
before *antes*
  before ... *antes de ...*
begin (to) *empezar, comenzar*
behind *detrás, atrás, retrasado/retrasada* (m./f.)
  behind ... *detrás de ...*
believe (to) *creer*
  not believe that ... (to) *no creer que ...*
below *bajo*
belt *cinturón* (m.)
benefit *beneficio* (m.), *provecho* (m.)
best (the) *el/la/los/las* (m. sg./f. sg./m. pl./f. pl.) *mejor*

bet *apuesta* (f.)
bet (to) *apostar*
bet that . . . (to) *apuesto a que . . .*
better *mejor* (m./f.)
It's better that . . . *Es mejor que . . .*
between *entre*
between . . . and . . . *entre . . . y . . .*
bicycle *bicicleta* (f.)
big *gran/grande* (before sg. nouns/all other cases), *gordo/gorda* (m./f.)
bigger *mayor* (m./f.)
biggest (the) *el/la/los/las* (m. sg./f. sg./m. pl./f. pl.) *mayor*
biking *ciclismo* (m.)
bill *cuenta* (f.)
billboard *cartelera* (f.)
billiards *billar* (m.)
biology *biología* (f.)
bitter *amargo/amarga* (m./f.)
black *negro/negra* (m./f.)
bleach *lejía* (f.)
blender *batidora* (f.)
block *cuadra* (f.), *manzana* (f.)
It's two blocks from here. *Está a dos cuadras de aquí.*
block (to) *bloquear*
blonde *rubio/rubia* (m./f.)
blood *sangre* (f.)
have blue blood (to) *ser de sangre azul (lit., to be of blue blood)*
have high/low blood pressure (to) *tener la tensión alta/baja*
take a blood test (to) *hacerse un examen de sangre*
take the blood pressure (to) *tomar la tensión*
blouse *blusa* (f.)
blue *azul* (m./f.)
color light blue (the) *azul* (m.) *claro*
dark blue *azul oscuro*
have blue blood (to) *ser de sangre azul (lit., to be of blue blood)*
light blue *azul claro*
navy blue *azul marino*
sky blue *celeste* (m./f.)
board *bordo* (m.), *tabla* (f.)
ironing board *tabla de planchar*
on board *a bordo*
Welcome aboard. *Bienvenidos a bordo.*
body *cuerpo* (m.)
Bolivia *Bolivia* (f.)
Bolivian *boliviano/boliviana* (m./f.)
bone *hueso* (m.)
book *libro* (m.)
bookshelf *estante* (m.)
bookstore *librería* (f.)
booth *cabina* (f.)
bore (to) *aburrir*
I'm bored by . . . *Me aburre/aburren . . .* (sg./pl.)
bored *aburrido/aburrida* (m./f.)
be bored (to) *aburrirse*
boring *aburrido/aburrida* (m./f.)
boss *jefe/jefa* (m./f.)
bottle *botella* (f.), *frasco* (m.)
bowl *cuenco* (m.), *tazón* (m.)
box *caja* (f.)
box office *taquilla* (f.)
boy *chico* (m.), *muchacho* (m.)
boyfriend *novio* (m.)
bracelet *pulsera* (f.)
brain *cerebro* (m.)
brake (automobile) *freno* (m.)
hit the brakes (to) *poner el pie en el freno*
Brazil *Brasil* (m.)
Brazilian *brasilero/brasilera* (m./f.) (adjective), *brasileño/brasileña* (m./f.) (noun)
bread *pan* (m.)
breakfast *desayuno* (m.)
breast *seno* (m.), *pecho* (m.)
bridge *puente* (m.)
bring (to) *traer*
brochure *folleto* (m.)
broom *escoba* (f.)
brother *hermano* (m.)
brothers, brothers and sisters *hermanos* (pl.)
brother-in-law *cuñado* (m.)
brown *marrón* (m./f.)
grayish brown *pardo/parda* (m./f.)
buckle up (to) *abrocharse el cinturón de seguridad*
building *edificio* (m.)
bunch *manojo* (m.)
bunch of grapes *racimo* (m.) *de uvas*
burnt *quemado/quemada* (m./f.)
bus *autobús* (m.)
tour bus *recorrido* (m.) *por autobús*
bus stop *parada* (f.)

business *negocio* (m.)
  businessman *hombre* (m.) *de negocios*
  businesswoman *mujer* (f.) *de negocios*
busy *ocupado/ocupada* (m./f.)
  The line is busy. *Está comunicando.*
but *pero, mas*
butcher shop *carnicería* (f.)
butter *mantequilla* (f.)
buy (to) *comprar*
  buy on sale (to) *comprar en rebaja*
by *por, en*
  by chance *por casualidad*
  by (a certain time) *para*
  go by (to) *pasar*
  I'm bored by . . . *Me aburre/aburren . . .* (sg./pl.)
  know by sight (to) *conocer de vista*
Bye. *Chao.*

C

cabin *cabina* (f.)
cable *cable* (m.)
café *cafetería* (f.)
cafeteria *cafetería* (f.)
cake *torta* (f.)
call (to) *llamar*
  be called (to) *llamarse*
  call . . . on the phone (to) *llamar por teléfono a . . .*
  make a phone call (to) *llamar por teléfono*
  Who's calling? *¿Quién lo llama?*
calm *tranquilo/tranquila* (m./f.)
camera *cámara* (f.)
camp *campo* (m.)
camping *cámping* (m.)
  go camping (to) *ir de cámping*
can *lata* (f.)
can *poder*
  Could you . . . ? *¿Podría . . . ?*
Canada *Canadá* (m.)
Canadian *canadiense* (m./f.)
cancel (to) *cancelar*
candidate *candidato/candidata* (m./f.)
capacity *capacidad* (f.)
car *auto* (m.), *automóvil* (m.), *carro* (m.), *coche* (m.)
card *tarjeta* (f.)
  playing cards *naipes* (m. pl.), *cartas* (f. pl.)
cardboard *cartón* (m.)
carefully *atentamente*
carnival *carnaval* (m.)
carpal tunnel syndrome *síndrome* (m.) *del túnel del carpio*
carpenter *carpintero/carpintera* (m./f.)
carpet *alfombra* (f.)
carpus *carpio* (m.)
carrot *zanahoria* (f.)
carry (to) *llevar*
carton *bote* (m.), *cartón* (m.)
case *caso* (m.)
cash *efectivo* (m.)
  pay cash (to) *pagar en efectivo*
cash register *caja* (f.)
casual *informal* (m./f.)
cat *gato* (m.)
catch (to) *coger*
cathedral *catedral* (f.)
CD *CD* (m.)
  CD player *lector* (m.) *de CD*
  CD-ROM *CD rom* (m.)
  CD-ROM drive *lector* (m.) *de CD rom*
ceiling *techo* (m.)
cell phone *celular* (m.)
center *centro* (m.)
century *siglo* (m.)
  this century *este siglo*
chair *silla* (f.)
champagne *champaña/champán* (f./m.)
champion *campeón/campeona* (m./f.)
championship *campeonato* (m.)
chance *casualidad* (f.)
  by chance *por casualidad*
change *cambio* (m.)
change (to) *cambiar*
channel *canal* (m.)
charm *encanto* (m.)
chat *charla* (f.)
  chat room *espacio* (m.) *para charla, chat* (m.)
cheap *barato/barata* (m./f.)
check *cheque* (m.), *cuenta* (f.)
check in (to) *registrarse*
check out (to) *pagar la cuenta*
cheek *mejilla* (f.)
cheer (to) *vitorear*
cheese *queso* (m.)
chemistry *química* (f.)
chess *ajedrez* (m.)
chest *pecho* (m.)

chicken *pollo* (m.)
child (male/female) *niño/niña* (m./f.)
child psychology *sicología* (f.) *infantil*
children (sons and daughters) *hijos* (pl.)
children's *infantil* (m./f.)
young child *párvulo/párvula* (m./f.)
Chile *Chile* (m.)
Chilean *chileno/chilena* (m./f.)
chin *barbilla* (f.)
Chinese (language) *chino* (m.)
chocolate *chocolate* (m.)
choir *coro* (m.)
choose (to) *elegir, escoger*
chop *chuleta* (f.)
lamb chop *chuleta de cordero*
Christmas Eve *Nochebuena*
church *iglesia* (f.)
cigarette *cigarrillo* (m.)
pack of cigarettes *cajetilla* (f.) *de cigarrillos*
circus *circo* (m.)
city *ciudad* (f.)
city hall *ayuntamiento* (m.)
class *clase* (f.)
classic *clásico/clásica* (m./f.)
classical music *música* (f.) *clásica*
classroom *aula* (m.)
claw *uña* (f.)
clean *limpio/limpia* (m./f.)
clearly *claramente, claro*
clinic *clínica* (f.)
clinical pharmacy *farmacia* (f.) *clínica*
clock *reloj* (m.)
close *cerca*
close to ... *cerca de ...*
close (to) *cerrar*
closet *armario* (m.)
clothing *ropa* (f.)
clothing store *tienda* (f.) *de ropa*
cloud *nube* (f.)
cloudy *nublado/nublada* (m./f.)
It's cloudy. *Está nublado.*
club *club* (m.)
coach *entrenador/entrenadora* (m./f.)
coal *carbón* (m.)
coca *coca* (f.)
code *código* (m.)
coffee *café* (m.)
coffee shop *cafetería* (f.)
coffee-colored *café* (m./f.)
coffeemaker *cafetera* (f.)
coincidence *coincidencia* (f.)
What a coincidence! *¡Qué coincidencia!*
coincidence *casualidad* (f.)
cold *frío/fría* (m./f.)
cold temperature/sensation *frío* (m.)
be cold (to) *tener frío*
It's cold. *Hace frío.*
colleague *colega/colega* (m./f.)
collect (to) *coleccionar*
collection *colección* (f.)
cologne *colonia* (f.)
Colombia *Colombia* (f.)
Colombian *colombiano/colombiana* (m./f.)
color *color* (m.)
color gray (the) *gris* (m.)
color light blue (the) *azul* (m.) *claro*
wear rose-colored glasses (to) *ver todo color de rosa (lit., to see everything pink)*
What color is ... ? *¿De qué color es ... ?*
column *columna* (f.)
combine (to) *combinar*
come (to) *venir*
comedy *comedia* (f.)
comfortable *cómodo/cómoda* (m./f.)
coming *entrante* (m./f.)
comma *coma* (f.)
commercial *comercial* (m./f.)
communicate (to) *comunicar*
company *compañía* (f.)
complete (to) *completar*
completely *completamente*
computer *computadora* (f.), *ordenador* (m.)
concert *concierto* (m.)
conference *conferencia* (f.)
conference room *sala de conferencias*
congratulate (to) *felicitar*
congratulations *enhorabuena* (f.)
Congratulations! *¡Felicitaciones!*
connect (to) *conectar*
connection *conexión* (f.)
construction worker *obrero/obrera* (m./f.)
consult (to) *consultar*
continue (to) *continuar*
Continue straight. *Continúa recto.*
contract *contrato* (m.)
contribution *contribución* (f.)

convenience store *tienda* (f.)
cook (to) *cocinar*
cookie *galleta* (f.)
cooking *cocina* (f.)
copy *copia* (f.)
copy (to) *copiar*
corncob *mazorca* (f.)
corner *esquina* (f.)
  around the corner *a la vuelta de la esquina*
cost (to) *costar*
  How much does it cost? *¿Cuánto cuesta?*
cotton *algodón* (m.)
couch *sofá* (m.)
cough *tos* (f.)
  have a cough (to) *tener tos*
count (to) *contar*
counter *mostrador* (m.)
country *país* (m.)
coupon *vale* (m.)
course *curso* (m.), *asignatura* (f.)
court *juzgado* (m.)
cousin *primo/prima* (m./f.)
  cousins *primos* (pl.)
craft *artesanía* (f.)
credit *crédito* (m.)
  credit card *tarjeta* (f.) *de crédito*
creme *crema* (f.)
crime *delito* (m.)
cross (to) *cruzar*
cry *grito* (m.)
cry (to) *llorar*
cucumber *pepino* (m.)
cup *taza* (f.)
cupboard *aparador* (m.)
curriculum *currículum* (m.)
  CV *currículum vítae*
curtain *cortina* (f.)
custom sew (to) *hacer a la medida*
customer *cliente* (m./f.)
cycling *ciclismo* (m.)

D

dad *papá* (m.), *papi* (m.)
daily *diario/diaria* (m./f.)
dairy store *lechería* (f.)
dance (to) *bailar*
dancing *baile* (m.)
dark *oscuro/oscura* (m./f.)
  dark blue *azul* (m./f.) *oscuro*
  dark green *verde* (m./f.) *oscuro*
  dark-skinned *moreno/morena* (m./f.)
date *fecha* (f.)
daughter *hija* (f.)
daughter-in-law *nuera* (f.)
dawn *amanecer* (m.)
  at dawn *al amanecer*
day *día* (m.)
  all day *todo el día*
  every day *todos los días*
  Have a nice day. *Que tenga un buen día.*
  special of the day *plato del día*
  spend the day (to) *pasar el día*
  this day *este día*
  working day *jornada* (f.)
dead person, dead *muerto/muerta* (m./f.)
decade *década* (f.)
December *diciembre* (m.)
decide (to) *decidir*
decision *decisión* (f.)
dedicate (to) *dedicar*
degree *grado* (m.), *título* (m.)
delay (to) *retrasar*
delete (to) *eliminar*
delicatessen *charcutería* (f.)
delicious *delicioso/deliciosa* (m./f.)
demand (to) *exigir*
demanding *exigente* (m./f.)
dentist *dentista* (m./f.)
deny (to) *negar*
  deny that . . . (to) *negar que . . .*
deodorant *desodorante* (m.)
department *departamento* (m.), *facultad* (f.) *(at a college/university)*
  department store *tienda* (f.) *por departamentos*
depend (to) *depender*
  depend on . . . (to) *depender de . . .*
describe (to) *describir*
description *descripción* (f.)
desert *desierto* (m.)
design *diseño* (m.)
desire *gana* (f.)
desk *escritorio* (m.)
dessert *postre* (m.)
detail *detalle* (m.)
detergent *detergente* (m.)

dishwashing detergent *detergente de vajilla*
laundry detergent *detergente de ropa*
detest (to) *detestar*
develop (to) *desarrollar*
dial (to) *marcar*
dial a phone number (to) *marcar un número de teléfono*
dial tone *tono* (m.)
diarrhea *diarrea* (f.)
diary *diario* (m.)
keep a diary (to) *llevar un diario*
die (to) *morir*
difference *diferencia* (f.)
different *diferente* (m./f.)
difficult *difícil* (m./f.)
difficult situation *apuro* (m.)
digital *digital* (m./f.)
diligently *diligentemente*
diner *cafetería* (f.)
dining room *comedor* (m.)
dinner *cena* (f.), *comida* (f.)
diploma *diploma* (m.), *título* (m.)
direct (to) *dirigir*
direction *dirección* (f.), *sentido* (m.)
dirty *sucio/sucia* (m./f.)
disaster *desastre* (m.)
discount *descuento* (m.), *rebaja* (f.)
give a discount (to) *hacer un descuento*
discuss (to) *discutir*
disease *enfermedad* (f.)
dish *plato* (m.)
do the dishes(to) *lavar los platos*
main dish *plato principal*
dishwasher *lavaplatos* (m.)
dishwashing detergent *detergente* (m.) *de vajilla*
disk *disco* (m.)
Disneyland *Disneylandia*
display window *escaparate* (m.)
dissertation *tesis* (f.)
diving *buceo* (m.)
divorce (someone) (to) *divorciarse de …*
get a divorce (to) *divorciarse*
divorced *divorciado/divorciada* (m./f.)
dizzy *mareado/mareada* (m./f.)
be dizzy (to) *tener mareo*
do (to) *hacer*
be not doing well (to) *estar mal*
Do me the favor of … *Hágame el favor de …*
do the dishes (to) *lavar los platos*
do the laundry (to) *lavar la ropa*
doctor *doctor/doctora* (m./f.), *médico/médica* (m./f.)
doctor's office *consultorio* (m.) *del médico*
document *documento* (m.)
documentary *documental* (m.)
dog *perro* (m.)
dollar *dólar* (m.)
dominate (to) *dominar*
done *hecho/hecha* (m./f.)
door *puerta* (f.)
doubt (to) *dudar*
doubt that … (to) *dudar que …*
download (to) *bajar*
drama *drama* (m.), *obra* (f.) *dramática*
dramatic *dramático/dramática* (m./f.)
draw (to) *empatar*
drawer *cajón* (m.)
dream (to) *soñar*
Don't even dream about it! *¡Ni lo sueñes!*
dream about … *soñar con …*
dress *vestido* (m.)
be dressed to the nines (to) *ir de punta en blanco (lit., to go from the tip in white)*
evening dress *vestido de noche*
dress (someone) (to) *vestir*
dressing room *probador* (m.)
drink *bebida* (f.)
drink (to) *beber*
drive (to) *conducir*
drugstore *farmacia* (f.)
drunk *borracho/borracha* (m./f.)
dry *seco/seca* (m./f.)
dry-clean (to) *lavar en seco*
dryer *secadora* (f.)
DSL *línea* (f.) *de suscriptor/abonado digital (DSL)*
due to *por*
during *durante*
dusk *atardecer* (m.)
at dusk *al atardecer*
dust *polvo* (m.)
duty *derecho* (m.)
DVD *DVD* (m.)
DVD player *lector* (m.) *de DVD*

E

each *cada* (m./f.)
ear *oreja* (f.)
early *temprano/temprana* (m./f.)
  early morning (from midnight till daybreak) *madrugada* (f.)
early (adverb) *temprano*
earn (to) *ganar*
earnings *ingreso* (m.)
earrings *pendientes* (m. pl.)
easily *fácilmente*
east *este* (m.), *oriente* (m.)
Easter *Pascua* (f.)
easy *fácil* (m./f.)
eat (to) *comer*
  eat dinner (to) *cenar*
economical *económico/económica* (m./f.)
economics *economía* (f.)
Ecuador *Ecuador* (m.)
Ecuadorian *ecuatoriano/ecuatoriana* (m./f.)
efficiently *eficientemente*
egg *huevo* (m.)
eight *ocho*
  at eight ten (8:10) *a las ocho y diez*
  eight hundred *ochocientos/ochocientas* (m./f.)
  twenty-eight *veintiocho*
eighteen *dieciocho, diez y ocho*
eighty *ochenta*
elbow *codo* (m.)
electric *eléctrico/eléctrica* (m./f.)
electrical *eléctrico/eléctrica* (m./f.)
  electrical appliance *electrodoméstico* (m.)
electrician *electricista/electricista* (m./f.)
electronic *electrónico/electrónica* (m./f.)
  electronics store *tienda* (f.) *de electrodomésticos*
elegant *elegante* (m./f.)
elementary school *colegio* (m.)
elephant *elefante* (m.)
eleven *once*
eliminate (to) *eliminar*
e-mail *correo* (m.) *electrónico, correo-e* (m.)
  e-mail address *dirección* (f.) *de correo electrónico*
  e-mail attachment *anexo* (m.) *al correo electrónico*
employee *empleado/empleada* (m./f.)
employment *empleo* (m.)
enchant (to) *encantar*
enclosed *adjunto/adjunta* (m./f.)
end *fin* (m.), *final* (m.), *punta* (f.)
engineer *ingeniero/ingeniera* (m./f.)
engineering *ingeniería* (f.)
  mechanical engineering *ingeniería mecánica*
England *Inglaterra* (f.)
English *inglés/inglesa* (m./f.)
English (language) *inglés* (m.)
  Do you speak English? (infml.) *¿Hablas inglés?*
  Do you speak English? (fml.) *¿Habla usted inglés?*
Enjoy the meal! *¡Buen provecho!*
enough *suficiente* (m./f.), *bastante*
enter (to) *entrar*
entertainment *entretenimiento* (m.)
entrance *entrada* (f.)
equal *igual* (m./f.)
  . . . equals (=) . . . *. . . es igual a . . .*
erase (to) *borrar*
especially *sobre todo*
even *hasta*
evening *noche* (f.)
  evening dress *vestido* (m.) *de noche*
  Good evening. *Buenas noches.*
  in the evening *de la noche*
  this evening *esta noche* (f.)
event *suceso* (m.)
every *todo/toda* (m./f.), *cada* (m./f.)
  every day *todos los días*
  every week *todas las semanas*
everything *todo* (m.)
  How is everything going? *¿Cómo va todo?*
ex- *ex*
exact *exacto/exacta* (m./f.), *en punto*
  Exactly. *Exacto.*
exceed (to) *exceder*
excellent *excelente* (m./f.)
exception *excepción* (f.)
exchange (to) *cambiar, intercambiar*
  in exchange for *por*
exciting *emocionante* (m./f.)
excuse *disculpa* (f.)
excuse (to) *disculpar*
  Excuse me. *Disculpa./Disculpe.* (infml./fml.)/ *Perdón.*
exercise *ejercicio* (m.)

exit *salida* (f.)
expense *gasto* (m.)
expensive *caro/cara* (m./f.), *costoso/costosa* (m./f.)
experience *experiencia* (f.)
explanation *explicación* (f.)
extra *extra* (m./f.)
 extra hours *horas* (f. pl.) *extras*
extraordinary *extraordinario/extraordinaria* (m./f.)
extroverted *extrovertido/extrovertida* (m./f.)
eye *ojo* (m.)
 an eye for an eye *ojo por ojo*
eyebrow *ceja* (f.)
eyeglasses *gafas* (f. pl.)
 wear rose-colored glasses (to) *ver todo color de rosa (lit., to see everything pink)*
eyelashes *pestañas* (f. pl.)

F

face *cara* (f.)
 face the circumstances (to) *dar la cara*
factory *fábrica* (f.)
faculty *profesorado* (m.)
fail (to) *suspender*
 fail a test (to) *suspender un examen*
fall *otoño* (m.)
fall (to) *caer*
 fall flat on one's face (to) *dar de narices*
fame *fama* (f.)
familiar *familiar* (m./f.)
family *familia* (f.)
 (of) family *familiar* (m./f.)
famous *famoso/famosa* (m./f.)
fan *aficionado/aficionada* (m./f.), *hincha* (m./f.)
fantastic *fantástico/fantástica* (m./f.)
far *lejos*
 far from ... *lejos de ...*
farmer *granjero/granjera* (m./f.)
fashion *moda* (f.)
 in fashion *de moda*
fast (adjective) *rápido/rápida* (m./f.)
fast (adverb) *rápidamente, rápido*
fasten (to) *abrochar*
fat *gordo/gorda* (m./f.)
father *padre* (m.)
father-in-law *suegro* (m.)
fatigue *consancio* (m.)
favor *favor* (m.)
 Do me the favor of ... *Hágame el favor de ...*
favorite *favorito/favorita* (m./f.)
fax machine *fax* (m.)
fear *miedo* (m.)
fear (to) *temer*
February *febrero* (m.)
feel (to) *sentir, sentirse*
 feel like ... (to) *tener ganas de ...*
fees *honorarios* (m. pl.)
festive *festivo/festiva* (m./f.)
fever *fiebre* (f.)
 have a fever (to) *tener fiebre*
few *pocos/pocas* (m. pl./f. pl.)
fiancé(e) *prometido/prometida* (m./f.)
field *campo* (m.)
fifteen *quince*
fifty *cincuenta*
file *archivo* (m.), *carpeta* (f.), *documento* (m.)
filing cabinet *armario* (m.)
fill (to) *llenar*
filler phrase *frase* (f.) *de relleno*
 filler word/phrase *muletilla* (f.)
filling *relleno* (m.)
film *película* (f.)
 adventure films *películas* (pl.) *de aventuras*
 horror films *películas de horror*
 romantic films *películas románticas*
 suspense films *películas de suspenso*
finally *por fin*
finance *finanzas* (f. pl.)
find (to) *encontrar*
 find (something) (to) *dar con*
fine (adjective) *estupendo/estupenda* (m./f.)
 Fine. *Pues bien.*
 I'm fine. *Estoy bien.*
fine (noun) *multa* (f.)
finger *dedo* (m.)
finish (to) *acabar, terminar*
first *primer/primero/primera* (before m. sg. nouns/m./f.)
fish *pescado* (m.)
 fish shop/market *pescadería* (f.)
fit (to) *quedar*
 fit (somebody) (to) *venir*
 It suits me fine. *Me viene bien.*
five *cinco*
 at a half past five *a las cinco y media*
 at five (o'clock) *a las cinco*

five hundred *quinientos/quinientas* (m./f.)
forty-five *cuarenta y cinco*
It's five to one. (12:55) *Es la una menos cinco.*
twenty-five *veinticinco*
fixed *fijo/fija* (m./f.)
flat *plano/plana* (m./f.)
flea market *mercadillo* (m.)
flight *vuelo* (m.)
floor *suelo* (m.), *piso* (m.)
flower *flor* (f.)
flowing *suelto/suelta* (m./f.)
fly (to) *volar*
fog *niebla* (f.)
follow (to) *seguir*
food *comida* (f.)
fool *bobo/boba* (m./f.)
foot *pie* (m.)
have both feet on the ground (to) *tener los pies en la tierra*
football *fútbol americano*
for *por, para*
For God's sake! *¡Por Dios!*
for this reason *por eso*
forbid (to) *prohibir*
forbid that/to ... (to) *prohibir que ...*
forehead *frente* (f.)
foreign *extranjero/extranjera* (m./f.)
forest *bosque* (m.)
forget (to) *olvidar*
fork *tenedor* (m.)
form *planilla* (f.)
form links (to) *vincularse*
form links with ... (to) *vincularse con ...*
forty *cuarenta*
forty-five *cuarenta y cinco*
forward (to) *retransmitir, pasar*
fossil *fósil* (m.)
four *cuatro*
at four p.m. *a las cuatro de la tarde*
four hundred *cuatrocientos/cuatrocientas* (m./f.)
twenty-four *veinticuatro*
fourteen *catorce*
free *gratis, libre* (m./f.)
freeway *autopista* (f.), *autovía* (f.), *carretera* (f.)
French *francés/francesa* (m./f.)
French (language) *francés* (m.)
I speak French fluently. *Domino el francés.*
frequency *frecuencia* (f.)
frequent *frecuente* (m./f.)
frequently *frecuentemente, con frecuencia*
Friday *viernes* (m.)
fried *frito/frita* (m./f.)
friend *amigo/amiga* (m./f.)
friendly *simpático/simpática* (m./f.)
from *de, desde*
across from ... *enfrente de ...*
far from ... *lejos de ...*
from the (m.) *del (de + el)*
from ... through ... *de ... a ...*
It's two blocks from here. *Está a dos cuadras de aquí.*
start from ... (to) *partir de ...*
Where are you from? *¿De dónde eres?*
fruit *fruta* (f.)
full *completo/completa* (m./f.)
full-time *a tiempo completo*
fun *divertido/divertida* (m./f.)
have fun (to) *divertirse*
function (to) *funcionar*
funny *gracioso/graciosa* (m./f.)
furnished *amueblado/amueblada* (m./f.)
furniture *muebles* (m. pl.)
future *futuro* (m.)

G

gallery *galería* (f.)
game *juego* (m.), *partido* (m.) *(sport)*
garage *garaje* (m.)
garden *jardín* (m.)
garment *prenda* (f.)
gas station *gasolinera* (f.)
gather (to) *reunir*
gel *gel* (m.)
generally *generalmente*
generous *generoso/generosa* (m./f.)
gentleman *caballero* (m.)
geography *geografía* (f.)
German *alemán/alemana* (m./f.)
German (language) *alemán* (m.)
get (to) *sacar, traer*
get a divorce (to) *divorciarse*
get angry (to) *enfadarse*
get dressed (to) *vestirse*
get good/bad grades (to) *sacar buenas/malas notas*

get married (to) *casarse*
get to . . . (to) *llegar a . . .*
get up (to) *levantarse, despertarse*
I get up. *Me levanto.*
gift *regalo* (m.)
girl *chica* (f.), *muchacha* (f.)
girlfriend *novia* (f.)
give (to) *dar*
give (a gift) (to) *regalar*
give a discount (to) *hacer un descuento*
give birth (to) *dar a luz*
give thanks (to) *dar (las) gracias*
glass *vaso* (m.)
gloves *guantes* (m. pl.)
go (to) *ir, marchar*
be going to (do) (to), go to (a place) (to) *ir a . . .*
go by (to) *pasar*
go camping (to) *ir de cámping*
go crazy (to), go out of one's mind (to) *pararse de cabeza*
go hiking (to) *hacer excursionismo, hacer senderismo*
go on a trip (to) *salir de viaje*
go out (to) *salir*
go shopping (to) *ir de compras*
go sightseeing (to) *visitar los lugares de interés*
Go straight. *Siga derecho.*
go through a light (to) *saltarse el semáforo*
go to bed (to) *acostarse*
go window-shopping (to) *ir de escaparates*
go with . . . (to) *combinar con . . .*
How's it going? *¿Qué pasa?*
What's going on? *¿Qué hay?*
goal *gol* (m.)
score a goal (to) *anotar/hacer/marcar un gol*
goalkeeper *portero* (m.)
God *Dios* (m.)
For God's sake! *¡Por Dios!*
gold (color) *dorado/dorada* (m./f.)
good *buen/bueno/buena* (before m. sg. nouns/ m./f.)
be in good hands (to) *estar en buenas manos*
Good afternoon. *Buenas tardes.*
Good evening./Good night. *Buenas noches.*
Good job! *¡Buen trabajo!*
Good morning. *Buenos días.*
Have a good trip. *Buen viaje.*
It's good that . . . *Es bueno que . . .*
The weather is good. *El tiempo es bueno.*
Good-bye. *Adiós.*
say good-bye (to) *despedirse*
grace *gracia* (f.)
grade *nota* (f.)
grades *calificaciones* (f. pl.)
get good/bad grades (to) *sacar buenas/malas notas*
graduate (to) *graduarse*
gram *gramo* (m.)
grandchildren *nietos* (pl.)
granddaughter *nieta* (f.)
grandfather *abuelo* (m.)
grandmother *abuela* (f.)
grandparents *abuelos* (pl.)
grandson *nieto* (m.)
grapes *uvas* (f. pl.)
bunch of grapes *racimo* (m.) *de uvas*
graphic *gráfico/gráfica* (m./f.)
grass *césped* (m.)
gray *gris* (m./f.)
gray (the color) *gris* (m.)
great *gran/grande* (before sg. nouns/all other cases), *magnífico/magnífica* (m./f.)
Great! *¡Estupendo!*
green *verde* (m./f.)
dark green *verde oscuro*
greeting *saludo* (m.)
grill *parrilla* (f.)
grilled *a la parrilla*
grill (to) *asar*
guava *guayaba* (f.)
guest *invitado/invitada* (m./f.)
guidebook *guía* (f.)
guided tour *visita guiada* (f.)
guitar *guitarra* (f.)
play the guitar (to) *tocar la guitarra*
gymnasium *gimnasio* (m.)
gymnastics *gimnasia* (f.)

H

hail (to) *granizar*
It's hailing. *Está granizando.*
hair *pelo* (m.)
hair salon *peluquería* (f.)
half *medio/media* (m./f.)
at a half past five *a las cinco y media*

halftime *medio tiempo* (m.)
hall *vestíbulo* (m.)
ham *jamón* (m.)
hand *mano* (f.)
at hand *a la mano*
be in good hands (to) *estar en buenas manos*
hand wash (to) *lavar a mano*
know like the back of one's hand (to) *conocer palmo a palmo*
on the left-hand side *a mano izquierda*
on the one hand *por una parte*
on the other hand *por otra parte*
on the right-hand side *a mano derecha*
shake hands (to) *dar la mano*
handbag *bolso* (m.), *cartera* (f.)
handful *manojo* (m.)
handle *manejar*
hang (to) *colgar*
hang up the phone (to) *colgar el teléfono*
happen (to) *pasar*
What's happening? *¿Qué tal?*
happening *suceso* (m.)
happily *felizmente*
happy *alegre* (m./f.), *contento/contenta* (m./f.), *feliz* (m./f.)
hard *duro/dura* (m./f.)
hardworking *trabajador* (m./f.)
hat *sombrero* (m.)
have (to) *tener, haber, tomar (food and drink)*
Do you have time? *¿Cómo estás de tiempo?*
have a cough (to) *tener tos*
have a fever (to) *tener fiebre*
Have a good trip. *Buen viaje.*
have a headache (to) *tener dolor de cabeza*
Have a nice day. *Que tenga un buen día.*
have a sore throat (to) *tener dolor de garganta*
have an operation (to) *operarse*
have an upset stomach (to) *estar mal del estómago*
have blue blood (to) *ser de sangre azul (lit., to be of blue blood)*
have both feet on the ground (to) *tener los pies en la tierra*
have fun (to) *divertirse*
have high/low blood pressure (to) *tener la tensión alta/baja*
have just . . . (done something) (to) *acabar de . . .*
have lunch (to) *almorzar*
have nausea (to) *tener náusea(s)*
have permission to (to) *poder*
have to . . . (to) *tener que . . .*
How have you been? *¿Cómo te ha ido?*
not have a clue about . . . (to) *no saber ni jota de . . .*
What time do you have? *¿Qué hora tiene?*
You have to . . . *Tienes que . . .*
he *él*
head *cabeza* (f.), *cabecera* (f.)
have a headache (to) *tener dolor de cabeza*
keep a cool head (to) *tener la cabeza fría*
lose one's head (to) *perder la cabeza*
headphones *audífonos* (m. pl.)
healthy *saludable* (m./f.)
hear (to) *oír*
heart *corazón* (m.)
heat *calor* (m.)
heel *tacón* (m.)
height *alto* (m.)
Hello. *Hola.*
Hello! *¡Saludos!*
Hello? (on the phone) *¿Aló?/¿Dígame?*
help *ayuda* (f.)
How may I help you? *¿En qué puedo servirle?*
Thank you for your help. *Le agradezco su ayuda.*
help (to) *ayudar*
Can you help me? *¿Puede ayudarme?*
her (before a noun) *su/sus* (sg./pl.)
her (direct object pronoun) *la*
(to/for) her (indirect object pronoun) *le, se (used in place of le when preceding lo/la/los/las)*
herb *hierba* (f.)
here *aquí*
Here is . . . *Aquí está . . .*
Here you are. *Aquí tiene.*
Here we are. *Pues, aquí estamos.*
It's two blocks from here. *Está a dos cuadras de aquí.*
hers *suyo/suya/suyos/suyas* (m. sg./f. sg./m. pl./f. pl.), *el de ella* (m. sg.), *la de ella* (f. sg.)
herself *se*
hey (filler word) *che (Argentina), oye*
hide-and-seek *escondidas* (f. pl.)
high *alto/alta* (m./f.)
have high blood pressure (to) *tener la tensión*

alta
highway *autopista* (f.), *autovía* (f.), *carretera* (f.)
hiking *excursionismo* (m.), *senderismo* (m.)
  go hiking (to) *hacer excursionismo, hacer senderismo*
hill *cerro* (m.), *colina* (f.)
him (direct object pronoun) *lo*
  (to/for) him (indirect object pronoun) *le, se* (*used in place of le when preceding lo/la/los/las*)
himself *se*
hip *cadera* (f.)
his *suyo/suya/suyos/suyas* (m. sg./f. sg./m. pl./f. pl.), *el de él* (m. sg.), *la de él* (f. sg.)
  his (before a noun) *su/sus* (sg./pl.)
history *historia* (f.)
Hmm . . . *Mire . . .*
hobby *afición* (f.), *pasatiempos* (m.)
hockey *hockey* (m.)
hold (to) *poseer*
  Hold on. *Un momento.*
  Hold on, please. *Espere, por favor.*
  put on hold (to) *poner en espera*
holiday *fiesta* (f.), *día* (m.) *festivo*
homeopathy *homeopatía* (f.)
homework *tarea* (f.)
honest *honesto/honesta* (m./f.)
honey *miel* (f.)
hope (to) *esperar*
  hope that . . . (to) *esperar que . . .*
  I hope . . . *Ojalá que . . .*
  I hope so! *¡Yo espero que sí!*
horror *horror* (m.)
  horror films *películas* (f. pl.) *de horror*
horse *caballo* (m.)
horseback riding *equitación* (f.)
hospital *hospital* (m.)
hot *caliente* (m./f.)
  be hot (to) *tener calor*
  It's hot. *Hace calor.*
hotel *hotel* (m.)
hour *hora* (f.)
  extra hours *horas* (pl.) *extras*
house *casa* (f.)
how *cómo*
  Do you know how to . . . ? *¿Sabe cómo . . . ?*
  How . . . ! *¡Qué . . . !*
  How about if . . . ? *¿Qué tal si . . . ?/¿Qué te parece si . . . ?*
  How are things? *¿Cómo van las cosas?*
  How are you doing for time? *¿Cómo estás de tiempo?*
  How are you? *¿Cómo está usted?* (fml.)/*¿Cómo estás (tú)?* (infml.)
  How do I know!?/How should I know!? *¡Yo qué sé!*
  How do you say " . . . " in . . . ? *¿Cómo se dice " . . . " en . . . ?*
  How have you been? *¿Cómo te ha ido?*
  How is everything going? *¿Cómo va todo?*
  how many *cuántos/cuántas* (m. pl./f. pl.)
  How may I help you? *¿En qué puedo servirle?*
  how much *cuánto/cuánta* (m./f.)
  How much does it cost? *¿Cuánto cuesta?*
  How much is it? *¿Cuánto es?/¿Cuánto vale?*
  How nice! *¡Qué bien!*
  How old are you (sg. fml.)**/is he/is she?** *¿Cuántos años tiene?*
  How's it going? *¿Qué pasa?*
  How's life treating you? *¿Cómo te trata la vida?*
  learn how to . . . (to) *aprender a . . .*
huge *enorme* (m./f.)
human *humano/humana* (m./f.)
  human body *cuerpo* (m.) *humano*
hundred *cien/ciento* (before a noun/before a number except mil)
  eight hundred *ochocientos/ochocientas* (m./f.)
  five hundred *quinientos/quinientas* (m./f.)
  four hundred *cuatrocientos/cuatrocientas* (m./f.)
  hundred thousand *cien mil*
  nine hundred *novecientos/novecientas* (m./f.)
  one hundred and three dollars *ciento tres dólares*
  one hundred people *cien personas*
  one hundred percent *cien por ciento*
  seven hundred *setecientos/setecientas* (m./f.)
  six hundred *seiscientos/seiscientas* (m./f.)
  three hundred *trescientos/trescientas* (m./f.)
  two hundred *doscientos/doscientas* (m./f.)
hunger *hambre* (f.)
hunting *caza* (f.)
hurricane *huracán* (m.)
hurry *prisa* (f.)
  be in a hurry (to) *tener prisa*

husband *esposo* (m.), *marido* (m.)
hygienic *higiénico/higiénica* (m./f.)

I

I *yo*
ice *hielo* (m.)
ice cream *helado* (m.)
  ice cream parlor *heladería* (f.)
idea *idea* (f.)
ideal *ideal* (m./f.)
idiot *bobo/boba* (m./f.)
if *si*
  How about if . . . ? *¿Qué tal si . . . ?/¿Qué te parece si . . . ?*
illness *enfermedad* (f.), *mal* (m.)
imagine (to) *imaginar*
immediate *inmediato/inmediata* (m./f.)
immediately *inmediatamente, de inmediato*
important *importante* (m./f.)
impossible *imposible* (m./f.)
  It is impossible that . . . *Es imposible que . . .*
impressive *impresionante* (m./f.)
in *en*
  be in a hurry (to) *tener prisa*
  be in good hands (to) *estar en buenas manos*
  be interested in . . . (to) *tener interés en . . .*
  check in (to) *registrarse*
  in exchange for *por*
  in fashion *de moda*
  in front *delante*
  in front of . . . *delante de . . . /enfrente de . . .*
  in love *enamorado/enamorada* (m./f.)
  in order to *para*
  in place of *por*
  in style *de moda*
  in the afternoon *de la tarde*
  in the early morning *de la madrugada*
  in the evening *de la noche*
  in the morning *de la mañana*
incentive *incentivo* (m.)
include (to) *incluir*
  Is service included? *¿Está incluido el servicio?*
information *información* (f.)
  information center *centro* (m.) *de información*
ingredient *ingrediente* (m.)
inherit (to) *heredar*
injury *lesión* (f.)
inside *dentro*
  inside of . . . *dentro de . . .*
insist (to) *insistir*
  insist that . . . (to) *insistir en que . . .*
instantaneous *instantáneo/instantánea* (m./f.)
instant message *mensaje* (m.) *instantáneo*
insurance *seguro* (m.)
intelligent *inteligente* (m./f.)
intended for *para*
interest *interés* (m.)
interest (to) *interesar*
  be interested in . . . (to) *tener interés en . . .*
  I'm interested in . . . (to) *Me interesa/ interesan . . .* (sg./pl.)
interesting *interesante* (m./f.)
intermediate *intermedio/intermedia* (m./f.)
international *internacional* (m./f.)
  international call *llamada* (f.) *internacional*
internet *Internet*
intersection *cruce* (m.), *intersección* (f.)
interview *entrevista* (f.)
interview (to) *entrevistar*
introduce (to) *presentar*
  Let me introduce you to . . . *Te presento a . . .*
investigation *investigación* (f.)
invitation *invitación* (f.)
invite (to) *invitar*
iron *plancha* (f.)
iron (to) *planchar*
  ironing board *tabla* (f.) *de planchar*
it (direct object pronoun) *lo/la* (m./f.)
  (to/for) it (indirect object pronoun) *le, se (used in place of le when preceding lo/la/los/las)*
  That's it. *Ya está.*
It is . . . *Es . . . /Está . . .*
  It's a pity that . . . *Es una lástima que . . .*
  It's a pleasure. *Mucho gusto.*
  It's beautiful. (weather) *Hace muy buen tiempo.*
  It's better that . . . *Es mejor que . . .*
  It's cloudy. *Está nublado.*
  It's cold. *Hace frío.*
  It's five to one. (12:55) *Es la una menos cinco.*
  It's good that . . . *Es bueno que . . .*
  It's hailing. *Está granizando.*
  It's hot. *Hace calor.*
  It's impossible that . . . *Es imposible que . . .*
  It's necessary that . . . *Es necesario que . . .*

It's necessary to . . . *Hay que . . .*
It's not bad. *No está mal.*
It's not true that . . . *No es cierto que . . .*
It's one o'clock. *Es la una.*
It's possible that . . . *Es posible que . . .*
It's preferable that . . . *Es preferible que . . .*
It's raining. *Está lloviendo.*
It's sad that . . . *Es triste que . . .*
It's snowing. *Está nevando.*
It's sunny. *Hace sol.*
It's ten after one in the morning. *Es la una y diez de la madrugada.*
It's three o'clock sharp. *Son las tres en punto.*
It's three o'clock. *Son las tres.*
It's twelve noon. *Son las doce del mediodía.*
It's two blocks from here. *Está a dos cuadras de aquí.*
It's windy. *Hace viento.*
Italian *italiano/italiana* (m./f.)
Italian (language) *italiano* (m.)
its *su/sus* (sg./pl.)
itself *se*

J

jacket *americana* (f.), *chaqueta* (f.), *saco* (m.)
jam *mermelada* (f.)
January *enero* (m.)
jar *frasco* (m.)
jazz *jazz* (m.)
jealous *celoso/celosa* (m./f.)
jeans *jeans* (m. pl.), *tejanos* (m. pl.), *vaqueros* (m. pl.)
job *trabajo* (m.), *empleo* (m.)
Good job! *¡Buen trabajo!*
summer job *trabajo de verano*
steady job *trabajo fijo*
jog (to) *trotar*
joke *chiste* (m.)
tell a dirty joke (to) (lit., to tell a green joke) *contar un chiste verde*
journalist *periodista* (m./f.)
judge *juez* (m.)
juice *jugo* (m.), *zumo* (m.)
July *julio* (m.)
June *junio* (m.)

K

keep (to) *llevar, guardar*
keep a cool head (to) *tener la cabeza fría*
keep a diary (to) *llevar un diario*
key *llave* (f.)
keyboard *teclado* (m.)
kid *crío/cría* (m./f.)
kilo, kilogram *kilo* (m.)
kilometer *kilómetro* (m.)
kind *clase* (f.)
all kinds *toda clase*
kiss (to) *besar*
kitchen *cocina* (f.)
knee *rodilla* (f.)
knife *cuchillo* (m.)
know (to) *saber (facts, information), conocer (people, places)*
as you already know *como ya sabes*
Do you know how to . . . ? *¿Sabe cómo . . . ?*
How do I know!?/How should I know!? *¡Yo qué sé!*
know by sight (to) *conocer de vista*
know like the back of one's hand (to) *conocer palmo a palmo*
make known (to) *dar a conocer*
not have a clue about . . . (to) *no saber ni jota de . . .*
not know (to) *desconocer*
Who knows? *¿Quién sabe?*

L

label *etiqueta* (f.)
lake *lago* (m.)
lamb *cordero/cordera* (m./f.)
lamb chop *chuleta* (f.) *de cordero*
lamp *lámpara* (f.)
lamppost *farola* (f.)
land *tierra* (f.)
lane *carril* (m.), *vía* (f.)
Stay in the right lane. *Siga por el carril de la derecha.*
language *idioma* (m.), *lengua* (f.)
large *gran/grande* (before sg. nouns/all other cases)
last *último/última* (m./f.)
at last *por fin*
last month *mes* (m.) *pasado*
last night *anoche*
last week *semana* (f.) *pasada*
last year *año* (m.) *pasado*
late *tarde*

I'll see you later. *Hasta luego.*
I'm late. *Se me hace tarde.*
late night (from midnight) *madrugada* (f.)
later *más tarde, luego*
Until later. *Hasta más tarde.*
very latest (the) *último grito* (m.)
laugh (to) *reír*
laugh very hard (to) (lit., to turn black with laughter) *estar negro de la risa*
laughter *risa* (f.)
laundry detergent *detergente* (m.) *de ropa*
law *derecho* (m.)
lawn *césped* (m.)
lawyer *abogado/abogada* (m./f.)
lazy *perezoso/perezosa* (m./f.)
be lazy (to) *ser perezoso*
learn (to) *aprender, saber*
learn how to ... (to) *aprender a ...*
I'm learning Spanish. *Estoy aprendiendo español.*
least ... in/of ... (the) *el/la/los/las* (m. sg./f. sg./m. pl./f. pl.) *menos ... de ...*
leather *cuero* (m.)
leave (to) *dejar, marchar, parar, partir, salir*
leave a message after the tone (to) *dejar un mensaje después de oír la señal*
lecture *conferencia* (f.)
lecture hall *sala* (f.) *de conferencias*
left side *izquierda* (f.)
on the left *a la izquierda*
Turn left. *Gira a la izquierda.*
left-hand *izquierdo/izquierda* (m./f.)
on the left-hand side *a mano izquierda*
leg *pierna* (f.)
lemon *limón* (m.)
lemonade *limonada* (f.)
less *menos*
least ... in/of ... (the) *el/la/los/las* (m. sg./f. sg./m. pl./f. pl.) *menos ... de ...*
less ... than ... *menos ... que ...*
more or less *más o menos*
lesson *lección* (f.)
Let's go ... *Vamos ...*
Let's see ... *A ver ...*
letter *cartas* (f. pl.)
lettuce *lechuga* (f.)
library *biblioteca* (f.)
lie (to) *mentir*
life *vida* (f.)
How's life treating you? *¿Cómo te trata la vida?*
lift (to) *levantar*
light *luz* (f.)
turn off the lights (to) *apagar las luces*
light *claro/clara* (m./f.), *ligero/ligera* (m./f.)
light blue *azul* (m./f.) *claro*
lightening *relámpago* (m.)
like *como*
like (to) *(se) gustar*
I like ... *Me gusta/gustan ...* (sg./pl.)
I really like ... *Me encanta/encantan ...* (sg./pl.)
I'd like ... *Me gustaría ...*
like (it) that ... (to) *gustar que ...*
What would you like? *¿Qué desea?*
likewise *igualmente*
limit *límite* (m.)
line *cola* (f.), *fila* (f.), *línea* (f.)
stand in line (to) *hacer una cola/fila*
The line is busy. *Está comunicando.*
linen *lino* (m.)
lip *labio* (m.)
list *lista* (f.)
list of plays *cartelera* (f.)
listen to (to) *escuchar*
liter *litro* (m.)
literature *literatura* (f.)
little *poco*
a little *un poco*
I speak a little Spanish. *Hablo un poco de español.*
live (to) *vivir*
What do you do for a living? *¿En qué trabaja?*
living room *sala* (f.)
loan *crédito* (m.), *préstamo* (m.)
lobster *langosta* (f.)
local *local* (m./f.)
local call *llamada* (f.) *local*
London *Londres*
long *largo/larga* (m./f.)
long weekend *puente* (m.)
look at (to) *mirar*
look for (to) *buscar*
look like (to) *parecer*
look up (to) *consultar*
loose *suelto/suelta* (m./f.)
Los Angeles *Los Ángeles*

lose (to) *perder*
  lose one's head (to) *perder la cabeza*
lottery *lotería* (f.)
love (to) *querer, amar*
  I love you. *Te quiero.*
  I'd love to! *¡Me encantaría!*
  in love *enamorado/enamorada* (m./f.)
low-cost *económico/económica* (m./f.)
low-cut *escotado/escotada* (m./f.)
lower (to) *bajar*
LP *disco de vinilo* (m.)
luck *suerte* (f.)
lunch *almuerzo* (m.)
  have lunch (to) *almorzar*
lungs *pulmones* (m. pl.)

M

made *hecho/hecha* (m./f.)
magazine *revista* (f.)
magical *mágico/mágica* (m./f.)
magnificent *magnífico/magnífica* (m./f.)
mailbox *buzón* (m.)
main *principal* (m./f.)
  main dish *plato* (m.) *principal*
major *carrera* (f.), *especialidad* (f.)
major in . . . (to) *especializarse en . . .*
  make (to) *hacer*
  make an international/local/national call (to) *hacer una llamada internacional/local/nacional*
  make known (to) *dar a conocer*
man *hombre* (m.), *tío (m., colloquial)*
manager *gerente* (m.)
manner *forma* (f.)
many *muchos/muchas* (m. pl./f. pl.)
  how many *cuántos/cuántas* (m. pl./f. pl.)
map *mapa* (m.), *plano* (m.)
March *marzo* (m.)
marine *marino/marina* (m./f.)
mark (to) *marcar*
market *mercado* (m.)
  flea market *mercadillo*
marriage *matrimonio* (m.)
married *casado/casada* (m./f.)
marry (someone) (to) *casarse con*
  get married (to) *casarse*
martini *martini* (m.)
martyr *mártir* (m./f.)
marvelous *estupendo/estupenda* (m./f.)
master (to) *dominar*
master's degree *maestría* (f.), *especialización* (f.)
match (to) *combinar*
material *material* (m.)
mathematics *matemáticas* (f. pl.)
matter (to) *importar*
  It doesn't matter. *No importa.*
May *mayo* (m.)
May I please . . . ? (fml.) *¿Me permite . . . ?* (fml.)/*¿Me permites . . . ?* (infml.)
  May you be well. *Que esté bien.*
mayor *alcalde* (m.)
me (after a proposition) *mí*
  me (direct object pronoun) *me*
  (to/for) me (indirect object pronoun) *me*
mean (to) *significar*
  What does that mean? *¿Qué quiere decir eso?*
meanwhile *mientras tanto*
measure (to) *medir*
measurement *medida* (f.)
meat *carne* (f.)
mechanical *mecánico/mecánica* (m./f.)
  mechanical engineering *ingeniería* (f.) *mecánica*
medication *medicamento* (m.)
  take medication (to) *tomar un medicamento*
medicine *medicina* (f.)
  medicine cabinet *botiquín* (m.)
medium *mediano/mediana* (m./f.), *término* (m.) *tres cuartos (cooked meat)*
  medium-rare *término* (m.) *medio*
meet (to) *conocer, reunirse*
  meet (somebody) (to) *conocer (a alguien), encontrarse con*
  meet up with (to) *encontrar*
  Pleased to meet you. *Gusto en conocerlo/la.*
meeting *reunión* (f.), *conferencia* (f.)
  meeting room *sala* (f.) *de conferencias*
memory *memoria* (f.)
menu *carta* (f.)
merely *sólo*
message *mensaje* (m.)
  instant message *mensaje instantáneo*
  leave a message after the tone (to) *dejar un mensaje después de oír la señal*
metro *metro* (m.)
Mexican *mexicano/mexicana* (m./f.)

Mexico *México* (m.)
microwave *microondas* (m.)
midnight *medianoche* (f.), *media noche* (f.)
  at midnight *a medianoche*
midway *medio/media* (m./f.)
milk *leche* (f.)
  powdered milk *leche en polvo*
  skim milk *leche descremada*
million *millón*
  one million houses *un millón de casas*
mind *mente* (f.)
  go out of one's mind (to) *pararse de cabeza*
mine *mío/mía/míos/mías* (m. sg./f. sg./m. pl./f. pl.)
minus (-) *menos*
minute *minuto* (m.)
miracle *maravilla* (f.)
mirror *espejo* (m.)
misfortune *desgracia* (f.)
miss (to) *perder, faltar*
mixed *mixto/mixta* (m./f.)
mobile phone *móvil* (m.)
modem *módem* (m.)
modern *moderno/moderna* (m./f.)
molar *muela* (f.)
mole *lunar* (m.)
mom *mamá* (f.), *mami* (f.)
moment *momento* (m.)
  at this moment *en este momento*
  One moment. *Un momento.*
Monday *lunes* (m.)
money *dinero* (m.)
monitor *monitor* (m.)
month *mes* (m.)
  last month *mes pasado*
  next month *mes entrante, mes que viene*
  this month *este mes*
monument *monumento* (m.)
moon *luna* (f.)
more *más*
  more or less *más o menos*
  more . . . /-er than . . . *más . . . que . . .*
moreover *además*
morning *mañana* (f.)
  early morning (from midnight till daybreak) *madrugada* (f.)
  Good morning. *Buenos días.*
  in the early morning *de la madrugada*
  in the morning *de la mañana*
  It's ten after one in the morning. *Es la una y diez de la madrugada.*
  this morning *esta mañana*
Moscow *Moscú*
mosque *mezquita* (f.)
most . . . in/of . . . (the) *el/la/los/las* (m. sg./f. sg./m. pl./f. pl.) *más . . . de . . .*
mother *madre* (f.)
mother-in-law *suegra* (f.)
mountain *montaña* (f.)
mouse *ratón* (m.)
mouth *boca* (f.)
move (to) *mover*
movie *película* (f.)
  movie listing *cartelera de cine*
  movie theater *cine* (m.)
Mr. *señor* (m.), *don* (m.)
Mrs. *señora* (f.), *doña* (f.)
much *mucho*
  how much *cuánto/cuánta* (m./f.)
municipal building *ayuntamiento* (m.), *alcaldía* (f.)
muscle *músculo* (m.)
museum *museo* (m.)
music *música* (f.)
  classical music *música clásica*
musical *musical* (m.)
musician *músico* (m.)
must *deber*
my *mi/mis* (sg./pl.)
myself *me*

N

nail *uña* (f.)
name *nombre* (m.)
  My name is . . . *Me llamo . . .*
  What's your name? *¿Cómo se llama usted?* (fml.)/*¿Cómo te llamas?* (infml.)
nap *siesta* (f.)
napkin *servilleta* (f.)
narrow *angosto/angosta* (m./f.), *estrecho/estrecha* (m./f.)
national *nacional* (m./f.)
  national call *llamada* (f.) *nacional*
nationality *nacionalidad* (f.)
natural *natural* (m./f.)
nature *naturaleza* (f.)
nausea *náusea* (f.)

be nauseated/have nausea (to) *tener náusea(s)*
navy blue *azul* (m./f.) *marino*
near *cerca, próximo/próxima* (m./f.)
near ... *cerca de ...*
necessary *necesario/necesaria* (m./f.)
be necessary (to) *faltar*
It's necessary that ... *Es necesario que ...*
It's necessary to ... *Hay que ...*
neck *cuello* (m.)
necklace *collar* (m.)
need (to) *necesitar*
needle *aguja* (f.)
neighbor *vecino/vecina* (m./f.)
neighborhood *barrio* (m.)
neither *tampoco*
neither ... nor *ni ... ni*
nephew *sobrino* (m.)
nerve *nervio* (m.)
never *nunca*
almost never *casi nunca*
new *nuevo/nueva* (m./f.)
news *noticias* (pl.)
a piece of news *noticia* (f.)
newspaper *periódico* (m.)
New York *Nueva York*
next *próximo/próxima* (m./f.)
next month *mes* (m.) *que viene*
next to ... *al lado de ...*
next week *próxima semana* (f.), *semana* (f.) *que viene*
next year *año* (m.) *que viene*
nice *bonito/bonita* (m./f.)
Have a nice day. *Que tenga un buen día.*
How nice! *¡Qué bien!*
niece *sobrina* (f.)
night *noche* (f.)
at night *de la noche*
Good night. *Buenas noches.*
last night *anoche*
late night (from midnight) *madrugada* (f.)
nine *nueve*
at about nine o'clock *a eso de las nueve*
at nine a.m. *a las nueve de la mañana*
be dressed to the nines (to) *ir de punta en blanco (lit., to go from the tip in white)*
nine hundred *novecientos/novecientas* (m./f.)
twenty-nine *veintinueve*
nineteen *diecinueve, diez y nueve*
ninety *noventa*
no *no, ningún/ninguno/ninguna* (before m. sg. nouns/m. sg./f. sg.)
no one *nadie*
No, not at all. *No, para nada.*
There's no ... that/who ... *No hay ningún ... que ...*
There's no one who/that ... *No hay nadie que ...*
nobody *nadie*
There's no one who/that ... *No hay nadie que ...*
none *ningún/ninguno/ninguna* (before m. sg. nouns/m. sg./f. sg.)
noon *mediodía* (m.)
at noon *a mediodía*
It's twelve noon. *Son las doce del mediodía.*
nor *ni*
neither ... nor *ni ... ni*
normal *normal* (m./f.)
normally *normalmente*
north *norte* (m.)
nose *nariz* (f.)
not *no*
absolutely not *en absoluto*
be not doing well (to) *estar mal*
It's not bad. *No está mal.*
No, not at all. *No, para nada.*
not either *tampoco*
note *nota* (f.)
take note (to) *tomar nota*
notebook *cuaderno* (m.)
nothing *nada*
nothing else *nada más*
There's nothing that ... *No hay nada que ...*
novel *novela* (f.)
romance novel *novela rosa*
November *noviembre* (m.)
now *ahora, ya*
right now *ahora mismo*
nowadays *hoy en día*
number *número* (m.)
telephone number *número de teléfono*

O

object *objeto* (m.)
objective *objetivo* (m.)

ocean *océano* (m.), *mar* (m.)
October *octubre* (m.)
of *de*
  because of *por*
  in place of *por*
  of course *por supuesto*
  Of course! *¡Claro que sí!*
  of the (m.) *del (de + el)*
  of which (relative pronoun) *cuyo/cuya/cuyos/cuyas* (m. sg./f. sg./m. pl./f. pl.)
  on top of *sobre*
  outside of . . . *fuera de . . .*
  Yes, of course. *Sí, claro.*
offer *oferta* (f.)
offer (to) *ofrecer*
office *oficina* (f.), *despacho* (m.), *estudio* (m.), *consultorio* (m.)
  doctor's office *consultorio del médico*
  office worker *oficinista* (m./f.)
often *con frecuencia*
oil *aceite* (m.)
(just) okay *más o menos*
old *viejo/vieja* (m./f.), *antiguo/antigua* (m./f.)
  be . . . years old (to) *tener . . . años*
  How old are you (sg. fml.)**/is he/is she?** *¿Cuántos años tiene?*
  older *mayor* (m./f.)
  oldest (the) *el/la/los/las* (m. sg./f. sg./m. pl./f. pl.) *mayor*
on *en*
  buy on sale (to) *comprar en rebaja*
  depend on . . . (to) *depender de . . .*
  go on a trip (to) *salir de viaje*
  Hold on, please. *Espere, por favor.*
  Hold on. *Un momento.*
  on board *a bordo*
  on the left *a la izquierda*
  on the left-hand side *a mano izquierda*
  on the one hand *por una parte*
  on the other hand *por otra parte*
  on the phone *por teléfono*
  on the radio *por la radio*
  on the right *a la derecha*
  on the right-hand side *a mano derecha*
  on the sidewalk *por el andén*
  on time *a tiempo*
  on top of *sobre*
  on vacation *de vacaciones*
  put on hold (to) *poner en espera*
  put something on (to) *ponerse*
  try on (clothes) (to) *probarse*
once again *nuevamente*
one *uno*
  It's five to one. (12:55) *Es la una menos cinco.*
  It's one o'clock. *Es la una.*
  no one *nadie*
  on the one hand *por una parte*
  one (o'clock) *una*
  One moment. *Un momento.*
  once *una vez*
  once again *nuevamente*
  one-piece *enterizo/enteriza* (m./f.)
  one-way *de sentido* (m.) *único*
  thirty-one *treinta y uno*
  twenty-one *veintiuno*
one (impersonal pronoun) *se*
onion *cebolla* (f.)
online *por Internet, en línea*
only (adjective) *único/única* (m./f.), *solo/sola* (m./f.)
only (adverb) *solamente, sólo, simplemente*
open (to) *abrir*
  open the door (to) *abrir la puerta*
opera *ópera* (f.)
operator *operadora* (f.)
opposite *opuesto/opuesta* (m./f.)
or *o*
  either . . . or *o . . . o*
  more or less *más o menos*
orange (color) *anaranjado/anaranjada* (m./f.)
orange (fruit) *naranja* (f.)
order (to) *pedir*
  in order to *para*
ounce *onza* (f.)
our *nuestro/nuestra/nuestros/nuestras* (m. sg./f. sg./m. pl./f. pl.)
ours *nuestro/nuestra/nuestros/nuestras* (m. sg./f. sg./m. pl./f. pl.)
ourselves *nos*
outbound journey *ida* (f.)
outdoor market *plaza de mercado*
outside (adverb) *afuera, fuera*
  outside of . . . *fuera de . . .*
outside (noun) *exterior* (m.)
outskirts *afueras* (f. pl.)
oven *horno* (m.)

over *sobre*
overcoat *abrigo* (m.)
overcooked *sobrecocido/sobrecocida* (m./f.)
overtime *horas* (f. pl.) *extras*
owe (to) *deber*
own (to) *poseer*

P

package *paquete* (m.)
packet *cajetilla* (f.)
  pack of cigarettes *cajetilla de cigarrillos*
page *página* (f.)
  yellow pages *páginas* (pl.) *amarillas*
  webpage *página web*
pain *dolor* (m.), *pena* (f.)
painter *pintor/pintora* (m./f.)
painting *pintura* (f.), *cuadro* (m.)
pajamas *pijama* (m.)
palace *palacio* (m.)
palm *palmo* (m.)
Panamanian *panameña/panameño* (m./f.)
pants *pantalones* (m. pl.)
papaya *papaya* (f.)
paper *papel* (m.)
  research paper *trabajo* (m.) *de investigación*
Paraguay *Paraguay* (m.)
Pardon me? *¿Cómo?*
parents *padres* (pl.)
Paris *París*
park *parque* (m.)
parking lot *parqueadero* (m.)
part *parte* (f.)
partial *parcial* (m./f.)
particular *particular* (m./f.)
part-time *a tiempo parcial*
party *fiesta* (f.)
pass (to) *aprobar, pasar*
  pass a course (to) *aprobar un curso*
  pass a test (to) *aprobar un examen*
passport *pasaporte* (m.)
past *pasado/pasada* (m./f.)
  at a half past five *a las cinco y media*
  at a quarter past six *a las seis y cuarto*
pastry *dulce* (m.)
path *camino* (m.)
patience *paciencia* (f.)
  be patient (to) *tener paciencia*
patterned, with a pattern *estampado/estampada* (m./f.)
pay *sueldo* (m.)
pay (to) *pagar*
  pay cash (to) *pagar en efectivo*
payment *pago* (m.)
pear *pera* (f.)
pedestrian *peatón* (m.)
pediatrician *pediatra* (m./f.)
  regular pediatrician *pediatra* (m./f.) *de cabecera*
pediatrics *pediatría* (f.)
pen *bolígrafo* (m.), *pluma* (f.)
pencil *lápiz* (m.)
penicillin *penicilina* (f.)
pension *pensión* (f.)
people *gente* (f.)
people (impersonal pronoun) *se*
pepper *pimienta* (f.) *(spice), pimiento* (m.) *(vegetable)*
perceive (to) *percibir*
percent *por ciento*
perceptibly *sensiblemente*
perfect *perfecto/perfecta* (m./f.)
perfume *perfume* (m.)
perhaps *tal vez*
period *período* (m.)
period *término* (m.)
permanent *fijo/fija* (m./f.)
person *persona* (f.)
Peru *Perú* (m.)
Peruvian *peruano/peruana* (m./f.)
peso *peso* (m.)
pharmacist *farmacéutico/farmacéutico* (m./f.)
pharmacy *farmacia* (f.)
philosophy *filosofía* (f.)
phone book *guía* (f.) *telefónica*
phone call *llamada* (f.)
  make an international/local/national call (to) *hacer una llamada internacional/local/nacional*
photograph *foto* (f.)
photography *fotografía* (f.)
phrase *frase* (f.)
physics *física* (f.)
piano *piano* (m.)
pick up (to) *recoger, coger, buscar*
picture *foto* (f.), *cuadro* (m.)
  take a picture (to) *hacer una foto*

piece *pieza* (f.)
  one-piece *enterizo/enteriza* (m./f.)
  two-piece *de dos piezas*
pig *cerdo/cerda* (m./f.)
piglet *chanchito/chanchita* (m./f.)
pill *pastilla* (f.)
pink *rosado/rosada* (m./f.)
pity *lástima* (f.), *pena* (f.)
  It's a pity that ... *Es una lástima que ...*
place *lugar* (m.), *sitio* (m.)
  in place of *por*
place (to) *poner*
plaid *a cuadros*
plan *plan* (m.)
plant *planta* (f.)
plastic *plástico* (m.)
plate *plato* (m.)
play (to) *jugar, practicar (sports), tocar (instrument)*
  play sports (to) *hacer deporte*
  play the piano (to) *tocar el piano*
  play the guitar (to) *tocar la guitarra*
play (theater) *obra* (f.)
player *jugador/jugadora* (m./f.)
plaza *plaza* (f.)
pleasant *agradable* (m./f.)
please (to) *gustar*
  Pleased to meet you. *Encantado./Encantada.* (said by a man/said by a woman)/*Gusto en conocerlo/la.*
Please. *Por favor.*
pleasure *placer* (m.), *gusto* (m.)
  It's a pleasure. *Mucho gusto.*
plumber *fontanero/fontanera* (m./f.)
plus (+) *más*
p.m. *de la tarde, de la noche*
  at four p.m. *a las cuatro de la tarde*
  at seven p.m. *a las siete de la noche*
pocket-knife *navaja* (f.)
point *punto* (m.), *término* (m.)
police officer *policía* (m./f.)
  policewoman *mujer* (f.) *policía*
polka-dot *de lunares*
polyester *poliéster* (m.)
pond *estanque* (m.)
pool *piscina* (f.)
poor, poor person *pobre* (m./f.)
  poor (the) *los pobres*
poorly *mal*
pork *cerdo* (m.), *carne* (f.) *de cerdo*
Portuguese *portugués/portuguesa* (m./f.)
position (job) *puesto* (m.)
possible *posible* (m./f.)
  as soon as possible *lo antes posible*
  It is possible that ... *Es posible que ...*
post (job) *puesto* (m.)
postage stamp *estampilla* (f.)
post office *correo* (m.)
postpone (to) *retrasar*
potato *papa* (f.), *patata* (f.)
pound *libra* (f.)
  half pound *media libra*
powder *polvo* (m.)
  powdered milk *leche* (f.) *en polvo*
practice (to) *practicar*
prayer *oración* (f.)
precisely *precisamente*
prefer (to) *preferir*
  prefer that ... (to) *preferir que ...*
preferable *preferible* (m./f.)
  It's preferable that ... *Es preferible que ...*
pregnant *embarazada* (f.)
prepared *preparado/preparada* (m./f.)
presentation *presentación* (f.)
president *presidente/presidenta* (m./f.)
pressure *presión* (f.)
  have high/low blood pressure (to) *tener la tensión alta/baja*
prestigious *prestigioso/prestigiosa* (m./f.)
pretty *bonito/bonita* (m./f.)
prevent (to) *impedir*
price *precio* (m.)
  price tag *etiqueta* (f.) *con el precio*
  reasonable price *precio económico*
printer *impresora* (f.)
prison *cárcel* (f.)
prize *premio* (m.)
probation *prueba* (f.)
  probationary period *período* (m.) *de prueba*
problem *problema* (m.)
produce (to) *producir*
product *producto* (m.)
profession *profesión* (f.)
professional *profesional* (m./f.)
professionally *profesionalmente*
professor *profesor/profesora* (m./f.)

program *programa* (m.)
  television program *programa de televisión*
prohibit (to) *prohibir*
project *proyecto* (m.)
promise (to) *prometer*
proof *prueba* (f.)
protect (to) *proteger*
psychology *sicología* (f.)
punctual *puntual* (m./f.)
purchase *compra* (f.)
purple *morado/morada* (m./f.), *púrpura* (m./f.)
put (to) *poner*
  I'm putting you through. (on the phone) *Lo paso.*
  put on hold (to) *poner en espera*
  put something on (to) *ponerse*

Q

qualification *cualificación* (f.)
qualified *cualificado/cualificada* (m./f.)
quarter *cuarto* (m.)
  at a quarter past six *a las seis y cuarto*
  at a quarter to six *a las seis menos cuarto*
question *pregunta* (f.)
questionnaire *cuestionario* (m.)
quick *rápido/rápida* (m./f.)
quickly *rápidamente, rápido, aprisa*
quiet *tranquilo/tranquila* (m./f.)
quietly *silenciosamente*
quite, quite a lot *bastante*

R

radio *radio* (f.)
  on the radio *por la radio*
railroad *ferrocarril* (m.)
rain *lluvia* (f.)
rain (to) *llover*
  It's raining. *Está lloviendo.*
raincoat *gabardina* (f.)
raise (to) *levantar*
ramp *rampa* (f.)
rash *brote* (m.)
razor *navaja* (f.) *de afeitar*
read (to) *leer*
reader *lector* (m.)
reading *lectura* (f.)
ready *listo/lista* (m./f.), *preparado/preparada* (m./f.)
  Ready? *¿Listos?/¿Preparados?*
realism *realismo* (m.)
realistic *realista* (m./f.)
Really? *No me digas.*
reason *razón* (f.)
reasonable price *precio* (m.) *económico*
receive (to) *recibir*
reception desk *recepción* (f.)
receptionist *recepcionista* (m./f.)
recess *receso* (m.)
recipe *receta* (f.)
recognize (to) *reconocer*
recommend (to) *recomendar*
  recommend that . . . (to) *recomendar que . . .*
record *registro* (m.), *historial* (m.), *disco* (m.)
record (to) *anotar*
recreation *recreo* (m.)
red *rojo/roja* (m./f.), *colorado/colorada* (m./f.)
  red wine *vino* (m.) *tinto*
reduce (to) *reducir*
reduced *rebajado/rebajada* (m./f.)
reference *referencia* (f.)
refrigerator *nevera* (f.)
regain strength (to) *coger fuerzas* (f. pl.)
regarding . . . *en cuanto a . . .*
region *región* (f.)
regional *regional* (m./f.)
register (to) *matricularse*
registration *matrícula* (f.)
regret that . . . (to) *sentir que . . .*
relationship *relación* (f.)
relative *pariente* (m./f.)
remain (to) *quedar*
remember (to) *recordar*
rent (to) *alquilar*
repayment *retribución* (f.)
repeat (to) *repetir*
  Repeat, please. *Repita, por favor*
reply to (to) *contestar*
report *informe* (m.)
  report card *calificaciones* (f. pl.)
representative *representante* (m.)
request (to) *solicitar*
  request that . . . (to) *pedir que . . .*
research *investigación* (f.)
  research paper *trabajo* (m.) *de investigación*
reservation *reserva* (f.), *reservación* (f.)
resolve (to) *resolver*

responsible *responsable* (m./f.)
rest *resto* (m.)
rest (to) *descansar*
restaurant *restaurante* (m.)
result *resultado* (m.)
résumé *historial* (m.) *de trabajo, currículum vítae, hoja* (f.) *de vida*
retain (to) *quedar*
retired, retired person *jubilado/jubilada* (m./f.)
return (to) *regresar, volver*
rice *arroz* (m.)
rich *rico/rica* (m./f.)
ride (to) *montar*
right *derecho* (m.), *ya*
  be right (to) *tener razón*
  right? *¿verdad?*
  on the right *a la derecha*
  on the right-hand side *a mano derecha*
  right now *en este momento, ahora mismo*
  right side *derecha* (f.)
  right-side *derecho/derecha* (m./f.)
  That's right. *Es verdad./Así es.*
  Turn right. *Gira a la derecha.*
ring *anillo* (m.)
ring (to) *sonar*
rise (to) *levantarse*
river *río* (m.)
robe *albornoz* (m.), *bata* (f.), *deshabillé* (m.)
rock *roca* (f.)
romance novel *novela* (f.) *rosa*
romantic *romántico/romántica* (m./f.)
  romantic films *películas* (f. pl.) *románticas*
room *alcoba* (f.), *cuarto* (m.), *habitación* (f.)
rose *rosa* (f.)
  wear rose-colored glasses (to) *ver todo color de rosa (lit., to see everything pink)*
rotten *podrido/podrida* (m./f.)
rough *agitado/agitada* (m./f.)
round *redondo/redonda* (m./f.)
route *recorrido* (m.)
run (to) *correr*
rural *rural* (m./f.)
Russian (language) *ruso* (m.)

S

sack *bolsa* (f.)
sad *triste* (m./f.)
  It's sad that . . . *Es triste que . . .*
sadly *tristemente*
safe *seguro/segura* (m./f.)
safety *seguridad* (f.)
salad *ensalada* (f.)
salary *salario* (m.)
sale *venta* (f.)
  buy on sale (to) *comprar en rebaja*
salesman/saleswoman *vendedor/vendedora* (m./f.)
salsa *salsa* (f.)
salt *sal* (f.)
salty *salado/salada* (m./f.)
same *mismo/misma* (m./f.)
  The same to you. *Igualmente.*
sand *arena* (f.)
sandals *sandalias* (f. pl.)
Saturday *sábado* (m.)
sauce *salsa* (f.)
save (to) *ahorrar, guardar*
say (to) *decir*
  How do you say " . . . " in . . . ? *¿Cómo se dice " . . . " en . . . ?*
  say good-bye (to) *despedirse*
scarf *bufanda* (f.)
scary *espantoso/espantosa* (m./f.)
schedule *horario* (m.)
scholarship *beca* (f.)
school *escuela* (f.), *academia* (f.)
  school subject *materia* (f.)
science *ciencia* (f.)
scoreboard *marcador* (m.)
scream *grito* (m.)
scream (to) *gritar*
screen *pantalla* (f.)
sculpture *escultura* (f.)
sea *mar* (m.)
season *estación* (f.)
seat *silla* (f.)
seat (to) *sentar*
  be seated (to) *estar sentado*
second *segundo/segunda* (m./f.)
  second year *segundo año*
secondary school *colegio* (m.)
secret *secreto* (m.)
secretary *secretaria* (m./f.)
section *sección* (f.)
security *seguridad* (f.)
see (to) *ver*

I'll see you later. *Hasta luego.*
Let's see ... *Vamos .../A ver ...*
See you. *Nos vemos. (lit., We see each other.)*
See you soon. *Hasta pronto.*
See you tomorrow. *Hasta mañana.*
seem (to) *parecer*
seldom *casi nunca*
sell (to) *vender*
semester *semestre* (m.)
send (to) *enviar*
sense *sentido* (m.)
sensibly *sensatamente*
September *septiembre* (m.)
series *serie* (f.)
serious *grave* (m./f.), *serio/seria* (m./f.)
serve (to) *servir, atender*
service *servicio* (m.)
Is service included? *¿Está incluido el servicio?*
session *sesión* (f.)
set off (to) *partir*
seven *siete*
at seven p.m. *a las siete de la noche*
seven hundred *setecientos/setecientas* (m./f.)
twenty-seven *veintisiete*
seventeen *diecisiete, diez y siete*
seventy *setenta*
several *varios/varias* (m./f.)
sewing *costura* (f.)
shake hands (to) *dar la mano*
shampoo *champú* (m.)
shave (to) *afeitar*
shave (oneself) (to) *afeitarse*
shaving cream *crema de afeitar*
she *ella*
sheet (of paper) *hoja* (f.)
shelf *estante* (m.)
shirt *camisa* (f.)
shoes *zapatos* (m. pl.)
shoe store *zapatería* (f.)
tennis shoes *zapatillas* (f. pl.) *deportivas*
What shoe size do you wear? *¿Qué número calza?*
shop (to) *comprar*
shopping mall *centro* (m.) *comercial*
short *bajo/baja* (m./f.), *corto/corta* (m./f.)
shoulder *hombro* (m.)
shout (to) *gritar*
show (to) *mostrar, dar*
shower *ducha* (f.)
shrimp *camarón* (m.), *gamba* (f.)
shy *tímido/tímida* (m./f.)
siblings *hermanos* (pl.)
sick *enfermo/enferma* (m./f.)
sickness *mareo* (m.), *náusea* (f.)
side *lado* (m.), *parte* (f.)
on the left-hand side *a mano izquierda*
on the right-hand side *a mano derecha*
sidewalk *andén* (m.), *acera* (f.)
on the sidewalk *por el andén/la acera*
signal *señal* (f.)
signature *firma* (f.)
silk *seda* (f.)
silver (color) *plateado/plateada* (m./f.)
simply *simplemente*
since *desde, pues*
sing (to) *cantar*
singer *cantante* (m./f.)
single *único/única* (m./f.), *soltero/soltera* (m./f.)
sink *lavabo* (m.), *fregadero* (m.) *(kitchen)*
sister *hermana* (f.)
sister-in-law *cuñada* (f.)
sit down (to) *sentarse*
situation *situación* (f.)
six *seis*
at a quarter past six *a las seis y cuarto*
at a quarter to six *a las seis menos cuarto*
six hundred *seiscientos/seiscientas* (m./f.)
twenty-six *veintiséis*
sixteen *dieciséis, diez y seis*
sixty *sesenta*
size *talla* (f.), *tamaño* (m.)
What shoe size do you wear? *¿Qué número calza?*
ski (to) *esquiar*
skill *destreza* (f.), *cualificación* (f.)
skimmed *descremado/descremada* (m./f.)
skim milk *leche* (f.) *descremada*
skin *piel* (f.)
skip (to) *saltar*
skirt *falda* (f.)
sky *cielo* (m.)
sky blue *celeste* (m./f.)
sleep *sueño* (m.)
be sleepy (to) *tener sueño*
sleep (to) *dormir*
sleepiness *sueño* (m.)

slice *rebanada* (f.), *tajada* (f.)
slippers *chinelas* (f. pl.), *pantuflas* (f. pl.), *zapatillas* (f. pl.)
slow *lento/lenta* (m./f.), *retrasado/retrasada* (m./f.)
slowly *despacio, lentamente*
Speak more slowly, please. *Hable más despacio, por favor.*
small *pequeño/pequeña* (m./f.)
smaller *menor* (m./f.)
smallest (the) *el/la/los/las* (m. sg./f. sg./m. pl./f. pl.) *menor*
smart *inteligente* (m./f.)
smell (to) *oler*
smile (to) *sonreír*
smog *niebla* (f.) *tóxica/con humo*
smoke (to) *fumar*
smoked *ahumado/ahumada* (m./f.)
snack time *merienda* (f.)
snake *serpiente* (f.)
sneakers *zapatillas* (f. pl.) *deportivas*
snow *nieve* (f.)
snow (to) *nevar*
It's snowing. *Está nevando.*
so *así, pues*
I hope so! *¡Yo espero que sí!*
I think so. *Creo que sí.*
so-so *más o menos*
So ... *Así que ...*
so to speak *por así decir*
so (very) *tan*
soap *jabón* (m.)
soccer *fútbol* (m.)
socks *calcetines* (m. pl.), *medias* (f. pl.)
soda *refresco* (m.)
sofa *sofá* (m.)
soft *suave* (m./f.)
soft drink *refresco* (m.)
sole *solo/sola* (m./f.)
solely *sólo*
solitude *soledad* (f.)
solution *solución* (f.)
some *unos/unas* (m. pl./f. pl.), *algún/alguno/alguna* (before m. sg. nouns/m. sg./f. sg.), *algunos/algunas* (m. pl./f. pl.)
somebody, someone *alguien*
somebody else *alguien más*
something *algo, algún/alguno/alguna* (before m. sg. nouns/m. sg./f. sg.), *algunos/algunas* (m. pl./f. pl.)
sometimes *a veces*
somewhat *algo*
son *hijo* (m.)
song *canción* (f.)
son-in-law *yerno* (m.)
soon *pronto*
as soon as possible *lo antes posible*
See you soon. *Hasta pronto.*
(I'm) sorry. *Lo siento.*
sound *sonido* (m.)
sound system *sistema* (m.) *de sonido*
sound (to) *sonar*
soup *sopa* (f.)
sour *agrio/agria* (m./f.), *cortado/cortada* (m./f.), *amargo/amarga* (m./f.)
south *sur* (m.)
South America *Sudamérica*
space *espacio* (m.)
Spain *España* (f.)
Spanish *español/española* (m./f.)
Spanish (language) *español* (m.)
I'm learning Spanish. *Estoy aprendiendo español.*
I speak a little Spanish. *Hablo un poco de español.*
speak (to) *hablar*
Do you speak English? (fml.) *¿Habla usted inglés?*
Do you speak English? (infml.) *¿Hablas inglés?*
I speak a little Spanish. *Hablo un poco de español.*
I speak French fluently. *Domino el francés.*
so to speak *por así decir*
Speak more slowly, please. *Hable más despacio, por favor.*
speak to ... (to) *hablar con ....*
specialization *especialización* (f.)
specialize (to) *especializarse*
special of the day *plato del día*
specialty *especialidad* (f.)
spectator *espectador/espectadora* (m./f.)
speed *velocidad* (f.)
spend (to) *pasar*
spend the day (to) *pasar el día*
spicy *condimentado/condimentada* (m./f.), *picante* (m./f.)

spinal column *columna* (f.) *vertebral*
spoiled *pasado/pasada* (m./f.)
spoon *cuchara* (f.)
sport *deporte* (m.)
  person who plays sports *deportista* (m./f.)
spot *pinta* (f.)
spring *primavera* (f.)
spy *espía* (m./f.)
square *cuadro* (m.), *plaza* (f.)
stadium *estadio* (m.)
staff *personal* (m.), *plantilla* (f.)
stairs *escaleras* (f. pl.)
stamp collecting *filatelia* (f.)
stand in line (to) *hacer una cola/fila*
star *estrella* (f.)
start (to) *comenzar*
  start . . . (doing something) (to) *comenzar a . . .*
  start from . . . (to) *partir de . . .*
state *estado* (m.)
station *estación* (f.)
  train station *estación de tren, estación de ferrocarril*
Stay in the right lane. *Siga por el carril de la derecha.*
steady job *trabajo* (m.) *fijo*
stepdaughter *hijastra* (f.)
stepfather *padrastro* (m.)
stepmother *madrastra* (f.)
stepson *hijastro* (m.)
stick *palo* (m.)
still *todavía*
stockings *pantymedias* (f. pl.), *medias* (f. pl.)
stomach *estómago* (m.)
  have an upset stomach (to) *tener mal de estómago*
stop *alto* (m.), *parada* (f.)
  Stop! *¡Alto!*
stop (to) *parar, cesar*
  stop . . . (doing something) (to) *cesar de . . .*
store *tienda* (f.)
  antique store *tienda de antigüedades*
  clothing store *tienda de ropa*
  convenience store *tienda* (f.)
  department store *tienda por departamentos*
  electronics store *tienda de electrodomésticos*
  store clerk *dependiente/dependienta* (m./f.)
storm *tormenta* (f.)
stove *cocina* (f.)
straight *recto, derecho*
  Continue straight. *Continúa recto.*
  Go straight. *Siga derecho.*
strange *extraño/extraña* (m./f.)
stranger *extranjero/extranjera* (m.)
street *calle* (f.)
streetlight *luz* (f.) *de la calle*
strength *fuerza* (f.)
  regain strength (to) *coger fuerzas* (f. pl.)
stressing, stressful *estresante* (m./f.)
stripe *raya* (f.)
striped *a rayas*
strong *fuerte* (m./f.)
student *estudiante/estudiante* (m./f.), *alumno/alumna* (m./f.)
study *estudio* (m.)
  studies *estudios* (pl.)
study (to) *estudiar*
stuffing *relleno* (m.)
style *estilo* (m.)
  in style *de moda*
subject *asignatura* (f.)
submit (to) *entregar*
subscriber *abonado/abonada* (m./f.)
suburban *suburbano/suburbana* (m./f.)
subway *subterráneo* (m.), *metro* (m.)
success *éxito* (m.)
such *tal*
suede *gamuza* (f.)
suffer (to) *sufrir*
sugar *azúcar* (m.)
suggest (to) *sugerir*
  suggest that . . . (to) *sugerir que . . .*
suit *traje* (m.)
suitcase *maleta* (f.)
summer *verano* (m.)
  summer job *trabajo* (m.) *de verano*
sun *sol* (m.)
  It's sunny. *Hace sol.*
Sunday *domingo* (m.)
sunglasses *gafas* (f. pl.) *de sol*
supermarket *supermercado* (m.)
supporter *hincha* (m./f.)
supposition *supuesto* (m.)
sure *seguro/segura* (m./f.)
  I'm sure. *Seguro/segura que sí.*
surprise *sorpresa* (f.)

be surprised (to) *sorprenderse*
be surprised that . . . (to) *sorprenderse de que . . .*
suspend (to) *suspender*
suspense *suspenso* (m.)
suspense films *películas* (f. pl.) *de suspenso*
sweater *suéter* (m.), *jersey* (m.)
sweet (adjective) *dulce* (m./f.)
sweet (noun) *dulce* (m.)
swell (to) *hincharse*
swim (to) *nadar*
swimming *natación* (f.)
swimming pool *piscina* (f.)
switchboard *centralita* (f.)
symptom *síntoma* (m.)
syndrome *síndrome* (m.)
carpal tunnel syndrome *síndrome del túnel del carpio*
system *sistema* (m.)
sound system *sistema de sonido*

T

table *mesa* (f.), *tabla* (f.)
tableware *vajilla* (f.)
tag *etiqueta* (f.)
price tag *etiqueta con el precio*
tail *cola* (f.)
take (to) *tomar, traer, coger, usar, llevar*
take a bath (to) *bañarse*
take a blood test (to) *hacerse un examen de sangre*
take a picture (to) *hacer una foto*
take a shower (to) *ducharse*
take a test (to) *hacer un examen, presentarse a un examen*
Take care. *Que estés bien.*
take care of (to) *atender*
take into acount (to) *tener en cuenta*
take medication (to) *tomar un medicamento*
take out (to) *sacar*
take the blood pressure (to) *tomar la tensión*
talented *dotado/dotada* (m./f.)
talk (to) *hablar*
talk show *programa* (m.) *de entrevistas*
tall *alto/alta* (m./f.)
taste *gusto* (m.)
taste (to) *saborear, probar, saber*
tax *impuesto* (m.)
tax return *planilla* (f.) *de impuestos*
taxi *taxi* (m.)
taxi driver *taxista* (m./f.)
tea *té* (m.)
teacher *maestro/maestra* (m./f.)
teakettle *tetera* (f.)
team *equipo* (m.)
technology *tecnología* (f.)
teenager *adolescente* (m.)
telephone *teléfono* (m.)
answer the phone (to) *contestar el teléfono*
call . . . on the phone (to) *llamar por teléfono a . . .*
dial a phone number (to) *marcar un número de teléfono*
hang up the phone (to) *colgar el teléfono*
make a phone call (to) *llamar por teléfono*
on the phone *por teléfono*
telephone booth *cabina* (f.) *telefónica*
telephone number *número* (m.) *de teléfono*
telephonic *telefónico/telefónica* (m./f.)
television *televisión* (f.)
television program *programa* (m.) *de televisión*
television set *televisor* (m.)
watch television (to) *mirar la televisón*
tell (to) *contar, decir*
tell a dirty joke (to) *contar un chiste verde (lit., to tell a green joke)*
tell time (to) *dar la hora*
temperature *temperatura* (f.)
temple *templo* (m.)
ten *diez*
at eight ten (8:10) *a las ocho y diez*
It's ten after one in the morning. *Es la una y diez de la madrugada.*
ten thousand *diez mil*
tendon *tendón* (m.)
tennis *tenis* (m.)
tennis shoes *zapatillas* (f. pl.) *deportivas*
tension *tensión* (f.)
term *término* (m.)
terrible *pésimo/pésima* (m./f.)
test *examen* (m.), *prueba* (f.)
fail a test (to) *suspender un examen*
pass a test (to) *aprobar un examen*
take a blood test (to) *hacerse un examen de sangre*

take a test (to) *hacer un examen, presentarse a un examen*
text *texto* (m.)
textbook *libro* (m.) *de texto*
than *que*
less ... than ... *menos ... que ...*
more ... /-er than ... *más ... que ...*
thanks *gracias* (pl.)
be thankful (to) *agradecer*
give thanks (to) *dar (las) gracias*
Thanks a lot. *Muchas gracias.*
Thank you. *Gracias.*
Thank you for your help. *Le agradezco su ayuda.*
that (demonstrative) *ese/esa* (m. sg./f. sg.) *(near the listener), aquel/aquella* (m. sg./f. sg.) *(far from the speaker and the listener)*
that (one) *ése/ésa* (m. sg./f. sg.) *(near the listener)*
that (one) over there *aquél/aquélla* (m. sg./f. sg.) *(far from the speaker and the listener)*
that (one, thing) (neuter) *eso* (m.) *(near the listener)*
that (one, thing) over there (neuter) *aquello* (m.) *(far from the speaker and the listener)*
That's it. *Ya está.*
That's right. *Es verdad./Así es.*
That's too bad! *¡Qué pena!*
that (conjunction, relative pronoun) *que*
the *el/la/los/las* (m. sg./f. sg./m. pl./f. pl.)
of the (m.)**/from the** (m.)**/about the** (m.) *del (de + el)*
to the (m.)**/at the** (m.) *al (a + el)*
theater *teatro* (m.)
their *su/sus* (sg./pl.)
theirs (m./f.) *suyo/suya/suyos/suyas* (m. sg./f. sg./m. pl./f. pl.)
theirs (f. pl.) *el de ellas* (m. sg.)*, la de ellas* (f. sg.)
theirs (m. pl./mixed group) *el de ellos* (m. sg.)*, la de ellos* (f. sg.)
them (direct object pronoun) *los/las* (m./f.)
(to/for) them (indirect object pronoun) *les, se* (used in place of les when preceding lo/la/los/las)
themselves *se*
then *entonces, luego, pues*
Until then. *Hasta entonces.*
there *ahí, allí*
There is ... /There are ... *Hay ...*
There's no ... that/who ... *No hay ningún ... que ...*
There's no one who/that ... *No hay nadie que ...*
There's nothing that ... *No hay nada que ...*
therefore *por lo tanto, pues*
these *estos/estas* (m. pl./f. pl.)
these (ones) *éstos/éstas* (m. pl./f. pl.)
they *ellos/ellas* (m. pl. & mixed group/f. pl.)
thick *espeso/espesa* (m./f.)
thief *ladrón* (m./f.)
thin *delgado/delgada* (m./f.)*, ligero/ligera* (m./f.)
thing *cosa* (f.)
How are things? *¿Cómo van las cosas?*
think (to) *creer, pensar*
Don't you think? *¿No crees?*
I think so. *Creo que sí.*
not think that ... (to) *no pensar que ...*
What do you think of ... ? *¿Qué te parece ... ?*
third *tercero/tercer/tercera* (m. sg./m. sg. before a noun/f. sg.)
third year *tercer año*
thirst *sed* (f.)
be thirsty (to) *tener sed*
thirteen *trece*
thirty *treinta*
thirty-one *treinta y uno*
thirty percent off *treinta por ciento de descuento*
this *este/esta* (m. sg./f. sg.)
this (one) *éste/ésta* (m. sg./f. sg.)
this (one, thing)(neuter) *esto* (m.)
this afternoon *esta tarde*
this day *este día*
this evening *esta noche* (f.)
those *aquellos/aquellas* (m. pl./f. pl.) *(far from the speaker and the listener)*
those (ones) over there *aquéllos/aquéllas* (m. pl./f. pl.) *(far from the speaker and the listener)*
thousand *mil*
hundred thousand *cien mil*
ten thousand *diez mil*
twenty thousand *veinte mil*
three *tres*
It's three o'clock. *Son las tres.*
It's three o'clock sharp. *Son las tres en punto.*
one hundred and three dollars *ciento tres dólares*
three hundred *trescientos/trescientas* (m./f.)

twenty-three *veintitrés*
throat *garganta* (f.)
have a sore throat (to) *tener dolor de garganta*
through *por*
from … through … *de … a …*
go through a light (to) *saltarse el semáforo*
I'm putting you through. (on the phone) *Lo paso.*
thunder *trueno* (m.)
Thursday *jueves* (m.)
ticket *billete* (m.), *boleto* (m.), *pasaje* (m.), *tiquete* (m.), *entrada* (f.)
tie *corbata* (f.)
tie (to) *empatar*
tied *empatado/empatada* (m./f.)
be tied (to) *quedar empatados*
tight *ajustado/ajustada* (m./f.)
time *hora* (f.), *tiempo* (m.), *vez* (f.)
at the present time *actualmente*
At what time is it? *¿A qué hora es?*
Do you have time?/How are you doing for time? *¿Cómo estás de tiempo?*
full-time *a tiempo completo*
on time, in time *a tiempo*
overtime *horas* (f. pl.) *extras*
part-time *a tiempo parcial*
tell time (to) *dar la hora*
What time is it? *¿Qué hora es?/¿Qué horas son?*
What time do you have? *¿Qué hora tiene?*
tingling feeling *cosquilleo* (m.)
tip *propina* (f.), *punta* (f.)
tired *cansado/cansada* (m./f.)
be tired (to) *tener cansancio*
to *a, con*
in order to *para*
It's five to one. (12:55) *Es la una menos cinco.*
to the (m.) *al (a + el)*
toast *tostada* (f.)
today *hoy*
toe *dedo del pie*
together *junto/junta* (m./f.)
toilet *inodoro* (m.)
toilet paper *papel* (m.) *higiénico*
toll *peaje* (m.)
tomato *tomate* (m.)
tomorrow *mañana* (f.)
Until tomorrow./See you tomorrow. *Hasta mañana.*
tone *tono* (m.), *señal* (f.)
leave a message after the tone (to) *dejar un mensaje después de oír la señal*
tongue *lengua* (f.)
tonight *esta noche*
too *también*
too much, too many *demasiado/demasiada* (m./f.)
tooth *diente* (m.)
touch (to) *tocar*
tour bus trip *recorrido por autobús*
tourism *turismo* (m.)
tourist *turista* (m./f.)
toward(s) *hacia, para*
towel *toalla* (f.)
town *ciudad* (f.), *pueblo* (m.)
around town *por la ciudad*
toxic *tóxico/tóxica* (m./f.)
traffic *tráfico* (m.)
go through a traffic light (to) *saltarse el semáforo*
traffic jam *embotellamiento* (m.)
traffic light *semáforo* (m.)
train *tren* (m.), *ferrocarril* (m.)
train station *estación* (f.) *de tren, estación* (f.) *de ferrocarril*
transfer (to) *trasladar*
translate (to) *traducir*
travel *viaje* (m.)
travel (to) *viajar*
treat (to) *tratar*
How's life treating you? *¿Cómo te trata la vida?*
treatment *tratamiento* (m.)
tree *árbol* (m.)
trip *viaje* (m.)
go on a trip (to) *salir de viaje*
Have a good trip. *Buen viaje.*
true *cierto/cierta* (m./f.)
It is not true that … *No es cierto que …*
truth *verdad* (f.)
try (to) *tratar, probar*
try … (to do something) (to) *tratar de …*
try on (clothes) (to) *probarse*
T-shirt *camiseta* (f.)
Tuesday *martes* (m.)
tuition *derechos* (m. pl.) *de matrícula*
tuna *atún* (m.)
tunnel *túnel* (m.)

turn *vuelta* (f.)
turn (to) *doblar, girar, volver, ponerse*
turn around (to) *dar la vuelta*
Turn left. *Gira a la izquierda.*
turn off (to) *apagar*
turn off the lights (to) *apagar las luces*
Turn right. *Gira a la derecha.*
twelve *doce*
It's twelve noon. *Son las doce del mediodía.*
twenty *veinte*
twenty-eight *veintiocho*
twenty-five *veinticinco*
twenty-four *veinticuatro*
twenty-nine *veintinueve*
twenty-one *veintiuno*
twenty-seven *veintisiete*
twenty-six *veintiséis*
twenty-three *veintitrés*
twenty-two *veintidós*
two *dos*
twenty-two *veintidós*
twice a week *dos veces por semana*
two hundred *doscientos/doscientas* (m./f.)
two-piece *de dos piezas*
type *tipo* (m.)
typical *típico/típica* (m./f.)

U

ugly *feo/fea* (m./f.)
umbrella *paraguas* (m.)
uncle *tío* (m.)
uncomfortable *incómodo/incómoda* (m./f.)
under *bajo*
undergarments (men's) *calzones* (m. pl.)
underneath *debajo*
underneath ... *debajo de ...*
underpants (men's) *calzoncillos* (m. pl.)
undershirt *camisilla* (f.), *camiseta* (f.)
understand (to) *comprender, entender*
underwear (women's) *bombachas* (f. pl.), *bragas* (f. pl.), *calzoncitos* (m. pl.), *pantis* (m. pl.)
unemployed *parado/parada* (m./f.)
unfortunately *desafortunadamente, por desgracia*
unfriendly *antipático/antipática* (m./f.)
union *sindicato* (m.)
unique *único/única* (m./f.)
united *unido/unida* (m./f.)
United States (the) *los Estados Unidos*
university *universidad* (f.)
university course *carrera* (f.)
unpleasant *desagradable* (m./f.)
until *hasta, para*
Till then. *Hasta entonces.*
Until later. *Hasta más tarde.*
Until then. *Hasta entonces.*
Until tomorrow. *Hasta mañana.*
urban *urbano/urbana* (m./f.)
urgently *urgentemente*
Uruguay *Uruguay* (m.)
Uruguayan *uruguayo/uruguaya* (m./f.)
us (direct object pronoun); **(to/for) us** (indirect object pronoun) *nos*
use (to) *usar*
use for the first time (to) *estrenar*

V

vacation *vacaciones* (f. pl.)
on vacation *de vacaciones*
variety *variedad* (f.)
vegetable *vegetal* (m.), *verdura* (f.)
Venezuela *Venezuela* (f.)
Venezuelan *venezolano/venezolana* (m./f.)
vertebral *vertebral* (m./f.)
very *muy, mucho*
veterinarian *veterinario/veterinaria* (m./f.)
view *vista* (f.)
village *aldea* (f.)
vinyl *vinilo* (m.)
vinyl record *disco* (m.) *de vinilo*
violet (color) *violeta* (m./f.)
violin *violín* (m.)
visit (to) *visitar*
visitor *visitante* (m./f.)
voice *voz* (f.)
voice mail *buzón* (m.) *de voz*
voucher *vale* (m.)

W

wage *paga* (f.), *jornal* (m.)
wait *espera* (f.)
wait (to) *esperar*
waiter *camarero* (m.), *mesero* (m.)
waitress *camarera* (f.), *mesera* (f.)
wake up (to) *despertarse*
walk (to) *andar, caminar, ir a pie/caminar*
wall *pared* (f.)

wallet *cartera* (f.)
want (to) *querer, desear*
  want that/to ... (to) *querer que ...*
wish (to) *desear*
  I wish ... *Ojalá que ...*
  wish that ... (to) *desear que ...*
wash (to) *lavar*
  hand wash (to) *lavar a mano*
  wash oneself (to) *lavarse*
wash basin *lavabo* (m.)
washing machine *lavadora* (f.)
watch *reloj* (m.)
watch (to) *mirar*
  watch television (to) *mirar la televisón*
water *agua* (f.)
  mineral water *agua mineral*
  water (the) *el agua*
  waters (the) *las aguas*
way *camino* (m.), *forma* (f.)
  one-way *de sentido* (m.) *único*
we *nosotros* (m. pl./mixed group), *nosotras* (f. pl.)
weak *débil* (m./f.)
wear (to) *llevar, calzar (shoes)*
  wear rose-colored glasses (to) *ver todo color de rosa (lit., to see everything pink)*
  What shoe size do you wear? *¿Qué número calza?*
weather *tiempo* (m.)
  The weather is good. *El tiempo es bueno.*
web (on the computer) *web* (f.)
  webpage *página* (f.) *web*
  website *sitio* (m.) *web*
Wednesday *miércoles* (m.)
week *semana* (f.)
  every week *todas las semanas*
  last week *semana pasada*
  next week *próxima semana, semana que viene*
  this week *esta semana*
  twice a week *dos días a la semana*
weekend *fin* (m.) *de semana*
  long weekend *puente* (m.)
weekly *semanal* (m./f.)
weigh (to) *pesar*
Welcome. *Bienvenido./Bienvenida.* (m./f.) (to a man/to a woman)
  You're welcome. *De nada.*
well *bien, pues*
  be not doing well (to) *estar mal*
  May you be well. *Que esté bien.*
  well-done *bien asada*
west *oeste* (m.), *occidente* (m.)
what *qué, cuál/cuáles* (sg./pl.)
  At what time is it? *¿A qué hora es?*
  What a coincidence! *¡Qué coincidencia!*
  What color is ... ? *¿De qué color es ... ?*
  What do you do for a living? *¿En qué trabaja?*
  What do you think of ... ? *¿Qué te parece ... ?*
  What does that mean? *¿Qué quiere decir eso?*
  What shoe size do you wear? *¿Qué número calza?*
  What time do you have? *¿Qué hora tiene?*
  What time is it? *¿Qué hora es?/¿Qué horas son?*
  What would you like? *¿Qué desea?*
  What?/Pardon me? *¿Cómo?*
  What's going on? *¿Qué hay?*
  What's happening? *¿Qué tal?*
  What's up?/What's going on? *¿Qué hay?*
  What's your name? *¿Cómo se llama usted?* (fml.)/*¿Cómo te llamas?* (infml.)
when *cuándo* (question), *cuando* (relative adverb)
where *dónde* (question), *donde* (relative adverb)
  Where are you from? *¿De dónde eres?*
which *cuál/cuáles* (sg./pl.) (question), *cual/cuales* (sg./pl.) (relative pronoun)
  of which (relative pronoun) *cuyo/cuya/cuyos/cuyas* (m. sg./f. sg./m. pl./f. pl.)
while *mientras*
white *blanco/blanca* (m./f.)
  white wine *vino* (m.) *blanco*
who *quién/quiénes* (sg./pl.) (question), *quien/quienes* (sg./pl.) (relative pronoun)
  Who knows? *¿Quién sabe?*
  Who's calling? *¿De parte de quién?/¿Quién lo llama?*
whole *entero/entera* (m./f.)
  whole milk *leche* (f.) *entera*
whom (question) *quién/quiénes* (sg./pl.)
  whom (relative pronoun) *quien/quienes* (sg./pl.)
whose (relative pronoun) *cuyo/cuya/cuyos/cuyas* (m. sg./f. sg./m. pl./f. pl.)
  Whose ... ? *¿De quién ... ?*
why *por qué*
wide *ancho/ancha* (m./f.)
wife *esposa* (f.), *mujer* (f.)
win (to) *ganar*
  I hope they win! *¡Ojalá que ganen!*

wind *viento* (m.)
It's windy. *Hace viento.*
window *ventana* (f.)
display window *escaparate* (m.)
wine *vino* (m.)
red wine *vino tinto*
white wine *vino blanco*
wineglass *copa* (f.)
glass of wine *copa de vino*
winter *invierno* (m.)
wish *deseo* (m.)
with *con*
with you *contigo*
without *sin*
woman *mujer* (f.), *tía* (f.)
businesswoman *mujer de negocios*
policewoman *mujer policía*
wonder *maravilla* (f.)
wonderful *estupendo/estupenda* (m./f.)
wood *madera* (f.)
wooden *de madera*
wool *lana* (f.)
word *palabra* (f.)
work *trabajo* (m.)
work (to) *trabajar, funcionar*
What do you do for a living? *¿En qué trabaja?*
working day *jornada* (f.)
world *mundo* (m.)
world championship *campeonato* (m.) *mundial*
worldly *mundial* (m./f.)
worldwide *mundial* (m./f.)
worry (to) *preocuparse*
Don't worry. *No se preocupe.*
worry that . . . (to) *preocuparse de que . . .*
worse *peor* (m./f.)
worst (the) *el/la/los/las* (m. sg./f. sg./m. pl./f. pl.) *peor*
wrist *muñeca* (f.)
write (to) *escribir*
write down (to) *anotar*
writer *escritor/escritora* (m./f.)
wrong *equivocado/equivocada* (m./f.)
wrong number *número* (m.) *equivocado*

Y

year *año* (m.)
be . . . years old (to) *tener . . . años*
fifties (the) *los años cicuenta*
last year *año pasado*
next year *año que viene*
second year *segundo año*
third year *tercer año*
this year *este año*
yellow *amarillo/amarilla* (m./f.)
yellow pages *páginas* (f. pl.) *amarillas*
yes *sí*
yesterday *ayer*
yet *todavía*
you (after a proposition) *ti* (infml. sg.)
you (direct object pronoun) *lo/la/te/los/las/os* (m. sg. fml./f. sg. fml./sg. infml./m. pl./f. pl./pl. infml)
you (impersonal pronoun) *se*
(to/for) you (indirect object pronoun) *le/les* (fml. sg./pl.), *se* (fml. sg./pl.) (used in place of le/les when preceding lo/la/los/las), *te/os* (infml. sg./pl.)
you (subject pronoun) *usted/tú/ustedes/vosotros/vosotras* (sg. fml./sg. infml./pl./m. pl. & mixed group infml. used in Spain/f. pl. infml. used in Spain)
young *joven* (m./f.)
young boy *niño* (m.)
young child *párvulo/párvula* (m./f.)
young girl *niña* (f.)
younger *menor* (m./f.)
youngest (the) *el/la/los/las* (m. sg./f. sg./m. pl./f. pl.) *menor*
your (pl. fml. & infml.) *su/sus* (sg./pl.)
your (pl. infml.) *vuestro/vuestra/vuestros/vuestras* (m. sg./f. sg./m. pl./f. pl.) (used in Spain)
your (sg. fml.) *su/sus* (sg./pl.)
your (sg. infml.) *tu/tus* (sg./pl.)
yours (pl. fml. & infml.) *suyo/suya/suyos/suyas* (m. sg./f. sg./m. pl./f. pl.), *el de ustedes* (m. sg.), *la de ustedes* (f. sg.)
yours (pl. infml.) *vuestro/vuestra/vuestros/vuestras* (m. sg./f. sg./m. pl./f. pl.) (used in Spain)
yours (sg. fml.) *suyo/suya/suyos/suyas* (m. sg./f. sg./m. pl./f. pl.), *el de usted* (m. sg.), *la de usted* (f. sg.)
yours (sg. infml.) *tuyo/tuya/tuyos/tuyas* (m. sg./f. sg./m. pl./f. pl.) (infml.)
yourself *se/te* (fml./infml.)
yourselves *se/os* (fml./infml.)
youth hostel *hostal* (m.)

Z

zero *cero*

Intermediate Spanish

Edited by
Enrique Montes

LIVING LANGUAGE®

Content in this program has been modified and enhanced from *Starting Out in Spanish* and *Complete Course Spanish: The Basics*, both published in 2008.

Published in the United States by Living Language, an imprint of Random House, Inc.

www.livinglanguage.com

Editor: Suzanne McQuade
Production Editor: Carolyn Roth
Production Manager: Tom Marshall
Interior Design: Sophie Chin
Illustrations: Sophie Chin

First Edition

Library of Congress Cataloging-in-Publication Data

Montes, Enrique.
Intermediate Spanish / edited by Enrique Montes.—1st ed.
p. cm.
ISBN 978-0-307-97163-0
1. Spanish language—Textbooks for foreign speakers—English. 2. Spanish language—Grammar.
3. Spanish language—Spoken Spanish. I. Montes, Enrique. II. Title.
PC4129.E5I58 2011
468.2'421—dc23 2011021881

PRINTED IN THE UNITED STATES OF AMERICA

10 9 8 7 6 5

Acknowledgments

Thanks to the Living Language team: Amanda D'Acierno, Christopher Warnasch, Suzanne McQuade, Laura Riggio, Erin Quirk, Amanda Munoz, Fabrizio LaRocca, Siobhan O'Hare, Sophie Chin, Sue Daulton, Alison Skrabek, Carolyn Roth, Ciara Robinson, and Tom Marshall.

COURSE

OUTLINE

COURSE

OUTLINE

How to Use This Course

¡Bienvenidos! Welcome to *Living Language Intermediate Spanish*!

Before we begin, let's take a quick look at what you'll see in this course.

CONTENT

Intermediate Spanish is a continuation of *Essential Spanish*. It will review, expand on, and add to the foundation that you received in *Essential Spanish*. In other words, this course contains:

- an in-depth review of important vocabulary and grammar from *Essential Spanish*;
- an expanded and more advanced look at some key vocabulary and grammar from *Essential Spanish*;
- an introduction to idiomatic language and more challenging Spanish grammar.

UNITS

There are five units in this course. Each unit has four lessons arranged in a "building block" structure: the first lesson will present essential *words*, the second will introduce longer *phrases*, the third will teach *sentences*, and the fourth will show how everything works together in everyday *conversations*.

At the beginning of each unit is an introduction highlighting what you'll learn in that unit. At the end of each unit you'll find the Unit Essentials, which reviews the key information from that unit, and a self-graded Unit Quiz, which tests what you've learned.

LESSONS

There are four lessons per unit for a total of 20 lessons in the course. Each lesson has the following components:

- **Introduction** outlining what you will cover in the lesson.
- **Word Builder 1** (first lesson of the unit) presenting key words and phrases.
- **Phrase Builder 1** (second lesson of the unit) introducing longer phrases and expressions.
- **Sentence Builder 1** (third lesson of the unit) teaching sentences.
- **Conversation 1** (fourth lesson of the unit) for a natural dialogue that brings together important vocabulary and grammar from the unit.
- **Take It Further** providing extra information about the new vocabulary you just saw, expanding on certain grammar points, or introducing additional words and phrases.
- **Word/Phrase/Sentence/Conversation Practice 1** practicing what you learned in Word Builder 1, Phrase Builder 1, Sentence Builder 1, or Conversation 1.
- **Grammar Builder 1** guiding you through important Spanish grammar that you need to know.
- **Work Out 1** for a comprehensive practice of what you saw in Grammar Builder 1.
- **Word Builder 2/Phrase Builder 2/Sentence Builder 2/Conversation 2** for more key words, phrases, or sentences, or a second dialogue.
- **Take It Further** for expansion on what you've seen so far and additional vocabulary.
- **Word/Phrase/Sentence/Conversation Practice 2** practicing what you learned in Word Builder 2, Phrase Builder 2, Sentence Builder 2, or Conversation 2.

- **Grammar Builder 2** for more information on Spanish grammar.
- **Work Out 2** for a comprehensive practice of what you saw in Grammar Builder 2.
- **Tip or Culture Note** for a helpful language tip or useful cultural information related to the lesson or unit.
- **Word Recall** reviewing important grammar and vocabulary from the lesson.
- **How Did You Do?** outlining what you learned in the lesson.

UNIT ESSENTIALS

You will see the **Unit Essentials** at the end of every unit. This section summarizes and reviews the key information from the unit, but with missing vocabulary information for you to fill in. In other words, each Unit Essentials works as both a study guide and a blank "cheat sheet." Once you complete it, you'll have your very own reference for the most essential vocabulary and grammar from the unit.

UNIT QUIZ

After each Unit Essentials, you'll see a **Unit Quiz**. The quizzes are self-graded so it's easy for you to test your progress and see if you should go back and review.

PROGRESS BAR

You will see a **Progress Bar** on each page that has course material. It indicates your current position within the unit and lets you know how much progress you're making. Each line in the bar represents a Grammar Builder section.

AUDIO

Look for the symbol ▶ to help guide you through the audio as you're reading the book. It will tell you which track to listen to for each section that has audio. When you see the symbol, select the indicated track and start listening! If you don't see the symbol, then there isn't any audio for that section. You'll also see ⏸, which will tell you where that track ends.

The audio can be used on its own—in other words, without the book—when you're on the go. Whether in your car or at the gym, you can listen to the audio on its own to brush up on your pronunciation or review what you've learned in the book.

PRONUNCIATION GUIDE, GRAMMAR SUMMARY, GLOSSARY

At the back of this book you will find a **Pronunciation Guide**, **Grammar Summary**, and **Glossary**. The Pronunciation Guide provides information on Spanish pronunciation and the phonetics system used in this course. The Grammar Summary contains a helpful, brief overview of key points in the Spanish grammar system. The Glossary (Spanish–English and English–Spanish) includes all of the essential words from the five units of *Intermediate Spanish*, as well as some additional vocabulary.

FREE ONLINE TOOLS

Go to **www.livinglanguage.com/languagelab** to access your free online tools. The tools are organized around the units in this course, with audiovisual flashcards, as well as interactive games and quizzes for each unit. These tools will help you review and practice the vocabulary and grammar that you've seen in the units, as well as provide some bonus words and phrases related to the unit's topic.

Unit 1:
Talking About Yourself and Your Family

In this unit, you'll learn how to talk about yourself and your family as well as how to describe where you live. You'll also expand your knowledge of Spanish grammar by reviewing gender, plurals, the forms of *to be*, the verb *to have*, and more. By the end of this unit, you should be able to:

- ☐ Understand how articles work
- ☐ Identify the gender of words
- ☐ Name some family members
- ☐ Name some rooms of the house and items found around the house
- ☐ Confidently conjugate **ser** and **estar**
- ☐ Count to 100 without difficulty, and combine some numbers and words
- ☐ Clearly understand the difference in usage between **ser** and **estar**
- ☐ Identify nationalities and professions
- ☐ Confidently conjugate the verb **tener** and use it in several idiomatic expressions
- ☐ Use the expression **Hay . . .** to express *there is, there are*

▶ Look for this symbol to help guide you through the audio as you're reading the book. It will tell you which track to listen to for each section that has audio. However, keep in mind that the audio can also be used on its own when you're on the go!

Lesson 1: Words

By the end of this lesson, you will be able to:

- ☐ Understand how articles work
- ☐ Identify the gender of words
- ☐ Name some family members
- ☐ Name some rooms of the house and items found around the house

Word Builder 1

Let's start by looking at a list of words that refer to family members.

1A Word Builder 1 (CD 4, Track 1)

la madre	*mother*
el padre	*father*
el/la niño/a	*boy/girl*
el/la hijo/a	*son/daughter*
el/la hermano/a	*brother/sister*
el/la abuelo/a	*grandfather/grandmother*
el/la tío/a	*aunt/uncle*
el/la primo/a	*cousin*
el/la sobrino/a	*nephew/niece*
el/la esposo/a	*husband/wife*
el/la nieto/a	*grandson/granddaughter*
el/la suegro/a	*father-in-law/mother-in-law*
la nuera	*daughter-in-law*

el yerno	*son-in-law*
el/la cuñado/a	*brother-in-law/sister-in-law*

Take It Further

Here are a few extra words that will appear in this lesson, either in the examples or in the exercises. Study them at your leisure, or return to this section when you come across them and want a review.

la tarjeta	*card*
el libro	*book*
el bolígrafo	*pen*
la carta	*letter*
el lápiz	*pencil*
la luz	*light*
la cafetera	*coffeemaker*
el premio	*prize*
el código	*code*
el nombre	*name*
el cheque	*check*
la nacionalidad	*nationality*
la profesión	*profession*

Word Practice 1

Match the Spanish word on the right with its English translation on the left.

1. *nephew* — a. **la nieta**
2. *granddaughter* — b. **el cuñado**
3. *brother-in-law* — c. **la sobrina**
4. *daughter-in-law* — d. **el sobrino**
5. *niece* — e. **la nuera**
6. *sister-in-law* — f. **la cuñada**

ANSWER KEY
1. d; 2. a; 3. b; 4. e; 5. c; 6. f

Grammar Builder 1

REVIEWING PLURALS

1B Grammar Builder 1 (CD 4, Track 2)

Let's review how the plural is formed in Spanish.

VOWEL ENDING	-S
un hombre (*a man*)	**unos hombres** (*some men*)
una abuela (*a grandmother*)	**unas abuelas** (*some grandmothers*)

CONSONANT ENDING (OTHER THAN -Z)	-ES
un señor (*a gentleman*)	**unos señores** (*some gentlemen*)
una mujer (*a woman*)	**unas mujeres** (*some women*)

-Z ENDING	DROP -Z, ADD -CES
un lápiz (*a pencil*)	**unos lápices** (*some pencils*)
una luz (*a light*)	**unas luces** (*some lights*)

Note that the plural of **padre** (*father*) means *parents*. Similarly, other masculine plural nouns referring to family members can take on a more general sense and do not necessarily refer to males only. This depends on context, of course.

hijos	*children (sons and daughters)*
abuelos	*grandparents*
hermanos	*brothers and sisters, siblings*
primos	*cousins*
nietos	*grandchildren*

Work Out 1

We'll give you one object; you give us back more than one by making the following nouns plural and translating your answers.

1. **tarjeta** ____________________
2. **hermano** ____________________
3. **señor** ____________________
4. **abogado** ____________________
5. **hija** ____________________
6. **premio** ____________________
7. **nombre** ____________________
8. **cafetera** ____________________
9. **madre** ____________________
10. **padre** ____________________

ANSWER KEY

1. **tarjetas** (*cards*); 2. **hermanos** (*brothers*); 3. **señores** (*gentlemen*); 4. **abogados** (*lawyers*); 5. **hijas** (*daughters*); 6. **premios** (*prizes*); 7. **nombres** (*names*); 8. **cafeteras** (*coffeemakers*); 9. **madres** (*mothers*); 10. **padres** (*fathers/parents*)

Word Builder 2

Here are some words that can be used when talking about where we live.

1C Word Builder 2 (CD 4, Track 3)

la casa	*house*
el edificio	*building*
el apartamento	*apartment*
la sala	*living room*
el comedor	*dining room*
la cocina	*kitchen*
el baño	*bathroom*
la habitación	*bedroom*
el jardín	*garden*
el balcón	*balcony*
el escritorio	*desk/study*
la puerta	*door*
la ventana	*window*
la silla	*seat*
la mesa	*table*

Word Practice 2

Fill in the floorplan below with as many room names as you can come up with based on the vocabulary you just learned.

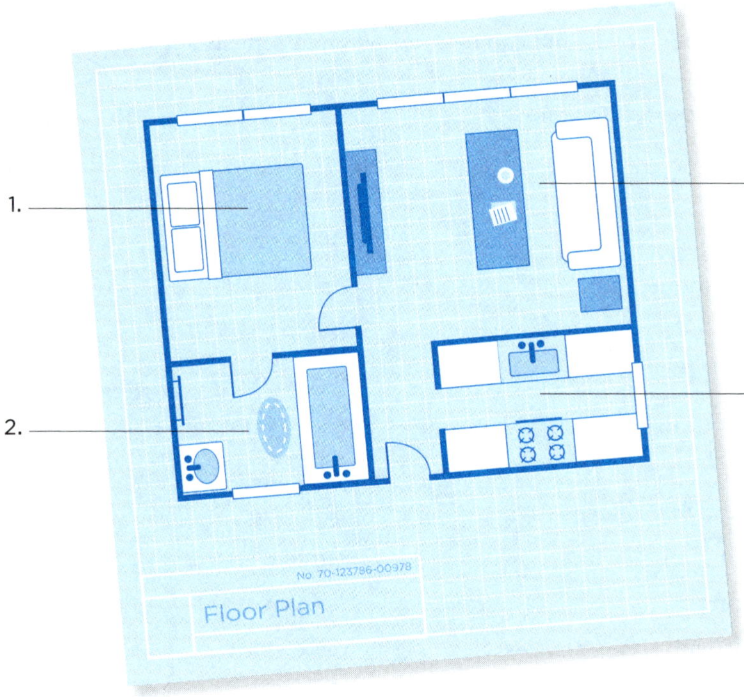

1. ______________________

2. ______________________

3. ______________________

4. ______________________

Grammar Builder 2

GENDER AND ARTICLES

1D Grammar Builder 2 (CD 4, Track 4)

You probably remember from *Essential Spanish* that all nouns and adjectives indicate gender, either masculine or feminine. You'll remember that for nouns with natural gender, this is easy: **hombre** (*man*), **muchacho** (*boy*), and **abogado** (*male lawyer*) are all masculine, while **mujer** (*woman*), **muchacha** (*girl*), and **abogada** (*female lawyer*) are all feminine. In cases where there is no natural gender, masculine nouns usually end in **-o**, and feminine nouns end in **-a**.

MASCULINE	FEMININE
libro (*book*)	**tarjeta** (*card*)
bolígrafo (*pen*)	**carta** (*letter*)

Take It Further

As a general rule, nouns and adjectives ending in **-dad** or **-ción** are feminine, and most nouns and adjectives that end in **-e** are masculine. For now, the best thing to do is simply memorize the gender of each new noun you learn. Let's look at the genders of some of the nouns you've learned so far.

MASCULINE	FEMININE
premio (*prize*)	**tarjeta** (*card*)
código (*code*)	**cafetera** (*coffeemaker*)
nombre (*name*)	**nacionalidad** (*nationality*)
cheque (*check*)	**profesión** (*profession*)

As in English, Spanish has articles that translate as *a*, *an*, *some*, and *the*. But remember that in Spanish, they have to match the gender and number of the noun they precede. Singular indefinite articles are translated as *a/an*, while plurals are translated as *some*.

	MASCULINE	FEMININE
singular	**un**	**una**
plural	**unos**	**unas**

un hombre (*a man*)	**unos niños** (*some boys/children*)
una mujer (*a woman*)	**unas niñas** (*some girls*)

Notice that the plural masculine form **unos** is used as long as at least one of the members of the group is male. The feminine plural form **unas** is used exclusively for groups with only female members.

The definite article in Spanish corresponds to *the* in English. And again, there are four forms that agree in gender and number with the nouns they modify.

	MASCULINE	FEMININE
singular	**el**	**la**
plural	**los**	**las**

el estudiante (*the male student*)	**la estudiante** (*the female student*)
el bebé (*the baby boy*)	**la bebé** (*the baby girl*)

Note that the plurals of the above words with their articles would be as follows:

los estudiantes (*the male students*)	**las estudiantes** (*the female students*)
los bebés (*the baby boys*)	**las bebés** (*the baby girls*)

Work Out 2

Replace the indefinite article with the definite article, and then translate your answers.

1. **unas habitaciones** ____________________

2. **un abuelo** ____________________

3. **unos padres** ____________________

4. **una cocina** ____________________

5. **una prima** ____________________

6. **unas hermanas** ____________________

7. **un niño** ____________________

8. **un jardín** ____________________

ANSWER KEY

1. **las habitaciones** (*the bedrooms*); 2. **el abuelo** (*the grandfather*); 3. **los padres** (*the fathers/parents*); 4. **la cocina** (*the kitchen*); 5. **la prima** (*the female cousin*); 6. **las hermanas** (*the sisters*); 7. **el niño** (*the boy*); 8. **el jardín** (*the garden*)

Culture Note

Spanish speakers around the world use slightly different words for the same things. Here are a few differences.

In Spain, for example, you will hear people talking about their **piso** when referring to **un apartamento** (*apartment*). They'll also refer to their parents as **madre** (*mother*) and **padre** (*father*). Spaniards usually talk about their young children as **el crío** (*kid, m.*) or **la cría** (*kid, f.*).

In Latin America, people will use the words **cuarto** and **dormitorio** to refer to **una habitación** (*bedroom*). There is also the word **estudio**, which is used instead of **escritorio**, in the sense of *study* or *office*. And you will hear Latin Americans use the words **mamá** (*mom*) and **papá** (*dad*), or even **mami** and **papi**, when talking about their parents. In some parts of Latin America, you'll hear the word **párvulo** in reference to young children.

The words **habitación** and **cuarto** are literally translated as *room*. However, in many countries they are used to mean specifically a *bedroom*. Spanish has two other words that literally mean *bedroom*: **alcoba** and **dormitorio**. But **habitación** is also commonly used to refer to rooms in a hotel.

How Did You Do?

Let's see how you did! By now, you should be able to:

- ☐ Understand how articles work
  (Still unsure? Jump back to page 21.)
- ☐ Identify the gender of words
  (Still unsure? Jump back to page 21.)
- ☐ Name some family members
  (Still unsure? Jump back to page 15.)
- ☐ Name some rooms of the house and items found around the house
  (Still unsure? Jump back to page 19.)

Word Recall

Place the appropriate indefinite article in front of each of the following nouns.

1. ______________________ **hermano**
2. ______________________ **amigo**
3. ______________________ **abuelo**
4. ______________________ **hermana**

5. ______________________ **amiga**

6. ______________________ **abuela**

7. ______________________ **hermanos**

8. ______________________ **amigos**

9. ______________________ **abuelos**

10. ______________________ **hermanas**

11. ______________________ **amigas**

12. ______________________ **abuelas**

ANSWER KEY

1–3: **un**; 4–6: **una**; 7–9: **unos**; 10–12: **unas**

Lesson 2: Phrases

By the end of this lesson, you should be able to:

- ☐ Confidently conjugate **ser** and **estar**
- ☐ Count to 100 without difficulty, and combine some numbers and words

Phrase Builder 1

Here are some phrases that can be used to talk about family and friends. You'll see them again in the dialogues in this unit.

2A Phrase Builder 1 (CD 4, Track 5)

como ya sabes	*as you already know*

el mayor	*the oldest (male)*
la menor	*the youngest (female)*
diferencia de edades	*difference in ages*
el centro de atracción	*center of attraction*
es natural	*it's natural*
y encima . . .	*and on top of that . . .*
situación familiar	*family situation*
tienes que . . .	*you have to . . .*
en un mismo apartamento	*in the same apartment*

Take It Further

In this lesson, you will also encounter several other words related to professions. Let's take a look at them briefly.

el/la abogado/a	*lawyer*
el/la artista	*artist*
el/la secretaria	*secretary*
el/la profesor/a	*professor*
la universidad	*university*

Phrase Practice 1

Translate the phrases you just learned from English into Spanish. Don't be ashamed to go back to the list of phrases for some help!

1. *as you already know* ____________________

2. *the oldest (male)* ____________________

3. *the youngest (female)* ______________________

4. *difference in ages* ______________________

5. *center of attraction* ______________________

6. *it's natural* ______________________

7. *and on top of that . . .* ______________________

8. *family situation* ______________________

9. *you have to . . .* ______________________

10. *in the same apartment* ______________________

ANSWER KEY

1. **como ya sabes**; 2. **el mayor**; 3. **la menor**; 4. **diferencia de edades**; 5. **el centro de atracción**; 6. **es natural**; 7. **y encima . . .** ; 8. **situación familiar**; 9. **tienes que . . .** ; 10. **en un mismo apartamento**

Grammar Builder 1

SER AND ESTAR (*TO BE*)

2B Grammar Builder 1 (CD 4, Track 6)

Before we go further into the differences between **ser** and **estar** in the next lesson, let's review their conjugations.

SER (*TO BE*)			
yo soy	*I am*	**nosotros/as somos**	*we are*
tú eres	*you are (infml.)*	**vosotros/as sois**	*(all of) you are (pl. infml.)*
él/ella/usted es	*he/she is, you are (fml.)*	**ellos/ellas/ustedes son**	*they are, (all of) you are (pl. fml.)*

ESTAR (TO BE)			
yo estoy	*I am*	**nosotros/as estamos**	*we are*
tú estás	*you are (infml.)*	**vosotros/as estáis**	*(all of) you are (pl. infml.)*
él/ella/usted está	*he/she is, you are (fml.)*	**ellos/ellas/ ustedes están**	*they are, (all of) you are (pl. fml.)*

Work Out 1

A. Fill in the blanks with the correct form of **ser**.

1. **Mi nombre ____________ Marliz Camargo.**
2. **Yo ____________ Ana Benavides. ____________ la secretaria de la universidad.**
3. **¿Cuál ____________ su número de teléfono, por favor?**
4. **Nosotros ____________ abogados, ¿y ustedes?**
5. **Vosotros ____________ de Bolivia y ellas ____________ de España.**
6. **Tú ____________ profesora de inglés.**
7. **Él ____________ soltero y ella ____________ casada.**
8. **Ellos ____________ venezolanos.**
9. **¿____________ usted casado o soltero?**
10. **Ustedes ____________ muy inteligentes.**

B. Now fill in the blanks with the correct form of the verb **estar**.

1. Yo __________ en el apartamento.

2. Vosotros ________________ felices.

3. Ellos ________________ en la casa.

4. ¿Cómo __________________ usted?

5. ¿Cómo ________________ vosotros?

6. Yo _________________ bien, ¿y tú?

ANSWER KEY

A. 1. es; 2. soy/Soy; 3. es; 4. somos; 5. sois/son; 6. eres; 7. es/es; 8. son; 9. Es; 10. son
B. 1. estoy; 2. estáis; 3. están; 4. está; 5. estáis; 6. estoy

Phrase Builder 2

Let's look at some common expressions using ser and estar.

2C Phrase Builder 2 (CD 4, Track 7)

¿Es usted también español?	*Are you also from Spain?*
¿Cuál es su profesión?	*What's your profession?*
Soy abogada.	*I'm a lawyer.*
¿Sois de Argentina?	*Are you from Argentina?*
No, somos colombianos.	*No, we're Colombian.*
Ustedes son artistas.	*You're artists.*
¿Cuál es su número de fax?	*What's your fax number?*
¿Cuál es su dirección de correo electrónico?	*What's your email address?*
Nosotros no somos de Brasil.	*We're not from Brazil.*
¿Cómo estás?	*How are you?*
Estoy bien, gracias.	*I'm fine, thanks.*
Estoy cansado.	*I'm tired. (male)*
Estoy cansada.	*I'm tired. (female)*

Estoy triste.	*I'm sad.*
Estás feliz.	*You're happy.*
Está mal.	*He/She is not doing well.*
¿Donde está la universidad?	*Where's the university?*
Está en la Avenida Palacios.	*It's on Avenida Palacios.*
El horno está caliente.	*The oven is hot.*
El agua está fría.	*The water is cold.*

Take It Further

Notice that you say el agua instead of la agua. That's because agua begins with a stressed vowel. If a feminine word begins with a stressed a- or ha-, use el instead of la. In the plural, though, use the regular las.

el agua/las aguas	*the water/the waters*
el hacha/las hachas	*the axe/the axes*

Phrase Practice 2

Match the Spanish sentence on the right with its English translation on the left.

1. *I'm tired. (male)*
2. *He/She is not doing well.*
3. *I'm tired. (female)*
4. *The water is cold.*
5. *You're happy.*
6. *I'm sad.*

a. **Estás feliz.**
b. **Estoy triste.**
c. **Estoy cansado.**
d. **Está mal.**
e. **El agua está fría.**
f. **Estoy cansada.**

ANSWER KEY

1. c; 2. d; 3. f; 4. e; 5. a; 6. b

Grammar Builder 2

REVIEWING NUMBERS 0-100

2D Grammar Builder 2 (CD 4, Track 8)

Before we move on to the next lesson, let's take a moment to review the numbers from 0 to 100 in Spanish. (Just remember: the more you practice, the better you'll be at recalling these when you need them!)

0	**cero**	*20*	**veinte**
1	**uno**	*21*	**veintiuno**
2	**dos**	*22*	**veintidós**
3	**tres**	*23*	**veintitrés**
4	**cuatro**	*24*	**veinticuatro**
5	**cinco**	*25*	**veinticinco**
6	**seis**	*26*	**veintiséis**
7	**siete**	*27*	**veintisiete**
8	**ocho**	*28*	**veintiocho**
9	**nueve**	*29*	**veintinueve**
10	**diez**	*30*	**treinta**
11	**once**	*31*	**treinta y uno**
12	**doce**	*32*	**treinta y dos**
13	**trece**	*40*	**cuarenta**
14	**catorce**	*50*	**cincuenta**
15	**quince**	*60*	**sesenta**
16	**dieciséis** (*or* **diez y seis**)	*70*	**setenta**
17	**diecisiete** (*or* **diez y siete**)	*80*	**ochenta**
18	**dieciocho** (*or* **diez y ocho**)	*90*	**noventa**
19	**diecinueve** (*or* **diez y nueve**)	*100*	**cien**

Notice that once you go above thirty, the numbers are formed with the tens followed by **y** (*and*) and then the number.

45	**cuarenta y cinco**	*(lit., forty and five)*
77	**setenta y siete**	*(lit., seventy and seven)*
82	**ochenta y dos**	*(lit., eighty and two)*

Work Out 2

Match the sequence of numbers on the left with the Spanish translations on the right. Be sure to say each number out loud as you answer.

1. 77, 11, 31
2. 45, 35, 25
3. 90, 100, 15
4. 67, 10, 21
5. 100, 81, 20
6. 45, 65, 19

a. **sesenta y siete, diez, veintiuno**
b. **cien, ochenta y uno, veinte**
c. **setenta y siete, once, treinta y uno**
d. **cuarenta y cinco, treinta y cinco, veinticinco**
e. **cuarenta y cinco, sesenta y cinco, diecinueve**
f. **noventa, cien, quince**

ANSWER KEY

1. c; 2. d; 3. f; 4. a; 5. b; 6. e

Culture Note

You'll hear the word **hombre** (*man*) used conversationally when two men are addressing each other. This is very similar to the conversational English use of *man*. Today, women are also beginning to use the word **mujer** (*woman*) in the same way. Also, many times, a Spanish speaker will refer to his wife as **mi mujer**, which literally means *my woman*. It is, however, not meant in a disrespectful way; that's just the word that's used. Women usually refer to their husbands as **mi marido**. The most commonly used expression for one's spouse in Latin America, however, is **mi esposa/esposo** (*my wife/husband*).

How Did You Do?

By now, you should be able to:

- ☐ Confidently conjugate **ser** and **estar**
  (Still unsure? Jump back to page 27.)
- ☐ Count to 100 without difficulty, and combine some numbers and words
  (Still unsure? Jump back to page 31.)

Word Recall

Fill in the blanks with the correct form of the verb **ser**.

1. **Yo** ______________________ **inteligente.**
2. **Tú** ______________________ **inteligente.**
3. **Él/Ella/Ud.** ______________________ **inteligente.**
4. **Nosotros** ______________________ **inteligentes.**
5. **Vosotros** ______________________ **inteligentes.**
6. **Ellos/Ellas/Uds.** ______________________ **inteligentes.**

ANSWER KEY

1. **soy**; 2. **eres**; 3. **es**; 4. **somos**; 5. **sois**; 6. **son**

Lesson 3: Sentences

By the end of this lesson, you will be able to:

- ☐ Clearly understand the difference in usage between **ser** and **estar**
- ☐ Identify nationalities and professions

Sentence Builder 1

3A Sentence Builder 1 (CD 4, Track 9)

¿Cuántos años tienen?	*How old are they?*
¿Cómo se llaman?	*What are their names?*
No me siento muy bien.	*I don't feel very well.*
Ella está un poco celosa.	*She's a bit jealous.*
Eso no es todo.	*That's not all.*
Hay cuatro alcobas.	*There are four rooms.*
Hay una cocina.	*There's a kitchen.*
Tengo dos hijos.	*I have two sons.*
No hay otra solución.	*There's no other solution.*
No me digas.	*Really? (lit., Don't tell me.)*

Take It Further

Notice that a few new words were introduced in the above sentences.

la solución	*solution*
decir	*to say*

todo/a	*all*
celoso/a	*jealous*

Don't forget the distinction in gender!

Sentence Practice 1

Fill in the blanks with the word that completes the sentence based on the English translations provided.

1. ____________ **muy bien.** *I don't feel very well.*
2. **Ella está un poco** ____________. *She's a bit jealous.*
3. **Eso no es** ____________. *That's not all.*
4. **Hay cuatro** ____________. *There are four rooms.*
5. **Tengo** ____________. *I have two sons.*
6. **No hay** ____________. *There's no other solution.*
7. ____________. *Really? (lit., Don't tell me.)*

ANSWER KEY

1. **No me siento**; 2. **celosa**; 3. **todo**; 4. **alcobas**; 5. **dos hijos**; 6. **otra solución**; 7. **No me digas.**

Grammar Builder 1

USING SER AND ESTAR

3B Grammar Builder 1 (CD 4, Track 10)

So, how are **ser** and **estar** used? The major difference, in a nutshell, is that **ser** expresses permanent, or at least long-lasting, qualities, while **estar** expresses qualities that are likely to change. **Estar** is also used to describe location, even of something that's not likely to move.

Let's start with **ser**, which is generally used in the following ways.

1. To express origin or nationality

Soy de Argentina.
I'm from Argentina.

Eres francesa.
You're French.

2. To identify people and things

¿Cuál es su nombre?
What's your name?

Mi nombre es Marta.
My name is Marta.

¿Cuál es su número de teléfono?
What's your phone number?

Es el tres dos cero tres cuatro cinco seis.
It's 320-3456.

3. To express occupation

Ella es profesora de matemáticas.
She's a professor of mathematics.

Ellos son ingenieros.
They're engineers.

4. To express permanent or inherent characteristics

El hielo es frío.
Ice is cold.

Las rosas son hermosas.
Roses are beautiful.

The verb **estar**, on the other hand, is used in the following circumstances.

1. To show location or place things in space and time

Mi hermana está en el apartamento.
My sister is in the apartment.

Londres está en Inglaterra.
London is in England.

2. To express what is temporal or accidental

El café está frío.
The coffee is cold (right now).

3. To express feelings and emotions

¡Estoy feliz!
I am happy (right now)!

As you can see, one of the main differences between **ser** and **estar** is the fact that **ser** expresses a permanent characteristic and **estar** a temporal condition or location. So, depending on the speaker's intention, in some cases either **ser** or **estar** can be used. Notice the differences.

Ella es bonita.
She's pretty (by nature).

Ella está bonita.
She looks pretty right now.

Es (un) borracho.
He's a drunk (as a characteristic).

Está borracho.
He's drunk right now.

Es triste.
He's gloomy (by nature).

Está triste.
He's feeling down.

¿Cómo eres?
What are you like? (Describe yourself.)

¿Cómo estás?
How are you? (How's your current state?)

Work Out 1

Choose the verb that best completes the sentence.

1. **Buenos Aires (es, está) en Argentina.** ____________________
2. **Juan, Pedro, y Miguel (están, son) profesores.** ____________________
3. **¡Hola! ¿Cómo (estás, eres)?** ____________________
4. **Tú y María (sois, estáis) portuguesas.** ____________________
5. **Yo (estoy, soy) en mi casa.** ____________________
6. **Mi tía y mi hermana (están, son) en el apartamento.** ____________________
7. **Yo (estoy, soy) un estudiante.** ____________________
8. **¡Hola! ¿Cómo (estáis, sois)?** ____________________

ANSWER KEY

1. **está**; 2. **son**; 3. **estás**; 4. **sois**; 5. **estoy**; 6. **están**; 7. **soy**; 8. **estáis**

Sentence Builder 2

You learned the most common greetings in *Essential Spanish*. Here are a few more informal ways to greet someone and a few sentences that can be used to make small talk.

3C Sentence Builder 2 (CD 4, Track 11)

¿Qué tal?	*What's up?*
¿Qué pasa?	*How's it going?*
¿Qué hay?	*What's up? What's going on?*
¿Cómo va todo?	*How's everything?*
Así, así.	*So-so.*
Pues, nada.	*Not much.*

Pues, aquí estamos.	*Here we are.*
Y la familia, ¿cómo está?	*How's your family doing?*
Y su esposa/o, ¿cómo va?	*How's your wife/husband?*
¿Y sus hijos?	*What about your children?*
¿Qué tal andan todos?	*How's everyone?*
Pues, bien.	*Fine.*
¿Cómo te trata la vida?	*How's life treating you?*

Sentence Practice 2

Translate the following English phrases into Spanish.

1. *How's everything?* __________
2. *So-so.* __________
3. *Not much.* __________
4. *Here we are.* __________
5. *How's your family doing?* __________
6. *How's your wife/husband?* __________
7. *What about your children?* __________
8. *How's everyone?* __________
9. *Fine.* __________
10. *How's life treating you?* __________

ANSWER KEY

1. **¿Cómo va todo?** 2. **Así, así.** 3. **Pues, nada.** 4. **Pues, aquí estamos.** 5. **Y la familia, ¿cómo está?** 6. **Y su esposa/o, ¿cómo va?** 7. **¿Y sus hijos?** 8. **¿Qué tal andan todos?** 9. **Pues, bien.** 10. **¿Cómo te trata la vida?**

Grammar Builder 2

COUNTRIES, NATIONALITIES, AND PROFESSIONS

3D Grammar Builder 2 (CD 4, Track 12)

Let's look at a list of a few nationalities and countries.

País (*country*)	**Nacionalidad** (*nationality*)
Argentina	**argentino/a**
Bolivia	**boliviano/a**
Brasil	**brasilero/a**
Canadá	**canadiense**
Chile	**chileno/a**
Colombia	**colombiano/a**
Ecuador	**ecuatoriano/a**
España	**español/a**
Estados Unidos	**estadounidense**
Inglaterra	**inglés/inglesa**
México	**mexicano/a**
Perú	**peruano/a**
Uruguay	**uruguayo/a**
Venezuela	**venezolano/a**

Take It Further

Let's also look at some common professions.

el periodista/la periodista	*journalist*
el abogado/la abogada	*lawyer*
el arquitecto/la arquitecta	*architect*

el médico/la médica	*doctor*
el policía/la policía	*police officer*
el profesor/la profesora	*teacher, professor*
el pintor/la pintora	*painter*

Work Out 2

We'll give you a country, an industry, and a gender; you tell us their nationality and profession.

1. *Spain, engineering, female* __________
2. *Uruguay, academia, male* __________
3. *Mexico, the arts, male* __________
4. *USA, law, female* __________
5. *Chile, law enforcement, female* __________

ANSWER KEY

1. **la arquitecta española**; 2. **el profesor uruguayo**; 3. **el pintor mexicano**; 4. **la abogada estadounidense**; 5. **la policía chilena**

Tip!

In trying to learn how to use **ser** and **estar**, don't get too hung up on the rules. Try to remember the basic differences and then experiment, and pay attention to how Spanish speakers use them. One way of exploring this difference is to type fragments like **"el presidente/la doctora/María es"** and **"el presidente/la doctora/María está"** into a search engine. See if you can decipher the results and identify the different nuances. You'll see that, with time, it will all start making more sense. Remember, be patient with yourself, and most of all, have fun learning the language.

How Did You Do?

By now, you should be able to:

- ☐ Clearly understand the difference in usage between **ser** and **estar**
  (Still unsure? Jump back to page 35.)
- ☐ Identify nationalities and professions
  (Still unsure? Jump back to page 41.)

Word Recall

Read each of the sentences below. Decide which form of *to be* you need to use, then write the appropriate form of **ser** or **estar** in the blank.

1. **Mi madre ________________ simpática y responsable.**
2. **Mi madre ________________ colombiana.**
3. **¿ ________________ mi madre estudiante de la universidad regional?**
4. **Mi madre ________________ buena estudiante.**
5. **Mi madre ________________ en España.**
6. **Mi madre ________________ muy contenta y feliz.**
7. **¿ ________________ mi madre enferma?**
8. **Mi madre ________________ en el restaurante nuevo.**

ANSWER KEY

1–4: **es**; 5–8: **está**

Lesson 4: Conversations

By the end of this lesson, you will be able to:

- ☐ Confidently conjugate the verb **tener** and use it in several idiomatic expressions
- ☐ Use the expression **Hay . . .** to express *there is, there are*

Conversation 1

Farina is on her third date with Fabio. She's telling him a little bit more about her personal life and her family.

4A Conversation 1 (CD 4, Track 13 - Spanish Only; Track 14 - Spanish and English)

Farina:	**Como ya sabes, estoy divorciada de mi segundo esposo y tengo dos hijos.**
Fabio:	**¿Cuántos años tienen?**
Farina:	**Bueno, el mayor tiene venticinco años y la menor tiene ocho años.**
Fabio:	**Es una diferencia de edades muy grande, ¿no? ¿Cómo se llaman?**
Farina:	**Carlos es de mi primer matrimonio y Carolina del segundo. Carlos está casado y tiene una bebita de dieciséis meses.**
Fabio:	**¡Así que eres abuela!**
Farina:	**Sí, soy abuela y me siento muy bien. ¡Estoy feliz!**
Fabio:	**¡Y tu hija ya es tía!**
Farina:	**Sí, pero ella está un poco celosa de mi nieta.**
Fabio:	**Es natural. La bebé es en este momento el centro de atracción de la familia.**

Farina:	*As you already know, I'm divorced from my second husband and I have two children.*
Fabio:	*How old are they?*

Farina:	*Well, the older one is twenty-five and the younger one is eight.*
Fabio:	*That's a big age difference, don't you think? What are their names?*
Farina:	*Carlos is from my first marriage and Carolina from the second. Carlos is married and has a sixteen-month-old baby.*
Fabio:	*So, you're a grandmother!*
Farina:	*Yes, I'm a grandmother and I feel good. I'm happy!*
Fabio:	*And your daughter is already an aunt!*
Farina:	*Yes, but she's a bit jealous of my granddaughter.*
Fabio:	*It's natural. Right now the baby is the center of attention of the whole family.*

Take It Further

In *Essential Spanish*, you learned how to ask for someone's name like this: **¿Cuál es su nombre?** That's one possibility, but Spanish speakers generally use the verb **llamarse** (*to be called*) instead.

¿Cómo se llaman?
What are their names?

¿Cómo se llama?
What is your name?

Me llamo María.
My name is María.

In the next unit, we'll learn how to conjugate regular verbs like this one.

Also remember from *Essential Spanish* that **mi** is the possessive adjective meaning *my*. We'll review the other possessive adjectives again in a later unit.

Conversation Practice 1

Fill in the blanks below with the appropriate word based on the English translations and the dialogue above.

1. **Estoy divorciada de mi segundo esposo y ________________.**

   I'm divorced from my second husband and I have two children.

2. **¿Cuántos años ________?** *How old are they?*

3. **El mayor tiene ________________ y la menor tiene ________________.** *The older one is twenty-five and the younger one is eight.*

4. **¡Así que eres ________!** *So, you're a grandmother!*

5. **¡Y tu ______ ya es ______!** *And your daughter is already an aunt!*

6. **Ella está un poco ________ de mi nieta.** *She's a bit jealous of my granddaughter.*

ANSWER KEY

1. **tengo dos hijos**; 2. **tienen**; 3. **venticinco años/ocho años**; 4. **abuela**; 5. **hija/tía**; 6. **celosa**

Grammar Builder 1

TENER (*TO HAVE*)

4B Grammar Builder 1 (CD 4, Track 15)

Let's learn more about the verb **tener** (*to have*). You'll remember from *Essential Spanish* that **tener** is an irregular verb, so let's review its forms.

TENER (*TO HAVE*)			
yo tengo	*I have*	**nosotros/as tenemos**	*we have*
tú tienes	*you have (infml.)*	**vosotros/as tenéis**	*(all of) you have (pl. fml.)*
él/ella/usted tiene	*he/she has, you have (fml.)*	**ellos/ellas/ ustedes tienen**	*they have, (all of) you have (pl. fml.)*

Remember that you use **tener** to tell a person's age.

¿Cuántos años tiene Pedro?

How old is Pedro? (lit., How many years does Pedro have?)

Pedro tiene veintitrés años.

Pedro is twenty-three years old.

It's also used to show possession, just as in English.

Tengo un apartamento en México y una casa en Paraguay.

I have an apartment in Mexico and a house in Paraguay.

The verb **tener** is also used to describe certain physical, mental, and emotional states. In most of the cases where Spanish uses **tener**, English uses *to be*.

tener frío	*to be cold*
tener calor	*to be warm*
tener sed	*to be thirsty*
tener hambre	*to be hungry*
tener sueño	*to be sleepy*
tener cansancio	*to be tired*
tener prisa	*to be in a hurry*
tener miedo	*to be scared*
tener razón	*to be right*

¿Tienes hambre?
Are you hungry?

Tengo sueño ahora.
I'm sleepy now.

Tenemos frío en enero.
We're cold in January.

Work Out 1

Fill in the blanks with the correct form of **tener**.

1. **Nosotros** ________________ **hambre y sed.**
2. **Ella** ________________ **veintisiete años y él** ________________ **cuarenta.**

3. **Vosotros ______________ una casa grande./Ustedes ______________ una casa grande.**

4. **Tú ______________ sueño.**

5. **¿Cuántos hijos ______________ tú?**

6. **¿Cuántos nietos ______________ Sara?**

7. **Yo ______________ tres primos.**

8. **Ella ______________ siete sobrinos.**

ANSWER KEY

1. **tenemos**; 2. **tiene**, **tiene**; 3. **tenéis**/**tienen**; 4. **tienes**; 5. **tienes**; 6. **tiene**; 7. **tengo**; 8. **tiene**

Conversation 2

A day after his date, Fabio meets up with his friend Jorge and tells him about the woman he's been dating.

4C Conversation 2 (CD 4, Track 16 - Spanish Only; Track 17 - Spanish and English)

Fabio:	**¡Está divorciada!**
Jorge:	**¿Tiene hijos?**
Fabio:	**Sí, dos. ¡Y encima es abuela!**
Jorge:	**¡No me digas!**
Fabio:	**Pero eso no es todo. Ella vive con sus hijos, su nuera y su nieta en un mismo apartamento.**
Jorge:	**¿Es un apartamento grande o pequeño?**
Fabio:	**Hay cuatro alcobas y una sala-comedor. Hay también una cocina y un balcón.**
Jorge:	**No está mal.**
Fabio:	**¿No está mal? ¡Los dos ex esposos viven en el edificio también!**
Jorge:	**Bueno, tienes razón. El problema es gordo.**

Fabio: **Farina es una mujer muy atractiva y divertida pero su situación familiar es difícil.**

Fabio: *She's divorced!*
Jorge: *Does she have children?*
Fabio: *Yes, two. And, on top of that, she's a grandmother!*
Jorge: *No kidding!*
Fabio: *But that's not all. She lives with her children, her daughter-in-law, and her granddaughter in the same apartment.*
Jorge: *Is it a big or a small apartment?*
Fabio: *There are four bedrooms and a living room–dining room. There's also a kitchen and a balcony.*
Jorge: *Not bad.*
Fabio: *Not bad? Her two ex-husbands are living in the building too!*
Jorge: *Well, you're right. That's a major problem.*
Fabio: *Farina is a very attractive and fun woman, but her family situation is very difficult.*

Take It Further

Notice that at the beginning of the dialogue, Fabio refers to the woman he's been on a date with as **la tía** (*the aunt*). In colloquial Spanish, the words **tío** and **tía** are used very frequently to refer to a man or a woman, just like we use the words *guy* and, less commonly, *gal* in English.

Conversation Practice 2

Fill in the blanks below with the appropriate word based on the English translations and the dialogue above.

1. **¡Y encima es ________________!** *And, on top of that, she's a grandmother!*

2. ________________ **cuatro alcobas y una sala-comedor.** *There are four bedrooms and a living room–dining room.*

3. **¡Los dos ex- ________________ viven en el edificio también!** *Her two ex-husbands are living in the building too!*

4. **Bueno, tienes ________________.** *Well, you're right.*

5. **Farina es una mujer muy ________________ y ________________ pero su situación familiar es difícil.** *Farina is a very attractive and fun woman, but her family situation is very difficult.*

ANSWER KEY

1. **abuela**; 2. **Hay**; 3. **esposos**; 4. **razón**; 5. **atractiva**, **divertida**

Grammar Builder 2

HAY (*THERE IS/THERE ARE*)

4D Grammar Builder 2 (CD 4, Track 18)

Let's review some sentences using the word **hay**, which means both *there is* and *there are*.

Hay una persona en la clase.
There's one person in the classroom.

En la casa hay tres habitaciones y un estudio.
There are three bedrooms and a study in the house.

¿Cuántas personas hay en su familia?
How many people are there in your family?

Work Out 2

Translate the following sentences, writing out the numbers in Spanish.

1. *There are seventy men and twenty women in the room.* ____________________

2. *The house has fifteen bathrooms.* ____________________

3. *I'm hungry.* ____________________
4. *The coffee is hot.* ____________________
5. *She's sleepy.* ____________________
6. *You (fml. sg.) are right.* ____________________
7. *We're hot.* ____________________
8. *They're scared.* ____________________

ANSWER KEY

1. **Hay setenta hombres y veinte mujeres en la habitación.** 2. **La casa tiene quince baños.** 3. **Tengo hambre.** 4. **El café está caliente.** 5. **Ella tiene sueño.** 6. **Usted tiene razón.** 7. **Tenemos calor.** 8. **Tienen miedo.**

Word Recall

Which **tener** expression would you use for each of the following? Answer using **Tengo** . . . .

1. *You are tired and need to sleep.* ____________________
2. *It's very hot.* ____________________

3. *It's cold.* ______________________________

4. *You are thirsty.* ______________________________

5. *You're hungry.* ______________________________

ANSWER KEY

1. **Tengo sueño.** 2. **Tengo calor.** 3. **Tengo frío.** 4. **Tengo sed.** 5. **Tengo hambre.**

How Did You Do?

By now, you should be able to:

- ☐ Confidently conjugate the verb **tener** and use it in several idiomatic expressions
(Still unsure? Jump back to page 47.)
- ☐ Use the expression **Hay . . .** to express *there is, there are*
(Still unsure? Jump back to page 51.)

Don't forget to practice and reinforce what you've learned by visiting **www.livinglanguage.com/languagelab** for flashcards, games, and quizzes for Unit 1!

Unit 1 Essentials

You're almost at the end of the first unit of *Intermediate Spanish*!

You will see Unit Essentials at the end of every unit. They are divided into two sections: Vocabulary Essentials and Grammar Essentials. The Vocabulary Essentials section is a blank "cheat sheet" for you to fill in and test yourself on the vocabulary you learned in the past four lessons. Once you've completed it, you will be able to use it along with the Grammar Essentials as your very own reference guide for all of the key material from each unit.

Vocabulary Essentials

FAMILY

	mother
	father
	boy/girl
	son/daughter
	brother/sister
	grandfather/grandmother
	aunt/uncle
	husband/wife

[Pg. 15] (If you're stuck, visit this page to review!)

OBJECTS

	book
	pen
	letter
	pencil

[Pg. 16]

HOME

	house
	building
	apartment
	living room
	dining room
	kitchen
	bathroom
	bedroom
	door
	window
	table

[Pg. 19]

PROFESSIONS

	lawyer
	artist
	secretary
	professor
	university

[Pg. 26]

EXPRESSIONS

	There is/There are . . .
	How are you?
	I'm fine, thanks.
	I'm tired. (male/female)
	to be cold
	to be warm
	to be thirsty
	to be hungry

[Pg. 48]

NUMBERS

	0		*20*
	1		*21*
	2		*22*
	3		*23*
	4		*24*
	5		*25*

	6		*26*
	7		*27*
	8		*28*
	9		*29*
	10		*30*
	11		*31*
	12		*32*
	13		*40*
	14		*50*
	15		*60*
	16		*70*
	17		*80*
	18		*90*
	19		*100*

[Pg. 31]

Grammar Essentials

ARTICLES

INDEFINITE ARTICLES	MASCULINE	FEMININE
singular	un	una
plural	unos	unas

DEFINITE ARTICLES	MASCULINE	FEMININE
singular	el	la
plural	los	las

VERBS

SER - *(TO BE)* (ORIGIN OR NATIONALITY; IDENTIFYING PEOPLE AND THINGS; OCCUPATION; PERMANENT OR INHERENT CHARACTERISTICS)			
soy	*I am*	somos	*we are*
eres	*you are (infml.)*	sois	*you are (pl. infml.)*
es	*he/she is, you are (fml.)*	son	*they are, you are (pl. fml.)*

ESTAR - *(TO BE)* (LOCATION IN SPACE AND TIME; TEMPORAL OR ACCIDENTAL; FEELINGS AND EMOTIONS)			
estoy	*I am*	estamos	*we are*
estás	*you are (infml.)*	estáis	*you are (pl. fml.)*
está	*he/she is, you are (fml.)*	están	*they are, you are (pl. fml.)*

TENER - *(TO HAVE)*			
tengo	*I have*	tenemos	*we have*
tienes	*you have (infml.)*	tenéis	*you have (pl. fml.)*
tiene	*he/she has, you have (fml.)*	tienen	*they have, you have (pl. fml.)*

Unit 1 Quiz

Let's put the most essential Spanish words and grammar points you've learned and reviewed so far to practice in a few exercises. It's essential that you have this mastered before you move on; score yourself at the end of the review and see if you need to go back for further review, or if you're ready to move on to more Spanish learning.

A. Finish the English sentence with the most appropriate word in Spanish using the proper definite article:

1. *My father's brother is my:* ______________________
2. *My mother's mother is my:* ______________________
3. *The room where we eat dinner is:* ______________________
4. *The room where we cook dinner is:* ______________________
5. *A woman who represents a defendant in court is:* ______________________

B. Fill in the blank in each sentence with the most appropriate word from the following list: **dirección**, **francesa**, **número**, **años**, **eres**

1. **¿Cuál es su** ______________________ **de teléfono?**
2. **Tú** ______________________ **profesora en la universidad.**
3. **¿Cuál es su** ______________________ **de correo electrónico?**
4. **La muchacha** ______________________ **es de París.**
5. **Carlos tiene treinta** ______________________**.**

C. Choose the best conjugation of the word in parentheses for each sentence below.

1. **Ella** ______________________ **(ser) bonita.**

2. **Usted** ______________________ **(tener) calor.**

3. **Yo** ______________________ **(estar) en Nueva York.**

4. **Nosotros** ______________________ **(ser) americanos.**

5. **¿**______________________ **(tener, tú) hambre?**

D. Blank Family Tree

Give the Spanish word for each of the family members below. Don't forget to include the definite article.

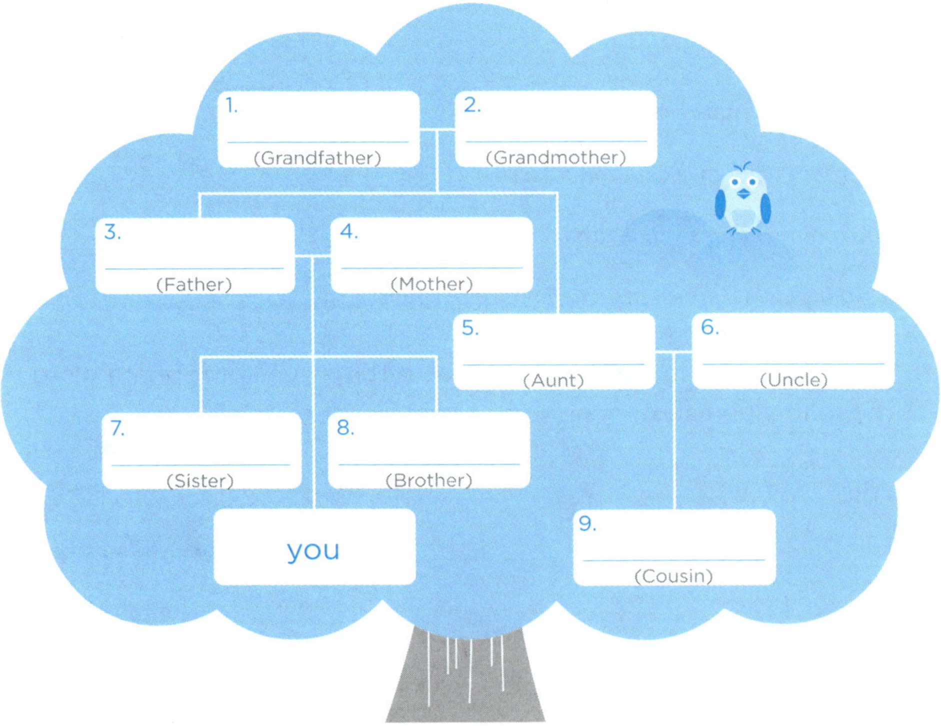

How Did You Do?

Give yourself a point for every correct answer, then use the following key to determine whether or not you're ready to move on:

0–7 points: It's probably best to go back and study the lessons again to make sure you understood everything completely. Take your time; it's not a race! Make sure you spend time reviewing vocabulary with the flashcards and reading through each grammar note carefully.

8–16 points: If the questions you missed were in sections A or B, you may want to review the vocabulary again; if you missed answers mostly in sections C or D, check the unit essentials to make sure you have your conjugations and other grammar basics down.

17–20 points: Feel free to move on to the next unit! You're doing a great job.

| | | points

ANSWER KEY

A. 1. el tío; 2. la abuela; 3. el comedor; 4. la cocina; 5. la abogada

B. 1. número; 2. eres; 3. dirección; 4. francesa; 5. años

C. 1. es; 2. tiene; 3. estoy; 4. somos; 5. tienes

D. 1. el abuelo; 2. la abuela; 3. el padre; 4. la madre; 5. la tía; 6. el tío; 7. la hermana; 8. el hermano; 9. el/la primo/a

Unit 2:
Everyday Life

In this unit you'll learn how to talk about your everyday life, what you do and when you do it, what you like to do, and what you don't like to do. You'll also learn how to ask someone about their everyday life.

By the end of this unit, you should be able to:

- ☐ Say the names of the days of the week
- ☐ Say the names of the months of the year
- ☐ Use numbers above 100
- ☐ Express the time
- ☐ Say good-bye in a variety of ways
- ☐ Talk about different times of the day
- ☐ Use adjectives to describe people and things
- ☐ Make plans with someone
- ☐ Ask questions using question words
- ☐ Tell someone what you do on certain days
- ☐ Ask yes/no questions and use tag questions
- ☐ Say what you like to do and what you don't like to do

Lesson 5: Words

By the end of this lesson, you should be able to:

- ☐ Say the names of the days of the week
- ☐ Say the names of the months of the year
- ☐ Use numbers above 100
- ☐ Express the time

Word Builder 1

5A Word Builder 1 (CD 4, Track 19)

Let's review the days of the week in Spanish and add some other useful vocabulary to your list.

la semana	*week*
el día	*day*
lunes	*Monday*
martes	*Tuesday*
miércoles	*Wednesday*
jueves	*Thursday*
viernes	*Friday*
sábado	*Saturday*
domingo	*Sunday*
el fin de semana	*weekend*
semanal	*weekly*
diario	*daily*
la mañana	*morning*

la tarde	*afternoon*
la noche	*evening, night*

Remember that in Spanish, the days of the week are not written with a capital letter.

Word Practice 1

Match the days of the week in Spanish to their English translations.

1. **miércoles**	a. *Sunday*
2. **viernes**	b. *Tuesday*
3. **domingo**	c. *Wednesday*
4. **sábado**	d. *Friday*
5. **martes**	e. *Monday*
6. **jueves**	f. *Thursday*
7. **lunes**	g. *Saturday*

ANSWER KEY

1. c; 2. d; 3. a; 4. g; 5. b; 6. f; 7. e

Grammar Builder 1

NUMBERS ABOVE 100

5B Grammar Builder 1 (CD 4, Track 20)

You already know the numbers 0 to 100. So, let's keep on counting and add some important information about using numbers above 100.

cien	*100*
ciento uno/una	*101*
ciento dos	*102*

doscientos/as	*200*
trescientos/as	*300*
cuatrocientos/as	*400*
quinientos/as	*500*
seiscientos/as	*600*
setecientos/as	*700*
ochocientos/as	*800*
novecientos/as	*900*
mil	*1,000*
mil novecientos noventa y ocho	*1,998*
diez mil	*10,000*
veinte mil	*20,000*
un millón	*1,000,000*

The hundreds not only have a masculine and a feminine form, but they are also plural.

doscientos hombres	*200 men*
cuatrocientas mujeres	*400 women*
quinientos treinta y tres niños	*533 boys (children)*
seiscientas quince niñas	*615 girls*

Usually the word **cien** is used before a noun, and the word **ciento** before any number except **mil** (*thousand*).

cien días	*100 days*
cien personas	*100 people*
ciento tres dólares	*103 dollars*
ciento setenta y siete años	*177 years*
cien mil pesos	*100,000 pesos*

Finally, the word **millón** (*million*) and others formed by using it are followed by the preposition **de** (*of*).

un millón de casas	*1,000,000 houses*
cuatro millones de personas	*4,000,000 people*

Work Out 1

Translate the following phrases. Write out the numbers in Spanish.

1. *365 days* ______
2. *52 weeks* ______
3. *10,000 people* ______
4. *1,565,000 houses* ______
5. *100 children* ______
6. *555 women* ______
7. *145 prizes* ______
8. *278 rooms* ______

ANSWER KEY

1. **trescientos sesenta y cinco días** 2. **cincuenta y dos semanas** 3. **diez mil personas** 4. **un millón quinientos sesenta y cinco mil casas**. 5. **cien niños** 6. **quinientas cincuenta y cinco mujeres** 7. **ciento cuarenta y cinco premios** 8. **doscientas setenta y ocho habitaciones**

Word Builder 2

5C Word Builder 2 (CD 4, Track 21)

Let's review the months of the year and add some other useful vocabulary.

el año	*year*
el mes	*month*
enero	*January*
febrero	*February*
marzo	*March*
abril	*April*
mayo	*May*
junio	*June*
julio	*July*
agosto	*August*
septiembre	*September*
octubre	*October*
noviembre	*November*
diciembre	*December*
la década	*decade*
el siglo	*century*
la estación	*season*
la primavera	*spring*
el verano	*summer*
el otoño	*fall*
el invierno	*winter*

Like the days of the week, the months and seasons are not capitalized in Spanish.

Word Practice 2

The months below are scrambled. Can you put them in their proper order?

septiembre	junio
diciembre	octubre
enero	mayo
noviembre	abril
marzo	febrero
agosto	julio

ANSWER KEY

enero; febrero; marzo; abril; mayo; junio; julio; agosto; septiembre; octubre; noviembre; diciembre

Grammar Builder 2

TELLING TIME

5D Grammar Builder 2 (CD 4, Track 22)

The verb **ser** comes in very handy when telling time. You can ask for the time using any of the following expressions.

¿Qué hora es?
What time is it?

¿Qué horas son?
What time is it?

¿Qué hora tiene?
What time do you have?

Usually, you answer by using the verb **ser + la(s)**, because the noun **hora** is feminine. Notice that with most hours you use **son las . . .**, but with one o'clock you use **es la . . .**

Son las doce (en punto).
12:00/It's twelve o'clock (sharp).

Es la una.
1:00/It's one o'clock.

Son las dos.
2:00/It's two o'clock.

Son las seis en punto.
6:00/It's six o'clock sharp.

Use **y** (*and*) to add minutes past the hour. Notice that you can use **cuarto** (*quarter*) or **quince** (*fifteen*) for a quarter of an hour and **media** (*half*) or **treinta** (*thirty*) for a half an hour.

Es la una y diez.
1:10/It's ten after one.

Son las cuatro y veinte.
4:20/It's twenty after four.

Es la una y quince.
1:15/It's one fifteen.

Son las tres y cuarto.
3:15/It's a quarter after three.

Son las nueve y treinta.
9:30/It's nine thirty.

Son las once y media.
11:30/It's eleven thirty.

Son las siete y cuarenta y cinco.
7:45/It's seven forty-five.

When telling time past the half hour, you subtract the minutes from the hour and use **menos** (*less*), like this.

Es la una menos cinco.
12:55/It's five to one.

Es la una menos cuarto.
12:45/It's a quarter to one.

Son las cuatro menos veinte.
3:40/It's twenty to four.

Son las ocho menos cuarto.
7:45/It's a quarter to eight.

You learned a few words for divisions of the day in your word list. Here they are again, with a few more expressions that will come in handy in telling the time.

la mañana	*morning*
el mediodía	*noon*
la tarde	*afternoon*
la noche	*evening, night*

la media noche	*midnight*
la madrugada	*late night, early morning (from midnight till daybreak)*

Because we normally don't use military time, you can specify the time of day when telling time with phrases like the following.

Es la una y diez de la madrugada.
1:10/It's ten after one in the morning.

Son las cuatro menos veinte de la mañana.
3:40/It's twenty to four in the morning.

Son las nueve y treinta de la noche.
9:30/It's nine thirty at night.

Es la una y diez de la tarde.
1:10/It's ten after one in the afternoon.

Notice that when the preposition **de** is followed by the masculine article **el**, it forms the contraction **del**.

Son las doce del mediodía.
It's twelve noon.

Work Out 2

What time is it? Write out your answers in complete words in Spanish.

1. *7:15 p.m.* ______________________________

____

2. *3:20 p.m.* ______

3. *1:45 a.m.* ______

4. *8:00 a.m.* ______

5. *2:30 p.m.* ______

6. *12:55 p.m.* ______

7. *6:45 a.m.* ______

8. *1:35 p.m.* ______

9. *9:10 a.m.* ______

ANSWER KEY

1. **Son las siete y cuarto (y quince) de la noche.** 2. **Son las tres y veinte de la tarde.** 3. **Es la una y cuarenta y cinco de la madrugada./Son las dos menos cuarto de la madrugada.** 4. **Son las ocho de la mañana.** 5. **Son las dos y treinta (y media) de la tarde.** 6. **Son las doce y cincuenta y cinco del medio día./Es la una menos cinco.** 7. **Son las seis y cuarenta y cinco de la mañana./Son las siete menos cuarto de la mañana.** 8. **Es la una y treinta y cinco de la tarde./Son las dos menos veinticinco de la tarde.** 9. **Son las nueve y diez de la mañana.**

Take It Further

Take a closer look at how numbers are written in Spanish and in English. Those little commas and periods we all love (especially when dealing with large amounts of money) signal something completely different.

5.000 (cinco mil)
5,000 (five thousand)

19,95 (diecinueve coma noventa y cinco)
19.95 (nineteen point ninety-five)

10.540,80 (diez mil quinientos cuarenta coma ochenta)
10,540.80 (ten thousand, five hundred forty point eighty)

Word Recall

What time is it? Below you will find different times; express what time it is in Spanish.

1. *1:00 p.m.* ______________________________

2. *1:15 p.m.* ______________________________

3. *1:30 p.m.* ______________________________

4. *1:45 p.m.* ______________________________

5. *2:00 p.m.* ______________________

____

ANSWER KEY

1. **Es la una de la tarde.** 2. **Es la una y cuarto/quince de la tarde.** 3. **Es la una y media de la tarde.** 4. **Es la una y cuarenta y cinco de la tarde./Son las dos menos cuarto de la tarde.** 5. **Son las dos de la tarde.**

How Did You Do?

By now you should be able to:

- ☐ Say the names of the days of the week
  (Still unsure? Jump back to page 63.)
- ☐ Say the names of the months of the year
  (Still unsure? Jump back to page 67.)
- ☐ Use numbers above 100
  (Still unsure? Jump back to page 64.)
- ☐ Express the time
  (Still unsure? Jump back to page 68.)

Lesson 6: Phrases

By the end of this lesson, you should be able to:

- ☐ Say good-bye in a variety of ways
- ☐ Talk about different times of the day
- ☐ Use adjectives to describe people and things

Phrase Builder 1

6A Phrase Builder 1 (CD 4, Track 23)

You've already seen a number of different ways to greet someone. How about saying good-bye? Here are a few phrases to help you out.

Adiós.	*Good-bye.*
Hasta luego.	*Until later.*
Hasta pronto.	*See you soon. (lit., Until soon).*
Hasta mañana.	*Until tomorrow.*
Hasta más tarde.	*Until later.*
Hasta entonces.	*Till then.*
Chao.	*Bye.*
Nos vemos.	*See you. (lit., We see each other.)*
Que estés bien. *(infml.)*	*Take care. (lit., May you be well.)*
Que esté bien. *(fml.)*	*Take care. (lit., May you be well.)*

Phrase Practice 1

Translate the phrases you just learned into Spanish.

1. *Good-bye.* __________
2. *Until later.* __________
3. *See you soon. (lit., Until soon).* __________
4. *Until tomorrow.* __________
5. *Till then.* __________
6. *See you. (lit., We see each other.)* __________

7. *Take care.(lit., May you be well.) (infml.)* ______________________

ANSWER KEY

1. **Adiós.** 2. **Hasta luego./Hasta más tarde.** 3. **Hasta pronto.** 4. **Hasta mañana.** 5. **Hasta entonces.** 6. **Nos vemos.** 7. **Que estés bien.** *(infml.)*

Grammar Builder 1

ADJECTIVE AGREEMENT

6B Grammar Builder 1 (CD 4, Track 24)

Remember that adjectives are words that you use to describe nouns. So *big, intelligent, interesting*, and *horrible* are adjectives in English. Don't forget that nouns in Spanish have gender (masculine or feminine) and number (singular or plural), and adjectives must agree with the nouns that they describe or modify.

un hombre panameño	*a Panamanian man*
una mujer panameña	*a Panamanian woman*
unos hombres panameños	*a few Panamanian men*
unas mujeres panameñas	*a few Panamanian women*

As you can see from the above examples, adjectives usually come after the nouns they modify. The typical adjective endings are **-o** for masculine singular, **-a** for feminine singular, **-os** for masculine plural, and **-as** for feminine plural. If an adjective ends in **-e**, (**grande,** *big*), then it has the same form in the singular for both genders (**grande**) and adds **-s** for both genders in the plural (**grandes**). There are a few irregularities that we'll get to, but that's the basic picture.

Here are some adjectives you can use to describe people and things. Notice that just the singular forms are given. You can make the plurals just by adding **-s** to the appropriate singular form.

alto(a)/bajo(a)	*tall/short*
gordo(a)/delgado(a)	*fat/thin*

largo(a)/corto(a)	*long/short*
ancho(a)/angosto(a)	*wide/narrow*
grande/pequeño(a)	*big/small*
rico(a)/pobre	*rich/poor*
costoso(a)/barato(a)	*expensive/cheap*
limpio(a)/sucio(a)	*clean/dirty*
libre/ocupado(a)	*free/busy*
bueno(a)/malo(a)	*good/bad*
agradable/desagradable	*pleasant/unpleasant*
temprano/tarde	*early/late*
divertido(a)/aburrido(a)	*fun/boring*
bonito(a)/feo(a)	*pretty/ugly*

Here are some examples using **ser**. Remember that the adjectives all agree with the person or thing they modify.

Soy alto.
I'm tall.

Eres delgada.
You're thin.

El apartamento es pequeño.
The apartment is small.

Ella es rica.
She's rich.

Somos pobres.
We are poor.

Vosotros sois divertidos.

You are fun.

Ellos son agradables.

They are pleasant.

Son bajos.

They are short.

Let's look at some more examples, this time with **tener**.

Tengo una casa grande.

I have a big house.

Tiene una abuela rica.

He/She has a rich grandmother.

Tenemos un día libre.

We have a free day.

Tienen un tío divertido.

They have a fun uncle.

Work Out 1

Connect each noun on the left with its appropriate matching adjective on the right and answer in a complete sentence using a form of **ser**.

1. **el día** — a. **larga**
2. **el libro** — b. **costosas**

3. las cafeteras c. divertida
4. la semana d. aburrido
5. los apartamentos e. corto
6. la comedia f. pequeños

ANSWER KEY
1. El día es corto. 2. El libro es aburrido. 3. Las cafeteras son costosas. 4. La semana es larga. 5. Los apartamentos son pequeños. 6. La comedia es divertida.

Phrase Builder 2

6C Phrase Builder 2 (CD 4, Track 25)

por la mañana	*in the morning*
por la tarde	*in the afternoon*
por la noche	*in the evening, at night*
al mediodía	*at noon*
a la medianoche	*at midnight*
a la madrugada	*in the early morning, at dawn*
al* amanecer	*at dawn*
al atardecer	*at dusk*
Se me hace tarde.	*I'm late.*
Es muy temprano.	*It's very early.*

*Remember how **de** + **el** = **del**? Well, the same thing happens with **a** (*to, at*) plus **el**: **a** + **el** = **al** (*to the, at the*) in the expressions **al amanecer** and **al atardecer**.

Phrase Practice 2

Translate the phrases below.

1. *in the morning* ______________________

2. *in the afternoon* ______________________

3. *in the evening, at night* ______________________

4. *at noon* ______________________

5. *at midnight* ______________________

6. *I'm late.* ______________________

7. *It's very early.* ______________________

ANSWER KEY

1. **por la mañana**; 2. **por la tarde**; 3. **por la noche**; 4. **al mediodía**; 5. **a la medianoche**; 6. **Se me hace tarde.** 7. **Es muy temprano.**

Grammar Builder 2

MORE ON ADJECTIVE AGREEMENT

6D Grammar Builder 2 (CD 4, Track 26)

Let's get back to adjectives and adjective agreement, so you know how to describe things in Spanish. Again, as with nouns, adjectives ending in **-o** are masculine, and the feminine is formed by changing the **-o** to **-a**. To form the plural, just add **-s** to the singular form.

	MASCULINE SINGULAR	FEMININE SINGULAR	MASCULINE PLURAL	FEMININE PLURAL
pretty	**bonito**	**bonita**	**bonitos**	**bonitas**
ugly	**feo**	**fea**	**feos**	**feas**

Es un jardín muy bonito.

It's a very pretty garden.

Es una foto muy fea.

It's a very ugly photo.

Tienen unos jardines bonitos.
They have some pretty gardens.

Tienen unas fotos feas.
They have some ugly pictures.

As you know, there are some adjectives that end in **-e**, like **grande** (*big*), **pobre** (*poor*), **libre** (*free*), and so on. These adjectives only have one singular form for both masculine and feminine. There are other adjectives that end in a consonant, like **difícil** (*difficult*) and **fácil** (*easy*). These adjectives also only have one singular form. Both of these types of adjectives end in **-es** in the plural.

Ella es una niña inteligente.
She's an intelligent girl.

Él es un chico inteligente.
He's an intelligent kid.

Son inteligentes.
They're intelligent.

Notice that **trabajador** (*hardworking*) ends in a consonant but has two singular forms.

Tienen un hermano trabajador.
They have a hardworking brother.

Ella es trabajadora.
She's hardworking.

Tienen unos padres trabajadores.
They have hardworking parents.

The exceptions to the above rule are those adjectives used to denote nationalities. Most of them end in a consonant, and the feminine is formed by adding **-a** to the end.

Yo soy española y él es alemán.
I'm Spanish and he's German.

Ella es alemana y ellos son franceses.
She's German and they're French.

Tú eres francesa y él es español.
You're French and he's Spanish.

Work Out 2

Form sentences using the words given. Make sure you use the correct form of the verb. Adjectives are given in the singular, masculine form, so you may have to change them.

1. **yo / tener / treinta / películas / divertido** ______

2. **casas / ser / feo** ______

3. **tú / tener / dos apartamentos / grande** ______

4. **ella / ser / inglés** ______

5. **las niñas / ser / alto y bonito** ______

6. **yo / tener / un día / libre** ______________________________

____

7. **vosotros / tener / unos tíos / rico** ______________________________

____

8. **ustedes / tener / unos tíos / rico** ______________________________

____

ANSWER KEY

1. **Yo tengo treinta películas divertidas.** 2. **Las casas son feas.** 3. **Tú tienes dos apartamentos grandes.** 4. **Ella es inglesa.** 5. **Las niñas son altas y bonitas.** 6. **Yo tengo un día libre.** 7. **Vosotros tenéis unos tíos ricos.** 8. **Ustedes tienen unos tíos ricos.**

Culture Note

You've probably heard the term **realismo mágico** (*magical realism*), which refers to a Latin American literary movement. The origin of the term has been attributed to the Cuban writer Alejo Carpentier, who first applied it to Latin American fiction in 1949. The main characteristic of magical realism is the matter-of-fact incorporation of fantastic or dreamlike elements into otherwise realistic fiction. The Colombian writer Gabriel García Márquez is probably the movement's best known proponent. His most famous novel is **Cien años de soledad** (*One Hundred Years of Solitude*). Other magic realist writers include Guatemala's Miguel Ángel Asturias, Argentina's Julio Córtazar, Mexico's Carlos Fuentes, and Chile's Isabel Allende.

Reading short stories by these writers might be a good way for you to get an introduction to Latin American literature and, in doing so, learn some adjectives!

Word Recall

Write the correct form of the adjective **bonito**.

1. **El apartamento es** ______________________________ .

2. **El niño es** ______________________________.

3. **La casa es** ______________________________.

4. **La niña es** ______________________________.

5. **Los apartamentos son** ______________________________.

6. **Los niños son** ______________________________.

7. **Las casas son** ______________________________.

8. **Las niñas son** ______________________________.

ANSWER KEY

1-2: **bonito**; 3-4: **bonita**; 5-6: **bonitos**; 7-8: **bonitas**

How Did You Do?

By now you should be able to:

- ☐ Say goodbye in a variety of ways
  (Still unsure? Jump back to page 75.)
- ☐ Talk about different times of the day
  (Still unsure? Jump back to page 79.)
- ☐ Use adjectives to describe people and things
  (Still unsure? Jump back to pages 76 and 80.)

Lesson 7: Sentences

By the end of this lesson, you should be able to:

- ☐ Make plans with someone

☐ Ask questions using question words

Sentence Builder 1

7A Sentence Builder 1 (CD 4, Track 27)

¿Cómo estás de tiempo?	*Do you have time?/How are you doing for time?*
¿Qué tal si nos encontramos para almorzar?	*How about if we meet for lunch?*
¿Qué te parece si nos reunimos al mediodía?	*How about if we meet at noon?*
¿Conoces el lugar?	*Do you know the place?*
¿Qué tal si vamos al cine?	*How about if we go to the movies?*
¿Tienes la cartelera de cine a la mano?	*Do you have the movie listings handy?*
Quedamos a las ocho, ¿no?	*We meet at eight, don't we?*
¿Por qué no escogemos una comedia?	*Why don't we choose a comedy?*

Sentence Practice 1

Translate the following questions into Spanish.

1. *Do you have time?/How are you doing for time?* ______________________________

____

2. *How about if we meet for lunch?* ______________________________

____

3. *How about if we meet at noon?* ___

4. *Do you know the place?* ___

5. *How about if we go to the movies?* ___

6. *Do you have the movie listings handy?* ___

7. *We meet at eight, don't we?* ___

8. *Why don't we choose a comedy?* ___

ANSWER KEY

1. **¿Cómo estás de tiempo?** 2. **¿Qué tal si nos encontramos para almorzar?** 3. **¿Qué te parece si nos reunimos al mediodía?** 4. **¿Conoces el lugar?** 5. **¿Qué tal si vamos al cine?** 6. **¿Tienes la cartelera de cine a la mano?** 7. **Quedamos a las ocho, ¿no?** 8. **¿Por qué no escogemos una comedia?**

Grammar Builder 1

QUESTION WORDS

7B Grammar Builder 1 (CD 4, Track 28)

You have seen examples of yes/no questions previously in this course, for instance: **¿Es Marta de Madrid o de Barcelona?** (*Is Marta from Madrid or Barcelona?*). We'll come back to yes/no questions in a moment. For now let's look at questions with question words like *who, what, where, when,* and so on. Here are a few question words in Spanish.

cómo	*how*
qué	*what*
quién	*who*
cuándo	*when*

You already know how to use **cómo** to greet people and to ask for a description of something or someone. It's also used when you don't understand what has been said. Notice that **cómo** comes at the beginning of the question and that the subject (if it's not dropped) and verb are reversed.

¿Cómo estás?
How are you?

¿Cómo es la película?
How's the movie?

¿Cómo se llama?
What is your name? (lit., How are you called?)

¿Cómo se llama la profesora?
What's the teacher's name?

¿Cómo?
What?/Pardon me?

The word **qué** is used to ask for an explanation or an identification. It's also used to ask when something is happening.

¿Qué es eso?
What is that?

¿Qué es la filosofía?
What is philosophy?

¿Qué hora es?
What time is it?

¿A qué hora es la película?
At what time is the movie?

Quién is used to request the identification of a person. In Spanish it has a plural form (**quiénes**).

¿Quién es ella?
Who is she?

¿Quiénes son ustedes?
Who are you?

¿Quién es su padre?
Who's your father?

¿Quiénes son sus padres?
Who are your parents?

Finally, **cuándo** is used to ask when something is taking place.

¿Cuándo es la película?
When is the movie?

¿Cuándo tienes el día libre?

When do you have a free day?

¿Cuándo está ocupada?

When is she busy?

Work Out 1

Translate the following sentences.

1. *When do you have time? (infml. sg.)* ____________________

2. *How are you doing? (infml. pl.)* ____________________

3. *At what time is the movie?* ____________________

4. *Who are the children?* ____________________

5. *How's the coffee?* ____________________

6. *What time is it?* ____________________

ANSWER KEY

1. ¿Cuándo tienes tiempo? 2. ¿Cómo estáis? 3. ¿A qué hora es la película? 4. ¿Quiénes son los niños? 5. ¿Cómo está el café? 6. ¿Qué hora es?

Sentence Builder 2

7C Sentence Builder 2 (CD 4, Track 29)

El lunes trabajo horas extras.	*On Monday I work extra hours.*
Los martes tengo clases en la universidad.	*On Tuesday I have classes at the university.*
Esa es una mejor idea.	*That's a better idea.*
No, al mediodía no me va bien.	*No, noontime is not good for me.*
Hablamos luego.	*We'll talk later.*
A mí tampoco me gustan.	*I don't like them either.*
Estoy muy ocupada.	*I'm very busy.*
¿Tienes la cartelera de cine a la mano?	*Do you have the movie listings handy?*

Sentence Practice 2

Translate the following sentences into Spanish.

1. *On Monday I work extra hours.* ______________________

2. *On Tuesday I have classes at the university.* ______________________

3. *That's a better idea.* ______________________

4. *No, noontime is not good for me.* ______________________

5. *We'll talk later.* ______________________

____

6. *I don't like them either.* ______________________

____

7. *I'm very busy.* ______________________

____

8. *Do you have the movie listings handy?* ______________________

____

ANSWER KEY

1. **El lunes trabajo horas extras.** 2. **Los martes tengo clases en la universidad.** 3. **Esa es una mejor idea.** 4. **No, al mediodía no me va bien.** 5. **Hablamos luego.** 6. **A mí tampoco me gustan.** 7. **Estoy muy ocupada.** 8. **¿Tienes la cartelera de cine a la mano?**

Grammar Builder 2

MORE QUESTION WORDS

7D Grammar Builder 2 (CD 5, Track 1)

Here are some more useful question words.

dónde	*where*
cuánto	*how much, how many*
cuál	*which*
por qué	*why*

Dónde is used with **estar** to ask for the location of something. In order to ask for the origin of something/someone, the phrase **de dónde** (*from where*) is used along with the verb **ser**.

¿Dónde está el restaurante?
Where is the restaurant?

¿Dónde están las niñas?
Where are the girls?

¿De dónde eres?
Where are you from?

Cuánto has a feminine form, **cuánta**, and the plural forms **cuántos/as**.

¿Cuánto es el apartamento?
How much is the apartment?

¿Cuánto dinero tienes?
How much money do you have?

¿Cuánta leche quieres?
How much milk do you want?

¿Cuántos días hay en una semana?
How many days are there in a week?

¿Cuántas horas tiene un día?
How many hours does a day have?

Cuál also has a plural form (**cuáles**) and is used when asking about something that belongs to a group.

¿Cuál es su casa?
Which is your house?

¿Cuáles son sus libros?
Which are your books?

Finally, there is **por qué**, which means *why*.

¿Por qué es delgado?
Why is he thin?

¿Por qué está María en Costa Rica?
Why is María in Costa Rica?

¿Por qué tienes sueño?
Why are you sleepy?

Work Out 2

Write a question for each of the following answers.

1. **El hotel tiene cuatrocientas cincuenta habitaciones.** ______________________

2. **La película es a las tres y media de la tarde.** ______________________

3. **Colombia está en Sudamérica.** ______________________

4. **Estoy cansado.** ______________________

5. **Tengo cinco hermanos.** ____________________

____

ANSWER KEY

1. **¿Cuántas habitaciones tiene el hotel?** 2. **¿A qué hora es la película?** 3. **¿Dónde está Colombia?** 4. **¿Cómo estás/está?** 5. **¿Cuántos hermanos tienes/tiene?**

Take It Further

In Spanish, the context of a sentence is very important, because speakers tend to drop the subject pronouns and only use them when they want to show emphasis or when they're absolutely necessary for clarity. In all cases, the verb ending helps you determine who the subject of the sentence is. But this is not the case with the third person singular and plural, because these verb endings are used with a few different subjects. Let's take a look at the following question.

¿Cuándo está libre?

This could be referring to **usted**, **él**, or **ella**.

And how about this one:

¿Cuándo están libres?

It could be referring to **ustedes**, **ellos**, or **ellas**.

When you need to use the pronoun for clarification, simply insert it after the verb.

¿Cuándo está usted libre?
When are you free?

¿Cuándo está ella libre?
When is she free?

¿Cuándo están ustedes libres?
When are you free?

¿Cuándo están ellos libres?
When are they free?

Word Recall

Fill in the blank according to the hint in parentheses.

1. ¿ ________________ **es la película?** *(when?)*
2. ¿ ________________ **es el almuerzo?** *(when?)*
3. ¿ ________________ **trabajas?** *(where?)*
4. ¿ ________________ **comes?** *(where?)*
5. ¿ ________________ **es el muchacho?** *(who?)*
6. ¿ ________________ **es la muchacha?** *(who?)*
7. ¿ ________________ **son los muchachos?** *(who?)*
8. ¿ ________________ **son las muchachas?** *(who?)*

ANSWER KEY

1-2: **Cuándo**; 3-4: **Dónde**; 5-6: **Quién**; 7-8: **Quiénes**

How Did You Do?

By now, you should be able to:

□ Make plans with someone
(Still unsure? Jump back to page 85.)

- ☐ Ask questions using question words
(Still unsure? Jump back to pages 86 and 91.)

Lesson 8: Conversations

By the end of this lesson, you should be able to:

- ☐ Tell someone what you do on certain days
- ☐ Ask yes/no questions and use tag questions
- ☐ Say what you like to do and what you don't like to do

Conversation 1

8A Conversation 1 (CD 5, Track 2 - Spanish Only; Track 3 - Spanish and English)

Clara and Margarita have been friends since high school. They haven't seen each other since graduation, and they're trying to set up a time to meet.

Clara: **¿Cómo estás de tiempo? Cualquier día después del trabajo me viene bien.**

Margarita: **Estoy muy ocupada. El lunes trabajo horas extras en la oficina. Los martes y jueves tengo clases en la universidad. Y los miércoles practico deporte. El único día que tengo libre es el viernes y generalmente se lo dedico a mi novio.**

Clara: **Sí, entiendo ... Bueno, y ¿qué tal si nos encontramos para almorzar?**

Margarita: **Esa es una mejor idea. ¿Qué te parece si nos reunimos este martes al mediodía?**

Clara: **No, el martes al mediodía no me va bien. Mejor por la tarde y tomamos un café. ¿Conoces un sitio que se llama "Chocolate y churros"?**

Margarita:	**Sí, es un lugar muy agradable. Me gustan mucho las tortas que tienen, pero son un poco costosas.**
Clara:	**Ay, lo siento Margarita, ya son las dos y media y se me hace tarde. Hablamos luego.**
Margarita:	**Bueno, que estés bien. Adiós.**
Clara:	**Chao.**

Clara:	*Do you have time? Any day after work is fine with me.*
Margarita:	*I'm very busy. On Monday I work extra hours in the office. On Tuesdays and Thursdays I have classes at school. And Wednesdays I play sports. The only day I have free is Friday, and I usually set that aside for my boyfriend (lit., dedicate it to him, to my boyfriend).*
Clara:	*Yes, I understand . . . Well, and how about if we meet for lunch?*
Margarita:	*That's a better idea. How about if we meet this Tuesday at noon?*
Clara:	*No, Tuesday at noon is not good for me. It'd be better in the afternoon for a coffee. Do you know a place called "Chocolate y churros"?*
Margarita:	*Yes, it's a very nice place. I like the cakes they have very much, but they're a bit expensive.*
Clara:	*Oh, sorry, Margarita, it's already two thirty and I'm running late. We'll talk later.*
Margarita:	*Okay . . . take care. Good-bye.*
Clara:	*Bye.*

Take It Further

Notice that the days of the week are masculine, so the masculine article is always used except after the verb **ser**.

Trabajo horas extras el lunes.

I work extra hours on Monday.

Hoy es martes.
Today is Tuesday.

Also notice that when talking about an activity that happens with a certain frequency on a certain day of the week, the plural is used.

Los miércoles hago deporte.
I play sports on Wednesdays.

Estudio los sábados.
I study on Saturdays.

There are plenty of examples of new verbs in this dialogue: trabajo (*I work*), practico (*I play, I practice*), dedico (*I dedicate*), and so on. You'll learn all about verb conjugation in the next unit.

Conversation Practice 1

Unscramble the sentences from the dialogue above. The English sentence is unscrambled.

1. **¿/estás/de/cómo/tiempo/?** *Do you have time?* ______________________

____

2. **una/idea/es/mejor/esa/.** *That's a better idea.* ______________________

____

3. **¿/un/llama/sitio/se/"Chocolate y churros"/que/conoces/?** *Do you know a place called "Chocolate y Churros"?* ______________________

____

4. **es/agradable/lugar/sí/muy/un/.** *Yes, it's a very nice place.* ________________

____

5. **gustan/costosas/mucho/las/me/son/tortas/que/poco/pero/tienen/un/.** *I like the cakes they have very much, but they're a bit expensive.* ________________

____

ANSWER KEY

1. ¿Cómo estás de tiempo? 2. Es una idea mejor. 3. Conoces un sitio que se llama "Chocolate y churros"? 4. Sí, es un lugar muy agradable. 5. Me gustan mucho las tortas que tienen, pero son un poco costosas.

Grammar Builder 1

YES/NO QUESTIONS

8B Grammar Builder 1 (CD 5, Track 4)

Question words like the ones we saw in Lesson 7 are one way of making questions. Yes/no questions are another type of question, and they're very simple to form. All you need to do is put the verb at the beginning of the sentence.

¿Eres boliviana?
Are you Bolivian?

¿Tienes hermanos?
Do you have brothers and sisters?

Notice that subject pronouns are often left out; they are only used for emphasis or to clarify. If they are used, or if a subject noun is used, they come after the verb.

¿Es (usted) profesora?
Are you a teacher?

¿Tiene (ella) el libro?
Does she have the book?

¿Es Marta de Costa Rica?
Is Marta from Costa Rica?

¿Tienen los niños tiempo?
Do the children have time?

Or-questions are formed in a similar way.

¿Eres soltero o casado?
Are you single or married?

¿Está Jorge en la casa o en la oficina?
Is Jorge at home or in the office?

In English, you can ask what's called a *tag question,* as in *He's a blast, isn't he?* or *They aren't much fun, are they?* In Spanish, the equivalents of tag questions can be formed with either **¿no?** (*no?*) or **¿verdad?** (*right?*) at the end of the question. Notice the difference in punctuation.

Eres soltera, ¿no?
You're single, aren't you?

Tienes dos hermanos, ¿verdad?
You have two brothers, don't you?

Él está en Londres y ella en Bogotá, ¿no?
He's in London and she's in Bogotá, right?

Work Out 1

Fill in the blank with the correct form of the verb in parentheses.

1. Ellos ______________ una casa en Madrid, ¿verdad? (tener)
2. ¿ ______________ usted colombiana? (ser)
3. Tú ______________ en la oficina, ¿verdad? (estar)
4. ¿Cuántas habitaciones ______________ el apartamento? (tener)
5. Nosotros ______________ solteros. (ser)
6. Vosotros ______________ en Quito, ¿verdad? (estar)
7. ¿Por qué ______________ usted sed? (tener)
8. ¡Nosotros ______________ hambre! (tener)

ANSWER KEY

1. tienen; 2. Es; 3. estás; 4. tiene; 5. somos; 6. estáis; 7. tiene; 8. tenemos

Conversation 2

8C Conversation 2 (CD 5, Track 5 - Spanish Only; Track 6 - Spanish and English)

Clara and Margarita had so much fun having coffee together and remembering the good old days that they have decided to get together over the weekend and go to the movies with their boyfriends. They're setting it all up over the phone.

Clara:	Bueno, y ¿qué tal si vamos los cuatro al cine este fin de semana?
Margarita:	Sí, sería divertido.
Clara:	¿Qué películas les gustan?
Margarita:	A mí me gustan mucho las películas de suspenso, pero Rafael las detesta.
Clara:	A mí tampoco me gustan. Prefiero las películas románticas o las comedias.

Margarita: **Bueno, ¿por qué no escogemos una comedia? ¿Tienes la cartelera de cine a la mano?**

Clara: **Sí, aquí la tengo. A ver ... Bueno, solamente hay dos películas: Dos bobos en apuros y Chanchitos en el espacio.**

Margarita: **No sé ... pero Chanchitos en el espacio suena divertida. La otra película parece aburrida, ¿no crees?**

Clara: **Sí, tienes razón.**

Margarita: **¿A qué hora la dan?**

Clara: **A las diez menos cuarto de la noche.**

Margarita: **Ya está ... Quedamos a las ocho en el bar que está al otro lado del teatro, ¿no?**

Clara: **A las ocho es muy temprano. Mejor a las nueve. Hasta entonces.**

Margarita: **Hasta luego.**

Clara: *Well, how about if the four of us go to the movies this weekend?*

Margarita: *Yes, that would be fun.*

Clara: *What movies do you like?*

Margarita: *I like suspense movies very much, but Rafael hates them.*

Clara: *I don't like them either. I prefer romantic or funny movies.*

Margarita: *Well, how about if we choose a comedy? Do you have the movie listings handy?*

Clara: *Yes, here they are. Let's see ... There are only two movies: Two Dummies in a Jam and Piglets in Space.*

Margarita: *I don't know ... but Piglets in Space sounds like fun. The other movie seems boring, don't you think?*

Clara: *Yes, you're right.*

Margarita: *What time is it playing?*

Clara: *At a quarter to ten.*

Margarita: *That's it. We're meeting at eight at the bar that's across from the theater, right?*

Clara: *Eight is too early. Nine is better. See you then.*

Margarita: *See you then.*

Take It Further

In Spanish, a simple **sí** or **no** is enough to answer short yes/no questions. However, because this way of answering is a bit brief, it is better to try to give a bit more information by using other short phrases or repeating the verb used in the question.

¿Tienes la cartelera de cine a la mano?
Do you have the movie listings handy?

Sí, aquí la tengo.
Yes, here they are (lit., Yes, I have it here.)

¿Están tus padres en casa?
Are your parents home?

Sí, sí están.
Yes, they are.

Conversation Practice 2

Fill in the blanks below with the appropriate word based on the English translations and the dialogue above.

1. **¿Qué películas les ____________________?** *What movies do you like?*
2. **A mí me gustan mucho las películas de suspenso, pero Rafael las __________.**

   I like suspense movies very much, but Rafael hates them.

3. ______________ **las películas románticas o las comedias.** *I prefer romantic or funny movies.*

4. **La otra película parece** ____________________, **¿no crees?** *The other movie seems boring, don't you think?*

5. **A las** ______________________________ **de la noche.** *At a quarter to ten.*

6. ________________________ **a las ocho en el bar que está al otro lado del teatro, ¿no?** *We're meeting at eight at the bar that's across from the theater, right?*

ANSWER KEY

1. **gustan**; 2. **detesta**; 3. **Prefiero**; 4. **aburrida**; 5. **diez menos cuarto**; 6. **Quedamos**

Grammar Builder 2

SAYING WHAT YOU LIKE TO DO

8D Grammar Builder 2 (CD 5, Track 7)

Here are some verbs that may come in handy when talking about things you usually do.

trabajar	*to work*
bailar	*to dance*
cantar	*to sing*
comer	*to eat*
beber	*to drink*
nadar	*to swim*
trotar	*to jog*
escribir	*to write*
dormir	*to sleep*

All of these verbs are in the infinitive, or basic, form, which corresponds to the *to* form in English. In the next unit, you'll learn how verbs are conjugated in Spanish—for example, how to say *I swim* or *she swims* instead of *to swim*. But before that, you can start using these infinitive forms with the very useful expression **me gusta** (*I like*).

Me gusta bailar.
I like to dance.

Me gusta nadar.
I like to swim.

Me gusta hablar español.
I like to speak Spanish.

Gusta is a form of the verb **gustar**, which literally means *to be pleasing*. In Spanish, when you say *I like X*, you say *X is pleasing to me*. If the thing you like is a verb, the form **gusta** is always used, as in the above examples. You also use **gusta** if you like a singular person or thing.

Me gusta el libro.
I like the book.

Me gusta el nuevo profesor.
I like the new teacher.

If you like more than one person or thing, you use **gustan**.

Me gustan los fines de semana.
I like weekends.

Me gustan los libros interesantes.
I like interesting books.

Me gustan los actores mexicanos.
I like Mexican actors.

To say that you don't like something, use **no me gusta** or **no me gustan** (*I don't like*).

No me gusta cantar.
I don't like to sing.

No me gusta trotar.
I don't like to jog.

No me gustan los lunes.
I don't like Mondays.

No me gustan las películas de horror.
I don't like horror movies.

Work Out 2

Fill in the blanks with the correct form of gustar.

1. **Me** ______________________________ **los apartamentos grandes.**
2. **No me** ______________________________ **los hombres altos.**
3. **Me** ______________________________ **los niños.**
4. **No me** ______________________________ **trabajar.**
5. **Me** ______________________________ **los viernes.**
6. **No me** ______________________________ **los libros largos.**

7. **Me** ________________________ **las comedias.**

ANSWER KEY
1. **gustan**; 2. **gustan**; 3. **gustan**; 4. **gusta**; 5. **gustan**; 6. **gustan**; 7. **gustan**

Take It Further

You may be wondering by now about accent marks on some words, like **cómo**. Accent marks are used for two purposes: to show where the stress or emphasis falls on a word when it's pronounced, and to help differentiate between identically spelled words. We won't get into all the rules here, but here are some general rules for when and why accents are used.

If a word ends in a vowel, **-n**, or **-s**, stress normally falls on the second-to-last syllable.

libro, hombre, España, computadora, gustan, tienen, cartas, tienes, estas

If a word ends in a consonant other than **-n** or **-s**, it is normally stressed on the last syllable.

mujer, español, celebrar, ciudad, escuchar

An accent mark overrides this rule:

fotografía, cárcel, tomó, sótano, estás

An accent mark is also used to distinguish between two words that are pronounced the same way but mean different things.

solo *(adjective: sole, only, alone)*	**sólo** *(adverb: merely, solely, only)*
que *(conjunction: that, that which)*	**qué** *(interrogative: what)*
si *(if)*	**sí** *(yes)*
el *(the, masc.)*	**él** *(he)*

Word Recall

Form sentences expressing your likes and dislikes based on the clues in parentheses.

1. **el actor americano** *(I like)* ______________________________

2. **la casa pequeña** *(I like)* ______________________________

3. **los actores americanos** *(I like)* ______________________________

4. **los sábados y los domingos** *(I like)* ______________________________

5. **el actor americano** *(I don't like)* ______________________________

6. **la casa pequeña** *(I don't like)* ______________________________

7. **los actores americanos** *(I don't like)* ______________________________

8. **los sábados ni los domingos** *(I don't like)* ______________________________

ANSWER KEY

1. **Me gusta el actor americano.** 2. **Me gusta la casa pequeña.** 3. **Me gustan los actores americanos.** 4. **Me gustan los sábados y los domingos.** 5. **No me gusta el actor americano.** 6. **No me gusta la casa pequeña.** 7. **No me gustan los actores americanos.** 8. **No me gustan los sábados ni los domingos.**

How Did You Do?

By now, you should be able to:

- ☐ Tell someone what you do on certain days
  (Still unsure? Jump back to page 97.)
- ☐ Ask yes/no questions and use tag questions
  (Still unsure? Jump back to page 99.)
- ☐ Say what you like to do and what you don't like to do
  (Still unsure? Jump back to page 104.)

Don't forget to practice and reinforce what you've learned by visiting **www.livinglanguage.com/languagelab** for flashcards, games, and quizzes for Unit 2!

Unit 2 Essentials

Vocabulary Essentials

DAYS OF THE WEEK

	Monday
	Tuesday
	Wednesday
	Thursday
	Friday
	Saturday
	Sunday

[Pg. 63]

MONTHS OF THE YEAR

	January
	February
	March
	April
	May
	June
	July
	August
	September
	October
	November

	December

[Pg. 67]

OTHER TIME AND SEASONAL EXPRESSIONS

	week
	day
	weekend
	weekly
	daily
	morning
	afternoon
	evening, night
	year
	month
	decade
	century
	season
	spring
	summer
	fall
	winter

[Pg. 63, Pg. 67]

PARTING EXPRESSIONS

	Good-bye.
	Until later.
	See you soon. (lit., Until soon).
	Until tomorrow.
	Until later.
	Till then.
	Bye.
	See you. (lit., We see each other.)
	Take care.(lit., May you be well.)
	May you be well.

[Pg. 75]

NUMBERS 100–1,000,000

	100
	101
	102
	200
	300
	400
	500
	600
	700
	800
	900
	1,000

	1,998
	10,000
	20,000
	1,000,000

[Pg. 64]

ADJECTIVES

	tall/short
	fat/thin
	long/short
	wide/narrow
	big/small
	rich/poor
	expensive/cheap
	clean/dirty
	free/busy
	good/bad
	pleasant/unpleasant
	early/late
	fun/boring
	pretty/ugly

[Pg. 76]

VERBS

	to work
	to dance

	to sing
	to eat
	to drink
	to swim
	to jog
	to write
	to sleep

[Pg. 104]

Grammar Essentials

ADJECTIVE AGREEMENT

	MASCULINE SINGULAR	FEMININE SINGULAR	MASCULINE PLURAL	FEMININE PLURAL
pretty	bonito	bonita	bonitos	bonitas
ugly	feo	fea	feos	feas

QUESTION WORDS

cómo	*how*
qué	*what*
quién/quiénes	*who*
cuándo	*when*
dónde	*where*
cuánto/cuánta/cuántos/cuántas	*how much, how many*
cuál/cuáles	*which*
por qué	*why*

YES/NO QUESTIONS

To form a yes/no question, put the verb at the beginning of the sentence. Subject pronouns are often omitted; they are only used for emphasis or to clarify. If they are used, or if a subject noun is used, they come after the verb.

TAG QUESTIONS

Tag questions are formed in Spanish by adding either **¿no?** (*no?*) or **¿verdad?** (*right?*) at the end of the question.

TO LIKE/TO NOT LIKE

	SINGULAR	PLURAL
I like	**me gusta**	**me gustan**
I don't like	**no me gusta**	**no me gustan**

Unit 2 Quiz

A. Give the day or month that follows the one listed below.

1. **abril:** ______________________
2. **martes:** ______________________
3. **julio:** ______________________
4. **sábado:** ______________________
5. **diciembre:** ______________________
6. **jueves:** ______________________
7. **septiembre:** ______________________
8. **viernes:** ______________________
9. **mayo:** ______________________
10. **lunes** ______________________

B. Fill in the blank in each sentence with the most appropriate word from the following list: **mañana**, **hora**, **es**, **son**, **quién**, **quiénes**

1. **¿Qué** ______________________ **es?**
2. ______________________ **las siete y media de la mañana.**
3. **Adiós, hasta** ______________________.
4. **¿** ______________________ **es ella?**
5. **¿** ______________________ **son ellas?**

6. ______________________________ **la una y veinte de la tarde.**

C. Give the number that goes before and after the number given below.

1. ____________________ **veintiocho** ____________________
2. ____________________ **noventa y nueve** ____________________
3. ____________________ **quinientos cuarenta y seis** ____________________
4. ____________________ **mil doscientos cincuenta y cuatro** ____________________
5. ____________________ **tres mil setecientos noventa y nueve** ____________________

D. Find the opposite of the word given.

1. **temprano**	a. **pequeño**
2. **gordo**	b. **malo**
3. **rico**	c. **sucio**
4. **grande**	d. **tarde**
5. **limpio**	e. **delgado**
6. **bueno**	f. **bajo**
7. **libre**	g. **ocupado**
8. **alto**	h. **pobre**

How Did You Do?

Give yourself a point for every correct answer, then use the following key to determine whether or not you're ready to move on:

0–7 points: It's probably best to go back and study the lessons again to make sure you understood everything completely. Take your time; it's not a race! Make sure you spend time reviewing vocabulary with the flashcards and reading through each grammar note carefully.

8–16 points: If the questions you missed were in sections A or B, you may want to review the vocabulary again; if you missed answers mostly in sections C or D, check the unit essentials to make sure you have your conjugations and other grammar basics down.

17–20 points: Feel free to move on to the next unit! You're doing a great job.

| | | points

ANSWER KEY

A. 1. mayo; 2. miércoles; 3. agosto; 4. domingo; 5. enero; 6. viernes; 7. octubre; 8. sábado; 9. junio; 10. martes

B. 1. hora; 2. son; 3. mañana; 4. quién; 5. quiénes; 6. es

C. 1. veintisiete/veintinueve; 2. noventa y ocho/cien; 3. quinientos cuarenta y cinco/quinientos cuarenta y siete; 4. mil doscientos cincuenta y tres/mil doscientos cincuenta y cinco ; 5. tres mil setecientos noventa y ocho/tres mil ochocientos

D. 1. d;. 2. e; 3. h; 4. a; 5. c; 6. b; 7. g; 8. f

Unit 3:
Health and the Human Body

In this unit you'll learn a lot of new and useful vocabulary related to the human body and health. By the end of the unit, you should know how to:

- ☐ Talk about parts of the body
- ☐ Express possession with possessive adjectives like *my* and *your*
- ☐ Talk about your physical state with a doctor
- ☐ Feel familiar with some idiomatic expressions using body parts
- ☐ Express possession using **de** + pronoun
- ☐ Express possession using **de** in other expressions
- ☐ Talk to a doctor about specific problems
- ☐ Use possessive pronouns to express *mine* and *yours*
- ☐ Use verbs like *to walk, to taste, to speak*
- ☐ Use verbs like *to run, to eat, to see*
- ☐ Use verbs like *to write, to live, to leave*
- ☐ Talk about the present tense using time expressions

Lesson 9: Words

By the end of this lesson, you should know how to:

- ☐ Talk about parts of the body
- ☐ Express possession with possessive adjectives like *my* and *your*

Word Builder 1

9A Word Builder 1 (CD 5, Track 8)

Let's learn a few words pertaining to the head and face.

la cabeza	*head*
la cara	*face*
el pelo	*hair*
la frente	*forehead*
la oreja	*ear*
el ojo	*eye*
la nariz	*nose*
la mejilla	*cheek*
la boca	*mouth*
el labio	*lip*
la lengua	*tongue*
el diente	*tooth*
la muela	*molar*
la garganta	*throat*
la barbilla	*chin*
el cuello	*neck*

Word Practice 1

Fill in the appropriate Spanish words in the illustration above.

ANSWER KEY

1. **el ojo**; 2. **la nariz**; 3. **la oreja**; 4. **la boca**

Grammar Builder 1

POSSESSIVE ADJECTIVES (SINGULAR)

9B Grammar Builder 1 (CD 5, Track 9)

Let's look at some useful little words called possessive adjectives, which correspond to the English *my*, *your*, *his*, *her*, *our*, and *their*. Because these are adjectives in Spanish, they must agree in gender and number with the nouns they modify. Let's start with the possessive adjectives that correspond to the singular personal pronouns (**yo, tú, él, ella, usted**).

mi(s)	*my*
tu(s)	*your (infml.)*
su(s)	*his, her, your (fml.)*

The possessive adjectives **mi**, **tu**, and **su** are used with singular possessions (**mi libro**, **tu casa**), and **mis**, **tus**, and **sus** are used with plural possessions (**mis libros**, **tus casas**). The gender of the possession doesn't make any difference in these cases. Let's see some more examples.

Mi pelo es rojo.
My hair is red.

Mis ojos son grandes.
My eyes are big.

Tu cara es bonita.
Your face is pretty.

Tus dientes son blancos.
Your teeth are white.

Su nariz es larga.
His/Her/Your nose is long.

Sus piernas son gordas.
His/Her/Your legs are fat.

Notice that there is only one form for *his, her,* and *your (fml.)*—**su**. The context will tell you what, exactly, **su** means.

Work Out 1

Translate the following sentences:

1. *I like your eyes.* ______________________

2. *His nose is long.* ______________________

3. *My family is in Caracas.* ______________________________

____

4. *Your (infml.) granddaughter is hungry.* ______________________________

____

5. *Her hair is short.* ______________________________

____

6. *My apartment is small.* ______________________________

____

7. *Your grandparents are tired.* ______________________________

____

8. *My house is your (fml.) house.* ______________________________

____

ANSWER KEY

1. **Me gustan tus ojos.** 2. **Su nariz es larga.** 3. **Mi familia está en Caracas.** 4. **Tu nieta tiene hambre.** 5. **Su pelo es corto.** 6. **Mi apartamento es pequeño.** 7. **Tus abuelos están cansados.** 8. **Mi casa es su casa.**

Word Builder 2

9C Word Builder 2 (CD 5, Track 10)

Here are some more words related to the rest of the human body.

el cuerpo	*the body*
el brazo	*arm*
la espalda	*back*
la columna vertebral	*backbone, spinal column*
el hombro	*shoulder*
el codo	*elbow*

la muñeca	*wrist*
la mano	*hand*
el dedo	*finger, toe*
el estómago	*stomach*
el pecho	*chest*
la pierna	*leg*
la rodilla	*knee*
el pie	*foot*
el corazón	*heart*
la cadera	*hip*

Word Practice 2

Fill in the appropriate body parts in the illustration.

ANSWER KEY

1. **la cabeza**; 2. **el brazo**; 3. **la pierna**; 4. **la mano**; 5. **el pie**

Grammar Builder 2

POSSESSIVE ADJECTIVES (PLURAL)

9D Grammar Builder 2 (CD 5, Track 11)

Let's take a look at the possessive adjectives that correspond to the plural subject pronouns (**nosotros**, **vosotros**, **ellos**, **ellas**, **ustedes**).

nuestro/a(s)	*our*
vuestro/a(s)	*your (infml.)*
su(s)	*their, your (fml.)*

Notice that the first two plural forms change depending on both the gender and the number of the possession—for example, **nuestro libro** (*our book*), **nuestra casa** (*our house*), **nuestros libros** (*our books*), and **nuestras casas** (*our houses*). Here are some more examples. Again, don't forget that the **vuestro** forms are not very common in Latin America, where **su(s)** is used instead.

Nuestra casa es grande.
Our house is big.

Nuestro apartamento está en Quito.
Our apartment is in Quito.

Vuestros/Sus hijos son altos.
Your children are tall.

Sus hijos son altos.
Their/Your children are tall.

Vuestras/Sus manos son pequeñas.
Your hands are small.

Sus manos son pequeñas.
Their/Your hands are small.

Su familia es boliviana.
Their/Your family is Bolivian.

Sus abuelos son italianos.
Their/Your grandparents are Italian.

Work Out 2

Fill in the blank with the correct form of the possessive adjective. The English possessive is given in parentheses.

1. ______ **primos son venezolanos.** *(their)*
2. **En** ______ **casa hay catorce habitaciones.** *(our)*
3. ______ **padres están divorciados.** *(your, fml.)*
4. ______ **familias son grandes.** *(our)*
5. **En** ______ **familia hay muchos niños.** *(your, infml.)*
6. ______ **apartamento está en Nueva York.** *(our)*
7. ______ **libros están en la oficina.** *(your, fml.)*
8. ______ **coche no es muy grande.** *(our)*

ANSWER KEY

1. **Sus**; 2. **nuestra**; 3. **Sus**; 4. **Nuestras**; 5. **vuestra**; 6. **Nuestro**; 7. **Sus**; 8. **Nuestro**

Take It Further

Although names of body parts are used in much the same manner in Spanish as in English, there is one significant difference—in Spanish, they are frequently preceded by a definite article (el, la, los, or las). In most cases, the possessive adjective is only used when it's not clear from the context to whose body something belongs. Here are a few examples.

Tengo la cara larga y los ojos azules.
I have a long face and blue eyes.

Tiene los dedos largos.
He/She has long fingers./You have long fingers.

Me gustan tus manos.
I like your hands.

Word Recall

Let's practice possession in Spanish. Tell whose item it is by writing the correct possessive adjective in the blank.

1. **Yo tengo un libro. Es ______ libro.**
2. **Yo tengo unos libros. Son ______ libros.**
3. **Tú tienes un libro. Es ______ libro.**
4. **Tú tienes unos libros. Son ______ libros.**
5. **Ella tiene un libro. Es ______ libro.**
6. **Ella tiene unos libros. Son ______ libros.**

ANSWER KEY

1. **mi**; 2. **mis**; 3. **tu**; 4. **tus**; 5. **su**; 6. **sus**

How Did You Do?

By now, you should know how to:

- ☐ Talk about parts of the body
  (Still unsure? Jump back to page 120.)
- ☐ Express possession with possessive adjectives like *my* and *your*
  (Still unsure? Jump back to pages 121 and 125.)

Lesson 10: Phrases

By the end of this lesson, you should be able to:

- ☐ Talk about your physical state with a doctor
- ☐ Feel familiar with some idiomatic expressions using body parts
- ☐ Express possession using **de** + pronoun
- ☐ Express possession using **de** in other expressions

Phrase Builder 1

10A Phrase Builder 1 (CD 5, Track 12)

Here are some phrases you can use when visiting the doctor or talking about your physical state. Notice the use of **tener**.

tener dolor de cabeza	*to have a headache*
tener dolor de garganta	*to have a sore throat*
tener fiebre	*to have a fever*

tener tos	*to have a cough*
tener mal de estómago	*to have an upset stomach*
tener mareo	*to be dizzy*
tener la tensión alta (tener la presión alta)	*to have high blood pressure*
tener la tensión baja (tener la presión baja)	*to have low blood pressure*
tener náusea	*to be nauseated, to have nausea*
hacer un examen de sangre	*to take a blood test*
tomar la tensión (tomar la presión)	*to take the blood pressure*
tomar un medicamento	*to take medication*

Phrase Practice 1

Match the Spanish phrase to its appropriate English translation.

1. **tener fiebre**	a. *to have a cough*
2. **tener mareo**	b. *to have a headache*
3. **tener náusea**	c. *to have an upset stomach*
4. **tener tos**	d. *to be nauseated, to have nausea*
5. **tener mal de estómago**	e. *to have a sore throat*
6. **tener dolor de garganta**	f. *to be dizzy*
7. **tener dolor de cabeza**	g. *to have a fever*

ANSWER KEY

1. g; 2. f; 3. d; 4. a; 5. c; 6. e; 7. b

Grammar Builder 1

POSSESSION WITH DE + PRONOUN

10B Grammar Builder 1 (CD 5, Track 13)

A definite article and the preposition **de** (*of*) can be used with a subject pronoun in place of the more ambiguous **su(s)**.

su pierna	*his/her/their/your leg*
la pierna de él	*his leg*
la pierna de ella	*her leg*
la pierna de ellos	*their leg*
la pierna de ellas	*their leg*
la pierna de usted	*your leg*
la pierna de ustedes	*your leg*

su cuerpo	*his/her/their/your body*
el cuerpo de él	*his body*
el cuerpo de ella	*her body*
el cuerpo de ellos	*their body*
el cuerpo de ellas	*their body*
el cuerpo de usted	*your body*
el cuerpo de ustedes	*your body*

In the plural form, simply use the plural feminine or masculine article, depending on the gender of the noun.

las piernas de él	*his legs*
los cuerpos de ustedes	*your bodies*

Work Out 1

Can you say each of the sentences below in another way? Follow the example:

Ex. **Son los padres de mis padres.**
Son mis abuelos.

1. **Es el hijo de mi hermano.** ______
2. **Son los hermanos de mi esposo.** ______
3. **Es la esposa de tu padre.** ______
4. **Son las hijas de nuestra hija.** ______
5. **Son los padres de Juan.** ______
6. **Son los hijos de nuestra tía.** ______

ANSWER KEY

1. **Es mi sobrino.** 2. **Son mis cuñados.** 3. **Es tu madre.** 4. **Son nuestras nietas.** 5. **Son sus padres.** 6. **Son nuestros primos.**

Phrase Builder 2

10C Phrase Builder 2 (CD 5, Track 14)

Just as in English, Spanish has a few idioms using words for parts of the body.

estar en buenas manos	*to be in good hands*
pararse de cabeza	*to go crazy, to go out of one's mind*
dar la cara	*to face the circumstances*
tener cara dura	*to be shameless*
tener los pies en la tierra	*to have both feet on the ground*
perder la cabeza	*to lose one's head*
tener la cabeza fría	*to keep a cool head*
ojo por ojo	*an eye for an eye*

Phrase Practice 2

Fill in the missing verb in each phrase.

1. ______________________ **en buenas manos** *to be in good hands*
2. ______________________ **de cabeza** *to go crazy, to go out of one's mind*
3. ______________________ **la cara** *to face the circumstances*
4. ______________________ **la cabeza** *to lose one's head*
5. ______________________ **la cabeza fría** *to keep a cool head*

ANSWER KEY

1. **estar** 2. **pararse** 3. **dar** 4. **perder** 5. **tener**

Grammar Builder 2

MORE POSSESSION WITH DE

10D Grammar Builder 2 (CD 5, Track 15)

The preposition **de** comes in very handy when talking about possession. While English uses apostrophe *-s,* Spanish uses a phrase with **de**. This is similar to another way of showing possession in English with *of.* Let's take a look at some examples.

el corazón de la señora Suárez

Mrs. Suárez's heart

los primos de María

María's cousins

el restaurante de Jorge
Jorge's restaurant

las ventanas de la casa
the windows of the house

la puerta de la oficina
the door of the office

Remember that when **de** is followed by the masculine article (**el**), it becomes **del**.

la casa del padre de Juan.
Juan's father's house

la cola del caballo
the horse's tail

Please be careful! When using **de** + the masculine pronoun **él**, there is no contraction.

La casa de él es grande.
His house is big.

Here's how you can ask questions about possession. Notice that **¿de quién?** means *whose*.

¿De quién es la casa?
Whose house is it?

¿De quién es el restaurante?
Whose restaurant is it?

¿De quién son los primos?
Whose cousins are they?

Work Out 2

Translate the following sentences:

1. *His parents are divorced.* ______________________________

____

2. *Whose heart is it?* ______________________________

____

3. *Roberto's mother has high blood pressure.* ______________________________

____

4. *It's María's sister's uncle.* ______________________________

____

5. *Their sister's husband has a headache.* ______________________________

____

ANSWER KEY

1. **Sus padres están divorciados.** 2. **¿De quién es el corazón?** 3. **La madre de Roberto tiene la presión alta.** 4. **Es el tío de la hermana de María.** 5. **El esposo de su hermana tiene dolor de cabeza.**

Take It Further

Here are some useful phrases you can use to describe yourself and others.

tener la cara larga	*to have a long face*
tener la cara redonda	*to have a round face*
ser rubio/a	*to be blond*
ser moreno/a	*to be dark skinned*
ser blanco/a	*to be white*

tener los ojos negros/azules/marrones/verdes	*to have black/blue/brown/green eyes*
tener el cabello largo/corto	*to have long/short hair*
ser calvo/a	*to be bald*
ser alto/a	*to be tall*
ser bajo/a	*to be short*

Let's take a look at some examples.

Soy bajo y rubio. Tengo los ojos verdes.
I'm short and blond. I have green eyes.

Soy morena de ojos azules.
I'm dark skinned with blue eyes.

Ella tiene el cabello largo y es alta.
She has long hair and is tall.

Word Recall

Let's practice possession using the preposition **de**.

1. *my mother's book* ____________
2. *my sister's book* ____________
3. *the boy's book* ____________
4. *Juan's book* ____________
5. *his book* ____________

6. *the man's book* ______________________

7. *Lina's book* ______________________

8. *their book* ______________________

ANSWER KEY

1. **el libro de mi madre**; 2. **el libro de mi hermana**; 3. **el libro del niño/chico**; 4. **el libro de Juan**; 5. **el libro de él**; 6. **el libro del hombre**; 7. **el libro de Lina**; 8. **el libro de ellos/ellas**

How Did You Do?

By now, you should be able to:

- ☐ Talk about your physical state with a doctor
  (Still unsure? Jump back to page 128.)
- ☐ Feel familiar with some idiomatic expressions using body parts
  (Still unsure? Jump back to page 131.)
- ☐ Express possession using **de** + pronoun
  (Still unsure? Jump back to page 130.)
- ☐ Express possession using **de** in other expressions
  (Still unsure? Jump back to page 132.)

Lesson 11: Sentences

By the end of this lesson, you should be able to:

- ☐ Talk to a doctor about specific problems
- ☐ Use possessive pronouns to express *mine* and *yours*
- ☐ Use verbs like *to walk, to taste, to speak*

Sentence Builder 1

11A Sentence Builder 1 (CD 5, Track 16)

Here are sentences that may come in handy at a doctor's office.

¿Cuál es el problema?	*What's the problem?*
Tengo dolor de garganta y tos.	*I have a sore throat and a cough.*
Me siento mareado.	*I feel dizzy.*
Tengo náusea y diarrea.	*I have nausea and diarrhea.*
¿Toma algún medicamento en este momento?	*Are you taking any medication right now?*
¿Sufre de alguna enfermedad?	*Do you suffer from any illnesses?*
¿Fuma usted?	*Do you smoke?*
¿Tiene la presión alta?	*Do you have high blood pressure?*
¿Lo han operado de algo?	*Have you had any operations?*
¿En dónde tiene dolor?	*Where do you have pain?*
¿Tiene problemas del corazón?	*Do you have heart problems?*
¿Tiene alergias?	*Do you have any allergies?*
Soy alérgico a la penicilina.	*I'm allergic to penicillin.*
¿Tiene hijos?	*Do you have children?*
¿Hace deporte con frecuencia?	*Do you play sports regularly?*

Sentence Practice 1

Fill in the missing word in the following sentences.

1. **¿Sufre de** ________________**?** *Do you suffer from any illnesses?*
2. **¿**________________ **usted?** *Do you smoke?*

3. **¿Tiene ________________?** *Do you have high blood pressure?*

4. **¿Tiene ________________?** *Do you have heart problems?*

5. **¿Tiene ________________?** *Do you have any allergies?*

6. **¿Tiene ________________?** *Do you have children?*

ANSWER KEY

1. **alguna enfermedad**; 2. **Fuma**; 3. **la presión alta**; 4. **problemas del corazón**; 5. **alergias**; 6. **hijos**

Grammar Builder 1

POSSESSIVE PRONOUNS

11B Grammar Builder 1 (CD 5, Track 17)

Another way to talk about the things we own is by using possessive pronouns, which are equivalent to the English *mine*, *yours*, *his*, *hers*, *ours*, and *theirs*. They usually take the place of a noun and are normally used with a definite article.

el mío/la mía, los míos/las mías	*mine*
el tuyo/la tuya, los tuyos/las tuyas	*yours (infml.)*
el suyo/la suya, los suyos/las suyas	*his, hers, yours (fml.)*
el nuestro/la nuestra, los nuestros/las nuestras	*ours*
el vuestro/la vuestra, los vuestro/las vuestras	*yours (infml.)*
el suyo/la suya, los suyos/las suyas	*theirs, yours (fml.)*

Notice that all of the possessive pronouns agree in both gender and number with the nouns they stand in for. Let's look at some examples to see how this works.

Mi cara es redonda y la tuya es larga.
My face is round and yours is long.

Tu cabello es rubio y el nuestro es negro.
Your hair is blond and ours is black.

Vuestros hijos están en Brasil y los suyos en Costa Rica.
Your children are in Brazil and hers/his/theirs/yours (are) in Costa Rica.

In the first example, **la tuya** is standing in for **la cara**. In the second, **el nuestro** is standing in for **el cabello**. In the third, **los suyos** is standing in for **los hijos**.

As we saw in Lesson 10, the use of the possessive adjective **su** can be clarified by using the preposition **de** and the corresponding pronoun. The same thing can be done with possessive pronouns, but in this case, only a definite article is used before the **de** phrase. Let's first take a look at the feminine.

Mi casa es grande y la suya es pequeña.
My house is big and his/hers/theirs/yours is small.

Mi casa es grande y la de él es pequeña.
My house is big and his is small.

Mi casa es grande y la de ella es pequeña.
My house is big and hers is small.

Mi casa es grande y la de ellos es pequeña.
My house is big and theirs is small.

Mi casa es grande y la de ellas es pequeña.
My house is big and theirs is small.

Mi casa es grande y la de usted es pequeña.
My house is big and yours is small.

Mi casa es grande y la de ustedes es pequeña.
My house is big and yours is small.

Now, let's take a look at the masculine.

Mi cabello es largo y el suyo es corto.
My hair is long and his/hers/theirs/yours is short.

Mi cabello es largo y el de él es corto.
My hair is long and his is short.

Mi cabello es largo y el de ella es corto.
My hair is long and hers is short.

Mi cabello es largo y el de ellos es corto.
My hair is long and theirs is short.

Mi cabello es largo y el de ellas es corto.
My hair is long and theirs is short.

Mi cabello es largo y el de usted es corto.
My hair is long and yours is short.

Mi cabello es largo y el de ustedes es corto.
My hair is long and yours is short.

Let's take a few examples with the plural feminine and masculine.

Nuestras manos son pequeñas y las de él son grandes.
Our hands are small and his are big.

Tus padres están en Londres y los de ellos en Guadalajara.
Your parents are in London and theirs are in Guadalajara.

When the possessive pronoun comes after the verb ser, the article is left out.

La casa grande es mía.
The big house is mine.

La habitación treinta y dos es tuya/suya.
Room 32 is yours.

Work Out 1

Join the two sentences by using a possessive pronoun. Follow the example:

Ex. **El padre de Juan está en La Paz. El padre de Margarita está en Francia.**
El padre de Juan está en La Paz y el suyo está en Francia.

1. **Nuestra profesora es alta. La profesora tuya y la de Luis es baja.** ____________
____
2. **Las manos de Ángela son bonitas. Mis manos son feas.** ____________
____
3. **La madre de Pedro tiene sesenta y siete años. La madre de Enrique y Sara tiene ochenta y ocho.** ____________
____
4. **Mi hermano es abogado. Tu hermano es astronauta.** ____________
____
5. **La habitación de María es grande. La habitación de Claudia es pequeña.** ____________
____

ANSWER KEY

1. **Nuestra profesora es alta y la vuestra es baja.** 2. **Las manos de Ángela son bonitas y las mías son feas.** 3. **La madre de Pedro tiene sesenta y siete años y la suya tiene ochenta y ocho.** 4. **Mi hermano es abogado y el tuyo es astronauta.** 5. **La habitación de María es grande y la suya es pequeña.**

Sentence Builder 2

11C Sentence Builder 2 (CD 5, Track 18)

Tengo un cosquilleo muy desagradable.	*I have a very unpleasant tingling feeling.*
¿Se le hinchan los pies y las manos?	*Do your feet and hands swell?*
Sí, con mucha frecuencia.	*Yes, very frequently.*
¿Y, qué quiere decir eso?	*So, what does that mean?*
¿Es grave?	*Is it serious?*
¿Cuál es el tratamiento a seguir?	*What is the treatment to be followed?*
Tiene un brote en todo el cuerpo.	*She has a rash all over her body.*
¿Es él su pediatra de cabecera?	*Is he your regular pediatrician?*
Él tiene paciencia con los niños.	*He is patient with children.*
Le gusta mucho la homeopatía.	*He likes homeopathy very much.*

Sentence Practice 2

Translate the following sentences.

1. *I have a very unpleasant tingling feeling.* ______________________________

2. *Do your feet and hands swell?* ______________________________

3. *So, what does that mean?* ______________________________

____

4. *Is it serious?* ______________________________

____

5. *She has a rash all over her body.* ______________________________

____

ANSWER KEY

1. **Tengo un cosquilleo muy desagradable.** 2. **¿Se le hinchan los pies y las manos?** 3. **¿Y, qué quiere decir eso?** 4. **¿Es grave?** 5. **Tiene un brote en todo el cuerpo.**

Grammar Builder 2

CONJUGATION OF -AR VERBS

11D Grammar Builder 2 (CD 5, Track 19)

Now let's look at how to conjugate verbs in Spanish. A conjugation is the pattern of endings (or other changes) that a verb undergoes to agree with a subject, as in the English *I sing, you sing, she sings,* etc. In Spanish, there are slightly different conjugations for different types of verbs. Verbs are grouped according to three different infinitive endings: **-ar** verbs, **-er** verbs, and **-ir** verbs. Examples from each group are **hablar** (*to speak*), **comer** (*to eat*), and **vivir** (*to live*). There are both regular and irregular verbs—that is, those that follow a regular pattern of conjugation and those that don't. But don't panic. Most verbs are regular!

Let's start with a list of some common **-ar** verbs.

caminar	*to walk*
hablar	*to talk, to speak*
tocar	*to touch, to play an instrument*
escuchar	*to listen to*

saborear	*to taste*
estudiar	*to study*

To conjugate any verb, take off the infinitive ending, which, in this case, is **-ar**. Then you're left with the verb stem, and you add certain endings to that stem depending on the subject. For regular **-ar** verbs, you will add the following endings:

yo	**-o**	**nosotros**	**-amos**
tú	**-as**	**vosotros**	**-áis**
él/ella/usted	**-a**	**ellos/ellas/ustedes**	**-an**

Let's look at the conjugation of a regular **-ar** verb, **caminar**:

CAMINAR ***(TO WALK)***			
yo camino	*I walk*	**nosotros caminamos**	*we walk*
tú caminas	*you walk (infml.)*	**vosotros camináis**	*you walk (pl. fml.)*
él/ella/usted camina	*he/she walks, you walk (fml.)*	**ellos/ellas/ustedes caminan**	*they walk, you walk (pl. fml.)*

All of the **-ar** verbs from the list above are conjugated in exactly this way. Here are some examples.

Los fines de semana nosotros caminamos en el parque.
We walk in the park on weekends.

Yolanda toca la guitarra muy bien.
Yolanda plays the guitar very well.

Ellos hablan cuatro idiomas.
They speak four languages.

Yo escucho música todas las noches.
I listen to music every night.

Notice that in English, you *listen to* something, but in Spanish, you don't need a preposition; **escuchar** is perfectly fine on its own. You'll see this sort of difference a lot when you compare two languages. Sometimes one language will use a preposition where the other won't, and sometimes the situation is reversed. As a general tip, be wary of translating prepositions literally; in fact, it's better not even to assume that you need one in another language just because your native language uses one. Prepositions are often used in very different ways from one language to another!

Work Out 2

Fill in the blank with the appropriate form of the verb in parentheses.

1. **Nosotros** ______________ **por la mañana. (caminar)**
2. **Ustedes** ______________ **el piano. (tocar)**
3. **Yo** ______________ **música clásica los fines de semana. (escuchar)**
4. **Tú** ______________ **el vino. (saborear)**
5. **Ellos** ______________ **español. (hablar)**
6. **Él** ______________ **por la mañana. (caminar)**
7. **Vosotras** ______________ **por teléfono. (hablar)**
8. **Yo** ______________ **la radio. (escuchar)**

ANSWER KEY

1. **caminamos**; 2. **tocan**; 3. **escucho**; 4. **saboreas**; 5. **hablan**; 6. **camina**; 7. **habláis**; 8. **escucho**

Take It Further

Don't forget that Spanish speakers tend to drop the subject pronouns because the verb endings indicate who the subject is. This is true for **yo**, **tú**, **nosotros/as**, and **vosotros/as**. In the case of **él**, **ella**, **usted**, **ellos**, **ellas**, and **ustedes**, it is not always clear who the subject is. Therefore, the pronoun may be used.

Hablas por teléfono.
You talk on the phone. (infml.)

Habla por teléfono.
He/She talks on the phone./You talk on the phone.

Él habla por teléfono.
He talks on the phone.

Word Recall

Rewrite the sentence in each line using the subject in parentheses. Make sure that you write the correct form of the **-ar** verb.

1. **Yo camino mucho. (Tú)** ______________________________

2. **Yo camino mucho. (Nosotros)** ______________________________

3. **Yo camino mucho. (Usted)** ______________________________

4. **Yo camino mucho. (Él)** ______________________________

____

5. **Roberto y Luisa hablan por teléfono. (Yo)** ______________________________

____

6. **Roberto y Luisa hablan por teléfono. (Roberto)** ______________________________

____

7. **Roberto y Luisa hablan por teléfono. (Tú)** ______________________________

____

8. **Roberto y Luisa hablan por teléfono. (Ustedes)** ______________________________

____

ANSWER KEY

1. **Tú caminas mucho.** 2. **Nosotros caminamos mucho.** 3. **Usted camina mucho.** 4. **Él camina mucho.** 5. **Yo hablo por teléfono.** 6. **Roberto habla por teléfono.** 7. **Tú hablas por teléfono.** 8. **Ustedes hablan por teléfono.**

How Did You Do?

By now, you should be able to:

- ☐ Talk to a doctor about specific problems
  (Still unsure? Jump back to page 137.)
- ☐ Use possessive pronouns to express *mine* and *yours*
  (Still unsure? Jump back to page 138.)
- ☐ Use verbs like *to walk, to taste, to speak*
  (Still unsure? Jump back to page 143.)

Lesson 12: Conversations

By the end of this lesson, you should know how to:

- ☐ Use verbs like *to run, to eat, to see*
- ☐ Use verbs like *to write, to live, to leave*
- ☐ Talk about the present tense using time expressions

Conversation 1

12A Conversation 1 (CD 5, Track 20 - Spanish Only; Track 21 - Spanish and English)

Listen in while Gloria visits the doctor.

Médico:	**Buenos días, Doña Solís, ¿cuál es el problema?**
Gloria:	**Tengo mucho dolor en las muñecas, sobre todo la derecha.**
Médico:	**¿Tiene dolor en el cuello o la espalda?**
Gloria:	**No, para nada. Pero por las noches tengo un cosquilleo muy desagradable en los dedos de mi mano derecha.**
Médico:	**¿Toma algún medicamento en este momento?**
Gloria:	**Sí, estoy tomando una pastilla para bajar la tensión.**
Médico:	**¿Se le hinchan los pies o las manos, sobre todo por las tardes?**
Gloria:	**Sí, con mucha frecuencia.**
Médico:	**Bueno, son los clásicos síntomas del síndrome del túnel del carpio.**
Gloria:	**¿Y, qué quiere decir eso? ¿Es grave?**
Médico:	**No, simplemente tiene bloqueados los nervios del carpio, que son los que conectan la muñeca con el resto de la mano.**
Gloria:	**¿Y cuál es el tratamiento a seguir?**
Médico:	**La acupuntura ayuda mucho. Así que vamos a comenzar con una sesión dos veces por semana por un mes.**

Doctor:	*Good morning, Mrs. Solís. What seems to be the problem?*
Gloria:	*I have a lot of pain in my wrists, especially the right one.*
Doctor:	*Do you have pain in your neck or your back?*
Gloria:	*No, not at all. But at nighttime I have a very unpleasant tingling sensation in the fingers of my right hand.*
Doctor:	*Are you taking any medication right now?*
Gloria:	*Yes, I'm taking a pill to lower my blood pressure.*
Doctor:	*Do your feet and hands swell, especially in the afternoons?*
Gloria:	*Yes, very frequently.*
Doctor:	*Well, those are the typical symptoms of carpal tunnel syndrome.*
Gloria:	*What does that mean? Is it serious?*
Doctor:	*No, it only means that the carpal nerves, which connect your wrist to the hand, are blocked.*
Gloria:	*What treatment is there?*
Doctor:	*Acupuncture helps a lot. So we're going to begin with one session twice a week for a month.*

Take It Further

Two polite titles that you may hear are **don** and **doña**, although they're dying out. They are usually used before the first name of a person who deserves respect on the basis of his or her age or status in society. They are usually accompanied by the given name of the person being addressed. You will very often see them used to address the Spanish king and queen: **Don Juan Carlos y Doña Sofía**. In Latin America, they are commonly used by workers to address their employers, especially in rural areas.

Notice that the doctor asked: **¿Toma algún medicamento en este momento?** The English translation is: *Are you taking any medication right now?* In Spanish, the present tense (**toma**, for example) can be translated into English as the simple present (*you take*), the present continuous or progressive (*you are taking*), or even the present emphatic (*you do take*). It all depends on the context.

Conversation Practice 1

Fill in the blanks below with the appropriate word based on the English translations and the dialogue above.

1. **¿Tiene dolor en el ________ o la ________?** *Do you have pain in your neck or your back?*
2. **Pero por las noches tengo un cosquilleo muy ________ en los dedos de mi mano derecha.** *But at nighttime I have a very unpleasant tingling sensation in the fingers of my right hand.*
3. **¿Y, qué ________ decir eso? ¿Es grave?** *What does that mean? Is it serious?*
4. **Sí, estoy tomando ________ para bajar la tensión.** *Yes, I'm taking a pill to lower my blood pressure.*
5. **No, simplemente tiene bloqueados los nervios del carpio, que son los que conectan la ________ con el resto de la ________.** *No, it only means that the carpal nerves, which connect your wrist to the hand, are blocked.*

ANSWER KEY

1. **cuello, espalda**; 2. **desagradable**; 3. **quiere**; 4. **una pastilla**; 5. **muñeca, mano**

Grammar Builder 1

CONJUGATION OF -ER VERBS AND VER (*TO SEE*)

12B Grammar Builder 1 (CD 5, Track 22)

Verbs with an **-er** infinitive ending are also very easy to conjugate. Here are some examples.

correr	*to run*
beber	*to drink*
comer	*to eat*
ver	*to see*
leer	*to read*

Let's take a closer look at the verb **correr**. First, remove the **-er** ending to get the stem, **corr-**. Then add the appropriate ending for each subject.

CORRER *(TO RUN)*			
yo corro	*I run*	**nosotros corremos**	*we run*
tú corres	*you run (infml.)*	**vosotros corréis**	*you run (pl. fml.)*
él/ella/usted corre	*he/she runs, you run (fml.)*	**ellos/ellas/ ustedes corren**	*they run, you run (pl. fml.)*

Here are those **-er** endings once again.

yo	**-o**	**nosotros**	**-emos**
tú	**-es**	**vosotros**	**-éis**
él/ella/usted	**-e**	**ellos/ellas/ustedes**	**-en**

If you take a closer look at the conjugation of **-ar** and **-er** verbs, you can see that they are almost identical except for one letter. Here are some more examples of **-er** verbs.

Ella bebe dos litros de agua a diario.
She drinks two litres of water a day.

Los niños comen dulces.
The children eat sweets.

Now, you may be a little bit puzzled when asked to conjugate the verb **ver**. Naturally so, because when you take the ending off, you're left with only one letter! Yes, that's actually the stem, and it's conjugated just like **correr**.

VER ***(TO SEE)***			
yo veo	*I see*	**nosotros vemos**	*we see*
tú ves	*you see (infml.)*	**vosotros veis**	*you see (pl. fml.)*
él/ella/usted ve	*he/she sees, you see (fml.)*	**ellos/ellas/ ustedes ven**	*they see, you see (pl. fml.)*

Vemos a nuestros amigos con frecuencia.
We see our friends often.

Sabina y Ana ven muchas películas.
Sabina and Ana see a lot of movies.

Take a look at that first example again. **Vemos a nuestros amigos ...** Did you notice that little **a** in between the verb **vemos** and the phrase **nuestros amigos**? This is called the **a** *personal*, and it's used when a direct object is a person. We'll come back to that later on in the course.

Work Out 1

Choose the verb that best completes the sentence.

1. **Nosotras (beben, bebemos, bebéis) mucha agua.** ____________
2. **Ella (lees, leen, lee) un libro.** ____________
3. **Tú (corro, corre, corres) por las tardes.** ____________
4. **Vosotros (vemos, veis, ven) televisión.** ____________

5. **Yo no (comes, coméis, como) carne.** ______________________

6. **Ustedes (bebéis, beben, bebés) vino tinto.** ______________________

7. **Yo (ve, ves, veo) a mi amigo.** ______________________

8. **¿Qué (leo, lee, lees), Ana?** ______________________

ANSWER KEY

1. **bebemos**; 2. **lee**; 3. **corres**; 4. **veis**; 5. **como**; 6. **beben**; 7. **veo**; 8. **lees**

Conversation 2

12C Conversation 2 (CD 5, Track 23 - Spanish Only; Track 24 - Spanish and English)

Isabel is at the pediatrician's office with her little daughter. She's talking to another mother in the waiting room.

Margarita:	**Mi hija tiene tres años, ¿y la suya?**
Isabel:	**Tiene veintidós meses. Se llama Catherina, ¿y la suya?**
Margarita:	**Sofía. ¿Qué le pasa a Catherina?**
Isabel:	**Tiene una fiebre muy alta y un brote en todo el cuerpo. No tiene apetito y llora mucho.**
Margarita:	**Mi hija también tiene una fiebre muy alta.**
Isabel:	**¿Es este su pediatra de cabecera?**
Margarita:	**Sí, es muy bueno. Estoy muy contenta. Sobre todo porque le gusta mucho la homeopatía.**
Isabel:	**Qué bien. No me gusta darle medicinas a Catherina cuando no es absolutamente necesario.**
Margarita:	**Si, además es un médico que escucha a los padres y tiene mucha paciencia con los niños.**
Isabel:	**Bueno, ya estoy más tranquila.**
Margarita:	**No se preocupe. Catherina está en buenas manos.**

Margarita:	*My daughter is three years old, and yours?*
Isabel:	*She's twenty-two months. Her name is Catherina. And yours?*

Margarita:	*Sofía. What's wrong with Catherina?*
Isabel:	*She has a very high fever and a rash all over her body. She has no appetite and cries a lot.*
Margarita:	*My daughter has a high fever, too.*
Isabel:	*Is this your regular pediatrician?*
Margarita:	*Yes, he's very good. I am very happy. Especially because he likes homeopathy very much.*
Isabel:	*That's good. I don't like to give Catherina medicine when it isn't absolutely necessary.*
Margarita:	*Yes, plus he's a doctor who listens to parents and has a lot of patience with the children.*
Isabel:	*Well, now I feel better.*
Margarita:	*Don't worry. Catherina is in good hands.*

Take It Further

Homeopathic medicine and other more natural approaches to treating illnesses are becoming the trend in Spanish-speaking countries. In most of Latin America, you'll find that people consider themselves much more in tune with nature and their bodies and prefer natural remedies and herbal teas to conventional Western medicine, which is considered by some to be very aggressive and hard on the body.

Some common herbs are **palo de aceite** (*oily stick*), which is used to treat intestinal problems, rheumatism, colic, and asthma; **cola de caballo** (*horse's tail*), which is used to treat wounds and infections of the gums; **uña de gato** (*cat's claw*), which is used to treat stomach and lung tumors; and **guayaba** (*guava*), which is a fruit whose parts are used to make an infusion to treat diarrhea.

You've probably also heard that in several South American countries, a tea made out of **mate de coca** (*coca leaf*) is a popular beverage. In fact, people living at very high altitudes either drink this tea or chew coca leaves to help fight altitude dizziness and sickness. The effects of this tea are similar to those of coffee. The tea is not considered a drug, and it is also used for medicinal and religious purposes.

Conversation Practice 2

Unscramble the sentences from the dialogue above. The English sentence is unscrambled.

1. **¿/Catherina/pasa/le/a/qué/?** *What's wrong with Catherina?* ____________________

2. **tiene/alta/también/mi/muy/una/hija/fiebre/.** *My daughter has a high fever, too.*

3. **gusta/le/sobre todo/homeopatía/mucho/la/porque/.** *Especially because he likes homeopathy very much.* ____________________

4. **ya/bueno/más/estoy/tranquila/.** *Well, now I feel better.* ____________________

5. **se/no/preocupe/.** *Don't worry.* ____________________

ANSWER KEY

1. **¿Qué le pasa a Catherina?** 2. **Mi hija también tiene una fiebre muy alta.** 3. **Sobre todo porque le gusta mucho la homeopatía.** 4. **Bueno, ya estoy más tranquila.** 5. **No se preocupe.**

Grammar Builder 2

CONJUGATION OF -IR VERBS

12D Grammar Builder 2 (CD 5, Track 25)

The third group of verbs end in **-ir** in the infinitive.

percibir	*to perceive*
escribir	*to write*
vivir	*to live*
partir	*to leave*

Here's the **-ir** conjugation.

ESCRIBIR *(TO WRITE)*			
yo escribo	*I write*	**nosotros escribimos**	*we write*
tú escribes	*you write (infml.)*	**vosotros escribís**	*you write (pl. fml.)*
él/ella/usted escribe	*he/she writes, you write (fml.)*	**ellos/ellas/ustedes escriben**	*they write, you write (pl. fml.)*

Let's look at the **-ir** endings one more time.

yo	**-o**	**nosotros**	**-imos**
tú	**-es**	**vosotros**	**-ís**
él/ella/usted	**-e**	**ellos/ellas/ustedes**	**-en**

If you take a closer look, you'll notice that the only difference between **-er** and **-ir** verbs is the ending used for **nosotros** and **vosotros**. Here are some example sentences with **-ir** verbs.

Nosotros escribimos muchas cartas.

We write a lot of letters.

Ellos viven en una ciudad grande, pero tú vives en una aldea pequeña.
They live in a big city, but you live in a little village.

Now you've learned how to conjugate all three types of Spanish verbs in the present tense. Don't forget that the Spanish present tense can be translated into English as the simple present (*she goes*), the present progressive or continuous (*she is going*), or the present emphatic (*she does go*). It can also be used to talk about something that will happen in the near future, as in the English *It's 3:00 now, and the train arrives in an hour*.

Here are some useful expressions of time that you can use with the simple present tense.

ahora	*now*
ahora mismo	*right now*
mañana	*tomorrow*
esta noche	*tonight*
siempre	*always*
con frecuencia	*frequently*
a veces	*sometimes*
casi nunca	*seldom, almost never*
nunca	*never*
todos los días	*every day*
todas las semanas	*every week*
una vez por semana	*once a week*
dos veces por semana	*twice a week*

Work Out 2

Translate the following sentences into Spanish.

1. *Right now she has a headache.* ______________________________

2. *My parents leave tomorrow in the afternoon.* ______________________________

3. *We live in a small apartment.* ______________________________

4. *I always drink coffee in the morning.* ______________________________

5. *She writes emails every day.* ______________________________

6. *Sometimes we listen to jazz.* ______________________________

7. *They never eat at night.* ______________________________

8. *My wife leaves this evening.* ______________________________

ANSWER KEY

1. **Ahora mismo ella tiene dolor de cabeza.** 2. **Mis padres parten mañana por la tarde.** 3. **Nosotros vivimos en un apartamento pequeño.** 4. **Yo siempre bebo café por la mañana.** 5. **Ella escribe emails todos los días.** 6. **A veces nosotros escuchamos jazz.** 7. **Ellos nunca comen por la noche.** 8. **Mi esposa parte esta noche.**

Tip!

Now that you've learned verbs in Spanish, you'll want to find plenty of creative ways to practice using them. The more you use them, the more automatic the verb conjugations will become for you. A simple way to lodge verb conjugations in your mind is repetition—listening to the audio, repeating aloud, reading the forms in the book, and writing them out. There's also a lot of information in the grammar summary on verbs, but for now it's probably best to stick with the present tense. To practice the present tense, make it a goal to learn three to five new and useful verbs every day, and write example sentences for them in your language journal. Tailor this exercise to your life and your routine, and look up any new vocabulary you need. Another activity that will help is to find a photo of people—in a magazine, in an old photo album, online—and write a few sentences describing what they're doing. Stick to regular verbs at first, because we'll cover the irregular ones in small groups as we move along.

Word Recall

Rewrite each sentence given using the subject in parentheses. Make sure that you write the correct form of the **-er** or **-ir** verb.

1. **Yo corro cinco kilómetros. (Ella)** ____________________

2. **Yo corro cinco kilómetros. (Nosotros)** ____________________

3. **Yo corro cinco kilómetros. (Vosotros)** ____________________

4. **Yo corro cinco kilómetros. (Ellos)** ____________________

5. **Patricia vive en Sevilla ahora. (Tú)** ______________________

____

6. **Patricia vive en Sevilla ahora. (Enrique y Catalina)** ______________________

____

7. **Patricia vive en Sevilla ahora. (Yo)** ______________________

____

8. **Patricia vive en Sevilla ahora. (Usted)** ______________________

____

ANSWER KEY

1. **Ella corre cinco kilómetros.** 2. **Nosotros corremos cinco kilómetros.** 3. **Vosotros corréis cinco kilómetros.** 4. **Ellos corren cinco kilómetros.** 5. **Tú vives en Sevilla ahora.** 6. **Enrique y Catalina viven en Sevilla ahora.** 7. **Yo vivo en Sevilla ahora.** 8. **Usted vive en Sevilla ahora.**

How Did You Do?

By now, you should know how to:

- ☐ Use verbs like *to run, to eat, to see*
  (Still unsure? Jump back to page 150.)
- ☐ Use verbs like *to write, to live, to leave*
  (Still unsure? Jump back to page 156.)
- ☐ Talk about the present tense using time expressions
  (Still unsure? Jump back to page 157.)

Don't forget to practice and reinforce what you've learned by visiting **www.livinglanguage.com/languagelab** for flashcards, games, and quizzes for Unit 3!

Unit 3 Essentials

Vocabulary Essentials

PARTS OF THE BODY (HEAD AND NECK)

	head
	face
	hair
	forehead
	ear
	eye
	nose
	cheek
	mouth
	lip
	tongue
	tooth
	molar
	throat
	chin
	neck

[Pg. 120]

PARTS OF THE BODY (BELOW THE NECK)

	the body
	arm
	back
	backbone, spinal column
	shoulder
	elbow
	wrist
	hand
	finger, toe
	stomach
	chest
	leg
	knee
	foot
	heart
	hip

[Pg. 123]

HEALTH EXPRESSIONS

	to have a headache
	to have a sore throat
	to have a fever
	to have a cough
	to have an upset stomach
	to be dizzy

	to have high blood pressure
	to have low blood pressure
	to be nauseated, to have nausea
	to take a blood test
	to take the blood pressure
	to take medication

[Pg. 128]

MORE HEALTH EXPRESSIONS

	What's the problem?
	I have a sore throat and a cough.
	I feel dizzy.
	I have nausea and diarrhea.
	Do you have high blood pressure?
	Have you had any operations?
	Where do you have pain?
	Do you have heart problems?
	Do you have any allergies?
	I'm allergic to penicillin.

[Pg. 137]

DESCRIBING PEOPLE

	to have a long face
	to have a round face
	to be blond
	to be dark skinned

	to be white
	to have black/blue/brown/green eyes
	to have long/short hair
	to be bald
	to be tall
	to be short

[Pg. 134]

-AR VERBS

	to walk
	to talk, to speak
	to touch, to play an instrument
	to listen to
	to taste
	to study

[Pg. 143]

-ER VERBS

	to run
	to drink
	to eat
	to see
	to read

[Pg. 151]

-IR VERBS

	to perceive
	to write
	to live
	to leave

[Pg. 156]

EXPRESSIONS OF FREQUENCY

	now
	right now
	tomorrow
	tonight
	always
	frequently
	sometimes
	seldom, almost never
	never
	every day
	every week
	once a week
	twice a week

[Pg. 157]

Grammar Essentials

POSSESSIVE ADJECTIVES

mi(s)	*my*
tu(s)	*your (infml.)*
su(s)	*his, her, your (fml.)*
nuestro/a(s)	*our*
vuestro/a(s)	*your (infml.)*
su(s)	*their, your (fml.)*

POSSESSION WITH DE + PRONOUN

su + noun; or, noun + **de él**	*his (noun)*
su + noun; or, noun + **de ella**	*her (noun)*
su + noun; or, noun + **de ellos/ellas**	*their (noun)*
su + noun; or, noun + **de usted/ustedes**	*your (noun)*

POSSESSIVE PRONOUNS

el mío/la mía, los míos/las mías	*mine*
el tuyo/la tuya, los tuyos/las tuyas	*yours (infml.)*
el suyo/la suya, los suyos/las suyas	*his, hers, yours (fml.)*
el nuestro/la nuestra, los nuestros/las nuestras	*ours*
el vuestro/la vuestra, los vuestros/las vuestras	*yours (infml.)*
el suyo/la suya, los suyos/las suyas	*theirs, yours (fml.)*

-AR VERB ENDINGS

yo	**-o**	**nosotros**	**-amos**
tú	**-as**	**vosotros**	**-áis**
él/ella/usted	**-a**	**ellos/ellas/ ustedes**	**-an**

CAMINAR *(TO WALK)*			
yo camino	*I walk*	**nosotros caminamos**	*we walk*
tú caminas	*you walk (infml.)*	**vosotros camináis**	*you walk (pl. fml.)*
él/ella/usted camina	*he/she walks, you walk (fml.)*	**ellos/ellas/ ustedes caminan**	*they walk, you walk (pl. fml.)*

-ER VERB ENDINGS

yo	**-o**	**nosotros**	**-emos**
tú	**-es**	**vosotros**	**-éis**
él/ella/usted	**-e**	**ellos/ellas/ ustedes**	**-en**

CORRER *(TO RUN)*			
yo corro	*I run*	**nosotros corremos**	*we run*
tú corres	*you run (infml.)*	**vosotros corréis**	*you run (pl. fml.)*
él/ella/usted corre	*he/she runs, you run (fml.)*	**ellos/ellas/ ustedes corren**	*they run, you run (pl. fml.)*

VER ***(TO SEE)***			
yo veo	*I see*	nosotros vemos	*we see*
tú ves	*you see (infml.)*	vosotros veis	*you see (pl. fml.)*
él/ella/usted ve	*he/she sees, you see (fml.)*	ellos/ellas/ ustedes ven	*they see, you see (pl. fml.)*

-IR **VERB ENDINGS**

yo	-o	nosotros	-imos
tú	-es	vosotros	-ís
él/ella/usted	-e	ellos/ellas/ ustedes	-en

ESCRIBIR ***(TO WRITE)***			
yo escribo	*I write*	nosotros escribimos	*we write*
tú escribes	*you write (infml.)*	vosotros escribís	*you write (pl. fml.)*
él/ella/usted escribe	*he/she writes, you write (fml.)*	ellos/ellas/ ustedes escriben	*they write, you write (pl. fml.)*

Unit 3 Quiz

A. Let's practice verbs. Write the correct form of the verb in parentheses. But watch out! There are **-ar**, **-er**, and **-ir** verbs combined.

1. **Camila ________________ en el parque todos los días. (correr)**
2. **Mis hermanos ________________ mucho y son muy atléticos. (caminar)**
3. **Ustedes ________________ en una casa muy bonita. (vivir)**
4. **En la sala de mi casa, yo ________________ mucho. (leer)**
5. **Mara y Emilio ________________ muy bien el español. (escribir)**
6. **¿A qué hora ________________ tú? (comer)**
7. **Tú y yo ________________ la televisión juntos. (ver)**
8. **¿Por qué tú no ________________ a tus padres? (escuchar)**

B. Give the Spanish name for each part of the human face below. Don't forget to include the definite article.

C. Select the correct possessive adjective that goes with each body part or object.

1. *our elbows* ______________________ **codos**
2. *my shoulder* ______________________ **hombro**
3. *our backs* ______________________ **espaldas**
4. *his knee* ______________________ **rodilla**
5. *their house* ______________________ **casa**
6. *your (infml. sing.) leg* ______________________ **pierna**
7. *your (fml. sing.) hands* ______________________ **manos**
8. *your (fml. pl.) feet* ______________________ **pies**

D. Look at the following list of words. One word from each list doesn't quite fit. Which is the odd one out?

1. **el diente, el corazón, el estómago, el pecho** ______________________
2. **la lengua, la boca, el diente, el cuello** ______________________
3. **la mano, la muñeca, la pierna, el dedo** ______________________
4. **el pie, la rodilla, la pierna, el codo** ______________________
5. **la columna vertebral, la espalda, el cuello, el pie** ______________________

How Did You Do?

Give yourself a point for every correct answer, then use the following key to determine whether or not you're ready to move on:

0–7 points: It's probably best to go back and study the lessons again to make sure you understood everything completely. Take your time; it's not a race! Make sure you spend time reviewing vocabulary with the flashcards and reading through each grammar note carefully.

8–16 points: If the questions you missed were in sections A or B, you may want to review the vocabulary again; if you missed answers mostly in sections C or D, check the unit essentials to make sure you have your conjugations and other grammar basics down.

17–20 points: Feel free to move on to the next unit! You're doing a great job.

points

ANSWER KEY

A. 1. corre; 2. caminan; 3. viven; 4. leo; 5. escriben; 6. comes; 7. vemos; 8. escuchas

B. 1. el ojo; 2. la nariz; 3. la oreja; 4. la boca

C. 1. nuestros codos; 2. mi hombro; 3. nuestras espaldas; 4. su rodilla; 5. su casa; 6. tu pierna; 7. sus manos; 8. sus pies

D. 1. el diente; 2. el cuello; 3. la pierna; 4. el codo; 5. el pie

Unit 4:
Using the Telephone and Making Appointments

In this unit, you'll learn common vocabulary and phrases used when talking on the phone, including how to make an appointment with someone.

By the end of this unit, you should be able to:

- ☐ Talk about the telephone and messages
- ☐ Talk a little bit about computers
- ☐ Use demonstrative adjectives to express *this book, that teacher*
- ☐ Use demonstrative pronouns to express *this one, that one*
- ☐ Talk about leaving a message or sending an e-mail
- ☐ Make a negative statement
- ☐ Understand some expressions used on the telephone
- ☐ Use indefinite pronouns to express *something, anything, either . . . or*
- ☐ Ask someone if they'd like to call back or leave a message
- ☐ Express *to make, to do, to put, to bring,* and *to fall*
- ☐ Express *to go out* and *to say*
- ☐ Feel comfortable with the verb *to go*
- ☐ Distinguish *yes* from *if*
- ☐ Say what you *want* or *would like*

Lesson 13: Words

By the end of this lesson, you should be able to:

- ☐ Talk about the telephone and messages
- ☐ Talk a little bit about computers
- ☐ Use demonstrative adjectives to express *this book, that teacher*
- ☐ Use demonstrative pronouns to express *this one, that one*

Word Builder 1

13A Word Builder 1 (CD 5, Track 26)

el contestador automático	*answering machine*
la llamada	*phone call*
la operadora	*operator*
la guía telefónica	*phone book*
las páginas amarillas	*yellow pages*
la cabina telefónica	*telephone booth*
el mensaje	*message*
el buzón de voz	*voice mail*
la centralita	*switchboard*
eliminar	*to eliminate*
borrar	*to erase*

Word Practice 1

Match the following Spanish words to their English translations.

1. **eliminar**	a. *phone call*
2. **borrar**	b. *to eliminate*
3. **la operadora**	c. *to erase*
4. **el mensaje**	d. *voice mail*
5. **el buzón de voz**	e. *operator*
6. **la llamada**	f. *message*

ANSWER KEY

1. b; 2. c; 3. e; 4. f; 5. d; 6. a

Grammar Builder 1

DEMONSTRATIVE ADJECTIVES

13B Grammar Builder 1 (CD 5, Track 27)

Demonstratives, or words like *this* and *that*, show or point to places, people, or things. When a demonstrative is used right before a noun, as in *this book*, it's called a demonstrative adjective. In Spanish, demonstrative adjectives must agree in gender and number with the nouns they point to. Also, Spanish distinguishes among three spatial relations, while English recognizes only two. Let's look at each one.

The first set of demonstratives is used to point to things that are relatively close to the speaker. It can be translated as *this* in the singular and *these* in the plural.

este libro	*this book (m. sg.)*
esta casa	*this house (f. sg.)*
estos profesores	*these teachers (m. pl.)*
estas computadoras	*these computers (f. pl.)*

The second set of demonstratives is used to point to things that are farther away from the speaker but perhaps closer to the listener. The translation is *that* or *those*.

ese niño	*that boy (m. sg.)*
esa mujer	*that woman (f. sg.)*
esos cuadernos	*those notebooks (m. pl.)*
esas llaves	*those keys (f. pl.)*

Finally, the third set is used to point to things that are relatively far away from both the speaker and the listener. The most appropriate English translation is *that (over) there* or *those (over) there*.

aquel edificio	*that building there (m. sg.)*
aquella oficina	*that office over there (f. sg.)*
aquellos coches	*those cars there (m. pl.)*
aquellas calles	*those streets over there (f. pl.)*

Let's see some more examples in sentences.

Este teléfono no funciona.
This phone doesn't work.

Esa línea está ocupada.
That line is busy.

Aquella cabina telefónica está libre.
That phone booth over there is free.

Work Out 1

Choose the correct demonstrative adjective to fill in the blank.

1. **(Este, Esta, Estos, Estas)** ______________________ **llamada es importante.**
2. **(Aquellos, Aquel, Aquella, Aquellas)** ____________ **oficinas están ocupadas.**
3. **(Esas, Esa, Ese, Esos)** ________________________ **contestador no funciona.**
4. **(Esas, Esa, Ese, Esos)** ________________ **télefonos son de la oficina de mi tío.**
5. **(Este, Esta, Estos, Estas)** ____________________ **mensajes son para Julián.**
6. **(Aquellos, Aquel, Aquella, Aquellas)** ________________ **hombre es mi padre.**

ANSWER KEY

1. **Esta**; 2. **Aquellas**; 3. **Ese**; 4. **Esos**; 5. **Estos**; 6. **Aquel**

Word Builder 2

13C Word Builder 2 (CD 5, Track 28)

el fax	*fax*
el móvil	*mobile phone*
el celular	*cell phone*
Internet	*internet*
la computadora	*computer*
el teclado	*keyboard*
la pantalla	*screen*
la impresora	*printer*
el ratón	*mouse*
los audífonos	*headphones*
la conexión	*connection*

Word Practice 2

Match the following Spanish words to their English translations.

1. **Internet**	a. *internet*
2. **el ratón**	b. *screen*
3. **el teclado**	c. *keyboard*
4. **la pantalla**	d. *mouse*
5. **la computadora**	e. *printer*
6. **la impresora**	f. *computer*

ANSWER KEY

1. a; 2. d; 3. c; 4. b; 5. f; 6. e

Grammar Builder 2

DEMONSTRATIVE PRONOUNS

13D Grammar Builder 2 (CD 5, Track 29)

Words like *this* and *that* not only function as adjectives in English, as in *this book* or *that house*, but can also be used as pronouns, as in *I like this (one) and you like that (one)*. In Spanish, demonstrative pronouns have an accent mark that distinguishes them from demonstrative adjectives.

éste/ésta	*this (one)*
éstos/éstas	*these (ones)*
ése/ésa	*that (one)*
ésos/ésas	*those (ones)*
aquél/aquélla	*that (one) over there*
aquéllos/aquéllas	*those (ones) over there*

Let's take a look at some examples. Notice the difference between demonstrative adjectives, which are used right before nouns, and demonstrative pronouns, which stand on their own in place of nouns.

Este número de fax es el mío y éste es el tuyo.
This fax number is mine and this one is yours.

Esa pantalla es plana y ésa no.
That screen is flat and that one is not.

Aquella computadora es nueva y aquélla no.
That computer is new and that one is not.

There are three neuter demonstrative pronouns that are used to refer to abstract concepts or unspecified objects. They're also used when the speaker doesn't necessarily have a specific noun in mind, so the gender is unknown; the neuter form is used instead.

esto	*this (one, thing)*
eso	*that (one, thing)*
aquello	*that (one, thing) further away*

Here are some examples.

Esto es un desastre.
This is a disaster.

Eso es verdad.
That's true.

Aquello no me gusta.
I don't like that.

Work Out 2

Choose either the demonstrative adjective or the demonstrative pronoun to complete the sentence.

1. **(Ese, Ése)** ____________________ **teléfono está ocupado.**
2. **(Este, Éste)** ____________________ **es mi número de celular.**
3. **(Estos, Éstos)** ____________________ **meses son largos.**
4. **(Esta, Ésta)** ____________________ **pantalla es oscura y (aquella, aquélla)** ____________________ **es pequeña.**
5. **(Estas, Éstas)** ____________________ **computadoras son costosas.**
6. **(Esta, Ésta)** ____________________ **semana tengo dos reuniones.**
7. **(Esas, Ésas)** ____________________ **son nuestras oficinas.**
8. **(Ese, Ése)** ____________________ **teclado no me gusta.**

ANSWER KEY

1. **Ese**; 2. **Éste**; 3. **Estos**; 4. **Esta**, **aquélla**; 5. **Estas**; 6. **Esta**; 7. **Ésas**; 8. **Ese**

Take It Further

Demonstrative adjectives can also be used with time expressions, just as they are in English.

esta mañana	*this morning*
esta tarde	*this afternoon*
esta noche	*tonight*
esta semana	*this week*
este día	*this day*
este mes	*this month*

este año	*this year*
este siglo	*this century*

Here are some examples.

Este mes tengo mucho trabajo.
I have a lot of work this month.

Esta tarde tenemos dos reuniones.
We have two meetings this afternoon.

Word Recall

Choose the appropriate demonstrative adjective or pronoun.

1. **(Éste/Este/Ésta/Esta) ________________ señor es el padre de Paquito.**
2. **(Éste/Este/Ésta/Esta) ________________ es el padre de Paquito.**
3. **(Éste/Este/Ésta/Esta) ________________ señora es la madre de Paquito.**
4. **(Éste/Este/Ésta/Esta) ________________ es la madre de Paquito.**
5. **(Aquél/Aquel/Aquélla/Aquella) ________________ coche es nuevo.**
6. **(Aquéllos/Aquellos/Aquéllas/Aquellas) ________________ coches son nuevos.**
7. **(Ésas/Esas/Ésos/Esos) ________________ cuadernos son para mi clase de español.**
8. **(Ésas/Esas/Ésos/Esos) ________________ plumas son para mi clase de español.**
9. **(Aquel/Aquél/Aquellos/Aquéllos) ________________ edificios son muy altos.**
10. **(Aquél/Aquél/Aquellos/Aquéllos) ________________ son edificios muy altos.**

ANSWER KEY

1. **Este**; 2. **Éste**; 3. **Esta**; 4. **Ésta**; 5. **Aquel**; 6. **Aquellos**; 7. **Esos**; 8. **Esas**; 9. **Aquellos**; 10. **Aquéllos**

How Did You Do?

By now, you should be able to:

- ☐ Talk about the telephone and messages
  (Still unsure? Jump back to page 173.)
- ☐ Talk a little bit about computers
  (Still unsure? Jump back to page 176.)
- ☐ Use demonstrative adjectives to express *this book, that teacher*
  (Still unsure? Jump back to page 174.)
- ☐ Use demonstrative pronouns to express *this one, that one*
  (Still unsure? Jump back to page 177.)

Lesson 14: Phrases

By the end of this lesson, you should be able to:

- ☐ Talk about leaving a message or sending an e-mail
- ☐ Make a negative statement
- ☐ Understand some expressions used on the telephone
- ☐ Use indefinite pronouns to express *something, anything, either … or*

Phrase Builder 1

14A Phrase Builder 1 (CD 5, Track 30)

Here are a few verb phrases you'll use when talking on the phone or sending e-mail. They're all regular verbs, except for **colgar**, which we'll come back to later.

llamar por teléfono	*to make a phone call*
contestar el teléfono	*to answer the phone*
colgar el teléfono	*to hang up the phone*
marcar un número de teléfono	*to dial a phone number*
dejar un mensaje después de oír la señal	*to leave a message after the tone*
enviar un mensaje	*to send a message*
borrar un mensaje	*to erase a message*
copiar un mensaje	*to copy a message*
recibir un fax	*to receive a fax*
hacer una llamada internacional	*to make an international call*
hacer una llamada nacional	*to make a national call*
enviar un correo electrónico	*to send an e-mail*
contestar* un correo electrónico	*to reply to an e-mail*
enviar un archivo	*to send a file*
bajar un archivo	*to download a file*

* Notice that in English, you need a preposition after *reply*, but in Spanish, you can use **contestar** on its own. This is very similar to what you saw with **escuchar** (*to listen to*).

Phrase Practice 1

Fill in the missing word or phrase.

1. **llamar** ______________________ *to make a phone call*

2. **contestar** ________________ *to answer the phone*

3. ________________ **el teléfono** *to hang up the phone*

4. **marcar** ________________ *to dial a phone number*

5. ________________ **un correo electrónico** *to send an e-mail*

6. ________________ **un correo electrónico** *to reply to an e-mail*

7. ________________ **un archivo** *to send a file*

8. ________________ **un archivo** *to download a file*

ANSWER KEY

1. **por teléfono**; 2. **el teléfono**; 3. **colgar**; 4. **un número de teléfono**; 5. **enviar**; 6. **contestar**; 7. **enviar**; 8. **bajar**

Grammar Builder 1

NEGATION

14B Grammar Builder 1 (CD 5, Track 31)

Making a negative statement in Spanish is very easy—simply place the word **no** (*not*) before the verb.

Tengo conexión de Internet en mi casa.
I have an internet connection at home.

No tengo conexión de Internet en mi casa.
I don't have an internet connection at home.

La línea está ocupada.
The line is busy.

La línea no está ocupada.
The line isn't busy.

Hay tono.
There's a dial tone.

No hay tono.
There's no dial tone.

Eres un arquitecto.
You are an architect.

No eres un arquitecto.
You're not an architect.

When the answer to a question is negative, the word **no** is used twice—once to mean *no*, and once to mean *not*.

¿Está la señora Ruiz en su oficina?
Is Mrs. Ruiz in her office?

No. Ella no está en su oficina.
No. She's not in her office.

¿Tienes tiempo para tomar un café?
Do you have time for a coffee?

No. No tengo tiempo.
No. I don't have time.

Work Out 1

Make the following statements negative.

1. **Éste es mi número de teléfono.** ________________

2. **Las secretarias hablan por teléfono.** ________________

3. **Tus padres tienen una casa pequeña.** ________________

4. **Yo escribo un correo electrónico.** ________________

5. **Tenemos tu número de celular.** ________________

6. **Leo un fax.** ________________

7. **Estas oficinas son muy grandes.** ________________

8. **La línea está ocupada.** ________________

ANSWER KEY

1. **Éste no es mi número de teléfono.** 2. **Las secretarias no hablan por teléfono.** 3. **Tus padres no tienen una casa pequeña.** 4. **Yo no escribo un correo electrónico.** 5. **No tenemos tu número de celular.** 6. **No leo un fax.** 7. **Estas oficinas no son muy grandes.** 8. **La línea no está ocupada.**

Phrase Builder 2

14C Phrase Builder 2 (CD 5, Track 32)

Here are some phrases you'll use when talking on the phone.

¿Dígame?	*Hello? (lit., Tell me?)*
¿Aló?	*Hello?*
Le paso.	*I'm putting you through.*
La línea está ocupada.	*The line is busy.*
Está comunicando.	*It's ringing.*
No hay tono.	*There is no dial tone.*
No cuelgue, por favor.	*Do not hang up, please.*
Espere, por favor.	*Hold on, please.*
poner en espera	*to put on hold*

Phrase Practice 2

Translate the following phrases.

1. *Hello? (lit., Tell me?)* ____________
2. *Hello?* ____________
3. *Do not hang up, please.* ____________
4. *Hold on, please.* ____________
5. *to put on hold* ____________

ANSWER KEY

1. **¿Dígame?** 2. **¿Aló?** 3. **No cuelgue, por favor.** 4. **Espere, por favor.** 5. **poner en espera**

Grammar Builder 2

INDEFINITE PRONOUNS

14D Grammar Builder 2 (CD 6, Track 1)

An indefinite pronoun is a pronoun that doesn't refer to anyone in particular. Here are some indefinite pronouns and other words that will come in handy in Spanish. Notice that they're all affirmative. We'll look at their negative counterparts in a moment.

algo	*something*
alguien	*somebody, someone*
algún(-o/-a/-os/-as)	*some, something*
siempre	*always*
también	*also, too*
o . . . o	*either . . . or*

Here's how they're used in a sentence.

Hay algo diferente en esta habitación.
There's something different in this room.

Alguien llama por teléfono.
Somebody's calling on the phone.

Algunos teléfonos no funcionan.
Some phones don't work.

Ella siempre escribe emails.
She always writes e-mails.

Nosotros también tocamos el piano.
We also play the piano.

Yo o corro o camino por las mañanas.
I either run or walk in the mornings.

Notice that **o ... o** is used to introduce two different options, and each **o** is placed in front of one of the options. In the example above, the two options are actions, so each **o** is placed before the verb. (Sometimes the first **o** is omitted.)

Here are their negative counterparts. **Ni ... ni** functions just like **o ... o**.

nada	*nothing*
nadie	*nobody, no one*
ningún(-o/-a/-os/-as)	*no, none*
nunca	*never*
tampoco	*neither, not either*
ni ... ni	*neither ... nor*

Negative words can be used alone, preceding the verb.

Jorge nunca come.
Jorge never eats.

Él tampoco canta.
He doesn't sing either.

Nadie habla italiano aquí.
No one here speaks Italian.

Double negation is perfectly correct in Spanish. Usually the word **no** immediately precedes the verb and another negative word follows the verb.

No funciona ni el teléfono ni el fax.
Neither the phone nor the fax works.

No hay conexión nunca.
There's never a connection.

No hay nadie en la oficina.
There's nobody in the office./There isn't anyone in the office.

Work Out 2

Translate the following sentences. When appropriate, use single (instead of double) negation.

1. *I always have a copy of my messages.* ____________________

2. *Nobody answers the phone.* ____________________

3. *They never erase their messages.* ____________________

4. *Someone receives a fax.* ____________________

5. *Someone also receives an e-mail.* ____________________

6. *He doesn't have a phone or a fax in his office.* ______________________

____

ANSWER KEY

1. **Siempre tengo una copia de mis mensajes.** 2. **Nadie contesta el teléfono.** 3. **Nunca borran sus mensajes.** 4. **Alguien recibe un fax.** 5. **Alguien también recibe un correo electrónico.** 6. **No tiene ni un teléfono ni un fax en su oficina.**

Take It Further

Later on in this unit, you'll be learning how to make polite requests. In doing so, the phrase **por favor** (*please*) comes in very handy. Another phrase that you'll often hear is **hágame el favor de** (*lit., do me the favor of*). You'll never be wrong to use **por favor**. However, you might be surprised not to hear the words when asking someone to do something that he or she is expected to do (as when ordering a meal from a server). As in English, your tone of voice can have as much to do with how your request is received as does its grammatical form.

Word Recall

The following are affirmative sentences. Say the opposite by turning each sentence into a negation according to the hints in parentheses.

1. **Yo tengo dos reuniones esta semana.** *(don't have)* ______________________

____

2. **La línea está ocupada.** *(isn't)* ______________________

____

3. **Este mes tengo mucho trabajo.** *(don't have)* ______________________

____

4. **Estela y yo hablamos francés.** *(don't speak)* ______________________________

____

5. **Hay muchas personas en mi oficina.** *(there aren't)* ______________________________

____

6. **Alguien llama por teléfono.** *(no one)* ______________________________

____

7. **Ella siempre bebe café.** *(never)* ______________________________

____

ANSWER KEY

1. **Yo no tengo dos reuniones esta semana.** 2. **La línea no está ocupada.** 3. **Este mes no tengo mucho trabajo.** 4. **Estela y yo no hablamos francés .** 5. **No hay muchas personas en mi oficina.** 6. **Nadie llama por teléfono.** 7. **Ella nunca bebe café.**

How Did You Do?

By now, you should be able to:

- □ Talk about leaving a message or sending an e-mail
(Still unsure? Jump back to page 182.)
- □ Make a negative statement
(Still unsure? Jump back to page 183.)
- □ Understand some expressions used on the telephone
(Still unsure? Jump back to page 186.)
- □ Use indefinite pronouns to express *something, anything, either . . . or*
(Still unsure? Jump back to page 187.)

Lesson 15: Sentences

By the end of this lesson, you should be able to:

- ☐ Ask someone if they'd like to call back or leave a message
- ☐ Express *to make*, *to do*, *to put*, *to bring*, and *to fall*
- ☐ Express *to go out* and *to say*

Sentence Builder 1

15A Sentence Builder 1 (CD 6, Track 2)

Quisiera hablar con . . .	*I'd like to talk to . . .*
Lo siento, tiene un número equivocado.	*Sorry, you have the wrong number.*
¿De parte de quién?	*Who's calling?*
¿Quién lo llama?	*Who's calling?*
¿Con quién hablo?	*Who am I talking to?*
Ahora no está.	*He/She isn't in right now.*
Está ocupado/a.	*He's/She's busy.*
Por favor, llame más tarde.	*Please call later.*
Llame en cinco minutos.	*Please call in five minutes.*
No está en su oficina.	*He/She is not in his/her office.*
Ya salió.	*He/She already left.*
¿Desea dejar un mensaje?	*Would you like to leave a message?*

Sentence Practice 1

Translate the following sentences.

1. *I'd like to talk to ...* ______________________
2. *Sorry, you have the wrong number.* ______________________

____

3. *Who's calling?* ______________________
4. *Who am I talking to?* ______________________
5. *He/She isn't in right now.* ______________________
6. *He's/She's busy.* ______________________
7. *Please call later.* ______________________

ANSWER KEY

1. **Quisiera hablar con ...** 2. **Lo siento, tiene un número equivocado.** 3.**¿De parte de quién?/¿Quién lo llama?** 4.**¿Con quién hablo?** 5. **Ahora no está.** 6. **Está ocupado/a.** 7. **Por favor, llame más tarde.**

Grammar Builder 1

IRREGULAR VERBS HACER (*TO MAKE, TO DO*), PONER (*TO PUT*), TRAER (*TO BRING*), AND CAER (*TO FALL*)

15B Grammar Builder 1 (CD 6, Track 3)

As you know, there are a few verbs in Spanish that are irregular. Most of the time, these verbs follow the pattern of endings you learned in Unit 4, but their stems change a bit when conjugated. For example, you already know the verb **tener**, which has a **g** before the ending for the first person singular (**yo tengo**), and the **e** in its stem changes to **ie** in several forms (**tienes, tiene, tienen**).

There are a few other verbs that add **g** in the first person singular: **hacer** (*to make, to do*), **poner** (*to put*), **traer** (*to bring*), and **caer** (*to fall*). For all other persons, they are conjugated just like regular **-er** verbs.

HACER *(TO MAKE, TO DO)*	
yo hago	nosotros/as hacemos
tú haces	vosotros/as hacéis
él/ella/usted hace	ellos/ellas/ustedes hacen

PONER *(TO PUT)*	
yo pongo	nosotros/as ponemos
tú pones	vosotros/as ponéis
él/ella/usted pone	ellos/ellas/ustedes ponen

The verb **traer** (*to bring*) also takes an **i** before the **g** in the **yo** form.

TRAER *(TO BRING)*	
yo traigo	nosotros/as traemos
tú traes	vosotros/as traéis
él/ella/usted trae	ellos/ellas/ustedes traen

The verb **caer** (*to fall*) is conjugated just like **traer**.

CAER *(TO FALL)*	
yo caigo	nosotros/as caemos
tú caes	vosotros/as caéis
él/ella/usted cae	ellos/ellas/ustedes caen

Work Out 1

Complete the following sentences with the correct form of the verb.

1. **Nosotros no** ______________________ **llamadas locales. (hacer)**
2. **Ustedes** ______________________ **los contratos. (traer)**
3. **Ella** ______________________ **a María en espera. (poner)**
4. **Yo** ______________ **llamadas internacionales todos los días. (hacer)**
5. **Ellas no** ______________________ **en la oficina en este momento. (estar)**
6. **Usted** ______________________ **la línea equivocada. (tener)**
7. **Ella** ______________________ **buenas noticias. (traer)**
8. **Tú** ______________________ **ocupado todos los días. (estar)**
9. **Vosotros** ______________________ **la computadora en la oficina. (poner)**
10. **Yo** ______________________ **una reunión el martes. (tener)**

ANSWER KEY

1. **hacemos**; 2. **traen**; 3. **pone**; 4. **hago**; 5. **están**; 6. **tiene**; 7. **trae**; 8. **estás**; 9. **ponéis**; 10. **tengo**

Sentence Builder 2

15C Sentence Builder 2 (CD 6, Track 4)

¿Quiere esperar un momento?	*Do you want to wait a moment?*
No hay nadie disponible en este momento.	*There's no one available at the moment.*
Por favor, anote mi número de teléfono.	*Please write down my telephone number.*
Necesito hablar con el señor Sánchez lo antes posible.	*I need to speak to Mr. Sánchez as soon as possible.*

Que tenga un buen día.	*Have a nice day.*
Casi no reconozco tu voz.	*I almost don't recognize your voice.*
Tengo los contratos listos, pero falta tu firma.	*I have the contracts ready, but your signature is missing.*
Salgo de viaje ese mismo día.	*I go on a trip that very same day.*
El martes por la mañana me viene bien.	*Tuesday morning suits me fine.*
Tengo una reunión muy temprano.	*I have a meeting very early.*
¿Cuál es su dirección de correo electrónico?	*What's your e-mail address?*
¿Su compañía tiene un sitio web?	*Does your company have a website?*
El informe está en un anexo al correo electrónico.	*The report is in an e-mail attachment.*

Sentence Practice 2

Fill in the missing words in Spanish.

1. ______________________ **el señor Sánchez lo antes posible.**

   I need to speak to Mr. Sánchez as soon as possible.

2. ______________________ **un buen día.** *Have a nice day.*

3. **El martes por la mañana** ______________________ . *Tuesday morning suits me fine.*

4. **Tengo** ______________________ **muy temprano.** *I have a meeting very early.*

5. **¿Cuál es** ______________________ **?**

   What's your e-mail address?

6. **¿Su compañía** ______________________________ **?**

Does your company have a website?

7. **El informe está en** ______________________________ **.**

The report is in an e-mail attachment.

ANSWER KEY

1. **Necesito hablar con**; 2. **Que tenga**; 3. **me viene bien**; 4. **una reunión**; 5. **su dirección de correo electrónico**; 6. **tiene un sitio web**; 7. **un anexo al correo electrónico**

Grammar Builder 2

IRREGULAR VERBS SALIR (*TO GO OUT*) AND DECIR (*TO SAY*)

15D Grammar Builder 2 (CD 6, Track 5)

Let's look at some more irregular verbs. The verbs **salir** (*to go out*) and **decir** (*to say*) are irregular **-ir** verbs that also have the **g** in the first person singular.

SALIR (*TO GO OUT*)	
yo salgo	**nosotros/as salimos**
tú sales	**vosotros/as salís**
él/ella/usted sale	**ellos/ellas/ustedes salen**

Notice that **decir** (*to say*) also has a vowel change from **e** to **i** in its stem.

DECIR (*TO SAY*)	
yo digo	**nosotros/as decimos**
tú dices	**vosotros/as decís**
él/ella/usted dice	**ellos/ellas/ustedes dicen**

Yo salgo del trabajo a las tres de la tarde.
I leave work at 3:00 p.m.

Ella dice siempre la verdad.

She always tells the truth.

So far you've learned two verbs that have vowel changes in their stems: **tener** and **decir**. In **tener**, **e** becomes **ie**, and in **decir**, **e** becomes **i**. Notice that these changes do not happen in the **nosotros/as** and **vosotros/as** forms. You'll learn more about stem changing verbs later, but for now keep in mind that if there is a stem change, it doesn't affect the first and second person plural forms, **nosotros/as** and **vosotros/as**.

Work Out 2

Rewrite the following sentences using the subject pronoun given in parentheses.

1. **Yo digo pocas palabras. (nosotros)** ______________________

2. **Tú sales de viaje el domingo. (yo)** ______________________

3. **Ustedes dicen la verdad. (ella)** ______________________

4. **Él sale de su oficina a las tres de la tarde. (tú)** ______________________

5. **Nosotros salimos de nuestra casa a las nueve de la mañana. (vosotros)** ______________________

6. **Ellos no dicen nada. (yo)** ______________________

ANSWER KEY

1. **Nosotros decimos pocas palabras.** 2. **Yo salgo de viaje el domingo.** 3. **Ella dice la verdad.** 4. **Tú sales de tu oficina a las tres de la tarde.** 5. **Vosotros salís de nuestra casa a las nueve de la mañana.** 6. **Yo no digo nada.**

Tip!

Don't get too worked up about learning irregular verbs. You'll see that the most frequently used verbs are the ones with the most irregularities—you'll hear them so often that you'll end up learning them very quickly. Also, the most irregular person in the conjugation of verbs is the first person singular, or **yo** form (*I*). So, even though a verb may be called irregular, it may only mean that the first person singular is irregular and the rest of the conjugation follows a regular pattern, as you saw with some of the verbs in this lesson. If you're a stickler for memorizing irregular forms, though, here are some suggestions. Make flash cards for each new irregular verb, following the two-column format in which the irregular verbs are presented in this lesson. Keep them in your pocket, and when you have a few spare moments, take them out, glance over them, and repeat the forms aloud to yourself. You'll have them memorized pretty quickly.

Word Recall

Let's practice those irregular verbs once again. Rewrite each sentence by using the suggested noun in parentheses.

1. **Ella hace muchas llamadas por teléfono. (Tú)** ______________________

____

2. **Ella hace muchas llamadas por teléfono. (Nosotros)** ______________________

____

3. **Ella hace muchas llamadas por teléfono. (Ustedes)** ______________________

____

4. **Yo siempre digo la verdad. (Tú)** ______________________

____

5. **Yo siempre digo la verdad. (Nosotros)** ______________________

____

6. **Yo siempre digo la verdad. (Ustedes)** ______________________

____

ANSWER KEY

1. **Tú haces muchas llamadas por teléfono.** 2. **Nosotros hacemos muchas llamadas por teléfono.** 3. **Ustedes hacen muchas llamadas por teléfono.** 4. **Tú siempre dices la verdad.** 5. **Nosotros siempre decimos la verdad.** 6. **Ustedes siempre dicen la verdad.**

How Did You Do?

By now, you should be able to:

- ☐ Ask someone if they'd like to call back or leave a message
(Still unsure? Jump back to page 192.)
- ☐ Express *to make, to do, to put, to bring*, and *to fall*
(Still unsure? Jump back to page 193.)
- ☐ Express *to go out* and *to say*
(Still unsure? Jump back to page 197.)

Lesson 16: Conversations

By the end of this lesson, you should be able to:

- ☐ Feel comfortable with the verb *to go*
- ☐ Distinguish *yes* from *if*

☐ Say what you *want* or *would like*

Conversation 1

16A Conversation 1 (CD 6, Track 6 - Spanish Only; Track 7 - Spanish and English)

Juan Fernández is calling Nova Limitada to speak with Miguel Sánchez. He dials the switchboard and gets the operator.

Operadora: **Nova Limitada, buenos días, ¿con quién desea hablar?**
Juan: **Buenos días. Me llamo Juan Fernández y necesito hablar con el gerente de ventas, el señor Miguel Sánchez.**
Operadora: **Le comunico. Un momento por favor.**

(after a moment)

Operadora: **La línea está ocupada. ¿Quiere esperar un momento?**
Juan: **No, no tengo tiempo. ¿Hay alguien más?**
Operadora: **No. Lo siento. En ese departamento no hay nadie disponible en este momento. Todos están en una reunión fuera de la ciudad.**
Juan: **Bueno, por favor anote mi número de teléfono. Necesito hablar con el señor Sánchez lo antes posible.**
Operadora: **¿Quiere su buzón de voz?**
Juan: **Buena idea.**
Operadora: **Ya le conecto. Que tenga un buen día.**
Juan: **Muchas gracias. Igualmente.**

Operator: *Nova Limitada, good morning; who would you like to speak to?*
Juan: *Good morning. My name is Juan Fernández, and I need to speak to the sales manager, Mr. Miguel Sánchez.*
Operator: *I'll put you through. One moment please.*

(after a moment)

Operator:	*The line is busy. Do you want to wait a moment?*
Juan:	*No, I don't have time. Is there anybody else?*
Operator:	*No. I'm sorry. There's no one available in that department at the moment. Everyone is at a meeting out of town.*
Juan:	*Well, please write down my phone number. I need to speak to Mr. Sánchez as soon as possible.*
Operator:	*Do you want his voice mail?*
Juan:	*Good idea.*
Operator:	*I'll put you through right now. Have a nice day.*
Juan:	*Thank you; same to you.*

Take It Further

As briefly mentioned in Lesson 12, when the direct object of a verb is a person, you must introduce it with the preposition **a**. This **a** has no real meaning, and when it's followed by the masculine article **el**, it forms the contraction **al**.

Invitamos al gerente de ventas.
We're inviting the sales manager.

Traigo a mis amigos.
I'm bringing my friends.

Veo a mis amigos todas las semanas.
I see my friends every week.

Quieren mucho a sus padres.
They love their parents very much.

The only exception is the verb **tener**. If **tener** has a person as a direct object, the preposition **a** is not used.

Tiene muchos amigos.
She/He has a lot of friends.

Tengo un hermano y una hermana.
I have a brother and a sister.

Conversation Practice 1

Fill in the blanks below with the appropriate word based on the English translations and the dialogue above.

1. **Nova Limitada, buenos días, ¿con quién ________________?**

   Nova Limitada, good morning; who would you like to speak to?

2. **¿________________ esperar un momento?** *Do you want to wait a moment?*

3. **¿Hay ________________ más?** *Is there anybody else?*

4. **En ese departamento no hay ________________ disponible en este momento.**

   There's no one available in that department at the moment.

5. **Todos están en una ________________ fuera de la ciudad.**

   Everyone is at a meeting out of town.

ANSWER KEY

1. **desea hablar**; 2. **Quiere**; 3. **alguien**; 4. **nadie**; 5. **reunión**

Grammar Builder 1

IR (*TO GO*)

16B Grammar Builder 1 (CD 6, Track 8)

The verb **ir** (*to go*) is used in many situations, and it is also an irregular verb.

IR (*TO GO*)	
yo voy	**nosotros/as vamos**
tú vas	**vosotros/as vais**
él/ella/usted va	**ellos/ellas/ustedes van**

Notice that we generally use the preposition **a** (*to*) with the verb **ir**. And remember that **a** + the masculine article **el** forms the contraction **al**.

Esta tarde voy a mi oficina.
This afternoon I'm going to my office.

Nosotros vamos al cine los fines de semana.
We go to the movies on the weekends.

Work Out 1

Match the sentences in the left column with the appropriate responses in the right column.

1. **¿Quién lo llama?**
2. **¿Cuál es su número?**
3. **¿Desea dejar un mensaje?**

a. **No, gracias, llamo más tarde.**
b. **Le paso.**
c. **Lo siento. Ella ya salió.**

4. **¿Es el tres, ocho, nueve, uno, dos?**
5. **Quisiera hablar con el señor Martínez, por favor.**
6. **Quisiera hablar son la señora Marcos.**
7. **Cienfuentes Abogados, ¿dígame?**

d. **Sí, gracias, necesito hablar con el señor Almirante.**
e. **Es el siete, tres, cero, nueve, dos, dos.**
f. **No. Tiene el número equivocado.**
g. **Soy Manuel Marcos, de Industrias Talía.**

ANSWER KEY

1. g; 2.e; 3. a; 4. f; 5. b; 6. c; 7. d

Conversation 2

16C Conversation 2 (CD 6, Track 9 - Spanish Only; Track 10 - Spanish and English)

Later that afternoon, Miguel returns Juan's call.

Secretaria:	**Trías y Trías Abogados, buenas tardes.**
Miguel:	**Buenas tardes. Soy Miguel Sánchez. Necesito hablar con el señor Fernández.**
Secretaria:	**Le paso.**
Juan:	**¿Dígame?**
Miguel:	**¿Con quién hablo?**
Juan:	**¡Hola, Miguel; soy yo, Juan!**
Miguel:	**Hola, Juan. Casi no reconozco tu voz. ¿Cómo van las cosas?**
Juan:	**Pues más o menos. Necesito reunirme contigo urgentemente. Tengo los contratos listos, pero falta tu firma.**
Miguel:	**¿Qué te parece si nos vemos el miércoles a eso de las nueve?**
Juan:	**Salgo de viaje ese mismo día. Y el lunes . . . ¿tienes tiempo?**
Miguel:	**Pero hombre, si es día festivo. Pero el martes por la mañana me viene bien.**
Juan:	**Listo. Voy primero a los juzgados y luego a tu oficina.**

Miguel: **Tengo una reunión muy temprano ... Si vienes después de las diez, mejor.**
Juan: **Perfecto. Entonces, nos vemos el martes.**
Miguel: **Hasta luego.**

Secretary: *Trías and Trías Lawyers, good afternoon.*
Miguel: *Good afternoon. I'm Miguel Sánchez. I need to speak to Mr. Fernández.*
Secretary: *I'll put you through.*
Juan: *Hello?*
Miguel: *Who am I speaking to?*
Juan: *Hi, Miguel; it's me, Juan!*
Miguel: *Hi, Juan. I almost don't recognize your voice. How are things?*
Juan: *Well, so-so. I need to meet with you urgently. I have the contracts ready, but your signature is missing.*
Miguel: *How about getting together on Wednesday at about nine?*
Juan: *I leave on a trip that same day. What about Monday ... Do you have time?*
Miguel: *Come on now, that's a holiday! But Tuesday morning is fine with me.*
Juan: *Good. I'll first go to court and then to your office.*
Miguel: *I have a meeting very early. If you come after ten, that's better.*
Juan: *Perfect. So, see you Tuesday.*
Miguel: *Till later.*

Take It Further

Don't confuse **sí** with **si**. When **sí** is spelled with an accent mark, it means *yes*; when it is spelled without the accent mark, it means *if*.

Notice that Miguel said: **Pero hombre, si es día festivo**. The words **hombre** and **si** are used as flavoring words, giving emphasis to what Miguel is saying. The sentence could be translated in a number of ways to capture the same sentiment, for example: *Come on now, that's a holiday!*

Conversation Practice 1

Fill in the blanks below with the appropriate word based on the English translations and the dialogue above.

1. ________________ **con el señor Fernández.** *I need to speak to Mr. Fernández.*
2. **¿Con quién** ________ **?** *Who am I speaking to?*
3. **Pues** ________________ . *Well, so-so.*
4. ________ **primero a los juzgados y luego** ________ . *I'll first go to court and then to your office.*
5. **Entonces,** ________ **el martes.** *So, see you Tuesday.*

ANSWER KEY
1. **Necesito hablar**; 2. **hablo**; 3. **más o menos**; 4. **Voy**, **a tu oficina**; 5. **nos vemos**

Grammar Builder 2

QUERER (*TO WANT, TO LOVE*)

16D Grammar Builder 2 (CD 6, Track 11)

When making polite requests you will very often use the verb **querer** (*to want*). This is an irregular verb, conjugated as follows.

QUERER (*TO WANT*)	
yo quiero	**nosotros/as queremos**

QUERER ***(TO WANT)***	
tú quieres	**vosotros/as queréis**
él/ella/usted quiere	**ellos/ellas/ustedes quieren**

Querer can be used right before another verb in the infinitive, just as *to want to* is in English.

Quiero una habitación grande, por favor.
I want a big room, please

Quiero hablar con Patricia.
I want to speak to Patricia.

Quiero escribir un correo electrónico.
I want to write an e-mail.

A much nicer and more polite way of making requests is by using the form **quisiera** (*would like*).

Quisiera una cerveza, por favor.
I would like a beer, please.

Quisiera hablar con Patricia.
I'd like to speak to Patricia.

Quisiera hacer una llamada internacional.
I'd like to make an international call.

Note that this verb is often used to mean *to love*. So, a common way of saying *I love you* is to say **Te quiero**. Spanish does have the verb **amar**, which means *to* *love,* but it is not used as often, and it is usually used strictly in a romantic way. Don't forget to use the preposition **a** if the direct object of **querer** is a person.

Gloria quiere mucho a su papá.
Gloria loves her daddy very much.

Queremos a nuestros amigos.
We love our friends.

Another verb that can be used to make a polite request is **gustar** (*to like*). Again, you would use the form **me gustaría** (*I would like*).

Me gustaría un café.
I would like a cup of coffee.

Me gustaría llamar por teléfono.
I'd like to make a phone call.

Work Out 2

Translate the following sentences into Spanish.

1. *I would like to speak to the manager, please.* ______________________

____

2. *We want a new computer.* ______________________

____

3. *I'd like to go to my brother's office.* ______________________

____

4. *He wants your telephone number.* ________________

____

5. *I'd like to leave a message.* ________________

____

ANSWER KEY

1. **Me gustaría**/**Quisiera hablar con el gerente, por favor.** 2. **Queremos una computadora nueva.** 3. **Me gustaría**/**Quisiera ir a la oficina de mi hermano.** 4. **Él quiere tu número de teléfono.** 5. **Me gustaría**/**Quisiera dejar un mensaje.**

Culture Note

Every country in the Spanish-speaking world celebrates different national, religious, and local **fiestas** or **días festivos** (*holidays*) depending on heritage and tradition. For economic reasons, in some countries the government has decided to move the celebration of religious holidays to the following Monday in order to avoid the very long **puentes** (*long weekends, lit., bridges*) that would result in a holiday being on a Tuesday or Thursday, for example.

You might want to check out the internet for information on holidays like **el Día de los Reyes Magos** (*Three Kings Day*), **el Día de los Muertos** (*All Souls Day*), **la Nochebuena** (*Christmas Eve*), **la Pascua** (*Easter*), or **el carnaval** (*carnival*) to learn more about Spanish and Latin American holidays and traditions.

Word Recall

Let's practice some phrases with the verb **querer**. Make sentences using **quisiera** (*I would like to*) followed by the action suggested. For example, *to speak on the phone*: **Quisiera hablar por teléfono**

1. *to drink coffee* ________________
2. *to speak to my brother* ________________

3. *to have more money* ____________________

4. *to study Spanish* ____________________

5. *to dance tango* ____________________

6. *to sleep more* ____________________

7. *to go to Spain* ____________________

8. *to walk every day* ____________________

ANSWER KEY

1. **Quisiera tomar café.** 2. **Quisiera hablar con mi hermano.** 3. **Quisiera tener más dinero.** 4. **Quisiera estudiar español.** 5. **Quisiera bailar tango.** 6. **Quisiera dormir más.** 7. **Quisiera ir a España.** 8. **Quisiera caminar todos los días.**

How Did You Do?

By now, you should be able to:

- ☐ Feel comfortable with the verb *to go*
  (Still unsure? Jump back to page 204.)
- ☐ Distinguish *yes* from *if*
  (Still unsure? Jump back to page 206.)
- ☐ Say what you *want* or *would like*
  (Still unsure? Jump back to page 207.)

Don't forget to practice and reinforce what you've learned by visiting **www.livinglanguage.com/languagelab** for flashcards, games, and quizzes for Unit 4!

Unit 4 Essentials

Vocabulary Essentials

TELEPHONE VOCABULARY

	answering machine
	phone call
	operator
	phone book
	yellow pages
	telephone booth
	message
	voice mail
	switchboard
	to eliminate
	to erase

[Pg. 173]

TELECOMMUNICATION VOCABULARY

	fax
	mobile phone
	cell phone
	internet
	computer
	keyboard

	screen
	printer
	mouse
	headphones
	connection

[Pg. 176]

TELECOMMUNICATION VERBS

	to make a phone call
	to answer the phone
	to hang up the phone
	to dial a phone number
	to leave a message after the tone
	to send a message
	to erase a message
	to copy a message
	to receive a fax
	to make an international call
	to make a national/local call
	to send an e-mail
	to reply to an e-mail
	to send a file
	to download a file

[Pg. 182]

TELEPHONE EXPRESSIONS

	Hello? (lit., Tell me?)
	Hello?
	I'm putting you through.
	The line is busy.
	The line is busy.
	There is no dial tone.
	Do not hang up, please.
	Hold on, please.
	to put on hold

[Pg. 186]

MORE TELEPHONE EXPRESSIONS

	I'd like to talk to …
	Sorry, you have the wrong number.
	Who's calling?
	Who's calling?
	Who am I talking to?
	He/She isn't in right now.
	He's/She's busy.
	Please call later.
	Please call in five minutes.
	He/She is not in his/her office.
	He/She already left.
	Would you like to leave a message?

[Pg. 192]

Grammar Essentials

DEMONSTRATIVE ADJECTIVES

este/esta *(m./f.)*	*this*
estos/estas *(m./f.)*	*these*
ese/esa *(m./f.)*	*that*
esos/esas *(m./f.)*	*those*
aquel/aquella *(m./f.)*	*that over there*
aquellos/aquellas *(m./f.)*	*those over there*

DEMONSTRATIVE PRONOUNS

éste/ésta *(m./f.)*, **esto** *(neuter)*	*this (one)*
éstos/éstas *(m./f.)*	*these (ones)*
ése/ésa *(m./f.)*, **eso** *(neuter)*	*that (one)*
ésos/ésas *(m./f.)*	*those (ones)*
aquél/aquélla *(m./f.)*, **aquello** *(neuter)*	*that (one) over there*
aquéllos/aquéllas *(m./f.)*	*those (ones) over there*

NEGATION

To make a negative statement in Spanish, place the word **no** (*not*) before the verb.

INDEFINITE PRONOUNS

POSITIVE	
algo	*something*
alguien	*somebody, someone*
algún(-o/-a/-os/-as)	*some, something*
siempre	*always*

POSITIVE	
también	*also, too*
o … o	*either … or*

NEGATIVE	
nada	*nothing*
nadie	*nobody, no one*
ningún(-o/-a/-os/-as)	*no, none*
nunca	*never*
tampoco	*neither, not either*
ni … ni	*neither … nor*

IRREGULAR VERBS

CAER ***(TO FALL)***	
yo caigo	nosotros/as caemos
tú caes	vosotros/as caéis
él/ella/usted cae	ellos/ellas/ustedes caen

DECIR ***(TO SAY)***	
yo digo	nosotros/as decimos
tú dices	vosotros/as decís
él/ella/usted dice	ellos/ellas/ustedes dicen

HACER ***(TO MAKE, TO DO)***	
yo hago	nosotros/as hacemos
tú haces	vosotros/as hacéis

HACER *(TO MAKE, TO DO)*	
él/ella/usted hace	ellos/ellas/ustedes hacen

IR *(TO GO)*	
yo voy	nosotros/as vamos
tú vas	vosotros/as vais
él/ella/usted va	ellos/ellas/ustedes van

PONER *(TO PUT)*	
yo pongo	nosotros/as ponemos
tú pones	vosotros/as ponéis
él/ella/usted pone	ellos/ellas/ustedes ponen

QUERER *(TO WANT)*	
yo quiero	nosotros/as queremos
tú quieres	vosotros/as queréis
él/ella/usted quiere	ellos/ellas/ustedes quieren

SALIR *(TO GO OUT)*	
yo salgo	nosotros/as salimos
tú sales	vosotros/as salís
él/ella/usted sale	ellos/ellas/ustedes salen

TRAER *(TO BRING)*	
yo traigo	nosotros/as traemos
tú traes	vosotros/as traéis
él/ella/usted trae	ellos/ellas/ustedes traen

Unit 4 Quiz

A. Let's practice irregular verbs. Write the correct form of the verb in parentheses.

1. **Nosotros ____________________ muchas llamadas internacionales. (hacer)**
2. **Él ____________________ la llamada en espera. (poner)**
3. **Ustedes ____________________ el pasaporte al aeropuerto. (traer)**
4. **Vosotros ____________________ de la oficina tarde. (salir)**
5. **Yo ____________________ que tú eres una persona muy simpática. (decir)**
6. **Tú ____________________ al trabajo a las ocho de la mañana. (ir)**
7. **Usted ____________________ mucho a su familia. (querer)**
8. **Mario y Lupita ____________________ dolor de cabeza. (tener)**

B. Choose the vocabulary word that best completes the blank.

1. **Esta ____________________ (teléfono/línea) está ocupada.**
2. **Aquella cabina telefónica está ____________________ (operadora/libre).**
3. **Este ____________________ (mensaje/teléfono) no funciona.**
4. **Yo necesito marcar el ____________________ (número/archivo).**
5. **Quisiera ____________________ (hablar/hacer) una llamada internacional.**
6. **Este teléfono no funciona y éste ____________________ (también/tampoco).**

7. **Nuestra compañía tiene un ________________ (sitio web/computadora) muy interesante.**
8. **La línea está ocupada y no tiene ________________ (tono/tiempo).**

C. Say the negative of each of the expressions below:

1. **Este teléfono funciona.** ________________
2. **Jorge come siempre.** ________________
3. **Esta semana tengo dos reuniones importantes.** ________________

   ____
4. **Hay alguien de Canadá en mi oficina.** ________________

   ____
5. **Hay tono.** ________________
6. **Hay conexión siempre.** ________________
7. **Alguien llama por teléfono.** ________________
8. **Yo tengo algo importante en mi computadora.** ________________

   ____

D. Fill out the following chart with the corresponding demonstrative adjective.

	CLOSE TO THE SPEAKER	FAR FROM SPEAKER CLOSE TO THE LISTENER	FAR FROM BOTH
masc. sing.	**este muchacho**	*1.* ________ **muchacho**	*2.* ________ **muchacho**
masc. plural	*3.* ________ **muchachos**	**esos muchachos**	*4.* ________ **muchachos**
fem. sing.	*5.* ________ **muchacha**	*6.* ________ **muchacha**	**aquella muchacha**

	CLOSE TO THE SPEAKER	FAR FROM SPEAKER CLOSE TO THE LISTENER	FAR FROM BOTH
fem. plural	estas muchachas	7. ________ muchachas	8. ________ muchachas

How Did You Do?

Give yourself a point for every correct answer, then use the following key to determine whether or not you're ready to move on:

0–7 points: It's probably best to go back and study the lessons again to make sure you understood everything completely. Take your time; it's not a race! Make sure you spend time reviewing vocabulary with the flashcards and reading through each grammar note carefully.

8–16 points: If the questions you missed were in sections A or B, you may want to review the vocabulary again; if you missed answers mostly in sections C or D, check the unit essentials to make sure you have your conjugations and other grammar basics down.

17–20 points: Feel free to move on to the next unit! You're doing a great job.

points

ANSWER KEY

A. 1. **hacemos**; 2. **pone**; 3. **traen**; 4. **salís**; 5. **digo**; 6. **vas**; 7. **quiere**; 8. **tienen**

B. 1. **línea**; 2. **libre**; 3. **teléfono**; 4. **número**; 5. **hacer**; 6. **tampoco**; 7. **sitio web**; 8. **tono**

C. 1. **Este teléfono no funciona.** 2. **Jorge no come nunca** *or* **Jorge nunca come.** 3. **Esta semana no tengo dos reuniones importantes.** 4. **No hay nadie de Canadá en mi oficina.** 5. **No hay tono.** 6. **No hay conexión nunca.** *or* **Nunca hay conexión.** 7. **Nadie llama por teléfono.** 8. **Yo no tengo nada importante en mi computadora.**

D. 1. **ese**; 2. **aquel**; 3. **estos**; 4. **aquellos**; 5. **esta**; 6. **esa**; 7. **esas**; 8. **aquellas**

Unit 5: Getting Around Town

In this unit, you'll learn how to ask for and give directions. You'll learn a lot of important vocabulary that will help you talk about running errands and getting around cities and towns.

By the end of this unit, you should be able to:

- ☐ Understand cardinal directions
- ☐ Distinguish between **saber** and **conocer** (*to know*)
- ☐ Name city landmarks
- ☐ Say *I can*, *I must*, and *I have to*
- ☐ Talk about traffic
- ☐ Express *to see*, *to come*, and *to give*
- ☐ Use phrases like *next to* and *across from* in directions
- ☐ Use the present progressive to express *I am eating, she is talking*
- ☐ Give someone directions and ask for directions
- ☐ Use some common prepositions to describe location
- ☐ Use some common prepositions of time
- ☐ Understand how other prepositions are used
- ☐ Use commands to tell someone to *go*, *see*, *work*, or *come*
- ☐ Understand the differences between **para** and **por**

Lesson 17: Words

By the end of this lesson, you should be able to:

- ☐ Understand cardinal directions
- ☐ Distinguish between **saber** and **conocer** (*to know*)
- ☐ Name city landmarks
- ☐ Say *I can*, *I must*, and *I have to*

Word Builder 1

17A Word Builder 1 (CD 6, Track 12)

norte	*north*
sur	*south*
este/oriente	*east*
oeste/occidente	*west*
izquierda	*left*
derecha	*right*
la carretera/la autopista/la autovía	*highway, freeway*
la salida	*exit*
el peaje	*toll*
el carril/la vía	*lane*
de sentido único	*one-way*
el mapa	*map*
el cruce	*intersection*
las afueras	*outskirts*
el pueblo	*town*

el subterráneo/el metro	*subway/metro*
el edificio	*building*
el edificio de apartamentos	*apartment building*

Word Practice 1

Match the following directional words in Spanish to their English counterparts.

1. **derecha** — a. *left*
2. **sur** — b. *right*
3. **izquierda** — c. *north*
4. **oeste** — d. *south*
5. **este** — e. *east*
6. **norte** — f. *west*

ANSWER KEY

1. b; 2. d; 3. a; 4. f; 5. e; 6. c

Grammar Builder 1

SABER AND CONOCER (*TO KNOW*)

17B Grammar Builder 1 (CD 6, Track 13)

As you may remember from *Essential Spanish*, there are two different verbs that can be translated as *to know*: **saber** and **conocer**. They have different meanings and are not interchangeable. Let's start our review of these verbs with **saber**.

SABER (*TO KNOW*)	
yo sé	**nosotros/as sabemos**
tú sabes	**vosotros/as sabéis**
él/ella/usted sabe	**ellos/ellas/ustedes saben**

Saber means *to know* as in to know a fact, to know something thoroughly, or to know how to do something. It can be followed by a noun like **su nombre** (*her name*) or **la respuesta** (*the answer*), by **que . . .** (*that . . .*), **donde . . .** (*where . . .*), and **cuando . . .** (*when . . .*) to introduce facts, or by another verb in the infinitive, in which case it's translated as *to know how to*.

Saben mi nombre.
They know my name.

No sé la respuesta.
I don't know the answer.

Yo sé hablar francés.
I know how to speak French.

Ella sabe mucho sobre geografía.
She knows a lot about geography.

Nosotros sabemos que tienes un secreto.
We know that you have a secret.

Tú sabes dónde está la salida.
You know where the exit is.

Ustedes no saben cuándo parte el tren.
You don't know when the train leaves.

Now let's look again at **conocer**.

CONOCER ***(TO KNOW)***	
yo conozco	**nosotros/as conocemos**
tú conoces	**vosotros/as conocéis**

CONOCER ***(TO KNOW)***	
él/ella/usted conoce	**ellos/ellas/ustedes conocen**

Conocer means to know as in to know a person or to be familiar with something—a city, a book, a film, a restaurant, and so on. If the direct object of **conocer** is a person, don't forget to use the preposition **a**.

Conocemos a tus padres.
We know your parents.

Pedro conoce un restaurante italiano estupendo.
Pedro knows an excellent Italian restaurant.

Marta no conoce Nueva York.
Marta doesn't know New York./Marta isn't familiar with New York.

Yo conozco a mucha gente famosa.
I know many famous people.

Sometimes **conocer** can even be used to mean *to meet*, especially in the past tense, which you'll learn a bit later. But for now, learn the following expression.

Gusto en conocerle.
Pleased to meet you.

Work Out 1

Complete the sentences with the correct form of either saber or conocer:

1. Nosotros no ______ la ciudad de Moscú.
2. Yo ______ bailar salsa.
3. ¿Vosotros ______ historia antigua?
4. Ella no ______ hablar alemán.
5. ¿(Tú) ______ a mi hermana Luisa?
6. Mi familia no ______ a mi esposo.
7. Ella no ______ esquiar.
8. Yo no ______ este restaurante.

ANSWER KEY

1. conocemos; 2. sé; 3. sabéis; 4. sabe; 5. Conoces; 6. conoce; 7. sabe; 8. conozco

Word Builder 2

17C Word Builder 2 (CD 6, Track 14)

la avenida	*avenue*
la calle	*street*
la cuadra/la manzana	*block*
la esquina	*corner*
la biblioteca	*library*
el restaurante	*restaurant*
la tienda	*store*
el parque	*park*
el banco	*bank*

la iglesia	*church*
el templo	*temple*
la mezquita	*mosque*
la acera/el anden	*sidewalk*
la panadería	*bakery*
la carnicería	*butcher shop*
la cafetería	*café/coffee shop*
la farmacia	*drugstore/pharmacy*
el supermercado	*supermarket*
la tienda de ropa	*clothing store*
la tienda por departamentos	*department store*
derecho	*straight*
el semáforo	*traffic light*
doblar	*to turn*
dar la vuelta	*to turn around*
ir a pie/caminar	*to walk*
seguir	*to follow*
el peatón	*pedestrian*

Word Practice 2

Match the following words in Spanish to their English counterparts.

1. **la tienda de ropa** — a. *bakery*
2. **el semáforo** — b. *café/coffee shop*
3. **la acera** — c. *butcher shop*
4. **la esquina** — d. *traffic light*
5. **la panadería** — e. *corner*

6. **la cafetería** f. *pedestrian*
7. **la carnicería** g. *sidewalk*
8. **el parque** h. *store*
9. **la tienda** i. *clothing store*
10. **el peatón** j. *park*

ANSWER KEY
1. i; 2. d; 3. g; 4. e; 5. a; 6. b; 7. c; 8. j; 9. h; 10. f

Grammar Builder 2

PODER (*CAN*), DEBER (*MUST*), AND TENER QUE (*TO HAVE TO*)

17D Grammar Builder 2 (CD 6, Track 15)

The verb **poder** means *can*, *to be able to*, or *to have permission to*.

PODER (*CAN*)	
yo puedo	**nosotros/as podemos**
tú puedes	**vosotros/as podéis**
él/ella/usted puede	**ellos/ellas/ustedes pueden**

Just like **querer** (*to want to*), it's followed by another verb in the infinitive.

¿Puedes esquiar?
Can you ski?

Yo puedo hablar chino.
I'm able to speak Chinese./I can speak Chinese.

¿Podemos usar su teléfono?
May we use your phone?

Aquí no podemos fumar.

We cannot smoke here.

Ella no puede trabajar con música.

She can't work while listening to music.

The verb **deber** means *must* or *to have to*. **Deber** is a regular **-er** verb.

DEBER *(MUST)*	
yo debo	**nosotros/as debemos**
tú debes	**vosotros/as debéis**
él/ella/usted debe	**ellos/ellas/ustedes deben**

Debo estudiar español.

I have to study Spanish.

Debemos entregar este informe hoy.

We have to submit this report today.

Spanish also uses the expression **tener que** + a verb in the infinitive, which is a bit stronger than using **deber**.

Tienen que comprar una nueva computadora.

They have to buy a new computer.

Tenéis que hacer las reservaciones de hotel esta tarde.

You have to make the hotel reservations this afternoon.

Work Out 2

Fill in the blanks with the correct form of the verb in parentheses.

1. ____________ ir a la oficina esta tarde. (yo - tener)
2. ¿____________ hacer una llamada internacional? (nosotros - poder)
3. ____________ partir a las siete y media. (nosotros - deber)
4. ____________ hacer las reservaciones por Internet. (ustedes - poder)
5. ____________ doblar a la izquierda. (usted - tener que)
6. ____________ hablar con nuestro jefe. (nosotros - tener que)
7. ¿____________ salir temprano de la oficina hoy? (ustedes - poder)
8. ____________ traer su pasaporte. (él - deber)
9. ____________ hablar por teléfono en este momento. (ella - no poder)
10. ____________ partir por la mañana. (usted - tener que)

ANSWER KEY

1. Tengo que; 2. Podemos; 3. Debemos; 4. Pueden; 5. Tiene que; 6. Tenemos que; 7. Pueden; 8. Debe; 9. No puede; 10. Tiene que

Take It Further

Here are a few expressions you'll often hear using saber and conocer.

no saber ni jota de algo

to not have a clue about something

¿Quién sabe?

Who knows?

¡Yo qué sé!
How do I know!?/How should I know!?

conocer palmo a palmo
to know like the back (lit., palm) of one's hand

No sé.
I don't know.

conocer de vista
to know by sight

dar a conocer
to make known

Conozco la ciudad de Nueva York palmo a plamo.
I know New York like the back of my hand.

Ella no sabe ni jota de álgebra.
She has no clue about algebra.

Conocemos a tu esposo de vista.
We know your husband by sight.

Word Recall

Fill in the blanks with the correct form of the verb in parentheses.

1. **Tú** ______________ **escuchar con atención. (deber)**
2. **Tú** ______________ **escuchar con atención. (poder)**
3. **Tú** ______________ **escuchar con atención. (saber)**
4. **Tú** ______________ **escuchar con atención (tener que)**
5. **Yo** ______________ **tocar la guitarra eléctrica. (deber)**
6. **Yo** ______________ **tocar la guitarra eléctrica. (poder)**
7. **Yo** ______________ **tocar la guitarra eléctrica. (saber)**
8. **Yo** ______________ **tocar la guitarra eléctrica. (tener que)**

ANSWER KEY

1. **debes**; 2. **puedes**; 3. **sabes**; 4. **tienes que**; 5. **debo**; 6. **puedo**; 7. **sé**; 8. **tengo que**

How Did You Do?

By now, you should be able to:

- ☐ Understand cardinal directions
  (Still unsure? Jump back to page 222.)
- ☐ Distinguish between **saber** and **conocer** (*to know*)
  (Still unsure? Jump back to page 223.)
- ☐ Name city landmarks
  (Still unsure? Jump back to page 226.)
- ☐ Say *I can*, *I must*, and *I have to*
  (Still unsure? Jump back to page 228.)

Lesson 18: Phrases

By the end of this lesson, you should be able to:

- ☐ Talk about traffic
- ☐ Express *to see, to come*, and *to give*
- ☐ Use phrases like *next to* and *across from* in directions
- ☐ Use the present progressive to express *I am eating, she is talking*

Phrase Builder 1

18A Phrase Builder 1 (CD 6, Track 16)

Here are some phrases you can use when traveling by car.

¡Pare!/¡Alto!	*Stop!*
el embotellamiento	*traffic jam*
apagar las luces	*to turn off the lights*
pagar el peaje	*to pay the toll*
abrocharse el cinturón de seguridad	*to buckle up*
poner el pie en el freno	*to hit the brakes*
exceder el límite de velocidad	*to exceed the speed limit*
saltarse el semáforo	*to go through a light*
ir en dirección opuesta	*to go in the opposite direction*
reducir la velocidad	*to slow down*
pagar una multa	*to pay a fine*

Phrase Practice 1

Fill in the appropriate Spanish verb in the following phrases.

1. ______________________ **las luces** *to turn off the lights*
2. ______________________ **el peaje** *to pay the toll*
3. ______________________ **el cinturón de seguridad** *to buckle up*
4. ______________________ **el pie en el freno** *to hit the brakes*
5. ______________________ **el límite de velocidad** *to exceed the speed limit*
6. ______________________ **el semáforo** *to go through a light*
7. ______________________ **en dirección opuesta** *to go in the opposite direction*
8. ______________________ **la velocidad** *to slow down*
9. ______________________ **una multa** *to pay a fine*

ANSWER KEY

1. **apagar**; 2. **pagar**; 3. **abrocharse**; 4. **poner**; 5. **exceder**; 6. **saltarse**; 7. **ir**; 8. **reducir**; 9. **pagar**

Grammar Builder 1

VER (*TO SEE*), VENIR (*TO COME*), AND DAR (*TO GIVE*)

18B Grammar Builder 1 (CD 6, Track 17)

In this section, we'll take a look at two more irregular verbs, **venir** (*to come*) and **dar** (*to give*). But first let's start with a review of **ver**, which you saw in Lesson 12.

VER (*TO SEE*)	
yo veo	nosotros/as vemos
tú ves	vosotros/as veis
él/ella/usted ve	ellos/ellas/ustedes ven

Ver means *to see*, but it is also used to mean *to watch*—for example, to watch TV, a play, a sports event, or a movie. You will also often hear Spanish speakers using the expression **a ver**, which literally means *let's see*.

A ella le gusta ver películas de horror.
She likes to watch horror movies.

Nosotros vemos televisión todas las noches.
We watch TV every evening.

A ver, la calle Alcalá está a dos cuadras de aquí.
Let's see, Alcalá Street is two blocks from here.

Veis/Ven un partido de tenis.
You are watching a tennis match.

The verb **venir** (*to come*) is an irregular verb.

VENIR ***(TO COME)***	
yo vengo	**nosotros/as venimos**
tú vienes	**vosotros/as venís**
él/ella/usted viene	**ellos/ellas/ustedes vienen**

Notice that it's often used with the preposition **de**—take a look.

Ellos vienen de Brasil.
They come from Brazil.

Nosotros venimos de trabajar.
We're coming from work.

¿Vienes del supermercado?
Are you coming from the supermarket?

The verb **dar** (*to give*) is also an irregular verb.

DAR (TO GIVE)	
yo doy	**nosotros/as damos**
tú das	**vosotros/as dais**
él/ella/usted da	**ellos/ellas/ustedes dan**

Dar is used in a variety of common expressions.

dar (las) gracias	*to give thanks*
dar a luz	*to give birth*
dar con algo	*to find something*
dar de narices	*to fall flat on one's face (lit., nose)*
dar la hora	*to tell time*
dar la mano	*to shake hands*

Ella no quiere dar a luz en el hospital.
She doesn't want to give birth in the hospital.

El reloj da la hora exacta.
The clock shows/gives the exact time.

No me gusta dar la mano a personas extrañas.
I don't like to shake hands with strangers.

Work Out 1

Fill in the blanks with the correct form of the verbs in parentheses.

1. **¿Disculpe, me _______________ la hora? (poder/dar)**
2. **Mis abuelos _______________ en el tren de las once. (venir)**
3. **Yo _______________ una comedia esta noche. (querer/ver)**
4. **En su país las personas no _______________ la mano. (dar)**
5. **No me _______________ televisión. (gustar/ver)**
6. **Los padres _______________ regalos a sus hijos en Navidad. (dar)**
7. **Yo _______________ de la universidad. (venir)**
8. **Ellos _______________ un partido de fútbol. (ver)**

ANSWER KEY

1. **puede dar**; 2. **vienen**; 3. **quiero ver**; 4. **dan**; 5. **gusta ver**; 6. **dan**; 7. **vengo**; 8. **ven**

Phrase Builder 2

18C Phrase Builder 2 (CD 6, Track 18)

The following phrases will help you get around town and ask for directions.

cruzar la calle	*to cross the street*
caminar dos cuadras/manzanas	*to walk two blocks*
al lado de	*next to*
enfrente de	*in front of*
a mano izquierda	*on the left-hand side*
a mano derecha	*on the right-hand side*
en la esquina	*at the corner*
a la vuelta de la esquina	*around the corner*

por el anden (por la acera)	*on the sidewalk*
por el callejón	*through the alley*

Phrase Practice 2

Match the Spanish phrase to its English counterpart.

1. **enfrente de**	a. *next to*
2. **a la vuelta de la esquina**	b. *in front of*
3. **a mano derecha**	c. *on the left-hand side*
4. **en la esquina**	d. *on the right-hand side*
5. **al lado de**	e. *at the corner*
6. **a mano izquierda**	f. *around the corner*

ANSWER KEY

1. b; 2. f; 3. d; 4. e; 5.a; 6. c

Grammar Builder 2

THE PRESENT PROGRESSIVE

18D Grammar Builder 2 (CD 6, Track 19)

We've seen a lot of verbs in the simple present tense. But Spanish, like English, also has a present progressive tense, which expresses actions happening at the very moment you are speaking. The formation is similar to English: use the verb **estar** (*to be*) followed by the present participle, which is like the *-ing* form of the verb in English. The present participle is formed as follows.

For **-ar** verbs, take off the **-ar** and add **-ando** to the stem.

For **-er** and **-ir** verbs, take off the **-er** or **-ir** and add **-iendo** to the stem.

Estoy caminando por el callejón.
I'm walking through the alley.

Estás hablando por teléfono.
You're talking on the phone.

Está comiendo churros.
He/She is eating churros.

¿Usted está viendo televisión?
Are you watching TV?

Estamos dando las gracias.
We're giving thanks.

Estáis conociendo la ciudad.
You're getting to know the city.

No están escribiendo cartas.
They/You aren't writing letters.

There are, of course, a few irregular verbs that you will learn as we go along, and those irregularities may include the present participle. Here are the present participles of the irregular verbs we have seen so far.

VERB		PRESENT PARTICIPLE	
traer	*to bring*	**trayendo**	*bringing*
decir	*to say*	**diciendo**	*saying*
ir	*to go*	**yendo**	*going*
venir	*to come*	**viniendo**	*coming*
poder	*to be able to*	**pudiendo**	*being able to*

Unlike English, Spanish does not use this tense to express a future action. It is only used to talk about an action that is happening at the moment of speech. Here are a few time expressions you're likely to use with this tense.

ahora	*now*
ahora mismo	*right now*
en este momento	*at this moment*

Work Out 2

Change the verbs in the following sentences from the simple present to the present progressive.

1. **Cantamos en el coro de la iglesia.** ____________________

2. **Él envía un fax.** ____________________

3. **Ustedes dicen pocas palabras.** ____________________

4. **Visito la ciudad de Nueva York.** ____________________

5. **Ellos salen de la oficina.** ____________________

6. **Vosotros habláis con vuestro jefe.** ____________________

7. **¿Lees el periódico?** ______________________________

____

8. **Él toma café.** ______________________________

____

ANSWER KEY

1. **Estamos cantando en el coro de la iglesia.** 2. **Él está enviando un fax.** 3. **Ustedes están diciendo pocas palabras.** 4. **Estoy visitando la ciudad de Nueva York.** 5. **Ellos están saliendo de la oficina.** 6. **Vosotros estáis hablando con vuestro jefe.** 7. **¿Estás leyendo el periódico?** 8. **Él está tomando café.**

Take It Further

Muletillas or **frases de relleno** (*filler words*) are used when the speaker doesn't know what to say next or is looking for a word. These phrases are the equivalents of the English filler words *well, um, you know, err,* and so on. Spanish speakers prefer to use words like **este**, **pues**, **a ver**, **por así decir**, **es decir**, **vamos**, or **bueno**. There is some regional variation in the use of Spanish filler phrases. People from Argentina, for example, are known around the world for using the word **che** at the beginning of their sentences, and Spaniards tend to use **vamos** fairly often. In many regions, the word **mira** or **mire** (*look*) is used to start a sentence.

Mire, el teatro queda a dos cuadras.
Look, the theater is two blocks away.

A ver, cruce la calle y doble a la derecha.
Let's see, cross the street and turn right.

Pues, es muy fácil.
Well, it's very easy.

Word Recall

Form the present progressive with the subject and verb suggested.

1. **Yo – hablar** ______________________
2. **Yo - beber** ______________________
3. **Yo - vivir** ______________________
4. **Yo - comer** ______________________
5. **Nosotros - bailar** ______________________
6. **Nosotros – poner** ______________________
7. **Nosotros - decir** ______________________
8. **Nosotros – traer** ______________________

ANSWER KEY

1. **Yo estoy hablando.** 2. **Yo estoy bebiendo.** 3. **Yo estoy viviendo.** 4. **Yo estoy comiendo.** 5. **Nosotros estamos bailando.** 6. **Nosotros estamos poniendo.** 7. **Nosotros estamos diciendo.** 8. **Nosotros estamos trayendo.**

How Did You Do?

By now, you should be able to:

- ☐ Talk about traffic
  (Still unsure? Jump back to page 233.)
- ☐ Express *to see*, *to come*, and *to give*
  (Still unsure? Jump back to page 234.)
- ☐ Use phrases like *next to* and *across from* in directions
  (Still unsure? Jump back to page 237.)
- ☐ Use the present progressive to express *I am eating, she is talking*
  (Still unsure? Jump back to page 238.)

Lesson 19: Sentences

By the end of this lessson, you should be able to:

- ☐ Give someone directions and ask for directions
- ☐ Use some common prepositions to describe location
- ☐ Use some common prepositions of time
- ☐ Understand how other prepositions are used

Sentence Builder 1

19A Sentence Builder 1 (CD 6, Track 20)

Siga derecho hasta ...	*Go straight till ...*
Le agradezco mucho su ayuda.	*Thanks a lot for your help. (lit., I thank you much for your help.)*
¿Sabe cómo llegar a ... ?	*Do you know how to get to ... ?*
Aquí en el mapa está muy claro.	*Here on the map, it is very clear.*
Buen viaje.	*Have a good trip.*
Siga por el carril de la derecha.	*Stay in the right lane.*
A más o menos dos kilómetros hay un peaje.	*At more or less two kilometers, there is a toll.*
Tome la rampa en dirección ...	*Take the ramp towards ...*

Sentence Practice 1

Fill in the blanks in the following sentences with the appropriate word or phrase.

1. ______________________ **hasta . . .** *Go straight till . . .*
2. ______________________ **su ayuda.** *Thanks for (lit., I thank you for) your help.*
3. **¿Sabe** ______________________ **. . . ?** *Do you know how to get to . . . ?*
4. **Aquí en el mapa está** ______________________. *Here on the map, it is very clear.*
5. ______________________. *Have a good trip.*
6. ______________________ **de la derecha.** *Stay in the right lane.*
7. ______________________ **hay un peaje.** *At more or less two kilometers, there is a toll.*
8. **Tome la rampa** ______________________ **. . .** *Take the ramp towards . . .*

ANSWER KEY

1. **Siga derecho**; 2. **Le agradezco mucho**; 3. **cómo llegar a**; 4. **muy claro**; 5. **Buen viaje**; 6. **Siga por el carril**; 7. **A más o menos dos kilómetros**; 8. **en dirección**

Grammar Builder 1

COMMON PREPOSITIONS OF LOCATION

19B Grammar Builder 1 (CD 6, Track 21)

Prepositions are those little words we use to connect other words in order to show spatial, temporal, or other kinds of relationships. Examples of prepositions are *on*, *in*, and *at*. In Spanish, prepositions function almost the same way as in

English, but their precise usage often has to be memorized. Let's first take a look at prepositions that show spatial relationships.

en	*in, on*
entre	*between*
delante de	*in front of*
enfrente de	*in front of*
detrás de	*behind*
debajo de	*underneath*
encima de	*on top of*
sobre	*above*
contra	*against*
cerca de	*close to*
lejos de	*far away from*
dentro de	*inside of*
fuera de	*outside of*

When showing spatial relationships, either **estar** or **hay** (*there is/are*) is typically used. Take a look at how the above prepositions are used in a sentence.

Madrid está en España.
Madrid is in Spain.

Antonio está sentado entre Marta y Alejandra.
Antonio is seated between Marta and Alejandra.

El teatro está delante de mi oficina.
The theater is in front of my office.

Hay un edificio alto enfrente de nuestra casa.
There's a tall building in front of our house.

La tienda está detrás del museo.
The shop is behind the museum.

Hay un gato debajo de la mesa.
There's a cat underneath the table.

El/La computador/a está encima del escritorio.
The computer is on top of the desk.

Hay dos lámparas sobre la cama.
There are two lamps above the bed.

El armario está contra la pared.
The closet is against the wall.

La universidad está cerca de aquí.
The university is close to here.

Su oficina está lejos de su casa.
His office is far away from his house.

Los huevos están dentro de la nevera.
The eggs are inside the refrigerator.

El museo está fuera de la ciudad.
The museum is outside of the city.

Work Out 1

Replace each of the underlined prepositions with one that means the opposite. For example, if you see **debajo de** (*underneath*), change it to **encima de** (*on top of*).

1. **Delante del armario hay una puerta.** ____________________

2. **Los turistas están dentro del museo.** ____________________

3. **Mi familia vive lejos de mi casa.** ____________________

4. **Enfrente de su casa hay un bar.** ____________________

5. **El niño está debajo de la cama.** ____________________

6. **Cerca de mi casa está la universidad.** ____________________

7. **Los archivos están detrás de esos libros.** ____________________

8. **Los documentos están dentro del sobre.** ____________________

ANSWER KEY

1. **Detrás del armario hay una puerta.** 2. **Los turistas están fuera del museo.** 3. **Mi familia vive cerca de mi casa.** 4. **Detrás de su casa hay un bar.** 5. **El niño está encima de la cama.** 6. **Lejos de mi casa está la universidad.** 7. **Los archivos están enfrente de esos libros.** 8. **Los documentos están fuera del sobre.**

Sentence Builder 2

19C Sentence Builder 2 (CD 6, Track 22)

El teatro está a mano izquierda.	*The theater is on the left-hand side.*
Seguid derecho por esta calle.	*Go straight down this street.*
¿Me puede decir cómo llegar a . . . ?	*Can you tell me how to get to . . . ?*
La entrada para visitantes está en la parte de atrás.	*The visitors' entrance is in back*
Queremos tomarnos un café para coger fuerzas.	*We want to have a cup of coffee to wake us up a bit (lit., to get some strength).*
En la esquina de la plaza hay un café.	*On the corner of the plaza there's a coffee place.*
Vamos, es muy fácil.	*Let's see—it's very easy.*
Ahí queda el teatro de la ópera.	*That's where the opera theater is located.*

Sentence Practice 2

Fill in the blanks below with the appropriate word or phrase.

1. ____________________ **a mano izquierda.** *The theater is on the left-hand side.*
2. **Seguid derecho** ____________________. *Go straight down this street.*
3. ¿____________________ **cómo llegar a . . . ?** *Can you tell me how to get to . . . ?*

4. **La entrada para visitantes está** ______________________________.

The visitors' entrance is in back.

5. ______________________________ **hay un café.**

On the corner of the plaza there's a coffee place.

ANSWER KEY

1. **El teatro está**; 2. **por esta calle**; 3. **Me puede decir**; 4. **en la parte de atrás**; 5. **En la esquina de la plaza**

Grammar Builder 2

COMMON PREPOSITIONS OF TIME

19D Grammar Builder 2 (CD 6, Track 23)

Now let's look at some prepositions and phrasal prepositions of time.

antes de	*before*
después de	*after*
desde	*since, from*
durante	*during*
hasta	*until, till*

Antes de salir, leo el periódico.
Before leaving, I read the newspaper.

Después del trabajo, hacemos deporte.
After work, we play sports.

Desde esta mañana estoy trabajando en este proyecto.
I've been working (lit., I am working) on this project since this morning.

Desde este edificio podemos ver toda la ciudad.
From this building, we can see the entire city.

Están de vacaciones desde enero hasta abril.

They are on vacation from January till April.

Generalmente tomo una siesta durante el día.

I usually take a nap during the day.

¡Hasta mañana!

See you tomorrow!/Until tomorrow!

Take It Further

19E Take It Further (CD 6, Track 24)

Here are other common prepositions, some of which you already know.

a	*to, at*
con	*with*
de	*of*
hacia	*toward*
sin	*without*
sobre	*about/on top of*

The preposition **a** has several uses. First, it's a common preposition of motion.

Vamos a Caracas.

We're going to Caracas.

Ellos viajan a Chile todos los veranos.

They travel to Chile every summer.

In the last unit, you learned about the preposition **a** when it introduces a direct object that is a person. **A** is also used to introduce an indirect object, like the English *to*.

Ella da su comida a los pobres.
She gives her food to the poor.

Enviamos muchos mensajes a nuestros amigos.
We send many messages to our friends.

A is also used after certain verbs, such as **aprender** and **comenzar**.

Tengo que aprender a escribir a máquina.
I need to learn how to type.

Tengo que comenzar a estudiar com más frecuencia.
I need to start studying more often.

Some verbs are followed by **de** before an infinitive. Here are a few examples of common expressions using **de** + an infinitive.

acabar de hacer algo	*to have just done something*
tratar de hacer algo	*to try to do something*
cesar de hacer algo	*to stop doing something*

Juan acaba de salir de la oficina.
Juan just left the office.

Ella trata de aprender a esquiar.
She tries to learn how to ski.

Mi hija no cesa de llorar.
My daughter doesn't stop crying.

Finally, here are examples of how to use **hacia**, **sin**, and **sobre**:

Ellos van hacia Madrid.

They are going towards Madrid.

Me gusta el café sin azúcar.

I like coffee without sugar.

El libro es sobre turismo en España.

The book is about tourism in Spain.

Work Out 2

Choose the preposition that best completes the sentence:

1. **No queremos ir de viaje ________________ nuestros hijos. (sobre, sin, a)**
2. **El mapa es ________________ Carlos. (de, hacia, a)**
3. ________________ **hoy estoy haciendo dieta. (hasta, antes de, desde)**
4. ________________ **partir, quiero ir a la catedral otra vez. (después de, antes de, durante)**
5. ________________ **la mañana bebo mucho café. (durante, sin, a)**
6. **Aprender ________________ hablar otro idioma no es fácil. (de, a, con)**
7. **Tenemos que comenzar ________________ preparar la presentación. (a, con, de)**
8. **El mensaje es ________________ algo personal. (de, sobre, a)**

ANSWER KEY

1. **sin**; 2. **de**; 3. **Desde**; 4. **Antes de**; 5. **Durante**; 6. **a**; 7. **a**; 8. **sobre**

Tip!

When you're learning another language, it's not always easy to meet native speakers. But it's important to give yourself the chance to hear native speakers, even if you can't interact with them. Listening to the radio provides one opportunity to do that. Here are a few links that will help you find different radio stations in Spanish. The phrase that you should look for is **escucha en vivo** (listen direct/live):

www.radiocentro.com.mx (Mexico)
www.continental.com.ar (Argentina)
www.caracol.com.co (Colombia)
www.rtve.es/rne/envivo.htm (Spain)

Newspapers are also a great way to practice Spanish. A single site that will direct you to a huge number of newspapers from around the world, including, of course, Spanish-speaking countries, is **www.onlinenewspapers.com**. Just select the country that you're interested in.

Of course, you won't be able to follow everything that you read or hear at this point, but a good strategy is to look for stories that you're already familiar with, perhaps from English-language media. Alternatively, focus on a very small piece of real Spanish, maybe a paragraph or a very short audio clip, and read or listen along with a dictionary as many times as it takes to really become familiar with it. Just be patient, and be adventurous. You'll be surprised at how easy it is to practice your new language online!

Word Recall

A. Give the opposite of the following prepositions:

1. **antes de** ______________________________

2. **lejos de** ______________________________

3. **encima de** ______________________________

4. **delante de** ______________________________

B. Now choose the preposition that best completes the sentence:

1. **California está** ____________________ **(en/encima de) México.**

2. **Yo voy al parque** ____________________ **(a/con) mi amigo.**

3. **Yo voy al gimnasio** ____________________ **(lejos de/durante) la tarde.**

4. **Mi casa está** ____________________ **(entre/fuera) la casa de la familia López y la casa de la familia Pérez.**

ANSWER KEY

A. 1. **después de**; 2. **cerca de**; 3. **debajo de**; 4. **detrás de**

B. 1. **encima de**; 2. **con**; 3. **durante**; 4. **entre**

How Did You Do?

By now, you should be able to:

☐ Give someone directions and ask for directions
(Still unsure? Jump back to page 243.)

☐ Use some common prepositions to describe location
(Still unsure? Jump back to page 244.)

☐ Use some common prepositions of time
(Still unsure? Jump back to page 249.)

☐ Understand how other prepositions are used
(Still unsure? Jump back to page 250.)

Lesson 20: Conversations

By the end of this lesson, you should be able to:

- ☐ Use commands to tell someone to go, see, work, or come
- ☐ Understand the differences between **para** and **por**

Conversation 1

20A Conversation 1 (CD 6, Track 25 - Spanish Only; Track 26 - Spanish and English)

Alfonso and Luisa are on their honeymoon in Madrid. Today they're going to visit the palace of **El Escorial**, in the foothills of the **Sierra de Guadarrama** to the northwest of Madrid. Alfonso is asking the hotel receptionist for driving directions.

Recepcionista:	**Este … ¿Sabe cómo llegar a la Gran Vía?**
Alfonso:	**Sí, claro que sí. Hasta ahí no me pierdo.**
Recepcionista:	**Bien. Pues siga derecho por la Gran Vía, luego tome la Avenida de la Victoria. Siga derecho hasta la salida número seis.**
Alfonso:	**Aquí tengo un mapa. A ver … sí, aquí está: salida seis, autovía del Noreste, ¿verdad?**
Recepcionista:	**Exactamente. Siga por ahí hasta la salida dieciocho. Siga por el carril de la derecha y tome la rampa en dirección Las Rosas/ El Escorial.**
Alfonso:	**Pues, es muy fácil. Aquí en el mapa está muy claro.**
Recepcionista:	**A más o menos dos kilómetros hay un peaje.**
Alfonso:	**¿Cuánto hay que pagar?**
Recepcionista:	**Mire … No sé. Pero no es mucho. Cuando pase el peaje, doble a la izquierda. El Escorial no está muy lejos de ahí.**
Alfonso:	**Bueno, le agradezco mucho su ayuda.**

Recepcionista: **De nada. Buen viaje.**
Alfonso: **Gracias.**

Hotel clerk: *Well . . . Do you know how to get to the Gran Vía?*
Alfonso: *Yes, of course. Up to there I won't get lost.*
Hotel clerk: *Good. Then, go straight along the Gran Vía, then take the Avenida de la Victoria. Go straight until exit number 6.*
Alfonso: *I have a map here. Let's see . . . yes, here it is: Exit 6, Northeast highway, is that right?*
Hotel clerk: *Exactly. Go down through there until exit 18. Take the right lane up the ramp towards "Las Rosas/El Escorial."*
Alfonso: *Well, it's very easy. Here on the map, it is very clear.*
Hotel clerk: *At about two kilometers, there's a toll.*
Alfonso: *How much is it?*
Hotel clerk: *Hmm, I don't know. But it's not much. Once you pass the toll, make a left turn. The Escorial is not far from there.*
Alfonso: *Well, thank you very much for your help.*
Hotel clerk: *Not at all. Have a good trip.*
Alfonso: *Thank you.*

Culture Note

The Royal Monastery of San Lorenzo del Escorial was built between 1563 and 1584 for Felipe II and is traditionally believed to have been built in honor of St. Lawrence. Its severe and non-ornamental style became one of the most influential in Spain. The palace is a monastery, a museum, a library, and the burial place of Spanish sovereigns. The complex is a UNESCO world heritage site.

There are many myths about the **Sierra de Guadarrama**, the mountains to the northwest of Madrid. One such myth, known as **La Sima de los Pastores** (*the Shepherd's Chasm*), tells of a hidden treasure buried in one of the mountains. It is believed that a certain Rafael Corraliza, who was in charge of the financial affairs of the monastery, decided one day to run off to Portugal with the treasure. He took a route that he thought would be less guarded towards the town of **Robledondo**. It was already dark, and when he reached the area known as **Sima de los Pastores**, he was swallowed by the earth, treasure and all. It is said that St. Lawrence had something to do with this, and with time, the abyss was covered with rocks and leaves to prevent something similar from ever happening again.

Conversation Practice 1

Fill in the blanks below with the appropriate word based on the English translation and the dialogue above.

1. **Pues por la Gran Vía, ________________ la Avenida de la Victoria.**

   Then, go straight along the Gran Vía, then take the Avenida de la Victoria.

2. **Siga derecho ________ la salida número seis.** *Go straight until exit number 6.*
3. **Aquí en ____________ está muy claro.** *Here on the map, it is very clear.*
4. **Cuando pase el peaje, ______________________________.**

   Once you pass the toll, make a left turn.

5. **El Escorial no está muy ________ de ahí.** *The Escorial is not far from there.*

ANSWER KEY

1. **luego tome**; 2. **hasta**; 3. **el mapa**; 4. **doble a la izquierda**; 5. **lejos**

Grammar Builder 1

THE IMPERATIVE

20B Grammar Builder 1 (CD 6, Track 27)

Let's look at the imperative, or command form, which you would use, for instance, when giving directions.

Because there are different ways of expressing *you* in Spanish, there are different command forms, informal and formal, corresponding to **tú**, **usted**, **vosotros**, and **ustedes**. For the **tú** (infml.) command forms, just take the final **-s** off the present **tú** form of a regular verb. For example, from **tú hablas** (*you speak*), the imperative is **habla** (*speak*). In the same way, **comer** (*to eat*) becomes **come** (*eat*) and **escribir** (*to write*) becomes **escribe** (*write*). There are, of course, some irregular verbs. Here are a few.

salir (*to leave, to go out*)	**sal** (*leave, go out*)
decir (*to say, to tell*)	**di** (*say, tell*)
venir (*to come*)	**ven** (*come*)
hacer (*to do, to make*)	**haz** (*do, make*)
tener (*to have*)	**ten** (*have*)
poner (*to put*)	**pon** (*put*)
ver (*to see*)	**ve** (*see*)
ir (*to go*)	**ve** (*go*)

The command with **vosotros** (also informal) is even easier. Just take the infinitive form of the verb, drop the final **-r**, and add a **-d**. This works for all verbs. So **hablar** becomes **hablad**, **comer** becomes **comed**, **escribir** becomes **escribid**, **decir** becomes **decid**, **poner** becomes **poned**, and so on.

Let's now take a look at how to make formal commands with **usted** and **ustedes**. Take the present form of the first person singular (**yo**) of the verb, drop the final **-o**, and add **-e** or **-en** for **-ar** verbs, and add **-a** or **-an** for **-er** and **-ir** verbs.

TRABAJAR ***(TO WORK)***	
(usted) trabajé	*work (sg.)*
(ustedes) trabajen	*work (pl.)*

COMER ***(TO EAT)***	
(usted) coma	*eat (sg.)*
(ustedes) coman	*eat (pl.)*

ESCRIBIR ***(TO WRITE)***	
(usted) escriba	*write (sg.)*
(ustedes) escriban	*write (pl.)*

As usual, there are a few irregular verbs.

saber *(to know)*	**sepa, sepan**
ser *(to be)*	**sea, sean**
ir *(to go)*	**vaya, vayan**
dar *(to give)*	**dé, den**
estar *(to be)*	**esté, estén**

Work Out 1

Rephrase each sentence as a command.

1. **Tienes que llamar a mi secretaria.** ____________________

2. **Tenéis que partir a las seis de la mañana.** ____________________

3. **Tienen que hacer las reservaciones por Internet.** ____________________

4. **Tienes que caminar dos cuadras y doblar a la derecha.** ____________________

____

5. **Tiene que enviar el informe hoy por la tarde.** ____________________

____

6. **Tenéis que decir la verdad.** ____________________

____

7. **Tienes que contestar el mensaje.** ____________________

____

8. **Tenéis que seguir derecho por esta calle.** ____________________

____

9. **Tiene que llamar a Marta a las diez en punto.** ____________________

____

10. **Tienen que regresar temprano.** ____________________

____

ANSWER KEY

1. **Llama a mi secretaria.** 2. **Partid a las seis de la mañana.** 3. **Hagan las reservaciones por Internet.** 4. **Camina dos cuadras y dobla a la derecha.** 5. **Envíe el informe hoy por la tarde.** 6. **Decid la verdad.** 7. **Contesta el mensaje.** 8. **Seguid derecho por esta calle.** 9. **Llame a Marta a las diez en punto.** 10. **Regresen temprano.**

Conversation 2

20C Conversation 2 (CD 6, Track 28 - Spanish Only; Track 29 - Spanish and English)

Alfonso and Luisa are now at **la Puerta del Sol** in Madrid. They are lost, and Luisa is asking a woman on the street for directions to **el Palacio Real**.

Luisa: **Disculpe, ¿nos puede decir cómo llegar al Palacio Real?**
Señora: **Vamos, es muy fácil. Está a unas pocas cuadras de aquí. Seguid derecho por esta calle que se llama Calle del Arenal hasta llegar a la plaza.**
Luisa: **Ahí queda el teatro de la ópera, ¿no?**
Señora: **Sí, el teatro está a mano izquierda. Tenéis que seguir por ahí e inmediatamente doblar a mano derecha y continuar por una calle muy pequeña ... no recuerdo el nombre.**
Luisa: **No importa. Podemos preguntar a alguien.**
Señora: **Desde allí se puede ver la Plaza de Oriente. El palacio está en frente. Y la entrada para visitantes está en la parte de atrás.**
Luisa: **Muchas gracias.**
Señora: **Si queréis tomar un café para coger fuerzas, hay una cafetería que está muy bien en la esquina de la plaza a mano izquierda.**
Luisa: **Con este frío, creo que un chocolate con churros es mejor idea.**
Señora: **¡Vamos, en este lugar los churros son deliciosos!**

Luisa: *Excuse me, could you please tell us how to get to the Royal Palace?*
Woman: *It's very easy. It's a few blocks away from here. Go straight down this street, which is called Calle del Arenal, until you reach the square.*
Luisa: *The opera theater is there, isn't it?*
Woman: *Yes, the theater is on the left-hand side. You have to go through there and immediately turn right and go along a very short street ... I don't remember its name.*
Luisa: *It doesn't matter. We can ask someone.*

Woman:	*From there, you can see the Plaza de Oriente. The palace is in front. And the visitors' entrance is in back.*
Luisa:	*Many thanks.*
Woman:	*If you'd like to have a coffee to pick yourself up (lit., regain strength) to go on, there's a café on the corner on the left-hand side that is pretty good.*
Luisa:	*It's so cold, I think a chocolate with churros is a better idea.*
Woman:	*Well, at this place, the churros are delicious!*

Culture Note

La Puerta del Sol (the Gateway of the Sun) is Madrid's center square, one of the busiest points and one of the city's most popular meeting places. The square marks the site of the original eastern entrance to the city through a gatehouse in a castle. These have long since disappeared, and in their place there has been a succession of churches. In the late nineteenth century, the area was turned into a square, becoming the center of café society. Shaped like a half-moon, the square features a red brick building with a clock tower, which is the focus of the city's New Year's Eve celebration. Crowds fill the square on that day, and at midnight, people swallow a single grape with each toll of the bell. According to tradition, this is supposed to bring good luck throughout the year.

The **Palacio Real** (Royal Palace) is no longer used as a residence for the royal family, who live instead in the **Palacio de la Zarzuela**, a more modest palace outside Madrid. The Royal Palace, lavish and built to impress, is used for state occasions. Construction lasted twenty-six years, and its decor reflects the exuberant tastes of two Bourbon kings: Charles III and Charles IV.

Conversation Practice 2

Fill in the blanks below with the appropriate word based on the English translation and the dialogue above.

1. ______________, **¿nos puede decir cómo llegar al Palacio Real?**

   Excuse me, could you please tell us how to get to the Royal Palace?

2. **Seguid derecho** ______________ **que se llama Calle del Arenal.**

   Go straight down this street, which is called Calle del Arenal.

3. **Tenéis que seguir por ahí e inmediatamente** ______________.

   You have to go through there and immediately turn right.

4. **El palacio está** ______________. *The palace is in front.*

5. **Hay una cafetería que está muy bien** ______________ **de la plaza a mano izquierda.** *There's a café on the corner on the left-hand side that is pretty good.*

ANSWER KEY

1. **Disculpe**; 2. **por esta calle**; 3. **doblar a mano derecha**; 4. **en frente**; 5. **en la esquina**

Grammar Builder 2

PARA AND POR (*FOR*)

▶ 20D Grammar Builder 2 (CD 6, Track 30)

You've probably already seen the prepositions **para** and **por** in the dialogues. Both of them are usually translated into English as *for*, but they have different uses.

Para indicates a purpose (*in order to*), an intention (*intended for*), a limit in time (*by/until a certain time*), or a destination (*towards*). Note that when used to show an intention, **para** is followed by a verb in the infinitive. Here are a few examples.

Esta carta es para Julián.
This letter is for Julián.

Este nuevo programa es para hacer diseños gráficos.
This new program is for making graphic designs.

Necesitamos el informe para mañana a las nueve en punto.
We need the report by tomorrow morning at nine o'clock.

Voy para Cuernavaca.
I'm going to Cuernavaca.

On the other hand, **por** is used to indicate cause or reason (*because of, due to*), a length of time (*for*), or to indicate exchange (*in place of, in exchange for*). It can also mean *through*.

El viaje está cancelado por la tormenta.
The trip is canceled because of the storm.

Necesito cambiar unos dólares por pesos.
I need to exchange some dollars for pesos.

El hombre salió por esa puerta.
The man left through that door.

Pasamos por Miami de camino a Chile.
We went through Miami on our way to Chile.

Queremos una habitación por diez noches.
We want a room for ten nights.

Work Out 2

Take a look at the following sentences and decide what preposition you would use in Spanish.

1. **Puedes cambiar el suéter __________ otro en una talla más grande.**

   (*You can exchange the sweater for another one in a bigger size.*)

2. **Tenemos que terminar el proyecto __________ la próxima semana.**

   (*We have to finish the project by next week.*)

3. **El regalo es __________ su hermana.** (*The present is for her sister.*)

4. **Ella está mirando __________ la ventana.** (*She is looking through the window.*)

5. **Ella está ahorrando __________ comprar una casa.**

   (*She is saving in order to buy a house.*)

6. **Ellos están partiendo __________ Londres.** (*They are leaving for London.*)

7. **__________ su retraso, no podemos empezar la conferencia.**

   (*Because of his delay, we cannot begin the conference.*)

8. **Queremos alquilar el apartamento __________ tres años.**

   (*We want to rent the apartment for three years.*)

ANSWER KEY

1. **por**; 2. **para**; 3. **para**; 4. **por**; 5. **para**; 6. **para**; 7. **Por**; 8. **por**

Take It Further

Learning **por** and **para** is, again, a question of practice and being very patient with yourself. Just remember that it is not a big deal if you get these prepositions wrong. Most people will appreciate your effort and won't mind the mistakes you make.

To help you a bit, here are some colloquial expressions that you will often hear using **por**. Try to familiarize yourself with them, and experiment with using them from time to time.

¡Por Dios!	*For God's sake!*
¡Por fin!	*At last!*
por lo visto	*apparently*
por eso	*for this reason*
por lo tanto	*therefore*
por desgracia	*unfortunately*
por una parte	*on the one hand*
por otra parte	*on the other hand*
por supuesto	*of course*
por casualidad	*by chance*

Por lo visto el vuelo está retrasado.
Apparently, the flight is delayed.

Nos encontramos con María por casualidad.
We bumped into María by chance.

Por desgracia no podemos viajar mañana.
Unfortunately, we can't travel tomorrow.

Word Recall

The following sentences are informal commands in the **tú** form. Turn them into formal commands by using the **usted** form.

1. **Habla español ahora.** ____________________
2. **Toma una siesta.** ____________________
3. **Camina hasta mi casa.** ____________________
4. **Trabaja más.** ____________________
5. **Escribe en la computadora.** ____________________
6. **Bebe más vino.** ____________________

ANSWER KEY

1. **Hable español ahora.** 2. **Tome una siesta.** 3. **Camine hasta mi casa.** 4. **Trabaje más.** 5. **Escriba en la computadora.** 6. **Beba más vino.**

How Did You Do?

By now, you should be able to:

- ☐ Use commands to tell someone to *go*, *see*, *work*, or *come*
(Still unsure? Jump back to page 257.)
- ☐ Understand the differences between **para** and **por**
(Still unsure? Jump back to page 263.)

Don't forget to practice and reinforce what you've learned by visiting **www.livinglanguage.com/languagelab** for flashcards, games, and quizzes for Unit 5!

Unit 5 Essentials

Vocabulary Essentials

DIRECTIONAL VOCABULARY

	north
	south
	east
	west
	left
	right

[Pg. 222]

DRIVING VOCABULARY

	highway, freeway
	exit
	toll
	lane
	one-way
	map
	intersection

[Pg. 222]

OTHER WORDS AROUND TOWN

	outskirts
	town
	subway/metro
	building
	apartment building

[Pg. 222]

TOWN FEATURES

	avenue
	street
	block
	corner
	traffic light
	pedestrian

[Pg. 226]

PLACES AROUND TOWN

	library
	restaurant
	store
	park
	bank
	church
	temple
	mosque

	sidewalk
	bakery
	butcher shop
	café/coffee shop
	drugstore/pharmacy
	supermarket
	clothing store
	department store

[Pg. 226]

VERBS AND ADJECTIVES FOR GETTING AROUND TOWN

	straight
	to turn
	to turn around
	to walk
	to follow

[Pg. 227]

DRIVING EXPRESSIONS

	Stop!
	traffic jam
	to turn off the lights
	to pay the toll
	to buckle up
	to hit the brakes
	to exceed the speed limit

	to go through a light
	to go in the opposite direction
	to slow down
	to pay a fine

[Pg. 233]

EXPRESSIONS USING DAR

	to give thanks
	to give birth
	to find something
	to fall flat on one's face (lit., nose)
	to tell time
	to shake hands

[Pg. 236]

DIRECTIONAL EXPRESSIONS

	to cross the street
	to walk two blocks
	next to
	in front of
	on the left-hand side
	on the right-hand side
	at the corner
	around the corner
	on the sidewalk
	through the alley

[Pg. 237]

MORE DIRECTIONAL EXPRESSIONS

	Go straight till ...
	Thanks for (lit., I thank you for) your help.
	Do you know how to get to ... ?
	Here on the map, it is very clear.
	Have a good trip.
	Stay in the right lane.
	At more or less two kilometers, there is a toll.
	Take the ramp towards ...
	The theater is on the left-hand side.
	Go straight down this street.
	Can you tell me how to get to ... ?
	The visitors' entrance is in back.

[Pg. 243, Pg. 248]

EXPRESSIONS USING POR

	For God's sake!
	At last!
	apparently
	for this reason
	therefore
	unfortunately
	on the one hand
	on the other hand
	of course

	by chance

[Pg. 266]

Grammar Essentials

THE PRESENT PROGRESSIVE

The present progressive is formed as follows in Spanish:

estar (*to be*) + present participle

To form the present participle:

For **-ar** verbs, take off the **-ar** and add **-ando** to the stem.

For **-er** and **-ir** verbs, take off the **-er** or **-ir** and add **-iendo** to the stem.

IRREGULAR PRESENT PARTICIPLES

VERB	PRESENT PARTICIPLE
traer (*to bring*)	**trayendo**
decir (*to say*)	**diciendo**
ir (*to go*)	**yendo**
venir (*to come*)	**viniendo**
poder (*to be able to*)	**pudiendo**

COMMON PREPOSITIONS OF LOCATION

en	*in, on*
entre	*between*
delante de	*in front of*
enfrente de	*in front of*
detrás de	*behind*
debajo de	*underneath*
encima de	*on top of*

sobre	*above*
contra	*against*
cerca de	*close to*
lejos de	*far away from*
dentro de	*inside of*
fuera de	*outside of*

COMMON PREPOSITIONS OF TIME

antes de	*before*
después de	*after*
desde	*since, from*
durante	*during*
hasta	*until, till*

OTHER COMMON PREPOSITIONS

a	*to, at*
con	*with*
de	*of*
hacia	*toward*
sin	*without*
sobre	*about/on top of*

THE IMPERATIVE

	FAMILIAR	SINGULAR POLITE	PLURAL POLITE
comer *(to eat)*	(tú) come	(usted) coma	(ustedes) coman
dar *(to give)*	da	dé	den

	FAMILIAR	SINGULAR POLITE	PLURAL POLITE
decir *(to say, to tell)*	**di**	**diga**	**digan**
escribir *(to write)*	**escribe**	**escriba**	**escriban**
estar *(to be)*	**está**	**esté**	**estén**
hacer *(to do, to make)*	**haz**	**haga**	**hagan**
ir *(to go)*	**ve**	**vaya**	**vayan**
poner *(to put)*	**pon**	**ponga**	**pongan**
saber *(to know)*	**sabe**	**sepa**	**sepan**
salir *(to leave, to go out)*	**sal**	**salga**	**salgan**
ser *(to be)*	**sé**	**sea**	**sean**
tener *(to have)*	**ten**	**tenga**	**tengan**
trabajar *(to work)*	**trabaja**	**trabaje**	**trabajen**
venir *(to come)*	**ven**	**venga**	**vengan**
ver *(to see)*	**ve**	**vea**	**vean**

PARA AND POR

1. **Para** indicates a purpose (*in order to*), an intention (*intended for*), a limit in time (*by/until a certain time*), a length of time (*for*), or a destination (*towards*). When used to show intention, **para** is followed by a verb in the infinitive.
2. **Por** is used to indicate cause or reason (*because of, due to*), or to indicate exchange (*in place of, in exchange for*). It can also mean *through*.

VERBS

CONOCER *(TO KNOW A PERSON OR TO BE FAMILIAR WITH SOMETHING)*	
yo conozco	**nosotros/as conocemos**
tú conoces	**vosotros/as conocéis**
él/ella/usted conoce	**ellos/ellas/ustedes conocen**

DAR *(TO GIVE)*	
yo doy	nosotros/as damos
tú das	vosotros/as dais
él/ella/usted da	ellos/ellas/ustedes dan

DEBER *(MUST)*	
yo debo	nosotros/as debemos
tú debes	vosotros/as debéis
él/ella/usted debe	ellos/ellas/ustedes deben

PODER *(CAN)*	
yo puedo	nosotros/as podemos
tú puedes	vosotros/as podéis
él/ella/usted puede	ellos/ellas/ustedes pueden

SABER *(TO KNOW A FACT, TO KNOW HOW TO DO SOMETHING)*	
yo sé	nosotros/as sabemos
tú sabes	vosotros/as sabéis
él/ella/usted sabe	ellos/ellas/ustedes saben

VENIR *(TO COME)*	
yo vengo	nosotros/as venimos
tú vienes	vosotros/as venís
él/ella/usted viene	ellos/ellas/ustedes vienen

Unit 5 Quiz

A. Match the column on the left with its appropriate English counterpart on the right.

1. **el peaje**	a. *right*
2. **la derecha**	b. *corner*
3. **las afueras**	c. *sidewalk*
4. **la biblioteca**	d. *toll*
5. **la esquina**	e. *lights*
6. **las luces**	f. *butcher shop*
7. **la carnicería**	g. *outskirts*
8. **la acera**	h. *library*

B. Form the present progressive of the following sentences.

1. **Mi amiga Brenda habla español.** ____________________

____

2. **Yo como churros.** ____________________

____

3. **Nosotros damos las gracias.** ____________________

____

4. **Usted ve la televisión con su familia.** ____________________

____

5. **Ustedes pagan el peaje.** ______________________________

____

6. **Ernesto y yo apagamos las luces.** ______________________________

____

7. **Mis amigos esquían muy bien.** ______________________________

____

8. **Su hija cruza la calle.** ______________________________

____

C. Translate each of the following sentences.

1. *The theater is in front of the bakery.* ______________________________

____

2. *There's a museum next to the library.* ______________________________

____

3. *The bank is at the corner.* ______________________________

____

4. *The pharmacy is behind the supermarket.* ______________________________

____

5. *There's a book under the table.* ______________________________

____

D. Choose the vocabulary word that best fits each sentence.

1. El opuesto del norte es el ______________________________ (este/sur).
2. El opuesto de la izquierda es la ______________________ (derecha/salida).
3. Tú vives en una ciudad grande pero yo vivo en un ______________________ (pueblo/cruce) pequeño.
4. Yo ______________________________ (sé/conozco) el nombre del artista.
5. Yo ____________________________________ (sé/conozco) al tío de Pepe.
6. La casa está en la ________________________________ (iglesia/esquina).
7. Yo compro ropa en ____________________________ (el parque/la tienda).
8. La comida es muy buena en ese ___________________ (restaurante/banco).

How Did You Do?

Give yourself a point for every correct answer, then use the following key to determine whether or not you're ready to move on:

0–7 points: It's probably best to go back and study the lessons again to make sure you understood everything completely. Take your time; it's not a race! Make sure you spend time reviewing vocabulary with the flashcards and reading through each grammar note carefully.

8–16 points: If the questions you missed were in sections A or B, you may want to review the vocabulary again; if you missed answers mostly in sections C or D, check the unit essentials to make sure you have your conjugations and other grammar basics down.

17–20 points: Feel free to move on to the next level! You're doing a great job.

points

ANSWER KEY

A. 1. d; 2. a; 3. g; 4. h; 5. b; 6. e; 7. f; 8. c

B. 1. **Mi amiga Brenda está hablando español.** 2. **Yo estoy comiendo churros.** 3. **Nosotros estamos dando las gracias.** 4. **Usted está viendo la televisión con su familia.** 5. **Ustedes están pagando el peaje.** 6. **Ernesto y yo estamos apagando las luces.** 7. **Mis amigos están esquiando muy bien.** 8. **Su hija está cruzando la calle.**

C. 1. **El teatro está enfrente de la panadería.** 2. **Hay un museo al lado de la biblioteca.** 3. **El banco está en la esquina.** 4. **La farmacia está detrás del supermercado.** 5. **Hay un libro debajo de la mesa.**

D. 1. **sur**; 2. **derecha**; 3. **pueblo**; 4. **sé**; 5. **conozco**; 6. **esquina**; 7. **la tienda**; 8. **restaurante**

Pronunciation Guide

If you've ever had trouble with English spelling, or if you've ever come across an unfamiliar word and had no idea how to pronounce it, you'll be happy to know that neither of these things is likely to be an issue in Spanish. Spanish spelling is phonetic, meaning that things are pronounced the way they're written. The rules for stress—which SYL-la-ble gets the EM-pha-sis—are very regular in Spanish, and any irregularities are marked in spelling with an accent mark. We'll cover all of that little by little, but let's get started with an overview of Spanish pronunciation.

1. VOWELS

Each vowel in Spanish is pronounced clearly and distinctly, and each vowel has one and only one pronunciation. A vowel may be written with an accent, as in **sí** or **América**, but this never changes the pronunciation of that vowel. It may mark stress, as in **América**, or it may only serve to distinguish between two words, as in **sí** (*yes*) and **si** (*if*). Let's look at each vowel, starting with simple vowels.

a	like *a* in *father*	**a, amigo, la, las, pan, habla, Santiago**
e	like *ay* in *day*, but cut off before the *ee*	**él, de, en, padre, tren, este, Mercedes**
i	like *i* in *police*	**mí, amiga, hiciste, cinco, Chile, Sevilla**
o	like *o* in *no*, but cut off before the *oo*	**no, dos, hombre, costar, ocho, teléfono, Colombia**
u	like *u* in *rule*	**uno, tú, mucho, azúcar, Honduras, puro**

Vowels can also appear in pairs, which are called diphthongs. A diphthong is usually a combination of a weaker vowel (**i** or **u**) and a more prominent one.

ai, ay	like *i* in *bide*	**aire, hay, traigo, ¡ay!**

au	like *ou* in *house*	**restaurante, autobús, automóvil, Mauricio**
ei, ey	like *ay* in *day*	**seis, ley, treinta, rey**
ia, ya	like *ya* in *yard*	**gracias, comercial, estudiar, ya**
ie, ye	like *ye* in *yet*	**pie, quiero, tiene, yerba, abyecto**
io, yo	like *yo* in *yoga*	**yo, acción, despacio, estudio**
iu, yu	like *u* in *united*	**ciudad, yuca, yugo, yunta**
oi, oy	like *oy* in *toy*	**estoy, hoy, oiga, voy**
ua	like *wa* in *want*	**cuatro, Juan, ¿cuál?, ¿cuánto?**
ue	like *we* in *west*	**nueve, fuego, puerta, cuesta, bueno**
uo	like *wo* in *woe*	**continuo, antiguo, mutuo, superfluo**
ui, uy	like *we* in *week*	**muy, ruido, cuidado, huir**

2. CONSONANTS

b	like *b* in *boy* at the beginning of a word	**bueno, brazo, bajo, barca, bocadillo**
b	between vowels for some speakers, as above, but the lips don't touch	**Cuba, haber, beber, cobayo, deber, ubicar**
c	like *k* in *kite* before consonants, **a**, **o**, and **u**	**Cristóbal, cosa, casa, cuánto, cuál, truco**

c	like *s* in *sea* before **e** and **i**	**cerca, servicio, cierto, fácil, posición**
ch	like *ch* in *choose*	**charlar, chico, muchacho, ocho, mucho**
d	at the beginning of a word or after **n**, like *d* in *day*, but with the tongue touching the back of the upper teeth	**día, despegar, durante, cuándo, donde, mando**
d	between vowels, like *th* in *thin*	**media, nada, todo, poder, freiduría, prometido**
f	like *f* in *father*	**familia, Francisco, Federico, formulario**
g	like *g* in *go* before consonants, **a**, **o**, and **u**	**grande, Gloria, gustar, gusano, goloso, ganar, vengo**
g	like the strong *h* in *hope* before **e** or **i**	**general, Gibraltar, girar, rígido, urgente**
gü	like *gw* in *Gwen*	**vergüenza, lengüeta, cigüeña**
h	silent	**hablo, hay, hubo, ahora, hombre, deshonroso**
j	like the strong *h* in *hope*	**julio, jabón, mejor, José, tarjeta, jefe, trujar**
ll	like *y* in *yes*	**llamo, pollo, llama, llover, allí, llaves, trulla**
m	like *m* in *met*	**mismo, Marco, mano, Manuel, pluma, mandar**

n	like *n* in *not*	**nunca, no, Nicaragua, Argentina, nombre**
ñ	like *ni* in *onion*	**español, mañana, muñeca, ñame, gañir**
p	like *p* in *pear*	**para, pueblo, postre, Panamá, Perú**
qu	like *k* in *kite*	**que, querer, paquete, saquen, quemar, quizás**
r	at the beginning of a word, a trilled sound made with the tongue against the ridge behind the upper teeth	**rico, rubio, Ramón, Rosa, rincón, red, risa**
r	otherwise like the tapped *d* in *ladder*	**América, pero, quisiera, aire, libre, brazo, caro**
rr	like word-initial **r**, a trilled sound made with the tongue against the ridge behind the upper teeth	**perro, carro, tierra, horror, irritar, terrible**
s	like *s* in *see* (never like *z* in *zone*)	**casa, sucio, San Salvador, soltero, vasto, rosa**
t	like *t* in *take*, but with the tongue touching the back of the upper teeth	**tocar, fruta, tú, teclado, traje, tener**
v	like *b* in *boy* at the beginning of a word	**vaso, veinte, vivir, vivo, veramente**
y	like *y* in *yes*; on its own, like *ee* in *teen*	**ayer, ayudo, Bayamo, poyo**

z	like *s* in *see*	**zona, diez, luz, marzo, azul, azúcar**

3. STRESS

There are three simple rules to keep in mind when it comes to stress. First, if a word ends in any consonant other than **-n** or **-s**, the last syllable receives the stress.

cuidad, capaz, notabilidad, navegar, familiar, refrigerador

Second, if a word ends in a vowel or in **-n** or **-s**, the penultimate (second-to-last) syllable receives the stress.

amigo, hablan, derechos, cubierto, portorriqueño, examen, libros

Note that diphthongs with the weak vowels **i** or **u** count as one syllable, so the stress will regularly fall before them.

academia, continuo, manubrio, sanitario, justicia

Combinations with two strong vowels count as two syllables.

tarea, menudeo, banqueteo, barbacoa

Any time stress doesn't follow these rules, an accent is used.

inglés, teléfono, tomó, práctico, drogaría, todavía, título, farmacéutico, petróleo, revés, apagón

4. REGIONAL SPANISH PRONUNCIATION

The Spanish pronunciation that you'll learn in this course is standard Latin American Spanish. There are certainly some local differences in pronunciation that you will probably come across, the most commonly known being the difference between Latin American and European Spanish. The major difference in pronunciation is that the sound *th*, as in *thin*, is much more common in Spain. In Latin America, this sound is typically only found in *d* when it comes between vowels.

media, nada, todo, poder, puedo

These words are pronounced with a *th* in Spain, too. But in Spain, **c** before **i** or **e** and **z** is also pronounced like *th* in *thin*.

cerca, servicio, cierto, fácil, docena, diez, voz, luz, marzo, azul, razón

There are some noticeable differences in local varieties of Spanish found in Latin America and Spain, as well. You don't need to worry about imitating these differences; the standard pronunciation you'll learn in this course will serve you perfectly well. But you may notice, for example, that in some countries or regions the combination **ll** is pronounced like the *lli* in *million*, the *j* in *juice*, the *sh* in *show*, or the *s* in *pleasure*. The semivowel **y** may have a similar range of pronunciation. In some countries, particularly in the Caribbean, final **s** may be dropped altogether, if not the entire last syllable! You may even hear **r** pronounced as something similar to **l**. There's certainly nothing wrong with any of these variations, although as a student, you'll probably find it useful to concentrate on the standard pronunciation offered in this course first.

Grammar Summary

Keep in mind that there are always at least some exceptions to every grammar rule.

1. ARTICLES

	DEFINITE		INDEFINITE	
	Singular	Plural	Singular	Plural
Masculine	el	los	un	unos
Feminine	la	las	una	unas

Note: El is used before a feminine noun beginning with stressed a (or ha). The article lo is used before parts of speech other than nouns when they are used as nouns. Unos (unas) is often used to mean *some* or *a few*.

2. CONTRACTIONS

de + el = del (*from/of the*)

a + el = al (*to the*)

3. PLURALS

a. Nouns ending in an unstressed vowel or diphthong add -s.

b. Nouns ending in a stressed vowel or diphthong add -es.

c. Nouns ending in a consonant add -es.

d. Nouns ending in -z change the z to c and then add -es.

4. POSSESSION

Possession is shown by the preposition de: el libro de Juan (*Juan's book*).

5. ADJECTIVES

Adjectives agree with the nouns they modify in both gender and number.

a. If the masculine singular ending is **-o**, the feminine singular is **-a**, the masculine plural is **-os**, and the feminine plural is **-as**.
b. If the masculine singular ending is not **-o**, there is no change in the feminine singular, and both genders are **-es** in the plural.

6. COMPARISON

The regular comparative is formed with **más** (*more*) or **menos** (*less*), and the regular superlative is formed with the definite article + **más** (*the most*) or **menos** (*the least*).

7. PRONOUNS

	SUBJECT	DIRECT OBJECT	INDIRECT OBJECT	PREPOSITIONAL	REFLEXIVE
1st sg.	**yo**	**me**	**me**	**mí**	**me**
2nd sg.	**tú**	**te**	**te**	**ti**	**te**
3rd m. sg.	**él**	**lo**	**le**	**él**	**se**
3rd f. sg.	**ella**	**la**	**le**	**ella**	**se**
2nd sg., fml.	**usted**	**lo/la**	**le**	**usted**	**se**
1st pl.	**nosotros/ nosotras**	**nos**	**nos**	**nosotros**	**nos**
2nd pl.	**vosotros/ vosotras**	**os**	**os**	**vosotros**	**os**
3rd m. pl.	**ellos**	**los**	**les**	**ellos**	**se**

	SUBJECT	DIRECT OBJECT	INDIRECT OBJECT	PREPOSITIONAL	REFLEXIVE
3rd f. pl.	ellas	las	les	ellas	se
2nd pl., fml.	ustedes	los/las	les	ustedes	se

8. QUESTION WORDS

¿Qué?	*What?*	¿Cuál? ¿Cuáles?	*What?/ Which one?*
¿Por qué?	*Why?*	¿Quién? ¿Quiénes?	*Who?*
¿Cómo?	*How?*	¿Dónde?	*Where?*
¿Cuánto? ¿Cuánta? ¿Cuántos? ¿Cuántas?	*How much?/How many?*	¿Cuándo?	*When?*

9. ADVERBS

Spanish **-mente** corresponds to *-ly* in English. It is added to the feminine form of the adjective.

10. DEMONSTRATIVES

ADJECTIVES		PRONOUNS			
Masculine	Feminine	Masculine	Feminine	Neuter	
este	esta	éste	ésta	esto	*this*
ese	esa	ése	ésa	eso	*that*
aquel	aquella	aquél	aquélla	aquello	*that (farther removed)*
estos	estas	éstos	éstas	estos	*these*
esos	esas	ésos	ésas	esos	*those*
aquellos	aquellas	aquéllos	aquéllas	aquellos	*those (farther removed)*

11. *IF* SENTENCES

IF THE MAIN CLAUSE HAS A VERB IN THE:	THE SI *(IF)* CLAUSE HAS A VERB IN THE:
Present	*Present/Future*
Future	*Present*
Imperfect	*Imperfect*
Preterite	*Preterite*
Conditional	*Imperfect Subjunctive* (-ra *or* -se)
Past Conditional	*Past Perfect Subjunctive* (hubiera *or* hubiese)

If the subject of the main clause and the subject of the *if* clause are the same, it's possible to replace a verb in the subjunctive with an infinitive. In this case si is replaced by de.

12. SUBJUNCTIVE

The subjunctive is used:

a. with verbs of desire, request, suggestion, permission, approval and disapproval, judgment, opinion, uncertainty, emotion, surprise, fear, denial, and so on. It is often used in a dependent clause introduced by **que** (*that*).

b. in affirmative or negative commands in the polite form, in negative commands in the familiar form, in *let's* suggestions, and in indirect or third person commands with *let (him/her/them)*.

c. in **si** (*if*) conditional clauses that are unreal or contrary to fact.

d. after impersonal verbs that do not express certainty.

e. after certain conjunctions that never introduce statements of accomplished fact (**antes de que**, **aunque**, **como si**, etc.). Other conjunctions may or may not introduce a statement of accomplished fact. When they do, they take the indicative; otherwise they take the subjunctive (**a menos que**, **a pesar de que**, etc.).

f. to refer to indefinites like **ningún** (*no*) or **alguien** (*someone*) when there's a doubt about that person's existence.

g. after compounds with **-quiera** (*-ever*): **quienquiera** (*whoever*), **dondequiera** (*wherever*), **cualquier** (*whatever, whichever*).

comer
to eat

yo	nosotros/as
tú	vosotros/as
él/ella/usted	ellos/ellas/ustedes

Present		Present Progressive	
como	comemos	estoy comiendo	estamos comiendo
comes	coméis	estás comiendo	estáis comiendo
come	comen	está comiendo	están comiendo

Preterite		Imperfect	
comí	comimos	comía	comíamos
comiste	comisteis	comías	comíais
comió	comieron	comía	comían

Future		Conditional	
comeré	comeremos	comería	comeríamos
comerás	comeréis	comerías	comeríais
comerá	comerán	comería	comerían

Imperative		Subjunctive	
		coma	comamos
come	comed	comas	comáis
coma		coma	coman

conducir
to drive

yo	nosotros/as
tú	vosotros/as
él/ella/usted	ellos/ellas/ustedes

Present		Present Progressive	
conduzco	conducimos	estoy conduciendo	estamos conduciendo
conduces	conducís	estás conduciendo	estáis conduciendo
conduce	conducen	está conduciendo	están conduciendo

Preterite		Imperfect	
conduje	condujimos	conducía	conducíamos
condujiste	condujisteis	conducías	conducíais
condujo	condujeron	conducía	conducían

Future		Conditional	
conduciré	conduciremos	conduciría	conduciríamos
conducirás	conduciréis	conducirías	conduciríais
conducirá	conducirán	conduciría	conducirían

Imperative		Subjunctive	
		conduzca	conduzcamos
conduce	conducid	conduzcas	conduzcáis
conduzca		conduzca	conduzcan

conocer
to know

yo	nosotros/as
tú	vosotros/as
él/ella/usted	ellos/ellas/ustedes

Present		Present Progressive	
conozco	conocemos	estoy conociendo	estamos conociendo
conoces	conocéis	estás conociendo	estáis conociendo
conoce	conocen	está conociendo	están conociendo

Preterite		Imperfect	
conocí	conocimos	conocía	conocíamos
conociste	conocisteis	conocías	conocíais
conoció	conocieron	conocía	conocían

Future		Conditional	
conoceré	conoceremos	conocería	conoceríamos
conocerás	conoceréis	conocerías	conoceríais
conocerá	conocerán	conocería	conocerían

Imperative		Subjunctive	
		conozca	conozcamos
conoce	conoced	conozcas	conozcáis
conozca		conozca	conozcan

dar
to give

yo	nosotros/as
tú	vosotros/as
él/ella/usted	ellos/ellas/ustedes

Present		Present Progressive	
doy	damos	estoy dando	estamos dando
das	dais	estás dando	estáis dando
da	dan	está dando	están dando

Preterite		Imperfect	
di	dimos	daba	dábamos
diste	disteis	dabas	dabais
dio	dieron	daba	daban

Future		Conditional	
daré	daremos	daría	daríamos
darás	daréis	darías	daríais
dará	darán	daría	darían

Imperative		Subjunctive	
		dé	demos
da	dad	des	deis
dé		dé	den

deber

to have to, must

yo	nosotros/as
tú	vosotros/as
él/ella/usted	ellos/ellas/ustedes

Present		Present Progressive	
debo	debemos	estoy debiendo	estamos debiendo
debes	debéis	estás debiendo	estáis debiendo
debe	deben	está debiendo	están debiendo

Preterite		Imperfect	
debí	debimos	debía	debíamos
debiste	debisteis	debías	debíais
debió	debieron	debía	debían

Future		Conditional	
deberé	deberemos	debería	deberíamos
deberás	deberéis	deberías	deberíais
deberá	deberán	debería	deberían

Imperative		Subjunctive	
		deba	debamos
debe	debed	debas	debáis
deba		deba	deban

escoger
to choose

yo	nosotros/as
tú	vosotros/as
él/ella/usted	ellos/ellas/ustedes

Present		Present Progressive	
escojo	escogemos	estoy escogiendo	estamos escogiendo
escoges	escogéis	estás escogiendo	estáis escogiendo
escoge	escogen	está escogiendo	están escogiendo

Preterite		Imperfect	
escogí	escogimos	escogía	escogíamos
escogiste	escogisteis	escogías	escogíais
escogió	escogieron	escogía	escogían

Future		Conditional	
escogeré	escogeremos	escogería	escogeríamos
escogerás	escogeréis	escogerías	escogeríais
escogerá	escogerán	escogería	escogerían

Imperative		Subjunctive	
		escoja	escojamos
escoge	escoged	escojas	escojáis
escoja		escoja	escojan

estar
to be

yo	nosotros/as
tú	vosotros/as
él/ella/usted	ellos/ellas/ustedes

Present		Present Progressive	
estoy	estamos	estoy estando	estamos estando
estás	estáis	estás estando	estáis estando
está	están	está estando	están estando

Preterite		Imperfect	
estuve	estuvimos	estaba	estábamos
estuviste	estuvisteis	estabas	estábais
estuvo	estuvieron	estaba	estaban

Future		Conditional	
estaré	estaremos	estaría	estaríamos
estarás	estaréis	estarías	estaríais
estará	estarán	estaría	estarían

Imperative		Subjunctive	
		esté	estemos
está	estad	estés	estéis
esté		esté	estén

hablar

to speak, to talk

yo	nosotros/as
tú	vosotros/as
él/ella/usted	ellos/ellas/ustedes

Present		Present Progressive	
hablo	hablamos	estoy hablando	estamos hablando
hablas	habláis	estás hablando	estáis hablando
habla	hablan	está hablando	están hablando

Preterite		Imperfect	
hablé	hablamos	hablaba	hablábamos
hablaste	hablasteis	hablabas	hablabais
habló	hablaron	hablaba	hablaban

Future		Conditional	
hablaré	hablaremos	hablaría	hablaríamos
hablarás	hablaréis	hablarías	hablaríais
hablará	hablarán	hablaría	hablarían

Imperative		Subjunctive	
		hable	hablemos
habla	hablad	hables	habléis
hable		hable	hablen

hacer
to do, to make

yo	nosotros/as
tú	vosotros/as
él/ella/usted	ellos/ellas/ustedes

Present		Present Progressive	
hago	hacemos	estoy haciendo	estamos haciendo
haces	hacéis	estás haciendo	estáis haciendo
hace	hacen	está haciendo	están haciendo

Preterite		Imperfect	
hice	hicimos	hacía	hacíamos
hiciste	hicisteis	hacías	hacíais
hizo	hicieron	hacía	hacían

Future		Conditional	
haré	haremos	haría	haríamos
harás	haréis	harías	haríais
hará	harán	haría	harían

Imperative		Subjunctive	
		haga	hagamos
haz	haced	hagas	hagáis
haga		haga	hagan

ir
to go

yo	nosotros/as
tú	vosotros/as
él/ella/usted	ellos/ellas/ustedes

Present		Present Progressive	
voy	vamos	estoy yendo	estamos yendo
vas	vais	estás yendo	estáis yendo
va	van	está yendo	están yendo

Preterite		Imperfect	
fui	fuimos	iba	íbamos
fuiste	fuisteis	ibas	ibais
fue	fueron	iba	iban

Future		Conditional	
iré	iremos	iría	iríamos
irás	iréis	irías	iríais
irá	irán	iría	irían

Imperative		Subjunctive	
		vaya	vayamos
ve	id	vayas	vayáis
vaya		vaya	vayan

pedir

to ask for

yo	nosotros/as
tú	vosotros/as
él/ella/usted	ellos/ellas/ustedes

Present		Present Progressive	
pido	pedimos	estoy pidiendo	estamos pidiendo
pides	pedís	estás pidiendo	estáis pidiendo
pide	piden	está pidiendo	están pidiendo

Preterite		Imperfect	
pedí	pedimos	pedía	pedíamos
pediste	pedisteis	pedías	pedíais
pidió	pidieron	pedía	pedían

Future		Conditional	
pediré	pediremos	pediría	pediríamos
pedirás	pediréis	pedirías	pediríais
pedirá	pedirán	pediría	pedirían

Imperative		Subjunctive	
		pida	pidamos
pide	pedid	pidas	pidáis
pida		pida	pidan

pensar

to think

yo	nosotros/as
tú	vosotros/as
él/ella/usted	ellos/ellas/ustedes

Present		Present Progressive	
pienso	pensamos	estoy pensando	estamos pensando
piensas	pensáis	estás pensando	estáis pensando
piensa	piensan	está pensando	están pensando

Preterite		Imperfect	
pensé	pensamos	pensaba	pensábamos
pensaste	pensasteis	pensabas	pensabais
pensó	pensaron	pensaba	pensaban

Future		Conditional	
pensaré	pensaremos	pensaría	pensaríamos
pensarás	pensaréis	pensarías	pensaríais
pensará	pensarán	pensaría	pensarían

Imperative		Subjunctive	
		piense	pensemos
piensa	pensad	pienses	penséis
piense		piense	piensen

poder

to be able to, can

yo	nosotros/as
tú	vosotros/as
él/ella/usted	ellos/ellas/ustedes

Present		Present Progressive	
puedo	podemos	estoy pudiendo	estamos pudiendo
puedes	podéis	estás pudiendo	estáis pudiendo
puede	pueden	está pudiendo	están pudiendo

Preterite		Imperfect	
pude	pudimos	podía	podíamos
pudiste	pudisteis	podías	podíais
pudo	pudieron	podía	podían

Future		Conditional	
podré	podremos	podría	podríamos
podrás	podréis	podrías	podríais
podrá	podrán	podría	podrían

Imperative		Subjunctive	
		pueda	podamos
puede	poded	puedas	podáis
pueda		pueda	puedan

poner
to put

yo	nosotros/as
tú	vosotros/as
él/ella/usted	ellos/ellas/ustedes

Present		Present Progressive	
pongo	ponemos	estoy poniendo	estamos poniendo
pones	ponéis	estás poniendo	estáis poniendo
pone	ponen	está poniendo	están poniendo

Preterite		Imperfect	
puse	pusimos	ponía	poníamos
pusiste	pusisteis	ponías	poníais
puso	pusieron	ponía	ponían

Future		Conditional	
pondré	pondremos	pondría	pondríamos
pondrás	pondréis	pondrías	pondríais
pondrá	pondrían	pondría	pondrían

Imperative		Subjunctive	
		ponga	pongamos
pon	poned	pongas	pongáis
ponga		ponga	pongan

querer
to want

yo	nosotros/as
tú	vosotros/as
él/ella/usted	ellos/ellas/ustedes

Present		Present Progressive	
quiero	queremos	estoy queriendo	estamos queriendo
quieres	queréis	estás queriendo	estáis queriendo
quiere	quieren	está queriendo	están queriendo

Preterite		Imperfect	
quise	quisimos	quería	queríamos
quisiste	quisisteis	querías	queríais
quiso	quisieron	quería	querían

Future		Conditional	
querré	querremos	querría	querríamos
querrás	querréis	querrías	querríais
querrá	querrán	querría	querrían

Imperative		Subjunctive	
		quiera	queramos
quiere	quered	quieras	queráis
quiera		quiera	quieran

saber
to know

yo	nosotros/as
tú	vosotros/as
él/ella/usted	ellos/ellas/ustedes

Present		Present Progressive	
sé	sabemos	estoy sabiendo	estamos sabiendo
sabes	sabéis	estás sabiendo	estáis sabiendo
sabe	saben	está sabiendo	están sabiendo

Preterite		Imperfect	
supe	supimos	sabía	sabíamos
supiste	supisteis	sabías	sabíais
supo	supieron	sabía	sabían

Future		Conditional	
sabré	sabremos	sabría	sabríamos
sabrás	sabréis	sabrías	sabríais
sabrá	sabrán	sabría	sabrían

Imperative		Subjunctive	
		sepa	sepamos
sabe	sabed	sepas	sepáis
sepa		sepa	sepan

salir
to go out

yo	nosotros/as
tú	vosotros/as
él/ella/usted	ellos/ellas/ustedes

Present		Present Progressive	
salgo	salimos	estoy saliendo	estamos saliendo
sales	salís	estás saliendo	estáis saliendo
sale	salen	está saliendo	están saliendo

Preterite		Imperfect	
salí	salimos	salía	salíamos
saliste	salisteis	salías	salíais
salió	salieron	salía	salían

Future		Conditional	
saldré	saldremos	saldría	saldríamos
saldrás	saldréis	saldrías	saldríais
saldrá	saldrán	saldría	saldrían

Imperative		Subjunctive	
		salga	salgamos
sal	salid	salgas	salgáis
salga		salga	salgan

ser
to be

yo	nosotros/as
tú	vosotros/as
él/ella/usted	ellos/ellas/ustedes

Present		Present Progressive	
soy	somos	estoy siendo	estamos siendo
eres	sois	estás siendo	estáis siendo
es	son	está siendo	están siendo

Preterite		Imperfect	
fui	fuimos	era	éramos
fuiste	fuisteis	eras	erais
fue	fueron	era	eran

Future		Conditional	
seré	seremos	sería	seríamos
serás	seréis	serías	seríais
será	serán	sería	serían

Imperative		Subjunctive	
		sea	seamos
sé	sed	seas	seáis
sea		sea	sean

tener
to have

yo	nosotros/as
tú	vosotros/as
él/ella/usted	ellos/ellas/ustedes

Present		Present Progressive	
tengo	tenemos	estoy teniendo	estamos teniendo
tienes	tenéis	estás teniendo	estáis teniendo
tiene	tienen	está teniendo	están teniendo

Preterite		Imperfect	
tuve	tuvimos	tenía	teníamos
tuviste	tuvisteis	tenías	teníais
tuvo	tuvieron	tenía	tenían

Future		Conditional	
tendré	tendremos	tendría	tendríamos
tendrás	tendréis	tendrías	tendríais
tendrá	tendrán	tendría	tendrían

Imperative		Subjunctive	
		tenga	tengamos
ten	tened	tengas	tengáis
tenga		tenga	tengan

traer
to bring

yo	nosotros/as
tú	vosotros/as
él/ella/usted	ellos/ellas/ustedes

Present		Present Progressive	
traigo	traemos	estoy trayendo	estamos trayendo
traes	traéis	estás trayendo	estáis trayendo
trae	traen	está trayendo	están trayendo

Preterite		Imperfect	
traje	trajimos	traía	traíamos
trajiste	trajisteis	traías	traíais
trajo	trajeron	traía	traían

Future		Conditional	
traeré	traeremos	traería	traeríamos
traerás	traeréis	traerías	traeríais
traerá	traerán	traería	traerían

Imperative		Subjunctive	
		traiga	traigamos
trae	traed	traigas	traigáis
traiga		traiga	traigan

venir
to come

yo	nosotros/as
tú	vosotros/as
él/ella/usted	ellos/ellas/ustedes

Present		Present Progressive	
vengo	venimos	estoy viniendo	estamos viniendo
vienes	venís	estás viniendo	estáis viniendo
viene	vienen	está viniendo	están viniendo

Preterite		Imperfect	
vine	vinimos	venía	veníamos
viniste	vinisteis	venías	veníais
vino	vinieron	venía	venían

Future		Conditional	
vendré	vendremos	vendría	vendríamos
vendrás	vendréis	vendrías	vendríais
vendrá	vendrán	vendría	vendrían

Imperative		Subjunctive	
		venga	vengamos
ven	venid	vengas	vengáis
venga		venga	vengan

ver
to see

yo	nosotros/as
tú	vosotros/as
él/ella/usted	ellos/ellas/ustedes

Present		Present Progressive	
veo	vemos	estoy viendo	estamos viendo
ves	veis	estás viendo	estáis viendo
ve	ven	está viendo	están viendo

Preterite		Imperfect	
vi	vimos	veía	veíamos
viste	visteis	veías	veíais
vio	vieron	veía	veían

Future		Conditional	
veré	veremos	vería	veríamos
verás	veréis	verías	veríais
verá	verán	vería	verían

Imperative		Subjunctive	
		vea	veamos
ve	ved	veas	veáis
vea		vea	vean

vivir
to live

yo	nosotros/as
tú	vosotros/as
él/ella/usted	ellos/ellas/ustedes

Present		Present Progressive	
vivo	vivimos	estoy viviendo	estamos viviendo
vives	vivís	estás viviendo	estáis viviendo
vive	viven	está viviendo	están viviendo

Preterite		Imperfect	
viví	vivimos	vivía	vivíamos
viviste	vivisteis	vivías	vivíais
vivió	vivieron	vivía	vivían

Future		Conditional	
viviré	viviremos	viviría	viviríamos
vivirás	viviréis	vivirías	viviríais
vivirá	vivirán	viviría	vivirían

Imperative		Subjunctive	
		viva	vivamos
vive	vivid	vivas	viváis
viva		viva	vivan

Glossary

Note that the following abbreviations will be used in this glossary: (m.) = masculine, (f.) = feminine, (sg.) = singular, (pl.) = plural, (fml.) = formal/polite, (infml.) = informal/familiar. If a word has two grammatical genders, (m./f.) or (f./m.) is used.

Spanish-English

A

a *to, at*
  a las cinco *at five (o'clock)*
  ¿A qué hora es? *At what time is it?*
  A ver ... *Let's see ...*
  de ... a ... *from ... through ...*
abdomen (m.) *abdomen*
abogado/abogada (m./f.) *lawyer*
abonado/abonada (m./f.) *subscriber*
  línea (f.) **de abonado digital (DSL)** *DSL*
abrigo (m.) *overcoat*
abril (m.) *April*
abrir *to open*
  abrir la puerta *to open the door*
abrochar *to fasten*
  abrocharse el cinturón de seguridad *to buckle up*
absolutamente *absolutely*
absoluto/absoluta (m./f.) *absolute*
  en absoluto *absolutely not*
absurdo/absurda (m./f.) *absurd*
abuela (f.) *grandmother*
abuelo (m.) *grandfather*
  abuelos (pl.) *grandfathers, grandparents*
aburrido/aburrida (m./f.) *bored, boring*
aburrir *to bore*
aburrirse *to be bored, to get bored*
  Me aburre/aburren ... (sg./pl.) *I'm bored by ...*
acabar *to finish*
  acabar de ... *to have just ... (done something)*
academia (f.) *school, academy*
académico/académica (m./f.) *academic*
accidente (m.) *accident*
aceite (m.) *oil*
aceptar *to accept*
acera (f.) *sidewalk*
aconsejar *to advise*
  aconsejar que ... *to advise that/to ...*
acostarse *to go to bed*
actor (m.) *actor*
actriz (f.) *actress*
actualmente *at the present time*
acuerdo (m.) *agreement*
  De acuerdo. *All right.*
acupuntura (f.) *acupuncture*
además *moreover*
Adiós. *Good-bye.*
adjuntar *to attach*
  adjuntar un documento *to attach a file*
adjunto/adjunta (m./f.) *enclosed*
  documento (m.) **adjunto** *attachment*
adolescente (m.) *adolescent, teenager*
adulto/adulta (m./f.) *adult*
aerolínea (f.) *airline*
aeropuerto (m.) *airport*
afeitar *to shave*
  navaja (f.) **de afeitar** *razor*
afeitarse *to shave (oneself)*
afición (f.) *hobby*
aficionado/aficionada (m./f.) *fan*
afuera *outside*
afueras (f. pl.) *outskirts*
agencia (f.) *agency*
agente (m./f.) *agent*
agitado/agitada (m./f.) *agitated, rough*
agosto (m.) *August*
agradable (m./f.) *pleasant*
agradecer *to be thankful*
  Le agradezco su ayuda. *Thank you for your help.*
agrio/agria (m./f.) *sour*
agua (f.) *water*

agua mineral *mineral water*
el agua *the water*
las aguas *the waters*
aguacate (m.) *avocado*
aguja (f.) *needle*
ahí *there*
ahora *now*
ahora mismo *right now*
ahorrar *to save*
ahumado/ahumada (m./f.) *smoked*
ajedrez (m.) *chess*
ajustado/ajustada (m./f.) *tight*
al (a + el) *to the* (m.)*/at the* (m.)
albornoz (m.) *robe*
alcalde (m.) *mayor*
alcaldía (f.) *municipal building*
alcoba (f.) *bedroom, room*
aldea (f.) *village*
alegrarse *to be glad*
alegrarse de que ... *to be glad that ...*
alegre (m./f.) *happy*
alemán (m.) *German (language)*
alemán/alemana (m./f.) *German*
alergia (f.) *allergy*
alérgico/alérgica (m./f.) *allergic*
alfombra (f.) *carpet*
álgebra (f.) *algebra*
algo *something, somewhat*
¿Algo más? *Anything else?*
algodón (m.) *cotton*
alguien *somebody, someone*
alguien más *somebody else*
algún/alguno/alguna (before m. sg. nouns/ m. sg./f. sg.) *some, something*
algunos/algunas (m. pl./f. pl.) *some, something*
allí *there*
almorzar *to have lunch*
almuerzo (m.) *lunch*
¿Aló? *Hello? (on the phone)*
alquilar *to rent*
alto (m.) *stop, height*
¡Alto! *Stop!*
alto/alta (m./f.) *tall, high*
tener la tensión alta *to have high blood pressure*
alumno/alumna (m./f.) *student*
amanecer (m.) *dawn*
al amanecer *at dawn*
amar *to love*
amargo/amarga (m./f.) *bitter, sour*
amarillo/amarilla (m./f.) *yellow*
páginas (f. pl.) **amarillas** *yellow pages*
americana (f.) *jacket*
americano/americana (m./f.) *American*
amigo/amiga (m./f.) *friend*
amueblado/amueblada (m./f.) *furnished*
anaranjado/anaranjada (m./f.) *orange (color)*
ancho/ancha (m./f.) *wide, baggy*
andar *to walk*
andén (m.) *sidewalk, platform*
por el andén *on the sidewalk*
anexo (m.) *attachment*
anexo al correo electrónico *e-mail attachment*
angosto/angosta (m./f.) *narrow*
anillo (m.) *ring*
año (m.) *year*
año pasado *last year*
año que viene *next year*
año entrante *next year*
¿Cuántos años tiene? *How old are you (sg. fml.)/is he/is she?*
este año *this year*
los años cincuenta *the fifties*
segundo año *second year*
tercer año *third year*
tener ... años *to be ... years old*
anoche *last night*
anotar *to record, to write down*
anotar un gol *to score a goal*
antes *before*
antes de ... *before ...*
lo antes posible *as soon as possible*
antigüedad (f.) *antique*
tienda (f.) **de antigüedades** *antique store*
antigüedades (f. pl.) *antiques*
antiguo/antigua (m./f.) *old*
antipático/antipática (m./f.) *unfriendly*
apagar *to turn off*
apagar las luces *to turn off the lights*
aparador (m.) *cupboard*
apartamento (m.) *apartment*
apetito (m.) *appetite*
apostar *to bet*
apuesto a que ... *to bet that ...*
aprender *to learn*

aprender a ... *to learn how to ...*
Estoy aprendiendo español. *I'm learning Spanish.*
aprobar *to pass*
aprobar un curso *to pass a course*
aprobar un examen *to pass a test*
apuesta (f.) *bet*
apuro (m.) *difficult situation*
aquel/aquella (m. sg./f. sg.) *that (far from the speaker and the listener)*
aquél/aquélla (m. sg./f. sg.) *that (one) over there (far from the speaker and the listener)*
aquello (neuter) *that (one, thing) over there (far from the speaker and the listener)*
aquellos/aquellas (m. pl./f. pl.) *those (far from the speaker and the listener)*
aquéllos/aquéllas (m. pl./f. pl.) *those (ones) over there (far from the speaker and the listener)*
aquí *here*
Aquí está ... *Here is ...*
Aquí tiene. *Here you are.*
árbol (m.) *tree*
archivo (m.) *file*
área (m.) *area*
arena (f.) *sand*
Argentina (f.) *Argentina*
argentino/argentina (m./f.) *Argentinian*
armario (m.) *closet, filing cabinet*
arquitecto/arquitecta (m./f.) *architect*
arquitectura (f.) *architecture*
arroz (m.) *rice*
arte (m.) *art*
artesanía (f.) *craft*
artista (m./f.) *artist*
asar *to grill*
bien asada *well-done*
así *so*
Así es. *That's right.*
Así que ... *So ...*
por así decir *so to speak*
asignatura (f.) *subject, course*
asistente (m./f.) *assistant*
asistir *to attend, to be present*
astronauta (m./f.) *astronaut*
atardecer (m.) *dusk*
al atardecer *at dusk*
atención (f.) *attention*
atender *to attend to, to serve, to take care of*
atentamente *carefully*
atleta (m./f.) *athlete*
atlético/atlética (m./f.) *athletic*
atracción (f.) *attraction*
atractivo/atractiva (m./f.) *attractive*
atrás *behind, back*
atún (m.) *tuna*
audífonos (m. pl.) *headphones*
aula (m.) *classroom*
auto (m.) *car*
autobús (m.) *bus*
recorrido (m.) **por autobús** *tour bus*
automático/automática (m./f.) *automatic*
contestador (m.) **automático** *answering machine*
automóvil (m.) *car*
autopista (f.) *highway, freeway*
autor/autora (m./f. less common) *author*
autovía (f.) *highway, freeway*
avenida (f.) *avenue*
aventura (f.) *adventure*
películas (pl.) **de aventuras** *adventure films*
avión (m.) *airplane*
ayer *yesterday*
ayuda (f.) *help*
Le agradezco su ayuda. *Thank you for your help.*
ayudar *to help*
¿Puede ayudarme? *Can you help me?*
ayuntamiento (m.) *city hall*
azúcar (m.) *sugar*
azul (m.) **claro** *the color light blue*
azul (m./f.) *blue*
azul claro *light blue*
azul marino *navy blue*
azul oscuro *dark blue*
ser de sangre azul *to have blue blood (lit., to be of blue blood)*

B

bailar *to dance*
baile (m.) *dancing*
bajar *to lower, to download*
bajo *under, below*
bajo/baja (m./f.) *short*
tener la tensión baja *to have low blood pressure*
balcón (m.) *balcony*

balón (m.) *ball*
baloncesto (m.) *basketball*
bañador (m.) *bathing trunks*
banana (f.) *banana*
bañarse *to take a bath, to bathe*
banco (m.) *bank*
banda (f.) *band*
bañera (f.) *bathtub*
baño (m.) *bathroom*
  traje (m.) **de baño** *bathing suit*
banquero/banquera (m./f.) *banker*
bar (m.) *bar*
barato/barata (m./f.) *cheap*
barbería (f.) *barbershop*
barbilla (f.) *chin*
barrio (m.) *neighborhood*
base (f.) *base*
bastante *quite, enough, quite a lot*
bata (f.) *robe*
batidora (f.) *blender*
bebé (m./f.) *baby*
beber *to drink*
bebida (f.) *drink*
bebito/bebita (m./f.) *little baby*
beca (f.) *scholarship*
béisbol (m.) *baseball*
  partido (m.) **de béisbol** *baseball game*
beneficio (m.) *benefit*
besar *to kiss*
biblioteca (f.) *library*
bicicleta (f.) *bicycle*
bien *well*
  Estoy bien. *I'm fine.*
  Que esté bien. *May you be well.*
  Que estés bien. *Take care.*
  ¡Qué bien! *How nice!*
Bienvenido./Bienvenida. (m./f.) *Welcome.* (to a man/to a woman)
billar (m.) *pool, billiards*
billete (m.) *ticket*
biología (f.) *biology*
blanco/blanca (m./f.) *white*
  ir de punta en blanco *to be dressed to the nines (lit., to go from the tip in white)*
  vino (m.) **blanco** *white wine*
bloquear *to block*
blusa (f.) *blouse*
bobo/boba (m./f.) *fool, idiot*
boca (f.) *mouth*
boleto (m.) *ticket*
bolígrafo (m.) *pen*
Bolivia (f.) *Bolivia*
boliviano/boliviana (m./f.) *Bolivian*
bolsa (f.) *bag, sack*
bolso (m.) *handbag*
bombachas (f. pl.) *women's underwear*
bonito/bonita (m./f.) *nice, pretty*
bordo (m.) *board*
  a bordo *on board*
  Bienvenidos a bordo. *Welcome aboard.*
borracho/borracha (m./f.) *drunk*
borrar *to erase*
bosque (m.) *forest*
bote (m.) *carton*
botella (f.) *bottle*
botiquín (m.) *medicine cabinet*
bragas (f. pl.) *women's underwear*
Brasil (m.) *Brazil*
brasileño/brasileña (m./f.) *Brazilian* (noun)
brasilero/brasilera (m./f.) *Brazilian* (adjective)
brazo (m.) *arm*
brote (m.) *rash*
buceo (m.) *diving*
buen/bueno/buena (before m. sg. nouns/m./f.) *good*
  Buenas noches. *Good evening./Good night.*
  Buenas tardes. *Good afternoon.*
  Buenos días. *Good morning.*
  ¡Buen provecho! *Enjoy the meal!*
  ¡Buen trabajo! *Good job!*
  El tiempo es bueno. *The weather is good.*
  Es bueno que ... *It's good that ...*
  Hace muy buen tiempo. *It's beautiful.*
  Nochebuena (f.) *Christmas Eve*
bufanda (f.) *scarf*
buscar *to look for, to pick up*
buzón (m.) *mailbox*
  buzón de voz *voice mail*

C

caballero (m.) *gentleman*
caballo (m.) *horse*
cabecera (f.) *head*
  pediatra (m./f.) **de cabecera** *regular pediatrician*
cabeza (f.) *head*

pararse de cabeza *to go crazy, to go out of one's mind*
perder la cabeza *to lose one's head*
tener dolor de cabeza *to have a headache*
tener la cabeza fría *to keep a cool head*
cabina (f.) *booth, cabin*
cabina telefónica *telephone booth*
cable (m.) *cable*
cada (m./f.) *each, every*
cadera (f.) *hip*
caer *to fall*
café (m.) *coffee*
café (m./f.) *coffee-colored*
cafetera (f.) *coffeemaker*
cafetería (f.) *café, coffee shop, cafeteria, diner*
caja (f.) *cash register, box*
cajetilla (f.) *packet*
cajetilla de cigarrillos *pack of cigarettes*
cajón (m.) *drawer*
calcetines (m. pl.) *socks*
caliente (m./f.) *hot*
calificaciones (f. pl.) *grades*
calle (f.) *street*
luz (f.) **de la calle** *streetlight*
callejón (m.) *alley*
calor (m.) *heat*
Hace calor. *It's hot.*
tener calor *to be hot, to be warm*
calvo/calva (m./f.) *bald*
calzar *to wear (shoes)*
¿Qué número calza? *What shoe size do you wear?*
calzoncillos (m. pl.) *men's underpants*
calzoncitos (m. pl.) *women's underwear*
calzones (m. pl.) *men's undergarments*
cama (f.) *bed*
cámara (f.) *camera*
camarera (f.) *waitress*
camarero (m.) *waiter*
camarón (m.) *shrimp*
cambiar *to change, to exchange*
cambio (m.) *change*
caminar *to walk*
camino (m.) *way, path*
camisa (f.) *shirt*
camiseta (f.) *T-shirt, undershirt*
camisilla (f.) *undershirt*
campeón/campeona (m./f.) *champion*
campeonato (m.) *championship*
camping (m.) *camping*
ir de camping *to go camping*
campo (m.) *field, camp*
Canadá (m.) *Canada*
canadiense (m./f.) *Canadian*
canal (m.) *channel*
cancelar *to cancel*
canción (f.) *song*
candidato/candidata (m./f.) *candidate*
cansado/cansada (m./f.) *tired*
cansancio (m.) *fatigue*
tener cansancio *to be tired*
cantante (m./f.) *singer*
cantar *to sing*
capacidad (f.) *capacity*
cara (f.) *face*
dar la cara *to face the circumstances*
ser caradura *to be shameless*
carbón (m.) *coal*
cárcel (f.) *prison*
carnaval (m.) *carnival*
carne (f.) *meat, beef*
carne de cerdo (f.) *pork*
carnicería (f.) *butcher shop*
caro/cara (m./f.) *expensive*
carpeta (f.) *file*
carpintero/carpintera (m./f.) *carpenter*
carpio (m.) *carpus*
síndrome (m.) **del túnel del carpio** *carpal tunnel syndrome*
carrera (f.) *major, university course*
carretera (f.) *highway, freeway*
carril (m.) *lane*
Siga por el carril de la derecha. *Stay in the right lane.*
carro (m.) *car*
carta (f.) *menu, letter*
cartas (f. pl.) *playing cards*
cartelera (f.) *billboard, list of plays*
cartelera de cine *movie listing*
cartera (f.) *wallet, handbag*
cartón (m.) *carton, cardboard*
casa (f.) *house*
casado/casada (m./f.) *married*
casarse *to get married*
casarse con *to marry (someone)*
casi *almost*

casi nunca *seldom, almost never*
caso (m.) *case*
casualidad (f.) *chance, coincidence*
por casualidad *by chance*
catedral (f.) *cathedral*
catorce *fourteen*
caza (f.) *hunting*
CD (m.) *CD*
CD rom (m.) *CD-ROM*
lector (m.) **de CD** *CD player*
lector (m.) **de CD rom** *CD-ROM drive*
cebolla (f.) *onion*
ceja (f.) *eyebrow*
celeste (m./f.) *sky blue*
celoso/celosa (m./f.) *jealous*
celular (m.) *cell phone*
cena (f.) *dinner*
cenar *to eat dinner*
centralita (f.) *switchboard*
centro (m.) *center*
centro comercial *shopping mall*
centro de información *information center*
cerca *close, near*
cerca de ... *close to/near ...*
cerdo (m.) *pork*
carne (f.) **de cerdo** *pork*
cerdo/cerda (m./f.) *pig*
carne (f.) **de cerdo** *pork*
cerebro (m.) *brain*
cero *zero*
cerrar *to close*
cerro (m.) *hill*
cerveza (f.) *beer*
cesar *to stop*
cesar de ... *to stop ... (doing something)*
césped (m.) *lawn, grass*
champaña (m.) *champagne*
champú (m.) *shampoo*
chanchito/chanchita (m./f.) *piglet*
Chao. *Bye.*
chaqueta (f.) *jacket*
charcutería (f.) *delicatessen*
charla (f.) *chat*
espacio (m.) **para charla** *chat room*
chat (m.) *chat room*
che *hey (filler word, Argentina)*
cheque (m.) *check*
chica (f.) *girl*
chico (m.) *boy*
Chile (m.) *Chile*
chileno/chilena (m./f.) *Chilean*
chinelas (f. pl.) *slippers*
chino (m.) *Chinese (language)*
chiste (m.) *joke*
contar un chiste verde *to tell an obscene joke (lit., to tell a green joke)*
chocolate (m.) *chocolate*
chuleta (f.) *chop*
chuleta de cordero *lamb chop*
ciclismo (m.) *biking, cycling*
cielo (m.) *sky*
cien/ciento (before a noun/before a number except mil) *one hundred*
cien personas *one hundred people*
cien por ciento *one hundred percent*
ciento tres dólares *one hundred and three dollars*
por ciento *percent*
ciencia (f.) *science*
cierto/cierta (m./f.) *true*
No es cierto que ... *It is not true that ...*
cigarrillo (m.) *cigarette*
cajetilla (f.) **de cigarrillos** *pack of cigarettes*
cinco *five*
a las cinco *at five (o'clock)*
cuarenta y cinco *forty-five*
cincuenta *fifty*
cine (m.) *movie*
cinturón (m.) *belt*
abrocharse el cinturón de seguridad *to buckle up*
circo (m.) *circus*
cita (f.) *appointment*
ciudad (f.) *city, town*
claramente *clearly*
claro *clearly*
¡Claro que sí! *Of course!*
Sí, claro. *Yes, of course.*
claro/clara (m./f.) *light*
azul (m./f.) **claro** *light blue*
clase (f.) *class, kind*
toda clase *all kinds*
clásico/clásica (m./f.) *classic*
música (f.) **clásica** *classical music*
cliente (m./f.) *customer*
clínica (f.) *clinic*

farmacia (f.) **clínica** *clinical pharmacy*
club (m.) *club*
coca (f.) *coca*
coche (m.) *car*
cocina (f.) *kitchen, stove, cooking*
cocinar *to cook*
código (m.) *code*
codo (m.) *elbow*
coger *to catch, to pick up, to take*
coger fuerzas (f. pl.) *to regain strength*
coger un examen *to take a test*
coincidencia (f.) *coincidence*
¡Qué coincidencia! *What a coincidence!*
cola (f.) *tail, line*
hacer una cola *to stand in line*
colección (f.) *collection*
coleccionar *to collect*
colega/colega (m./f.) *colleague*
colegio (m.) *elementary/secondary school*
colgar *to hang*
colgar el teléfono *to hang up the phone*
colina (f.) *hill*
collar (m.) *necklace*
Colombia (f.) *Colombia*
colombiano/colombiana (m./f.) *Colombian*
colonia (f.) *cologne*
color (m.) *color*
¿De qué color es . . . ? *What color is . . . ?*
ver todo color de rosa *to be an optimist, to wear rose colored glasses*
colorado/colorada (m./f.) *red*
ponerse colorado *to be embarrassed (lit., to turn red)*
columna (f.) *column*
columna vertebral *backbone, spinal column*
coma (f.) *comma*
combinar *to combine, to match*
combinar con . . . *to go with . . .*
comedia (f.) *comedy*
comedor (m.) *dining room*
comenzar *to start, to begin*
comenzar a . . . *to start . . . (doing something)*
comer *to eat*
comercial (m./f.) *commercial*
centro (m.) **comercial** *shopping mall*
comida (f.) *food, dinner*
como *as, like*
como ya sabes *as you already know*
cómo *how* (question)
¿Cómo? *What?/Pardon me?*
¿Cómo estás (tú)? *How are you?* (infml.)
¿Cómo estás de tiempo? *Do you have time?/How are you doing for time?*
¿Cómo está usted? *How are you?* (fml.)
¿Cómo se llama usted? *What's your name?* (fml.)
¿Cómo te llamas? *What's your name?* (infml.)
¿Cómo te trata la vida? *How's life treating you?*
¿Cómo va todo? *How is everything going?*
¿Sabe cómo . . . ? *Do you know how to . . . ?*
cómodo/cómoda (m./f.) *comfortable*
compañía (f.) *company*
completamente *completely*
completar *to complete*
completo/completa (m./f.) *full*
a tiempo completo *full-time*
compra (f.) *purchase*
ir de compras *to go shopping*
comprar *to buy, to shop*
comprar en rebaja *to buy on sale*
comprender *to understand*
computadora (f.) *computer*
comunicar *to communicate*
Está comunicando. *The line is busy.*
con *with, to*
concierto (m.) *concert*
condimentado/condimentada (m./f.) *spicy*
conducir *to drive*
conectar *to connect*
conexión (f.) *connection*
conferencia (f.) *conference, meeting, lecture*
sala (f.) **de conferencias** *meeting room*
conjunto (m.) *band (music)*
conocer *to know (people, places), to meet*
conocer de vista *to know by sight*
conocer palmo a palmo *to know like the back of one's hand*
dar a conocer *to make known*
Gusto en conocerlo/la. *Pleased to meet you.* (to a man/to a woman)
consultar *to look up, to consult*
consultorio (m.) *office*
consultorio del médico *doctor's office*
contable (m./f.) *accountant*
contar *to count, to tell*

contar un chiste verde *to tell an obscene joke (lit., to tell a green joke)*
contento/contenta (m./f.) *happy*
contestador (m.) **(automático)** *answering machine*
contestar *to reply to, to answer*
contestar el teléfono *to answer the phone*
contigo *with you*
continuar *to continue*
Continúa recto. *Continue straight.*
contra *against*
contrato (m.) *contract*
contribución (f.) *contribution*
copa (f.) *wineglass*
copa de vino *glass of wine*
copia (f.) *copy*
copiar *to copy*
corazón (m.) *heart*
corbata (f.) *tie*
cordero/cordera (m./f.) *lamb*
chuleta (f.) **de cordero** *lamb chop*
coro (m.) *choir*
correo (m.) *post office*
correo electrónico (correo-e) *e-mail*
dirección (f.) **de correo electrónico** *e-mail address*
correr *to run*
cortado/cortada (m./f.) *sour*
cortina (f.) *curtain*
corto/corta (m./f.) *short*
cosa (f.) *thing*
¿Cómo van las cosas? *How are things?*
cosquilleo (m.) *tingling feeling*
costar *to cost*
¿Cuánto cuesta? *How much does it cost?*
costoso/costosa (m./f.) *expensive*
costura (f.) *sewing*
crédito (m.) *loan, credit*
tarjeta (f.) **de crédito** *credit card*
creer *to believe, to think*
Creo que sí. *I think so.*
no creer que ... *not to believe that ...*
¿No crees? *Don't you think?*
crema (f.) *creme*
crema de afeitar *shaving cream*
crío/cría (m./f.) *kid*
cruce (m.) *intersection*
cruzar *to cross*
cuaderno (m.) *notebook*
cuadra (f.) *block*
Está a dos cuadras de aquí. *It's two blocks from here.*
cuadro (m.) *painting, picture, square*
a cuadros *plaid*
cual/cuales (sg./pl.) *which* (relative pronoun)*, as*
cuál/cuáles (sg./pl.) *which, what* (question)
cualificación (f.) *qualification, skill*
cualificado/cualificada (m./f.) *qualified*
cualquier *any*
cuando *when* (relative adverb)
cuándo *when* (question)
cuanto/cuanta/cuantos/cuantas (m. sg./f. sg./m. pl./f. pl.) *as much, as many*
en cuanto a ... *regarding ...*
cuánto/cuánta/cuántos/cuántas (m. sg./f. sg./m. pl./f. pl.) *how much, how many*
¿Cuántos años tiene? *How old are you* (sg. fml.)*/is he/is she?*
¿Cuánto cuesta? *How much does it cost?*
¿Cuánto es? *How much is it?*
cuarenta *forty*
cuarenta y cinco *forty-five*
cuarto (m.) *quarter, room, bedroom*
a las seis menos cuarto *at a quarter to six*
a las seis y cuarto *at a quarter past six*
término (m.) **tres cuartos** *medium (cooked meat)*
cuatro *four*
cuatrocientos/cuatrocientas (m./f.) *four hundred*
cuchara (f.) *spoon*
cuchillo (m.) *knife*
cuello (m.) *neck*
cuenco (m.) *bowl*
cuenta (f.) *bill, check, account*
tener en cuenta *to take into account*
pagar la cuenta *to check out*
cuero (m.) *leather*
cuerpo (m.) *body*
cuerpo humano *human body*
cuestionario (m.) *questionnaire*
cuñada (f.) *sister-in-law*
cuñado (m.) *brother-in-law*
currículum (m.) *curriculum*
currículum vítae *résumé, CV*
curso (m.) *course*

cuyo/cuya/cuyos/cuyas (m. sg./f. sg./m. pl./f. pl.) *whose, of which* (relative pronoun)

D

dar *to give, to show*
dar a conocer *to make known*
dar a luz *to give birth*
dar con *to find (something)*
dar de narices *to fall flat on one's face*
dar la cara *to face the circumstances*
dar la hora *to tell time*
dar la mano *to shake hands*
dar la vuelta *to turn around*
dar (las) gracias *to give thanks*
de *of, from, about*
de … a … *from … through …*
¿De dónde eres? *Where are you from?*
de la madrugada *in the early morning (before daybreak)*
de la mañana *in the morning*
de la noche *in the evening, at night*
de la tarde *in the afternoon*
De nada. *You're welcome.*
¿De qué color es … ? *What color is … ?*
debajo *underneath*
debajo de … *underneath …*
deber *must, to owe*
débil (m./f.) *weak*
década (f.) *decade*
decidir *to decide*
decir *to tell, to say*
¿Cómo se dice " … " en … ? *How do you say " … " in … ?*
¿Díga(me)? *Hello? (on the phone)*
No me digas. *Really?*
por así decir *so to speak*
¿Qué quiere decir eso? *What does that mean?*
decisión (f.) *decision*
dedicar *to dedicate*
dedo (m.) *finger*
dedo del pie *toe*
dejar *to leave*
dejar un mensaje después de oír la señal *to leave a message after the tone*
del (de + el) *of the* (m.), *from the* (m.), *about the* (m.)
delante *in front*
delante de … *in front of …*
delgado/delgada (m./f.) *thin*
delicioso/deliciosa (m./f.) *delicious*
delito (m.) *crime*
demasiado/demasiada (m./f.) *too much, too many*
dentista (m./f.) *dentist*
dentro *inside*
dentro de … *inside of …*
departamento (m.) *department*
tienda (f.) **por departamentos** *department store*
depender *to depend*
depender de … *to depend on …*
dependiente/dependienta (m./f.) *store clerk*
deporte (m.) *sport*
deportista (m./f.) *person who plays sports*
deportivo/deportiva (m./f.) *athletic*
zapatillas (f. pl.) **deportivas** *sneakers, tennis shoes*
derecha (f.) *right side*
a la derecha *on the right*
Gira a la derecha. *Turn right.*
derecho *straight*
Siga derecho. *Go straight.*
derecho (m.) *law, right, duty*
derechos (pl.) **de matrícula** *tuition*
derecho/derecha (m./f.) *right-side*
a mano derecha *on the right-hand side*
desafortunadamente *unfortunately*
desagradable (m./f.) *unpleasant*
desarrollar *to develop*
desastre (m.) *disaster*
desayuno (m.) *breakfast*
descansar *to rest*
desconocer *not to know*
descremado/descremada (m./f.) *skimmed*
leche (f.) **descremada** *skim milk*
describir *to describe*
descripción (f.) *description*
descuento (m.) *discount*
hacer un descuento *to give a discount*
treinta por ciento de descuento *thirty percent off*
desde *since, from*
desear *to want, to wish*
desear que … *to wish that …*
¿Qué desea? *What would you like?*
desgracia (f.) *misfortune*
por desgracia *unfortunately*

deshabillé (m.) *robe*
desierto (m.) *desert*
desodorante (m.) *deodorant*
despacho (m.) *office*
despacio *slowly*
  Hable más despacio, por favor. *Speak more slowly, please.*
despedirse *to say good-bye*
despertarse *to wake up, to get up*
después *afterwards*
  después de . . . *after . . .*
detalle (m.) *detail*
detergente (m.) *detergent*
  detergente de ropa *laundry detergent*
  detergente de vajilla *dishwashing detergent*
detestar *to detest*
detrás *behind*
  detrás de . . . *behind . . .*
día (m.) *day*
  Buenos días. *Good morning.*
  día festivo *holiday*
  dos días a la semana *twice a week*
  este día *this day*
  hoy en día *nowadays*
  Que tenga un buen día. *Have a nice day.*
  todo el día *all day*
  todos los días *every day*
diario (m.) *diary*
  llevar un diario *to keep a diary*
diario/diaria (m./f.) *daily*
diarrea (f.) *diarrhea*
diciembre (m.) *December*
diecinueve *nineteen*
dieciocho *eighteen*
dieciséis *sixteen*
diecisiete *seventeen*
diente (m.) *tooth*
diez *ten*
  a las ocho y diez *at eight ten (8:10)*
  diez mil *ten thousand*
  diez y seis *sixteen*
  diez y siete *seventeen*
  diez y ocho *eighteen*
  diez y nueve *nineteen*
diferencia (f.) *difference*
diferente (m./f.) *different*
difícil (m./f.) *difficult*
digital (m./f.) *digital*
  línea (f.) **de suscriptor/abonado digital (DSL)** *DSL*
diligentemente *diligently*
dinero (m.) *money*
Dios (m.) *God*
  ¡Por Dios! *For God's sake!*
diploma (m.) *diploma*
dirección (f.) *address, direction*
  dirección de correo electrónico *e-mail address*
dirigir *to direct*
disco (m.) *disk, record*
  disco de vinilo *vinyl record, LP*
disculpa (f.) *excuse, apology*
disculpar *to excuse*
  Disculpa./Disculpe. *Excuse me.* (infml./fml.)
discutir *to discuss*
diseño (m.) *design*
Disneylandia *Disneyland*
disponible (m./f.) *available*
diversión (f.) *amusement*
  parque (m.) **de diversiones** *amusement park*
divertido/divertida (m./f.) *fun*
divertirse *to have fun*
divorciado/divorciada (m./f.) *divorced*
divorciarse *to get a divorce*
  divorciarse de . . . *to divorce (someone)*
doblar *to turn*
doce *twelve*
doctor/doctora (m./f.) *doctor*
documental (m.) *documentary*
documento (m.) *document, file*
  documento adjunto *attachment*
dólar (m.) *dollar*
dolor (m.) *pain*
  tener dolor de cabeza *to have a headache*
  tener dolor de garganta *to have a sore throat*
dominar *to dominate, to master*
  Domino el francés. *I speak French fluently.*
domingo (m.) *Sunday*
don (m.) *Mr.*
doña (f.) *Mrs.*
donde *where* (relative adverb)
dónde *where* (question)
  ¿De dónde eres? *Where are you from?*
dorado/dorada (m./f.) *gold (color)*
dormir *to sleep*
dormitorio (m.) *bedroom*

dos *two*
  dos días a la semana *twice a week*
doscientos/doscientas (m./f.) *two hundred*
dotado/dotada (m./f.) *talented*
drama (m.) *drama*
dramático/dramática (m./f.) *dramatic*
  obra (f.) **dramática** *drama*
ducha (f.) *shower*
ducharse *to take a shower/bath*
dudar *to doubt*
  dudar que ... *to doubt that ...*
dulce (m.) *sweet, pastry*
dulce (m./f.) *sweet*
durante *during*
duro/dura (m./f.) *hard*
  ser caradura *to be shameless*
DVD (m.) *DVD*
  lector (m.) **de DVD** *DVD player*

E

economía (f.) *economics*
económico/económica (m./f.) *economical, low-cost*
  precio (m.) **económico** *reasonable price*
Ecuador (m.) *Ecuador*
ecuatoriano/ecuatoriana (m./f.) *Ecuadorian*
edad (f.) *age*
edificio (m.) *building*
efectivamente *actually*
efectivo (m.) *cash*
  pagar en efectivo *to pay cash*
eficientemente *efficiently*
ejercicio (m.) *exercise*
el *the* (m. sg.)
  el de ella *hers*
  el de ellas *theirs* (f. pl.)
  el de ellos *theirs* (m. pl./mixed group)
  el de él *his*
  el de usted *yours* (sg. fml.)
  el de ustedes *yours* (pl.)
él *he*
  el de él (m. sg.) *his*
  la de él (f. sg.) *his*
eléctrico/eléctrica (m./f.) *electric, electrical*
electricista/electricista (m./f.) *electrician*
electrodoméstico (m.) *electrical appliance*
  tienda (f.) **de electrodomésticos** *electronics store*
electrónico/electrónica (m./f.) *electronic*
  correo (m.) **electrónico** *e-mail*
  dirección (f.) **de correo electrónico** *e-mail address*
elefante (m.) *elephant*
elegante (m./f.) *elegant*
elegir *to choose*
eliminar *to delete, to eliminate*
ella *she*
  el de ella (m. sg.) *hers*
  la de ella (f. sg.) *hers*
ellas *they* (f. pl.)
  el de ellas (m. sg.) *theirs* (f. pl.)
  la de ellas (f. sg.) *theirs* (f. pl.)
ellos *they* (m. pl./mixed group)
  el de ellos (m. sg.) *theirs* (m. pl./mixed group)
  la de ellos (m. sg.) *theirs* (m. pl./mixed group)
embarazada (f.) *pregnant*
embotellamiento (m.) *traffic jam*
emocionante (m./f.) *exciting*
empatado/empatada (m./f.) *tied*
  quedar empatados *to be tied*
empatar *to draw, to tie*
empezar *to begin*
empleado/empleada (m./f.) *employee*
empleo (m.) *job, employment*
en *in, at, by (means), on*
enamorado/enamorada (m./f.) *in love*
encantar *to enchant*
  Encantado./Encantada. *Pleased to meet you.* (said by a man/said by a woman)
  Me encanta/encantan ... (sg./pl.) *I really like ...*
  ¡Me encantaría! *I'd love to!*
encanto (m.) *charm*
encima *above*
  encima de ... *above ...*
  y encima ... *and on top of that ...*
encontrar *to meet up with, to find*
  encontrarse con ... *to meet ... (somebody)*
enero (m.) *January*
enfadarse *to get angry*
  enfadarse de que ... *to be angry that ...*
enfermedad (f.) *illness, disease*
enfermo/enferma (m./f.) *sick*
enfrente *opposite*
  enfrente de ... *across from ... , in front of ...*
enhorabuena (f.) *congratulations*

enorme (m./f.) *huge*
ensalada (f.) *salad*
entender *to understand*
enterizo/enteriza (m./f.) *one-piece*
entero/entera (m./f.) *whole*
leche (f.) **entera** *whole milk*
entonces *then*
Hasta entonces. *Until then.*
entrada (f.) *entrance, ticket, appetizer*
entrante (m./f.) *coming*
mes (m.) **entrante** *next month*
entrar *to enter*
entre *between*
entre … y … *between … and …*
entregar *to submit*
entrenador/entrenadora (m./f.) *coach*
entretenimiento (m.) *entertainment*
entrevista (f.) *interview*
programa (m.) **de entrevistas** *talk show*
entrevistar *to interview*
enviar *to send*
equipo (m.) *team*
equitación (f.) *horseback riding*
equivocado/equivocada (m./f.) *wrong*
número (m.) **equivocado** *wrong number*
escaleras (f. pl.) *stairs*
escaparate (m.) *display window*
ir de escaparates *to go window-shopping*
escoba (f.) *broom*
escoger *to choose*
escondidas (f. pl.) *hide-and-seek*
escotado/escotada (m./f.) *low-cut*
escribir *to write*
escritor/escritora (m./f.) *writer*
escritorio (m.) *desk, study*
escuchar *to listen to*
escuela (f.) *school*
escultura (f.) *sculpture*
ese/esa (m. sg./f. sg.) *that (near the listener)*
ése/ésa (m. sg./f. sg.) *that (one) (near the listener)*
eso (neuter) *that (one, thing) (near the listener)*
a eso de *about, around*
a eso de las nueve *at about nine o'clock*
por eso *for this reason*
esos/esas (m. pl./f. pl.) *those (near the listener)*
ésos/ésas (m. pl./f. pl.) *those (ones) (near the listener)*
espacio (m.) *space*
espacio para charla *chat room*
espalda (f.) *back*
España (f.) *Spain*
español (m.) *Spanish (language)*
Estoy aprendiendo español. *I'm learning Spanish.*
Hablo un poco de español. *I speak a little Spanish.*
español/española (m./f.) *Spanish*
espantoso/espantosa (m./f.) *scary*
especialidad (f.) *specialty, major*
especialización (f.) *specialization, master's degree*
especializarse *to specialize*
especializarse en … *to major in …*
espectador/espectadora (m./f.) *spectator*
espejo (m.) *mirror*
espera (f.) *wait*
poner en espera *to put on hold*
esperar *to hope, to wait*
esperar que … *to hope that …*
Espere, por favor. *Hold on, please.*
¡Yo espero que sí! *I hope so!*
espeso/espesa (m./f.) *thick*
espía (m./f.) *spy*
esposa (f.) *wife*
esposo (m.) *husband*
esquiar *to ski*
esquina (f.) *corner*
a la vuelta de la esquina *around the corner*
estación (f.) *station*
estación de ferrocarril *train station*
estación de tren *train station*
estación (f.) *season*
estadio (m.) *stadium*
estado (m.) *state*
los Estados Unidos *the United States*
estadounidense (m./f.) *American*
estampado/estampada (m./f.) *with a pattern, patterned*
estampilla (f.) *postage stamp*
estanque (m.) *pond*
estante (m.) *shelf, bookshelf*
estar *to be*
Aquí está … *Here is …*
¿Cómo estás (tú)? *How are you?* (infml.)
¿Cómo estás de tiempo? *Do you have time?/ How are you doing for time?*

¿Cómo está usted? *How are you?* (fml.)
Está granizando. *It's hailing.*
Está lloviendo. *It's raining.*
Está nevando. *It's snowing.*
Está nublado. *It's cloudy.*
estar en buenas manos *to be in good hands*
estar mal *to be not doing well*
Estoy aprendiendo español. *I'm learning Spanish.*
Estoy bien. *I'm fine.*
No está mal. *It's not bad.*
Que esté bien. *May you be well.*
Que estés bien. *Take care.*
este (m.) *east*
este/esta (m. sg./f. sg.) *this (near the speaker)*
esta noche (f.) *this evening, tonight*
éste/ésta (m. sg./f. sg.) *this (one) (near the speaker)*
estilo (m.) *style*
esto (neuter) *this (one, thing) (near the speaker)*
estómago (m.) *stomach*
tener mal de estómago *to have an upset stomach*
estos/estas (m. pl./f. pl.) *these (near the speaker)*
éstos/éstas (m. pl./f. pl.) *these (ones) (near the speaker)*
estrecho/estrecha (m./f.) *narrow*
estrella (f.) *star*
estrenar *to use for the first time*
estresante (m./f.) *stressing, stressful*
estudiante/estudiante (m./f.) *student*
estudiar *to study*
estudio (m.) *study, office*
estudios (pl.) *studies*
estupendo/estupenda (m./f.) *fine, wonderful, marvelous*
¡Estupendo! *Great!*
etiqueta (f.) *tag, label*
etiqueta con el precio *price tag*
ex *ex-*
exacto/exacta (m./f.) *exact*
Exacto. *Exactly.*
examen (m.) *test*
aprobar un examen *to pass a test*
hacer un examen, presentarse a un examen *to take a test*
hacerse un examen de sangre *to take a blood test*
suspender un examen *to fail a test*
exceder *to exceed*
excelente (m./f.) *excellent*
excepción (f.) *exception*
excursionismo (m.) *hiking*
hacer excursionismo *to go hiking*
exigente (m./f.) *demanding*
exigir *to demand*
éxito (m.) *success*
experiencia (f.) *experience*
explicación (f.) *explanation*
exterior (m.) *outside*
extra (m./f.) *extra*
horas (f. pl.) **extras** *extra hours, overtime*
extranjero/extranjera (m./f.) *foreign, foreigner*
extraño/extraña (m./f.) *strange*
persona (f.) **extraña** *strange person*
extraordinario/extraordinaria (m./f.) *extraordinary*
extrovertido/extrovertida (m./f.) *extroverted*

F

fábrica (f.) *factory*
fácil (m./f.) *easy*
fácilmente *easily*
facultad (f.) *department (at college/university)*
falda (f.) *skirt*
faltar *to miss, to be lacking, to be necessary*
fama (f.) *fame*
familia (f.) *family*
familiar (m./f.) *(of) family, familiar*
famoso/famosa (m./f.) *famous*
fantástico/fantástica (m./f.) *fantastic*
farmacéutico/farmacéutico (m./f.) *pharmacist*
farmacia (f.) *drugstore, pharmacy*
farmacia clínica *clinical pharmacy*
farola (f.) *lamppost*
favor (m.) *favor*
Hágame el favor de ... *Do me the favor of ...*
Por favor. *Please.*
favorito/favorita (m./f.) *favorite*
fax (m.) *fax machine*
febrero (m.) *February*
fecha (f.) *date*
felicitar *to congratulate*
¡Felicitaciones! *Congratulations!*
feliz (m./f.) *happy*
felizmente *happily*

feo/fea (m./f.) *ugly*
ferrocarril (m.) *railroad, train*
  estación (f.) **de ferrocarril** *train station*
festivo/festiva (m./f.) *festive*
  día (m.) **festivo** *holiday*
fiebre (f.) *fever*
  tener fiebre *to have a fever*
fiesta (f.) *party, holiday*
fijo/fija (m./f.) *fixed, permanent*
  trabajo (m.) **fijo** *steady job*
fila (f.) *line*
  hacer una fila *to stand in line*
filatelia (f.) *stamp collecting*
filosofía (f.) *philosophy*
fin (m.) *end*
  fin de semana *weekend*
  por fin *finally, at last*
final (m.) *end*
finanzas (f. pl.) *finance*
firma (f.) *signature*
física (f.) *physics*
flor (f.) *flower*
folleto (m.) *brochure*
fontanero/fontanera (m./f.) *plumber*
forma (f.) *way, manner*
fósil (m.) *fossil*
foto (f.) *picture, photograph*
  hacer una foto *to take a picture*
fotografía (f.) *photography*
francés (m.) *French (language)*
francés/francesa (m./f.) *French*
frasco (m.) *jar, bottle*
frase (f.) *phrase*
frecuencia (f.) *frequency*
  con frecuencia *frequently, often*
frecuente (m./f.) *frequent*
frecuentemente *frequently*
fregadero (m.) *(kitchen) sink*
freno (m.) *brake (automobile)*
  poner el pie en el freno *to hit the brakes*
frente (f.) *forehead*
fríjol (m.) *bean*
frío (m.) *cold temperature/sensation*
  Hace frío. *It's cold.*
  tener frío *to be cold*
frío/fría (m./f.) *cold*
  tener la cabeza fría *to keep a cool head*
frito/frita (m./f.) *fried*
fruta (f.) *fruit*
fuera *outside*
  fuera de ... *outside of ...*
fuerte (m./f.) *strong*
fuerza (f.) *strength*
  coger fuerzas (f. pl.) *to regain strength*
fumar *to smoke*
funcionar *to work, to function*
fútbol (m.) *soccer*
  fútbol americano *football*
futuro (m.) *future*

G

gabardina (f.) *raincoat*
gafas (f. pl.) *eyeglasses*
  gafas de sol *sunglasses*
galería (f.) *gallery*
galleta (f.) *cookie*
gamba (f.) *shrimp*
gamuza (f.) *suede*
gana (f.) *wish, desire*
  tener ganas de ... *to feel like ...*
ganar *to earn, to win*
  ¡Ojalá que ganen! *I hope they win!*
ganga (f.) *bargain*
garaje (m.) *garage*
garganta (f.) *throat*
  tener dolor de garganta *to have a sore throat*
gasolinera (f.) *gas station*
gasto (m.) *expense*
gato (m.) *cat*
gel (m.) *gel*
generalmente *generally*
generoso/generosa (m./f.) *generous*
gente (f.) *people*
geografía (f.) *geography*
gerente (m.) *manager*
gimnasia (f.) *gymnastics*
gimnasio (m.) *gymnasium*
girar *to turn*
  Gira a la derecha. *Turn right.*
  Gira a la izquierda. *Turn left.*
gol (m.) *goal*
  anotar/hacer/marcar un gol *to score a goal*
gordo/gorda (m./f.) *fat, big*
gracia (f.) *grace, appeal*
  dar (las) gracias *to give thanks*
  gracias (pl.) *thanks*

Gracias. *Thank you.*
Muchas gracias. *Thanks a lot.*
gracioso/graciosa (m./f.) *funny*
grado (m.) *degree*
graduarse *to graduate*
gráfico/gráfica (m./f.) *graphic*
gramo (m.) *gram*
gran/grande (before sg. nouns/all other cases) *big, large, great*
granizar *to hail*
Está granizando. *It's hailing.*
granjero/granjera (m./f.) *farmer*
gratis *free*
grave (m./f.) *serious*
gris (m.) *the color gray*
gris (m./f.) *gray*
gritar *to shout, to scream*
grito (m.) *cry, scream*
último grito *the very latest*
guantes (m. pl.) *gloves*
guardar *to save, to keep*
guayaba (f.) *guava*
guía (f.) *(guide) book*
guía telefónica *phone book*
guitarra (f.) *guitar*
tocar la guitarra *to play the guitar*
gustar *to please*
gustar que ... *to like (it) that ...*
Me gusta/gustan ... (sg./pl.) *I like ...*
Me gustaría ... *I'd like ...*
gusto (m.) *pleasure, taste*
Gusto en conocerlo/la. *Pleased to meet you.* (to a man/to a woman)
Mucho gusto. *It's a pleasure.*

H

haber *to have*
¿Cómo te ha ido? *How have you been?*
Hay ... *There is .../There are ...*
Hay que ... *It is necessary to ...*
No hay nada que ... *There's nothing that ...*
No hay nadie que ... *There's no one who/that ...*
No hay ningún ... que ... *There's no ... that/who ...*
¿Qué hay? *What's up?/What's going on?*
habitación (f.) *room, bedroom*
hablar *to speak, to talk*
hablar con .... *to speak to ...*
¿Hablas inglés? *Do you speak English?* (infml.)
¿Habla usted inglés? *Do you speak English?* (fml.)
Hable más despacio, por favor. *Speak more slowly, please.*
Hablo un poco de español. *I speak a little Spanish.*
hacer *to do, to make*
Hace calor. *It's hot.*
Hace frío. *It's cold.*
Hace muy buen tiempo. *It's beautiful.*
hacer a la medida *to custom sew*
hacer deporte *to play sports*
hacer una cola/fila *to stand in line*
hacer un descuento *to give a discount*
hacer excursionismo *to go hiking*
hacer senderismo *to go hiking*
hacer una foto *to take a picture*
hacer una llamada internacional/local/nacional *to make an international/local/national call*
hacerse un examen de sangre *to take a blood test*
Hace sol. *It's sunny.*
Hace viento. *It's windy.*
Hágame el favor de ... *Do me the favor of ...*
Se me hace tarde. *I'm late.*
hacha (f.) *axe*
hacia *toward*
hambre (f.) *hunger*
tener hambre *to be hungry*
hasta *until, even*
Hasta entonces. *Till then.*
Hasta luego. *I'll see you later.*
Hasta mañana. *Until tomorrow./See you tomorrow.*
Hasta más tarde. *Until later.*
Hasta pronto. *See you soon.*
hecho/hecha (m./f.) *made, done*
heladería (f.) *ice cream parlor*
helado (m.) *ice cream*
heredar *to inherit*
hermana (f.) *sister*
hermano (m.) *brother*
hermanos (pl.) *brothers, brothers and sisters, siblings*
hielo (m.) *ice*

hierba (f.) *herb*
higiénico/higiénica (m./f.) *hygienic*
papel (m.) **higiénico** *toilet paper*
hija (f.) *daughter*
hijastra (f.) *stepdaughter*
hijastro (m.) *stepson*
hijo (m.) *son*
hijos (pl.) *sons, children (sons and daughters)*
hincha (m./f.) *fan, supporter*
hincharse *to swell*
historia (f.) *history*
historial (m.) *background, record*
historial de trabajo *résumé*
hockey (m.) *hockey*
hoja (f.) *sheet (of paper)*
hoja de vida *résumé*
Hola. *Hello.*
hombre (m.) *man*
hombre de negocios *businessman*
hombro (m.) *shoulder*
homeopatía (f.) *homeopathy*
honesto/honesta (m./f.) *honest*
honorarios (m. pl.) *fees*
hora (f.) *time, hour*
¿A qué hora es? *At what time is it?*
dar la hora *to tell time*
horas (f. pl.) **extras** *extra hours, overtime*
¿Qué hora es? *What time is it?*
¿Qué horas son? *What time is it?*
¿Qué hora tiene? *What time do you have?*
horario (m.) *schedule*
horno (m.) *oven*
horror (m.) *horror*
hospital (m.) *hospital*
hostal (m.) *youth hostel*
hotel (m.) *hotel*
hoy *today*
hoy en día *nowadays*
hueso (m.) *bone*
huevo (m.) *egg*
humano/humana (m./f.) *human*
cuerpo (m.) **humano** *human body*
huracán (m.) *hurricane*

I

ida (f.) *outbound journey*
idea (f.) *idea*
ideal (m./f.) *ideal*
idioma (m.) *language*
iglesia (f.) *church*
igual (m./f.) *equal*
... es igual a ... *... equals (=) ...*
igualmente *also, likewise*
Igualmente. *The same to you.*
imaginar *to imagine*
impedir *to prevent*
importante (m./f.) *important*
importar *to matter*
No importa. *It doesn't matter.*
imposible (m./f.) *impossible*
Es imposible que ... *It is impossible that ...*
impresionante (m./f.) *impressive*
impresora (f.) *printer*
impuesto (m.) *tax*
planilla (f.) **de impuestos** *tax return*
incentivo (m.) *incentive*
incluir *to include*
¿Está incluido el servicio? *Is service included?*
incómodo/incómoda (m./f.) *uncomfortable*
infantil (m./f.) *children's*
sicología (f.) **infantil** *child psychology*
información (f.) *information*
centro (m.) **de información** *information center*
informal (m./f.) *casual*
informe (m.) *report*
ingeniería (f.) *engineering*
ingeniería mecánica *mechanical engineering*
ingeniero/ingeniera (m./f.) *engineer*
Inglaterra (f.) *England*
inglés (m.) *English (language)*
¿Hablas inglés? *Do you speak English?* (infml.)
¿Habla usted inglés? *Do you speak English?* (fml.)
inglés/inglesa (m./f.) *English*
ingrediente (m.) *ingredient*
ingreso (m.) *earnings*
inmediatamente *immediately*
inmediato/inmediata (m./f.) *immediate*
de inmediato *immediately*
inodoro (m.) *toilet*
insistir *to insist*
insistir en que ... *to insist that ...*
instantáneo/instantánea (m./f.) *instantaneous*
mensaje (m.) **instantáneo** *instant message*

inteligente (m./f.) *intelligent, smart*
intercambiar *to exchange*
interés (m.) *interest*
  tener interés en ... *to be interested in ...*
  visitar los lugares de interés *to go sightseeing*
interesante (m./f.) *interesting*
interesar *to interest*
  Me interesa/interesan ... (sg./pl.) *I'm interested in ...*
intermedio/intermedia (m./f.) *intermediate*
internacional (m./f.) *international*
  llamada (f.) **internacional** *international call*
Internet *internet*
  por Internet *online*
intersección (f.) *intersection*
investigación (f.) *research, investigation*
  trabajo (m.) **de investigación** *research paper*
invierno (m.) *winter*
invitación (f.) *invitation*
invitado/invitada (m./f.) *guest*
invitar *to invite*
ir *to go*
  ¿Cómo te ha ido? *How have you been?*
  ¿Cómo van las cosas? *How are things?*
  ir a ... *to go to (a place), to be going to (do)*
  ir a pie/caminar *to walk*
  ir de camping *to go camping*
  ir de compras *to go shopping*
  ir de escaparates *to go window-shopping*
  ir de punta en blanco *to be dressed to the nines (lit., to go from the tip in white)*
ira (f.) *anger*
  estar rojo de la ira *to be very angry (lit., to be red with fury)*
italiano (m.) *Italian (language)*
italiano/italiana (m./f.) *Italian*
izquierda (f.) *left side*
  a la izquierda *on the left*
  Gira a la izquierda. *Turn left.*
izquierdo/izquierda (m./f.) *left*
  a mano izquierda *on the left-hand side*

J

jabón (m.) *soap*
jamón (m.) *ham*
jardín (m.) *garden*
jazz (m.) *jazz*
jeans (m. pl.) *jeans*
jefe/jefa (m./f.) *boss*
jersey (m.) *sweater*
jornada (f.) *working day*
jornal (m.) *wage*
jota (f.) *the letter j*
  no saber ni jota de ... *to not have a clue about ...*
joven (m./f.) *young*
jubilado/jubilada (m./f.) *retired, retired person*
juego (m.) *game*
jueves (m.) *Thursday*
juez (m.) *judge*
jugador/jugadora (m./f.) *player*
jugar *to play*
jugo (m.) *juice*
julio (m.) *July*
junio (m.) *June*
junto/junta (m./f.) *together*
juzgado (m.) *court*

K

kilo (m.) *kilo, kilogram*
kilómetro (m.) *kilometer*

L

la *the* (f. sg.)*; it* (f.)*, her, you (f. sg. fml.)* (direct object pronoun)
  la de ella *hers*
  la de ellas *theirs* (f. pl.)
  la de ellos *theirs* (m. pl./mixed group)
  la de él *his*
  la de usted *yours* (sg. fml.)
  la de ustedes *yours* (pl.)
labio (m.) *lip*
lado (m.) *side*
  al lado de ... *next to ...*
ladrón (m./f.) *thief*
lago (m.) *lake*
lámpara (f.) *lamp*
lana (f.) *wool*
langosta (f.) *lobster*
lápiz (m.) *pencil*
largo/larga (m./f.) *long*
las *the* (f. pl.)*; them* (f.)*, you* (f. pl.) (direct object pronoun)
lástima (f.) *pity*
  Es una lástima que ... *It's a pity that ...*
lata (f.) *can*

lavabo (m.) *sink, wash basin*
lavadora (f.) *washing machine*
lavaplatos (m.) *dishwasher*
lavar *to wash*
lavar a mano *to hand wash*
lavar en seco *to dry-clean*
lavar la ropa *to do the laundry*
lavar los platos *to do the dishes*
lavarse *to wash oneself*
le *(to/for) him, her, it, you* (fml. sg.) (indirect object pronoun)
lección (f.) *lesson*
leche (f.) *milk*
leche en polvo *powdered milk*
lechería (f.) *dairy store*
lechuga (f.) *lettuce*
lector (m.) *reader*
lector de CD *CD player*
lector de CD rom *CD-ROM drive*
lector de DVD *DVD player*
lectura (f.) *reading*
leer *to read*
lejía (f.) *bleach*
lejos *far*
lejos de . . . *far from . . .*
lengua (f.) *tongue, language*
lentamente *slowly*
lento/lenta (m./f.) *slow*
les *(to/for) them, you* (fml. pl.) (indirect object pronoun)
lesión (f.) *injury*
levantar *to raise, to lift*
levantarse *to get up, to rise*
Me levanto. *I get up.*
libra (f.) *pound*
media libra *half pound*
libre (m./f.) *free*
librería (f.) *bookstore*
libro (m.) *book*
libro de texto *textbook*
licenciatura (f.) *bachelor's degree*
ligero/ligera (m./f.) *light, thin*
límite (m.) *limit*
limón (m.) *lemon*
limonada (f.) *lemonade*
limpio/limpia (m./f.) *clean*
línea (f.) *line*
línea de suscriptor/abonado digital (DSL) *DSL*
lino (m.) *linen*
lista (f.) *list*
listo/lista (m./f.) *ready*
¿Listos? *Ready?*
literatura (f.) *literature*
litro (m.) *liter*
llamada (f.) *phone call*
hacer una llamada internacional/local/nacional *to make an international/local/national call*
llamar *to call*
llamar por teléfono *to make a phone call*
llamar por teléfono a . . . *to call . . . on the phone*
¿Quién lo llama? *Who's calling?*
llamarse *to be called*
¿Cómo se llama usted? *What's your name?* (fml.)
¿Cómo te llamas? *What's your name?* (infml.)
Me llamo . . . *My name is . . .*
llave (f.) *key*
llegar *to arrive*
llegar a . . . *to get to . . . , to arrive at . . .*
llenar *to fill*
llevar *to wear, to carry, to take, to keep*
llevar un diario *to keep a diary*
llorar *to cry*
llover *to rain*
Está lloviendo. *It's raining.*
lluvia (f.) *rain*
lo *it* (m.)*, him, you (m. sg. fml.)* (direct object pronoun)
Lo siento. *I'm sorry.*
local (m./f.) *local*
llamada (f.) **local** *local call*
Londres *London*
los *the* (m. pl.)*; them* (m.)*, you* (m. pl.) (direct object pronoun)
Los Ángeles *Los Angeles*
lotería (f.) *lottery*
luego *later, then*
Hasta luego. *I'll see you later.*
lugar (m.) *place*
visitar los lugares de interés *to go sightseeing*
luna (f.) *moon*
lunar (m.) *mole, beauty mark*
de lunares *polka-dotted*

lunes (m.) *Monday*
luz (f.) *light*
  apagar las luces *to turn off the lights*
  dar a luz *to give birth*
  luz de la calle *streetlight*

M

madera (f.) *wood*
  de madera *wooden*
madrastra (f.) *stepmother*
madre (f.) *mother*
madrugada (f.) *late night, early morning (from midnight till daybreak)*
  de la madrugada *in the early morning*
  Es la una y diez de la madrugada. *It's ten after one in the morning.*
maestro/maestra (m./f.) *teacher*
mágico/mágica (m./f.) *magical*
magnífico/magnífica (m./f.) *magnificent, great*
mal *bad(ly), poorly*
  estar mal *to be not doing well*
  No está mal. *It's not bad.*
mal (m.) *illness*
  estar mal del estómago *to have an upset stomach*
maleta (f.) *suitcase*
malo/mala (m./f.) *bad*
mamá (f.) *mom*
mami (f.) *mom*
mañana (f.) *morning, tomorrow*
  a las nueve de la mañana *at nine a.m.*
  de la mañana *in the morning*
  esta mañana *this morning*
  Hasta mañana. *Until tomorrow./See you tomorrow.*
manejar *handle*
mano (f.) *hand*
  a la mano *at hand*
  a mano derecha *on the right-hand side*
  a mano izquierda *on the left-hand side*
  dar la mano *to shake hands*
  estar en buenas manos *to be in good hands*
  lavar a mano *to hand wash*
manojo (m.) *handful, bunch*
mantequilla (f.) *butter*
manzana (f.) *apple, block*
mapa (m.) *map*
mar (m.) *sea, ocean*
maravilla (f.) *wonder, miracle*
marcador (m.) *scoreboard*
marcar *to mark, to dial*
  marcar un gol *to make a goal*
  marcar un número de teléfono *to dial a phone number*
marchar *to go, to leave*
mareado/mareada (m./f.) *dizzy*
mareo (m.) *sickness*
  tener mareo *to be dizzy*
marido (m.) *husband*
marino/marina (m./f.) *marine*
  azul (m./f.) **marino** *navy blue*
marrón (m./f.) *brown*
martes (m.) *Tuesday*
martini (m.) *martini*
mártir (m./f.) *martyr*
marzo (m.) *March*
mas *but*
más *more, plus (+)*
  alguien más *somebody else*
  el/la/los/las (m. sg./f. sg./m. pl./f. pl.) **más ... de ...** *the most ... in/of ...*
  Hasta más tarde. *Until later.*
  más o menos *more or less, so-so, just okay*
  más ... que ... *more .../-er than ...*
  más tarde *later*
matemáticas (f. pl.) *mathematics*
materia (f.) *school subject*
material (m.) *material*
matrícula (f.) *registration*
  derechos (m. pl.) **de matrícula** *tuition*
matricularse *to register*
matrimonio (m.) *marriage*
mayo (m.) *May*
mayor (m./f.) *older, bigger*
  el/la/los/las (m. sg./f. sg./m. pl./f. pl.) **mayor** *the oldest, the biggest*
mazorca (f.) *corncob*
me *me* (direct object pronoun)*; (to/for) me* (indirect object pronoun)*; myself*
  Me aburre/aburren ... (sg./pl.) *I'm bored by ...*
  Me encanta/encantan ... (sg./pl.) *I really like ...*
  Me gusta/gustan ... (sg./pl.) *I like ...*
  Me gustaría ... *I'd like ...*
  Me interesa/interesan ... (sg./pl.) *I'm interested in ...*
  Me levanto. *I get up.*

Me llamo ... *My name is ...*
¿Me permite ... ? *May I please ... ?* (fml.)
¿Me permites ... ? *May I please ... ?* (infml.)
mecánico/mecánica (m./f.) *mechanical*
ingeniería (f.) **mecánica** *mechanical engineering*
mediano/mediana (m./f.) *medium*
medianoche (f.) *midnight*
a medianoche *at midnight*
medias (f. pl.) *stockings, socks*
medicamento (m.) *medication*
tomar un medicamento *to take medication*
medicina (f.) *medicine*
médico/médica (m./f.) *doctor*
consultorio (m.) **del médico** *doctor's office*
medida (f.) *measurement*
hacer a la medida *to custom sew*
medio/media (m./f.) *half, midway*
a las cinco y media *at five thirty*
medianoche (f.) *midnight*
medio tiempo (m.) *halftime*
término (m.) **medio** *medium-rare*
mediodía (m.) *noon*
a mediodía *at noon*
Son las doce del mediodía. *It's twelve noon.*
medir *to measure*
mejilla (f.) *cheek*
mejor (m./f.) *better*
el/la/los/las (m. sg./f. sg./m. pl./f. pl.) **mejor** *the best*
Es mejor que ... *It's better that ...*
memoria (f.) *memory*
menor (m./f.) *younger, smaller*
el/la/los/las (m. sg./f. sg./m. pl./f. pl.) **menor** *the youngest, the smallest*
menos *less, minus (-)*
a las seis menos cuarto *at a quarter to six*
el/la/los/las (m. sg./f. sg./m. pl./f. pl.) **menos ... de ...** *the least ... in/of ...*
Es la una menos cinco. *It's five to one. (12:55)*
más o menos *more or less, so-so, just okay*
menos ... que ... *less ... than ...*
mensaje (m.) *message*
dejar un mensaje después de oír la señal *to leave a message after the tone*
mensaje instantáneo *instant message*
mente (f.) *mind*
mentir *to lie*
mercadillo (m.) *flea market*
mercado (m.) *market*
merienda (f.) *snack time*
mermelada (f.) *jam*
mes (m.) *month*
este mes *this month*
mes entrante *next month*
mes pasado *last month*
mes que viene *next month*
mesa (f.) *table*
mesera (f.) *waitress*
mesero (m.) *waiter*
metro (m.) *metro, subway*
mexicano/mexicana (m./f.) *Mexican*
México (m.) *Mexico*
mezquita (f.) *mosque*
mí *me* (after a preposition)
mi/mis (sg./pl.) *my*
microondas (m.) *microwave*
miedo (m.) *fear*
tener miedo *to be scared/afraid*
tener miedo de que ... *to be scared/afraid that ...*
miel (f.) *honey*
mientras *while*
mientras tanto *meanwhile*
miércoles (m.) *Wednesday*
mil *one thousand*
cien mil *hundred thousand*
diez mil *ten thousand*
veinte mil *twenty thousand*
millón *one million*
un millón de casas *one million houses*
minuto (m.) *minute*
mío/mía/míos/mías (m. sg./f. sg./m. pl./f. pl.) *mine*
mirar *to watch, to look at*
mirar la televisón *to watch television*
Mire ... *Hmm .../Look ...*
mismo/misma (m./f.) *same*
ahora mismo *right now*
mixto/mixta (m./f.) *mixed*
moda (f.) *fashion*
de moda *in fashion, in style*
módem (m.) *modem*
moderno/moderna (m./f.) *modern*
molestarse *to be bothered*
molestarse de que ... *to be bothered that ...*

momento (m.) *moment*
en este momento *at this moment, right now*
Un momento. *Hold on./One moment.*
monitor (m.) *monitor*
montaña (f.) *mountain*
montar *to ride*
monumento (m.) *monument*
morado/morada (m./f.) *purple*
moreno/morena (m./f.) *dark-haired, dark-skinned*
morir *to die*
Moscú *Moscow*
mostrador (m.) *counter*
mostrar *to show*
mover *to move*
móvil (m.) *mobile phone*
muchacha (f.) *girl*
muchacho (m.) *boy*
mucho *a lot, much, very*
mucho/mucha (m./f.) *a lot of*
Mucho gusto. *It's a pleasure.*
muchos/muchas (m. pl./f. pl.) *many, a lot of*
Muchas gracias. *Thanks a lot.*
muebles (m. pl.) *furniture*
muela (f.) *molar*
muerto/muerta (m./f.) *dead person, dead*
mujer (f.) *woman, wife*
mujer de negocios *businesswoman*
mujer policía *policewoman*
muletilla (f.) *filler word/phrase*
multa (f.) *fine*
mundial (m./f.) *worldwide, worldly*
campeonato (m.) **mundial** *world championship*
mundo (m.) *world*
muñeca (f.) *wrist*
músculo (m.) *muscle*
museo (m.) *museum*
música (f.) *music*
música clásica *classical music*
musical (m.) *musical*
músico (m./f.) *musician*
muy *very*

N

nacional (m./f.) *national*
llamada (f.) **nacional** *national call*
nacionalidad (f.) *nationality*
nada *nothing*
De nada. *You're welcome.*
nada más *nothing else*
No hay nada que ... *There's nothing that ...*
No, para nada. *No, not at all.*
nadar *to swim*
nadie *nobody, no one*
No hay nadie que ... *There's no one who/that ...*
naipes (m. pl.) *(playing) cards*
naranja (f.) *orange (fruit)*
nariz (f.) *nose*
dar de narices *to fall flat on one's face*
natación (f.) *swimming*
natural (m./f.) *natural*
naturaleza (f.) *nature*
náusea (f.) *nausea, sickness*
tener náusea(s) *to be nauseated, to have nausea*
navaja (f.) *pocket-knife*
navaja de afeitar *razor*
necesario/necesaria (m./f.) *necessary*
Es necesario que ... *It's necessary that ...*
necesitar *to need*
negar *to deny*
negar que ... *to deny that ...*
negocio (m.) *business*
hombre (m.) **de negocios** *businessman*
mujer (f.) **de negocios** *businesswoman*
negro/negra (m./f.) *black*
estar negro de la risa *to laugh very hard (lit., to turn black with laughter)*
ver todo negro *to be a pessimist (lit., to see everything as black)*
nervio (m.) *nerve*
nevar *to snow*
Está nevando. *It's snowing.*
nevera (f.) *refrigerator*
ni *nor*
ni ... ni *neither ... nor*
niebla (f.) *fog*
niebla tóxica/con humo *smog*
nieta (f.) *granddaughter*
nieto (m.) *grandson*
nietos (pl.) *grandsons, grandchildren*
nieve (f.) *snow*
niña (f.) *young girl, female child*
ningún/ninguno/ninguna (before m. sg.

nouns/m. sg./f. sg.) *no, none*
No hay ningún . . . que . . . *There's no . . . that/who . . .*
niño (m.) *young boy, male child*
no *not, no*
No, para nada. *No, not at all.*
noche (f.) *evening, night*
a las siete de la noche *at seven p.m.*
Buenas noches. *Good evening./Good night.*
de la noche *at night, in the evening*
esta noche *tonight*
medianoche *midnight*
Nochebuena *Christmas Eve*
por la noche *at night*
nombre (m.) *name*
normal (m./f.) *normal*
normalmente *normally*
norte (m.) *north*
nos *us* (direct object pronoun)*; (to/for) us* (indirect object pronoun)*; ourselves*
nosotras *we* (f. pl.)
nosotros *we* (m. pl./mixed group)
nota (f.) *note, grade*
sacar buenas/malas notas *to get good/bad grades*
tomar nota *to take note*
noticia (f.) *a piece of news*
noticias (pl.) *news*
novecientos/novecientas (m./f.) *nine hundred*
novela (f.) *novel*
novela rosa *romance novel*
noventa *ninety*
novia (f.) *girlfriend, fiancée*
noviembre (m.) *November*
novio (m.) *boyfriend, fiancé*
nube (f.) *cloud*
nublado/nublada (m./f.) *cloudy*
Está nublado. *It's cloudy.*
nuera (f.) *daughter-in-law*
nuestro/nuestra/nuestros/nuestras (m. sg./f. sg./m. pl./f. pl.) *our*
nuestro/nuestra/nuestros/nuestras (m. sg./f. sg./m. pl./f. pl.) *ours*
Nueva York *New York*
nuevamente *once again*
nueve *nine*
nuevo/nueva (m./f.) *new*
número (m.) *number*
número de teléfono *telephone number*
nunca *never*
casi nunca *seldom, almost never*

O

o *or*
más o menos *more or less, so-so, just okay*
o . . . o *either . . . or*
objetivo (m.) *objective, aim*
objeto (m.) *object*
obra (f.) *play (theater)*
obra dramática *drama*
obrero/obrera (m./f.) *construction worker*
occidente (m.) *west*
océano (m.) *ocean*
ochenta *eighty*
ocho *eight*
a las ocho y diez *at eight ten (8:10)*
ochocientos/ochocientas (m./f.) *eight hundred*
octubre (m.) *October*
ocupado/ocupada (m./f.) *busy*
oeste (m.) *west*
oferta (f.) *offer*
oficina (f.) *office*
oficinista (m./f.) *office worker*
ofrecer *to offer*
oír *to hear*
Ojalá que . . . *I hope/wish . . .*
ojo (m.) *eye*
ojo por ojo *an eye for an eye*
oler *to smell*
olvidar *to forget*
once *eleven*
onza (f.) *ounce*
ópera (f.) *opera*
operadora (f.) *operator*
operarse *to have an operation*
opuesto/opuesta (m./f.) *opposite*
oración (f.) *prayer*
ordenador (m.) *computer*
oreja (f.) *ear*
oriente (m.) *east*
os *all of you* (infml.) (direct object pronoun)*; (to/for) you* (infml. pl.)*(indirect object pronoun); yourselves* (infml.)
oscuro/oscura (m./f.) *dark*
azul (m./f.) **oscuro** *dark blue*
verde (m./f.) **oscuro** *dark green*

otoño (m.) *fall*
otro/otra (m./f.) *another*

P

paciencia (f.) *patience*
  tener paciencia *to be patient*
padrastro (m.) *stepfather*
padre (m.) *father*
  padres (pl.) *fathers, parents*
paga (f.) *wage*
pagar *to pay*
  pagar en efectivo *to pay cash*
  pagar la cuenta *to check out, to pay the bill/check*
página (f.) *page*
  páginas (pl.) **amarillas** *yellow pages*
  página web *webpage*
pago (m.) *payment*
país (m.) *country*
palabra (f.) *word*
palacio (m.) *palace*
palmo (m.) *palm*
  conocer palmo a palmo *to know like the back of one's hand*
palo (m.) *stick*
pan (m.) *bread*
panadería (f.) *bakery*
panameño/panameña (m./f.) *Panamanian*
pantalla (f.) *screen*
pantalones (m. pl.) *pants*
pantis (m. pl.) *women's underwear*
pantuflas (f. pl.) *slippers*
pantymedias (f. pl.) *stockings*
papa (f.) *potato*
papá (m.) *dad*
papi (m.) *dad*
papaya (f.) *papaya*
papel (m.) *paper*
  papel higiénico *toilet paper*
paquete (m.) *package*
para *for, towards, in order to, intended for, by/until a certain time*
  espacio (m.) **para charla** *chat room*
  No, para nada. *No, not at all.*
parada (f.) *stop, bus stop*
parado/parada (m./f.) *unemployed*
paraguas (m.) *umbrella*
Paraguay (m.) *Paraguay*
parar *to stop, to leave*
  pararse de cabeza *to go crazy, to go out of one's mind*
parcial (m./f.) *partial*
  a tiempo parcial *part-time*
pardo/parda (m./f.) *grayish brown*
parecer *to look like, to seem*
  ¿Qué te parece . . . ? *What do you think of . . . ?*
  ¿Qué te parece si . . . ? *How about if . . . ?*
pared (f.) *wall*
pariente (m./f.) *relative*
París *Paris*
parque (m.) *park*
parqueadero (m.) *parking lot*
parrilla (f.) *grill*
  a la parrilla *grilled*
parte (f.) *part, side*
  ¿De parte de quién? *Who's calling?*
  por otra parte *on the other hand*
  por una parte *on the one hand*
particular (m./f.) *particular*
partido (m.) *(sport) game*
  partido de béisbol *baseball game*
partir *to leave, to set off*
  partir de . . . *to start from . . .*
párvulo/párvula (m./f.) *young child*
pasado/pasada (m./f.) *spoiled*
pasado/pasada (m./f.) *past*
  año (m.) **pasado** *last year*
  mes (m.) **pasado** *last month*
  semana (f.) **pasada** *last week*
pasaje (m.) *ticket*
pasaporte (m.) *passport*
pasar *to pass, to forward, to go by, to happen, to spend*
  Le paso. *I'm putting you through. (on the phone)*
  pasar el día *to spend the day*
  ¿Qué pasa? *How's it going?*
pasatiempos (m.) *hobby*
Pascua (f.) *Easter*
pastelería (f.) *bakery (for pastries, etc.)*
pastilla (f.) *pill*
patata (f.) *potato*
patio (m.) *backyard*
peaje (m.) *toll*
peatón (m.) *pedestrian*
pecho (m.) *breast, chest*

pediatra (m./f.) *pediatrician*
pediatría (f.) *pediatrics*
pedir *to order, to ask for*
  pedir que ... *to request that ...*
película (f.) *movie, film*
  películas (pl.) **de aventuras** *adventure films*
  películas de horror *horror films*
  películas de suspenso *suspense films*
  películas románticas *romantic films*
pelo (m.) *hair*
pelota (f.) *ball*
peluquería (f.) *hair salon*
pena (f.) *pain, pity*
  ¡Qué pena! *That's too bad!*
pendientes (m. pl.) *earrings*
penicilina (f.) *penicillin*
pensar *to think*
  no pensar que ... *not to think that ...*
pensión (f.) *pension*
peor (m./f.) *worse*
  el/la/los/las (m. sg./f. sg./m. pl./f. pl.) **peor** *the worst*
pepino (m.) *cucumber*
pequeño/pequeña (m./f.) *small*
pera (f.) *pear*
percibir *to perceive*
perder *to lose, to miss*
  perder la cabeza *to lose one's head*
Perdón. *Excuse me.*
perezoso/perezosa (m./f.) *lazy*
  ser perezoso *to be lazy*
perfecto/perfecta (m./f.) *perfect*
perfume (m.) *perfume*
periódico (m.) *newspaper*
periodista (m./f.) *journalist*
período (m.) *period*
  período de prueba *probationary period*
permitir *to allow*
  ¿Me permite ... ? *May I please ... ?* (fml.)
  ¿Me permites ... ? *May I please ... ?* (infml.)
pero *but*
perro (m.) *dog*
persona (f.) *person*
  persona extranjero *stranger*
personal (m.) *staff*
Perú (m.) *Peru*
peruano/peruana (m./f.) *Peruvian*
pesar *to weigh*
pescadería (f.) *fish shop, fish market*
pescado (m.) *fish*
pésimo/pésima (m./f.) *terrible*
peso (m.) *peso*
pestañas (f. pl.) *eyelashes*
piano (m.) *piano*
picante (m./f.) *spicy*
pie (m.) *foot*
  dedo (m.) **del pie** *toe*
  ir a pie *to walk*
  poner el pie en el freno *to hit the brakes*
  tener los pies en la tierra *to have both feet on the ground*
piel (f.) *skin*
pierna (f.) *leg*
pieza (f.) *piece*
  de dos piezas *two-piece*
pijama (m.) *pajamas*
pimienta (f.) *pepper (spice)*
pimiento (m.) *pepper (vegetable)*
pinta (f.) *spot, appearance*
pintor/pintora (m./f.) *painter*
pintura (f.) *painting*
piscina (f.) *swimming pool*
piso (m.) *floor, apartment*
placer (m.) *pleasure*
plan (m.) *plan*
plancha (f.) *iron*
planchar *to iron*
  tabla (f.) **de planchar** *ironing board*
planilla (f.) *form*
  planilla de impuestos *tax return*
plano (m.) *map*
plano/plana (m./f.) *flat*
planta (f.) *plant*
plantilla (f.) *staff*
plástico (m.) *plastic*
plátano (m.) *banana*
plateado/plateada (m./f.) *silver (color)*
plato (m.) *plate, dish*
  lavar los platos *to do the dishes*
  plato del día *special of the day*
  plato principal *main dish*
playa (f.) *beach*
plaza (f.) *plaza, square*
  plaza de mercado *outdoor market*
pluma (f.) *pen*
pobre (m./f.) *poor, poor person*

los pobres *the poor*
poco *little*
Hablo un poco de español. *I speak a little Spanish.*
un poco *a little*
pocos/pocas (m. pl./f. pl.) *few*
poder *can, to be able to, to have permission to*
¿Podría . . . ? *Could you . . . ?*
podrido/podrida (m./f.) *bad, rotten*
policía (m./f.) *police officer*
mujer (f.) **policía** *policewoman*
poliéster (m.) *polyester*
pollo (m.) *chicken*
polvo (m.) *dust, powder*
leche (f.) **en polvo** *powdered milk*
poner *to put, to place*
poner el pie en el freno *to hit the brakes*
poner en espera *to put on hold*
ponerse *to become, to turn, to put something on*
ponerse colorado *to be embarrassed (lit., to turn red)*
por *for, by, around, at, because of, due to, in place of, in exchange for, through*
por casualidad *by chance*
por desgracia *unfortunately*
¡Por Dios! *For God's sake!*
por eso *for this reason*
Por favor. *Please.*
por fin *finally, at last*
por la noche *at night*
por la radio *on the radio*
por lo tanto *therefore*
por lo visto *apparently*
por otra parte *on the other hand*
por qué *why*
por supuesto *of course*
por teléfono *on the phone*
por una parte *on the one hand*
porque *because*
portero (m.) *goalkeeper*
portugués/portuguesa (m./f.) *Portuguese*
poseer *to own, to hold*
posible (m./f.) *possible*
Es posible que . . . *It is possible that . . .*
lo antes posible *as soon as possible*
postre (m.) *dessert*
practicar *to practice, to play (sports)*
precio (m.) *price*
etiqueta (f.) **con el precio** *price tag*
precio económico *reasonable price*
precisamente *precisely*
preferible (m./f.) *preferable*
Es preferible que . . . *It's preferable that . . .*
preferir *to prefer*
preferir que . . . *to prefer that . . .*
pregunta (f.) *question*
preguntar *to ask*
premio (m.) *prize*
prenda (f.) *garment*
preocuparse *to worry*
No se preocupe. *Don't worry.*
preocuparse de que . . . *to worry that . . .*
preparado/preparada (m./f.) *ready, prepared*
¿Preparados? *Ready?*
presentación (f.) *presentation*
presentar *to introduce*
Te presento a . . . *Let me introduce you to . . .*
presidente/presidenta (m./f.) *president*
presión (f.) *pressure*
prestigioso/prestigiosa (m./f.) *prestigious*
primavera (f.) *spring*
primer/primero/primera (before m. sg. nouns/m./f.) *first*
primo/prima (m./f.) *cousin*
primos (pl.) *cousins*
principal (m./f.) *main*
plato (m.) **principal** *main dish*
prisa (f.) *hurry*
aprisa *quickly*
tener prisa *to be in a hurry*
probador (m.) *dressing room*
probar *to try, to taste*
probarse *to try on (clothes)*
problema (m.) *problem*
producir *to produce*
producto (m.) *product*
profesión (f.) *profession*
profesional (m./f.) *professional*
profesionalmente *professionally*
profesor/profesora (m./f.) *professor*
profesorado (m.) *faculty*
programa (m.) *program*
programa de entrevistas *talk show*
programa de televisión *television program*
prohibir *to forbid, to prohibit*
prohibir que . . . *to forbid that/to . . .*

prometer *to promise*
prometido/prometida (m./f.) *fiancé(e)*
pronto *soon*
propina (f.) *tip*
proteger *to protect*
provecho (m.) *benefit*
  ¡Buen provecho! *Enjoy the meal!*
próximo/próxima (m./f.) *near, next*
  próxima semana (f.) *next week*
proyecto (m.) *project*
prueba (f.) *proof, test, probation*
  período (m.) **de prueba** *probationary period*
pueblo (m.) *town*
puente (m.) *bridge, long weekend*
puerta (f.) *door*
  abrir la puerta *to open the door*
pues *so, since, therefore, well, then*
  Pues, aquí estamos. *Here we are.*
  Pues bien. *Fine.*
  Pues, nada. *Not much.*
puesto (m.) *(job) position, post*
pulmones (m. pl.) *lungs*
pulsera (f.) *bracelet*
punta (f.) *tip, end*
  ir de punta en blanco *to be dressed to the nines (lit., to go from the tip in white)*
punto (m.) *point*
  en punto *exactly*
  Son las tres en punto. *It's three o'clock sharp.*
puntual (m./f.) *punctual*
púrpura (m./f.) *purple*

Q

que *which, that* (relative pronoun, conjunction)
qué *what* (question)
  ¿A qué hora es? *At what time is it?*
  ¿De qué color es . . . ? *What color is . . . ?*
  por qué *why*
  ¡Qué . . . ! *How . . . !*
  ¡Qué bien! *How nice!*
  ¿Qué hay? *What's up?/What's going on?*
  ¿Qué hora es? *What time is it?*
  ¿Qué horas son? *What time is it?*
  ¿Qué pasa? *How's it going?*
  ¡Qué pena! *That's too bad!*
  ¿Qué quiere decir eso? *What does that mean?*
  ¿Qué tal? *What's happening?*
  ¿Qué tal si . . . ? *How about if . . . ?*
  ¿Qué te parece si . . . ? *How about if . . . ?*
  ¡Yo qué sé! *How do I know!?/How should I know!?*
quedar *to remain, to retain, to fit*
  quedar empatados *to be tied*
quemado/quemada (m./f.) *burnt*
querer *to want, to love*
  querer que . . . *to want that/to . . .*
  ¿Qué quiere decir eso? *What does that mean?*
  Quisiera . . . *I'd like . . .*
  Te quiero. *I love you.*
queso (m.) *cheese*
quien/quienes (sg./pl.) *who, whom* (relative pronoun)
quién/quiénes (sg./pl.) *who, whom* (question)
  ¿De parte de quién? *Who's calling?*
  ¿De quién . . . ? *Whose . . . ?*
  ¿Quién lo llama? *Who's calling?*
química (f.) *chemistry*
quince *fifteen*
quinientos/quinientas (m./f.) *five hundred*

R

racimo (m.) *bunch (of grapes)*
  racimo de uvas *bunch of grapes*
radio (f.) *radio*
  por la radio *on the radio*
rampa (f.) *ramp*
rápidamente *fast, quickly*
rápido *fast, quickly*
rápido/rápida (m./f.) *fast, quick*
ratón (m.) *mouse*
raya (f.) *stripe*
  a rayas *striped*
razón (f.) *reason*
  tener razón *to be right*
realismo (m.) *realism*
realista (m./f.) *realistic*
realmente *actually*
rebaja (f.) *discount*
  comprar en rebaja *to buy on sale*
rebajado/rebajada (m./f.) *reduced*
rebanada (f.) *slice*
recepción (f.) *reception desk*
recepcionista (m./f.) *receptionist*
receso (m.) *recess*
receta (f.) *recipe*
recibir *to receive*

recoger *to pick up*
recomendar *to recommend*
recomendar que ... *to recommend that ...*
reconocer *to recognize*
recordar *to remember*
recorrido (m.) *route*
recorrido por autobús *tour bus trip*
recreo (m.) *recreation*
recto *straight*
Continúa recto. *Continue straight.*
redondo/redonda (m./f.) *round*
reducir *to reduce*
referencia (f.) *reference*
refresco (m.) *soft drink, soda*
regalar *to give (a gift)*
regalo (m.) *gift*
región (f.) *region*
regional (m./f.) *regional*
registrarse *to check in*
regresar *to return*
reír *to laugh*
relación (f.) *relationship*
relámpago (m.) *lightening*
relleno (m.) *stuffing, filling*
frase (f.) **de relleno** *filler phrase*
reloj (m.) *watch, clock*
repetir *to repeat*
Repita, por favor *Repeat, please.*
representante (m.) *representative*
reserva (f.) *reservation*
reservación (f.) *reservation*
resolver *to resolve*
responder *to answer*
responsable (m./f.) *responsible*
respuesta (f.) *answer*
restaurante (m.) *restaurant*
resto (m.) *rest*
resultado (m.) *result*
retransmitir *to forward*
retrasado/retrasada (m./f.) *slow, behind*
retrasar *to delay, to postpone*
retribución (f.) *repayment*
reunión (f.) *meeting*
reunir *to gather, to meet*
revista (f.) *magazine*
rico/rica (m./f.) *rich*
río (m.) *river*
risa (f.) *laughter*
estar negro de la risa *to laugh very hard (lit., to turn black with laughter)*
roca (f.) *rock*
rodilla (f.) *knee*
rojo/roja (m./f.) *red*
estar rojo de la ira *to be very angry (lit., to be red with fury)*
romántico/romántica (m./f.) *romantic*
ropa (f.) *clothing*
detergente (m.) **de ropa** *laundry detergent*
lavar la ropa *to do the laundry*
tienda (f.) **de ropa** *clothing store*
rosa (f.) *rose*
novela (f.) **rosa** *romance novel*
ver todo color de rosa *to be an optimist, to wear rose colored glasses (lit., to see everything pink)*
rosado/rosada (m./f.) *pink*
rubio/rubia (m./f.) *blonde*
rural (m./f.) *rural*
ruso (m.) *Russian (language)*

S

sábado (m.) *Saturday*
saber (intransitive verb) *to taste*
saber (transitive verb) *to know (facts, information), to learn*
no saber ni jota de ... *to not have a clue about ...*
¿Quién sabe? *Who knows?*
¿Sabe cómo ... ? *Do you know how to ... ?*
¡Yo qué sé! *How do I know!?/How should I know!?*
saborear *to taste*
sacar *to take out, to get*
sacar buenas notas *to get good grades*
sacar malas notas *to get bad grades*
saco (m.) *jacket*
sal (f.) *salt*
sala (f.) *living room*
sala de conferencias *meeting room, conference room, lecture hall*
salado/salada (m./f.) *salty*
salario (m.) *salary*
salida (f.) *exit*
salir *to leave, to go out*
salir de viaje *to go on a trip*
salsa (f.) *sauce, salsa*

saltar *to skip*
saltarse el semáforo *to go through a light*
saludable (m./f.) *healthy*
saludo (m.) *greeting*
¡Saludos! *Hello!*
sandalias (f. pl.) *sandals*
sangre (f.) *blood*
hacerse un examen de sangre *to take a blood test*
ser de sangre azul *to have blue blood (lit., to be of blue blood)*
se *himself, herself, itself, yourself* (fml.), *themselves, yourselves* (fml.); *(to/for) him, her, it, you* (fml. sg./pl.), *them* (indirect object pronoun, used in place of le/les when preceding lo/la/los/las); *you, people, one* (impersonal pronoun)
secadora (f.) *dryer*
sección (f.) *section*
seco/seca (m./f.) *dry*
lavar en seco *to dry-clean*
secretaria (m./f.) *secretary*
secreto (m.) *secret*
sed (f.) *thirst*
tener sed *to be thirsty*
seda (f.) *silk*
seguir *to follow*
Siga derecho. *Go straight.*
Siga por el carril de la derecha. *Stay in the right lane.*
segundo/segunda (m./f.) *second*
segundo año *second year*
seguridad (f.) *safety, security*
abrocharse el cinturón de seguridad *to buckle up*
seguro (m.) *insurance*
seguro/segura (m./f.) *sure, safe*
Seguro/Segura que sí. *I'm sure.*
seis *six*
seiscientos/seiscientas (m./f.) *six hundred*
semáforo (m.) *traffic light*
saltarse el semáforo *to go through a light*
semana (f.) *week*
dos días a la semana *twice a week*
esta semana *this week*
fin (m.) **de semana** *weekend*
próxima semana *next week*
semana pasada *last week*
semana que viene *next week*
todas las semanas *every week*
semanal (m./f.) *weekly*
semestre (m.) *semester*
señal (f.) *signal*
dejar un mensaje después de oír la señal *to leave a message after the tone*
senderismo (m.) *hiking*
hacer senderismo *to go hiking*
seno (m.) *breast*
señor (m.) *Mr.*
señora (f.) *Mrs.*
sensatamente *sensibly*
sensiblemente *perceptibly*
sentar *to seat*
estar sentado *to be seated*
sentarse *to sit down*
sentido (m.) *sense, direction*
de sentido único *one-way*
sentir *to feel*
Lo siento. *I'm sorry.*
sentir que ... *to regret that ...*
sentirse *to feel*
septiembre (m.) *September*
ser *to be*
Es la una. *It's one o'clock.*
Son las tres. *It's three o'clock.*
Son las tres en punto. *It's three o'clock sharp.*
ser caradura *to be shameless*
serie (f.) *series*
serio/seria (m./f.) *serious*
serpiente (f.) *snake*
servicio (m.) *service*
¿Está incluido el servicio? *Is service included?*
servilleta (f.) *napkin*
servir *to serve*
¿En qué puedo servirle? *How may I help you?*
sesenta *sixty*
sesión (f.) *session*
setecientos/setecientas (m./f.) *seven hundred*
setenta *seventy*
si *if*
¿Qué tal si ...? *How about if ...?*
¿Qué te parece si ...? *How about if ...?*
sí *yes*
¡Claro que sí! *Of course!*
Creo que sí. *I think so.*
Seguro/segura que sí. *I'm sure.*

¡**Yo espero que sí!** *I hope so!*
sicología (f.) *psychology*
siempre *always*
siesta (f.) *nap*
siete *seven*
siglo (m.) *century*
este siglo *this century*
significar *to mean*
silenciosamente *quietly*
silla (f.) *chair, seat*
simpático/simpática (m./f.) *friendly*
simplemente *simply, only*
sin *without*
sindicato (m.) *union*
síndrome (m.) *syndrome*
síndrome del túnel del carpio *carpal tunnel syndrome*
síntoma (m.) *symptom*
sistema (m.) *system*
sistema de sonido *sound system*
sitio (m.) *place*
sitio web *website*
situación (f.) *situation*
sobre *on top of, over, above, about*
sobre todo *especially*
sobrecocido/sobrecocida (m./f.) *overcooked*
sobremesa (f.) *after-dinner conversation*
sobrina (f.) *niece*
sobrino (m.) *nephew*
sofá (m.) *sofa, couch*
sol (m.) *sun*
gafas (f. pl.) **de sol** *sunglasses*
Hace sol. *It's sunny.*
solamente *only*
soledad (f.) *solitude*
solicitar *to apply for, to request*
solicitud (f.) *application*
sólo *merely, solely, only*
solo/sola (m./f.) *sole, only, alone*
soltero/soltera (m./f.) *single*
solución (f.) *solution*
sombrero (m.) *hat*
sonar *to sound, to ring*
soñar *to dream*
¡Ni lo sueñes! *Don't even dream about it!*
soñar con ... *to dream about ...*
sonido (m.) *sound*
sistema (m.) **de sonido** *sound system*
sonido (m.) *sound*
sonreír *to smile*
sopa (f.) *soup*
sorprenderse *to be surprised*
sorprenderse de que ... *to be surprised that ...*
sorpresa (f.) *surprise*
sótano (m.) *basement*
su/sus (sg./pl.) *his, her, its, their, your* (pl./sg. fml.)
suave (m./f.) *soft*
subasta (f.) *auction*
subterráneo (m.) *subway*
suburbano/suburbana (m./f.) *suburban*
suceso (m.) *event, happening*
sucio/sucia (m./f.) *dirty*
Sudamérica *South America*
suegra (f.) *mother-in-law*
suegro (m.) *father-in-law*
sueldo (m.) *pay*
suelo (m.) *floor*
suelto/suelta (m./f.) *loose, flowing*
sueño (m.) *sleepiness, sleep*
tener sueño *to be sleepy*
suerte (f.) *luck*
suéter (m.) *sweater*
suficiente (m./f.) *enough*
sufrir *to suffer*
sugerir *to suggest*
sugerir que ... *to suggest that ...*
supermercado (m.) *supermarket*
supuesto (m.) *supposition*
por supuesto *of course*
sur (m.) *south*
suscriptor/suscriptora (m./f.) *subscriber*
línea (f.) **de suscriptor digital (DSL)** *DSL*
suspender *to fail, to suspend*
suspender un examen *to fail a test*
suspenso (m.) *suspense*
películas (f. pl.) **de suspenso** *suspense films*
suyo/suya/suyos/suyas (m. sg./f. sg./m. pl./f. pl.) *his, hers, theirs, yours*

T

tabla (f.) *table, board*
tabla de planchar *ironing board*
tacón (m.) *heel*
tajada (f.) *slice*
tal *such*

¿Qué tal? *How's it going?*
¿Qué tal si . . . ? *How about if . . . ?*
tal vez *perhaps*
talla (f.) *size*
tamaño (m.) *size*
también *also, too*
tampoco *neither, not either*
tan *so (very)*
tan . . . como *as . . . as* (comparison)
tanto *in such a manner*
mientras tanto *meanwhile*
por lo tanto *therefore*
tanto/tanta (m./f.) *as much, as many*
tanto/tanta/tantos/tantas (m. sg./f. sg./m. pl./f. pl.) **. . . como** *as . . . as* (comparison)
taquilla (f.) *box office*
tarde *late*
Hasta más tarde. *Until later.*
más tarde *later*
Se me hace tarde. *I'm late.*
tarde (f.) *afternoon*
a las cuatro de la tarde *at four p.m.*
Buenas tardes. *Good afternoon.*
de la tarde *in the afternoon*
esta tarde *this afternoon*
tarea (f.) *homework*
tarjeta (f.) *card*
tarjeta de crédito *credit card*
taxi (m.) *taxi*
taxista (m./f.) *taxi driver*
taza (f.) *cup*
tazón (m.) *bowl*
te *you* (infml. sg.) (direct object pronoun); *(to/for) you* (infml. sg.) (indirect object pronoun); *yourself* (infml.)
Te presento a . . . *Let me introduce you to . . .*
té (m.) *tea*
teatro (m.) *theater*
techo (m.) *ceiling*
teclado (m.) *keyboard*
tecnología (f.) *technology*
tejanos (m. pl.) *jeans*
telefónico/telefónica (m./f.) *(of) telephone, telephonic*
cabina (f.) **telefónica** *telephone booth*
guía (f.) **telefónica** *phone book*
teléfono (m.) *telephone*
colgar el teléfono *to hang up the phone*
contestar el teléfono *to answer the phone*
llamar por teléfono *to make a phone call*
llamar por teléfono a . . . *to call . . . on the phone*
marcar un número de teléfono *to dial a phone number*
número (m.) **de teléfono** *telephone number*
televisión (f.) *television*
mirar la televisón *to watch television*
programa (m.) **de televisión** *television program*
televisor (m.) *television (set)*
temer *to fear, to be afraid of*
temperatura (f.) *temperature*
templo (m.) *temple*
temprano *early* (adverb)
temprano/temprana (m./f.) *early*
tendón (m.) *tendon*
tenedor (m.) *fork*
tener *to have*
Aquí tiene. *Here you are.*
¿Cuántos años tiene? *How old are you* (sg. fml.)*/is he/is she?*
Que tenga un buen día. *Have a nice day.*
tener . . . años *to be . . . years old*
tener calor *to be hot, to be warm*
tener cansancio *to be tired*
tener dolor de cabeza *to have a headache*
tener dolor de garganta *to have a sore throat*
tener fiebre *to have a fever*
tener frío *to be cold*
tener ganas de . . . *to feel like . . .*
tener hambre *to be hungry*
tener interés en . . . *to be interested in . . .*
tener la cabeza fría *to keep a cool head*
tener la tensión alta/baja *to have high/low blood pressure*
tener los pies en la tierra *to have both feet on the ground*
tener mareo *to be dizzy*
tener miedo *to be scared*
tener náusea(s) *to be nauseated, to have nausea*
tener paciencia *to be patient*
tener prisa *to be in a hurry*
tener que . . . *to have to . . .*
tener razón *to be right*
tener sed *to be thirsty*

tener sueño *to be sleepy*
tener tos *to have a cough*
tenis (m.) *tennis*
tensión (f.) *tension*
tener la tensión alta/baja *to have high/low blood pressure*
tomar la tensión *to take the blood pressure*
tercero/tercer/tercera (m. sg./m. sg. before a m. noun/f.) *third*
tercer año *third year*
terminar *to finish*
término (m.) *term, period, point*
término medio *medium-rare*
término tres cuartos *medium*
tesis (f.) *dissertation*
tetera (f.) *teakettle*
texto (m.) *text*
libro (m.) **de texto** *textbook*
ti *you* (infml. sg.) (after a preposition)
tía (f.) *aunt, woman*
tiempo (m.) *time, weather*
a tiempo *on time, in time*
a tiempo completo *full-time*
a tiempo parcial *part-time*
El tiempo es bueno. *The weather is good.*
¿Cómo estás de tiempo? *Do you have time?/ How are you doing for time?*
Hace muy buen tiempo. *It's beautiful.*
medio tiempo *halftime*
tienda (f.) *store, convenience store*
tienda de antigüedades *antique store*
tienda de electrodomésticos *appliances store*
tienda de ropa *clothing store*
tienda por departamentos *department store*
Tienes que ... *You have to ...*
tierra (f.) *land*
tener los pies en la tierra *to have both feet on the ground*
tímido/tímida (m./f.) *shy*
tinto/tinta (m./f.) *dark red*
vino (m.) **tinto** *red wine*
tío (m.) *uncle, man*
típico/típica (m./f.) *typical*
tipo (m.) *type*
tiquete (m.) *ticket*
título (m.) *degree, diploma*
toalla (f.) *towel*
tobillo (m.) *ankle*
tocar *to touch, to play an instrument*
tocar el piano *to play the piano*
tocar la guitarra *to play the guitar*
todavía *still, yet*
todo (m.) *everything*
sobre todo *especially*
todo/toda (m./f.) *all, every*
todas las semanas *every week*
todo el día *all day*
todos los días *every day*
tomar *to take, to have (food and drink)*
tomar la tensión *to take the blood pressure*
tomar un medicamento *to take medication*
tomate (m.) *tomato*
tono (m.) *tone, dial tone*
tormenta (f.) *storm*
torta (f.) *cake*
tos (f.) *cough*
tener tos *to have a cough*
tostada (f.) *toast*
totalmente *absolutely*
tóxico/tóxica (m./f.) *toxic*
niebla (f.) **tóxica** *smog*
trabajador/trabajadora (m./f.) *hardworking*
trabajar *to work*
¿En qué trabaja? *What do you do for a living?*
trabajo (m.) *job, work*
¡Buen trabajo! *Good job!*
historial (m.) **de trabajo** *résumé*
trabajo de investigación *research paper*
trabajo de verano *summer job*
trabajo fijo *steady job*
traducir *to translate*
traer *to bring, to get, to take*
tráfico (m.) *traffic*
traje (m.) *suit*
traje de baño *bathing suit*
tranquilo/tranquila (m./f.) *quiet, calm*
trasladar *to transfer*
tratamiento (m.) *treatment*
tratar *to treat*
¿Cómo te trata la vida? *How's life treating you?*
tratar *to try*
tratar de ... *to try ... (to do something)*
trece *thirteen*
treinta *thirty*
tren (m.) *train*

estación (f.) **de tren** *train station*
tres *three*
trescientos/trescientas (m./f.) *three hundred*
triste (m./f.) *sad*
Es triste que … *It's sad that …*
tristemente *sadly*
trotar *to jog*
trueno (m.) *thunder*
tú *you* (sg. infml.) (subject pronoun)
tu/tus (sg./pl.) *your* (sg. infml.)
túnel (m.) *tunnel*
síndrome (m.) **del túnel del carpio** *carpal tunnel syndrome*
turismo (m.) *tourism*
turista (m./f.) *tourist*
tuyo/tuya/tuyos/tuyas (m. sg./f. sg./m. pl./f. pl.) *yours* (infml.)

U

último/última (m./f.) *last*
último grito (m.) *the very latest*
un *a* (m.)
una *a* (f.), *one (o'clock)*
Es la una. *It's one o'clock.*
It's one o'clock.
uña (f.) *nail, claw*
unas *some* (f. pl.)
único/única (m./f.) *only, unique, single*
de sentido (m.) **único** *one-way*
unido/unida (m./f.) *united*
los Estados Unidos *the United States*
universidad (f.) *university*
uno *one*
unos *some* (m. pl.)
urbano/urbana (m./f.) *urban*
urgentemente *urgently*
Uruguay (m.) *Uruguay*
uruguayo/uruguaya (m./f.) *Uruguayan*
usar *to use, to take*
usted *you* (sg. fml.) (subject pronoun)
el de usted (m. sg.) *yours* (sg. fml.)
la de usted (f. sg.) *yours* (sg. fml.)
ustedes *you* (pl.) (subject pronoun)
el de ustedes (m. sg.) *yours* (pl.) (referring to a masculine singular object)
la de ustedes (f. sg.) *yours* (pl.) (referring to a feminine singular object)
uvas (f. pl.) *grapes*
racimo (m.) **de uvas** *bunch of grapes*

V

vacaciones (f. pl.) *vacation*
de vacaciones *on vacation*
vajilla (f.) *tableware*
detergente (m.) **de vajilla** *dishwashing detergent*
vale (m.) *coupon, voucher*
¿Cuánto vale? *How much is it?*
Vamos … *Let's go …*
vaqueros (m. pl.) *jeans*
variedad (f.) *variety*
varios/varias (m./f.) *several*
vaso (m.) *glass*
vecino/vecina (m./f.) *neighbor*
vegetal (m.) *vegetable*
veinte *twenty*
veinticinco *twenty-five*
veinticuatro *twenty-four*
veintidós *twenty-two*
veintinueve *twenty-nine*
veintiocho *twenty-eight*
veintiséis *twenty-six*
veintisiete *twenty-seven*
veintitrés *twenty-three*
veintiuno *twenty-one*
velocidad (f.) *speed*
vendaje (m.) *bandage*
vendedor/vendedora (m./f.) *salesman/saleswoman*
vender *to sell*
venezolano/venezolana (m./f.) *Venezuelan*
Venezuela (f.) *Venezuela*
venir *to come, to fit (somebody)*
año (m.) **que viene** *next year*
mes (m.) **que viene** *next month*
Me viene bien. *It suits me fine.*
semana (f.) **que viene** *next week*
venta (f.) *sale*
ventana (f.) *window*
ver *to see*
A ver … *Let's see …*
Nos vemos. *See you. (lit., We see each other.)*
por lo visto *apparently*
ver todo negro *to be a pessimist (lit., to see everything as black)*
verano (m.) *summer*

trabajo (m.) **de verano** *summer job*
verdad (f.) *truth*
Es verdad. *That's right.*
No es verdad que … *It is not true that …*
¿verdad? *right?*
verde (m./f.) *green*
contar un chiste verde *to tell a dirty joke (lit., to tell a green joke)*
verde oscuro *dark green*
verdura (f.) *vegetable*
vertebral (m./f.) *vertebral*
columna (f.) **vertebral** *backbone, spinal column*
vestíbulo (m.) *hall*
vestido (m.) *dress*
vestido de noche *evening dress*
vestir *to dress (someone)*
vestirse *to get dressed*
veterinario/veterinaria (m./f.) *veterinarian*
vez (f.) *time*
a veces *sometimes*
dos veces por semana *twice a week*
una vez *once*
tal vez *perhaps*
vía (f.) *lane*
viajar *to travel*
viaje (m.) *travel, trip*
Buen viaje. *Have a good trip.*
salir de viaje *to go on a trip*
vida (f.) *life*
¿Cómo te trata la vida? *How's life treating you?*
hoja (f.) **de vida** *résumé*
viejo/vieja (m./f.) *old*
viento (m.) *wind*
Hace viento. *It's windy.*
viento (m.) *wind*
viernes (m.) *Friday*
vincularse *to form links*
vincularse con … *to form links with …*
vinilo (m.) *vinyl*
disco (m.) **de vinilo** *vinyl record*
vino (m.) *wine*
vino blanco *white wine*
vino tinto *red wine*
violeta (m./f.) *violet (color)*
violín (m.) *violin*
visita guiada (f.) *guided tour*
visitante (m./f.) *visitor*
visitar *to visit*
visitar los lugares de interés *to go sightseeing*
vista (f.) *view*
conocer de vista *to know by sight*
vitorear *to cheer*
vivir *to live*
volar *to fly*
volver *to turn, to return*
vosotras *you* (f. pl. infml.) (subject pronoun) *(used in Spain)*
vosotros *you* (m. pl. infml./mixed group infml.) (subject pronoun) (used in Spain)
voz (f.) *voice*
buzón (m.) **de voz** *voice mail*
vuelo (m.) *flight*
vuelta (f.) *turn*
a la vuelta de la esquina *around the corner*
vuestro/vuestra/vuestros/vuestras (m. sg./f. sg./m. pl./f. pl.) *your/yours* (pl. infml.) (used in Spain)

W

web (f.) *web (internet)*
página (f.) **web** *webpage*
sitio (m.) **web** *website*

Y

y *and*
a las ocho y diez *at eight ten (8:10)*
a las cinco y media *at a half past five*
treinta y uno *thirty-one*
ya *already, now, right*
Ya está. *That's it.*
yerno (m.) *son-in-law*
yo *I*

Z

zanahoria (f.) *carrot*
zapatería (f.) *shoe store*
zapatillas (f. pl.) *slippers*
zapatillas deportivas *sneakers, tennis shoes*
zapatos (m. pl.) *shoes*
zumo (m.) *juice*

English-Spanish

A

a *un/una* (m./f.)
a lot *mucho*
a lot of *mucho/mucha* (m./f.), *muchos/muchas* (m. pl./f. pl.)
abdomen *abdomen* (m.)
about *de, sobre, a eso de*
about the (m.) *del (de + el)*
at about nine o'clock *a eso de las nueve*
dream about . . . *soñar con . . .*
How about if . . . ? *¿Qué tal si . . . ?/¿Qué te parece si . . . ?*
not have a clue about . . . (to) *no saber ni jota de . . .*
above *encima, sobre*
above . . . *encima de . . .*
absolute *absoluto/absoluta* (m./f.)
absolutely *absolutamente, totalmente*
absolutely not *en absoluto*
absurd *absurdo/absurda* (m./f.)
academic *académico/académica* (m./f.)
academy *academia* (f.)
accept (to) *aceptar*
accident *accidente* (m.)
account *cuenta* (f.)
accountant *contable* (m./f.)
across from . . . *enfrente de . . .*
actor *actor* (m.)
actress *actriz* (f.)
actually *efectivamente, realmente*
acupuncture *acupuntura* (f.)
address *dirección* (f.)
adult *adulto/adulta* (m./f.)
adventure *aventura* (f.)
adventure films *películas* (pl.) *de aventuras*
advise (to) *aconsejar*
advise that/to . . . (to) *aconsejar que . . .*
after . . . *después de . . .*
after-dinner conversation *sobremesa* (f.)
It's ten after one in the morning. *Es la una y diez de la madrugada.*
afternoon *tarde* (f.)
Good afternoon. *Buenas tardes.*
in the afternoon *de la tarde*
this afternoon *esta tarde*
afterwards *después*
against *contra*
age *edad* (f.)
agency *agencia* (f.)
agent *agente* (m./f.)
agitated *agitado/agitada* (m./f.)
agreement *acuerdo* (m.)
aim *objetivo* (m.)
airline *aerolínea* (f.)
airplane *avión* (m.)
airport *aeropuerto* (m.)
algebra *álgebra* (f.)
all *todo/toda* (m./f.)
all day *todo el día*
All right. *De acuerdo.*
No, not at all. *No, para nada.*
allergic *alérgico/alérgica* (m./f.)
allergy *alergia* (f.)
alley *callejón* (m.)
allow (to) *permitir*
almost *casi*
almost never *casi nunca*
alone *solo/sola* (m./f.)
already *ya*
as you already know *como ya sabes*
also *igualmente, también*
always *siempre*
a.m. *de la mañana, de la madrugada*
at nine a.m. *a las nueve de la mañana*
American *americano/americana* (m./f.), *estadounidense* (m./f.)
amusement *diversión* (f.)
amusement park *parque* (m.) *de diversiones*
and *y*
and on top of that . . . *y encima . . .*
anger *ira* (f.)
ankle *tobillo* (m.)
another *otro/otra* (m./f.)
answer *respuesta* (f.)
answer (to) *responder, contestar*
answer the phone (to) *contestar el teléfono*
answering machine *contestador* (m.) *(automático)*
antique *antigüedad* (f.)
antiques *antigüedades* (f. pl.)
antique store *tienda* (f.) *de antigüedades*
any *cualquier*
Anything else? *¿Algo más?*

apartment *apartamento* (m.), *piso* (m.)
apology *disculpa* (f.)
apparently *por lo visto*
appeal *gracia* (f.)
appearance *pinta* (f.)
appetite *apetito* (m.)
appetizer *entrada* (f.)
apple *manzana* (f.)
application *solicitud* (f.)
apply for (to) *solicitar*
appointment *cita* (f.)
April *abril* (m.)
architect *arquitecto/arquitecta* (m./f.)
architecture *arquitectura* (f.)
area *área* (m.)
Argentina *Argentina* (f.)
Argentinian *argentino/argentina* (m./f.)
arm *brazo* (m.)
around *por, a eso de*
  around the corner *a la vuelta de la esquina*
  around town *por la ciudad*
arrive (to) *llegar*
  arrive at . . . (to) *llegar a . . .*
art *arte* (m.)
artist *artista* (m./f.)
as *como, cual/cuales* (sg./pl.)
  as . . . as *tan . . . como (comparisons), tanto/tanta/tantos/tantas* (m. sg./f. sg./m. pl./f. pl.) *. . . como (comparisons)*
  as many/much *cuanto/cuanta/cuantos/cuantas* (m. sg./f. sg./m. pl./f. pl.), *tanto/tanta* (m./f.)
  as soon as possible *lo antes posible*
  as you already know *como ya sabes*
ask (to) *preguntar*
ask for (to) *pedir*
assistant *asistente* (m./f.)
astronaut *astronauta* (m./f.)
at *a, en, por*
  arrive at . . . (to) *llegar a . . .*
  at a quarter to six *a las seis menos cuarto*
  at about nine o'clock *a eso de las nueve*
  at dawn *al amanecer*
  at dusk *al atardecer*
  at five (o'clock) *a las cinco*
  at hand *a la mano*
  at last *por fin*
  at midnight *a medianoche*
  at night *por la noche*
  at noon *a mediodía*
  at the (m.) *al (a + el)*
  at the present time *actualmente*
  at this moment *en este momento*
  At what time is it? *¿A qué hora es?*
  look at (to) *mirar*
  No, not at all. *No, para nada.*
athlete *atleta* (m./f.)
athletic *atlético/atlética* (m./f.), *deportivo/deportiva* (m./f.)
attach (to) *adjuntar*
  attach a file (to) *adjuntar un documento/archivo*
attachment *anexo* (m.), *archivo* (m.), *documento* (m.) *adjunto*
attend (to) *asistir*
  attend to (to) *atender*
attention *atención* (f.)
attraction *atracción* (f.)
attractive *atractivo/atractiva* (m./f.)
auction *subasta* (f.)
August *agosto* (m.)
aunt *tía* (f.)
author *autor* (m.)
automatic *automático/automático* (m./f.)
available *disponible* (m./f.)
avenue *avenida* (f.)
avocado *aguacate* (m.)
axe *hacha* (f.)

B

baby *bebé* (m./f.)
  little baby *bebito/bebita* (m./f.)
bachelor's degree *licenciatura* (f.)
back *espalda* (f.), *atrás*
  know like the back of one's hand (to) *conocer palmo a palmo*
backbone *columna* (f.) *vertebral*
background *historial* (m.)
backyard *patio* (m.)
bad *malo/mala* (m./f.), *podrido/podrida* (m./f.)
  It's not bad. *No está mal.*
bad(ly) *mal*
bag *bolsa* (f.)
baggy *ancho/ancha* (m./f.)
bakery *panadería* (f.), *pastelería* (f.) *(for pastries, etc.)*

balcony *balcón* (m.)
bald *calvo/calva* (m./f.)
ball *balón* (m.), *pelota* (f.)
banana *plátano* (m.), *banana* (f.)
band *banda* (f.), *conjunto* (m.) *(music)*
bandage *vendaje* (m.)
bank *banco* (m.)
banker *banquero/banquera* (m./f.)
bar *bar* (m.)
barbershop *barbería* (f.)
bargain *ganga* (f.)
base *base* (f.)
baseball *béisbol* (m.)
  baseball game *partido* (m.) *de béisbol*
basement *sótano* (m.)
basketball *baloncesto* (m.)
bathe (to) *bañarse*
bathing suit *traje* (m.) *de baño*
bathing trunks *bañador* (m.)
bathroom *baño* (m.)
bathtub *bañera* (f.)
be (to) *estar, ser*
  be ... years old (to) *tener ... años*
  be a pessimist (to) *ver todo negro (lit., to see everything as black)*
  be able to (to) *poder*
  be afraid (to) *tener miedo*
  be afraid of (to) *temer*
  be afraid that ... (to) *tener miedo de que ...*
  be an optimist (to) *ver todo color de rosa (lit., to see everything pink)*
  be angry that ... (to) *enfadarse de que ...*
  be bored (to) *aburrirse*
  be bothered (to) *molestarse*
  be bothered that ... (to) *molestarse de que ...*
  be called (to) *llamarse*
  be cold (to) *tener frío*
  be dizzy (to) *tener mareo*
  be dressed to the nines (to) *ir de punta en blanco (lit., to go from the tip in white)*
  be embarrassed (to) *ponerse colorado (lit., to turn red)*
  be glad (to) *alegrarse*
  be glad that ... (to) *alegrarse de que ...*
  be going to (do) (to) *ir a ...*
  be hot (to) *tener calor*
  be hungry (to) *tener hambre*
  be in a hurry (to) *tener prisa, tener cansancio*
  be in good hands (to) *estar en buenas manos*
  be interested in ... (to) *tener interés en ...*
  be lacking (to) *faltar*
  be lazy (to) *ser perezoso*
  be nauseated (to) *tener náusea(s)*
  be necessary (to) *faltar*
  be not doing well (to) *estar mal*
  be patient (to) *tener paciencia*
  be present (to) *asistir*
  be right (to) *tener razón*
  be scared (to) *tener miedo*
  be scared that ... (to) *tener miedo de que ...*
  be seated (to) *estar sentado*
  be shameless (to) *ser caradura*
  be sleepy (to) *tener sueño*
  be surprised (to) *sorprenderse*
  be surprised that ... (to) *sorprenderse de que ...*
  be thankful (to) *agradecer*
  be thirsty (to) *tener sed*
  be tied (to) *quedar empatados*
  be tired (to) *tener consancio*
  be very angry (to) *estar rojo de la ira (lit., to be red with fury)*
  be warm (to) *tener calor*
  May you be well. *Que esté bien.*
beach *playa* (f.)
bean *fríjol* (m.)
beauty mark *lunar* (m.)
because *porque*
  because of *por*
become (to) *ponerse*
bed *cama* (f.)
bedroom *dormitorio* (m.), *alcoba* (f.), *cuarto* (m.)
beef *carne* (f.)
beer *cerveza* (f.)
before *antes*
  before ... *antes de ...*
begin (to) *empezar, comenzar*
behind *detrás, atrás, retrasado/retrasada* (m./f.)
  behind ... *detrás de ...*
believe (to) *creer*
  not believe that ... (to) *no creer que ...*
below *bajo*
belt *cinturón* (m.)
benefit *beneficio* (m.), *provecho* (m.)
best (the) *el/la/los/las* (m. sg./f. sg./m. pl./f. pl.) *mejor*

bet *apuesta* (f.)
bet (to) *apostar*
bet that … (to) *apuesto a que …*
better *mejor* (m./f.)
It's better that … *Es mejor que …*
between *entre*
between … and … *entre … y …*
bicycle *bicicleta* (f.)
big *gran/grande* (before sg. nouns/all other cases), *gordo/gorda* (m./f.)
bigger *mayor* (m./f.)
biggest (the) *el/la/los/las* (m. sg./f. sg./m. pl./f. pl.) *mayor*
biking *ciclismo* (m.)
bill *cuenta* (f.)
billboard *cartelera* (f.)
billiards *billar* (m.)
biology *biología* (f.)
bitter *amargo/amarga* (m./f.)
black *negro/negra* (m./f.)
bleach *lejía* (f.)
blender *batidora* (f.)
block *cuadra* (f.), *manzana* (f.)
It's two blocks from here. *Está a dos cuadras de aquí.*
block (to) *bloquear*
blonde *rubio/rubia* (m./f.)
blood *sangre* (f.)
have blue blood (to) *ser de sangre azul (lit., to be of blue blood)*
have high/low blood pressure (to) *tener la tensión alta/baja*
take a blood test (to) *hacerse un examen de sangre*
take the blood pressure (to) *tomar la tensión*
blouse *blusa* (f.)
blue *azul* (m./f.)
color light blue (the) *azul* (m.) *claro*
dark blue *azul oscuro*
have blue blood (to) *ser de sangre azul (lit., to be of blue blood)*
light blue *azul claro*
navy blue *azul marino*
sky blue *celeste* (m./f.)
board *bordo* (m.), *tabla* (f.)
ironing board *tabla de planchar*
on board *a bordo*
Welcome aboard. *Bienvenidos a bordo.*
body *cuerpo* (m.)
Bolivia *Bolivia* (f.)
Bolivian *boliviano/boliviana* (m./f.)
bone *hueso* (m.)
book *libro* (m.)
bookshelf *estante* (m.)
bookstore *librería* (f.)
booth *cabina* (f.)
bore (to) *aburrir*
I'm bored by … *Me aburre/aburren …* (sg./pl.)
bored *aburrido/aburrida* (m./f.)
be bored (to) *aburrirse*
boring *aburrido/aburrida* (m./f.)
boss *jefe/jefa* (m./f.)
bottle *botella* (f.), *frasco* (m.)
bowl *cuenco* (m.), *tazón* (m.)
box *caja* (f.)
box office *taquilla* (f.)
boy *chico* (m.), *muchacho* (m.)
boyfriend *novio* (m.)
bracelet *pulsera* (f.)
brain *cerebro* (m.)
brake (automobile) *freno* (m.)
hit the brakes (to) *poner el pie en el freno*
Brazil *Brasil* (m.)
Brazilian *brasilero/brasilera* (m./f.) (adjective), *brasileño/brasileña* (m./f.) (noun)
bread *pan* (m.)
breakfast *desayuno* (m.)
breast *seno* (m.), *pecho* (m.)
bridge *puente* (m.)
bring (to) *traer*
brochure *folleto* (m.)
broom *escoba* (f.)
brother *hermano* (m.)
brothers, brothers and sisters *hermanos* (pl.)
brother-in-law *cuñado* (m.)
brown *marrón* (m./f.)
grayish brown *pardo/parda* (m./f.)
buckle up (to) *abrocharse el cinturón de seguridad*
building *edificio* (m.)
bunch *manojo* (m.)
bunch of grapes *racimo* (m.) *de uvas*
burnt *quemado/quemada* (m./f.)
bus *autobús* (m.)
tour bus *recorrido* (m.) *por autobús*
bus stop *parada* (f.)

business *negocio* (m.)
businessman *hombre* (m.) *de negocios*
businesswoman *mujer* (f.) *de negocios*
busy *ocupado/ocupada* (m./f.)
The line is busy. *Está comunicando.*
but *pero, mas*
butcher shop *carnicería* (f.)
butter *mantequilla* (f.)
buy (to) *comprar*
buy on sale (to) *comprar en rebaja*
by *por, en*
by chance *por casualidad*
by (a certain time) *para*
go by (to) *pasar*
I'm bored by ... *Me aburre/aburren ...* (sg./pl.)
know by sight (to) *conocer de vista*
Bye. *Chao.*

C

cabin *cabina* (f.)
cable *cable* (m.)
café *cafetería* (f.)
cafeteria *cafetería* (f.)
cake *torta* (f.)
call (to) *llamar*
be called (to) *llamarse*
call ... on the phone (to) *llamar por teléfono a ...*
make a phone call (to) *llamar por teléfono*
Who's calling? *¿Quién lo llama?*
calm *tranquilo/tranquila* (m./f.)
camera *cámara* (f.)
camp *campo* (m.)
camping *cámping* (m.)
go camping (to) *ir de cámping*
can *lata* (f.)
can *poder*
Could you ... ? *¿Podría ... ?*
Canada *Canadá* (m.)
Canadian *canadiense* (m./f.)
cancel (to) *cancelar*
candidate *candidato/candidata* (m./f.)
capacity *capacidad* (f.)
car *auto* (m.), *automóvil* (m.), *carro* (m.), *coche* (m.)
card *tarjeta* (f.)
playing cards *naipes* (m. pl.), *cartas* (f. pl.)
cardboard *cartón* (m.)
carefully *atentamente*
carnival *carnaval* (m.)
carpal tunnel syndrome *síndrome* (m.) *del túnel del carpio*
carpenter *carpintero/carpintera* (m./f.)
carpet *alfombra* (f.)
carpus *carpio* (m.)
carrot *zanahoria* (f.)
carry (to) *llevar*
carton *bote* (m.), *cartón* (m.)
case *caso* (m.)
cash *efectivo* (m.)
pay cash (to) *pagar en efectivo*
cash register *caja* (f.)
casual *informal* (m./f.)
cat *gato* (m.)
catch (to) *coger*
cathedral *catedral* (f.)
CD *CD* (m.)
CD player *lector* (m.) *de CD*
CD-ROM *CD rom* (m.)
CD-ROM drive *lector* (m.) *de CD rom*
ceiling *techo* (m.)
cell phone *celular* (m.)
center *centro* (m.)
century *siglo* (m.)
this century *este siglo*
chair *silla* (f.)
champagne *champaña/champán* (f./m.)
champion *campeón/campeona* (m./f.)
championship *campeonato* (m.)
chance *casualidad* (f.)
by chance *por casualidad*
change *cambio* (m.)
change (to) *cambiar*
channel *canal* (m.)
charm *encanto* (m.)
chat *charla* (f.)
chat room *espacio* (m.) *para charla, chat* (m.)
cheap *barato/barata* (m./f.)
check *cheque* (m.), *cuenta* (f.)
check in (to) *registrarse*
check out (to) *pagar la cuenta*
cheek *mejilla* (f.)
cheer (to) *vitorear*
cheese *queso* (m.)
chemistry *química* (f.)
chess *ajedrez* (m.)
chest *pecho* (m.)

chicken *pollo* (m.)
child (male/female) *niño/niña* (m./f.)
  child psychology *sicología* (f.) *infantil*
  children (sons and daughters) *hijos* (pl.)
  children's *infantil* (m./f.)
  young child *párvulo/párvula* (m./f.)
Chile *Chile* (m.)
Chilean *chileno/chilena* (m./f.)
chin *barbilla* (f.)
Chinese (language) *chino* (m.)
chocolate *chocolate* (m.)
choir *coro* (m.)
choose (to) *elegir, escoger*
chop *chuleta* (f.)
  lamb chop *chuleta de cordero*
Christmas Eve *Nochebuena*
church *iglesia* (f.)
cigarette *cigarrillo* (m.)
  pack of cigarettes *cajetilla* (f.) *de cigarrillos*
circus *circo* (m.)
city *ciudad* (f.)
city hall *ayuntamiento* (m.)
class *clase* (f.)
classic *clásico/clásica* (m./f.)
  classical music *música* (f.) *clásica*
classroom *aula* (m.)
claw *uña* (f.)
clean *limpio/limpia* (m./f.)
clearly *claramente, claro*
clinic *clínica* (f.)
  clinical pharmacy *farmacia* (f.) *clínica*
clock *reloj* (m.)
close *cerca*
  close to ... *cerca de ...*
close (to) *cerrar*
closet *armario* (m.)
clothing *ropa* (f.)
  clothing store *tienda* (f.) *de ropa*
cloud *nube* (f.)
cloudy *nublado/nublada* (m./f.)
  It's cloudy. *Está nublado.*
club *club* (m.)
coach *entrenador/entrenadora* (m./f.)
coal *carbón* (m.)
coca *coca* (f.)
code *código* (m.)
coffee *café* (m.)
  coffee shop *cafetería* (f.)
coffee-colored *café* (m./f.)
coffeemaker *cafetera* (f.)
coincidence *coincidencia* (f.)
  What a coincidence! *¡Qué coincidencia!*
coincidence *casualidad* (f.)
cold *frío/fría* (m./f.)
cold temperature/sensation *frío* (m.)
  be cold (to) *tener frío*
  It's cold. *Hace frío.*
colleague *colega/colega* (m./f.)
collect (to) *coleccionar*
collection *colección* (f.)
cologne *colonia* (f.)
Colombia *Colombia* (f.)
Colombian *colombiano/colombiana* (m./f.)
color *color* (m.)
  color gray (the) *gris* (m.)
  color light blue (the) *azul* (m.) *claro*
  wear rose-colored glasses (to) *ver todo color de rosa (lit., to see everything pink)*
  What color is ... ? *¿De qué color es ... ?*
column *columna* (f.)
combine (to) *combinar*
come (to) *venir*
comedy *comedia* (f.)
comfortable *cómodo/cómoda* (m./f.)
coming *entrante* (m./f.)
comma *coma* (f.)
commercial *comercial* (m./f.)
communicate (to) *comunicar*
company *compañía* (f.)
complete (to) *completar*
completely *completamente*
computer *computadora* (f.), *ordenador* (m.)
concert *concierto* (m.)
conference *conferencia* (f.)
  conference room *sala de conferencias*
congratulate (to) *felicitar*
congratulations *enhorabuena* (f.)
  Congratulations! *¡Felicitaciones!*
connect (to) *conectar*
connection *conexión* (f.)
construction worker *obrero/obrera* (m./f.)
consult (to) *consultar*
continue (to) *continuar*
  Continue straight. *Continúa recto.*
contract *contrato* (m.)
contribution *contribución* (f.)

convenience store *tienda* (f.)
cook (to) *cocinar*
cookie *galleta* (f.)
cooking *cocina* (f.)
copy *copia* (f.)
copy (to) *copiar*
corncob *mazorca* (f.)
corner *esquina* (f.)
  around the corner *a la vuelta de la esquina*
cost (to) *costar*
  How much does it cost? *¿Cuánto cuesta?*
cotton *algodón* (m.)
couch *sofá* (m.)
cough *tos* (f.)
  have a cough (to) *tener tos*
count (to) *contar*
counter *mostrador* (m.)
country *país* (m.)
coupon *vale* (m.)
course *curso* (m.), *asignatura* (f.)
court *juzgado* (m.)
cousin *primo/prima* (m./f.)
  cousins *primos* (pl.)
craft *artesanía* (f.)
credit *crédito* (m.)
  credit card *tarjeta* (f.) *de crédito*
creme *crema* (f.)
crime *delito* (m.)
cross (to) *cruzar*
cry *grito* (m.)
cry (to) *llorar*
cucumber *pepino* (m.)
cup *taza* (f.)
cupboard *aparador* (m.)
curriculum *currículum* (m.)
  CV *currículum vítae*
curtain *cortina* (f.)
custom sew (to) *hacer a la medida*
customer *cliente* (m./f.)
cycling *ciclismo* (m.)

D

dad *papá* (m.), *papi* (m.)
daily *diario/diaria* (m./f.)
dairy store *lechería* (f.)
dance (to) *bailar*
dancing *baile* (m.)
dark *oscuro/oscura* (m./f.)
  dark blue *azul* (m./f.) *oscuro*
  dark green *verde* (m./f.) *oscuro*
  dark-skinned *moreno/morena* (m./f.)
date *fecha* (f.)
daughter *hija* (f.)
daughter-in-law *nuera* (f.)
dawn *amanecer* (m.)
  at dawn *al amanecer*
day *día* (m.)
  all day *todo el día*
  every day *todos los días*
  Have a nice day. *Que tenga un buen día.*
  special of the day *plato del día*
  spend the day (to) *pasar el día*
  this day *este día*
  working day *jornada* (f.)
dead person, dead *muerto/muerta* (m./f.)
decade *década* (f.)
December *diciembre* (m.)
decide (to) *decidir*
decision *decisión* (f.)
dedicate (to) *dedicar*
degree *grado* (m.), *título* (m.)
delay (to) *retrasar*
delete (to) *eliminar*
delicatessen *charcutería* (f.)
delicious *delicioso/deliciosa* (m./f.)
demand (to) *exigir*
demanding *exigente* (m./f.)
dentist *dentista* (m./f.)
deny (to) *negar*
  deny that . . . (to) *negar que . . .*
deodorant *desodorante* (m.)
department *departamento* (m.), *facultad* (f.) *(at a college/university)*
  department store *tienda* (f.) *por departamentos*
depend (to) *depender*
  depend on . . . (to) *depender de . . .*
describe (to) *describir*
description *descripción* (f.)
desert *desierto* (m.)
design *diseño* (m.)
desire *gana* (f.)
desk *escritorio* (m.)
dessert *postre* (m.)
detail *detalle* (m.)
detergent *detergente* (m.)

dishwashing detergent *detergente de vajilla*
laundry detergent *detergente de ropa*
detest (to) *detestar*
develop (to) *desarrollar*
dial (to) *marcar*
dial a phone number (to) *marcar un número de teléfono*
dial tone *tono* (m.)
diarrhea *diarrea* (f.)
diary *diario* (m.)
keep a diary (to) *llevar un diario*
die (to) *morir*
difference *diferencia* (f.)
different *diferente* (m./f.)
difficult *difícil* (m./f.)
difficult situation *apuro* (m.)
digital *digital* (m./f.)
diligently *diligentemente*
diner *cafetería* (f.)
dining room *comedor* (m.)
dinner *cena* (f.), *comida* (f.)
diploma *diploma* (m.), *título* (m.)
direct (to) *dirigir*
direction *dirección* (f.), *sentido* (m.)
dirty *sucio/sucia* (m./f.)
disaster *desastre* (m.)
discount *descuento* (m.), *rebaja* (f.)
give a discount (to) *hacer un descuento*
discuss (to) *discutir*
disease *enfermedad* (f.)
dish *plato* (m.)
do the dishes(to) *lavar los platos*
main dish *plato principal*
dishwasher *lavaplatos* (m.)
dishwashing detergent *detergente* (m.) *de vajilla*
disk *disco* (m.)
Disneyland *Disneylandia*
display window *escaparate* (m.)
dissertation *tesis* (f.)
diving *buceo* (m.)
divorce (someone) (to) *divorciarse de …*
get a divorce (to) *divorciarse*
divorced *divorciado/divorciada* (m./f.)
dizzy *mareado/mareada* (m./f.)
be dizzy (to) *tener mareo*
do (to) *hacer*
be not doing well (to) *estar mal*
Do me the favor of … *Hágame el favor de …*
do the dishes (to) *lavar los platos*
do the laundry (to) *lavar la ropa*
doctor *doctor/doctora* (m./f.), *médico/médica* (m./f.)
doctor's office *consultorio* (m.) *del médico*
document *documento* (m.)
documentary *documental* (m.)
dog *perro* (m.)
dollar *dólar* (m.)
dominate (to) *dominar*
done *hecho/hecha* (m./f.)
door *puerta* (f.)
doubt (to) *dudar*
doubt that … (to) *dudar que …*
download (to) *bajar*
drama *drama* (m.), *obra* (f.) *dramática*
dramatic *dramático/dramática* (m./f.)
draw (to) *empatar*
drawer *cajón* (m.)
dream (to) *soñar*
Don't even dream about it! *¡Ni lo sueñes!*
dream about … *soñar con …*
dress *vestido* (m.)
be dressed to the nines (to) *ir de punta en blanco (lit., to go from the tip in white)*
evening dress *vestido de noche*
dress (someone) (to) *vestir*
dressing room *probador* (m.)
drink *bebida* (f.)
drink (to) *beber*
drive (to) *conducir*
drugstore *farmacia* (f.)
drunk *borracho/borracha* (m./f.)
dry *seco/seca* (m./f.)
dry-clean (to) *lavar en seco*
dryer *secadora* (f.)
DSL *línea* (f.) *de suscriptor/abonado digital (DSL)*
due to *por*
during *durante*
dusk *atardecer* (m.)
at dusk *al atardecer*
dust *polvo* (m.)
duty *derecho* (m.)
DVD *DVD* (m.)
DVD player *lector* (m.) *de DVD*

E

each *cada* (m./f.)
ear *oreja* (f.)
early *temprano/temprana* (m./f.)
early morning (from midnight till daybreak) *madrugada* (f.)
early (adverb) *temprano*
earn (to) *ganar*
earnings *ingreso* (m.)
earrings *pendientes* (m. pl.)
easily *fácilmente*
east *este* (m.), *oriente* (m.)
Easter *Pascua* (f.)
easy *fácil* (m./f.)
eat (to) *comer*
eat dinner (to) *cenar*
economical *económico/económica* (m./f.)
economics *economía* (f.)
Ecuador *Ecuador* (m.)
Ecuadorian *ecuatoriano/ecuatoriana* (m./f.)
efficiently *eficientemente*
egg *huevo* (m.)
eight *ocho*
at eight ten (8:10) *a las ocho y diez*
eight hundred *ochocientos/ochocientas* (m./f.)
twenty-eight *veintiocho*
eighteen *dieciocho, diez y ocho*
eighty *ochenta*
elbow *codo* (m.)
electric *eléctrico/eléctrica* (m./f.)
electrical *eléctrico/eléctrica* (m./f.)
electrical appliance *electrodoméstico* (m.)
electrician *electricista/electricista* (m./f.)
electronic *electrónico/electrónica* (m./f.)
electronics store *tienda* (f.) *de electrodomésticos*
elegant *elegante* (m./f.)
elementary school *colegio* (m.)
elephant *elefante* (m.)
eleven *once*
eliminate (to) *eliminar*
e-mail *correo* (m.) *electrónico, correo-e* (m.)
e-mail address *dirección* (f.) *de correo electrónico*
e-mail attachment *anexo* (m.) *al correo electrónico*
employee *empleado/empleada* (m./f.)
employment *empleo* (m.)
enchant (to) *encantar*
enclosed *adjunto/adjunta* (m./f.)
end *fin* (m.), *final* (m.), *punta* (f.)
engineer *ingeniero/ingeniera* (m./f.)
engineering *ingeniería* (f.)
mechanical engineering *ingeniería mecánica*
England *Inglaterra* (f.)
English *inglés/inglesa* (m./f.)
English (language) *inglés* (m.)
Do you speak English? (infml.) *¿Hablas inglés?*
Do you speak English? (fml.) *¿Habla usted inglés?*
Enjoy the meal! *¡Buen provecho!*
enough *suficiente* (m./f.), *bastante*
enter (to) *entrar*
entertainment *entretenimiento* (m.)
entrance *entrada* (f.)
equal *igual* (m./f.)
. . . equals (=) . . . *. . . es igual a . . .*
erase (to) *borrar*
especially *sobre todo*
even *hasta*
evening *noche* (f.)
evening dress *vestido* (m.) *de noche*
Good evening. *Buenas noches.*
in the evening *de la noche*
this evening *esta noche* (f.)
event *suceso* (m.)
every *todo/toda* (m./f.), *cada* (m./f.)
every day *todos los días*
every week *todas las semanas*
everything *todo* (m.)
How is everything going? *¿Cómo va todo?*
ex- *ex*
exact *exacto/exacta* (m./f.), *en punto*
Exactly. *Exacto.*
exceed (to) *exceder*
excellent *excelente* (m./f.)
exception *excepción* (f.)
exchange (to) *cambiar, intercambiar*
in exchange for *por*
exciting *emocionante* (m./f.)
excuse *disculpa* (f.)
excuse (to) *disculpar*
Excuse me. *Disculpa./Disculpe.* (infml./fml.)/ *Perdón.*
exercise *ejercicio* (m.)

exit *salida* (f.)
expense *gasto* (m.)
expensive *caro/cara* (m./f.), *costoso/costosa* (m./f.)
experience *experiencia* (f.)
explanation *explicación* (f.)
extra *extra* (m./f.)
  extra hours *horas* (f. pl.) *extras*
extraordinary *extraordinario/extraordinaria* (m./f.)
extroverted *extrovertido/extrovertida* (m./f.)
eye *ojo* (m.)
  an eye for an eye *ojo por ojo*
eyebrow *ceja* (f.)
eyeglasses *gafas* (f. pl.)
  wear rose-colored glasses (to) *ver todo color de rosa (lit., to see everything pink)*
eyelashes *pestañas* (f. pl.)

F

face *cara* (f.)
  face the circumstances (to) *dar la cara*
factory *fábrica* (f.)
faculty *profesorado* (m.)
fail (to) *suspender*
  fail a test (to) *suspender un examen*
fall *otoño* (m.)
fall (to) *caer*
  fall flat on one's face (to) *dar de narices*
fame *fama* (f.)
familiar *familiar* (m./f.)
family *familia* (f.)
  (of) family *familiar* (m./f.)
famous *famoso/famosa* (m./f.)
fan *aficionado/aficionada* (m./f.), *hincha* (m./f.)
fantastic *fantástico/fantástica* (m./f.)
far *lejos*
  far from ... *lejos de ...*
farmer *granjero/granjera* (m./f.)
fashion *moda* (f.)
  in fashion *de moda*
fast (adjective) *rápido/rápida* (m./f.)
fast (adverb) *rápidamente, rápido*
fasten (to) *abrochar*
fat *gordo/gorda* (m./f.)
father *padre* (m.)
father-in-law *suegro* (m.)
fatigue *consancio* (m.)
favor *favor* (m.)
  Do me the favor of ... *Hágame el favor de ...*
favorite *favorito/favorita* (m./f.)
fax machine *fax* (m.)
fear *miedo* (m.)
fear (to) *temer*
February *febrero* (m.)
feel (to) *sentir, sentirse*
  feel like ... (to) *tener ganas de ...*
fees *honorarios* (m. pl.)
festive *festivo/festiva* (m./f.)
fever *fiebre* (f.)
  have a fever (to) *tener fiebre*
few *pocos/pocas* (m. pl./f. pl.)
fiancé(e) *prometido/prometida* (m./f.)
field *campo* (m.)
fifteen *quince*
fifty *cincuenta*
file *archivo* (m.), *carpeta* (f.), *documento* (m.)
filing cabinet *armario* (m.)
fill (to) *llenar*
filler phrase *frase* (f.) *de relleno*
  filler word/phrase *muletilla* (f.)
filling *relleno* (m.)
film *película* (f.)
  adventure films *películas* (pl.) *de aventuras*
  horror films *películas de horror*
  romantic films *películas románticas*
  suspense films *películas de suspenso*
finally *por fin*
finance *finanzas* (f. pl.)
find (to) *encontrar*
  find (something) (to) *dar con*
fine (adjective) *estupendo/estupenda* (m./f.)
  Fine. *Pues bien.*
  I'm fine. *Estoy bien.*
fine (noun) *multa* (f.)
finger *dedo* (m.)
finish (to) *acabar, terminar*
first *primer/primero/primera* (before m. sg. nouns/m./f.)
fish *pescado* (m.)
  fish shop/market *pescadería* (f.)
fit (to) *quedar*
  fit (somebody) (to) *venir*
  It suits me fine. *Me viene bien.*
five *cinco*
  at a half past five *a las cinco y media*
  at five (o'clock) *a las cinco*

five hundred *quinientos/quinientas* (m./f.)
forty-five *cuarenta y cinco*
It's five to one. (12:55) *Es la una menos cinco.*
twenty-five *veinticinco*
fixed *fijo/fija* (m./f.)
flat *plano/plana* (m./f.)
flea market *mercadillo* (m.)
flight *vuelo* (m.)
floor *suelo* (m.), *piso* (m.)
flower *flor* (f.)
flowing *suelto/suelta* (m./f.)
fly (to) *volar*
fog *niebla* (f.)
follow (to) *seguir*
food *comida* (f.)
fool *bobo/boba* (m./f.)
foot *pie* (m.)
have both feet on the ground (to) *tener los pies en la tierra*
football *fútbol americano*
for *por, para*
For God's sake! *¡Por Dios!*
for this reason *por eso*
forbid (to) *prohibir*
forbid that/to … (to) *prohibir que …*
forehead *frente* (f.)
foreign *extranjero/extranjera* (m./f.)
forest *bosque* (m.)
forget (to) *olvidar*
fork *tenedor* (m.)
form *planilla* (f.)
form links (to) *vincularse*
form links with … (to) *vincularse con …*
forty *cuarenta*
forty-five *cuarenta y cinco*
forward (to) *retransmitir, pasar*
fossil *fósil* (m.)
four *cuatro*
at four p.m. *a las cuatro de la tarde*
four hundred *cuatrocientos/cuatrocientas* (m./f.)
twenty-four *veinticuatro*
fourteen *catorce*
free *gratis, libre* (m./f.)
freeway *autopista* (f.), *autovía* (f.), *carretera* (f.)
French *francés/francesa* (m./f.)
French (language) *francés* (m.)
I speak French fluently. *Domino el francés.*
frequency *frecuencia* (f.)
frequent *frecuente* (m./f.)
frequently *frecuentemente, con frecuencia*
Friday *viernes* (m.)
fried *frito/frita* (m./f.)
friend *amigo/amiga* (m./f.)
friendly *simpático/simpática* (m./f.)
from *de, desde*
across from … *enfrente de …*
far from … *lejos de …*
from the (m.) *del (de + el)*
from … through … *de … a …*
It's two blocks from here. *Está a dos cuadras de aquí.*
start from … (to) *partir de …*
Where are you from? *¿De dónde eres?*
fruit *fruta* (f.)
full *completo/completa* (m./f.)
full-time *a tiempo completo*
fun *divertido/divertida* (m./f.)
have fun (to) *divertirse*
function (to) *funcionar*
funny *gracioso/graciosa* (m./f.)
furnished *amueblado/amueblada* (m./f.)
furniture *muebles* (m. pl.)
future *futuro* (m.)

G

gallery *galería* (f.)
game *juego* (m.), *partido* (m.) *(sport)*
garage *garaje* (m.)
garden *jardín* (m.)
garment *prenda* (f.)
gas station *gasolinera* (f.)
gather (to) *reunir*
gel *gel* (m.)
generally *generalmente*
generous *generoso/generosa* (m./f.)
gentleman *caballero* (m.)
geography *geografía* (f.)
German *alemán/alemana* (m./f.)
German (language) *alemán* (m.)
get (to) *sacar, traer*
get a divorce (to) *divorciarse*
get angry (to) *enfadarse*
get dressed (to) *vestirse*
get good/bad grades (to) *sacar buenas/malas notas*

get married (to) *casarse*
get to ... (to) *llegar a ...*
get up (to) *levantarse, despertarse*
I get up. *Me levanto.*
gift *regalo* (m.)
girl *chica* (f.), *muchacha* (f.)
girlfriend *novia* (f.)
give (to) *dar*
give (a gift) (to) *regalar*
give a discount (to) *hacer un descuento*
give birth (to) *dar a luz*
give thanks (to) *dar (las) gracias*
glass *vaso* (m.)
gloves *guantes* (m. pl.)
go (to) *ir, marchar*
be going to (do) (to), go to (a place) (to) *ir a ...*
go by (to) *pasar*
go camping (to) *ir de cámping*
go crazy (to), go out of one's mind (to) *pararse de cabeza*
go hiking (to) *hacer excursionismo, hacer senderismo*
go on a trip (to) *salir de viaje*
go out (to) *salir*
go shopping (to) *ir de compras*
go sightseeing (to) *visitar los lugares de interés*
Go straight. *Siga derecho.*
go through a light (to) *saltarse el semáforo*
go to bed (to) *acostarse*
go window-shopping (to) *ir de escaparates*
go with ... (to) *combinar con ...*
How's it going? *¿Qué pasa?*
What's going on? *¿Qué hay?*
goal *gol* (m.)
score a goal (to) *anotar/hacer/marcar un gol*
goalkeeper *portero* (m.)
God *Dios* (m.)
For God's sake! *¡Por Dios!*
gold (color) *dorado/dorada* (m./f.)
good *buen/bueno/buena* (before m. sg. nouns/m./f.)
be in good hands (to) *estar en buenas manos*
Good afternoon. *Buenas tardes.*
Good evening./Good night. *Buenas noches.*
Good job! *¡Buen trabajo!*
Good morning. *Buenos días.*
Have a good trip. *Buen viaje.*
It's good that ... *Es bueno que ...*
The weather is good. *El tiempo es bueno.*
Good-bye. *Adiós.*
say good-bye (to) *despedirse*
grace *gracia* (f.)
grade *nota* (f.)
grades *calificaciones* (f. pl.)
get good/bad grades (to) *sacar buenas/malas notas*
graduate (to) *graduarse*
gram *gramo* (m.)
grandchildren *nietos* (pl.)
granddaughter *nieta* (f.)
grandfather *abuelo* (m.)
grandmother *abuela* (f.)
grandparents *abuelos* (pl.)
grandson *nieto* (m.)
grapes *uvas* (f. pl.)
bunch of grapes *racimo* (m.) *de uvas*
graphic *gráfico/gráfica* (m./f.)
grass *césped* (m.)
gray *gris* (m./f.)
gray (the color) *gris* (m.)
great *gran/grande* (before sg. nouns/all other cases), *magnífico/magnífica* (m./f.)
Great! *¡Estupendo!*
green *verde* (m./f.)
dark green *verde oscuro*
greeting *saludo* (m.)
grill *parrilla* (f.)
grilled *a la parrilla*
grill (to) *asar*
guava *guayaba* (f.)
guest *invitado/invitada* (m./f.)
guidebook *guía* (f.)
guided tour *visita guiada* (f.)
guitar *guitarra* (f.)
play the guitar (to) *tocar la guitarra*
gymnasium *gimnasio* (m.)
gymnastics *gimnasia* (f.)

H

hail (to) *granizar*
It's hailing. *Está granizando.*
hair *pelo* (m.)
hair salon *peluquería* (f.)
half *medio/media* (m./f.)
at a half past five *a las cinco y media*

halftime *medio tiempo* (m.)
hall *vestíbulo* (m.)
ham *jamón* (m.)
hand *mano* (f.)
at hand *a la mano*
be in good hands (to) *estar en buenas manos*
hand wash (to) *lavar a mano*
know like the back of one's hand (to) *conocer palmo a palmo*
on the left-hand side *a mano izquierda*
on the one hand *por una parte*
on the other hand *por otra parte*
on the right-hand side *a mano derecha*
shake hands (to) *dar la mano*
handbag *bolso* (m.), *cartera* (f.)
handful *manojo* (m.)
handle *manejar*
hang (to) *colgar*
hang up the phone (to) *colgar el teléfono*
happen (to) *pasar*
What's happening? *¿Qué tal?*
happening *suceso* (m.)
happily *felizmente*
happy *alegre* (m./f.), *contento/contenta* (m./f.), *feliz* (m./f.)
hard *duro/dura* (m./f.)
hardworking *trabajador* (m./f.)
hat *sombrero* (m.)
have (to) *tener, haber, tomar (food and drink)*
Do you have time? *¿Cómo estás de tiempo?*
have a cough (to) *tener tos*
have a fever (to) *tener fiebre*
Have a good trip. *Buen viaje.*
have a headache (to) *tener dolor de cabeza*
Have a nice day. *Que tenga un buen día.*
have a sore throat (to) *tener dolor de garganta*
have an operation (to) *operarse*
have an upset stomach (to) *estar mal del estómago*
have blue blood (to) *ser de sangre azul (lit., to be of blue blood)*
have both feet on the ground (to) *tener los pies en la tierra*
have fun (to) *divertirse*
have high/low blood pressure (to) *tener la tensión alta/baja*
have just . . . (done something) (to) *acabar de . . .*
have lunch (to) *almorzar*
have nausea (to) *tener náusea(s)*
have permission to (to) *poder*
have to . . . (to) *tener que . . .*
How have you been? *¿Cómo te ha ido?*
not have a clue about . . . (to) *no saber ni jota de . . .*
What time do you have? *¿Qué hora tiene?*
You have to . . . *Tienes que . . .*
he *él*
head *cabeza* (f.), *cabecera* (f.)
have a headache (to) *tener dolor de cabeza*
keep a cool head (to) *tener la cabeza fría*
lose one's head (to) *perder la cabeza*
headphones *audífonos* (m. pl.)
healthy *saludable* (m./f.)
hear (to) *oír*
heart *corazón* (m.)
heat *calor* (m.)
heel *tacón* (m.)
height *alto* (m.)
Hello. *Hola.*
Hello! *¡Saludos!*
Hello? (on the phone) *¿Aló?/¿Dígame?*
help *ayuda* (f.)
How may I help you? *¿En qué puedo servirle?*
Thank you for your help. *Le agradezco su ayuda.*
help (to) *ayudar*
Can you help me? *¿Puede ayudarme?*
her (before a noun) *su/sus* (sg./pl.)
her (direct object pronoun) *la*
(to/for) her (indirect object pronoun) *le, se (used in place of le when preceding lo/la/los/las)*
herb *hierba* (f.)
here *aquí*
Here is . . . *Aquí está . . .*
Here you are. *Aquí tiene.*
Here we are. *Pues, aquí estamos.*
It's two blocks from here. *Está a dos cuadras de aquí.*
hers *suyo/suya/suyos/suyas* (m. sg./f. sg./m. pl./f. pl.), *el de ella* (m. sg.), *la de ella* (f. sg.)
herself *se*
hey (filler word) *che (Argentina), oye*
hide-and-seek *escondidas* (f. pl.)
high *alto/alta* (m./f.)
have high blood pressure (to) *tener la tensión*

alta
highway *autopista* (f.), *autovía* (f.), *carretera* (f.)
hiking *excursionismo* (m.), *senderismo* (m.)
go hiking (to) *hacer excursionismo, hacer senderismo*
hill *cerro* (m.), *colina* (f.)
him (direct object pronoun) *lo*
(to/for) him (indirect object pronoun) *le, se (used in place of le when preceding lo/la/los/las)*
himself *se*
hip *cadera* (f.)
his *suyo/suya/suyos/suyas* (m. sg./f. sg./m. pl./f. pl.), *el de él* (m. sg.), *la de él* (f. sg.)
his (before a noun) *su/sus* (sg./pl.)
history *historia* (f.)
Hmm . . . *Mire . . .*
hobby *afición* (f.), *pasatiempos* (m.)
hockey *hockey* (m.)
hold (to) *poseer*
Hold on. *Un momento.*
Hold on, please. *Espere, por favor.*
put on hold (to) *poner en espera*
holiday *fiesta* (f.), *día* (m.) *festivo*
homeopathy *homeopatía* (f.)
homework *tarea* (f.)
honest *honesto/honesta* (m./f.)
honey *miel* (f.)
hope (to) *esperar*
hope that . . . (to) *esperar que . . .*
I hope . . . *Ojalá que . . .*
I hope so! *¡Yo espero que sí!*
horror *horror* (m.)
horror films *películas* (f. pl.) *de horror*
horse *caballo* (m.)
horseback riding *equitación* (f.)
hospital *hospital* (m.)
hot *caliente* (m./f.)
be hot (to) *tener calor*
It's hot. *Hace calor.*
hotel *hotel* (m.)
hour *hora* (f.)
extra hours *horas* (pl.) *extras*
house *casa* (f.)
how *cómo*
Do you know how to . . . ? *¿Sabe cómo . . . ?*
How . . . ! *¡Qué . . . !*
How about if . . . ? *¿Qué tal si . . . ?/¿Qué te parece si . . . ?*
How are things? *¿Cómo van las cosas?*
How are you doing for time? *¿Cómo estás de tiempo?*
How are you? *¿Cómo está usted?* (fml.)/*¿Cómo estás (tú)?* (infml.)
How do I know!?/How should I know!? *¡Yo qué sé!*
How do you say " . . . " in . . . ? *¿Cómo se dice " . . . " en . . . ?*
How have you been? *¿Cómo te ha ido?*
How is everything going? *¿Cómo va todo?*
how many *cuántos/cuántas* (m. pl./f. pl.)
How may I help you? *¿En qué puedo servirle?*
how much *cuánto/cuánta* (m./f.)
How much does it cost? *¿Cuánto cuesta?*
How much is it? *¿Cuánto es?/¿Cuánto vale?*
How nice! *¡Qué bien!*
How old are you (sg. fml.)**/is he/is she?** *¿Cuántos años tiene?*
How's it going? *¿Qué pasa?*
How's life treating you? *¿Cómo te trata la vida?*
learn how to . . . (to) *aprender a . . .*
huge *enorme* (m./f.)
human *humano/humana* (m./f.)
human body *cuerpo* (m.) *humano*
hundred *cien/ciento* (before a noun/before a number except mil)
eight hundred *ochocientos/ochocientas* (m./f.)
five hundred *quinientos/quinientas* (m./f.)
four hundred *cuatrocientos/cuatrocientas* (m./f.)
hundred thousand *cien mil*
nine hundred *novecientos/novecientas* (m./f.)
one hundred and three dollars *ciento tres dólares*
one hundred people *cien personas*
one hundred percent *cien por ciento*
seven hundred *setecientos/setecientas* (m./f.)
six hundred *seiscientos/seiscientas* (m./f.)
three hundred *trescientos/trescientas* (m./f.)
two hundred *doscientos/doscientas* (m./f.)
hunger *hambre* (f.)
hunting *caza* (f.)
hurricane *huracán* (m.)
hurry *prisa* (f.)
be in a hurry (to) *tener prisa*

husband *esposo* (m.), *marido* (m.)
hygienic *higiénico/higiénica* (m./f.)

I

I *yo*
ice *hielo* (m.)
ice cream *helado* (m.)
ice cream parlor *heladería* (f.)
idea *idea* (f.)
ideal *ideal* (m./f.)
idiot *bobo/boba* (m./f.)
if *si*
How about if . . . ? *¿Qué tal si . . . ?/¿Qué te parece si . . . ?*
illness *enfermedad* (f.), *mal* (m.)
imagine (to) *imaginar*
immediate *inmediato/inmediata* (m./f.)
immediately *inmediatamente, de inmediato*
important *importante* (m./f.)
impossible *imposible* (m./f.)
It is impossible that . . . *Es imposible que . . .*
impressive *impresionante* (m./f.)
in *en*
be in a hurry (to) *tener prisa*
be in good hands (to) *estar en buenas manos*
be interested in . . . (to) *tener interés en . . .*
check in (to) *registrarse*
in exchange for *por*
in fashion *de moda*
in front *delante*
in front of . . . *delante de . . . /enfrente de . . .*
in love *enamorado/enamorada* (m./f.)
in order to *para*
in place of *por*
in style *de moda*
in the afternoon *de la tarde*
in the early morning *de la madrugada*
in the evening *de la noche*
in the morning *de la mañana*
incentive *incentivo* (m.)
include (to) *incluir*
Is service included? *¿Está incluido el servicio?*
information *información* (f.)
information center *centro* (m.) *de información*
ingredient *ingrediente* (m.)
inherit (to) *heredar*
injury *lesión* (f.)
inside *dentro*
inside of . . . *dentro de . . .*
insist (to) *insistir*
insist that . . . (to) *insistir en que . . .*
instantaneous *instantáneo/instantánea* (m./f.)
instant message *mensaje* (m.) *instantáneo*
insurance *seguro* (m.)
intelligent *inteligente* (m./f.)
intended for *para*
interest *interés* (m.)
interest (to) *interesar*
be interested in . . . (to) *tener interés en . . .*
I'm interested in . . . (to) *Me interesa/ interesan . . .* (sg./pl.)
interesting *interesante* (m./f.)
intermediate *intermedio/intermedia* (m./f.)
international *internacional* (m./f.)
international call *llamada* (f.) *internacional*
internet *Internet*
intersection *cruce* (m.), *intersección* (f.)
interview *entrevista* (f.)
interview (to) *entrevistar*
introduce (to) *presentar*
Let me introduce you to . . . *Te presento a . . .*
investigation *investigación* (f.)
invitation *invitación* (f.)
invite (to) *invitar*
iron *plancha* (f.)
iron (to) *planchar*
ironing board *tabla* (f.) *de planchar*
it (direct object pronoun) *lo/la* (m./f.)
(to/for) it (indirect object pronoun) *le, se (used in place of le when preceding lo/la/los/las)*
That's it. *Ya está.*
It is . . . *Es . . . /Está . . .*
It's a pity that . . . *Es una lástima que . . .*
It's a pleasure. *Mucho gusto.*
It's beautiful. (weather) *Hace muy buen tiempo.*
It's better that . . . *Es mejor que . . .*
It's cloudy. *Está nublado.*
It's cold. *Hace frío.*
It's five to one. (12:55) *Es la una menos cinco.*
It's good that . . . *Es bueno que . . .*
It's hailing. *Está granizando.*
It's hot. *Hace calor.*
It's impossible that . . . *Es imposible que . . .*
It's necessary that . . . *Es necesario que . . .*

It's necessary to . . . *Hay que . . .*
It's not bad. *No está mal.*
It's not true that . . . *No es cierto que . . .*
It's one o'clock. *Es la una.*
It's possible that . . . *Es posible que . . .*
It's preferable that . . . *Es preferible que . . .*
It's raining. *Está lloviendo.*
It's sad that . . . *Es triste que . . .*
It's snowing. *Está nevando.*
It's sunny. *Hace sol.*
It's ten after one in the morning. *Es la una y diez de la madrugada.*
It's three o'clock sharp. *Son las tres en punto.*
It's three o'clock. *Son las tres.*
It's twelve noon. *Son las doce del mediodía.*
It's two blocks from here. *Está a dos cuadras de aquí.*
It's windy. *Hace viento.*
Italian *italiano/italiana* (m./f.)
Italian (language) *italiano* (m.)
its *su/sus* (sg./pl.)
itself *se*

J

jacket *americana* (f.), *chaqueta* (f.), *saco* (m.)
jam *mermelada* (f.)
January *enero* (m.)
jar *frasco* (m.)
jazz *jazz* (m.)
jealous *celoso/celosa* (m./f.)
jeans *jeans* (m. pl.), *tejanos* (m. pl.), *vaqueros* (m. pl.)
job *trabajo* (m.), *empleo* (m.)
Good job! *¡Buen trabajo!*
summer job *trabajo de verano*
steady job *trabajo fijo*
jog (to) *trotar*
joke *chiste* (m.)
tell a dirty joke (to) (lit., to tell a green joke) *contar un chiste verde*
journalist *periodista* (m./f.)
judge *juez* (m.)
juice *jugo* (m.), *zumo* (m.)
July *julio* (m.)
June *junio* (m.)

K

keep (to) *llevar, guardar*
keep a cool head (to) *tener la cabeza fría*
keep a diary (to) *llevar un diario*
key *llave* (f.)
keyboard *teclado* (m.)
kid *crío/cría* (m./f.)
kilo, kilogram *kilo* (m.)
kilometer *kilómetro* (m.)
kind *clase* (f.)
all kinds *toda clase*
kiss (to) *besar*
kitchen *cocina* (f.)
knee *rodilla* (f.)
knife *cuchillo* (m.)
know (to) *saber (facts, information), conocer (people, places)*
as you already know *como ya sabes*
Do you know how to . . . ? *¿Sabe cómo . . . ?*
How do I know!?/How should I know!? *¡Yo qué sé!*
know by sight (to) *conocer de vista*
know like the back of one's hand (to) *conocer palmo a palmo*
make known (to) *dar a conocer*
not have a clue about . . . (to) *no saber ni jota de . . .*
not know (to) *desconocer*
Who knows? *¿Quién sabe?*

L

label *etiqueta* (f.)
lake *lago* (m.)
lamb *cordero/cordera* (m./f.)
lamb chop *chuleta* (f.) *de cordero*
lamp *lámpara* (f.)
lamppost *farola* (f.)
land *tierra* (f.)
lane *carril* (m.), *vía* (f.)
Stay in the right lane. *Siga por el carril de la derecha.*
language *idioma* (m.), *lengua* (f.)
large *gran/grande* (before sg. nouns/all other cases)
last *último/última* (m./f.)
at last *por fin*
last month *mes* (m.) *pasado*
last night *anoche*
last week *semana* (f.) *pasada*
last year *año* (m.) *pasado*
late *tarde*

I'll see you later. *Hasta luego.*
I'm late. *Se me hace tarde.*
late night (from midnight) *madrugada* (f.)
later *más tarde, luego*
Until later. *Hasta más tarde.*
very latest (the) *último grito* (m.)
laugh (to) *reír*
laugh very hard (to) (lit., to turn black with laughter) *estar negro de la risa*
laughter *risa* (f.)
laundry detergent *detergente* (m.) *de ropa*
law *derecho* (m.)
lawn *césped* (m.)
lawyer *abogado/abogada* (m./f.)
lazy *perezoso/perezosa* (m./f.)
be lazy (to) *ser perezoso*
learn (to) *aprender, saber*
learn how to . . . (to) *aprender a . . .*
I'm learning Spanish. *Estoy aprendiendo español.*
least . . . in/of . . . (the) *el/la/los/las* (m. sg./f. sg./m. pl./f. pl.) *menos . . . de . . .*
leather *cuero* (m.)
leave (to) *dejar, marchar, parar, partir, salir*
leave a message after the tone (to) *dejar un mensaje después de oír la señal*
lecture *conferencia* (f.)
lecture hall *sala* (f.) *de conferencias*
left side *izquierda* (f.)
on the left *a la izquierda*
Turn left. *Gira a la izquierda.*
left-hand *izquierdo/izquierda* (m./f.)
on the left-hand side *a mano izquierda*
leg *pierna* (f.)
lemon *limón* (m.)
lemonade *limonada* (f.)
less *menos*
least . . . in/of . . . (the) *el/la/los/las* (m. sg./f. sg./m. pl./f. pl.) *menos . . . de . . .*
less . . . than . . . *menos . . . que . . .*
more or less *más o menos*
lesson *lección* (f.)
Let's go . . . *Vamos . . .*
Let's see . . . *A ver . . .*
letter *cartas* (f. pl.)
lettuce *lechuga* (f.)
library *biblioteca* (f.)
lie (to) *mentir*
life *vida* (f.)
How's life treating you? *¿Cómo te trata la vida?*
lift (to) *levantar*
light *luz* (f.)
turn off the lights (to) *apagar las luces*
light *claro/clara* (m./f.), *ligero/ligera* (m./f.)
light blue *azul* (m./f.) *claro*
lightening *relámpago* (m.)
like *como*
like (to) *(se) gustar*
I like . . . *Me gusta/gustan . . .* (sg./pl.)
I really like . . . *Me encanta/encantan . . .* (sg./pl.)
I'd like . . . *Me gustaría . . .*
like (it) that . . . (to) *gustar que . . .*
What would you like? *¿Qué desea?*
likewise *igualmente*
limit *límite* (m.)
line *cola* (f.), *fila* (f.), *línea* (f.)
stand in line (to) *hacer una cola/fila*
The line is busy. *Está comunicando.*
linen *lino* (m.)
lip *labio* (m.)
list *lista* (f.)
list of plays *cartelera* (f.)
listen to (to) *escuchar*
liter *litro* (m.)
literature *literatura* (f.)
little *poco*
a little *un poco*
I speak a little Spanish. *Hablo un poco de español.*
live (to) *vivir*
What do you do for a living? *¿En qué trabaja?*
living room *sala* (f.)
loan *crédito* (m.), *préstamo* (m.)
lobster *langosta* (f.)
local *local* (m./f.)
local call *llamada* (f.) *local*
London *Londres*
long *largo/larga* (m./f.)
long weekend *puente* (m.)
look at (to) *mirar*
look for (to) *buscar*
look like (to) *parecer*
look up (to) *consultar*
loose *suelto/suelta* (m./f.)
Los Angeles *Los Ángeles*

lose (to) *perder*
lose one's head (to) *perder la cabeza*
lottery *lotería* (f.)
love (to) *querer, amar*
I love you. *Te quiero.*
I'd love to! *¡Me encantaría!*
in love *enamorado/enamorada* (m./f.)
low-cost *económico/económica* (m./f.)
low-cut *escotado/escotada* (m./f.)
lower (to) *bajar*
LP *disco de vinilo* (m.)
luck *suerte* (f.)
lunch *almuerzo* (m.)
have lunch (to) *almorzar*
lungs *pulmones* (m. pl.)

M

made *hecho/hecha* (m./f.)
magazine *revista* (f.)
magical *mágico/mágica* (m./f.)
magnificent *magnífico/magnífica* (m./f.)
mailbox *buzón* (m.)
main *principal* (m./f.)
main dish *plato* (m.) *principal*
major *carrera* (f.), *especialidad* (f.)
major in . . . (to) *especializarse en . . .*
make (to) *hacer*
make an international/local/national call (to) *hacer una llamada internacional/local/nacional*
make known (to) *dar a conocer*
man *hombre* (m.), *tío (m., colloquial)*
manager *gerente* (m.)
manner *forma* (f.)
many *muchos/muchas* (m. pl./f. pl.)
how many *cuántos/cuántas* (m. pl./f. pl.)
map *mapa* (m.), *plano* (m.)
March *marzo* (m.)
marine *marino/marina* (m./f.)
mark (to) *marcar*
market *mercado* (m.)
flea market *mercadillo*
marriage *matrimonio* (m.)
married *casado/casada* (m./f.)
marry (someone) (to) *casarse con*
get married (to) *casarse*
martini *martini* (m.)
martyr *mártir* (m./f.)
marvelous *estupendo/estupenda* (m./f.)
master (to) *dominar*
master's degree *maestría* (f.), *especialización* (f.)
match (to) *combinar*
material *material* (m.)
mathematics *matemáticas* (f. pl.)
matter (to) *importar*
It doesn't matter. *No importa.*
May *mayo* (m.)
May I please . . . ? (fml.) *¿Me permite . . . ?* (fml.)/*¿Me permites . . . ?* (infml.)
May you be well. *Que esté bien.*
mayor *alcalde* (m.)
me (after a proposition) *mí*
me (direct object pronoun) *me*
(to/for) me (indirect object pronoun) *me*
mean (to) *significar*
What does that mean? *¿Qué quiere decir eso?*
meanwhile *mientras tanto*
measure (to) *medir*
measurement *medida* (f.)
meat *carne* (f.)
mechanical *mecánico/mecánica* (m./f.)
mechanical engineering *ingeniería* (f.) *mecánica*
medication *medicamento* (m.)
take medication (to) *tomar un medicamento*
medicine *medicina* (f.)
medicine cabinet *botiquín* (m.)
medium *mediano/mediana* (m./f.), *término* (m.) *tres cuartos (cooked meat)*
medium-rare *término* (m.) *medio*
meet (to) *conocer, reunirse*
meet (somebody) (to) *conocer (a alguien), encontrarse con*
meet up with (to) *encontrar*
Pleased to meet you. *Gusto en conocerlo/la.*
meeting *reunión* (f.), *conferencia* (f.)
meeting room *sala* (f.) *de conferencias*
memory *memoria* (f.)
menu *carta* (f.)
merely *sólo*
message *mensaje* (m.)
instant message *mensaje instantáneo*
leave a message after the tone (to) *dejar un mensaje después de oír la señal*
metro *metro* (m.)
Mexican *mexicano/mexicana* (m./f.)

Mexico *México* (m.)
microwave *microondas* (m.)
midnight *medianoche* (f.), *media noche* (f.)
  at midnight *a medianoche*
midway *medio/media* (m./f.)
milk *leche* (f.)
  powdered milk *leche en polvo*
  skim milk *leche descremada*
million *millón*
  one million houses *un millón de casas*
mind *mente* (f.)
  go out of one's mind (to) *pararse de cabeza*
mine *mío/mía/míos/mías* (m. sg./f. sg./m. pl./f. pl.)
minus (-) *menos*
minute *minuto* (m.)
miracle *maravilla* (f.)
mirror *espejo* (m.)
misfortune *desgracia* (f.)
miss (to) *perder, faltar*
mixed *mixto/mixta* (m./f.)
mobile phone *móvil* (m.)
modem *módem* (m.)
modern *moderno/moderna* (m./f.)
molar *muela* (f.)
mole *lunar* (m.)
mom *mamá* (f.), *mami* (f.)
moment *momento* (m.)
  at this moment *en este momento*
  One moment. *Un momento.*
Monday *lunes* (m.)
money *dinero* (m.)
monitor *monitor* (m.)
month *mes* (m.)
  last month *mes pasado*
  next month *mes entrante, mes que viene*
  this month *este mes*
monument *monumento* (m.)
moon *luna* (f.)
more *más*
  more or less *más o menos*
  more . . . /-er than . . . *más . . . que . . .*
moreover *además*
morning *mañana* (f.)
  early morning (from midnight till daybreak) *madrugada* (f.)
  Good morning. *Buenos días.*
  in the early morning *de la madrugada*
  in the morning *de la mañana*
  It's ten after one in the morning. *Es la una y diez de la madrugada.*
  this morning *esta mañana*
Moscow *Moscú*
mosque *mezquita* (f.)
most . . . in/of . . . (the) *el/la/los/las* (m. sg./f. sg./m. pl./f. pl.) *más . . . de . . .*
mother *madre* (f.)
mother-in-law *suegra* (f.)
mountain *montaña* (f.)
mouse *ratón* (m.)
mouth *boca* (f.)
move (to) *mover*
movie *película* (f.)
  movie listing *cartelera de cine*
  movie theater *cine* (m.)
Mr. *señor* (m.), *don* (m.)
Mrs. *señora* (f.), *doña* (f.)
much *mucho*
  how much *cuánto/cuánta* (m./f.)
municipal building *ayuntamiento* (m.), *alcaldía* (f.)
muscle *músculo* (m.)
museum *museo* (m.)
music *música* (f.)
  classical music *música clásica*
musical *musical* (m.)
musician *músico* (m.)
must *deber*
my *mi/mis* (sg./pl.)
myself *me*

N

nail *uña* (f.)
name *nombre* (m.)
  My name is . . . *Me llamo . . .*
  What's your name? *¿Cómo se llama usted?* (fml.)/*¿Cómo te llamas?* (infml.)
nap *siesta* (f.)
napkin *servilleta* (f.)
narrow *angosto/angosta* (m./f.), *estrecho/estrecha* (m./f.)
national *nacional* (m./f.)
  national call *llamada* (f.) *nacional*
nationality *nacionalidad* (f.)
natural *natural* (m./f.)
nature *naturaleza* (f.)
nausea *náusea* (f.)

be nauseated/have nausea (to) *tener náusea(s)*
navy blue *azul* (m./f.) *marino*
near *cerca, próximo/próxima* (m./f.)
near . . . *cerca de . . .*
necessary *necesario/necesaria* (m./f.)
be necessary (to) *faltar*
It's necessary that . . . *Es necesario que . . .*
It's necessary to . . . *Hay que . . .*
neck *cuello* (m.)
necklace *collar* (m.)
need (to) *necesitar*
needle *aguja* (f.)
neighbor *vecino/vecina* (m./f.)
neighborhood *barrio* (m.)
neither *tampoco*
neither . . . nor *ni . . . ni*
nephew *sobrino* (m.)
nerve *nervio* (m.)
never *nunca*
almost never *casi nunca*
new *nuevo/nueva* (m./f.)
news *noticias* (pl.)
a piece of news *noticia* (f.)
newspaper *periódico* (m.)
New York *Nueva York*
next *próximo/próxima* (m./f.)
next month *mes* (m.) *que viene*
next to . . . *al lado de . . .*
next week *próxima semana* (f.), *semana* (f.) *que viene*
next year *año* (m.) *que viene*
nice *bonito/bonita* (m./f.)
Have a nice day. *Que tenga un buen día.*
How nice! *¡Qué bien!*
niece *sobrina* (f.)
night *noche* (f.)
at night *de la noche*
Good night. *Buenas noches.*
last night *anoche*
late night (from midnight) *madrugada* (f.)
nine *nueve*
at about nine o'clock *a eso de las nueve*
at nine a.m. *a las nueve de la mañana*
be dressed to the nines (to) *ir de punta en blanco (lit., to go from the tip in white)*
nine hundred *novecientos/novecientas* (m./f.)
twenty-nine *veintinueve*
nineteen *diecinueve, diez y nueve*
ninety *noventa*
no *no, ningún/ninguno/ninguna* (before m. sg. nouns/m. sg./f. sg.)
no one *nadie*
No, not at all. *No, para nada.*
There's no . . . that/who . . . *No hay ningún . . . que . . .*
There's no one who/that . . . *No hay nadie que . . .*
nobody *nadie*
There's no one who/that . . . *No hay nadie que . . .*
none *ningún/ninguno/ninguna* (before m. sg. nouns/m. sg./f. sg.)
noon *mediodía* (m.)
at noon *a mediodía*
It's twelve noon. *Son las doce del mediodía.*
nor *ni*
neither . . . nor *ni . . . ni*
normal *normal* (m./f.)
normally *normalmente*
north *norte* (m.)
nose *nariz* (f.)
not *no*
absolutely not *en absoluto*
be not doing well (to) *estar mal*
It's not bad. *No está mal.*
No, not at all. *No, para nada.*
not either *tampoco*
note *nota* (f.)
take note (to) *tomar nota*
notebook *cuaderno* (m.)
nothing *nada*
nothing else *nada más*
There's nothing that . . . *No hay nada que . . .*
novel *novela* (f.)
romance novel *novela rosa*
November *noviembre* (m.)
now *ahora, ya*
right now *ahora mismo*
nowadays *hoy en día*
number *número* (m.)
telephone number *número de teléfono*

O

object *objeto* (m.)
objective *objetivo* (m.)

ocean *océano* (m.), *mar* (m.)
October *octubre* (m.)
of *de*
  because of *por*
  in place of *por*
  of course *por supuesto*
  Of course! *¡Claro que sí!*
  of the (m.) *del (de + el)*
  of which (relative pronoun) *cuyo/cuya/cuyos/cuyas* (m. sg./f. sg./m. pl./f. pl.)
  on top of *sobre*
  outside of . . . *fuera de . . .*
  Yes, of course. *Sí, claro.*
offer *oferta* (f.)
offer (to) *ofrecer*
office *oficina* (f.), *despacho* (m.), *estudio* (m.), *consultorio* (m.)
  doctor's office *consultorio del médico*
  office worker *oficinista* (m./f.)
often *con frecuencia*
oil *aceite* (m.)
(just) okay *más o menos*
old *viejo/vieja* (m./f.), *antiguo/antigua* (m./f.)
  be . . . years old (to) *tener . . . años*
  How old are you (sg. fml.)**/is he/is she?** *¿Cuántos años tiene?*
  older *mayor* (m./f.)
  oldest (the) *el/la/los/las* (m. sg./f. sg./m. pl./f. pl.) *mayor*
on *en*
  buy on sale (to) *comprar en rebaja*
  depend on . . . (to) *depender de . . .*
  go on a trip (to) *salir de viaje*
  Hold on, please. *Espere, por favor.*
  Hold on. *Un momento.*
  on board *a bordo*
  on the left *a la izquierda*
  on the left-hand side *a mano izquierda*
  on the one hand *por una parte*
  on the other hand *por otra parte*
  on the phone *por teléfono*
  on the radio *por la radio*
  on the right *a la derecha*
  on the right-hand side *a mano derecha*
  on the sidewalk *por el andén*
  on time *a tiempo*
  on top of *sobre*
  on vacation *de vacaciones*
  put on hold (to) *poner en espera*
  put something on (to) *ponerse*
  try on (clothes) (to) *probarse*
once again *nuevamente*
one *uno*
  It's five to one. (12:55) *Es la una menos cinco.*
  It's one o'clock. *Es la una.*
  no one *nadie*
  on the one hand *por una parte*
  one (o'clock) *una*
  One moment. *Un momento.*
  once *una vez*
  once again *nuevamente*
  one-piece *enterizo/enteriza* (m./f.)
  one-way *de sentido* (m.) *único*
  thirty-one *treinta y uno*
  twenty-one *veintiuno*
one (impersonal pronoun) *se*
onion *cebolla* (f.)
online *por Internet, en línea*
only (adjective) *único/única* (m./f.), *solo/sola* (m./f.)
only (adverb) *solamente, sólo, simplemente*
open (to) *abrir*
  open the door (to) *abrir la puerta*
opera *ópera* (f.)
operator *operadora* (f.)
opposite *opuesto/opuesta* (m./f.)
or *o*
  either . . . or *o . . . o*
  more or less *más o menos*
orange (color) *anaranjado/anaranjada* (m./f.)
orange (fruit) *naranja* (f.)
order (to) *pedir*
  in order to *para*
ounce *onza* (f.)
our *nuestro/nuestra/nuestros/nuestras* (m. sg./f. sg./m. pl./f. pl.)
ours *nuestro/nuestra/nuestros/nuestras* (m. sg./f. sg./m. pl./f. pl.)
ourselves *nos*
outbound journey *ida* (f.)
outdoor market *plaza de mercado*
outside (adverb) *afuera, fuera*
  outside of . . . *fuera de . . .*
outside (noun) *exterior* (m.)
outskirts *afueras* (f. pl.)
oven *horno* (m.)

over *sobre*
overcoat *abrigo* (m.)
overcooked *sobrecocido/sobrecocida* (m./f.)
overtime *horas* (f. pl.) *extras*
owe (to) *deber*
own (to) *poseer*

P

package *paquete* (m.)
packet *cajetilla* (f.)
pack of cigarettes *cajetilla de cigarrillos*
page *página* (f.)
yellow pages *páginas* (pl.) *amarillas*
webpage *página web*
pain *dolor* (m.), *pena* (f.)
painter *pintor/pintora* (m./f.)
painting *pintura* (f.), *cuadro* (m.)
pajamas *pijama* (m.)
palace *palacio* (m.)
palm *palmo* (m.)
Panamanian *panameña/panameño* (m./f.)
pants *pantalones* (m. pl.)
papaya *papaya* (f.)
paper *papel* (m.)
research paper *trabajo* (m.) *de investigación*
Paraguay *Paraguay* (m.)
Pardon me? *¿Cómo?*
parents *padres* (pl.)
Paris *París*
park *parque* (m.)
parking lot *parqueadero* (m.)
part *parte* (f.)
partial *parcial* (m./f.)
particular *particular* (m./f.)
part-time *a tiempo parcial*
party *fiesta* (f.)
pass (to) *aprobar, pasar*
pass a course (to) *aprobar un curso*
pass a test (to) *aprobar un examen*
passport *pasaporte* (m.)
past *pasado/pasada* (m./f.)
at a half past five *a las cinco y media*
at a quarter past six *a las seis y cuarto*
pastry *dulce* (m.)
path *camino* (m.)
patience *paciencia* (f.)
be patient (to) *tener paciencia*
patterned, with a pattern *estampado/estampada* (m./f.)
pay *sueldo* (m.)
pay (to) *pagar*
pay cash (to) *pagar en efectivo*
payment *pago* (m.)
pear *pera* (f.)
pedestrian *peatón* (m.)
pediatrician *pediatra* (m./f.)
regular pediatrician *pediatra* (m./f.) *de cabecera*
pediatrics *pediatría* (f.)
pen *bolígrafo* (m.), *pluma* (f.)
pencil *lápiz* (m.)
penicillin *penicilina* (f.)
pension *pensión* (f.)
people *gente* (f.)
people (impersonal pronoun) *se*
pepper *pimienta* (f.) *(spice), pimiento* (m.) *(vegetable)*
perceive (to) *percibir*
percent *por ciento*
perceptibly *sensiblemente*
perfect *perfecto/perfecta* (m./f.)
perfume *perfume* (m.)
perhaps *tal vez*
period *período* (m.)
period *término* (m.)
permanent *fijo/fija* (m./f.)
person *persona* (f.)
Peru *Perú* (m.)
Peruvian *peruano/peruana* (m./f.)
peso *peso* (m.)
pharmacist *farmacéutico/farmacéutico* (m./f.)
pharmacy *farmacia* (f.)
philosophy *filosofía* (f.)
phone book *guía* (f.) *telefónica*
phone call *llamada* (f.)
make an international/local/national call (to) *hacer una llamada internacional/local/nacional*
photograph *foto* (f.)
photography *fotografía* (f.)
phrase *frase* (f.)
physics *física* (f.)
piano *piano* (m.)
pick up (to) *recoger, coger, buscar*
picture *foto* (f.), *cuadro* (m.)
take a picture (to) *hacer una foto*

piece *pieza* (f.)
  one-piece *enterizo/enteriza* (m./f.)
  two-piece *de dos piezas*
pig *cerdo/cerda* (m./f.)
piglet *chanchito/chanchita* (m./f.)
pill *pastilla* (f.)
pink *rosado/rosada* (m./f.)
pity *lástima* (f.), *pena* (f.)
  It's a pity that ... *Es una lástima que ...*
place *lugar* (m.), *sitio* (m.)
  in place of *por*
place (to) *poner*
plaid *a cuadros*
plan *plan* (m.)
plant *planta* (f.)
plastic *plástico* (m.)
plate *plato* (m.)
play (to) *jugar, practicar (sports), tocar (instrument)*
  play sports (to) *hacer deporte*
  play the piano (to) *tocar el piano*
  play the guitar (to) *tocar la guitarra*
play (theater) *obra* (f.)
player *jugador/jugadora* (m./f.)
plaza *plaza* (f.)
pleasant *agradable* (m./f.)
please (to) *gustar*
  Pleased to meet you. *Encantado./Encantada.* (said by a man/said by a woman)*/Gusto en conocerlo/la.*
Please. *Por favor.*
pleasure *placer* (m.), *gusto* (m.)
  It's a pleasure. *Mucho gusto.*
plumber *fontanero/fontanera* (m./f.)
plus (+) *más*
p.m. *de la tarde, de la noche*
  at four p.m. *a las cuatro de la tarde*
  at seven p.m. *a las siete de la noche*
pocket-knife *navaja* (f.)
point *punto* (m.), *término* (m.)
police officer *policía* (m./f.)
  policewoman *mujer* (f.) *policía*
polka-dot *de lunares*
polyester *poliéster* (m.)
pond *estanque* (m.)
pool *piscina* (f.)
poor, poor person *pobre* (m./f.)
  poor (the) *los pobres*
poorly *mal*
pork *cerdo* (m.), *carne* (f.) *de cerdo*
Portuguese *portugués/portuguesa* (m./f.)
position (job) *puesto* (m.)
possible *posible* (m./f.)
  as soon as possible *lo antes posible*
  It is possible that ... *Es posible que ...*
post (job) *puesto* (m.)
postage stamp *estampilla* (f.)
post office *correo* (m.)
postpone (to) *retrasar*
potato *papa* (f.), *patata* (f.)
pound *libra* (f.)
  half pound *media libra*
powder *polvo* (m.)
  powdered milk *leche* (f.) *en polvo*
practice (to) *practicar*
prayer *oración* (f.)
precisely *precisamente*
prefer (to) *preferir*
  prefer that ... (to) *preferir que ...*
preferable *preferible* (m./f.)
  It's preferable that ... *Es preferible que ...*
pregnant *embarazada* (f.)
prepared *preparado/preparada* (m./f.)
presentation *presentación* (f.)
president *presidente/presidenta* (m./f.)
pressure *presión* (f.)
  have high/low blood pressure (to) *tener la tensión alta/baja*
prestigious *prestigioso/prestigiosa* (m./f.)
pretty *bonito/bonita* (m./f.)
prevent (to) *impedir*
price *precio* (m.)
  price tag *etiqueta* (f.) *con el precio*
  reasonable price *precio económico*
printer *impresora* (f.)
prison *cárcel* (f.)
prize *premio* (m.)
probation *prueba* (f.)
  probationary period *período* (m.) *de prueba*
problem *problema* (m.)
produce (to) *producir*
product *producto* (m.)
profession *profesión* (f.)
professional *profesional* (m./f.)
professionally *profesionalmente*
professor *profesor/profesora* (m./f.)

program *programa* (m.)
  television program *programa de televisión*
prohibit (to) *prohibir*
project *proyecto* (m.)
promise (to) *prometer*
proof *prueba* (f.)
protect (to) *proteger*
psychology *sicología* (f.)
punctual *puntual* (m./f.)
purchase *compra* (f.)
purple *morado/morada* (m./f.), *púrpura* (m./f.)
put (to) *poner*
  I'm putting you through. (on the phone) *Lo paso.*
  put on hold (to) *poner en espera*
  put something on (to) *ponerse*

Q

qualification *cualificación* (f.)
qualified *cualificado/cualificada* (m./f.)
quarter *cuarto* (m.)
  at a quarter past six *a las seis y cuarto*
  at a quarter to six *a las seis menos cuarto*
question *pregunta* (f.)
questionnaire *cuestionario* (m.)
quick *rápido/rápida* (m./f.)
quickly *rápidamente, rápido, aprisa*
quiet *tranquilo/tranquila* (m./f.)
quietly *silenciosamente*
quite, quite a lot *bastante*

R

radio *radio* (f.)
  on the radio *por la radio*
railroad *ferrocarril* (m.)
rain *lluvia* (f.)
rain (to) *llover*
  It's raining. *Está lloviendo.*
raincoat *gabardina* (f.)
raise (to) *levantar*
ramp *rampa* (f.)
rash *brote* (m.)
razor *navaja* (f.) *de afeitar*
read (to) *leer*
reader *lector* (m.)
reading *lectura* (f.)
ready *listo/lista* (m./f.), *preparado/preparada* (m./f.)
  Ready? *¿Listos?/¿Preparados?*
realism *realismo* (m.)
realistic *realista* (m./f.)
Really? *No me digas.*
reason *razón* (f.)
reasonable price *precio* (m.) *económico*
receive (to) *recibir*
reception desk *recepción* (f.)
receptionist *recepcionista* (m./f.)
recess *receso* (m.)
recipe *receta* (f.)
recognize (to) *reconocer*
recommend (to) *recomendar*
  recommend that . . . (to) *recomendar que . . .*
record *registro* (m.), *historial* (m.), *disco* (m.)
record (to) *anotar*
recreation *recreo* (m.)
red *rojo/roja* (m./f.), *colorado/colorada* (m./f.)
  red wine *vino* (m.) *tinto*
reduce (to) *reducir*
reduced *rebajado/rebajada* (m./f.)
reference *referencia* (f.)
refrigerator *nevera* (f.)
regain strength (to) *coger fuerzas* (f. pl.)
regarding . . . *en cuanto a . . .*
region *región* (f.)
regional *regional* (m./f.)
register (to) *matricularse*
registration *matrícula* (f.)
regret that . . . (to) *sentir que . . .*
relationship *relación* (f.)
relative *pariente* (m./f.)
remain (to) *quedar*
remember (to) *recordar*
rent (to) *alquilar*
repayment *retribución* (f.)
repeat (to) *repetir*
  Repeat, please. *Repita, por favor*
reply to (to) *contestar*
report *informe* (m.)
  report card *calificaciones* (f. pl.)
representative *representante* (m.)
request (to) *solicitar*
  request that . . . (to) *pedir que . . .*
research *investigación* (f.)
  research paper *trabajo* (m.) *de investigación*
reservation *reserva* (f.), *reservación* (f.)
resolve (to) *resolver*

responsible *responsable* (m./f.)
rest *resto* (m.)
rest (to) *descansar*
restaurant *restaurante* (m.)
result *resultado* (m.)
résumé *historial* (m.) *de trabajo, currículum vítae, hoja* (f.) *de vida*
retain (to) *quedar*
retired, retired person *jubilado/jubilada* (m./f.)
return (to) *regresar, volver*
rice *arroz* (m.)
rich *rico/rica* (m./f.)
ride (to) *montar*
right *derecho* (m.), *ya*
  be right (to) *tener razón*
  right? *¿verdad?*
  on the right *a la derecha*
  on the right-hand side *a mano derecha*
  right now *en este momento, ahora mismo*
  right side *derecha* (f.)
  right-side *derecho/derecha* (m./f.)
  That's right. *Es verdad./Así es.*
  Turn right. *Gira a la derecha.*
ring *anillo* (m.)
ring (to) *sonar*
rise (to) *levantarse*
river *río* (m.)
robe *albornoz* (m.), *bata* (f.), *deshabillé* (m.)
rock *roca* (f.)
romance novel *novela* (f.) *rosa*
romantic *romántico/romántica* (m./f.)
  romantic films *películas* (f. pl.) *románticas*
room *alcoba* (f.), *cuarto* (m.), *habitación* (f.)
rose *rosa* (f.)
  wear rose-colored glasses (to) *ver todo color de rosa (lit., to see everything pink)*
rotten *podrido/podrida* (m./f.)
rough *agitado/agitada* (m./f.)
round *redondo/redonda* (m./f.)
route *recorrido* (m.)
run (to) *correr*
rural *rural* (m./f.)
Russian (language) *ruso* (m.)

S

sack *bolsa* (f.)
sad *triste* (m./f.)
  It's sad that … *Es triste que …*
sadly *tristemente*
safe *seguro/segura* (m./f.)
safety *seguridad* (f.)
salad *ensalada* (f.)
salary *salario* (m.)
sale *venta* (f.)
  buy on sale (to) *comprar en rebaja*
salesman/saleswoman *vendedor/vendedora* (m./f.)
salsa *salsa* (f.)
salt *sal* (f.)
salty *salado/salada* (m./f.)
same *mismo/misma* (m./f.)
  The same to you. *Igualmente.*
sand *arena* (f.)
sandals *sandalias* (f. pl.)
Saturday *sábado* (m.)
sauce *salsa* (f.)
save (to) *ahorrar, guardar*
say (to) *decir*
  How do you say " … " in … ? *¿Cómo se dice " … " en … ?*
  say good-bye (to) *despedirse*
scarf *bufanda* (f.)
scary *espantoso/espantosa* (m./f.)
schedule *horario* (m.)
scholarship *beca* (f.)
school *escuela* (f.), *academia* (f.)
  school subject *materia* (f.)
science *ciencia* (f.)
scoreboard *marcador* (m.)
scream *grito* (m.)
scream (to) *gritar*
screen *pantalla* (f.)
sculpture *escultura* (f.)
sea *mar* (m.)
season *estación* (f.)
seat *silla* (f.)
seat (to) *sentar*
  be seated (to) *estar sentado*
second *segundo/segunda* (m./f.)
  second year *segundo año*
secondary school *colegio* (m.)
secret *secreto* (m.)
secretary *secretaria* (m./f.)
section *sección* (f.)
security *seguridad* (f.)
see (to) *ver*

I'll see you later. *Hasta luego.*
Let's see ... *Vamos .../A ver ...*
See you. *Nos vemos. (lit., We see each other.)*
See you soon. *Hasta pronto.*
See you tomorrow. *Hasta mañana.*
seem (to) *parecer*
seldom *casi nunca*
sell (to) *vender*
semester *semestre* (m.)
send (to) *enviar*
sense *sentido* (m.)
sensibly *sensatamente*
September *septiembre* (m.)
series *serie* (f.)
serious *grave* (m./f.), *serio/seria* (m./f.)
serve (to) *servir, atender*
service *servicio* (m.)
Is service included? *¿Está incluido el servicio?*
session *sesión* (f.)
set off (to) *partir*
seven *siete*
at seven p.m. *a las siete de la noche*
seven hundred *setecientos/setecientas* (m./f.)
twenty-seven *veintisiete*
seventeen *diecisiete, diez y siete*
seventy *setenta*
several *varios/varias* (m./f.)
sewing *costura* (f.)
shake hands (to) *dar la mano*
shampoo *champú* (m.)
shave (to) *afeitar*
shave (oneself) (to) *afeitarse*
shaving cream *crema de afeitar*
she *ella*
sheet (of paper) *hoja* (f.)
shelf *estante* (m.)
shirt *camisa* (f.)
shoes *zapatos* (m. pl.)
shoe store *zapatería* (f.)
tennis shoes *zapatillas* (f. pl.) *deportivas*
What shoe size do you wear? *¿Qué número calza?*
shop (to) *comprar*
shopping mall *centro* (m.) *comercial*
short *bajo/baja* (m./f.), *corto/corta* (m./f.)
shoulder *hombro* (m.)
shout (to) *gritar*
show (to) *mostrar, dar*
shower *ducha* (f.)
shrimp *camarón* (m.), *gamba* (f.)
shy *tímido/tímida* (m./f.)
siblings *hermanos* (pl.)
sick *enfermo/enferma* (m./f.)
sickness *mareo* (m.), *náusea* (f.)
side *lado* (m.), *parte* (f.)
on the left-hand side *a mano izquierda*
on the right-hand side *a mano derecha*
sidewalk *andén* (m.), *acera* (f.)
on the sidewalk *por el andén/la acera*
signal *señal* (f.)
signature *firma* (f.)
silk *seda* (f.)
silver (color) *plateado/plateada* (m./f.)
simply *simplemente*
since *desde, pues*
sing (to) *cantar*
singer *cantante* (m./f.)
single *único/única* (m./f.), *soltero/soltera* (m./f.)
sink *lavabo* (m.), *fregadero* (m.) *(kitchen)*
sister *hermana* (f.)
sister-in-law *cuñada* (f.)
sit down (to) *sentarse*
situation *situación* (f.)
six *seis*
at a quarter past six *a las seis y cuarto*
at a quarter to six *a las seis menos cuarto*
six hundred *seiscientos/seiscientas* (m./f.)
twenty-six *veintiséis*
sixteen *dieciséis, diez y seis*
sixty *sesenta*
size *talla* (f.), *tamaño* (m.)
What shoe size do you wear? *¿Qué número calza?*
ski (to) *esquiar*
skill *destreza* (f.), *cualificación* (f.)
skimmed *descremado/descremada* (m./f.)
skim milk *leche* (f.) *descremada*
skin *piel* (f.)
skip (to) *saltar*
skirt *falda* (f.)
sky *cielo* (m.)
sky blue *celeste* (m./f.)
sleep *sueño* (m.)
be sleepy (to) *tener sueño*
sleep (to) *dormir*
sleepiness *sueño* (m.)

slice *rebanada* (f.), *tajada* (f.)
slippers *chinelas* (f. pl.), *pantuflas* (f. pl.), *zapatillas* (f. pl.)
slow *lento/lenta* (m./f.), *retrasado/retrasada* (m./f.)
slowly *despacio, lentamente*
  Speak more slowly, please. *Hable más despacio, por favor.*
small *pequeño/pequeña* (m./f.)
  smaller *menor* (m./f.)
  smallest (the) *el/la/los/las* (m. sg./f. sg./m. pl./f. pl.) *menor*
smart *inteligente* (m./f.)
smell (to) *oler*
smile (to) *sonreír*
smog *niebla* (f.) *tóxica/con humo*
smoke (to) *fumar*
smoked *ahumado/ahumada* (m./f.)
snack time *merienda* (f.)
snake *serpiente* (f.)
sneakers *zapatillas* (f. pl.) *deportivas*
snow *nieve* (f.)
snow (to) *nevar*
  It's snowing. *Está nevando.*
so *así, pues*
  I hope so! *¡Yo espero que sí!*
  I think so. *Creo que sí.*
  so-so *más o menos*
  So . . . *Así que . . .*
  so to speak *por así decir*
so (very) *tan*
soap *jabón* (m.)
soccer *fútbol* (m.)
socks *calcetines* (m. pl.), *medias* (f. pl.)
soda *refresco* (m.)
sofa *sofá* (m.)
soft *suave* (m./f.)
soft drink *refresco* (m.)
sole *solo/sola* (m./f.)
solely *sólo*
solitude *soledad* (f.)
solution *solución* (f.)
some *unos/unas* (m. pl./f. pl.), *algún/alguno/alguna* (before m. sg. nouns/m. sg./f. sg.), *algunos/algunas* (m. pl./f. pl.)
somebody, someone *alguien*
  somebody else *alguien más*
something *algo, algún/alguno/alguna* (before m. sg. nouns/m. sg./f. sg.), *algunos/algunas* (m. pl./f. pl.)
sometimes *a veces*
somewhat *algo*
son *hijo* (m.)
song *canción* (f.)
son-in-law *yerno* (m.)
soon *pronto*
  as soon as possible *lo antes posible*
  See you soon. *Hasta pronto.*
(I'm) sorry. *Lo siento.*
sound *sonido* (m.)
  sound system *sistema* (m.) *de sonido*
sound (to) *sonar*
soup *sopa* (f.)
sour *agrio/agria* (m./f.), *cortado/cortada* (m./f.), *amargo/amarga* (m./f.)
south *sur* (m.)
South America *Sudamérica*
space *espacio* (m.)
Spain *España* (f.)
Spanish *español/española* (m./f.)
Spanish (language) *español* (m.)
  I'm learning Spanish. *Estoy aprendiendo español.*
  I speak a little Spanish. *Hablo un poco de español.*
speak (to) *hablar*
  Do you speak English? (fml.) *¿Habla usted inglés?*
  Do you speak English? (infml.) *¿Hablas inglés?*
  I speak a little Spanish. *Hablo un poco de español.*
  I speak French fluently. *Domino el francés.*
  so to speak *por así decir*
  Speak more slowly, please. *Hable más despacio, por favor.*
  speak to . . . (to) *hablar con . . . .*
specialization *especialización* (f.)
specialize (to) *especializarse*
special of the day *plato del día*
specialty *especialidad* (f.)
spectator *espectador/espectadora* (m./f.)
speed *velocidad* (f.)
spend (to) *pasar*
  spend the day (to) *pasar el día*
spicy *condimentado/condimentada* (m./f.), *picante* (m./f.)

spinal column *columna* (f.) *vertebral*
spoiled *pasado/pasada* (m./f.)
spoon *cuchara* (f.)
sport *deporte* (m.)
  person who plays sports *deportista* (m./f.)
spot *pinta* (f.)
spring *primavera* (f.)
spy *espía* (m./f.)
square *cuadro* (m.), *plaza* (f.)
stadium *estadio* (m.)
staff *personal* (m.), *plantilla* (f.)
stairs *escaleras* (f. pl.)
stamp collecting *filatelia* (f.)
stand in line (to) *hacer una cola/fila*
star *estrella* (f.)
start (to) *comenzar*
  start ... (doing something) (to) *comenzar a ...*
  start from ... (to) *partir de ...*
state *estado* (m.)
station *estación* (f.)
  train station *estación de tren, estación de ferrocarril*
Stay in the right lane. *Siga por el carril de la derecha.*
steady job *trabajo* (m.) *fijo*
stepdaughter *hijastra* (f.)
stepfather *padrastro* (m.)
stepmother *madrastra* (f.)
stepson *hijastro* (m.)
stick *palo* (m.)
still *todavía*
stockings *pantymedias* (f. pl.), *medias* (f. pl.)
stomach *estómago* (m.)
  have an upset stomach (to) *tener mal de estómago*
stop *alto* (m.), *parada* (f.)
  Stop! *¡Alto!*
stop (to) *parar, cesar*
  stop ... (doing something) (to) *cesar de ...*
store *tienda* (f.)
  antique store *tienda de antigüedades*
  clothing store *tienda de ropa*
  convenience store *tienda* (f.)
  department store *tienda por departamentos*
  electronics store *tienda de electrodomésticos*
  store clerk *dependiente/dependienta* (m./f.)
storm *tormenta* (f.)
stove *cocina* (f.)
straight *recto, derecho*
  Continue straight. *Continúa recto.*
  Go straight. *Siga derecho.*
strange *extraño/extraña* (m./f.)
stranger *extranjero/extranjera* (m.)
street *calle* (f.)
streetlight *luz* (f.) *de la calle*
strength *fuerza* (f.)
  regain strength (to) *coger fuerzas* (f. pl.)
stressing, stressful *estresante* (m./f.)
stripe *raya* (f.)
striped *a rayas*
strong *fuerte* (m./f.)
student *estudiante/estudiante* (m./f.), *alumno/alumna* (m./f.)
study *estudio* (m.)
  studies *estudios* (pl.)
study (to) *estudiar*
stuffing *relleno* (m.)
style *estilo* (m.)
  in style *de moda*
subject *asignatura* (f.)
submit (to) *entregar*
subscriber *abonado/abonada* (m./f.)
suburban *suburbano/suburbana* (m./f.)
subway *subterráneo* (m.), *metro* (m.)
success *éxito* (m.)
such *tal*
suede *gamuza* (f.)
suffer (to) *sufrir*
sugar *azúcar* (m.)
suggest (to) *sugerir*
  suggest that ... (to) *sugerir que ...*
suit *traje* (m.)
suitcase *maleta* (f.)
summer *verano* (m.)
  summer job *trabajo* (m.) *de verano*
sun *sol* (m.)
  It's sunny. *Hace sol.*
Sunday *domingo* (m.)
sunglasses *gafas* (f. pl.) *de sol*
supermarket *supermercado* (m.)
supporter *hincha* (m./f.)
supposition *supuesto* (m.)
sure *seguro/segura* (m./f.)
  I'm sure. *Seguro/segura que sí.*
surprise *sorpresa* (f.)

be surprised (to) *sorprenderse*
be surprised that . . . (to) *sorprenderse de que . . .*
suspend (to) *suspender*
suspense *suspenso* (m.)
suspense films *películas* (f. pl.) *de suspenso*
sweater *suéter* (m.), *jersey* (m.)
sweet (adjective) *dulce* (m./f.)
sweet (noun) *dulce* (m.)
swell (to) *hincharse*
swim (to) *nadar*
swimming *natación* (f.)
swimming pool *piscina* (f.)
switchboard *centralita* (f.)
symptom *síntoma* (m.)
syndrome *síndrome* (m.)
carpal tunnel syndrome *síndrome del túnel del carpio*
system *sistema* (m.)
sound system *sistema de sonido*

T

table *mesa* (f.), *tabla* (f.)
tableware *vajilla* (f.)
tag *etiqueta* (f.)
price tag *etiqueta con el precio*
tail *cola* (f.)
take (to) *tomar, traer, coger, usar, llevar*
take a bath (to) *bañarse*
take a blood test (to) *hacerse un examen de sangre*
take a picture (to) *hacer una foto*
take a shower (to) *ducharse*
take a test (to) *hacer un examen, presentarse a un examen*
Take care. *Que estés bien.*
take care of (to) *atender*
take into acount (to) *tener en cuenta*
take medication (to) *tomar un medicamento*
take out (to) *sacar*
take the blood pressure (to) *tomar la tensión*
talented *dotado/dotada* (m./f.)
talk (to) *hablar*
talk show *programa* (m.) *de entrevistas*
tall *alto/alta* (m./f.)
taste *gusto* (m.)
taste (to) *saborear, probar, saber*
tax *impuesto* (m.)
tax return *planilla* (f.) *de impuestos*
taxi *taxi* (m.)
taxi driver *taxista* (m./f.)
tea *té* (m.)
teacher *maestro/maestra* (m./f.)
teakettle *tetera* (f.)
team *equipo* (m.)
technology *tecnología* (f.)
teenager *adolescente* (m.)
telephone *teléfono* (m.)
answer the phone (to) *contestar el teléfono*
call . . . on the phone (to) *llamar por teléfono a . . .*
dial a phone number (to) *marcar un número de teléfono*
hang up the phone (to) *colgar el teléfono*
make a phone call (to) *llamar por teléfono*
on the phone *por teléfono*
telephone booth *cabina* (f.) *telefónica*
telephone number *número* (m.) *de teléfono*
telephonic *telefónico/telefónica* (m./f.)
television *televisión* (f.)
television program *programa* (m.) *de televisión*
television set *televisor* (m.)
watch television (to) *mirar la televisón*
tell (to) *contar, decir*
tell a dirty joke (to) *contar un chiste verde (lit., to tell a green joke)*
tell time (to) *dar la hora*
temperature *temperatura* (f.)
temple *templo* (m.)
ten *diez*
at eight ten (8:10) *a las ocho y diez*
It's ten after one in the morning. *Es la una y diez de la madrugada.*
ten thousand *diez mil*
tendon *tendón* (m.)
tennis *tenis* (m.)
tennis shoes *zapatillas* (f. pl.) *deportivas*
tension *tensión* (f.)
term *término* (m.)
terrible *pésimo/pésima* (m./f.)
test *examen* (m.), *prueba* (f.)
fail a test (to) *suspender un examen*
pass a test (to) *aprobar un examen*
take a blood test (to) *hacerse un examen de sangre*

take a test (to) *hacer un examen, presentarse a un examen*
text *texto* (m.)
textbook *libro* (m.) *de texto*
than *que*
less . . . than . . . *menos . . . que . . .*
more . . . /-er than . . . *más . . . que . . .*
thanks *gracias* (pl.)
be thankful (to) *agradecer*
give thanks (to) *dar (las) gracias*
Thanks a lot. *Muchas gracias.*
Thank you. *Gracias.*
Thank you for your help. *Le agradezco su ayuda.*
that (demonstrative) *ese/esa* (m. sg./f. sg.) *(near the listener), aquel/aquella* (m. sg./f. sg.) *(far from the speaker and the listener)*
that (one) *ése/ésa* (m. sg./f. sg.) *(near the listener)*
that (one) over there *aquél/aquélla* (m. sg./f. sg.) *(far from the speaker and the listener)*
that (one, thing) (neuter) *eso* (m.) *(near the listener)*
that (one, thing) over there (neuter) *aquello* (m.) *(far from the speaker and the listener)*
That's it. *Ya está.*
That's right. *Es verdad./Así es.*
That's too bad! *¡Qué pena!*
that (conjunction, relative pronoun) *que*
the *el/la/los/las* (m. sg./f. sg./m. pl./f. pl.)
of the (m.)**/from the** (m.)**/about the** (m.) *del (de + el)*
to the (m.)**/at the** (m.) *al (a + el)*
theater *teatro* (m.)
their *su/sus* (sg./pl.)
theirs (m./f.) *suyo/suya/suyos/suyas* (m. sg./f. sg./m. pl./f. pl.)
theirs (f. pl.) *el de ellas* (m. sg.), *la de ellas* (f. sg.)
theirs (m. pl./mixed group) *el de ellos* (m. sg.), *la de ellos* (f. sg.)
them (direct object pronoun) *los/las* (m./f.)
(to/for) them (indirect object pronoun) *les, se* (used in place of les when preceding lo/la/los/las)
themselves *se*
then *entonces, luego, pues*
Until then. *Hasta entonces.*
there *ahí, allí*
There is . . . /There are . . . *Hay . . .*
There's no . . . that/who . . . *No hay ningún . . . que . . .*
There's no one who/that . . . *No hay nadie que . . .*
There's nothing that . . . *No hay nada que . . .*
therefore *por lo tanto, pues*
these *estos/estas* (m. pl./f. pl.)
these (ones) *éstos/éstas* (m. pl./f. pl.)
they *ellos/ellas* (m. pl. & mixed group/f. pl.)
thick *espeso/espesa* (m./f.)
thief *ladrón* (m./f.)
thin *delgado/delgada* (m./f.), *ligero/ligera* (m./f.)
thing *cosa* (f.)
How are things? *¿Cómo van las cosas?*
think (to) *creer, pensar*
Don't you think? *¿No crees?*
I think so. *Creo que sí.*
not think that . . . (to) *no pensar que . . .*
What do you think of . . . ? *¿Qué te parece . . . ?*
third *tercero/tercer/tercera* (m. sg./m. sg. before a noun/f. sg.)
third year *tercer año*
thirst *sed* (f.)
be thirsty (to) *tener sed*
thirteen *trece*
thirty *treinta*
thirty-one *treinta y uno*
thirty percent off *treinta por ciento de descuento*
this *este/esta* (m. sg./f. sg.)
this (one) *éste/ésta* (m. sg./f. sg.)
this (one, thing)(neuter) *esto* (m.)
this afternoon *esta tarde*
this day *este día*
this evening *esta noche* (f.)
those *aquellos/aquellas* (m. pl./f. pl.) *(far from the speaker and the listener)*
those (ones) over there *aquéllos/aquéllas* (m. pl./f. pl.) *(far from the speaker and the listener)*
thousand *mil*
hundred thousand *cien mil*
ten thousand *diez mil*
twenty thousand *veinte mil*
three *tres*
It's three o'clock. *Son las tres.*
It's three o'clock sharp. *Son las tres en punto.*
one hundred and three dollars *ciento tres dólares*

three hundred *trescientos/trescientas* (m./f.)
twenty-three *veintitrés*
throat *garganta* (f.)
have a sore throat (to) *tener dolor de garganta*
through *por*
from … through … *de … a …*
go through a light (to) *saltarse el semáforo*
I'm putting you through. (on the phone) *Lo paso.*
thunder *trueno* (m.)
Thursday *jueves* (m.)
ticket *billete* (m.), *boleto* (m.), *pasaje* (m.), *tiquete* (m.), *entrada* (f.)
tie *corbata* (f.)
tie (to) *empatar*
tied *empatado/empatada* (m./f.)
be tied (to) *quedar empatados*
tight *ajustado/ajustada* (m./f.)
time *hora* (f.), *tiempo* (m.), *vez* (f.)
at the present time *actualmente*
At what time is it? *¿A qué hora es?*
Do you have time?/How are you doing for time? *¿Cómo estás de tiempo?*
full-time *a tiempo completo*
on time, in time *a tiempo*
overtime *horas* (f. pl.) *extras*
part-time *a tiempo parcial*
tell time (to) *dar la hora*
What time is it? *¿Qué hora es?/¿Qué horas son?*
What time do you have? *¿Qué hora tiene?*
tingling feeling *cosquilleo* (m.)
tip *propina* (f.), *punta* (f.)
tired *cansado/cansada* (m./f.)
be tired (to) *tener cansancio*
to *a, con*
in order to *para*
It's five to one. (12:55) *Es la una menos cinco.*
to the (m.) *al (a + el)*
toast *tostada* (f.)
today *hoy*
toe *dedo del pie*
together *junto/junta* (m./f.)
toilet *inodoro* (m.)
toilet paper *papel* (m.) *higiénico*
toll *peaje* (m.)
tomato *tomate* (m.)
tomorrow *mañana* (f.)
Until tomorrow./See you tomorrow. *Hasta mañana.*
tone *tono* (m.), *señal* (f.)
leave a message after the tone (to) *dejar un mensaje después de oír la señal*
tongue *lengua* (f.)
tonight *esta noche*
too *también*
too much, too many *demasiado/demasiada* (m./f.)
tooth *diente* (m.)
touch (to) *tocar*
tour bus trip *recorrido por autobús*
tourism *turismo* (m.)
tourist *turista* (m./f.)
toward(s) *hacia, para*
towel *toalla* (f.)
town *ciudad* (f.), *pueblo* (m.)
around town *por la ciudad*
toxic *tóxico/tóxica* (m./f.)
traffic *tráfico* (m.)
go through a traffic light (to) *saltarse el semáforo*
traffic jam *embotellamiento* (m.)
traffic light *semáforo* (m.)
train *tren* (m.), *ferrocarril* (m.)
train station *estación* (f.) *de tren, estación* (f.) *de ferrocarril*
transfer (to) *trasladar*
translate (to) *traducir*
travel *viaje* (m.)
travel (to) *viajar*
treat (to) *tratar*
How's life treating you? *¿Cómo te trata la vida?*
treatment *tratamiento* (m.)
tree *árbol* (m.)
trip *viaje* (m.)
go on a trip (to) *salir de viaje*
Have a good trip. *Buen viaje.*
true *cierto/cierta* (m./f.)
It is not true that … *No es cierto que …*
truth *verdad* (f.)
try (to) *tratar, probar*
try … (to do something) (to) *tratar de …*
try on (clothes) (to) *probarse*
T-shirt *camiseta* (f.)
Tuesday *martes* (m.)

tuition *derechos* (m. pl.) *de matrícula*
tuna *atún* (m.)
tunnel *túnel* (m.)
turn *vuelta* (f.)
turn (to) *doblar, girar, volver, ponerse*
  turn around (to) *dar la vuelta*
  Turn left. *Gira a la izquierda.*
  turn off (to) *apagar*
  turn off the lights (to) *apagar las luces*
  Turn right. *Gira a la derecha.*
twelve *doce*
  It's twelve noon. *Son las doce del mediodía.*
twenty *veinte*
  twenty-eight *veintiocho*
  twenty-five *veinticinco*
  twenty-four *veinticuatro*
  twenty-nine *veintinueve*
  twenty-one *veintiuno*
  twenty-seven *veintisiete*
  twenty-six *veintiséis*
  twenty-three *veintitrés*
  twenty-two *veintidós*
two *dos*
  twenty-two *veintidós*
  twice a week *dos veces por semana*
  two hundred *doscientos/doscientas* (m./f.)
  two-piece *de dos piezas*
type *tipo* (m.)
typical *típico/típica* (m./f.)

U

ugly *feo/fea* (m./f.)
umbrella *paraguas* (m.)
uncle *tío* (m.)
uncomfortable *incómodo/incómoda* (m./f.)
under *bajo*
undergarments (men's) *calzones* (m. pl.)
underneath *debajo*
  underneath . . . *debajo de . . .*
underpants (men's) *calzoncillos* (m. pl.)
undershirt *camisilla* (f.), *camiseta* (f.)
understand (to) *comprender, entender*
underwear (women's) *bombachas* (f. pl.), *bragas* (f. pl.), *calzoncitos* (m. pl.), *pantis* (m. pl.)
unemployed *parado/parada* (m./f.)
unfortunately *desafortunadamente, por desgracia*
unfriendly *antipático/antipática* (m./f.)
union *sindicato* (m.)
unique *único/única* (m./f.)
united *unido/unida* (m./f.)
United States (the) *los Estados Unidos*
university *universidad* (f.)
  university course *carrera* (f.)
unpleasant *desagradable* (m./f.)
until *hasta, para*
  Till then. *Hasta entonces.*
  Until later. *Hasta más tarde.*
  Until then. *Hasta entonces.*
  Until tomorrow. *Hasta mañana.*
urban *urbano/urbana* (m./f.)
urgently *urgentemente*
Uruguay *Uruguay* (m.)
Uruguayan *uruguayo/uruguaya* (m./f.)
us (direct object pronoun); **(to/for) us** (indirect object pronoun) *nos*
use (to) *usar*
  use for the first time (to) *estrenar*

V

vacation *vacaciones* (f. pl.)
  on vacation *de vacaciones*
variety *variedad* (f.)
vegetable *vegetal* (m.), *verdura* (f.)
Venezuela *Venezuela* (f.)
Venezuelan *venezolano/venezolana* (m./f.)
vertebral *vertebral* (m./f.)
very *muy, mucho*
veterinarian *veterinario/veterinaria* (m./f.)
view *vista* (f.)
village *aldea* (f.)
vinyl *vinilo* (m.)
  vinyl record *disco* (m.) *de vinilo*
violet (color) *violeta* (m./f.)
violin *violín* (m.)
visit (to) *visitar*
visitor *visitante* (m./f.)
voice *voz* (f.)
  voice mail *buzón* (m.) *de voz*
voucher *vale* (m.)

W

wage *paga* (f.), *jornal* (m.)
wait *espera* (f.)
wait (to) *esperar*
waiter *camarero* (m.), *mesero* (m.)

waitress *camarera* (f.), *mesera* (f.)
wake up (to) *despertarse*
walk (to) *andar, caminar, ir a pie/caminar*
wall *pared* (f.)
wallet *cartera* (f.)
want (to) *querer, desear*
  want that/to . . . (to) *querer que . . .*
wish (to) *desear*
  I wish . . . *Ojalá que . . .*
  wish that . . . (to) *desear que . . .*
wash (to) *lavar*
  hand wash (to) *lavar a mano*
  wash oneself (to) *lavarse*
wash basin *lavabo* (m.)
washing machine *lavadora* (f.)
watch *reloj* (m.)
watch (to) *mirar*
  watch television (to) *mirar la televisón*
water *agua* (f.)
  mineral water *agua mineral*
  water (the) *el agua*
  waters (the) *las aguas*
way *camino* (m.), *forma* (f.)
  one-way *de sentido* (m.) *único*
we *nosotros* (m. pl./mixed group), *nosotras* (f. pl.)
weak *débil* (m./f.)
wear (to) *llevar, calzar (shoes)*
  wear rose-colored glasses (to) *ver todo color de rosa (lit., to see everything pink)*
  What shoe size do you wear? *¿Qué número calza?*
weather *tiempo* (m.)
  The weather is good. *El tiempo es bueno.*
web (on the computer) *web* (f.)
  webpage *página* (f.) *web*
  website *sitio* (m.) *web*
Wednesday *miércoles* (m.)
week *semana* (f.)
  every week *todas las semanas*
  last week *semana pasada*
  next week *próxima semana, semana que viene*
  this week *esta semana*
  twice a week *dos días a la semana*
weekend *fin* (m.) *de semana*
  long weekend *puente* (m.)
weekly *semanal* (m./f.)
weigh (to) *pesar*
Welcome. *Bienvenido./Bienvenida.* (m./f.) (to a man/to a woman)
  You're welcome. *De nada.*
well *bien, pues*
  be not doing well (to) *estar mal*
  May you be well. *Que esté bien.*
  well-done *bien asada*
west *oeste* (m.), *occidente* (m.)
what *qué, cuál/cuáles* (sg./pl.)
  At what time is it? *¿A qué hora es?*
  What a coincidence! *¡Qué coincidencia!*
  What color is . . . ? *¿De qué color es . . . ?*
  What do you do for a living? *¿En qué trabaja?*
  What do you think of . . . ? *¿Qué te parece . . . ?*
  What does that mean? *¿Qué quiere decir eso?*
  What shoe size do you wear? *¿Qué número calza?*
  What time do you have? *¿Qué hora tiene?*
  What time is it? *¿Qué hora es?/¿Qué horas son?*
  What would you like? *¿Qué desea?*
  What?/Pardon me? *¿Cómo?*
  What's going on? *¿Qué hay?*
  What's happening? *¿Qué tal?*
  What's up?/What's going on? *¿Qué hay?*
  What's your name? *¿Cómo se llama usted?* (fml.)/*¿Cómo te llamas?* (infml.)
when *cuándo* (question), *cuando* (relative adverb)
where *dónde* (question), *donde* (relative adverb)
  Where are you from? *¿De dónde eres?*
which *cuál/cuáles* (sg./pl.) (question), *cual/cuales* (sg./pl.) (relative pronoun)
  of which (relative pronoun) *cuyo/cuya/cuyos/cuyas* (m. sg./f. sg./m. pl./f. pl.)
while *mientras*
white *blanco/blanca* (m./f.)
  white wine *vino* (m.) *blanco*
who *quién/quiénes* (sg./pl.) (question), *quien/quienes* (sg./pl.) (relative pronoun)
  Who knows? *¿Quién sabe?*
  Who's calling? *¿De parte de quién?/¿Quién lo llama?*
whole *entero/entera* (m./f.)
  whole milk *leche* (f.) *entera*
whom (question) *quién/quiénes* (sg./pl.)
  whom (relative pronoun) *quien/quienes* (sg./pl.)
whose (relative pronoun) *cuyo/cuya/cuyos/cuyas* (m. sg./f. sg./m. pl./f. pl.)
  Whose . . . ? *¿De quién . . . ?*

why *por qué*
wide *ancho/ancha* (m./f.)
wife *esposa* (f.), *mujer* (f.)
win (to) *ganar*
  I hope they win! *¡Ojalá que ganen!*
wind *viento* (m.)
  It's windy. *Hace viento.*
window *ventana* (f.)
  display window *escaparate* (m.)
wine *vino* (m.)
  red wine *vino tinto*
  white wine *vino blanco*
wineglass *copa* (f.)
  glass of wine *copa de vino*
winter *invierno* (m.)
wish *deseo* (m.)
with *con*
  with you *contigo*
without *sin*
woman *mujer* (f.), *tía* (f.)
  businesswoman *mujer de negocios*
  policewoman *mujer policía*
wonder *maravilla* (f.)
wonderful *estupendo/estupenda* (m./f.)
wood *madera* (f.)
wooden *de madera*
wool *lana* (f.)
word *palabra* (f.)
work *trabajo* (m.)
work (to) *trabajar, funcionar*
  What do you do for a living? *¿En qué trabaja?*
working day *jornada* (f.)
world *mundo* (m.)
  world championship *campeonato* (m.) *mundial*
worldly *mundial* (m./f.)
worldwide *mundial* (m./f.)
worry (to) *preocuparse*
  Don't worry. *No se preocupe.*
  worry that … (to) *preocuparse de que …*
worse *peor* (m./f.)
worst (the) *el/la/los/las* (m. sg./f. sg./m. pl./f. pl.) *peor*
wrist *muñeca* (f.)
write (to) *escribir*
  write down (to) *anotar*
writer *escritor/escritora* (m./f.)
wrong *equivocado/equivocada* (m./f.)
  wrong number *número* (m.) *equivocado*

Y

year *año* (m.)
  be … years old (to) *tener … años*
  fifties (the) *los años cicuenta*
  last year *año pasado*
  next year *año que viene*
  second year *segundo año*
  third year *tercer año*
  this year *este año*
yellow *amarillo/amarilla* (m./f.)
  yellow pages *páginas* (f. pl.) *amarillas*
yes *sí*
yesterday *ayer*
yet *todavía*
you (after a proposition) *ti* (infml. sg.)
  you (direct object pronoun) *lo/la/te/los/las/os* (m. sg. fml./f. sg. fml./sg. infml./m. pl./f. pl./pl. infml)
  you (impersonal pronoun) *se*
  (to/for) you (indirect object pronoun) *le/les* (fml. sg./pl.), *se* (fml. sg./pl.) (used in place of le/les when preceding lo/la/los/las), *te/os* (infml. sg./pl.)
  you (subject pronoun) *usted/tú/ustedes/vosotros/vosotras* (sg. fml./sg. infml./pl./m. pl. & mixed group infml. used in Spain/f. pl. infml. used in Spain)
young *joven* (m./f.)
  young boy *niño* (m.)
  young child *párvulo/párvula* (m./f.)
  young girl *niña* (f.)
  younger *menor* (m./f.)
  youngest (the) *el/la/los/las* (m. sg./f. sg./m. pl./f. pl.) *menor*
your (pl. fml. & infml.) *su/sus* (sg./pl.)
  your (pl. infml.) *vuestro/vuestra/vuestros/vuestras* (m. sg./f. sg./m. pl./f. pl.) (used in Spain)
  your (sg. fml.) *su/sus* (sg./pl.)
  your (sg. infml.) *tu/tus* (sg./pl.)
yours (pl. fml. & infml.) *suyo/suya/suyos/suyas* (m. sg./f. sg./m. pl./f. pl.), *el de ustedes* (m. sg.), *la de ustedes* (f. sg.)
  yours (pl. infml.) *vuestro/vuestra/vuestros/vuestras* (m. sg./f. sg./m. pl./f. pl.) (used in Spain)
  yours (sg. fml.) *suyo/suya/suyos/suyas* (m. sg./f. sg./m. pl./f. pl.), *el de usted* (m. sg.), *la de usted* (f. sg.)

yours (sg. infml.) *tuyo/tuya/tuyos/tuyas* (m. sg./f. sg./m. pl./f. pl.) (infml.)
yourself *se/te* (fml./infml.)
yourselves *se/os* (fml./infml.)
youth hostel *hostal* (m.)

Z

zero *cero*

Join the Conversation

Join the Conversation

Join the Conversation

Join the Conversation

Join the Conversation

Join the Conversation

Join the Conversation

Join the Conversation

Join the Conversation

Join the Conversation

Join the Conversation

Join the Conversation

Join the Conversation

Join the Conversation

Join the Conversation

Join the Conversation

Join the Conversation

Join the Conversation

Join the Conversation

LIVING LANGUAGE®

Join the Conversation

Join the Conversation

Join the Conversation

Join the Conversation

Join the Conversation

Join the Conversation

LIVING LANGUAGE®

Join the Conversation

Join the Conversation

Join the Conversation

Join the Conversation

Join the Conversation

Join the Conversation

LIVING LANGUAGE®

Join the Conversation

Join the Conversation

Join the Conversation

LIVING LANGUAGE®

Join the Conversation

Join the Conversation

Join the Conversation

Join the Conversation

Join the Conversation

Join the Conversation

Join the Conversation

Join the Conversation

Join the Conversation

Join the Conversation

Join the Conversation

Join the Conversation

Join the Conversation

Join the Conversation

Join the Conversation

Join the Conversation

LIVING LANGUAGE®

Join the Conversation

Join the Conversation

LIVING LANGUAGE®

Join the Conversation

Join the Conversation

Join the Conversation

Join the Conversation

Join the Conversation

Join the Conversation

Join the Conversation

LIVING LANGUAGE®

Join the Conversation

Join the Conversation

Join the Conversation

Join the Conversation

Join the Conversation

LIVING LANGUAGE®